300 YEARS OF JEWISH LIFE
IN THE UNITED STATES

THE JEWISH PEOPLE — PAST AND PRESENT

We dedicate this volume on 300 years of Jew-ish life in the UNITED STATES *to the Jewish Labor Committee which saved the lives of many of our editors and contributors by bringing them to this country in the years 1940-1942, and which enabled us to achieve this work.*

COMMITTEE FOR JEWISH
ENCYCLOPEDIC HANDBOOKS

THE JEWISH PEOPLE

PAST AND PRESENT

VOLUME IV

JEWISH ENCYCLOPEDIC HANDBOOKS

NEW YORK

PRINTED IN THE UNITED STATES OF AMERICA
BY MARSTIN PRESS, NEW YORK, N. Y.
I. LONDON, *President*

 438

PREFACE

IN THE PREFACE to the third volume of the series *The Jewish People—Past and Present* we announced our new plan to publish a second three-volume set making a systematic presentation of the history of the Jewish communities on the various continents and in the most important countries of the globe, where Jews live or had lived. The original intention was to start the new series with a volume dedicated to the history of the Jewish communities in Europe, then to take the continent of America and, finally, to conclude the series with a special volume devoted to the State of Israel.

But the great interest exhibited by a considerable sector of American Jewry in the 300th anniversary of Jewish life in the United States led the publishers to shift the sequence of the planned volumes, and to begin with a volume presenting the various aspects of the Jewish population in the USA, that is to say, its activities in diverse fields—religious, cultural, socio-economic, national—during the last three hundred years. It is natural, however, that the emphasis should fall on the last 70-odd years when the Jewish community in the USA received an influx of about two and one half millions from the countries of Eastern and Central Europe. And quite a number of monographs are devoted to the analysis of the sociological processes which accompanied the adjustment of the gigantic masses of new Jewish immigrants to the social and political pattern of this country and the description of the unique role of the Jewish community in the economic and social life of the country, and of the impact of the American way of life and institutions on the collective and individual development of the Jewish citizens in the USA.

This project could not have been realized without the selfless and devoted labors of our editors, contributors, translators, and technical staff. We take great pleasure in expressing our warmest gratitude to these men and women.

Cordial acknowledgement is also due to the Yiddish Scientific Institute (YIVO), the Jewish Theological Seminary of America, the American Jewish Historical Society and Rabbi I. S. Meyer, librarian of the Society, Yeshiva University, New York Public Library (Jewish Division), the American Jewish Committee, Joint Distribution Committee, the Union of American Hebrew Congregations, Jewish Institute of Religion, Union of Orthodox Jewish Congregations, Zionist Organization of America, National Jewish Welfare Board, The Jewish Daily Forward; and to L. M. Stein, Chicago, B. Levin, Los Angeles and the late Sholem Perlmutter for their generous permission to use valuable documents, photographs and other materials in their possession.

In conclusion, we wish to thank the Workmen's Circle, Farband —Labor Zionist Order, International Ladies' Garment Workers' Union and Amalgamated Clothing Workers of America and the individuals whose generous support has made the present series possible.

THE PUBLISHERS

CONTENTS

ILLUSTRATIONS

THE HISTORY OF THE JEWS IN THE UNITED STATES

Anita Libman Lebeson

I.   A DREAM IS BORN

The history of Jews in America began as a dream. For in the heart of a hunted and pursued man the dream of sanctuary always exists. It is the spark that keeps him alive in the midst of terror. Fenced in physically by ghetto walls, hemmed in spiritually by proscriptive laws and the hatred of his neighbors, the Jew of the age of exploration and discovery dreamed of a sanctuary, an island to which to escape from the persecution and darkness that surrounded him. For more than a hundred years the major preoccupation of Jewish scholars and scientists was in the realm of cosmography and geography. They studied the stars. They charted the seas and the oceans. The stars gave them hope. The seas gave them avenues of escape. The twin sciences were related. Jews became famous as astronomers, mapmakers, navigators, pilots. The *portolani* they made were the most acceptable. They briefed explorers and travelers before they set out on their travels. Cresques *lo Juheu* drew the most famous maps in the world. At the School of Navigation at Sagres, Prince Henry the Navigator gathered a group of learned Jews to perfect the knowledge then available.

It was an age of darkness and persecution. It was a time of learning and scholarship.

That Columbus knew both Jewish scientists and Jewish scholars is a matter of history. That he addressed himself to influential Jews at the courts of the rulers of Portugal and Spain is a well-established fact. His own antecedents are still in dispute. No one can tell with absolute certainty who his people were or where his birthplace was. Although he is claimed by the Italians, it is a matter of record that he never used the Italian language and certainly failed to honor a single place in the new world with a geographic name connected with Italy. Spanish was his language and Spain's geography is reproduced in the New World. For it was part of the unresolved puzzle of Columbus that in subtle hints to Marrano friends in Spain, he seemed to ally himself with them, intimating that he was persecuted by Christians and dreaded them, even as did his friends to whom he addressed himself.

Columbus began his significant voyage on *Tisheah be-Ab*, the Ninth Day of Ab (August 3, 1492). The landfall was made on *Hoshana Rabbah,* the twenty-first day of Tishri (October 12, 1492). Of the men who composed his crews, there are many names which are found on Inquisition lists. Several Jews have been definitely identified. Luis de Torres, linguist, was one. There were two ship's surgeons and two crew members who were Jews. It was Luis de Torres who with another sailor was chosen to go ashore by Columbus. Luis knew both Hebrew and Arabic, languages which were considered invaluable in making arrangements with the natives of the newly discovered land. Luis de Torres was thus the first European in Columbus' party to set foot in America. To him also goes the credit for becoming the first settler. Recently in a Bulletin of the Department of Agriculture, Luis de Torres was also credited with having been the first European who learned about the cultivation of maize from the Indians and grew the first corn in the New World that was planted by a white man.

After Spain, Portugal entered the race for discovery of new lands. Two years after Columbus' historic discovery, a treaty had divided the spheres of influence of the two rival Iberian nations. Now Cabral headed an armada to the Western hemisphere. Abraham Zacuto, noted Jewish astronomer and scientist, was called in to serve as a technical expert. He lectured to the men who were about to sail westward. Among those who listened and later sailed with Cabral was a Polish Jew, named Gaspar Judeo, later known, in honor of Vasco da Gama, as Gaspar da Gama. To Gaspar Judeo goes the honor of being the first Jew in South American history. On this voyage Gaspar could, if he chose, speak Hebrew to several of the sailors. Another hero who emerges from the documents of those days was a New Christian of noble bearing and many attainments whose household and possessions made him acceptable in the court of the King of Portugal. Fernando de Loronha, or Fernão Noronha, was an ambitious, active, imaginative fellow. He conceived the plan of an enterprise of his own and enlisted a group of fellow-converts. One of his ships was named the *Judea*. A harbor in South America was named by him Cananea. He leased some lands from King Manuel of Portugal. He undertook to establish a settlement in the newly found lands. The first voyage was made by Loronha in 1501-1502. A year later, a handful of New Christian settlers built a fort there which they called Cape Frio.

To this day, on every navigator's map may be seen a little island off the coast of Brazil which was the King's gift to one of his favorites at court. It is the island of Fernando Noronha.

There was no escaping the terrors of the Inquisition. If a man became a convert and practiced his Judaism in secret, he was hunted down and burned at the stake. A crypto-Jew had no peace of mind and no safety for himself or his descendants. So New Christians or Marranos undertook to emigrate. But even in the New World they were not safe. The Inquisition set up a branch office in the Western hemisphere. By 1537 it was doing a land office business and had to appeal for help to the Pope. Crypto-Jews were caught and hounded wherever they went. In South and Central America, in Mexico and the Philippine Islands, the Inquisitorial sleuths were busy ferreting out secret Jews. No disguise, no secret practice was unknown to these agents of the Inquisition. Men and women and children were burned at the stake, languished in many prisons, were tortured in secret trials. Yet they persisted. With courage unmatched in human annals, with a devotion that burned in crypts and basements and caves, Jews continued to adhere to their faith, even though nominally they were counted as Catholics. There was no end to Jewish martyrdom and no limit to their heroism.

Brazil was like a magnet attracting secret Jews from many lands. They came from the Iberian peninsula and from as far north as Holland. There were scholars and artisans, educated and ignorant among these immigrants. Jews became planters. They had sugar plantations in Brazil and were agents in dyewood which was much in demand. They exported parrots and tropical plants and lumber. There were merchants and financiers and ship owners among them. Jews had relatives in every port in Europe. They watched with keen interest the development of commerce and industry in the New World. In growing numbers they crossed the South Atlantic to Brazil.

Their lot depended on the home government. The epic story of their fortunes fluctuated with the policies of the European nations under whose domination they lived. As economic pressure increased in Europe, America furnished the safety valve which removed the acute pressure, the economic insecurity, the shortages of raw materials. Governments looked to the New World for new lands, for essential metals, for fur and wood and dyestuffs. They also sought to find room for the unemployed and the insecure, for debtors and for convicted criminals. And the people, oppressed, persecuted, jailed for minor offences, undernourished and overworked, or homeless and without permanent addresses — these too looked to the New World for amelioration and change, for security or relief from the dull and unutterable grind of poverty. And then there were always the courageous and brave in quest of physical adventure, eager to explore and to pioneer, or in search of religious freedom and the right to worship God according to their own conscience.

Brazil is a perfect example of the fluctuation of colonial fortune under varying rule. Under the Portuguese there was oppression and severe control. Under the Dutch who gained a temporary foothold there was a flowering of commerce, a measure of freedom of worship, development of friendly ties with both government and economic ruling class at home. But when in 1654 the Portuguese regained their land in Brazil and drove the Dutch out—it was the end of orderly economic pursuits, the end of religious tolerance, the end of openly acknowledged profession of Judaism.

II.   THE DAWN OF AN ERA—1654

The year 1654 marked a turning point in American Jewish history. It was the end of an era in Brazil and South America and the beginning of Jewish community life in North America. For in that year, twenty-three Jews, refugees from South America, arrived in New Amsterdam and with one other Jew who had preceded them by a few weeks, Jacob Barsimson, began a narrative which is still unfolding. Individual Jews had already made their way to North America. Their presence in Mexico, in Central America, in the Caribbean is a matter of record. Jews are known to have found their way to various points along the Atlantic seaboard. The significance of the arrival to New Amsterdam of these refugees from Brazil lies in the fact that it was a *group* arrival. There must have been children among them, for the record tells us that the settlers were "big and little." We know, too, that they were penniless. They relied on promises of help from their coreligionists in Holland. It was slow in reaching New Amsterdam. Three of their number were thrown into a debtor's jail. Needless to say these new arrivals were unpopular. Peter Stuyvesant and his subordinates were up in arms against these "godless rascals." To have the Jews was bad enough—but to discover they were poor Jews—that added insult to injury. The Jews remained. First because the Dutch Jewish community, prosperous and enterprising, had a voice in the affairs of the Dutch West India Company. Second, because of the drive, energy and will-to-succeed with which the little immigrant group in New Amsterdam attacked its own problems. They insisted on their rights to trade, to bear arms, to take part in the common defense. They succeeded in wresting these rights from the reluctant officials. They remained. They established themselves. They conducted religious services, at first privately, later in the open. The original group was augmented by newer settlers. To the North of them in Newport, Rhode Island, another little group of Jews made its impact on the life of the colony. Fifteen Jewish families came there in 1658. In Boston, by 1674, a Jew's name appeared on the tax list. In Virginia, Elias Legardo was found as early as 1621. And in neighboring colonies Jews were mentioned in letters and official records. South Carolina and the Barbados had commercial interests in common. When John Locke drew up a constitution for the Carolinas, he made provision for Jewish and other dissenters. In this he had had a noble precedent. For many years before, Roger Williams had advocated toleration for the Jews.

When Roger Williams went to England in 1643 to get a charter for his colony, he did some writing as well. He "joined the liberal cause as a pamphleteer and in 1644 published his famous book, *The Bloudy Tenent of Persecution . . ."* John Cotton, who like Williams was a Cambridge University man, but unlike the great liberal was of the unyielding Puritan tradition, answered this plea for tolerance by a pamphlet in rebuttal. This in turn inspired Williams in 1652 to answer Cotton's argument by writing *The Bloudy Tenent Yet More Bloudy.* It was the contention of Roger Williams that God does not require religious uniformity. Among other pleas Williams included one for the rights of Jews. That this noble plea had its influence on the cause of resettlement of Jews in England which was to take place in the next few years is obvious. Three years after the first Jewish group established itself in New Amsterdam, Jews were officially accepted under the Protectorate in England. The year 1654 and the year 1657 are significant dates in America and in England respectively.

The history of the Puritans in America is a saga of strange contradiction. That men who were preoccupied with Old Testament concepts and exhibited a psychological predilection for the Prophetic teachings, who named their children after Old Testament heroes and introduced as the early legal code to follow a set of laws called "Draft of the Model of Moses, his Judicials"—that such men should regard with suspicion a champion of the Jews—is one of the contradictions of history. We know that the Book of Psalms was published in Cambridge, Massachusetts, in 1640. The Bay Psalm Book with a preface by Richard Mather was the first book to be published in the English settlements and it was translated directly from the Hebrew, using Hebrew type for the first time on the Western continent. The Puritans used every blandishment possible to persuade the Jews to join with them. Cotton Mather wrote a tract "to engage the Jewish Nation, unto the religion of their Patriarch . . ." Another of his books described the "conversion of a Jew." In the diary of Samuel Sewall, February 7, 1685/6 he describes attending a church service: ". . . went to the first Meeting House . . . Mr. Moodey preached from Isa: 12, 1 . . . Shewing that 'twas chiefly a Directory of Thanksgiving for the Conversion of the Jews. . . ."

Yet intolerance flourished and rigidity held sway. Roger Williams was banished from Massachusetts in 1635 for his beliefs —maintaining that he would not have liberty of conscience for himself which he would not freely share with others. He vowed that from the colony he founded none should be turned away, neither "Papists and Protestants, Jews and Turks." Wrote Williams:

> I have desired to labor in Europe, in America, with English, with Barbarians, yea, and also I have longed for some trading with Jews themselves, for whose hard measure, I fear the nations and England have yet a score to pay. I desire not that liberty to myself, which I would not freely

and impartially weigh out to all the consciences of the world besides. . . . Brave words, implemented by courageous practice.

So Jews found their way to Newport. By 1677 they had purchased a cemetery, always a sign of the existence of a community. Fragmentary though our knowledge still is about the early days of Newport and meager as are the records, a few facts stand out. Some fifteen families were among the earliest group of settlers. They came from Holland. They were of diverse occupations. They brought with them the first three degrees of Masonry. Mordecai Campanal at whose home the historic meeting of the Masonic order took place, was elected the head of the *Kahal Kadosh,* the religious community that they organized. The first services were read in the home of Campanal.

Shortly after the death of Roger Williams, an associate, Major William Dyre had the estates of several Jews seized and had them brought to "a Tryall as Aliens." But the Williams tradition triumphed even after his death. The court found for the defendants and the Major was ordered to pay the costs of litigation. Still the Jews of Newport wanted more. They wanted legal assurance of their status. They petitioned the General Assembly on June 24th, 1684, and were given the following Delphic answer: "We declare that they may expect as good protection here, as any stranger, being not of our nation, residing amongst us in this his Majesty's Colony ought to have, being obedient to his Majesty's laws." With this the Jews were perforce content. More Jews came from the West Indies. They had correspondents in many places—Holland, England, the West Indies, other North American colonies. Families broken up by persecution and oppression maintained ties which eventually reunited them — psychologically, emotionally and economically.

A battle won in one colony was a yardstick for other colonists. A community founded in one town gave heart and courage to the Jews of other cities. The building of a synagogue in one place spurred the Jews of other outposts. Fellowship and rivalry, competition and mutual assistance may be seen again and again, dominant patterns in Jewish communal organization. The Jews had, despite dispersion, despite generations of flight and terror, a common culture, a common tradition, an abiding sense of kinship, folkways and mores which knit them together.

III. COMMERCE AND COLONIZATION

Commerce was the spur to empire building. Trade was the life blood of expansion. In the absence of other forms of communication, correspondence with kinsmen and friends formed vital links which facilitated exchange of commodities, development of new markets. Addison, aware of the importance of Jews in the development of commerce, wrote ". . . they are become the instruments by which the most distant nations converse with one another and by which mankind are knit together in general correspondence." Yet toward the close of the seventeenth century, the economic activities of Jews were jeopardized by proscriptive measures. As early as 1660, the Navigation Act carried a provision which limited the economic activities in the British provinces. For the law provided that to be a merchant or factor, a man must be born on British soil or be endenizened there. The law of 1696 caused a protest to be addressed to Parliament from the "Hebrew Nation Residing at London." In this petition they referred to their peculiar situation "Because that most of them were by the Rigour of the Spanish and Portuguese Inquisition forced to Renounce their Native-Countries, and to shelter themselves under the Merciful Protection of the English Government. . . ." They stressed the fact that their commercial enterprises were ". . . to the great advantage of the said Plantations. . . ." They averred that "those of the Hebrew

Nation do look upon what ever Countrey they Retire to, from the Rigour of the Inquisition, as their Native-Countrey by reason of the Protection they meet with there. . ."

It is possible that even before formal relief was granted them, Jews in the American colonies had evolved a formula for trade, for partnership with Christians, for trans-Atlantic commerce. In 1678 Asser Levy entered into a partnership with a Christian and was permitted to build a slaughter-house. Excluded from retail trade, Jews were permitted to engage in wholesale commerce. So Jews became importers of tobacco and Negro slaves. One Jew callously exchanged merchandise for Negroes brought on his own vessel from Guinea. Jews sent ships to Calcutta, Malabar and China. Lewis Gomez, by 1710, was able to secure the repeal of laws which restricted the exportation of wheat. He sent wheat to Madeira. They sold rum by the hogshead, pins and needles, Scotch snuff, Cheshire cheese, loaf sugar, grindstones, pewter, pimento, army equipment, knee buckles, looking glasses and pier glasses, raisins, oil and every kind of cloth. They traded extensively with the Indians and became important factors in the fur trade. They bought and sold vast stretches of land and names like Rachel's Way and Aaronsburgh could be found on surveyors' maps. Circumscribed they may have been, but their ingenuity and resourcefulness matched their frustrations.

The Atlantic seaboard knew them, and soon the hinterland was to be penetrated by intrepid Jewish traders and their brokers and agents. That in a nutshell is the importance of Jewish history in America and elsewhere.

Along the Atlantic seaboard, certain Jewish group enterprises stand out. In New Amsterdam, later New York, in Newport, in Pennsylvania, in the Carolinas and in Georgia,—from the seventeenth century to the eve of the Revolutionary War—these settlements possessed a unity, a pattern, a history. Briefly, let us retrace it.

In September of 1654, a group of twenty-three Sephardim landed in New Amsterdam. Unable to pay their fare, a judgment was obtained against them. All their meager possessions were sold and three of their number were thrown into debtors' jail. Peter Stuyvesant, hard-headed and hard-hearted, found them "repugnant" and made many protests to the home office. Fortunately for the Jews, the Directors of the Dutch West India Company did not accede to the wishes of Stuyvesant and his associates that the Jews be driven out of the colony. Among the shareholders in the home company were wealthy Dutch Jews. Also the directors insisted in their letters to New Amsterdam that Jews had suffered grievously in Brazil and had lost all their possessions in the war and in the confiscations which followed. Jews were to be allowed to remain, to trade and to travel about—that was the edict from home. The New Amsterdam gentry yielded.

It was hoped that they would be as shadows in the land, inconspicuous, unobtrusive, self-effacing. But they reckoned without their Jews. They were in a fever of activity, of buying and selling, of building and trading, of litigation and constant vigilance in the definition and clarification of their rights. The colonial record both under Dutch and later under English rule is not the record of negative toleration, of supine acquiescence, of knuckling under to rigid officials of proven hostility. It was an open fight, honorably waged, tenaciously undertaken. With vigor and courage they demanded that they be allowed to perform their civic duties like other settlers. Every right had to be negotiated. The right to bake bread, to operate a butcher shop, to trade, to travel. In 1655, a Jew bought a house. Objections were raised because Jews could not own real estate. An appeal to the home office reversed that decision. When they petitioned in the same year to buy a burial ground, that request was denied until such time as a death should occur in their midst. On the 22nd day of February, 1656, they complied with the requirement and effected the purchase of a cemetery. As Rabbi David de Sola Pool points out in his brilliant *Portraits Etched in Stone,* it was in that same year that the Jews of Curaçao acquired a cemetery and a year later that the Jews of London were given title to their cemetery at Mile End. So the living and the dead made history.

Typical of the spirit of early Jewish settlers of this colony was an energetic butcher named Asser Levy. With Jacob Barsimson, the first Jewish settler of the colony, Levy petitioned for the right to do guard duty. Jews had been given the privilege of paying a fee for this exemption, because of "the disinclination and unwillingness" of Christian burghers "to be on guard with them in the same guardhouse." Such squeamishness and fastidiousness was intolerable. Barsimson and Levy "request to keep guard with other burghers, or be free from the tax which others of their nation pay, as they must earn their living by manual labor." The right was won. The next petition which we meet in the climb to equality is the request for citizenship: "Asser Levy, a Jew, appears in Court; requests to be admitted a Burgher; claims that such ought not be refused him as he keeps watch and ward like other Burghers. . ." Such crass boldness astonished the officials. The plea was rejected. Nothing daunted, Levy argued eloquently. The entire Jewish community was backing their battling butcher. After some holding back, the ultimate victory was won. On April 20, 1657, the burgomaster was ordered to admit Jews to citizenship. The order was signed by Stuyvesant and two lesser officials. And the Jews continued to arrive in New Amsterdam.

In 1664, the English conquered New Amsterdam. It became New York. The Dutch province had been a barrier between the New England colonies of the British in the North and their Southern colonies. Now the flag of England waved over an unbroken Atlantic coast line. The Jews had nothing to fear from the change. They must have known about the readmission of Jews to England which was effected under the Lord Protector, Oliver Cromwell. The Stuarts continued the policy of acceptance.

IV. THE FOUNDING OF SHEARITH ISRAEL

The records the Jewish pioneers left are meager. One reconstructs the history of this and other communities from their petitions and lawsuits, from their wills and tombstones, from their letters and inventories. And of course from their congregational records. A few will suffice.

We know that at first New York Jews worshipped in private homes. When in September, 1685, they petitioned for the right to worship in public, this request was denied. Nevertheless a map published in 1695 located a synagogue on Beaver Street. By 1700, a piece of land was identified as adjoining the synagogue. Those restrictions which continued in effect were often more honored in the breach than in observance. Although Jews were restricted to wholesale trade only by a decision of the Council in 1685, they achieved as merchants, artisans and traders, a measure of financial security. In 1700, Lord Bellamont of New York wrote to the Lords of Trade that but for a Dutch merchant and two or three Jews who advanced him money, he "should have been undone." In just one decade, we find the impoverished Asser Levy attending a meeting of the wealthiest citizens of his city. By 1671, this former resident of a debtor's prison was advancing money to the Lutherans for the purpose of building a church. From 1700 on, Jews were active in international trade. The accounts of Crown revenues received at the Port of New York list many Jews as active factors, and strangely, women as well as men were engaged in commerce and contributed revenue to the royal coffers.

That there were poor people among the Jews, many records attest. As early as 1708, "the poor of the Jewish nation" were remembered in a will. Widows and orphans and mendicants are the concern of the community. Delinquents are found among them as among their neighbors and the heavy hand of the law falls upon them mercilessly. There were men and women of substance among them, conspicuous for their wealth and charities. They were elected to public office and even paid fines in order to be excused from their duties. Many were undergoing the costly process of endenization. So in 1705, Lewis Gomez paid £57 for "Denization". Between 1705 and 1769, forty-four Jews became freemen in New York. Christians were aware of the growing number and importance of their Jewish neighbors. In 1712, the Reverend John Sharpe wrote: "It is possible also to learn Hebrew here as well as in Europe, there being a synagogue of Jews, and many ingenious men of that nation from Poland, Hungary, Germany, etc." The testimony is important because it calls attention to the early representation of Ashkenazim in American Jewish history, a fact which is coming to light more and more with the unearthing of new records. They worshipped under the same roof with the Sephardim and there are many records of "intermarriage" among them. The Congregation Shearith Israel (The Remnant of Israel) is known to have existed in 1700 in a rented house on Mill Street. A lot for a synagogue was bought in 1728 and the work of building was undertaken in the following year. Although the little community was heavily taxed for the building, the congregational records for the year 1729-1730, show an expenditure of £53 for *obras pias* (works of charity).

The Congregation Shearith Israel, oldest synagogue in North America, is a pattern for other synagogues. Its records are happily preserved and a continuing stream of invaluable data has been made available to scholars and historians. The latest and most significant book is *Portraits Etched in Stone*. Here the tombstones in the earliest Jewish cemetery of that part of the country are identified and their subjects are fully described. So that a full and priceless series of biographies is recalled to life.

It was a simple little brick edifice, yet it was a symbol of privileges won and status established. The extant records begin in 1727, the earlier ones having been lost. The Minute Books of the Congregation contain the religious and social history of the Congregation. A community is organized. Justice is administered. Charity is dispensed. Morals are supervised. Housewives are watched as to observance of *kashruth*. Attendance records are kept. Internal squabbles are settled. Financial obligations are determined and a system of fines announced for non-performance of duties. A school is established in 1731. From the first it was decreed that the children of the poor be taught without paying tuition. Hebrew education was stressed. Classes were in session daily, Fridays, Holy Days and Fast days excepted. In addition to Hebrew, the school curriculum was early expanded to include also Spanish, English, writing and arithmetic (in the order given). The schoolmaster was not to be left to his own devices. For the *Parnassim* and *Elders* were required to visit the school monthly and to examine the children to see that satisfactory progress was made.

Administrative affairs were rigidly handled. Discipline was sternly maintained. Every aspect of daily life came within the orbit of the synagogue. As early as 1737, we find proof in the following sentence culled from a letter of Abigail Franks to her son: "Our little congregation affords a variety of news and tattle." It is true that congregational dicta, meetings, regulations, observances, political struggles, internal squabbles and differences of opinion all constituted the climate in which the Jews of early New York and of other congregations as well lived and had their being.

The early record of the Minute Books of Shearith Israel is terminated by the Revolutionary War. From September 27, 1775, until December 8, 1783, there are, significantly, no entries.

Briefly we trace the pre-Revolutionary history of several other colonies. Rhode Island, Pennsylvania, the Carolinas and Georgia are communities worthy of greater attention.

V. THE FOUNDING OF THE JEWISH COMMUNITIES IN NEWPORT, PHILADELPHIA, CHARLESTON AND OTHER PLACES

We have noted the early Jewish arrivals in Rhode Island and spoken of some population additions made in the ensuing years. It was in the eighteenth century that the little Jewish community of Newport made history as a community. Even prior to 1759, the year when Newport Jewry appealed to Shearith Israel for help in building a synagogue, a small building fund was in existence. This argues two facts. First, that they had faith in their future, their continuing existence in Newport. Second, that they had both group life and leadership.

The Jewish immigrants brought many skills to Newport. By 1705, Jacob Rodrigues Rivera introduced the sperm oil industry to Newport. Soap-making and candle-making were developed there. Jews are credited with developing other industries, such as sugar refineries, distilleries,

Courtesy Kerschner, Newport, R. I.

INTERIOR OF THE HISTORIC TOURO SYNAGOGUE AT NEWPORT, R. I.,
NOW A NATIONAL SHRINE

"rope walks". Shipping was one of their major group enterprises. The Lopez Papers housed now in the archives of the American Jewish Historical Society are packed with inventories of goods shipped, with accounts of every type of business transaction. The members of the Polock, Hart, Rivera families threw themselves eagerly into diverse activities, all of which brought prosperity not only to them but to the larger community as well. So growing financial success and stability persuaded the Jews of Newport that the time to build a synagogue was at hand. The task of designing the building was given to an architectural genius, Peter Harrison. The beautiful synagogue he designed, now a National Shrine, has embodied within its framework all the poetry of rededication in sunlight and openly of what was once cherished in dark crypts. It stands, eloquent edifice, as an enduring monument to faith and hope and ultimate triumph over adversity.

To Newport came a visiting scholar, Haym Isaac Carigal. He was a native of Hebron, Palestine, and had preached in England and other European capitals as well as in Curaçao. Not only did he quicken the life of the Jewish community there, but to his friendship with Ezra Stiles, outstanding Christian scholar who was to become President of his Alma Mater, Yale, we are indebted for a vivid graphic account of the thought and practice, the activities and the psychological insights of the Jews of eighteenth century Newport. In his *Diaries* are reflected detailed reports of conversations which Stiles had with Carigal and other Newport Jews. When Carigal departed, Stiles sadly wrote that since a future meeting in their lifetime was unlikely, he hoped that "after Death [they] meet together in the Garden of Eden."

In Pennsylvania, a Philadelphia directory of 1703 lists a Jewish resident. Nearby lived Benjamin Levy. Little groups of Jews could be found in Easton, Lancaster and Reading. Lancaster was the home of one of the most enterprising, dynamic colonial Jews, Joseph Simon. He was an Indian trader, merchant and a land speculator on a vast scale. He was also a devout Jew in whose home a room was set aside to be used as a synagogue. He was one of the first two Jews to be naturalized in Lancaster. This was in 1749. He was an important factor in the development of trade in the Mississippi valley and shared in the formation of giant land companies which dealt in Mississippi Valley land, during two decades, 1748–1768. Others were associated in the land ventures with Joseph Simon. The Gratz brothers, Michael and Barnard, were among them.

But it was Philadelphia which dominated the Jewish scene in the Quaker colony. By 1740, the Jews of that city met for regular worship. They also owned a cemetery. From the first there were Ashkenazim as well as Sephardim among them. Two men who came from Silesia soon came to be considered among the most respected of that city. The brothers Gratz knew Hebrew and Yiddish as well as German and had in an extended stay in London learned English as well. They were dandies in dress and manner and their ambition was matched by a great capacity for work. In the counting house of David Franks, the rudiments of a business training were acquired and then they were on their own. Between 1759 and 1763, the ledgers of Michael Gratz recorded business transactions with Georgia, Halifax, Guadalupe, St. Christopher and London. They had friends in every important colony where other Jews lived and worked. Lopez and Rivera of Newport, like other correspondents of the Gratz brothers, always added a note of personal greeting to their business letters. In 1768, these enterprising brothers sent a Scotsman as their agent to the Illinois country. There a thriving Indian trading post was established. In numerous letters to his employers this agent complains jokingly about the suspension of business during Jewish Holy Days.

*Courtesy Miss Henrietta Clay and Frick
Art Reference Library*

REBECCA GRATZ (1781-1869). AFTER A
PAINTING BY THOMAS SULLY

One of the major accomplishments of the younger of these two brothers was his marriage with the daughter of Joseph Simon, Miriam. Her letters to her husband are delightful and afford the historian an invaluable glimpse of the folkways and *mores* of Colonial Jewry. Her devotion to her large family is well known. The most famous of the children of Michael and Miriam Gratz was Rebecca Gratz. Her beauty and social grace endeared her to many. Her letters became famous commentaries on the life and times of her generations—for she lived to a ripe old age. But it was as the original of Rebecca in *Ivanhoe* that she gained literary immortality. Like so many famous Jewesses she was destined never to marry and whether it was because intermarriage was a hurdle she could not take, we do not really know. What we know with certainty is that the flower of our young men and women intermarried with Christians and were lost to their people ever after. And many descendants of the dynamic Gratz brothers are among that number.

Down the Atlantic seaboard the steady trickle of Jewish immigration continued. Maryland was largely composed of Catholics who sought refuge there. Under the Naturalization Act of 1740, several Jews became citizens there. Scattered Jewish names are found in early Virginia history. Both the Carolinas and Georgia from their earliest days became host colonies to Jews. As early as 1665 Jews came from the Barbados to the Carolinas. Thirty years later the Governor of South Carolina mentioned that he had a Jewish interpreter. Simon Valentine is mentioned in Carolinian records from 1696 on. He is the earliest known Jewish landholder in South Carolina. By 1709 he was already endenizened.

Charleston ranks first, however, in the history of South Carolina. It is to this day a beautiful city of grace and charm. From the first those qualities must have been in evidence. According to Reznikoff's study —*The Jews of Charleston*—it was very likely the first community in the world where Jews were permitted to vote. Simon Valentine's name is found on a list of petitioners in 1697, requesting the rights of British subjects. By 1721, the passage of an election law seems to have changed this and abrogated Jewish rights. Nevertheless the new law apparently was not put into effect. Early in the eighteenth century, in 1703, the ubiquitous Valentine is appointed one of the town commissioners, in charge of the guard and patrol.

Other proscriptive laws were also ignored. The Jews of Charleston lived openly, had their *minyan* and by midcentury, their congregation. *Kahal Kadosh Beth Elohim,* organized 1749-1750, was in all likelihood the fifth Jewish congregation in what is now the United States. New York, Newport, Savannah in Georgia, and Philadelphia having preceded Beth Elohim. Originally no special building was erected. A dwelling house was occupied for religious purposes. The synagogue organization was modeled on Bevis Marks Synagogue in London. Moses Cohen was elected *haham* or rabbi and Isaac Da Costa served as *hazzan* or reader. The first Parnass *Presidente* was Joseph Tobias whose descendant, Thomas Jefferson Tobias, was at the head of this historic congregation when in 1950, the two-hundredth anniversary of *Kahal Kadosh Beth Elohim* was celebrated in Charleston. Elsewhere in two centuries there was a loss of descendants of early settlers through intermarriage and conversion. Charleston Jews kept their integrity to a certain extent.

From the first, although most Carolinian Jews were merchants, there was occupational diversity among them. So one merchant, advertising a variety of goods for sale, adds that he deals also in Negroes, bonds and papers, as well as "land all o'er the State." Rice and rum, sugar and staples could be found at the business establishments of Jewish merchants. One man was an expert judge of indigo and cochineal. Moses Lindo came to Charleston from London "to purchase Indico . . . and to remit the same to his Constituents in London." So proficient did he become that he was appointed in 1762 as Surveyor and Inspector-General of indigo for the province. Not only as a public official but as a student of various dyes, Lindo gained a fine reputation. A letter of his appeared in the *Philosophical Transactions* of 1763 in which he analyzes the merits of a new dye made of a native weed. He used various chemicals with satisfactory results in the perfection of dyes. Lindo's standards were exacting. He attained a measure of financial success. He owned a ship—*The Lindo Packett*. He was instrumental also in securing a favorable clause in the admission provisions of Brown University of Rhode Island because of a contribution he made to its funds. The record of 1770 reads "Voted, That the children of Jews may be admitted into this Institution. . ." He died four years later before fulfilling

his promise of additional benefactions to that school.

A Jewish pioneer of South Carolina who captured the imagination of historians is Francis Salvador. For in him the Jews of America have a dedicated Revolutionary hero, a patriot of high courage and burning zeal. Francis Salvador came of an opulent background. His family name was Jessurun. His great-grandfather was a prosperous Amsterdam merchant. His grandfather was endenizened in London where the family prospered, he was one of a committee which sent Jews to Georgia. His two sons, Jacob and Joseph, inherited wealth and position. Jacob's son was Francis Salvador. Francis came into a very large fortune which was augmented by his marriage to his cousin, daughter of Joseph Salvador. After an educational sojourn in France, on his return to London, Francis became involved, disastrously, in a couple of business ventures which induced him to seek his fortune again, this time in South Carolina. His uncle and father-in-law had a vast tract of land there. This was later called "Jews' Lands". In 1773, Francis Salvador bought a thousand acres of Joseph Salvador's land and five thousand more acres were purchased subject to a mortgage. He settled down to the life of a gentleman-planter. By 1774 Francis Salvador was elected to the first Provincial Congress of South Carolina. He may well be the first colonial Jew to have been elected to so important a post—and by his Christian neighbors at that! He served in both the first and the second Provincial Congress. Salvador was a key member of important committees. Revolutionary measures were the business of the day and when the new constitution was completed, Salvador became, automatically, a member of the first General Assembly of the newly created State of South Carolina. Francis Salvador was killed in one of the first preliminary skirmishes of the Revolutionary War. He was the first Jew to give his life in the struggle from which was to evolve the United States of America. In a report submitted by Major Andrew Williamson to John Rutledge, President of South Carolina, dated August 4, 1776, the death of this gallant Jewish soldier is described in detail. As he lay dying on the ground, Salvador asked Williamson "whether I had beat the enemy? I told him. He said he was glad of it, and shook me by the hand—and bade me farewell—and said, he would die in a few minutes." In 1950, the Jews of South Carolina with the aid of other civic groups, placed a commemorative tablet in the City Park of Charleston honoring Francis Salvador.

VI. ASHKENAZIM AND SEPHARDIM OF GEORGIA

Poverty lay like a fog over London and many other cities of England at this time. The colonies were regarded by the mother country as a sponge for the absorption of the poor and insecure. In every way the colonies were hampered by restrictive measures, by the application of the mercantile theory of trade, by the Navigation Acts. The miser's yardstick, the accumulation of gold, was both a national and a personal objective. Debts accumulated. Prisons overflowed with unfortunates whose only crime was that they were in financial arrears. James Oglethorpe, philanthropist and member of Parliament, investigated debtors' prisons and was aroused to a crusade of moral indignation. He proposed a colony for the rehabilitation of English debtors. In this he was aided by the Society for the Propagation of the Gospel, the Bank of England and many private citizens. So a colony named for George II, forbidding slavery and the notorious rum trade, was created and the prison population was readied for the transatlantic crossing. Hospitality was the rule, except to Catholics. Among those who volunteered to collect money for the charitable enterprise were three Jews,— one of the Salvadors, grandfather of the Revolutionary War hero, DaCosta and a Baron Suasso. Now it happened that these "elite" Sephardim were concerned about the presence of German Jews, recent arrivals, in their midst. A bold plan was conceived and executed. The money was collected, twelve Ashkenazic families were assembled, a ship was chartered and they set sail for the American wilderness. Destination Georgia. This was shortly after Oglethorpe and a group of colonists had left England. Oglethorpe was not too happy about their arrival. He did, however, give them land in Savannah. Soon they were augmented by forty Portuguese Jewish settlers. There was a doctor in this group, Samuel Nunez. At least some of these men were escaping the Portuguese Inquisition. By the year 1733 Jews were at home in Georgia.

From Palace Court came a number of paper threats and communications that "the settling of Jews in Georgia will be prejudicial to the Colony." The Jews remained.

They were allowed to buy land and did. Their farms were cultivated and their vineyards became show places. The rich Portuguese Jews prospered and the poor German Jews often had to look to fellow-Germans who were Christians, for acceptance. The Reverend Bolzius wrote that they "are so honest and faithful that the like is hardly to be found . . . " It is a fact to be noted that in this era of continuing persecution by the Inquisition, refugees from the Portuguese auto-da-fé were so rigid socially. A generation later even Voltaire was constrained to protest against the auto-da-fé of September 20, 1761, crying "O God, who hast created us all . . . accomplish Thou that there be no longer on this globe, in this least of all the worlds, either fanatics or persecutors." The colonial Jews had not learned that lesson. They refused to worship in one synagogue in Georgia. While the German Jews conducted their religious services in a decrepit cabin, their Portuguese fellow-immigrants rented a house on Market Street. The petitions were addressed to the same God, only in accents that differed.

Gradually, owing to many economic reasons, there was a trickle of settlers moving out of Georgia. This was a non-sectarian exodus. Restrictions which were in effect in Georgia and not in other colonies were largely responsible. Jewish settlers moved to the Carolinas, to Pennsylvania, to New York and elsewhere. In 1741, the Trustees' Journal noted how deserted had become the area once inhabited by Jews. But nine years later many of them found their way back to Georgia. As conditions improved in the colony, group tensions subsided.

To summarize the history of Jews up to the outbreak of the Revolutionary War, one must be aware of two types of migrants, Ashkenazim and Sephardim, differing in birthplace and custom, yet subtly united by a common heritage, by knowledge of Hebrew, by their religious calendar. They came singly or in groups. Their occupations were diversified. Their energies were boundless. They owned ships and were active in shipping of goods, in the import and export business. They owned and tilled land. They were artisans and craftsmen. They owned factories and made candles and furniture and refined sugar. They baked bread and they butchered meat. They were peddlers and professional men. Among them were highly educated scholarly men and those whose learning was limited to the reading of a few Hebrew prayers. They had no fear of travel, of trading with Indians. They were found in fringe communities, at the very edge of the wilderness, as well as in the cities. Different from their Christian neighbors they must have been in countless ways. Yet they overcame their differences and interfaith partnerships, friendships and memberships in groups like the Masonic order were numerous. While they were active in establishing synagogues and acquiring cemeteries and administering *Sedaka* and supervising both group and individual activities peculiar to their own needs, we find that they were elected to office, that they entered into partnerships, that they were executors of estates and un-

dertook the education and apprenticing of Christians as well as of Jews.

So the eve of the Revolutionary War saw American Jews inexorably drawn into the conflict. Like their neighbors, they had some Tories among them. Yet withal, considering the many merchants in their ranks, it is important to note the prevalence of patriots and their adherence to the cause of the Revolution.

VII. ON THE EVE OF THE AMERICAN REVOLUTION

Glimpses into the inner life of early American Jews are found in their family letters, in postscripts to business letters, in descriptions of them by Christian diarists and travelers who visited their homes and synagogues. From a sentence or a few words much may be deduced. So an agent in the heart of the Indian country complains in a business letter to the Brothers Gratz about the suspension of business during Passover. So a friend of the Christian faith writes to one of the Sheftalls telling him to be sure to bring his special knife, else he will go hungry. Immediately the laws of *kashruth* are inferred. Masters of portraiture like Gilbert Stuart and Thomas Sully paint their portraits and their features are forever caught and their inner thoughts sometimes conveyed. We see them proud and imperious, or quietly brooding and withdrawn. Occasionally when a cache of long-forgotten or lost letters is discovered a completely new vista of life is vouchsafed.

Loneliness, isolation, desperate homesickness, the feeling of oppression which comes from being outnumbered, the yearning for contact with fellow-Jews—all of these conditions we infer or reconstruct from the fragments that have come down to us. And of those who married Christians and were lost to Judaism forever, only their tombstones are eloquent.

Nevertheless there are some personalities that emerge from the records and we make the most of them. We can recall them to life, feel their problems, rejoice at their victories, grieve when sorrow befalls them. We know not only their primary drives but also their accommodation to their immediate environment. We see them functioning within a series of concentric spheres of influence,—family, close associates in synagogue and business, contacts with the larger circle around them,—eventually some of them reach an eminence which is of national importance. Let us consider a few of these influential men.

We have noted Asser Levy who arrived in New Amsterdam penniless in 1654 and by 1660 had achieved a substantial position in his community, reaching a self-importance which caused him to sign his name Asser Levy Van Swellem. By 1664 when the need arose for defending the community from approaching British attack, Asser was among the wealthiest men in the town who were assembled to raise money for defense. In a decade he made the transition from a penniless immigrant to tycoon. Acquiring wealth, possessions, real estate, he was frequently embroiled in lawsuits involving accounts, customs, contracts, apprenticeships. He extended his operations to reach as far as Albany, later even to Connecticut. In addition to real estate and a slaughter-house, he owned a famous tavern in the neighborhood of what is now Wall Street. He argued his own cases and was called in by Christian business men to arbitrate their disputes. He was named as executor of Jewish and Christian estates. An inventory of his personal possessions includes pictures, looking-glasses, lace tablecloths, swords and pistols, a spice box and a Sabbath lamp.

Another important figure was Aaron Lopez. Although he became a respected inhabitant of Newport, a man of substance and great wealth, owner of thirty ships which carried goods to and from Europe and the West Indies and Newport, he was, like other Jews, denied the right of becoming a citizen in the colony founded by Roger Williams. He was endenizened in Massachusetts. A Portuguese crypto-Jew,

Aaron Lopez, escaped to Newport with his family. Seven years after his arrival in Newport he was chosen to lay the first cornerstone of the synagogue being built there. That was in 1759, the year in which the Newport congregation addressed itself to the sister congregation in New York, Shearith Israel: " . . . intreating you to . . . supplicate for us their charitable assistance . . . " Upon his death Ezra Stiles, famous diarist, described Lopez as

> that amiable benevolent, most hospitable and very respectable Gentleman . . . a Merchant of the first Eminence; for Honor and Extent of Commerce probably surpassed by no Mercht in America. He did Business with the greatest Ease and Clearness—always carried about with him a Sweetness of Behav. a calm Urbanity an agreeable and unaffected Politeness of Manners. Without a single Enemy and the most universally beloved by an extensive Acquaintance of any man I ever knew. His Beneficence to his Famy Connexions, to his Nation, and to all the World is almost without a Parallel.

The catalogue of outstanding men is too impressive for quick condensation. To name a man like Joseph Simon, is to be aware of a dynamic, energetic, bustling personality, an Indian trader, merchant and landowner on a vast scale. To recall the brothers Gratz is to dip into a reservoir of documents running to hundreds of thousands of transactions. The Calendar of Gratz Papers alone is a thick volume. Their erstwhile employer, David Franks, combined interests that would easily fill a volume. Hart, Sheftall, Rivera, Nunez, Salvador—names to recall and to remember.

In 1765 nine Jewish merchants signed the Non-Importation agreement protesting British mercantile policy. This was but a preliminary gesture on the part of Jews. Inexorably they were drawn into the approaching conflict. As merchants, Jews cooperated with the economic policy of the Patriots. They were bankers, victualers and provisioners for the military forces and they fought in the ranks as officers and men. One of the ways in which Jews found that they could serve their country in its fight for Independence was through privateering. Congress had legalized the capture of enemy vessels in 1775. Among Jews who were owners or part-owners of armed ships were Moses Michael Hays of Boston; Isaac Moses and Benjamin Seixas of Philadelphia; Moses Levy of Philadelphia was in partnership with Robert Morris, famous financier of the Revolution and a non-Jew. And many others. In 1776, Aaron Lopez sold a whale boat and gunpowder to his colony. The Gratz brothers too owned shares in privateers. They sustained serious losses in the Revolutionary War as did Aaron Lopez. The British raid on Newport proved disastrous. The British forces burned ships, cut down trees and orchards, destroyed 480 houses, pillaged the town's library. Jews and other residents had to flee. So the rich communal life of Newport Jewry was ended and never again came to life in the same way. They moved to Leicester and Boston in Massachusetts, to Norwalk in Connecticut and to other places. In Connecticut Jews were active in collaborating with their Christian neighbors in hunting down Tories. For there were Jewish Tories as well as Patriots. In 1776 a Petition was signed by Jacob and Abraham Pinto with one hundred other signatories. In the same year Jewish Loyalists were found among those who addressed a testimonial of loyalty to the British conquerors. Of the nearly thousand signatories, sixteen were Jews.

Too impressive for summary condensation is the record of Jews in the Revolutionary War. Jews fought in the ranks and as officers. They had their losses in dead and prisoners. Women smuggled supplies and food to the captives. There are many manuscripts attesting to their courage and devotion. Aaron Lopez sacrificed his possessions, both of ships and goods. The Pinto brothers left Yale College to enlist as soldiers. David Salisbury Franks, who served under Benedict Arnold, asked General Washington for a complete inquiry into his military record. His request was granted and his military record found to be without a blemish. He was later sent to Madrid and Paris with confidential messages from Robert Morris. But if one major figure be singled out for attention at this time, it must unquestionably be that of Haym Salomon. Haym Salomon was a Polish Jew. He was thirty-two years old when in 1772 on arriving here he opened his Broad Street office as broker and commission merchant. He joined the Sons of Liberty. He was arrested by the British and imprisoned in 1776. After his release he married Rachel Franks. After less than a year, he was reimprisoned by the British. He was charged as a spy, court-martialed, sentenced to die. In his own words, he "made his happy escape" and fled. His wife and child were perforce left behind in New York. He came to Philadelphia penniless in 1778. During the next seven years, prior to his death, he managed to become a financier of importance. Into those seven years he packed seemingly impossible activities. He was broker to the Office of Finance. He represented France, Spain, Holland in financial transactions with the new nation. Prominent names figure in his correspondence. Entries in the diary of Robert Morris attest to his sense of indebtedness to Haym Salomon. He refers to himself as "the pensioner on the favor of Haym Salomon" and writes of "the kindness of our little friend in Front Street."

The note books of Haym Salomon, happily preserved in the collections of the American Jewish Historical Society, are fascinating accounts. His personality is apprehended in little personal notes that creep in—his insistence on religious observances, his concern for his poor relatives still in Europe, his offers of help both financial and moral, his desire that his "Relations . . . learn Hebrew" as well as secular subjects—all these things reveal a man of action, compassion, humility and loyalty.

Courtesy Columbia University, New York
GERSHOM MENDEZ SEIXAS (1745-1816)

Of Mordecai Sheftall, Deputy Commissary-General of Issues for the Georgian troops, much could be written. Perhaps he can best be remembered by a simple phrase which the British used to designate Sheftall: "a very great rebel." How the Jews fought and how they died in many battles, how quickly merchants were converted into soldiers can be seen in capsule form by looking at the Jews of Charleston, then Charles Town. The Jews of that city, augmented by some who had fled from Georgia, rushed to join up. Abraham Mendez Seixas, brother of the Reverend Gershom Mendez Seixas of New York, had been a lieutenant in the Continental Line in Georgia. But on reaching Charles Town he served again as a private in Captain Lushington's Company where most of the Jews of that city served. His company was called the "Jew Company" although less than half of it were actually Jews. It numbered men like Jacob Tobias, son of the first president of Congre-

gation Beth Elohim of that city. Names like Cardozo, De Lyon, Lazarus, Alexander, Levy are also recorded. Two Jewish soldiers, mercenaries in the British Hessian troops, remained in Charleston after the War. Myer Moses was especially commended by General Sumter for his "extremely friendly and humane" treatment of both wounded and prisoners.

Taking no less a heroic part in the Revolutionary War was the patriotic rabbi of the Congregation Shearith Israel of New York. To begin with, he was the first "native son" to serve as *hazzan*.

Gershom Mendes Seixas was born in New York City in 1745, became the *hazzan* of the congregation in 1768. Of his sentiments there was no doubt from the first. Even though he prayed, on the eve of hostilities, that "Thou mayest once more plant an everlasting peace between Great Brittain and her Colonies . . ."—he pleaded with his congregation that they close the synagogue and disperse rather than remain under British rule. So it was done. Most of the congregation followed the lead of their rabbi and when the British occupied the city, its members had scattered and the Torah scrolls and ceremonial objects had also gone into exile with Rabbi Seixas. During the occupation occasional services were held at the synagogue but congregational life did not resume until his return to New York in 1784. Notable too was his postwar record. From 1803 on he served as teacher of the Polonies Talmud Torah School. As teacher and counselor, as communal leader, as rabbi, Gershom Mendes Seixas had many occasions to stress the joys of life in a free nation at a time and in an era when the Jews of many other parts of the world lived under the yoke of intolerance and prejudice. His fame as a preacher was recognized by non-Jews as when he was asked to deliver a sermon at St. Paul's Church of his city. He was said to be in attendance at the inauguration of our first President, George Washington. The fact is not borne out by the extant historical documents. For thirty years he

THE DECLARATION COMMITTEE. LEFT TO RIGHT: THOMAS JEFFERSON,
ROGER SHERMAN, BENJAMIN FRANKLIN, ROBERT R. LIVINGSTON,
JOHN ADAMS

was a trustee of Columbia College and also was elected to serve as a member of the first Board of Regents of the University of the State of New York. When he died in 1816 his record was one in which all who knew him and all who came after him, could take pride.

VIII. THE REPUBLIC IS BORN

There were titans in the land when the republic was born. The leaders had noble goals. They understood the meaning of democracy. The strength of their convictions is forever preserved in those exalted documents which are the framework of our republic. "Nothing hereditary ever existed in the country, nor will the country require or admit of any such thing," wrote John Adams in 1775. "We hold these truths to be self-evident," wrote Thomas Jefferson in

The Declaration of Independence, "that all men are created equal . . ." The Virginia Bill of Rights declared: " . . . That no man, or set of men, are entitled to exclusive or separate emoluments or priveleges from the community . . . " "It is on this system that the American government is founded. It is representation ingrafted upon democracy," wrote Thomas Paine in *The Rights of Man*. "Interwoven as is the love of liberty with every ligament of your hearts," said George Washington in his Farewell Address, "no recommendation of mine is necessary to fortify or confirm the attachment." How these words must have sounded in the ears of recent Jewish refugees from terror it is not necessary to describe. Did not the Bible urge them "To proclaim liberty throughout the land"—and were not those cherished Hebrew sentiments inscribed on the Liberty Bell? Every phrase dedicated to

LIBERTY BELL.

THE INSCRIPTION ON
THE BELL IS FROM
LEV. XXV, 10:
PROCLAIM LIBERTY
THROUGHOUT THE
LAND UNTO ALL THE
INHABITANTS
THEREOF

Courtesy National Park Service, Philadelphia

liberty and democracy found quick room in the hearts of men who had known their bitter absence.

The American Jew was integrated. He won his place within the democratic framework. The qualities that were demanded in the carving out of a new nation—courage, energy, faith—all these were not lacking. The Founding Fathers of our land were not mere names to the early American Jew. Franklin, Jefferson, Madison, Monroe were not mere abstractions. Religious freedom for which Jefferson fought and for which law in Virginia he could claim authorship, influenced the French Encyclopedists. America was more than a noble experiment. It was a noble example.

The Jews were ever vigilant in the insistence on their rights. In an address to the President and to Congress drafted by Thomas Paine on behalf of Philadelphia citizens, some ten Jewish names were among the signers. This was in July of 1783. Some months later a group of Jews petitioned the Council of Censors in behalf of Pennsylvania Jews: "The Memorial of Rabbi Ger. Seixas of the Synagogue of the Jews at Philadelphia, Simon Nathan, their Parnass

Courtesy Ewing Galloway

GEORGE WASHINGTON

Courtesy Ewing Galloway

THOMAS JEFFERSON

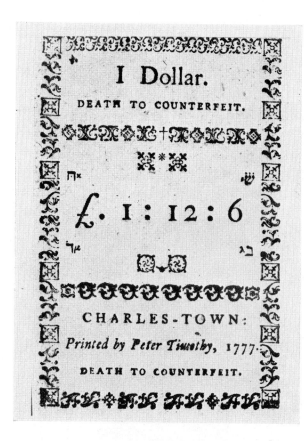
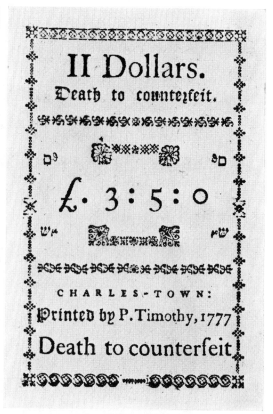

PAPER MONEY WITH HEBREW CHARACTERS—ISSUED BY SOUTH CAROLINA

or President, Asher Myers, Barnard Gratz and Haym Salomon the *Mahamad* . . . in behalf of themselves and their brethren Jews, residing in Pennsylvania"—to ask that reference to both Old and New Testament be amended, inasmuch as it excludes Jews from taking oath of office. "But certainly," they argued, "this religious test deprives the Jews of the most eminent rights of freemen . . . " The only letter sent to the Constitutional Convention in 1787 dealing with religious freedom was by a Jew, Jonas Phillips. He wrote: " . . . to swear and believe that the new testament was given by divine inspiration is absolutely against the Religious principle of a Jew . . . " This fight was carried on in Maryland and other states. There the law was not changed until 1825. North Carolina

had to wait until 1868 and a new state constitution for the removal of civil disabilities. To New Hampshire goes the dubious honor of carrying disability clauses directed against Jews and Catholics until 1876. One of the first objectives of the Board of Delegates of American Israelites formed in 1859 was to mobilize against proscriptive measures at home and abroad.

From the first the question of Jewish statistics in America has been in the realm of speculation. Individual biographies integrated in synagogal or communal affairs are easily identified. But the unattached, casual sojourner is forever lost. There are biographies the sum of whose lives are contained in a tombstone sketch giving the date of birth and the date of exit from life. The facts between are forever blotted out. A scientific study published in 1943 —*Jewish Population Studies*—by Sophia M. Robison, states:

> A great many persons believe that the extent of the Jewish population of the United States is reliably known. Some even labor under the illusion that the figures have been determined by a Federal census. This false impression is strengthened by the prevailing practice of citing precise totals rather than round numbers regarding the Jewish population of the country . . .

In a democracy only voluntary identification is possible. Under other forms of government where passports and identifications require declaration of race and nationality and religion, statistical studies flourish while freedom languishes. In America to be a Jew is not to be summarily ordered to declare himself. It is a matter of personal choice. So from the first the known Jews were the self-chosen ones. They made it possible to be counted.

At the beginning of the nineteenth century, in the first years of our Republic, it is estimated that there were about three thousand Jews in the United States.

This figure is conjectural and no more accurate than subsequent statistical summaries concerning the Jews in America. We may note trends. In the daily press, in legislative references, in petitions of Jewish groups addressed to authorities, in the formation of new congregations where none existed before—so is increase of numbers noted and a swelling census implied. An advertisement in a Philadelphia newspaper containing the announcement that Hebrew lessons were offered in Cherry Alley; a scrap of paper containing unflattering references to Jews; a broken tombstone calling attention to the demise of a Jewish patriot; a letter indicating participation by Jews in the westward movement; an exchange of letters in the press on the subject of Jews— these are the signs of population growth in the absence of reliable statistics. The time came, when it was possible for a Jew to boast that he had a large family "soberly and decently brought up. They have not been taught to revile a Christian, because his religion is not so *old* as theirs . . ." Jews may have been a minority, but it was one that dared to speak its mind. The numbers were being rapidly augmented by the increased immigration which the new century brought. So that by 1847, contemporary guessers were putting the number of Jews in America at fifty thousand. Again it is important to state that these were crude statistics, since all scientific checks were lacking. On the other hand, many immigrants were so completely anonymous that they managed to get lost. As an example one might cite the case of "le Juif, Elias Stultheus" whose record, since 1720, sank into the ooze of oblivion until this writer unearthed his history through a combination of happy circumstances and a persistent search of records.

The case "le Juif" well illustrates the "lost Jews" in American history. He was known as a Jew all of his life and still managed to disappear from history, although he played a prominent part in the development of a Mississippi Valley land project. Elias Stultheus was the chief director of a vast land colonization project conceived by John Law which was to become known as the Mississippi Bubble. It was known as "the most stupendous financial fabric that has ever been presented to the world." Briefly, it was a vast colonization project involving the lands at the mouth of the Mississippi River and the Arkansas River, extending about forty miles up the Mississippi on both banks. Several thousand immigrants were brought over on seven ships *"tant François qu'Allemands et Juifs."* The project failed, the immigrants were scattered, their identity forever lost. So much for "statistics."

Two significant factors may be noted with the advent of the nineteenth century. The number of native-born American Jews is markedly on the increase. Also Jewish religion in America subtly undergoes a process of psychological adaptation to the

To the Hebrew Congregation in Newport
Rhode Island.

Gentlemen.

While I receive, with much satisfaction, your Address replete with expressions of affection and esteem; I rejoice in the opportunity of assuring you, that I shall always retain a grateful remembrance of the cordial welcome I experienced in my visit to Newport, from all classes of Citizens.

The reflection on the days of difficulty and danger which are past is rendered the more sweet, from a consciousness that they are succeeded by days of uncommon prosperity and security. If we have wisdom to make the best use of the advantages with which we are now favored, we cannot fail, under the just administration of a good Government, to become a great and a happy people.

The Citizens of the United States of America have a right to applaud themselves for having given to mankind examples of an enlarged and liberal policy: a policy worthy of imitation. All possess alike liberty of conscience and immunities of citizenship. It is now no more that toleration is spoken of, as if it was by the indulgence of one class of people, that another enjoyed the exercise of their inherent natural rights. For happily

the

the Government of the United States, which gives to bigotry no sanction, to persecution no assistance requires only that they who live under its protection should demean themselves as good citizens, in giving it on all occasions their effectual support.

It would be inconsistent with the frankness of my character not to avow that I am pleased with your favorable opinion of my administration, and fervent wishes for my felicity. May the children of the Stock of Abraham, who dwell in this land, continue to merit and enjoy the good will of the other Inhabitants; while every one shall sit in safety under his own vine and figtree, and there shall be none to make him afraid. May the father of all mercies scatter light and not darkness in our paths, and make us all in our several vocations useful here, and in his own due time and way everlastingly happy.

G. Washington

GEORGE WASHINGTON'S LETTER TO THE HEBREW CONGREGATION
OF NEWPORT

new environment. Even in the eighteenth century the foundation for change was laid by that zealous patriot, Isaac Pinto. In 1766 there appeared English translations of the prayers used by Spanish and Portuguese Jews.

Issac Pinto was frank in stating that he prepared these translations to aid his co-religionists in their devotions. Could it be that already he had detected a diminishing knowledge of Hebrew among the Ya-hidim—as the Sephardim were called? No other answer is possible. As one generation of native-born Jews gave way to another, changes were introduced affecting both usage of Hebrew and ceremonial practices. So in Charleston, Solomon Harby was fined twenty pounds by the Elders of Beth El-ohim for an unspecified offence, probably an evasion of synagogue duties. His famous son, Isaac Harby, was educated in Charleston in the best liberal tradition. He became a famous journalist and teacher, mingling freely with the Christians of his city. He was one of the moving spirits of the "Re-formed Society of Israelites" which was the first organized group in America dedicated to changing the practices and ritual of Judaism in America. "America is the land of promise," said Harby in his famous "Discourse on the Jewish Synagogue." He interpreted the "promise" in terms of change. It was this tendency toward secu-larization that Isaac Leeser was to fight so bitterly. It was this movement toward con-formity with their Christian environment that Isaac M. Wise was to decry vehe-mently: "there were Episcopal Jews in New York, Quaker Jews in Philadelphia, Huguenot Jews in Charleston . . . every-where according to the prevailing sect." And Leeser who differed radically with Wise on so many issues was in agreement on this one, deploring the fact that Jews in America were seeking a way of life and religion "which is to be acceptable to gen-tiles." As their numbers increased, so did their accommodation to prevailing customs in America.

Changing too was the economic pattern of Jewish life in America. While the earliest settlers often were poor, their educational background, social presence, adaptability and ease of carrying on financial opera-tions were marked from the first. They were not strangers to agriculture. Their plantations were among the most thriving in Brazil. They were vintners in Georgia and had large estates in South Carolina, Pennsylvania and New York and other colonies. They were ship-owners and im-porters and exporters. They were brokers, often with London training. They owned factories and foundries and shops. In New-port alone, the Jewish community was a significant factor in the sperm oil industry which Jacob Rivera introduced in America. They made candles and rope and furni-ture, as well as soap. In other places they owned distilleries. They traded with In-dians, made ornamental silver objects, as well as perukes. They mined gold and bought and sold land. They raised tobacco and sold it. They practiced law and medi-cine. They were elected and appointed to important posts, serving as translators and advisers and negotiators. They owned schools and seminaries and contributed to local and national papers. But with in-creased migration there came marked changes. Poverty was more prevalent. Hawkers and walkers, peddlers carrying their merchandise on their backs, eking out a bare and meager living, became more common in the land. Laborers and appren-tices huddled in inadequate dwellings in seaboard cities. Factory workers began their sweatshop sagas. "Young ladies" in their teens were advertised for in the local papers. Opportunities were more re-stricted. And the immigrant felt the yawn-ing gap of "social distance" between him-self and his native-born employer. It is not surprising to find that an American Jew speaking before the House of Representa-tives on Naturalization Laws in the year 1845 can suddenly identify himself with "Nativist" sentiments. In the words of a demagogue, Lewis C. Levin states: "As Native Americans, we desire to erect additional bulwarks for the protection of American institutions from foreign influence . . . " and again: "Is our constitution placed above the danger of subversion by the influx of that horde of aliens, who combine to break down its barriers, that they may command in the citadel, or overrun the land?" Also "No alien has a right to naturalization," thundered this nineteenth century rabble-rouser. Fortunately there were other voices among Jews and they were on the side of "the huddled masses yearning to breathe free."

It is a fact not to be overlooked or minimized that with increasing numbers, the Jews in America developed separationist tendencies based on European geographic origins or economic stability. The old clichés and bromides about the exclusiveness of Sephardim and their unwillingness to mingle with Ashkenazim will have to be revised. For the records of our earliest communities from Shearith Israel down, show that German and Polish Jews were not as repugnant to the Yahidim as were East European Jews to the descendants of German-Jewish peddlers who had attained the dignity of an address and a non-movable store a century later. The favorite son-in-law of Gershom Mendes Seixas was Israel Baer Kursheedt of Germany who came to the United States in 1796.

Numbers swelled. Pressure of proscriptive marriage laws in Europe, economic and educational barriers left only one channel of escape—migration. So entire families, often even groups of families, made the westward journey. In a provocative study titled *In Search of Freedom,* Guido Kisch traces the impact of America, almost from the time of discovery, upon the residents of the Prague Jewish community. At first arousing interest as a subject for intellectual speculation and even fantasy, America gradually loomed large as a means of escape. The Thirty Years' War which began in 1618 initiated a troubled era for the Jews of Prague which saw its culmination in their expulsion from Prague in 1745. It took more than a century, however, for Bohemian Jews to begin their migrations in anything like significant numbers. In 1848 anti-Jewish riots broke out in Prague. In that crucial year Leopold Kompert wrote his plea titled "On to America". This theme with variations in other times and places was to become the theme song of oppressed European Jews.

Nor were the Jews of America unaware of impending tragedy in Europe. They had rallied in horror at the Damascus Blood Libel which sought to fasten upon the Jews the most repugnant and malicious of lies that Jews killed Christians for ritual purposes. This monstrous accusation which festered in ignorant minds at Passover time has cost the Jews untold misery and loss of life in pogroms. To the deluge of protests issued from London and Paris and other aroused communities, the Jews of New York added their voices. But our State Department which has followed a noble policy again and again in the interest of humanity had antedated the New York Jews' protest and had declared a week earlier that " . . . the President has learned with profound feelings of surprise and pain, the atrocious cruelties which have been practiced on the Jews of Damascus . . . " Committees to foster emigration were active in many cities. America was enriched by the Brandeis, Busch, Felsenthal and many other noted families whose eyes were fixed on the Western hemisphere whence would come their deliverance.

Men of substance might plan an ordered and considered campaign of emigration sending emissaries on ahead to survey the situation. But there were also those who were driven in haste, who had neither family nor friends to uphold them, who faced poverty, ill health, economic exploitation and abysmal, unmitigated, stark loneliness. Unfortunately such men do not engage in a voluminous correspondence, keep no diaries recording their thoughts and activities. We can only glimpse an occasional note of black despair from a newspaper clipping (one such can be found in Schappes) which tells the sorry narrative and the bitter end of one unhappy life. The New York *Sun* for May 7, 1849 carried the story of a Jewish carpenter named Marcus Cohen, who "in a fit of desperation on account of pecuniary embarrassments . . . with a hair trigger pistol terminated his existence." There were other desperates who barely survived. It is little wonder that from the first mutual assistance was an important branch of synagogue activity. *Obras pias* are prominently noted in the records of Shearith Israel and other congregations. Indeed Jewish group life has certain marked patterns of activity. A place to worship. A place to bury the dead. Committees or benevolent societies to administer charity, to care for the widow and orphan, the poor and the sick. There were funds for the providing of dowries for young brides and funds for the dispatching of beggars to other places.

Groups which Rabbi Pool describes in *Portraits Etched in Stone* as the "Dispensers of Kindness" so named for the Society for Dispensing Kindness to the Dead, developed into Mutual Aid societies which were influenced by similar groups in existence in the Christian society which surrounded them. Formation of other synagogues led to variants of this type of assistance group. One such group, described by Grinstein in his *The Rise of the Jewish Community in New York* was formed in 1826 and became known as the Hebrew Mutual Benefit Society. Here financial allowances were made in time of sickness. Such benefits were limited to its own members however. Soon other groups were added, doing business under such high-sounding names as the Society of Brotherly Love, the New York Assistance Society for Widows and Orphans, the Society Gates of Hope, the Montefiore Society. Loan funds were created to be used by worthy applicants. As early as 1813 the building of a poor-house for Jews was proposed. "In 1822," writes Grinstein, "Ashkenazic immigrant members of Shearith Israel formed

the celebrated Hebrew Benevolent Society." Straws in the wind! All of these organizations are eloquent proof of the presence of impoverished Jews in every period of American history. In Philadelphia, the beautiful Rebecca Gratz became noted for her "good works." Not only is she credited with founding the Hebrew Sunday School of Philadelphia in 1838, which was the oldest institution of its kind in the country, but she was also a founder of the Female Hebrew Benevolent Society, the Jewish Foster Home, the Fuel Society and the Sewing Society. She also aided in the work of communal, non-sectarian philanthropies. Among them were the Philadelphia Orphan Asylum and the Widows' Asylum.

In other cities, the same pattern is discernible. In Charleston, to give but one more example, the Hebrew Benevolent Society dating from 1784 was founded for the avowed purpose of assisting sick immigrants. They nursed the sick, fed the hungry, buried the dead, made clothing for the indigent. By the year 1801 there was an apparent need for the Hebrew Orphan Society. The purpose was high-minded. The trustees were on the alert for signs of exceptional ability in their charges or special aptitudes in the arts and sciences. Children were at first boarded in foster homes. This practice was due both to the lack of orphans and lack of an orphanage. But the condition was remedied by 1860, at which time they had a home.

All of these philanthropic activities did not preclude membership in non-sectarian groups. Many instances of active participation in communal philanthropies have come down to us. Rebecca Gratz was Secretary of the Female Association for the Relief of Women and Children in Reduced Circumstances. In Georgia as early as 1750, a member of the Sheftall family was one of the five founders of the Union Society; the other founders being three Protestants and one Catholic. In one way or another the presence of "a very great number of our nation, in very indigent circumstances" is revealed. Appeals for funds were frequent. Through wills and bequests, through circulating appeals, through minutes of Benevolent Societies, the impact of crushing poverty is made clear. Food, fuel and clothing were disbursed. Money was distributed only "under special circumstances of the applicant." No use coddling beggars! There was charity. But little compassion was evinced.

When the fraternal order of B'nai B'rith was organized in 1843, it was stated as one of its avowed purposes that "alleviating the wants of the poor and needy" was high on its agenda. "Inculcating the purest principles of philanthropy" was another of the objectives of this group. In the same year, in a report of the Society for the Education of Poor Children and Relief of Indigent Persons of the Jewish Persuasion, it was stated that they were overwhelmed by the conditions under which some Jews were compelled to live and work. Housing was worse than inadequate. Crowding was appalling. Many "charitable females" were restrained from visiting the poor because of the wretched conditions in which indigent Jews found themselves. The report reads:

> ...come with us and visit the abode of the poor—see them with their baskets but poorly furnished with a few articles, whereby they can realize a few paltry cents. Follow them a day, through all kinds of weather, and watch their return at night, exhausted ... look at their rooms, bare and unfurnished, without fuel, their children without clothing ...

All this was five years before 1848, a year when acceleration of immigration was to begin in earnest. It was a preview of things to come.

IX. MORDECAI MANUEL NOAH

Ease of communication with neighbors because there were no linguistic barriers, relative economic stability because the ups and downs had been weathered by their immigrant ancestors, increasing participa-

JUDAH TOURO (1775-1854)

tion in local and national affairs, psychological integration—these were but a few advantages enjoyed by native-born Jews over their immigrant coreligionists. If we look at some of them their position becomes obvious. There was Judah Touro who was born in Newport in 1775, who became a highly successful merchant and philanthropist. His name is to this day much respected in the city of his benefactions, New Orleans. Rebecca Gratz who was born in Philadelphia in 1781 has already been mentioned for her philanthropies.

Another Philadelphia-born Jew was Mordecai Manuel Noah whose birthdate is 1785. His family had been associated with South Carolina from 1750 on. His father was a Patriot. His mother was Zipporah Phillips, daughter of a Philadelphia Patriot. By 1811 Noah was well-enough known to be offered the post of United States Consul to Riga, Russia. This he declined, but he did accept the position of Consul to Tunis with a special mission to

Courtesy Moshe Davis

MORDECAI MANUEL NOAH (1785-1851)

Algiers. He took a vigorous stand against Moroccan pirates and succeeded in rescuing several Americans who were held as slaves in the Barbary States. Recalled by Monroe, he was received with open arms by Tammany in New York. He became an active journalist and either founded or edited a number of newspapers of a proslavery tinge. He wrote plays, some of which were very successful.

Noah was influenced by the post-Revolutionary ideologies, those nurtured in France and at the time of the birth of the United States of America. What he saw and learned about the conditions of Jews in Europe and Africa, galvanized him into action. "My faith does not rest wholly in miracles," he declared. He was a man of tremendous vitality and energy. He evolved a bold plan to solve the Jewish problem. The ultimate solution, he felt, was resettlement in Palestine. But first two steps had to be taken. An immediate refuge had to be found for persecuted Jews. An agricultural training colony was to be set up where future Palestinian colonists would be trained to agrarian pursuits. His plans

were known as early as 1820. John Quincy Adams wrote in his diary in that year that Noah had plans to colonize Jews in the United States and that he wished to be appointed Chargé d'Affaires in Vienna to further his undertaking. Next the legislature of the State of New York received a petition from Noah for a grant of land on Grand Island. Although reported on favorably by the legislative committee which considered the petition, the measure did not pass.

Five years were to go by without Noah's relinquishing his program for his colonization project. Troubles piled up at home. Noah outrode them. He became enamored of the theory that the American Indians were the Ten Lost Tribes of Israel. This idea was a source of unclouded pleasure to our protagonist. He soon convinced himself and tried to convince others that they need entertain no doubts on the subject. But his dearest daydream was ever the colonization project. He was to be the redeemer of his oppressed brethren, leader on a grand scale, an incomparable hero like unto the Prophets and Judges of ancient days. His fantasy was Biblical in orientation. It was both sublime and ludicrous. When in 1825 Grand Island was opened for settlement, Noah persuaded a friend, Samuel Leggett, to buy 2,500 acres of land to serve as a beginning for a Jewish city which was eventually to include the entire island.

This Jewish Don Quixote had his Sancho Panza, a single follower, named A. B. Seixas of New York. At ten o'clock on the morning of September 2, 1825, a parade was formed. In its midst was Noah, "the Judge of Israel," dressed in sumptuous robes. His escort garbed in Masonic and military accouterments, fringed by a crowd of curious onlookers, made his way to the Episcopal Church which had tendered its building for the occasion. To the strains of *Judas Maccabeus* they took their places. Noah delivered an imposing oration in his role as "Governor and Judge of Israel." His "Proclamation to the Jews" offered them asylum, peace, comfort and happiness. The city of refuge was to be called Ararat.

On a gray stone slab, now in the basement of the Buffalo Historical Society, there is the following inscription:

ARARAT
A City of Refuge for the Jews
Founded by Mordecai Manuel Noah
in the month of Tizri
Sept. 1825 & in the 50th year of
American Independence

The project failed. The dream remained. The name of Mordecai Manuel Noah is now beloved in Israel and his "prophecies" then seemingly ridiculous, strangely contain a predictive pattern of events he had once dimly foreseen. Some of these "prophetic" utterances have been realized.

There were others, and their biographies are available, who because they did not undergo the traumatic experience of persecution and transplantation, flowered on their native American soil. In many instances their identification with the local folkways and *mores* was so great as to make them outwardly indistinguishable from their Christian neighbors. Yet they kept their faith. Many American Jews did not marry because the very thought of intermarriage implied assimilation and ultimate obliteration. In social usage they conformed. Inwardly they were steadfast.

What of those lost to us? All things considered, one is aware of the continual trickle of lost souls who in one way or another were intent on anonymity. Through occasional conversion, through more frequent intermarriage, through separation by change of name or geographic isolation, Jewish ranks in America were being depleted. So today many of the descendants of our "first" families are lost in the limbo of the forgotten ones. So we cherish those who remain to us and salute those who spent their lives as celibates because they were Jews.

Bleak and lonely was the life of one such person and she may serve as an example.

Her name was Penina Moïse. She was born in Charleston in 1797 and died there in 1880. Her mouldering tombstone in the old cemetery records merely her name and her life's major accomplishment, that she died in her eighty-third year. The years between were packed with poignant experiences and the sum of her days was the arithmetic of desolation and sadness. "I have always lived in the shadow," she said on her deathbed and across the years the words become a dirge.

Here was a woman whose hymns were more prolific and more used in temples and synagogues than any other writer's, a dedicated Jewess who was adamant in her stand against intermarriage, to whom religious experience was a vital part of her life, yet she has been consigned for some strange reason to oblivion and is so little known today that when her name is spoken aloud, the average American Jew responds without recognition or recall. She deserves better of American Jewry.

When she was twelve Penina lost her father. It was a great emotional blow. It was an economic disaster to the family. There were twelve orphaned children. Penina became a breadwinner before she was in her teens. Like other women of her day, she took to lace-making. She was an avid reader and her education went on through intensive study and reading. It was but a step from self-education to self-expression. She began to write poetry and soon her name was known not only in her native Charleston but in other places as well. The *Charleston Courier,* the *Boston Daily Times, Godey's Lady's Book,* the *Occident* listed her as contributor. As her fame spread she began to hold a *salon* in her home on Friday afternoons. She wrote on many subjects. But she was at her best when she responded to the Jewish motif. Her religious fervor was deep and abiding. She was asked by her Christian friends for poems which marked the passing of a bishop, the building of a cathedral.

Penina Moïse became blind. Yet despite her blindness she conducted a successful girls' school and gave oral lessons. Her students read aloud to her from the works of George Eliot, Charlotte Brontë, Sir Walter Scott and many others. At heart she was an "unreconstructed rebel"— Southern in sympathy from first to last. Like other Jews her sentiments reflected her geographic environment. But she is best remembered for her poems on Jewish subjects. "The Jews of Damascus" were her kin and the disinherited and oppressed and disfranchised Jews in every section of the world were near and dear to Penina Moïse.

She had exhorted herself and others in stern words:

Pilgrim! Thy house in order set!
Thy soul for sudden change prepare,
Ere thou, to cancel nature's debt,
Art forced into an unknown sphere.

Soon on Coming Street in the city of Charleston, the Jews of that city will meet in reverence at the old Jewish cemetery and mark the grave of Penina Moïse with a monument more worthy of her role. But will the living remember? Will they read her verses, feel her sorrows, applaud her moral grandeur?

X. ECONOMIC RISE OF IMMIGRANTS

Now let us look at the other side of the coin. Let us meet a few of those men and women who despite their handicap of birth and language rose to positions of eminence. For just as one may characterize this period from the founding of the nation to the close of the Civil War as a time when native sons and daughters made their mark, so we are challenged by the fact that the great leaders in the field of religion and journalism numbered many immigrants. Jews were arriving in steadily increasing numbers. They came largely as urban people, changing one urban setting for another. It was in European cities that the news of America and its opportunities was discussed. And it was from the crowded and poverty-ridden areas that most of the

recruits for immigration were obtained. In 1819 there was circulated in London a pamphlet written by a Christian, W. D. Robinson, titled "Memoir Addressed to Persons of the Jewish Religion in Europe, on the Subject of Emigration to, and Settlement in, One of the Most Eligible Parts of the United States of North America." The settlement proposed was in the Upper Mississippi and Missouri regions,—areas that have since become prosperous states. "If," says Robinson, "a Jewish settlement should be established in the United States . . . it does not require the gift of prophecy to foresee the result. In a very few years such a settlement would become known to the Jews in every quarter of the globe, and we should find thousands flocking to it . . ." No such grandiose plan resulted in mass migration and agricultural settlements had to wait for later years to be recorded. We do not know why "the sparrows of the London streets"—to use a phrase of Stephen Vincent Benét—failed to follow the Western star. We can only record the failure. Nor was this the only appeal that failed to bring results. We know of Noah's. Later in the pages of the *Occident* a similar plea was to be made. What the reasons were belongs in the realm of speculation. Were the Jews waiting for a Divine deliverer? For a miracle? Or did these pleas fail to penetrate the murk and darkness which enveloped them in the narrow streets of the ghettos of Europe? Did centuries of urban life adjacent to their synagogues make them look askance at the vast prairies of America? Did separation from the soil and agricultural pursuits in their centuries of crowding and wandering make an insuperable barrier? They came—and lodged in cities under conditions that were appalling, almost unbearable, spent themselves in relentless labor in the hope that their children might find a place in the sun.

They brought their leaders with them. And it was from one of them that another colonization attempt was to come. The immigrant we speak of originally came from Sweden. The Reverend Dr. Morris Jacob Raphall, to give him his full title, was born in 1798 and so he was a contemporary of the "native sons and daughters" like Noah, Gratz, Moïse, Touro. He studied at a Jewish School in Copenhagen, then in 1812 was sent to England where he continued his secular studies. He traveled through Europe, studied in Germany, returned to England where he married and where his scholarship and literary ability brought him a measure of fame among English Jews. In 1841 he was called to serve as rabbi to the Jewish community of Birmingham in England. In 1849 he joined the growing stream of Jewish immigrants on their way to America and became Rabbi of Bnai Jeshurun of New York. Just three years after his arrival in New York, Raphall became interested in a colonization plan for Jews. He met Simon Berman, a colonization zealot, and was favorably impressed by his plans for land settlement. A meeting was held at Raphall's home where a plan was presented for the selling of stock at $25 per share. Prominent Jews like Isaac Leeser were deeply interested. But the plan failed as did all the others and Berman gave up his dream of Jewish colonization. It died hard. For next, a scant three years later, under the auspices of the B'nai B'rith, "A Call to Establish a Hebrew Agricultural Society" went forth. Sigismund Waterman was its author. Among the signers was a gentleman called Henry American. The elaborate plan to give the immigrants "a comparatively happy living and to wean them from beggary and from becoming a burden to our charitable institutions," was to collapse like other plans. Nevertheless it gives us a glimpse of what immigrant leaders were thinking.

One who knew Dr. Raphall, Henry Samuel Morais, describes his "comely and venerable appearance." He was an orator of note and much in demand. His literary labors were indefatigable. He wrote a two-volume Post-Biblical History of the Jews. He compiled "Devotional Exercises for the Daughters of Israel." He was the author of "The Path to Immortality." Despite his earliest association with his native Sweden, despite his years of residence in England where slavery was both unknown and unpopular—this learned and well-intentioned leader of his people came out with the full force of argument and eloquence (he was "one of the most celebrated orators in the American rabbinate of his time," says Korn)—for slavery and against abolitionism. "How dare you," he thundered, "denounce slavery as a sin?" and mustered Biblical citations to bolster his stand. His sermon "The Bible View of Slavery" was widely circulated and much praised in the South. We know that such views were repugnant to most Northern Jews. The most heated reply came from another immigrant, a Polish Jew, Michael Heilprin, who was "outraged" by Raphall's stand and his "sacrilegious words."

Yet Raphall's services to his congregation went on. He made a wartime journey to Washington to ask Lincoln to promote his son from a second to a first lieutenancy, a request which the President granted without hesitation.

The life of Rabbi Raphall dramatically calls attention to one of the burning issues of the time, an issue which was to split the country, to cause a civil war, to leave lasting scars many of which persist to this day. Before continuing the analysis of the Jewish leaders and their contribution to the problems of their day, it is well to summarize briefly the pre-war years, the time of accelerated migration. Then to indicate how some of their leaders faced the numerous problems—psychological, emotional, economic, that confronted their generation.

Much had happened since the day in 1775 when Ethan Allen and his Green Mountain Boys stormed Fort Ticonderoga and ordered the British garrison to surrender "in the name of the Great Jehovah and the Continental Congress." Two wars were won. Gradually the population of the Atlantic seaboard was pushing westward. We have noted that Jews were land speculators

Courtesy American Jewish Historical
Society and Frick Art Reference Library

JACOB FRANKS (1688-1769), COLONIAL MER-
CHANT-SHIPPER, PRESIDENT OF THE
SHEARITH ISRAEL CONGREGATION
(1730)

and played a part in developing trade with the Indians in river-born and overland commerce. Now Jews too were a part of the tide of settlers that left behind the "crowded" seaboard. Peddlers, fur traders, Indian traders, real estate promoters were within their ranks. In 1786 Aaron Levy conducted a lottery to sell land in his town in Pennsylvania—*Aaronsburgh,* whose two main intersections were named "Aaron's Square" and "Rachel's Way." David Salisbury Franks was connected with the Scioto Company, an unsuccessful project for settlement in the Ohio Valley. There was a Jacob Franks in Green Bay in 1794 and Jews are found in Canada, in northern Wisconsin and Michigan. Michael and Barnard Gratz were among the owners of a tract of 321,000 acres of land drained by the tributaries of the Ohio River. In

October of 1816, Joseph Jonas of Plymouth, England, came to America and in March of 1817 settled in Cincinnati. In his own words "for a while solitude was his portion." He writes of his happiness when another Jewish settler, David Israel Johnson, also of Plymouth, England, paused briefly in Cincinnati on his way to Indiana. He describes his delight at the addition of members of his family and a few other Jewish settlers. Adding "and now were our hearts rejoiced, for the prospects of a permanent congregation were near at hand." B'ne Israel was organized in 1824. In a letter written the following year we read "It is worthy of remark that there is not a congregation within 500 miles of this city. . . "

And far to the south, a Jewish promoter, Moses Elias Levy, was buying up vast tracts of land in Florida. One of his acquisitions embraced 36,000 acres of land, some of it bought while Spain still owned it. Settlers were being brought to Florida at Levy's expense. By 1823 fifty people were settled there.

So Jews were a part of the inexorable growth of the land. Yet in numbers the group was small. In 1818 Noah estimated the Jewish population of the United States at about 3,000. In 1826 Isaac Harby placed the number at 6,000. The *American Almanach* of 1840 estimated Jews at 15,000. By 1848, a published history numbered American Jews at 50,000. Israel Joseph Benjamin who wrote *Drei Jahre in America* noted that Bavarian marriage laws were responsible for the coming of Jewish immigrants from 1836 on. A non-Jewish observer, Gerstaeker, who traveled extensively in the United States in 1837 met Jews everywhere —in lonely outposts on the Wabash River, on the Ohio and Mississippi. He bought clothing from German Jews in New Orleans. Another Christian author, ten years later, wrote that Jews in America numbered fifty thousand, that they were found largely in cities, that they were as good citizens as the Christians and added " . . . *der Yankee sei selbst dem Juden zu Jüdisch im Handel und Religion . . .*" A Jewish poet surveying the situation in a poem titled "Ein traurieges Lied" called upon his readers to come to America:

Dort wohnt kein Vorurtheil,
   kein Hass, kein Neid,
Kein Henker weilet dort
   und kein Tyrann!

(Neither prejudice, nor hate, nor poverty is to be found there, no executioner dwells there, and no tyrant.)

So they came, the unknown and illustrious. Honored names among them—Max Lilienthal, Abraham Bettman, a pioneer Cincinnati physician. Religious leaders like Bernhard Felsenthal, Isaac M. Wise, Liebmann Adler, Isaac Leeser, David Einhorn, Samuel Myer Isaacs—and many others. Came and brought their talents and laid them freely before the Jews of America. Felsenthal was born in Germany. Isaac M. Wise was a native of Bohemia. Liebmann Adler was of German birth. Isaac Leeser came from Prussia. David Einhorn from Bavaria. S. M. Isaacs first saw light of day in Friesland, Holland. We have already noted that Raphall came from Sweden. One of the most noted immigrants from England was Robert Lyon. He was one of a very small group of men whose contribution lay in the field of journalism.

XI. AMERICAN JEWS ON THE ISSUE OF SLAVERY VERSUS ABOLITION

The American Jewish scene was not characterized by homogeneity. There were many issues to divide and inflame them. The immigrants took sides.

The secure versus the insecure. The Dispensers of Kindness versus the Recipients of Charity. Assimilation and gradual disappearance as against cultural pluralism and personal integrity. Urban concentration as against colonization and agricultural pursuits. Slavery as opposed to abolition.

On some points native and foreign-born Jews were in agreement. They were united in resenting all attacks upon Jews, at home

Courtesy American Jewish Historical Society and Frick Art Reference Library

MOSES LEVY (ca. 1665-1728), PRESIDENT OF THE NEW YORK JEWISH COMMUNITY (1728)

or abroad. All political and civil discrimination aroused them.

By and large the home life of Jews had much to distinguish it from that of their neighbors. Even in the outposts, there was the Sabbath bringing its dignified and reverent pause in the week's occupation. Often when distance from a synagogue made religious services impossible, a room in one's home served as a substitute. There the family would gather, augmented by a neighbor's family and any visiting or traveling Jew. There prayers would be read and the portion of the Torah chanted. The women living in these lonely areas transformed their homes into sanctuaries. In the cities, observance was easier and the acceptance of the Sabbath ritual and its sanctification a weekly phenomenon. Countless writers of all faiths have testified to the sense of immigrant unity, the closeness of parents and children. Whatever the sense of isolation and cultural difference which existed outside the home, all that constituted the phenomenon of "social distance" from one's Christian neighbors fell away when the individual returned home to his own. The host culture of the circumferent community had its own customs and holidays and calendar rhythms. The Jews, especially in the ranks of the immigrants, held to their own. Physicians and social workers who worked in the developing urban communities, where crowding and poverty and lack of sanitation bred disease, have commented on the relative freedom from epidemic diseases in Jewish homes.

Periodic housecleanings, the pre-Sabbath scrubbing, cleaning and bathing, insured a measure of cleanliness which aided health. Psychologically the Friday evening ritual served to transform the poor, awkward immigrant into an honored patriarch. Saturday synagogue attendance continued this health-giving pause. It was a salutary change from the long, degrading days of overwork and exposure to taunts, insults, or even simple misunderstanding because of the language barrier. Besides, the synagogue served as a forum where worshippers, after the prayers were over, could talk about their common problems. Both group and individual benefited. So in 1805 aroused members of the Congregation Shearith Israel sued Caleb Vandenburg for falsely affixing a seal on meat which resembled one that the Jews of New York used as a symbol of *kashruth*. Eleven years later a Pennsylvania Jew, as spokesman for other Jews as well as for himself, won exemption from the Sunday statute. In 1834, on her visit to America, Harriet Martineau was so impressed by the rights Jews had won in the United States that on her return to England, she joined in a campaign to secure them similar rights. Many of these rights were first dreamed of and then discussed in the journeyings to and from the synagogue by pious Jews.

So the synagogue was an umbrella under which Jews took shelter to meet their religious needs, to give them companionship, to assure their survival, to enforce Jewish customs and rituals, to fortify their morale. It is little to be wondered at, therefore, that the rabbis became the spokesmen for their adherents on matters religious and secular. The sermons dealt with many aspects of daily living. Often these sermons found their way into print where they were read and quoted. So Rabbi Felsenthal's *Juden und die Sclaverei* called attention to the fact that the majority of the Jews of America were antislavery. Of course, there were more Jews in the North than in the South and geographic location was largely the determining factor in a man's belief. Raphall in his sermons could twist Biblical meaning to proslavery ends. The synagogue served as a meetingplace when the Jews of New York gathered to see how they could help the Irish during the potato famine. In the course of his remarks Reverend Jacques Judah Lyons said that "sadness and gloom pervade the land . . . Aid and assistance to an unhappy Ireland—raiment, food and *life* itself to her destitute people are now invoked at your hands . . . " He ended by insisting that "the sufferings of our fellow-men, wheresoever and howsoever situated, demand from us alleviation, assistance and relief . . . " So much did pulpit sermons come to be in demand that the gifted Max Lilienthal circulated among three synagogues, preaching in rotation once every three weeks. Although in the earlier years the sermons were considered of secondary importance and placed at the conclusion of the services to permit those who chose to leave at the conclusion of prayers, gradually the sermon achieved greater importance. For many years, the rabbi's discourse was classified as a "lecture" rather than as a sermon. But no matter where it was placed nor what importance was attached to the lecture-sermon, the pulpit offered an excellent opportunity for the propagation of ideas. Courageous men took advantage of it. David Einhorn had to flee from an angry mob because he spoke against slavery. Bernhard Felsenthal carried on the campaign

Courtesy The Jewish Theological Seminary of America

SABATO MORAIS (1823-1897), ONE OF THE FOUNDERS OF CONSERVATIVE JUDAISM

for abolition at every opportunity. Sabato Morais delivered burning denunciations against slavery. A contemporary describing the influence of the Reverend S. M. Isaacs states that "the weekly sermons of Mr. Isaacs aroused the lethargic spirit of the community, and greatly added to the number of attendants at his Synagogue."

It was within the orbit of the synagogue that the Board of Delegates of American Israelites germinated. Leeser, Raphall, S. M. Isaacs were among the organizers of this group. For a generation, from 1859 to 1878, this group maintained a vigilant watch over all matters concerning the Jews. Although the Board of Delegates was organized primarily as a fact-finding body, it had an emotional appeal that acted as the catalytic agent. A little Italian Jewish boy, Edgar Mortara, was taken by a Catholic nursemaid to a church of her own faith and there baptized. With the knowl-

edge of the Pope the child was taken away from his parents. The case shocked not only Jews the world over, but Christians in every land. A French Catholic clergyman published a pamphlet disagreeing with the Pope. When a delegation of Philadelphia Jews called on President Buchanan, however, he refused to intervene. The Jewish press was indefatigable in urging American intervention. Isaac Leeser who had headed the Washington delegation kept his readers informed of developments in the pages of the *Occident*. Isaac M. Wise did likewise in his *Israelite*. So did S. M. Isaacs in *The Jewish Messenger*. The Reverend Sabato Morais of Philadelphia stated that he would not pray for a government that refused to intervene or take a stand against such an outrage. In the city of New York, Jews were joined by Protestants in an indignation meeting which numbered two thousand people.

Edgar Mortara was lost to his parents. That tragic loss united Jews of France, of England, of the United States, into a solid front determined to be on the alert against all such threats to Jews everywhere.

It was fortunate that, thanks to their European-born leaders, the Jews of America had a number of publications that kept them informed. As early as 1823 when *The Jew* began its two-year existence under the editorship of English-born Solomon H. Jackson, the need for a paper serving American Jews was obvious. Although married to the daughter of a Presbyterian minister, his five children were brought up in the Jewish faith. One of his daughters even brought a convert to Judaism when she married Dr. Peter Donovan who became a Jew. Another short-lived effort, *Israel's Herold,* was begun by a Bohemian Jew, Isidor Busch, later spelled Bush. Shortly after his arrival to New York in 1849, he began this German-language periodical. In all, twelve numbers appeared. A more lasting publication was begun by English-born Robert Lyon. The *Asmonean* was a sprightly, educational, interesting publication whose pages make good reading even

ISAAC LEESER (1806-1868)

after a century of dustgathering. Its editor was born in London in 1810. From the first he showed a marked aptitude for scholarship and business. At the age of thirty-four he emigrated to America. He considered the large numbers of Jews in New York and other cities and was convinced that they needed to be unified by means of a publication in English which could stress their many common interests. In October, 1849, the *Asmonean* was born. It ceased to appear shortly after the death of its brilliant editor who was stricken with a fatal illness in March of 1858. His enduring monument is contained in the pages of the magazine he edited.

Another European-born editor and one who more than any Jew in America is associated with its developing journalism in the Anglo-Jewish field is Isaac Leeser. He came to Richmond, Virginia, in 1824. A serious, plain-looking boy of eighteen. He had but recently graduated from the Münster Gymnasium in his native Germany. He was shy, brooding, quiet, pious. For a short time he attended school but necessity drove

him to earn a living. Like other immigrants before and after Leeser, he managed to work all day and study half the night. He became an unpaid teacher of Jewish children in Richmond. He taxed his health, his eyes. It was some articles which he read in the *London Quarterly Review* that determined his future. In 1828 there had appeared a series of defamatory articles, attacking both Jews and Judaism. This twenty-two year old boy with only a four-year knowledge of English undertook their vindication. His answer was published in a Richmond newspaper and attracted wide attention. He was summoned to Philadelphia to become the rabbi of Mikveh Israel Congregation. His first English sermon, somewhat of an innovation in America, was preached in June, 1830. He continued to write and to translate into English. Then in 1834 came the blow which was to mark him for life and which kept him a lonely, introverted bachelor until his death. In one of her witty letters Rebecca Gratz describes Isaac Leeser in 1829 and adds "wisdom is safest with ugliness." What he must have looked like when nearly blinded by small-pox and heavily pitted, we can only guess. It was a deeply traumatic experience.

Driven back into himself he found the strength to work, the wisdom to reflect, the resources of spirit to develop. He became a towering spokesman for the Jews of America. We can only refer briefly to but one facet of his life—his editorial career as founder and editor of the *Occident* and *American Jewish Advocate*.

XII.   TRADITION VERSUS *MINHAG AMERICA*

In the twenty-six volumes of the *Occident*, we have a summary of all that the Jews of America and of the world were then experiencing and thinking, dreaming and hoping. No one can even attempt to chronicle the events of these years without steeping himself deeply into its volumes. It is a mirror which reflects the passing scene.

From the very first issue our interest is held. A German Jew, Julius Stern, suggests that the Jews of Germany escape their unhappy lot by emigrating to America and founding a colony in the West. The year was 1843. The imagination, even more than a hundred years later, is aroused by the vast possibilities implied in such a program. In the same issue there is an unsigned editorial refuting the plan. Other controversial subjects are attacked and some non-controversial subjects are elaborated. Leeser objects to the "foolish attempts at conversion" made by The American Society for Meliorating Conditions of the Jews and by other missionary groups. For twenty-five years, until Leeser's death, and for one year after he died, the *Occident* was a great unifying and uplifting forum for American Jews. But it was only one of Leeser's activities. He traveled and lectured throughout the breadth and length of the United States. He reported each new congregation with the pride of a father announcing the birth of a child. He was one of the founders of the Board of Delegates of American Israelites, of the American Jewish Publication Society, of the Hebrew Education Society, of the Board of Hebrew Ministers, of the Jewish Hospital of Philadelphia, of Maimonides College. It was at his request that after his death the splinter charitable societies of Philadelphia were welded into the United Hebrew charities.

Of his major works, the most significant was his translation of the Bible into English. The clear, vigorous prose, the rhythm and beauty of his language are amazing. After all, he had learned it after he had mastered Hebrew and German. He translated a book on the geography of Palestine and finally Moses Mendelssohn's *Jerusalem*.

But in many ways, the project nearest and dearest to him was the founding of Maimonides College in 1867. It was "the darling of his heart." He was elected President of the college whose student body numbered four. The faculty counting Leeser were six in number. Although four

Courtesy Jewish Institute of Religion, New York

RABBI ISAAC MAYER WISE (1819-1900)

members of the teaching staff worked without salary, funds were desperately needed. Leeser worked without rest or respite. His heart and weakened body could not stand the strain. On the first of February, in the year 1868, that gallant Jewish heart that had lavished its outpourings upon every Jewish cause, was stilled forever. And Isaac Leeser to whom the Jews of America owed so much, had joined other immortals.

Of the men who figure prominently in Leeser's life, with whom he was to wage a heroic struggle, one especially stands out, this man was Isaac Mayer Wise. An immigrant from Bohemia, Rabbi Wise was to leave a lasting record of his coming to America. He was born in 1819 and emigrated to America in 1846. His first pulpit was in Albany, New York. His second and more significant move came in 1854 when he was called to Congregation Bne Jeshurun in Cincinnati. There the rest of his life was spent. He died in 1900.

It was a long life and crowned with lasting achievement and enduring successes, a complete contrast in many ways to the bleak career of Isaac Leeser. Yet the two men were to come to grips with problems of vital concern to every Jew in America.

One of the issues that was to rend the fabric of Jewish unity was in the field of religious reform. To those who lined up in opposite camps, it was not a battle of words. It was a war of deeply-felt ideologies. It left psychological scars which have not healed to this day. It reached both sides of the Atlantic. It had ancient roots. For the French Revolution and the Napoleonic Reforms directly affected the Jews of Europe, opening the tightly closed ghetto doors to the fresh air of political reform, of hope, that the slogans so often chanted of "liberty, equality and fraternity" might be translated into expanding horizons for the Jews as well. News of the American Revolution, of the Declaration of Independence, the Constitution and the new Republic was manna to those who were starved for elemental human rights. In the letters which American Jews sent to their transatlantic brethren, there was dawning hope. So the seeds were planted at the beginning of the nineteenth century. A letter of Haym Salomon's to his relatives in Poland stressing the need for secular as well as Hebrew education is but one of many such documents which pointed to a new day. In a history of Jews published in Germany in 1821, great stress is placed on the manners and customs of the Jews of Charleston who "do not differ from other citizens." Emancipation, accomplished in one spot on earth, was a tonic uplifting Jews in many places. The pendulum began to beat new rhythms, striking now west, now east.

In 1796, a congregation in Amsterdam introduced sermons in Dutch. In 1810 a Reform Temple was dedicated in Germany headed by Israel Jacobson. In 1818 a Reform Temple was opened in Hamburg.

The impact of new ideas, the desire to adapt Jewish practice and religion to new conditions, the need for plugging up those loopholes through which restive Jews were escaping from the constrictions of ancient law and lore—all of these factors were ferments at work. So it came to pass that in Charleston, in the year 1824, forty-seven Jews petitioned the vestry of Kahal Kadosh Beth Elohim for some changes in ritual practices and in services. This daring plea was branded an outrage by those who wished to adhere to historic practices and procedures. By those who sought a change it was considered a step in the direction of improving decorum, holding its youth, adding to the preservation of Judaism in America. The reformers stressed the fact that many congregants knew little if any Hebrew and thus much was incomprehensible to them. They pointed to new trends in Holland and Germany. They pleaded for sermons in English based on Biblical texts. They stressed the need for curtailing services. The petition was rejected but reform in Charleston did not languish and die. The Reformed Society of Israelites came into being. In the diary of a young Jew written in 1833, we read: "This is the day preceding the day of Atonement and everybody but myself and Mr. D. Lyon have gone to prayers . . . I have not gone, and why, because there I should have to remain seated, listening to Hebrew chaunted by a voice very well adapted to the pronunciation of that guttural harsh barbarous tongue . . . " Others loved that language and thrilled to its cadences even if they could not understand them. The issue was joined.

Those who longed for reform had been strengthened by the arrival in America of Isaac M. Wise and a number of like-minded colleagues. Within one short year after arriving here, Wise published a prayer book titled *Minhag America*. It was more than a set of rules for deviation from ancient practice. It constituted a new orientation, a revolutionary psychological approach to faith and tradition. He saw Judaism as a religion symbolic of the new freedom, adapted to the spirit of rationalism and science, political and social reform which was abroad in Europe and America—"without mysteries or miracles, rational, self-evident..." It was a tall order. It involved major surgery from the past. In order to understand the importance of what Wise proposed, we must consider the social implications involved in such departure from the usages of the past. We must study the nature and character of the immigrants who came to America and analyze the goals which were behind their migration. Jews have always been a mobile people. Of necessity, and not always self-imposed. Edicts of expulsion were primary causes of mobility. Economic and social discrimination acted as spurs to the search for new homes. Freedom and hope were the magnets. Mendelssohn, Wessely and many others brought news of enlightenment. Christians like Dohm and Lessing were propagating new attitudes toward Jews. Now Jews and Christians were side by side in seeking the general amelioration of the masses. Often Christians and Jews came to America at the same time, in the same boat, for much the same reason. Their first measures of acculturation paralleled those of their non-Jewish companions. Rationalism was a heady draught. For the Jews who quaffed it, *Minhag America* was the answer. Judaism was evolving in patterns of interaction and integration on American soil.

In addition to a broad program, the Reform Movement had many transplanted leaders,—Lilienthal, Einhorn, Adler, Felsenthal, Wise, Hirsch, among others,—who felt that the defection and indifference which characterized some American Jews was due to outworn ceremonials, lack of understanding of Hebrew, failure to adjust to new ideas and the new critical approach to the Bible and to religious concepts. So with adequate leadership, a vigorous modern approach, some legitimate reasons for criticism, the new program was launched. Isaac Mayer Wise was the titular head of the ranks of those seeking reform. Opposed

to him was an equally determined, often equally brilliant, force of those who appealed to tradition, to the love of the past, to time-honored observances of *Minhag Sephardit* or *Minhag Askenaz*. Isaac Leeser became a circuit-rider. He traveled widely through the United States advocating his ideas. He writes often in the *Occident* describing conditions among Jews as he found them. He pleads again and again for loyalty to the past. He advocates the beauty of Hebrew and the potency of traditionalism.

The adversaries, Leeser and Wise, were powerful leaders. Says Kisch in his *In Search of Freedom,* "Wise traveled throughout the United States, lecturing, dedicating synagogues, and arousing the interest of the Jewish communities in his plans and projects." Wise, like Leeser, became a factor in American-Jewish journalism. He edited the *American Israelite* and the *Deborah.* When American Jews found themselves the objects of discrimination in Switzerland in 1857, Wise was already a national figure and led the vigorous opposition to these laws. Yet the *Occident* continued its campaign against the despised innovators and found that Reform was "so hateful," savoring "of radical change and gentile innovation."

Again and again, Leeser thundered that Wise and his cohorts were trying to make religion more palatable to the secure and wealthy Jews and were turning their backs on the wage-earners, the poor and the insecure. There was some truth in this accusation. But Leeser was himself no less guilty of seeking the support of men of means. He hedged on slavery when the issue divided Jews of America as it did their Christian neighbors much along the line of the *haves* and *have-nots.* He was frank in stating that he could not afford to take sides on this question, for more than anything he wanted subscribers and supporters. Leeser could discuss "the terrific hatred" between North and South and maintain calmly that slavery was no more controversial than polygamy. He lacked the forthright courage of S. M. Isaacs whose famous editorial in the *Jewish Messenger* titled "Stand By the Flag" left no doubt in the minds of his readers where he stood. The *Jewish Messenger* fought both Reform and slavery!

Stratification in Jewish life was becoming a reality and was a deciding factor in the Jews' attitude toward the problems that were crucial and demanding. There were plantation Jews and Jews of large landed estates whose grandparents had secured by their happy timing, sizable possessions for their descendants. Especially in the South, Jewish material success had helped Jews become integrated in American society. The amenities of life were assured. Manners and possessions conferred status. The newer immigrants had little in common with the easy life and established routine of life in wealthy households. Here servants or slaves performed menial tasks and visitors could be accommodated in large homes where money and means were abundant. Into the Northern vortex with its developing industries, many immigrants of the forties were drawn. Their beliefs, their pattern of life, their goals and objectives, their identification with the rank and file, were marked from the first. Although the peddlers were soon siphoned off into the ranks of storekeepers, their sympathies and political associations were of the North, largely. Geography and occupation were the determining factors. Machines were creating a social revolution whose echoes were heard in the synagogues of the land. In the decade before the Civil War machine-made matzot were introduced in New York, not without some dissension in the ranks of New York Jews, many of whom clung to the manual method as more in keeping with religious practice. By 1855, the bakers were opposed by a matzoh "trust" in which five synagogues took a hand. Since there were in 1860, seventeen synagogues in New York, it is obvious that the issues involved were not vital. It simply shows the gradual incursion of the machine age.

New elements were to be found in the larger cities, especially in New York. A trickle of Jews from Russia was finding its way to America. In 1852 there were enough Russian Jews there to establish a congregation of their own. In a little garret on Bayard Street, for the sum of eight dollars a month, they met and conducted services. One of their leaders, Rabbi Ash, added to his rabbinical pittance by becoming a partner in a hoop-skirt factory. He alternated his two occupations, depending on the success of his business venture, being now a manufacturer and now a rabbi. Life was full of contradictions.

XIII. NO MORE FRONTIERS

For many reasons,—pressure in seaboard areas, limited opportunities where so many immigrants lived side by side, the lure of wider spaces and of employment possibilities, favorable reports from those who had joined the westward trek,—Jews like others were on the move. New states were being added to the United States. Following the War of 1812, five states were added in rapid succession (1816-1821). By 1848, the year of the great flood of immigration, the population flowed inexorably westward. Competing ideologies, antislavery and proslavery, caused rival factions to spur settlers. By 1836, Texas won its independence from Mexico. In March, 1845, Texas was annexed to the United States. The following year the United States was at war with Mexico.

We know that from the very earliest times Jews were associated with the development of the West. Michigan, Wisconsin, Illinois, Indiana were more than geographic terms. In Indian outposts, in frontier towns, in struggling new townships, there were Jewish pioneers. From New Orleans to the upper reaches of the Mississippi they could be found, sometimes as solitary traders, sometimes with their families. When Pike visited Iowa in 1804, he had Jewish soldiers among his men. When Des Moines was an outpost of not more than twenty settlers called Raccoon Forks, William Krause, a Jew, was one of that small band of settlers. In Chicago, Jews are known since 1841. Six years later the Congregation of the Men of the West, *Kehillah Anshe Maariv,* came into being. It took strong men to meet rugged conditions. They were found.

When Leopold Mayer reached Chicago in 1850, he found that "the two previous years, 1848-1849, had been trying for the Jewish colony, on account of the cholera... To the praise of the Jews then there, I must say that they clung together in sorrow and in joy." They clung together in Europe also. When anti-Jewish riots broke out in Prague. When mass migrations were advocated in Vienna. When committees met and deliberated as to the best way of planning an orderly exodus. One of the most energetic advocates of the "On to America" crusade, Isidor Bush, landed here in 1849, a symbol of the new type of immigrant, cultured, well educated, dynamic. His great-grandfather was the first Jew to become a member of the nobility in Austria. His childhood was sheltered and protected. He was surrounded by men and women of education and culture. He was employed in his father's printinghouse. He wrote and published many articles. He was twenty-six years old when the Revolution of 1848 cut short his security and hopes. Penniless he landed in New York, opened a little bookstore and began a publishing business. He founded *Israel's Herold* which lasted only three months. But it was a brave effort. The editorial policy stated in the first issue "that we serve no color, that we shall be impartial, and further only the interchange of ideas . . ." The twelfth number sadly marking the suspension of publication because, among other causes, "parties oppose one another so bitterly that they desire no reconciliation and understanding—yet, let that not excuse me or deter others." Bush faced westward toward St. Louis. He became first a storekeeper and then a landowner. He bought a hundred acres of land in Jeffer-

son County which he called "Bushberg." He raised grapes and published a grape manual which was translated into many languages. Grocer, vintner, railroad freight agent, hardware merchant, landowner, bank president—that was the protean Isidor Bush. Yet this did not sum up all of his activities. Because of a childhood physical injury he could not become a soldier in the ranks. Nevertheless he did become secretary to General John Charles Frémont. He held many civic posts. He identified himself with the Abolitionist cause. As a member of the Board of Education, the Library Committee, the City Council, the German Immigrant Aid Society, he was a force for good in his community. When the Union Party was organized, he was one of fifteen men proposed for the Party ticket. He did all he could to avoid "dismemberment" of the Union when Civil War threatened. When the inevitable split occurred, he championed "speedy emancipation."

Another Jew whose name looms large in the opening up of the West was Solomon Nunes Carvalho. Here too was a man of exceptional talents and abilities. By the time he was twenty, Carvalho was a portrait painter of note. He painted many notables of his day, as well as numerous religious subjects. He wrote a book on religion and married a Sunday School teacher who once taught under Rebecca Gratz. One day he met John Charles Frémont and his life underwent a complete change. From 1838 on, Frémont had persistently added to our knowledge of our land. He had explored the Upper Mississippi and the Missouri River areas. He had traveled with Kit Carson to the Oregon country. In 1845 he headed an exploring party to California. He helped win California and was rewarded by being made governor of that area. When gold was found on his land, he became rich as well as famous. He married Jessie Benton, daughter of Senator Benton, and became a champion of the Free-Soil Party. Later Carvalho was to dedicate one of his books to Jessie Benton Frémont.

Frémont invited Carvalho to join him on his next expedition. Carvalho completely captivated by Frémont's personality, impulsively accepted. In September, 1853, Carvalho "having in charge the daguerreo-type apparatus, painting materials . . ." left New York. He was to be the official artist of the expedition. There began an epic journey, which happily Carvalho recorded for posterity, during the course of which "travelling on foot over mountains of snow, I have stopped on the trail, made pictures of the country . . . The great secret, however, of my untiring perseverance was that my honor was pledged to Col. Frémont to perform certain duties, and I would rather have died than not have redeemed it." Carvalho describes in shocking detail the terrible privations which they all underwent. He was one of those who reached California. There, being a good Jew, one of his first activities was the organization of a Hebrew philanthropic society.

So in one way or another, Jews were part of the westward expansion, helping to conquer one frontier after another. As always they were in a numerical minority. Yet here and there an individual would manage in a way significant or dramatic or vital to call attention to his presence and to the presence of his anonymous brethren. In California which was our last frontier, spurred by the gold rush and by the call of high adventure, little Jewish communities sprang into being in Los Angeles, San Francisco, Sacramento, Stockton. Jews came overland and by boat. In one of her eloquent letters Rebecca Gratz laments the loss of friends who perished in a shipwreck on their way to California.

Less spectacular, but nonetheless important, was the Jewish story in Texas. As early as 1821, a Samuel Isaacs was a landholder in Texas, having come there with Stephen Austin's colony. For his services in the Texan Army during the crucial year of 1836-1837, he was given an additional grant of 320 acres. Soon there were little communities of Jews, at Velasco, at Nacogdoches. The Mayor of Nacogdoches was Adolphus Sterne, friend of General Sam Houston and a resident of Texas since 1824.

They fought in all the major battles for Texas liberation and independence. San Jacinto. Buena Vista. Alamo. Dr. Moses Albert Levy was Surgeon-General of Houston's Army. Dr. Isaac Lyons held a similar post under General Tom Green. A French Jew, Michael De Young, was victualer and provisioner, and after the Lone Star Republic was established, he was rewarded for his outstanding services by a gift of a large tract of land. Two brothers came from Jamaica and made their mark as early pioneers in Texas. They were Phineas and Jacob De Cordova. Simon Weiss, a German Jew, lent his name to Weiss Bluff. A Moravian immigrant, Moritz Kopperl, became president of the National Bank of Texas and president of the Colorado and Santa Fé Railroad. German-born Isidore Dyer made Galveston his home since 1840. Here in his home the first religious services were held by the Jews of Galveston. Another French Jew, Henry Castro, was appointed by the President of the Republic of Texas as Consul-General to France and was given the additional task of procuring German immigrants for Texas. So enthusiastic was Castro for the colonization program for Texas that he spent a huge sum of his own money to further this plan. He printed circulars in French and German, lauding the opportunities of his adopted land in such terms that he procured five thousand immigrants in three years and many of them settled in the town of Castroville to do him honor.

So the Jewish participation in the growth and development of Texas is traced. Cemeteries were acquired and synagogues established, twin proofs of Jewish existence. In Houston, a cemetery in 1844 and within ten years a synagogue. San Antonio, cemetery in 1854, congregation in 1872. Austin, cemetery in 1866, congregation in 1876. Waco, cemetery, 1869, congregation in 1881. Dallas, cemetery in 1872, congregation in 1876. It was a pattern repeated in every city—first a permanent home for the dead, then the formation of a congregation in which to worship. And often in the early years, a room in a private home would serve as an intermediate stage in communal organization.

No issue divided the Jews of America as much as the hydra-headed one of slavery and secession. Eloquent is the record of participation of Jews in both camps of the fratricidal struggle. From the first there were Jews who owned slaves and were slave-traders. There were others, like Judah Touro and Rebecca Gratz, who acquiesced and accepted the enslavement of fellow-creatures without outward conflict or inward qualms. They seemed as a group to lack religious scruples as to owning slaves. As early as 1661 there are records of Jewish importers of slaves. In 1720 a Jew exchanged merchandise for slaves he had brought in his own ship from Guinea. In the insurrection of 1741, in New York, a large number of Negroes had planned to sack and burn the city. They were discovered and many of them were transported or condemned to death. Some of these slaves belonged to Jewish owners.

It was not unusual, however, for Jews, when contemplating death to consider the need for freeing their slaves. Was this an admission of a sense of guilt on the eve of departure from life? Was it due to a basic ambivalence in attitude, that in life they condoned slavery and in death wished to be free of the stigma of slave ownership? Too many wills contained such clauses for the gesture to be taken lightly. The Negro servants in the Shepherd household where Judah Touro lived for many years, were all freed with his help. An interesting will, listed by Schappes in his *Documentary History* (pp. 100 ff.), is that of Isaiah Isaacs of Virginia, dated 1803 and 1806. The will contains the following provision: "Being of opinion that all men are by nature equally free, and being possessed of some of those beings who are unfortunate doomed to slavery . . . My slaves hereafter named are hereby manumitted and made free . . . " However, such principles did not prevent him from securing the economic benefits of slave labor during his lifetime. He wanted to be sure that his heirs were spared such burdening of conscience and to be himself unencumbered in eternity. Such qualms were rare and seemed to be almost completely confined to the North. There seem to have been no Abolitionists in the South. Not even in Charleston where the Grimké sisters, famous for their antislavery views, lived, were there Jewish voices raised against slavery. Until it became unlawful to free them, Jews of Charleston often liberated their slaves in their wills. Others got around the legal hurdle by allowing Negroes to work for wages as if they were free.

We learn that the Jews of Charleston did not try to convert their Negro slaves to Judaism, but provision seems to have been made for seating them in the gallery. Beth Elohim refused to accept colored converts to membership. We have no way of knowing to what extent Jews were in their hearts opposed to slavery and afraid to speak out for fear of jeopardizing their own position as a tolerated minority. We do know that Penina Moïse, whose moral sensibilities were highly developed, left no poem in lament for slavery.

It is when we move North and turn the spotlight upon the Jews of the North that the situation changes.

In a well-documented study Bertram W. Korn includes this interesting statement from the Annual Report of the American and Foreign Anti-slavery Society: "The Jews of the United States have never taken any steps whatever with regard to the Slavery question . . . Some of the Jews who reside in slave States, have refused to have any property in man, or even to have any slaves about them . . . " The year was 1853. Korn finds that this summary is "substantially correct." He adds "The records of the Manumission Society of New York City preserve the names of many Jews who emancipated their Negroes." In Congress the two Jewish senators, Judah P. Benjamin and David Yulee, were pro-slavery. In the North, Isidor Bush, Moritz Penner, Michael Heilprin were pronounced and outspoken foes of slavery. We have already noted that Rabbi Felsenthal insisted that the majority of American Jews were opposed to slavery; that Rabbi Raphall took the opposite point of view. Ernestine Rose, a Polish Jewess who became known as "Queen of the Platforms" lent all of her talents to the cause of emancipation of women and of slaves.

In the journalistic field, there was division. While the New York newspapers owned by Mordecai Manuel Noah were identified with the pro-slavery group, the *Kansas Post* owned by Pinner fought for emancipation. In Pinner, noted Abolitionist leaders found an ally of talent and fiery energy. In 1860 Missouri Republicans chose Pinner to the convention which nominated Lincoln. Among the followers of John Brown were three Jews, from Poland, from Bohemia and from Vienna. The last of the three, August Bondi, in a manuscript titled "With John Brown in Kansas" describes the association with that noted zealot in considerable detail. In 1861 Bondi was fighting as a sergeant in the Fifth Kansas Cavalry.

Enough facts have been cited to show that there was no unanimity among the Jews in America as they entered the momentous years which were to exact so bitter a price from all Americans. As other families were divided, so were some Jews separated in ideology and loyalty. Abraham Jonas, English-born Jew who was a friend of Abraham Lincoln and as postmaster of Quincy, Illinois, wielded considerable political influence, headed a divided family. Although one of his sons fought with the Fiftieth Illinois Infantry, his other sons were soldiers in the Confederate Army. As he was dying, Abe Jonas kept calling for his son Charles, who was a prisoner of war. President Lincoln arranged that he be allowed to visit his father. It was an act of compassion typical of Lincoln.

In the *Autobiography of Alfred Mordecai* another tragic family rift is revealed. North Carolina born, Major Alfred Mordecai, valedictorian of his class of 1823 at West Point, who made the Army his life's work, and became, to quote Simon Wolf, "a recognized authority in the military world in the field of scientific research," resigned his commission. He writes: "When Civil War became inevitable, unwilling to engage in it, for reasons peculiar to myself, I resigned my commission in the army . . . " With a heavy heart he severed his family ties as well. His son and namesake, graduated from West Point in the same year, 1861, that his father left the army. The son fought for the Union with distinction. The cost of the separation of father and son in anguish and loneliness leaves a stark record in the father's autobiography.

XIV. JEWISH PARTICIPATION IN THE CIVIL WAR

As in every period of history, the events of the critical years from 1861-1865 are to be viewed against the wider frame of reference. It is to be assumed that the reader is familiar with the inexorable logic, with the succession of events, that led to the costly Civil War. The campaigns of the war and its leaders, the battles and "incidents" on land and sea, are common knowledge. There are thousands of volumes of official documents, histories, biographies, analyses and narratives. All that can be done here, and very briefly, is to show to what extent the Jews of that period were involved in the Civil War. We know that they were ideologically identified in attitude, speech and printed word, with one side or another. That they helped in the formation of the Republican Party and the election of Lincoln. They fought on land and on sea as well. Briefly, let us examine the record.

Momentous events followed each other in quick succession. The election of Abraham Lincoln was a signal to the South that the Union had ceased to exist. A little more than a month after the election, South Carolina by unanimous vote determined that the Union "is dissolved." Nearly two hundred Jews of Charleston served in the war. Some twenty-five are known to have lost their lives. It was the same in other cities and states. A large proportion of the Jewish population of America was directly or indirectly involved in every phase of the bitter struggle. On February 4, 1861, the Confederacy was organized. On the same day, Judah P. Benjamin, a Jew who was to become known as "the brains of the Confederacy," made one of his ablest speeches in the United States Congress where he had served as the junior Senator from Louisiana. Born in the West Indies, educated in Charleston and in the schools of North Carolina and Yale, he achieved fame as a lawyer and wealth as a citizen, becoming a slave-holder and plantation owner. So high was the esteem in which Judah P. Benjamin was held that to this day the Daughters of the Confederacy maintain as a shrine to his memory the mansion in Ellenton, Florida, which was the last home he occupied before he fled for safety, after the war, to England. In New York, in April of the same year, S. M. Isaacs wrote in *The Jewish Messenger* calling on his readers to be loyal to the Union:— "Then stand by the flag! What death can be so glorious as that of the patriot, surrendering up life in defense of his country . . . Whether native or foreign-born, Christian or Israelite, stand by it . . ." To this the Jews of Shreveport, Louisiana, replied by a series of resolutions repudiating the sentiments voiced in *The Jewish Messenger* and pledging to boycott the paper.

Geography dictated to conscience. There were twenty-four Jewish staff officers in the Confederate Army. The ranking person among them was Judah P. Benjamin who was first called to take part in the Cabinet of Jefferson Davis as Attorney-General. Later he became Acting Secretary of War. On resigning the Justice Portfolio he became regular Secretary of War. Then in 1862, he was elevated to the position of Secretary of State, a post which he held to the end. The South had a Jewish Surgeon-General, David Camden De Leon. The North had its Jonathan Phineas Horwitz who was elevated to a similar position. Horwitz received a unanimous commendation from Congress for the way he administered the hospital program. It was a strange combination of circumstances which placed the care of the wounded, North and South, in the hands of Jewish doctors. The claims of conscience needed to be served by chaplains as well as by doctors. The Confederacy provided for clergymen, affiliation unspecified, to minister to its soldiers. The North was less liberal. Regimental Chaplains were to be members of a "Christian denomination." A Christian member of Congress denounced this as an offence to ". . . the large body of men in this country . . . of the Hebrew faith . . ." Rabbi Issac M. Wise also vigorously attacked such discrimination. Even without official sanction, a Jew, Michael Allen, was acting as regimental chaplain. He was "exposed" and resigned his post, to which he had been elected by the 65th Regiment of the 5th Pennsylvania Cavalry, a military unit whose commanding officer was Colonel Max Friedman and whose roster of officers and men counted many Jews. Determined to test the legality of such an indefensible law, Colonel Friedman's men next elected a rabbi to the post, the Reverend Arnold Fischel. He too was rejected.

In the ensuing outcry, all factions of Jewry were united. In December of 1861, Reverend Arnold Fischel addressing himself to the Senate Chairman of the Military Committee wrote that he had been chosen by the Board of Delegates of American Israelites at their own expense "to attend to the spiritual welfare of the Jewish soldiers in the Camps and Hospitals of the Army of the Potomac . . . " Many newspapers came to the assistance of the Jewish cause, some calling attention to "the alacrity" with which the Jews enlisted. Petitions flooded Congress. Christians aided Jews by appending their signatures. In December of 1861, President Lincoln in a letter to the Rev. Dr. A. Fischel stated: "I shall try to have a new law broad enough to cover what is desired by you in behalf of the Israelites." The law, after many delays, was amended to permit Jews and other minorities, by implication, to have the services of chaplains of their own faith. The first military chaplain duly to be appointed in 1862 was Rabbi Jacob Frankel.

Two more aspects of the war need to be briefly summarized—the military record and the struggle of civilian Jews against prejudicial attitudes and measures of men in high places.

The difficulties of gauging the number of Jews in the armies of the Civil War are inestimable. All scholars agree that the Jewish minority was submerged and outnumbered, that some Jews found it easier to fight without identifying themselves as Jews. Yet thanks to the researches of Simon Wolf and others, many Jews have been identified. We know that on both sides there were multiple enlistments by members of the same family. Of the five Jonas brothers, four fought for the Confederacy and one for the Union. North Carolina had six Cohen brothers. Among the troops of South Carolina there were five brothers Moses. There were three Cohen brothers from Arkansas and three Goldsmith brothers from Georgia and South Carolina. Virginia and Louisiana each had three Levy brothers. There were three Wolf brothers from Alabama. In the Union Army there were five Wenk brothers. Also a father and three sons named Levy. There were three Feder brothers. Three brothers Emanuel and three named Koch. Many

are lost because of their failure to identify themselves as Jews, a sure way to obliterate one's record from history. We must therefore rely on Simon Wolf's figures which estimate around 6,000 Jewish soldiers in the Union Armies and between 1200 and 1,500 in the Confederate Army. A Jewish soldier with the Army of the Potomac, writing in 1862, says—"Some of our brethren fear that were they known as Hebrews, it would expose them to the taunts and sneers of those among their comrades, who have been in the habit of associating with the name of Jew, everything that is mean and contemptible . . . " Nevertheless there are others who "meet together for worship on Sabbath, in some secluded spot, and I know a young soldier, who was on Kippore morning ordered to take part in a skirmish, near Harper's Ferry, which he had to go through, without having tasted food, and as soon as the enemy retreated, he retired to the woods, where he remained until sunset, reading his prayers."

Serving in the Confederate Congress was the son of the real estate promoter of Florida's earliest history, Moses Elias Levy. His son David who later was to change his name to Yulee, took no part in military action. As David Levy he was elected Senator from Florida in 1845 and so was the first Jew to serve in the United States Senate. Later with his Christian wife he severed all connection with Jews and spent his days as a gentleman planter and president of the Gulf Railroad.

Space does not permit more than a cursory survey of the role of Jews in the Confederacy. A South Carolina newspaper wrote "When the history of South Carolina's part in the great struggle is written . . . the Hebrew soldiers of this State, who wore grey, will have their full mead of praise." That history has not yet been written. The bombardment of Charleston necessitated the moving of the scrolls of the Law and other objects to Columbia. When Sherman reduced that city to ashes in 1865, only one scroll and a little bell were found in the debris. These

MONUMENT IN MEMORY OF THE JEWISH
SOLDIERS WHO DIED IN THE CIVIL WAR,
BROOKLYN, N. Y.

So we learn of Major Leopold Blumenberg, a veteran of the Prussian-Danish War who helped organize the Fifth Regiment of Maryland Volunteers. Captain Isidor Bush was aide-de-camp to General Frémont. A Jew from Hungary, Frederick Knefler, rose from private to colonel of the 79th Indiana Infantry. Others were: Colonel Henry Boernstein, Colonel Max Friedman, Colonel Marcus M. Spiegel, Colonel Max Einstein, Colonel Simon Levy. Among lieutenant-colonels were: Leopold C. Newman, Philip J. Joachimsen, Edward Selig Salomon, Isaac Moses. There were seven Jews who won the Congressional Medal of Honor: Leopold Karpeles, Benjamin B. Levy, Abraham Cohn, David Obranski, Henry Heller, Abraham Grunwalt and Isaac Gans. There were Naval heroes too, men like sailor William Durst who was aboard the *Monitor*. The commander of the vessel twice received the thanks of Congress, yet Admiral John L. Worden insisted that Durst was worthy of Congressional recognition for his gallantry in combat, on the ninth of March, 1862. So many records of individual acts of courage and valor have come down that it would take a sizable volume to record them. One officer wrote: "So many of the German officers and men, the Poles and the Hungarians, were of Jewish lineage that I am unable to designate them."

And there the record rests.

Of Lincoln's relationship with the Jews much, too, can be said. Korn's excellent book deals adequately with the subject. All that can be done here is to indicate briefly something of the mood and tempo of that period and of the symbol that Abraham Lincoln had become to the Jews of America.

As was pointed out earlier, because the Jews of the Diaspora often could not think of their earliest homes without recalling scenes of horror, of mob violence, of humility and degradation, they had learned early in their wanderings to substitute the image of some revered sage or teacher around whom they spun their loving leg-

were returned to Beth Elohim after the war. Dr. I. Baruch, assistant to Surgeon-General De Lyon, was also a Jew. Dr. Marx E. Cohen died a hero's death at the Battle of Bentonville. Joseph Frankland rose from private to assistant provost marshall. Randolph Mordecai from private to assistant adjutant-general. Colonel Raphael J. Moses was on the staff of General James Longstreet.

A Jewish architect of Charleston, David Lopez, was the inventor of a modern torpedo boat, called the *Little David*. Louis P. Levy enlisted as a midshipman at fifteen. The *Merrimac* had a Jewish officer aboard named Lieutenant R. J. Moses. Captain Levi M. Harby commanded the *Neptune*. Jews named Moïse, De Lyon, Lyons and many others served in the Confederate Navy.

In the Union armies their names are more numerous and their services better chronicled.

ends. On these revered heroes they lavished legend and loving anecdote. Toward such a figure they could look as to a father. Such a man and such a figure was the quiet, brooding, mystical, humorous man in the White House, who was leading his country through its darkest hour since its founding days. He was a symbol around whom they could rally in the hope of ultimate victory. To him they could look and did look for redress when their loyalty was assailed by one of the great generals of this period. We refer to the infamous slur on Jews contained in General Ulysses S. Grant's Order No. 11. There were other indications in the press, in speeches and in overt acts of hostility pointing to a latent antisemitism. The very fact that some Jewish soldiers felt constrained to deny their faith, indicates a strong undercurrent of prejudice. The military mind to this day is often similarly beclouded. It did not help the Jews of the North that the "Brains" of the Confederacy was a Jew, that many of its officers and soldiers were Jews. It was easy for some befuddled minds to call all Jews copperheads and rebels. When a Jew of Charleston presented his state, South Carolina, with a gift of $10,000 to help the cause he believed in,—it was fuel to the flame of latent Jew-hatred in the North. The editorial barb directed at Mordecai did not fail to include Judah P. Benjamin and Senator Yulee "whose name has been changed from the more appropriate one of Levy." Rabbi Raphall and others came in for their share of attacks. Those European bankers who made loans to the South were played up in the press because they were Jews. While the activities of the Seligman brothers, New York bankers, whose aid was described by William E. Dodd as "scarcely less important to the Union cause than the Battle of Gettysburg"—were overlooked in the heat of acrimonious feeling.

To get back to General Grant. There was great heroism displayed during the years of the war. There was also much greed and corruption. The Beards in their classic study titled *The Rise of American Civilization* describe "the corruption in high places, cold and cynical profiteering, extravagance and heartless frivolity." The North had imposed a blockade against the South. That blockade was repeatedly violated. There were some Jews among the blockade-runners. Some of them were newly arrived immigrants and could be easily recognized by their dress and language. In 1862, Grant wrote a letter, on the ninth of November, which read: "Refuse all permits to come south of Jackson for the present. The Israelites especially should be kept out." This was followed the next day by a letter, which read: "Give orders to all conductors on the road that no Jews are to be permitted to travel on the railroad southward from any point. They may go north and be encouraged in it; but they are such an intolerable nuisance that the department must be purged of them."

In December there came the infamous Order No. 11. In part it read: "The Jews, as a class violating every regulation of trade established by the Treasury Department . . . are hereby expelled within twenty-four hours from the receipt of this order . . . "

The deepest indignation followed in a torrential outburst. Christians joined with Jews in deploring and decrying this outrage. Parents of soldiers were up in arms. *The New York Times* called it "one of the deepest sensations of the war." Protest meetings were held. The press was inundated with angry letters. Captain Ferdinand Levy of the New York Volunteers wrote to the *Jewish Messenger* demanding that the President compel Grant to apologize or be dismissed from the service. In the *Congressional Globe* the case was discussed of "thirty Jewish gentlemen, residents of Paducah, [who] were driven from their homes and their business by virtue of this order of General Grant." The rabbis were aroused to a man. The Jews of Paducah petitioned their President. Rabbi Wise was burning up the pages of the *Israelite*. In the meanwhile the Jews of

Courtesy Ewing Galloway

ABRAHAM LINCOLN

THE STATUE OF LIBERTY

Paducah elected one of their number, Cesar Kaskel, a vice-president of the Paducah Union League Club, to represent them in Washington. He arrived in Washington bearing a number of letters of introduction to the President. He presented his case to the President who listened most attentively. Then with a characteristic twinkle in his eye, Lincoln said, "And so the children of Israel were driven from the happy land of Canaan?" and Cesar Kaskel replied, "Yes. They have come to Father Abraham's bosom to seek protection." Father Abraham rose to the occasion. "And this protection they shall have." The order was rescinded.

Order No. 11 was to dog General Grant the rest of his life. *The New York Times* wrote: "The order, to be sure, was promptly set aside by the President, but the affront to the Jews conveyed by its issue, was not so easily effaced."

"Father Abraham" in whom the Jews had found a staunch friend, was shot by an assassin on the fourteenth day of April in 1865. The Jews of the land mourned him as they would a father. Seven thousand Jews of New York marched in a procession of fifty thousand mourners. On the next day, the Sabbath following his death, in the oldest synagogue in North America, Shearith Israel, the *Hashkabah,* the Sephardic prayer for the dead, was recited for the first time for one not of the stock of Abraham. Abraham Lincoln had achieved an honorary membership in the ranks of the children of Abraham.

An era had closed. A new chapter was about to begin for the Jews of America. For soon after the war, before the mourning was over and the bereaved could forget, before the scars of war could be eradicated and the traumatic experiences healed, in less than a generation, the Jews of Russia and Poland and Rumania became the target for brutal attacks. A mighty cry of protest went up. Once more the driven and persecuted Jews looked to America for help. The movement for emancipation of slaves in America aided emancipation of the Russian serfs. The echo of events in one place always reverberated in another. Indeed the Russian freeing of serfs came in 1861, two years before the Emancipation Proclamation. But the handwriting on the wall was already legible. The Jewish historian is baffled at the strange patterns of history. No sooner does pressure ease up for the Jews in one part of the globe than it breaks out in another. There is never a respite.

When General Grant became President of the United States, the persecution of the Jews in Rumania was the despair of Jews in other lands. Simon Wolf who was a friend of President Grant (Order No. 11 was a thing of the past)—called on him and persuaded him to call a special meeting of his Cabinet to consider the expulsion of Jews from Russian Bessarabia. In all fairness it must be stated that the man who had issued his own expulsion order but seven years before, was now as President prepared to make amends. Our State Department was then headed by Hamilton Fish who upheld the best and most humanitarian American tradition. "The people of this country," he wrote, "universally abhor persecution." An eminent American Jew, Benjamin Franklin Peixotto, was appoined United States Consul to Rumania. He was an able lawyer who had studied for the bar under the noted Stephen A. Douglas. He was president of the Supreme Lodge of the B'nai B'rith, an organization founded in 1843. He plunged into a study of relief measures for persecuted Jews of Rumania. Three International Jewish Conferences were held in Europe at Peixotto's insistence. The inclusion of the Jewish question on the agenda of the Congress of Berlin was partly the result of his efforts. Other Americans representing our State Department were deeply concerned about the tragic, desperate, hopeless plight of the persecuted Jews. "It would be to the honor of the United States Government," read a report from Vienna, to Mr. W. M. Evarts, Secretary of State under President Hayes, "if it could

EMMA LAZARUS (1849-1887)

initiate a plan by which at once the condition of American Hebrews resident or travelling in Roumania, and the conditions of natives of the same race, could be ameliorated and their equality before the law at least partially assured." James G. Blaine, Thomas F. Bayard, John Hay, Elihu Root carried on the same noble, humanitarian work for the State Department.

XV. EMMA LAZARUS

If we were to consider the one person in American Jewish history whose life forms a bridge between all that was best in America and all the tragic experiences which now befell the Jews of Europe, it would be in the person of Emma Lazarus that we would find the perfect synthesis. For she was the harp upon whose strings the song of the persecuted was played. She was the crucible within whose fragile circumference the brimming distillation of Jewish experience could be found.

Emma Lazarus was born in New York City on July 22nd, 1849. She died November 19, 1887. Her family was in excellent circumstances and showered every advantage upon her. She came of a Sephardic family of status, whose identification with Shearith Israel was an important influence in her life. Her father supervised her education. There was a deep affection between them. He died in 1885 and she failed in health thereafter, surviving her father by just two years.

Emma Lazarus' initial published work brought her considerable national acclaim. Her poetry was at first Hellenic in mood. It was when she tapped the Hebraic strain that she reached her highest attainment. It was when she visited Ward's Island, when she saw the poverty and misery of the victims of oppression, when she identified herself as a Jewess with the refugees from terror, that her genius reached its heights. With passion she pleaded the cause of the oppressed. With zeal she identified herself with everything Jewish. She studied Hebrew. She translated Hebrew poets. She was indefatigable in her zeal for her brethren.

In 1882 she began a series of articles titled "Epistles to the Hebrews." She was the first in America to advocate industrial training for Jews. She helped found the Hebrew Technical Institute of New York. She found the courage to surmount her shyness and organized relief and protest meetings of Jews. And always, in poetry and prose, she insisted and demanded and pleaded for the rights of Jews everywhere. She became a disciple of George Eliot and her *Zionides*, songs of Zion, are the quintessence of her art and of her love for her people and for Zion.

It was she who wrote on a single sheet of paper, in words that still are potent today, the immortal poem which is the theme song of the immigrant in America. She wrote:

> *Give me your tired, your poor,*
> *Your huddled masses yearning to*
> *breathe free,*

The wretched refuse of your
teeming shore,
Send these, the homeless,
tempest-tost to me,
I lift my lamp beside the
golden door.

These words engraved at the base of the Statue of Liberty epitomize the longing and the yearning of every storm-battered traveler to find haven at last.

For whether the crossing of the Atlantic was undertaken in 1654 or three hundred years later—the motives were the same. It was closing the door on one chapter of personal history and opening the door on another. It was a search, a quest, the following of a dream. It was the end of one chapter in history and the beginning of a tale that is not yet told.

BIBLIOGRAPHY

FRIEDMAN, LEE M., *Early American Jews.* Cambridge, Mass., 1934.

GRINSTEIN, HYMAN B., *The Rise of the Jewish Community of New York.* Philadelphia, 5707—1947.

KISCH, GUIDO, *In Search of Freedom,* A History of American Jews from Czechoslovakia. London, 1949.

KORN, BERTRAM W., *American Jewry and the Civil War.* Philadelphia, 1951.

LEBESON, ANITA LIBMAN, *Jewish Pioneers in America.* New York, 1931. *Pilgrim People.* New York, 1950. The bibliography included in this book runs to almost a thousand titles. "American Jewish Chronicle" in *The Jews,* ed. Louis Finkelstein. New York, 1949. "Jewish Cartographers: A Forgotten Chapter of Jewish History," in *Historia Judaica,* Vol. X, No. 2.

MARCUS, JACOB RADER, *Early American Jewry,* 2 vols. Philadelphia, 1951-1953.

POOL, DAVID DE SOLA, *Portraits Etched in Stone.* New York, 1952.

Publications of the American Jewish Historical Society, 1950-1954.

REZNIKOFF, CHARLES, *The Jews of Charleston.* Philadelphia, 1950. (URIAH Z. ENGELMAN, co-author)

ROSENBERG, STUART E., *The Jewish Community in Rochester,* 1843-1925. New York, 1954.

SCHAPPES, MORRIS U., *A Documentary History of the Jews in the United States,* 1654-1875. New York, 1950.

ECONOMIC AND SOCIAL DEVELOPMENT OF AMERICAN JEWRY*

Jacob Lestschinsky

1. GROWTH AND CONCENTRATION OF THE JEWISH POPULATION

The rise of the great Jewish center in the United States has taken place in the last hundred years, and for the most part in the last fifty years. It is basically an immigrant community, although today two-thirds of American Jews are native-born.

* We must rely chiefly on estimates and conjectures for the most important statistical data because in the United States there are no official figures even for such basic questions as the number of Jews. In so far as we have more or less useful data, they are mostly the result of private, partial surveys, which are necessarily less than exact. We shall therefore usually employ round numbers. Notwithstanding the paucity of our data, we believe that the general picture of Jewish life in the United States given in this paper is reasonably accurate.

TABLE 1

GROWTH OF JEWISH POPULATION IN THE UNITED STATES, 1820 to 1953

Year	Number of Jews	Percent of Total Population in the U.S.	Percent of Jewish People in the World
1820......	5,000	0.05	0.16
1850......	50,000	0.21	1.06
1880......	275,000	0.55	3.44
1900......	1,100,000	1.45	10.00
1925......	3,800,000	3.25	27.14
1945......	4,700,000	3.35	44.80
1953......	5,100,000	3.25	44.00

This table shows the rapid growth of the Jewish population in the United States: from an insignificant number of some five thousand souls to upward of five millions in 130 years. The most rapid increase occurred in the quarter-century from 1900 to 1925. This was the period of the largest wave of immigration, and also of the highest natural increase. Because the immigrants were young and vigorous, their birth rate was high and their death rate low.

The proportion of American Jewry to the total population has climbed from 0.05 percent in 1820 to over three percent today. To be sure, even the latter figure is not high, and it is no longer rising as it was before 1925, but is stationary or even falling. This may be explained, first, by the fact that the natural increase among Jews is much smaller than among the American population as a whole; and second, by the fact that in recent years the proportion of Jews among all immigrants to America has declined, as we shall see below.

Of great interest and significance is the last column, showing the ratio of American Jewry to world Jewry: from one-sixth of one percent in 1820 it has risen to over 44 percent, or nearly one-half of the Jewish people. But here it should be borne in mind that this sharp rise was largely the result not only of organic growth—through immigration or a high natural increase—but also of the great Jewish catastrophe in Europe. In 1939 American Jewry constituted barely 30 percent of the Jewish people.

The American Jewish Year Book for 1954 has a listing of 795 localities, with the Jewish population of each. By adding up the figures, we arrive at the total Jewish population of the United States—5,065,000. The compilers of these statistical data point out that some areas with very small Jewish populations have been omitted because of difficulties in reaching them, and that the aggregate number of Jews in the United States must therefore be estimated at a *minimum* of 5,100,000.

On the basis of these figures, we have prepared the following table, which offers a clear picture of the distribution of American Jews in the United States:

The number of Jews in the five largest American cities (New York, Chicago, Los Angeles, Philadelphia and Boston) is 3,295,000. This constitutes 65 percent of all the Jews in the United States. Throughout our history, there has never been such a concentration of Jews in so small a number of localities, and in the largest cities. The non-Jewish population of these cities, according to the 1950 census, is 13,060,000 persons (16,355,000, less the 3,295,000 Jews), i.e., not more than 8.6 percent of the total population of the country. The percentage of Jews in the big cities is almost eight times higher.

This big-city concentration plays an important part in the life of American Jewry. To begin with, from the purely economic viewpoint, the average income of families living in big cities is almost double that of the average American family. Politically, the big cities, with their press and their leading position in the country's economic life, exert great influence on politics. And, of course, from the purely Jewish viewpoint, the compactness of the Jewish population facilitates the development of institutions and strengthens the sense of being a part of a large Jewish group.

TABLE 2

**DISTRIBUTION OF JEWS IN THE UNITED STATES
BY SIZE OF COMMUNITY, 1953**

Size of Community	Number of Communities	Number and Proportion of Jews			Average Jewish Population of each Community
		Absolute Number	% of Total Population	% of all Jews in the U.S.	
With a Jewish population of more than 100,000	5	3,295,000	20.1	65.0	659,000
With a Jewish population of 50 to 100 thousand	7	451,000	7.1	8.9	64,430
With a Jewish population of 25 to 50 thousand	5	164,000	5.5	3.2	32,800
With a Jewish population of 10 to 25 thousand	26	385,000	7.2	7.6	14,800
With a Jewish population of 5 to 10 thousand	36	250,000	. . .	4.9	7,000
With a Jewish population of 1 to 5 thousand	156	331,000	. . .	6.6	2,120
With a Jewish population less than 1,000	560	189,000	. . .	3.8	340
Total	**795**	**5,065,000**	. . . .	**100.0**	. . . . .

The second type of community, with a Jewish population of 50 to 100 thousand, comprises seven localities with a total of 451,000 Jews and an average Jewish population of more than 64,000—again a large enough number for Jewish community life. Altogether, we thus have approximately 3,750,000—almost 75% of the total Jewish population of America—concentrated in twelve of the largest communities.

A certain number of American Jews, however, are scattered over hundreds of localities. The average Jewish populations of the 560 smallest communities consist of not more than 340 persons. This number is certainly insufficient for the development of a community life or the establishment of institutions, particularly educational institutions. In the group of cities with Jewish populations of 1 to 5 thousand, the average number of Jews is not more than a little over 2,000—a number that is also not very favorable to the establishment and maintenance of community institutions.

The following table lists the cities with Jewish populations of more than 25,000.

The percentage of all American Jews living in these 16 cities, each with 25,000 or more Jewish inhabitants in 1953, was as follows:

Year	Percent
1900	75.1
1925	70.2
1953	77.0

This is a density never attained by European Jewry, except in countries with small numbers of Jews, such as the Scandinavian, where virtually the entire Jewish population lives in the capital cities.

In New York city alone there live more than 43 percent of all the Jews in the United States—2,300,000. This is five times the number of Jews in Moscow and six times the number of Jews in Warsaw in 1939, on the eve of World War II. And these were then the largest Jewish communities in Europe. Today New York City contains more Jews than the combined Jewish population of the nine largest Jewish communities in Europe in 1939—Berlin, Budapest, Kiev, Lodz, London, Moscow, Odessa, Vienna, Warsaw.

TABLE 3
NUMBER AND PROPORTION OF JEWS IN THE LARGEST CITIES OF THE UNITED STATES

City	Number of Jews			Percent of Total Population
	1900	1925	1953	1953
New York	500,000	1,600,000	2,300,000	29.0
Los Angeles	2,000	40,000	325,000	16.5
Chicago	60,000	270,000	325,000	9.0
Philadelphia	75,000	250,000	245,000	11.8
Boston	40,000	70,000	140,000	17.5
Detroit	10,000	45,000	72,000	4.0
Baltimore	25,000	55,000	78,000	8.0
Cleveland	20,000	70,000	85,000	9.0
Newark	15,000	50,000	56,000	12.0
Pittsburgh	10,000	50,000	54,000	8.0
San Francisco	15,000	25,000	51,000	8.0
St. Louis	25,000	45,000	48,000	6.0
Miami	1,000	5,000	55,000	20.0
Milwaukee	7,000	12,000	30,000	5.0
Washington	1,000	20,000	35,000	5.0
Hartford	2,000	10,000	26,000	13.0
Total	**808,000**	**2,617,000**	**3,925,000**	....

The relative weight of Jews in the cities of the United States is, however, much smaller than it was in pre-war Europe. There the Jews constituted between 30 and 40 percent of the total population in several major cities, while in the medium-sized and smaller cities of several East European countries the percentage of Jews often exceeded 50. In the very small towns the percentage of Jews frequently was as high as 80 or 90. In many cities and towns, moreover, the non-Jewish population was divided into two and often three ethnic groups, and the Jews consequently were a plurality. In Eastern Europe the smaller the town, the larger the percentage of Jews. In the United States the situation is reversed: the smaller the town, the smaller the percentage of Jews. In the United States it may be assumed that about 100,000 Jews live in rural areas, many of them with only a handful of Jews each; and some 200,000 Jews live in very small towns having less than five thousand inhabitants, and a very low ratio of Jews to the general population. While in Eastern Europe the village and small-town Jew was the most conservative and pious, and hence the most loyal to Jewish tradition, the contrary is true in the United States: here assimilation is much stronger in the small localities with few Jewish inhabitants than in the medium-sized and large cities with greater numbers of Jews.

2. JEWISH IMMIGRATION TO THE UNITED STATES

The eminent sociologist Franz Oppenheimer says in one of his works that the whole history of mankind is a history of migrations; history is the movement of masses of people. Whether or not this formula is true for humanity in general, it is true for the Jews, especially during the last one hundred years.

From 1840 till the end of 1953 there migrated overseas, mainly from Europe, more than five million Jews. This is more than the entire Jewish population in the world in 1840. The figure of more than five million Jews who emigrated to overseas countries does not include those who migrated within the confines of Europe itself, from the dense East European Jewish communities to the sparser Central and West European Jewish settlements. The latter movement involved about half a million Jews.

Over and above the usual political and economic causes that lead people to immigrate, the quest for sheer physical safety has been especially important in causing Jewish migration. The move from Europe to the Western Hemisphere saved millions of Jewish lives.

Of the five million Jewish migrants in the period under review, approximately three million went to the United States. Of these three million, only some 150,000 came from Asiatic and African countries. About 2,850,000 Jewish immigrants to the United States, or approximately 97 percent, came from Europe. It is this immigration that will be discussed here at some length, because in order to understand the development of American Jewry not only economically and socially, but also intellectually and culturally, it is necessary to know where the immigrants came from and what spiritual baggage they brought with them.

The countries of origin of European Jewish immigrants are as follows:

TABLE 4

ORIGINS OF JEWISH IMMIGRANTS TO THE UNITED STATES

Country of Origin	Number of Jews	Percent
Germany	250,000	8.8
England	150,000	5.3
France	50,000	1.7
Other West European countries	50,000	1.7
East and South European countries	2,350,000	82.5
Total	**2,850,000**	**100.0**

Even if we assume that all the immigrants from the West European countries

were natives of those countries (and therefore vocationally and culturally equipped
to cope with conditions in the new lands)
we must still conclude that American Jewry
is essentially East European in origin, since
82.5 percent is a large enough majority to
decide the basic character of a community.

In reality, however, even of the 500,000
immigrants from the West European countries most were by origin East European.
It was not native English Jews who emigrated to America but East Europeans, who
remained in London or Manchester only
long enough to earn enough money for the
last lap of the voyage to America. And
this was also true of the migration from
Paris and Antwerp and the Scandinavian
countries. These were all wayside stops for
the East European Jews, who constituted
the bulk of Jewish immigrants to the
United States from these countries. It was
different with Germany: in that country
there was also a purely German Jewish
emigration; but even there the Posen Jews,
in the main Polish, made up a considerable
percentage of all Jewish emigrants. We are
therefore inclined to assume that, of the
half-million Jewish immigrants from the
West European countries, at least 250,000
were East European Jews. This leads to the
conclusion that the East European Jews
constituted no less than 93 or 94 percent
of all Jewish immigrants to the United
States.

But it would be erroneous to assume
that the East European Jews who came by
way of the West European countries were
the same as those who came directly from
Russia and Poland, or Rumania and Hungary. The yeshiva student or middle-class
youth in general who did not go to America
directly from his home town or city, but
who first spent three or four years in London, learned to speak English, straightened
his back, had a taste of Western culture,
and mastered a trade—this typical Jewish
emigrant from England during the period
1870 to 1900 had already begun to change.
His London experience gave him not only

a good deal of needed knowledge and skill,
but also more courage and confidence in
himself, together with greater flexibility
and bolder ambitions. Even the immigrant
who was already a skilled worker in Eastern Europe, and who on the way to his
final destination spent a number of years
in a large city of Western Europe, notably
in London, could more easily find his bear-
ings in America and move more rapidly up
the social and economic ladder.

We reach the conclusion that there were
three types of Jewish immigrants to America: (a) East Europeans as such, (b) East
Europeans who had been exposed to vocational and cultural influences in a large
West European city *en route* to America,
and finally (c) West Europeans with a different culture and a different social background. (In reality, of course, even the
East European immigrants were not all of
a piece, especially in the twentieth century.
In the second half of the nineteenth century differences had arisen within East
European Jewry itself with respect to language and to secular and Jewish culture.
These differences played an exceedingly
important part in shaping the socio-economic, cultural, and spiritual physiognomy
of American Jewry.)

Let us turn to the distribution of Jewish
immigration to the United States by
periods of time. We have figures on the
distribution of the total immigration by
decades from 1820 to 1946.[1] From this data
it appears that of the 6,717,000 immigrants
to the United States from 1820 to 1870,
not more than 69,000 came from Eastern
and Southern Europe, or barely one percent. It is evident that during those fifty
years very few Jews came to the United
States from East European countries. And
while we know that there was a Jewish
influx in those years, by far the great
majority of it came from the West European countries, above all Germany. Subsequently the proportion of the immigrants
from Eastern and Southern Europe grew
apace, and of the 26,110,000 immigrants in

the years 1870-1946, 14,060,000, or about 54 percent, came from those regions. From Eastern Europe there were 8,319,000 immigrants.[2] Of these, no fewer than 2,500,000 were Jews. This is about 30 percent, or three times the percentage of Jews in the total East European population.

TABLE 5

DISTRIBUTION OF JEWISH IMMIGRATION BY PERIODS, 1840 to 1953

Years	Number	Percent of all Jewish Immigrants	Percent of Total Immigration
1840–1870	150,000	5.0	2.3
1871–1890	250,000	8.4	3.1
1891–1925	2,200,000	73.3	10.5
1926–1953	400,000	13.3	13.6
Total.....	**3,000,000**	**100.0**	**7.9**

Nearly three-fifths of all Jewish immigrants arrived in the 35 years from 1891 to 1925 inclusive. These were the years of unrestricted immigration in the United States, when the East European Jews surged forth from their old homes, from their ghettos and poverty-stricken towns, and flocked, not infrequently at the rate of a hundred thousand a year, to America. It should be remembered that of these 35 years, seven or eight were war years, with migration virtually impossible. (From August 1914 to the end of 1920, Russia was at war with Germany and later with Poland; in the six years 1915-1920, a total of only 76,450 Jews immigrated to the United States.) In part this massive immigration was made possible by the fact that by 1890 the United States already contained an East European Jewish community of a couple of hundreds of thousands, who were in a position to finance the immigration of relatives and friends. For poverty was for a long time one of the major obstacles to Jewish emigration from Eastern Europe.

Further large-scale Jewish immigration, from Europe in general and from Eastern Europe in particular, was checked by the immigration quota law of 1924. In the ensuing years, a period almost as long as that from 1891 to 1925, minus the war years, only about 400,000 Jews arrived in the United States, or less than a fifth of those who entered during virtually the same number of years before 1925. And surely there is no comparison between the tragic plight of the Jews in Europe from 1926 to 1953 and their lot in the preceding period.

The last column shows the proportion of Jewish immigration to the total immigration to the United States. From slightly over 2 percent in the period ending in 1870, the eve of mass Jewish emigration from Eastern Europe, the Jewish proportion rose to more than 10 percent in the period from 1891 to 1925. Since the immigration was mostly European and the Jews constituted a scant two percent of the population of Europe, it may be inferred that the Jewish population of Europe sought a haven of refuge in the United States five times as intensively as the non-Jewish population of that continent.

The large percentage of Jewish immigrants in the quota years (1926-1953) may be explained by the fact that during the depression (1929-1937) there was even a reemigration movement among many European ethnic groups in the United States, whereas for the Jews the situation in Europe was so dangerous that they were far less concerned with material prosperity than with saving their lives. Fortunately the German Jews, then most imminently threatened, were able to make use of the large German quota, which is second only to the British and exceeds 25,000 a year. In the years immediately preceding and during Second World War many Jews, often at great personal risk, made their way to America. Between 1936 and 1940 Jews were 68.3 percent of all immigrants to the United States, and between 1941 and 1945, 44.8 percent.

Before turning to a socio-economic analysis of the Jewish immigrants, let us first ascertain the distribution of the Jewish immigrants by periods *and* countries of origin. It must be borne in mind that in the course of the more than one hundred years of Jewish immigration to America, the social and economic structure of the Jews in the countries of emigration changed radically. One cannot compare the German Jewish immigrant of the 30-year period 1840-1870 with the German Jewish immigrant of the years 1933-1953, just as one cannot compare the East European Jewish immigrant of the first 20 years of the mass immigration—1871-1890—with the East European immigrant of the recent decades of the twentieth century.

Of the 250,000 Jewish immigrants from Germany, approximately 200,000 were natives, including those from Posen. Of these 200,000 German Jewish immigrants, nearly 100,000 arrived here in the period from 1840 to 1870, and an equal number from 1925 to 1953. The small numbers of Jewish immigrants from Germany in the interval between 1870 and 1925 had little impact on American Jewry.

Of the other 250,000 Jewish immigrants from West European countries, at least 200,000 were East European by origin. On arriving in America they identified themselves socially, economically, culturally and spiritually with the East European Jewish community. There was only a difference of tempo; those who came by way of Western Europe ascended the social ladder more quickly and had less difficulty in penetrating even the liberal professions, let alone commerce.

The 250,000 Jewish immigrants who arrived in the period 1871-1890 were nearly all East European, with a small admixture from Germany and from the Arab countries, chiefly Lebanon and Syria. The tidal waves of Jewish immigration from Eastern Europe occurred between 1891 and 1925. The subsequent Jewish immigration reflected to a lesser degree the character of the Jewish communities in the East European countries, since it was regulated by the quota law and included a relatively considerable percentage of non-quota immigrants in special categories, such as rabbis and students, spouses of American citizens, and the like.

3. "INGATHERING AND AMALGAMATION OF THE EXILES" IN THE DIASPORA

Migrations, which are so characteristic of the whole history of the Jews, have played a major part in the struggle for existence of the Jewish people in many alien environments these two thousand years. Sojourning long in a country, the Jew became attached to it, became acclimated, adopted the language of the majority and in many cases was so deeply imbued with it as not only to use it as a technical medium of communication with the surrounding non-Jewish world, but also to employ it in recording purely Jewish experiences and dreams. And Jews on their long wanderings adopted many non-Jewish customs, folkways, melodies, dances.

Expulsion and emigration would interrupt the natural process of assimilation. In the new Diaspora country, the basically Jewish tradition and values would revive with fresh vigor. What is more, many alien customs and values, brought over from the country of expulsion but transplanted in a new environment, would lose their former character and acquire a distinctly Jewish flavor. The transformation consisted in this, that the once alien phenomenon, which in its original country furthered the process of assimilation, became a force for Jewish survival. The history of Yiddish—a language which in the Slavic countries was transformed into a highly and remarkably developed national tongue and played, and still plays, a tremendous role in the struggle against assimilation—is an apt illustration.

Expulsions coincided in several Diaspora countries, as in Western and Central Europe at the time of the Crusades and later of the Black Plague; Jews were expelled from England, France, Switzerland, South and Central Germany, and also parts of Austria, from the thirteenth century to the fifteenth. In Poland diverse types of Jews, of different languages and backgrounds, blended and fused together and produced that most pronounced, nationally integrated Jewish community which played so vast a part in all Jewish social and cultural movements. It is probable that Polish Jewry also absorbed a Slavicized Jewish element from the south of Russia and also small groups of Spanish Jews.

Before our eyes there is taking place a gigantic amalgamation of over five million Jews in a country of a size and strength unexampled in Jewish history. In the United States there have met Jews from all parts of the world: from some thirty European countries and about half a score Oriental lands. For purely methodological reasons, we are accustomed to speak and write of the millions of Jews as West European, East European, and Oriental. Until the second half of the nineteenth century, such a division was perhaps correct and in accord with the objective situation: all the Jews of Eastern Europe spoke Yiddish and were very similar in many other aspects of culture and in way of life. Jews of the West European type lived for the most part in the German states and could also be considered as an entity. But the differentiation which began in the second half of the nineteenth century, as a result of emancipation in some countries and of auto-emancipation in others, drove a wedge between the Jews of different countries. So it was in Western Europe, and so also in Eastern Europe.

The German Jew at the turn of the twentieth century no longer could communicate so easily with the English Jew as in the first half of the nineteenth century, when the majority of English Jews were only one or two generations removed from immigration from Germany. In the first quarter of the present century, the linguistic differentiation and cultural alienation reached such a point that many ordinary Rumanian or Hungarian Jews no longer understood Lithuanian, White Russian, Ukrainian or Galician Jews.

The amalgamation on American soil began, naturally, among groups more or less culturally and economically akin. If one studies the origin and growth of various organizations and institutions among American Jewry, one is struck by the fact that the amalgamation of the severed and alienated Jewish groups proceeded according to the principle of majority rule. The German Jewish group, which represented the great majority of the West European immigrants, absorbed the small number of English and French, Dutch and Belgian, Swiss and Scandinavian Jews. Among the East European Jews, the Russian-Polish wing, which furnished over 70 percent of all Jewish immigrants, played the leading role in the amalgamative process.

Amalgamation proceeded in different ways among the diverse groups of Jews, and also at different tempos. The first and most elementary role in the process of welding together the severed members of the people was played by religion. The synagogue or temple was less concerned with the country of origin than with the form of the ritual or the degree of piety. At least within the framework of each religious trend, the naturally different and mutually aloof Jews from Germany and those from Eastern Europe met. But this was not the only way.

The German Jews, who in the nineteenth century were the pioneers of Jewish immigration, at first engaged almost exclusively in peddling; they were therefore scattered over all those states in which there was a substantial German Christian settlement. They formed no *landsmanshaften,* which had so great a role among the East European Jews, if only because the numbers from individual German provinces or cities were too small for the formation of *landsmanshaften.* Their first important organization, apart, naturally, from congregations and charitable institutions, was B'nai B'rith, which has already celebrated its centennial.

The East European Jews also had their share of peddlers, but they were incomparably fewer than those who flocked to the shops and factories. In the shops and factories *landsleit* very often met. Very often a manufacturer would import workers from his old home town in Eastern Europe. Their first organizations, again apart from the congregations and the benevolent societies connected with the synagogues, were the landsmanshaften.

The landsmanshaften played an exceedingly important part in the immigration itself: the indigent in their old home towns were provided with money for the voyage, and with loans after their arrival in this country. We cannot dwell here in greater detail on the manifold functions of the landsmanshaften and on their role in the great relief work of the American Jews for their European brethren. A few figures will suffice to give an idea of the prevalence of this unique folk organization. A study made in 1938 established that there were nearly three thousand landsmanshaften in New York, with approximately half a million members. Almost every fourth Jew belonged to a landsmanshaft. In the whole country there were then more than four thousand landsmanshaften, with about 750,000 members. The members of the New York landsmanshaften were roughly distributed as follows: 75 percent were wage earners, 15 percent retailers, and about 10 percent white-collar workers and professionals. Here is proof, though scarcely needed, that working people are particularly inclined to organization and mutual aid. Eighty-five percent of all the members were immigrants and only 15 percent native-born. Eighty percent of the landsmanshaften societies sprang up between 1903 and 1909, that is, after the Kishinev pogrom.

The most important role in the amalgamative process has in recent years been played by the fund-raising campaigns, especially the United Jewish Appeal. Here the differences between countries of origin are subordinated and American Jewry emerges as such. The campaigns of the United Jewish Appeal, for example, depend primarily on organization by trades, and only secondarily by the landsmanshaften and similar associations based on difference of origin and background.

4. NATURAL INCREASE AMONG THE JEWISH POPULATION OF THE UNITED STATES

The population trend in the United States has been the same as in all civilized countries during the last few decades. The rate of decline in birth greatly exceeded the rate of decline in mortality and, in consequence, the rate of natural increase diminished sharply. The Jews of the United States underwent this development, but at a quicker tempo. This is because Jews include a high percentage of city dwellers and a large proportion of professional persons and families in the higher income groups—all of whom are everywhere noted for a low rate of natural increase.

This development, characteristic of all civilized nations, had for a long time been counteracted in the United States, and among the Jewish population as well, by the tremendous influx of immigrants from countries with a high birth rate. With the establishment of quotas in 1924 and the consequent falling off of immigration from Southern and Eastern Europe, the situation stabilized and the decline of births assumed dangerous proportions, especially among Jews.

The process just described continued until World War II and after, when the birth rate suddenly began to soar, on a far greater scale than is usual in such times, and has continued for a much longer period. The mortality is still falling, so that the natural increase is quite considerable. Here are a few figures on the population trend in the United States.

TABLE 6

NATURAL INCREASE OF THE AMERICAN POPULATION (PER THOUSAND)

1900	13.8
1915	11.8
1930	7.6
1940	6.7
1946	13.3
1951-1952	17.5

In 1889 the Census Bureau of the Central Statistical Office[3] made a survey of 10,618 Jewish families, comprising 60,630 individuals, of whom 40,666, or 67.1 percent, were natives of America. These families had lived in the United States for more than 15 years. About three-fourths of all the families surveyed seem to have been of German origin. The survey embraced Jews in all parts of the country.

What did these figures show? First, that the natural increase among these families was about 13.7 per thousand, approximately the same as among the total population in the year 1900. Children up to 14 years of age made up 32.1 percent of the total number. This, too, coincides with the percentage of such children in the total population of the United States, according to the census.

Of interest are the figures showing the average number of children per family among Jews from various countries, according to the mother's country of origin. Whereas for mothers from Russia and Poland the average number of children per family was 5.63, it was 5.24 for mothers born in Germany, and only 3.56 for mothers born in America. The general conclusion from these figures must be that toward the end of the nineteenth century the natural increase among Jews in the United States was still quite high but with a suggestion of decline: mothers born in America bore a smaller number of children per family than immigrant mothers.

An attempt to compute the natural increase among American Jews was made by the famous Jewish scholar Joseph Jacobs in the *American Jewish Year Book*, Vol. 15 (1914-1915), p. 357. He reached the conclusion that the natural increase at that time (1910-1914) was 19 per thousand. This high figure was no doubt quite correct, because from 1900 to 1914 there came to the United States a million and a half Jews, at least 90 per cent of them from Eastern Europe.

There are no current direct vital statistics for American Jewry; we must therefore approach an estimate indirectly. The most important criterion of the natural increase among a population is the percentage of children; if a people has many live children, its biological future is assured. We say "live" children, because it is not enough that many children are born —they must live.

We have figures on the age structure of 25 Jewish communities with an aggregate population of about 700,000. Ten cities supply data on the age structure of their Jewish population in the Thirties, mostly for the years 1937 and 1938, while 15 communities offer figures for the Forties, mainly for the year 1948. We are thus in a position to estimate the changes which took place in the course of about ten years.

If we take the age class of children up to 4 years of age, we find that it constitutes at the most 8 percent among the first group, and in a majority of the first ten cities in the Thirties it is between 5.3 and 6 percent. Among the fifteen cities in the Forties, the minimum is 7.5 percent, the maximum 12.5 percent, and the average about 9 percent. From these figures it is evident that among the Jewish population, as among the non-Jewish, a radical change has taken place in the birth rate. And since there is little doubt that the mortality rate among Jews is declining even more sharply than among non-Jews, it may be inferred that the natural increase has risen among Jews in recent years. But the natural increase among Jews still falls considerably short of the non-Jewish increase. There is considerable evidence for this assertion. In a very thorough study made in Annapolis, Md., in 1941, the number of children for every hundred women between the age of 25 and 29 was as follows: among Catholics,

128; among Protestants, 120; among Jews, 79. The number of children for every hundred women between 35 and 39 was: among Catholics, 243; among Protestants, 199; among Jews, 178.

I am inclined to assume that, if among the total population the natural increase has lately amounted to 17-18 per thousand, among Jews it is 9 to 10 per thousand, possibly a little higher. The pre-war fear that American Jewry, which in its economic development resembles pre-Hitler German Jewry, playing a disproportionately large part in trade and the liberal professions, might fall victim to the two-child or one-child system, is gone. We do not know how long this will be true, just as we cannot tell how long the high natural increase will continue among the total population of the United States and in many other countries, including even France, which before World War II had a biological deficit.

I find evidence of the higher natural increase among American Jews in recent years in the data on Canada, where we have official and therefore exact figures.

TABLE 7

ANNUAL NATURAL INCREASE, PER THOUSAND, IN CANADA, 1936 to 1950

Years	Total Population	Jewish Population
1936-1940	10.6	6.5
1946-1950	18.2	13.1

American Jewry is older and economically more advanced, has a higher percentage of professionals, and consequently tends to a lower birth rate. I therefore assume a natural increase of 9 to 10 per thousand. I believe that American Jewry now has a natural increase of 45,000 to 50,000 a year.

The Jewish increase, however, is exposed to still another danger than the two-child system—a danger not yet acute, but capable of becoming so: intermarriage. In this respect a wide gulf already existed several decades ago between different types of Jews. Here are a few interesting figures covering the years 1908-1912. At that time the percentage of mixed marriages among various Jewish groups in New York was as follows:

TABLE 8[4]

PERCENTAGE OF MIXED MARRIAGES AMONG JEWS, NEW YORK CITY, 1908 TO 1912

Group	Percentage
French Jews	6.54
German Jews	5.16
Hungarian Jews	2.24
Russian-Polish Jews	0.62
Rumanian Jews	0.45

Of late, however, there has been virtually no difference between Jews of different countries of origin: intermarriage has become a common occurrence and no longer produces tragedies in Jewish families.

In 1870 there was not a single case of intermarriage among the Jews of New Haven; in 1931, 5.6 percent of the marriages among the Jews were mixed marriages; in 1940, they constituted 9 percent.

In Stamford, Conn., there were 59 mixed marriages in 1942 as against 823 endogamous ones, or 7.2 percent. Intermarriage is here not a "prerogative" of the upper and more educated and assimilated strata of Jewish society. On the contrary, mixed marriages occur more frequently among Jews of the middle class than of the upper class.

In the *Jewish Frontier* for March 1953, an anonymous Jewish mother, whose son is about to marry a Christian girl, writes as follows: "In my immediate family, including first cousins, there have been ten intermarriages. Among my friends and acquaintances there are at least a score more. Among the Jewish boys who have taken Christian wives there are professional men, white collar workers, manual workers, all types and all degrees of mentality." After expressing a fear that "his children, if any, would be brought up as Christians and, who knows, perhaps as Christians who hate and despise Jews," she concludes with these highly interesting and significant words: "Of course, it is silly for me to entertain thoughts like this . . . I, my thoughts and memories are of *yesterday*. My children, their hopes and dreams are of *tomorrow*" (italics added, J. L.).

What becomes of the children of mixed marriages? There are many cases where the Christian wife rears the children of the Jewish husband more in harmony with Jewish tradition than the average Jewish mother does. These are exceptions, however, and in the majority of cases the offspring of mixed marriages are raised as Christians. In the small towns intermarriage is more common than in the large cities. In an article entitled "The Disappearing Small-Town Jews," in *Commentary* for August 1952, Lee J. Levinger, a well-known Reform rabbi and author, writes that about twenty years earlier he attended a reunion of a group of his father's cousin's family in a little town in the Middle West. The sons of a large family had come back from their widely scattered homes. The writer paints the following picture:

> In the whole *mishpocho,* the only Jewish wife, besides my own, was Emil's—he kept a delicatessen store in St. Louis. The children of the mixed marriages were Lutherans, Methodists, Christian Scientists, according to the churches of their mothers. Frank from Texas boasted that his son, brought up by a pious Catholic mother, resembled him in appearance, and was nicknamed "the little Jew"; Frank also told me that he subscribes to an anti-Catholic paper just in order to read it ostentatiously when the priest comes to visit.

A mass-circulation magazine, *Women's Home Companion*, published in March 1953 the results of an opinion poll among Jewish and Christian women about intermarriages. Two of the questions asked were as follows:

> Do you think mature intelligent people of basically different religious background can have a happy marriage?

> If your son or daughter wished to marry someone of basically different religious views, would you approve or disapprove of the marriage?

Eighty-seven percent of the Jewish women, 83 percent of the Catholics, and 78 percent of the Protestants answered the first of these two questions in the affirmative.

Why were the Proestant women, whose religion is more tolerant than Catholicism, stricter than the Catholic women? The explanation is to be sought in the ethnic aspect of these religions. The Protestants are mostly of English, German, or generally Nordic stock, and keep rather aloof from the Catholics, the more recent immigrants from Eastern and Southern Europe, and the Jews. The great majority of the Jews, moreover, live among or near Catholics, and they also meet and mingle more with Catholics in school and at work. And it has been proved that mixed marriages among Jews more often than not involve Catholic spouses. In America opposition to intermarriage is losing its traditional power not only among Jews but also among the non-Jewish population, Catholics included.

There is a gap between theory and practice, as the answers to the second and more concrete question show. This time the Jewish women were more cautious: while the Catholics approved by 61 percent and the Protestants by 58, only 42 percent of the Jewish women voiced approval. Nevertheless, this is still a high percentage.

On the basis of many studies it may be assumed that the percentage of mixed marriages among Jews in the United States fluctuates between 8 and 10, but is steadily, though slowly, rising. Approximately three-fourths of the Jewish intermarriages are between Jewish men and Christian women, and about one-fourth between Jewish women and Christian men.

5. CRIME AMONG JEWS

It is generally known that the percentage of criminals among Jews is lower than among non-Jews and that Jews are rarely involved in serious crimes of violence. But it has likewise been proved that the more Jews become assimilated, the more they resemble the non-Jewish population with respect to incidence and types of crime.

Figures for the city of New York for the years 1902, 1903 and 1904 show the following number of prisoners in the city jails: in 1902, 4,115, including 381 Jews, or 9.2 percent; in 1903, 4,015, including 378 Jews, or 9.4 percent; in 1904, 3,251, including 479 Jews, or 14.7 percent. The percentage of Jews in New York at that time was about 17 or 18. The percentage of Jews among lawbreakers in the first two years was thus half of the percentage of Jews in the total population of the city. Even in the last year, with its rise in the percentage of Jews among the inmates of jails, the proportion of Jewish criminals is still lower than the Jewish proportion in the total population. Unfortunately, we have no data on the crimes for which they were convicted. This is an important point, bacause a jail sentence can be imposed for killing a person or for picking a pocket.

In the course of a decade—1920 to 1929 inclusive—the average prison population of the United States was 394,080. Of this number, 6,846, or 1.74 percent, were Jews. This is one-half of the percentage of Jews in the United States at that time. The number of offenders declined in the course of the decade, but more sharply among Jews than among non-Jews. Thus, the first three years accounted for more than 35 percent of all Jewish offenders, and the last three years for only 22.8 percent. For non-Jews the respective figures were 36.54 and 27.40 percent.

In the spring of 1947, the total prison population of New York State was 15,225. Of this number, 722 were Jews, or 4.7 percent, which is approximately one fourth the percentage of Jews in the State. Among Jews, major offenses, such as murder, rape, mayhem and the like, constituted only 25 percent of all offenses; among non-Jews, 50 percent. Sex offenses among Jews were 2.4 percent of all Jewish crimes; among non-Jews, 6.2 percent, nearly three times as high. In the summer of 1949 there was a convention in New York of Jewish prison chaplains, at which it was reported that the jails of New York City then had 5,000 inmates, of whom only 174 were Jews, or altogether 3.5 percent, which was one-eighth of the percentage of Jews in the city. This small percentage of Jews among the prisoners is to be explained by the great improvement in the economic condition of the Jewish population, and by the extensive and excellent educational and social work carried on in recent years by the special Jewish institutions for juveniles.

All the data set forth thus far are undoubtedly of some value; but they are too general, which greatly diminishes their significance. We do have detailed official information on Jewish lawbreakers in Los Angeles over a long period, however.

TABLE 9
JEWISH POPULATION OF LOS ANGELES, 1933 to 1947

Year	Number	Percentage
1933	75,000	5.8
1941	130,000	8.4
1947	225,000	11.6

The percentage of Jews among those arrested in Los Angeles (exclusive of drunkards) was:

Period	Percentage
1933–1936	3.35
1939–1941	3.54
1945–1947	1.88

The percentage of arrested Jews thus declined. In every period it was considerably less than the Jewish percentage in the total population, but in the last period it was only one sixth as large. Of the women arrested, Jewish women constituted a very small percentage: in the years 1933-1936, 1.97, and in the years 1945-1947, only 0.89.

If we examine the figures for white prisoners, the Jewish proportion rises a little, but it is still far below the percentage of Jews in the city's population. Thus the percentage of Jews among the white prisoners in the years 1933-1936 was 4.68; the Jews then constituted no less than 10 percent of the total white population. In the years 1945-1947, the percentage of Jews among the white prisoners was 3.93, but the percentage of Jews in the white population of the city was probably 17 to 18. Thus the proportion of Jewish offenders was still less than a fourth of the proportion of Jews among the white inhabitants of the city.

Of at least equal interest is the analysis of the categories of offenses. The following table gives us unusually precise information.

TABLE 10

PERCENTAGE OF JEWS AMONG WHITE PRISONERS IN LOS ANGELES, 1933 to 1947[5]

Offense	Percentage of Jews		
	Total White Prisoners	White Male Prisoners	White Female Prisoners
Murder	3.3	3.4	2.4
Assault	3.0	3.0	2.9
Rape	2.8	2.8	0.0
Robbery	3.8	4.0	1.3
Burglary	3.0	2.9	3.1
Theft	3.9	3.8	4.7
Forgery	5.2	5.3	4.5
Narcotic law violations	6.8	8.2	1.5
Liquor law violations	8.9	7.5	2.7
Drunkenness	0.5	0.5	0.4
Drunken driving	0.7	0.8	0.5
Traffic violations	1.7	1.6	1.9
Sex offenses	2.8	4.1	1.4
Desertion (of family)	3.1	3.2	1.0
Illegal possession of weapons	2.7	2.8	0.0
Begging	1.4	1.4	1.9
Breach of peace	3.6	3.4	4.8
Violation of municipal ordinances	10.8	11.4	5.7
Miscellaneous	8.4	8.7	4.7

Let us make a very conservative estimate and assume that in all the given years (1933-1947) the Jews averaged between 10 and 12 percent of the white inhabitants of the city. It will then appear that in only one category did they have an equal percentage of offenders: violations of municipal ordinances. This probably refers to keeping one's place of business open on Sunday, the Christian Sabbath. In the majority of other offenses, the percentage of Jews involved was on the average one-third or one-fourth of their percentage among the city's white residents. In arrests for drunkenness, the Jewish proportion was one-twentieth of the Jewish proportion in the white population. For begging, the Jewish proportion was about one-eighth; for rape, about one-third. It is interesting to note that on the charge of drunkenness Jews constituted only one half of one percent of all the white offenders, whereas in liquor law violations they made up 8.9 percent and, in narcotic law violations, 6.8 percent. The higher figures are explained by illegal traffic in liquor and narcotics.

The difference between males and females was not very marked, yet it is noteworthy that even in those categories in which Jewish men constituted quite a high percentage of all male offenders, the proportion of Jewish female offenders was low. Of the violators of municipal ordinances Jewish men were 11.4 percent, and Jewish women only 5.7; of dealers in narcotics, Jewish men constituted 8.2 percent, and Jewish women only 1.5.

Of extreme interest are the figures on Jewish alcoholics. In a hospital for the treatment of alcoholics in the State of New York it was estimated, on the basis of the number of patients admitted in the years 1929-1931, that the incidence of alcoholism per 100,000 persons was as follows: among the Irish, 25.6; among Scandinavians, 7.8; among Italians, 4.8; among Britishers, 4.3; among Germans, 3.8; and among Jews, only 0.5. Some believe that among Jews such a patient is not sent to the hospital but is treated at home. There probably is some truth in this, but the difference in the admission rates is so great that there must be proportionately far fewer alcoholics among Jews than among other groups. This conclusion is in harmony with the figures given above on the percentage of Jews arrested for drunkenness in Los Angeles.

We conclude this section with some very interesting data on juvenile offenders in the city of New York.[6]

TABLE 11

PERCENTAGE OF JEWISH TEEN-AGERS (Under 17 Years) AMONG THOSE TRIED AND AMONG THOSE SENTENCED TO A HOUSE OF CORRECTION, NEW YORK CITY

Year	Percent of Jews Among Those Tried	Percent of Jews Among Those Sentenced
1930	20.6	10.8
1933	15.4	5.9
1935	12.2	6.4
1938	9.8	5.3
1941	8.8	3.9

During these years the percentage of Jews in New York City was between 27 and 28. The proportion of Jewish to all teen-agers brought to trial in 1930, at the beginning of the great depression, was quite high, being over 20 percent, but thereafter it declined and at the end of the depression it was under 9 percent, or one-third of the percentage of Jews in the city. The figures on convictions, rather than trials, are even more striking. The percentage of those convicted is rarely more and usually less than one-half of those tried. The proportion of Jewish to all teen-agers convicted falls as low as 3.9 percent, or one-seventh of the percentage of Jews in the city's population.

6. SOCIAL AND ECONOMIC DEVELOPMENT OF AMERICAN JEWRY

There were three prime factors in the social and economic development of American Jewry. In the order of their importance, these were:

(a) The coincidence of mass Jewish immigration with the rapid economic expansion and industrialization of the United States.

(b) The social and psychological heritage and the economic skills brought over by the Jewish immigrants from the old country, which were highly appropriate to America's stage of development.

(c) The large-scale immigration into America of backward non-Jewish peasants and common laborers from the same East European countries from which the great mass of Jewish immigration came.

The population of the United States was 39,818,000 in 1870, reaching 150,697,-000 by 1950. Toward the end of 1953, it was estimated as being close to 160,000,000. The population has thus quadrupled in little more than eighty years.

In 1870 there were employed in agriculture 18,200,000, somewhat more than 45 percent; in 1950 it was 23,331,000, or a little more than 15 percent. And according to the latest reports, the shift to the cities has not slowed down.

This tremendous growth of the urban population, which is the clearest sign of industrial progress, also indicates an increased need for service occupations—i.e., retailing, transportation, entertainment, and professional and other services required by our complex city life.

Parallel with the enormous growth of industry, there was intensive technical progress, which powerfully affected the character of the economic development. While the percentage of industrial workers remained stable, the proportion of those engaged in the service occupations, technicians, and office personnel, grew apace.

In 1870 those employed in industry and mining numbered 3,787,000, or 30.3 percent of all the gainfully employed; in 1950 they numbered 18,300,000, or 30 percent of all the gainfully employed. But in trade the number employed in 1870 was 727,000, or 5.7 percent of all the gainfully employed; while in 1950 it was 9,700,000, or 15 percent of all the gainfully employed—a relative increase of almost 300 percent.

Even more striking is the growth in the professions and the white-collar occupations. In 1870 these pursuits employed 402,-000 people, or not more than 3.2 percent of all the gainfully employed; in 1950 the figure was 11,200,000, or 18.3 percent of all the gainfully employed—a relative increase of almost 600 percent.

This is how one of the best students of American development describes these trends:[7]

> ...Since 1900 the proportion of Americans engaged in farming has taken a big drop; the proportion engaged in industry, overall, has changed very little; the proportion engaged in the "services" has jumped upward. Take this fact in conjunction with the facts about the shift within industry and we emerge with a general finding: At the mid-century there are fewer and fewer people working with their hands, more and more people working at desks; fewer workers with brawn, more workers with brain; fewer whose jobs require only a limited education, more who need an advanced education.

No economic development could have been more favorable for the Jewish immigrants from Europe.

A few figures on the economic advance of New York City will be useful here. To be sure, the figures are general, but, as we know, the Jews constitute in trade no less than two-thirds of the proprietors and a very large percentage of the employees in general, and of the office workers in particular. There is also a large proportion of Jewish entrepreneurs in many of the industries of New York, amounting in some of them, such as wearing apparel, fur, and jewelry, to over 80 percent. Data concerning New York have therefore much bearing on the economic status of American Jews with respect not only to employers, but to employees as well. If there is a Jewish working class in the United States, one that is at the same time highly differentiated by trades, it is to be found, in its great majority, primarily in New York. For the smaller the locality, the smaller the proportion of Jewish workers.

The population of New York City in 1940 was 7,445,000, and in 1951, 7,960,000, an increase of barely 7 percent. The number of industrial enterprises in 1939 was 227,265; in 1951, 237,000, a very slight increase. The number of employees in 1939 was 2,839,000; in 1951, 3,200,000, an increase of nearly 13 percent. Of particular interest to us are the data on trade, in which there is a high proportion of Jews, whether as proprietors or as workers. The number of those employed in wholesale trades in New York in 1939 was 241,000; in 1948, 315,000, an increase of 30 percent. In the retail trades, the Jewish proportion is especially high. The number of retail stores in 1939 was 115,000; in 1948, 104,-000, a drop of 11,000. But the number of those employed in the retail trade in 1939 was 336,000 and in 1948, 428,000, an increase of 92,000. The United States Department of Commerce says that this is not a phenomenon peculiar to New York, but a general one, "owing to the rise of super-markets and the merger of small businesses." (At one time it was predicted that these rapidly multiplying super-markets would eliminate the small grocers, who are particularly numerous among Jews. But modernization of the premises and competition with respect to quality and service have enabled the individual proprietors to hold their own rather successfully so far.)

Gross sales in the retail trade in New York in 1939 totaled $3,191,000,000, in 1951, $10,000,000,000! This accounts for the rise in the number of those employed in the retail trade. Among the new additions to the ranks of those employed in the retail trade we find many Jews who were formerly garment workers or carpenters and also a certain percentage of "retired" workers.

We now turn to the social and psychological character of the Jewish immigrant group in the United States.

Every considerable immigrant ethnic group brings with it, besides certain material assets, social, cultural and psychological values. These consist not only of individual economic and technical skills, but also of a certain cultural development and mental alertness. Only in the third or fourth, or perhaps even the fifth generation, are the transplanted cultural and mental qualities and traits generally obliterated by the new milieu and submerged by the new characteristics engendered by the new conditions—provided, of course, that the new conditions are such as to afford no opportunity to preserve the heritage and cultivate it, but force its bearers more and more to renounce the past and adapt themselves to the demands of the present. But the contrary is also possible: the new conditions may favor further and even deeper development and enhancement of the transplanted heritage, in its essence rather than its outward forms.

Among the European immigrants to the United States, the Jews were the most urban, as they had been for centuries; the most given to trade, even compared with the most advanced people of Europe; intellectually and culturally the most alert and flexible, thanks to the unique training they had received in the *hadarim* and *yeshivas;* finally, as a result of centuries of persecution, oppression, political restriction and economic discrimination, the best equipped to adjust to new conditions. Mendele Mocher Seforim in his day spoke caustically of the ability to scent a business opportunity miles away, but it stood the Jewish immigrants in the United States in very good stead. Because of all these reasons the Jews were bolder, and more venturesome. Under favorable conditions in a young country, these are very useful qualities. The successes were more frequent than the failures.

As we have seen, the Jewish immigrants did not consist of one social and cultural group; there were differences among them depending on their countries and time of emigration. The Sephardic immigrants of the 17th and 18th centuries had little influence on shaping the character of American Jewry. By the time of the mass Jewish immigrations the Sephardim had virtually disappeared. It was the German Jews who

until 1870 furnished the great bulk of Jewish immigrants.

Here is the occupational distribution, in percentages, of the Jews of Prussia (including Posen) at two different points of time.

TABLE 12

OCCUPATIONAL DISTRIBUTION OF PRUSSIAN JEWRY, 1834 and 1852[8]

Occupation	1834		1852	
Trade and Credit...	51.0	(60.8)	51.5	(58.0)
Handicraft and Industry..........	17.7	(9.8)	19.4	(14.8)
Liberal Professions..	3.2	(4.2)	3.5	(4.2)
Miscellaneous.......	28.0	(25.2)	25.6	(23.0)
Total.............	**100.0**	**(100.0)**	**100.0**	**(100.0)**

These figures give an idea of the occupational structure in the Jewish community which from 1830 to 1870 supplied the great majority of Jewish immigrants to the United States. We have no information on the occupational distribution of the immigrants themselves, but there is very little doubt that traders constituted a high proportion of the immigrants to the United States. In turn, a very large proportion of the Jewish traders in Germany at that time were peddlers.

A large non-Jewish emigration from Germany to the United States was then in progress, and the German emigrants were almost exclusively peasants. From 1820 to 1840, 900,000 Germans immigrated to America from Germany. From 1840 to 1910 about 5,000,000 immigrated to America from Germany. At the time of the Jewish emigration from Germany, that country was in the initial stages of capitalist development. There was a movement of people from the villages to the cities of Germany itself and across the sea. These people were used to the Jewish peddler from the villages of the old country.

Rudolf Glanz[9] quotes the *Deutsche Monatsschrift* of 1855 as saying that "the majority of them [the German Jews in the United States] became peddlers and dealers in clothes." Cecil Roth, after commenting in his *The Jewish Contribution to*

Civilization (Cincinnati, 1940, p. 282) on the great part played by the peddlers in the development of the American Middle West, adds: "And, in most cases, these peddlers were Jews—to a large extent, Jewish refugees from the intolerant policies of Central Europe." A detailed account of the Jewish peddlers toward the end of the 1850's is given by the famous traveler Israel Joseph Benjamin in his German book, *Drei Jahre in Amerika— 1859-1862* (Hannover, 1862). On page 45 he writes: "The previously arrived *Landesleute* assisted the newcomers with words of advice and deeds, helped them obtain merchandise and advised them to peddle their wares to the farmers. This business is not looked down upon in America; the farmer, who at that time could not yet purchase the necessary goods nearby, readily paid the peddler a good price. The Jewish immigrant, with his inherited business instinct, threw himself most eagerly into this trade and prospered." The famous Reform rabbi, Dr. Max Lilienthal, wrote in the *Allgemeine Zeitung des Judenthums* (1874, p. 23): "We have in this city [New York] a large number of storekeepers who have establishments valued at $100,000 and $200,000—and these men, on their arrival in this country six years ago, did not have a cent to their name. They carried on their backs all day a pack of merchandise weighing 100 to 120 pounds in order to earn something. When they had earned 'something,' they began to transport their wares by horse and cart. Later they opened small shops in country places, and now they own stores in New York."

It must not be inferred from the foregoing that there were no artisans among the German Jewish immigrants. There were, and they were the initiators in the establishment of workshops and afterwards of factories producing ready-to-wear clothing. The usual procedure was somewhat as follows: A tailor would emigrate from Posen to Berlin and embark upon the production of ready-made clothes by means of cheap homework by non-Jewish workers who were then flocking to Berlin from the small towns and villages. A relative or friend, who had gone to the United States, would import the ready-to-wear clothes manufactured in Berlin. Before very long the American, either in partnership with his Berlin kin or independently, would open a shop in New York and begin to manufacture ready-to-wear garments here. This, however, was the later stage of the development, when penniless Jewish masses had begun to pour in from Eastern Europe and sold their labor cheaply.

Here we halt our account of the first wave of German Jewish immigration. We shall treat the second wave of Jewish immigration from Germany (1933-1953) after we have described the Jewish immigration from Eastern Europe.

If the East European Jews, especially those from Russia and Poland—which means the Polish, Ukrainian, Lithuanian, and Latvian Jews—began to emigrate in large numbers later than the German Jews, it was not because they were better off. Actually, their lot was a thousand times harder in every respect; their legal status was worse and so was their economic condition. It was for this very reason that they ventured across the ocean decades later. Strictly speaking, it cannot be said that they did not emigrate at all, because there were Russian-Polish Jews in London and Paris as early as the 1840's. But emigration as a mass movement did not start among the Jews of Eastern Europe until the 1870's.

Emigration, especially to so remote a country as America, is, to begin with, a financial problem. In the second place, it requires a certain degree of culture, of knowledge of the world, of courage, to dare to set out on a journey to a far-off land where one has no kith or kin. This explains why in the 1840's, when the lot of the Russian Jews had become desperate in the extreme and there was much talk of removing the Jews from Russia, these Jews themselves hardly made a move to leave the country.

About 50 to 55 percent of the Russian-Polish Jews were employed in trade, tavern-keeping, brokerage, makeshift occupations, as rabbis and other religious functionaries; about 25 percent artisans, and the rest were servants and declassed persons, beggars and paupers. This was the general picture, with the exception of an upper crust of wealthy or fairly well-to-do Jews. The bulk of Russian-Polish Jewry seemed outwardly as though petrified in the forms molded by the feudal system of Poland in the 18th century. Underneath, however, disintegration was setting in, accompanied by the germination of new patterns of living and new cultural trends. These did not come to light until the emancipation of the serfs (1861) and the reforms inaugurated by Tsar Alexander II, which stirred the Pale of Settlement, awakened the spiritual energies of the heads of Russian Jewry, shook the young men of the yeshivas and houses of study out of their lethargy, and set in motion that epoch-making emigration which ultimately gave rise to both the present American Jewish community and the State of Israel.

Parallel with the rise of the Haskalah movement, and under its influence, many young men who possessed considerable Jewish education sought to escape both from the poverty of the Pale and from its backwardness in secular culture. Individuals went to the Russian secondary schools and universities, and to the Russian revolutionary parties. The masses went to the larger cities of the Pale of Settlement, where small-scale and medium industry had begun to spring up and employment could be found, and also to faraway lands in quest of a broader future.

The growth of the Jewish population in the middle and large cities of Russia proceeded very rapidly, exceeding the rate of the cities' economic development. Increasingly large numbers of Jews were forced into the working class, but they too did not find enough opportunities for employment in the Pale. Still, the growth of industry and handicraft was quite considerable. In

some twenty years it radically changed the character of Russian-Polish Jewry.

The emigration overseas reflected these processes. The first wave of emigrants, whether to England, France, or the United States, comprised a majority of lower middle class and declassed elements with a small admixture of skilled workers, for the most part tailors and seamstresses. The subsequent waves of Jewish migrants consisted of a majority of artisans and workers and of a smaller percentage of traders and declassed persons. "Declassed" must be taken here in a slightly different sense from the usual meaning of the word, which signifies elements which have dropped out of certain classes. Here it rather refers to middle-class youths who did not yet possess a clearcut social character: yeshivah students who had been preparing to become rabbis or occupy other religious functions, but, having strayed from the path of Orthodoxy, went to distant places in search of a career; *kestniks* (i.e., young men supported for a time by their fathers-inlaw) who had looked forward to a comfortable and easy life with their wives' families, but who were forced, or chose voluntarily, to go out into the wide world, conscious of new energies and stirred by new ambitions.

They were a peculiar, a unique lot. Landless and rootless, economically bare, wandering souls, they had great energy and potential talent. Though without a secular education, they were equipped with razor-edge minds, as the Jewish studies at the heder and the yeshivah are better calculated to sharpen the intellect than to furnish it with practical information. In addition, they were hungry not only physically and materially, but also for secular culture. Accordingly, they applied themselves to the new studies even after a twelve-hour workday at the sweatshop. Their will, moreover, was spurred on by their memories of the individual and collective humiliations and vexations of the whole Jewish people.

The shift to working-class occupations proceeded intensively in Russia. It was further intensified in the countries of transit, England, France and other West and Central European countries. But it reached its peak in the United States.

Beginning in the 1890's, and especially with the turn of the twentieth century, we already encounter a Jewish immigrant mass with a majority of workers, but having a unique character. In its majority it was probably a first generation of workers, in the sense of belonging to the working class. Many had had their first taste of manual labor only a short time before their departure for America: they had sat down at a Singer sewing machine and after a few weeks' practice felt more confident in setting out for so remote a place as New York. Or else they had journeyed to Lodz or Bialystok and worked for months or even a couple of years at weaving and then, as experienced weavers, joined a relative who was a weaver in Paterson, N. J. Some first learned a little carpentry or locksmithing in Warsaw and then went overseas with more confidence and courage than they would have had if they had set out for a faraway place directly from the yeshivah or the family market-stall. It was not necessary in those days for admission to America to prove that one had a trade, but many Jews wanted the experience to bolster their own confidence.

This was a generation decidedly petty bourgeois; imbued with a business tradition of many centuries; from an environment where trade was virtually a monopoly of Jews, where even Jewish labor was concentrated in certain crafts, and where the artisans also had to engage in business operations. Tailors, shoemakers and capmakers had to purchase their raw materials and enter into combination and competition with others—in short, to transact business and not merely to work.

Here is one account of the pioneer period of the East European Jewish immigration to America:[10]

> Among those who became cloak operators were former yeshivah students, store clerks, insurance agents, semi-intellectuals, teachers, *kestniks*,

storekeepers, traders, etc., an element individualistic, undisciplined, but rather capable, agile, impatient. All these men, who in the old country had been strangers to physical labor, here harnessed themselves to a machine which rushed the life out of them.

One of the best authorities on the immigrants of the 1880's, who personally experienced the first stages of the new life in New York, writes as follows in the course of reminiscences:[11]

> Fortunate were those who had learned a trade in the old country; the tailors, the carpenters, and other artisans would very quickly obtain employment. But the great majority of the Jewish immigrants consisted of nonworkers. The committeemen and their friends used to take the newly arrived immigrants to work in their shops, where they were taught a trade. Many immigrants hired out as unskilled laborers, working for stevedore companies, for the railroads, and also in large factories.

A colorful picture of the social background of the first Jewish immigrants is to be found in the Hebrew-language miscellany *Haasif* (Warsaw, 1886) in a letter from Judah D. Eisenstein, who came to the United States in 1872, and who thus describes the first generation of immigrants from Russian Poland: "former yeshivah students, *kestniks*, Hebrew teachers, *shochtim*, cantors, preachers, agents, tavern keepers." He writes further that many of them took to peddling, "which is terribly hard and trying." He adds: "nearly all the great merchants here were formerly peddlers. Even the big banker Joseph Seligman, one of the richest Jews in America, was forty years ago a country peddler."

According to the Russian census of 1897, the occupational structure of Russian Jewry was already far different from what it had been half a century earlier. Trade and credit now comprised only 31 percent of all the gainfully employed, and in this category are included the tavern-keepers, whose numbers had decreased sharply after the Tsarist government had instituted a state monopoly on the sale of liquor. Those employed in industry and handicraft now came to 36.3 percent; and if farmers, servants, common laborers, and transportation workers (wagoners and porters) are added, workers constituted 50 percent of all gainfully employed. Moreover, the proportion of artisans and industrial workers grew from year to year. That is why the statistics on the background of the Jewish immigrants to America from 1900 to 1925 give us a totally different picture from the earlier period.

From 1900 to 1925, according to the official figure of the Bureau of Immigration, 596,043 Jewish skilled workers came to the United States, making up 61.3 percent of all gainfully employed Jewish immigrants. In addition, there arrived 102,739 Jewish unskilled workers, 24,792 farmers, and 123,820 domestic servants, for a total of 847,394 workers, who constituted 85 percent of all the gainfully employed Jewish immigrants.

By social origin, as has been said, a very large proportion of this mass of working people belonged to the middle class. Consequently, a shift to business was not only a dream but also a possibility that could be realized. In addition, they felt more deeply and painfully the wretched lot of the sweatshop worker and reacted more sharply to it than the worker of peasant or worker origin.

Following the introduction of immigration quotas, the proportion of skilled workers decreased; in the years 1925 to 1927, it already constituted only 47.8 percent of all the gainfully employed Jewish immigrants; and in the years 1931 and 1932, only 40.0 percent. As against this, there was a large increase in the proportion of professionals, for the most part clergymen, who were admitted as non-quota immigrants.

A radical change in the economic composition of the Jewish immigrants took place in 1933: the German Jews began to constitute the great majority of the Jewish immigrants, and the gainfully employed among them consisted almost exclusively of professionals and merchants. Among the immigrants from Europe admitted to the United States between 1933 and 1944, there were 25,535 professionals (5,516 physicians, 3,569 professors and teachers, 2,818 engineers [technical], 2,489 clergymen, 1,989 lawyers, 1,900 scientists and literary persons, 1,501 musicians, 767 actors, 507 chemists, 457 editors, etc.).[12] In the same period (1933 to 1944) there also arrived in the United States over 30,000 immigrants following commercial pursuits,[13] more than 90 percent of them Jews, for the most part German Jews.

We turn now to the non-Jewish East European immigration to America. From 1899 to 1927, 2,300,000 persons emigrated from Poland to America. Of this number, 800,000 were Jews.[14] It follows that for every Jewish immigrant there were two non-Jews. And more than 80 percent of the latter were peasants and unskilled workers. They settled mostly in the cities, living, like the Jews, in separate districts of their own. Among the non-Jewish East European immigrants the Poles and the Czechs were socially and culturally the most advanced. The Ukrainians, White Russians, Lithuanians, Latvians, Slovaks and Carpatho-Ruthenians were more backward and included an even larger percentage of peasants and unskilled workers. American industry absorbed millions of workers from Eastern Europe: they were not only inexpensive labor power, but also very docile and submissive. (According to the Russian census of 1897, only 16.8 percent of the total population of Russia was literate, including the 24.6 percent of Russian Jews who were literate in *Russian*.)

The peasant and working-class background of the non-Jewish East European immigrants had a certain influence on the economic pursuits of the Jews in America.

In Detroit about ten years ago, I visited the Polish quarter. It was a district containing more than 100,000 Polish workers, nearly all of them employed in the automobile industry, and it greatly resembled a medium-sized city in Poland. It is traversed by a broad and attractive street, where all the major businesses—food, clothing, radio, furniture stores, etc.—are located. In the side streets there are very small grocery stores. More than 90 percent of the stores in the main street were Jewish. I witnessed the same thing in Chicago, Buffalo and in several smaller cities with Ukrainian quarters. In Chicago, however, a Swedish section that I visited has practically no Jewish stores. From conversations with Jewish doctors it appears that Jewish physicians have a large practice among Poles, Ukrainians, Rumanians, etc. In the old country people were accustomed to dealing with Jewish merchants and professional men, and they continued to do so after immigrating to America.

7. THE EUROPEAN ANTECEDENTS FOR AMERICANIZATION

In seeking the causes of the very rapid and relatively easy integration of the immigrant Jewish population into the American economy, we must bear in mind that their economic advancement here was an organic process which also had scored like successes in the old countries—not always on the same scale as in America, to be sure, but still of the same character.

The first German Jewish immigration, predominantly one of retailers and peddlers, came to America when the population was essentially rural and scattered. Peddling was at this juncture an important and useful calling—and the German Jews made brilliant use of the situation. Their further advancement was no greater, relatively perhaps even smaller, than the wonderful economic rise of the Jews of Germany beginning with the 1870's, when capitalism began to make great strides in that country. It may well be that the departure of more than 150,000 Jews from a Jewish community which in 1850 numbered altogether 340,000 (or nearly a half of the total) was one of the factors which greatly contributed to the remarkable prosperity of the Jews remaining in Germany. The pursuits of the German Jews who came here did not require of them a difficult adaptation, but were for the most part an organic continuation of their previous careers. There was even greater smoothness in the case of the second wave of German Jewish immigration in the 1930's and 1940's.

Not equally smooth, perhaps, but smooth enough, was the economic adjustment of the Jewish mass immigration from Eastern Europe. By the 1870's and 1880's the intensive development of industry in America had already begun. The growth of the urban population accelerated with every passing decade. The demand for consumers' goods kept mounting. Tailoring, shoemaking, hatmaking, carpentry—all these trades had been widespread among the Jews of Eastern Europe for centuries. These were the trades that the Jewish masses here in America could continue to pursue.

To the Jewish middle-class and declassed elements handicraft was better suited and more appealing than work in a factory: handicraft is more individual and therefore better adapted to the historical psychology of the Jews. Handicraft offers far greater prospects of setting up shop for one's self. Becoming one's own master—this, too, typically appeals strongly to Jews. All this was quite similar to the processes at work in the East European countries.

Even the next stage of development, from handicraft and factory work to trade and the professions—a return, so to speak, to the roots, to the vocations which are historically more deeply rooted in the Jewish experience and more in line with the high average education of the Jews—has its counterpart in Soviet Russia. There many Jews who had entered the working class seized the first opportunity, when industry began to develop intensively and the urban population doubled in the brief space of 13 years (1926-1939), to shift to trade and the professions. It does not matter that the Jew running a store in Moscow or Leningrad is called a Socialist official and that the Jewish staff physician of a Soviet hospital is also called a Socialist official; in reality they perform the same economic function as the storekeeper and the doctor in the United States, and their status, as compared with the workers, is also about the same as in the capitalist countries. And even the high percentage of Jews in the ranks of Soviet officialdom properly so called has its parallel in America. In the last twenty years there has been a marked growth in the number of Jews employed by Federal, State and municipal governments. And this is true not only of the higher posts occupied by exceptional individuals, but also of the intermediate and even lower ranks of officialdom.

Similar, however, does not mean absolutely alike. The experience of American Jewry has been in many respects different from German or East European Jewry.

In Central, and partly also in Western Europe, Jews stood at the cradle of infant capitalism. They were the possessors of liquid capital and for this reason, as well as for others, they were the pioneers and innovators in many fields of capitalist development, particularly in banking and credit, railroad building, export and import, etc. German Jews came to America when the native capitalists already had important and firmly entrenched positions in these branches of the economy. They came here without capital, with the natural consequence that they have remained to this day outside the top positions of the economic life of the country. As we shall see, Jews achieved a certain success in these pursuits, too, but a rather modest one. The refugees of the 1930's and 1940's did bring certain amounts of capital, but by American standards these were paltry sums. They sufficed for small, and in rare cases for medium-sized, enterprises, but not for the top places of the American economy.

Many individual Jews from the East European countries caught up with the German Jewish immigrants and were integrated into the Jewish upper class, which in its majority is still decidedly German Jewish in composition. If we take into account not wealth and power, but income and profits, it is easy to find many Jews who occupy places not far below the highest peaks of the American upper class.

Further parallels between the fate of the East European Jewish immigrants and the lot of those who remained in Europe are impossible not only for the recent catastrophic years, but also for the interval between the two World Wars. The dismemberment of Austria-Hungary and of Russia created different and wholly new conditions for the Jews of Europe.

8. OCCUPATIONS OF AMERICAN JEWS IN THE LATE NINETEENTH CENTURY

In Section 4 above we quoted Census Bureau figures for the year 1889 concerning more than ten thousand Jewish families, three-fourths of which consisted of German Jewish immigrants or of their American-born offspring. The statistical table on occupations which follows is derived from the same source.

TABLE 13

OCCUPATIONS OF GAINFULLY EMPLOYED JEWS IN THE UNITED STATES, 1889

Occupation	Number	Percent
Retailers	8,796	45.1
Wholesalers and Financiers	2,571	13.2
Office Workers	3,842	19.7
Artisans and Wage Earners	2,800	14.3
Professional Persons	1,105	5.7
Farmers	383	2.0
Total	**19,497**	**100.0**

If we add three-fourhts of the office workers to those employed in trade, it will follow that over 72 percent were engaged in trade and finance, and a bare 20 percent in handicraft and labor generally. This is in full accord with what we know of the occupational distribution of German Jewry. The percentage of professional persons was quite considerable: at that time it was no higher among the German Jews in the old country.

The survey from which the table above is derived was confined to families, and among the East European Jews, who at that time were already numerous in America. There were many bachelors or married men whose wives and children were still in Europe. Nevertheless, there is little doubt that the majority of the nearly three thousand artisans and wage earners were Jewish immigrants from Eastern Europe.

Occupation does not fully determine income or wealth. However, we possess another gauge for the more than ten thousand families in question which quite clearly reflects differentiation with respect to material well-being. The Census Bureau presents figures on the number of house-maids in these families.

TABLE 14
DISTRIBUTION OF JEWISH FAMILIES ACCORDING TO NUMBER OF SERVANTS, 1889

Servants	Families	
	Number	Percent
No servants	3,996	37.6
One servant	3,743	35.3
Two servants	1,958	18.4
Three or more servants	921	8.7
Total	10,618	100.0

Three or more servants in a family is unquestionably proof of considerable wealth. Most of such families were those of wholesalers and financiers. Families with two servants, amounting to almost a fifth, must be assigned to the upper middle class. The more than one-third of the families without any servants must have been the families of small storekeepers, artisans, and wage earners.

The data just cited give us some idea of the occupational structure of American Jewry at a time when the Jewish immigration from Germany had stopped and the Jewish immigration from Eastern Europe was getting under way. All or nearly all of the large Jewish firms at that time belonged to German Jews. Here are a few

figures on the annual volume of business of certain lines of the Jewish wholesale trade in New York which afford an idea both of the types of business establishments and of their size and scope.

TABLE 15
ESTIMATED ANNUAL TRANSACTIONS OF JEWISH FIRMS IN VARIOUS INDUSTRIES IN NEW YORK, 1888

Manufacturers of clothing	$55,000,000
Jobbers of jewelry	30,000,000
Wholesale butchers	25,000,000
Wines, spirits and beer	25,000,000
Jobbers of leaf tobacco	15,000,000
Manufacturers of cigars	15,000,000
Manufacturers of cloaks	15,000,000
Importers of diamonds	12,000,000
Leather and hides	12,000,000
Manufacturers of overshirts	10,000,000

We took only the largest concerns from the source quoted,[15] which lists many other manufacturers and importers with smaller annual transactions. But the picture will become clearer if we let the author speak for himself:

In the cities of New York and Brooklyn there are 4,000 retail and 300 wholesale butchers, one-half of whom are Hebrews, including several millionaires and many whose wealth is represented by six figures. They employ in this business an army of 6,000 men, and their annual trade is $25,-000,000. The abattoir of Schwarzschild & Sulzberger occupies an entire block and they employ 500 men. Joseph Stern's establishment covers half a block.

The manufacture of hats and caps, the importation and manufacture of hides and leather, furs, laces and embroideries, artificial flowers and feathers, is largely controlled by Hebrews, while the wine and liquor trade is one of the most extensive in which they are engaged. It is estimated that the Hebrew capital represented on the New York Cotton Exchange is not far from $6,000,000.

The holdings of real estate by the Hebrews of New York, is estimated at $150,000,000. Five-eighths of the transfers in real estate, in the city of New York, are for their account.

An enumeration of the occupations of the Jews of Berlin or Vienna before the Great Catastrophe would have yielded a very similar picture. And again there is little doubt that if the occupations—not necessarily the trades—of the Jews of New York were recorded today, they, too, would greatly resemble those of 1888. The figures would be different, but the general picture would be the same.

The firms enumerated above were even then not among the largest in the country but among the intermediate ones—and so the picture remains to this day. The scale has changed, but the place occupied by Jews, including the German Jews, in the economic life of America remains the same as formerly in Europe, with one exception: in Europe Jews played a dominant role in banking and on the stock exchange. Even in England, where the Jews were not dominant in these fields, they played a much greater role than in the United States. The bankers Kuhn, Loeb & Co., Lehman Bros., Speyer & Co. (dissolved a few years ago), J. & W. Seligman & Co.,—these are all German Jews. But they do not now have and never had nearly as much importance here as Jewish bankers in England, let alone Germany and Austria, Russia and Poland, Hungary and Rumania, where Jews pioneered and dominated in these branches of the economy throughout the nineteenth century and until the First World War. A thorough study by the editors of a well-known American magazine[16] presented the following picture:

> First of all and very definitely, they [the Jews] do not run banking. They play little or no part in the great commercial houses. Of the 420 listed directors of the nineteen members of the New York Clearing House in 1933 only thirty were Jews and about half of these were in the commercial National Bank & Trust Co. and the Public National Bank & Trust. There were none in the Bank of New York & Trust Co., National City, Guaranty Trust, Central Hanover, First National, Chase, Bankers Trust, or New York Trust. Indeed, there are practically no Jewish employees of any kind in the largest commercial banks—and this in spite of the fact that many of their customers are Jews. In the investment field although there are of course Jewish houses, of which Kuhn, Loeb & Co., Speyer & Co., J. & W. Seligman & Co., Ladenburg, Thalmann & Co., and Lehman Bros. are the best known, they do not compare with the great houses owned by non-Jews ... If these houses are ranked upon the amount of foreign loans outstanding on March 1, 1935, J. P. Morgan with 19.87 percent, National City Co. with 11.71, Dillon, Read with 11.44, Chase, Harris, Forbes with 8.45, Guaranty Trust with 6.68 percent, and Lee Higginson with 4.25 percent all rank above the highest Jewish house, which is Kuhn, Loeb with 2.88 percent. Ranked on the basis of domestic activity, Kuhn, Loeb, which *has been very active* of late in the steel industry and which has a long and honorable record of general activity in American business, would of course stand very near the top, but even in the domestic field non-Jewish interests are still far and away the most influential ...

> On the New York Stock Exchange, 252 of the 1,375 members, or 18 percent, are Jews, while fifty-five of the 637 firms listed by the Exchange directory are Jewish, twenty-four are half-Jewish, and thirty-nine have dominant Jewish influence. The absence of Jews in the insurance business is noteworthy. Herman A. Behrens, President of Continental Assurance Co., and J. B. Levison, President of the Fireman's Fund Insurance Co. in San Francisco, are two of the few Jewish executives of large insurance companies. In the insurance-agency field, however, about half the business is Jewish in New York. And the New York insurance-brokerage business is predominantly Jewish although the three or four nationwide brokerage houses with New York offices are non-Jewish. Outside New York Jewish representation follows the Jewish population proportion.

A later survey of Jews in banking established that "not quite 600 of the 93,000 bankers and banking officials in this country are Jews." This is "little more than one-half of one percent!"[17]

In this respect, therefore, the development in America was different from Europe. However, in the year 1885, of 241 garment factories in New York, Jews owned 234, or more than 97 percent. At that time the great majority of the garment manufacturers were German Jews; but a good many were undoubtedly Posen Jews, i.e., politically German but culturally more East European. And even now the percentage of Jews among wearing apparel manufacturers is probably not much smaller than it was in 1885. A few figures on how this industry has grown will give an idea of the tremendous progress of a branch of the American economy which was founded mostly by Jewish entrepreneurs and has remained largely in Jewish hands. In 1880 the output of the wearing apparel industry totaled $60,000,000; in 1920, $900,000,000, or fifteen times as much; and in 1950, more than four billion dollars, an increase of 450 percent over 1920. The nearer we come to the present, the more the differences in origin of the various groups of Jews become blurred. The blurring is effected with particular thoroughness in two spheres: in religion, where the synagogues are increasingly differentiated by theological preference, and in the economic sphere, where the differentiation is according to industries and the amount of capital invested.

We have seen what the economic structure of American Jewry was like in 1888, when German Jews constituted the great majority. Not more than twelve years later the picture was quite different. In the interim there had arrived about 450,000 Jews, all directly or ultimately from Eastern Europe. (See Table 16).

The following statistical table on Boston gives us information not only about Jews, but about several other ethnic groups as well.

In Boston more than half of the Jewish immigrants were employed in manufacturing. Nevertheless, the percentage of Jews in trade was far from small: more than a third of all the gainfully employed, a larger percentage than that of the Britons, a people who must feel quite at home in America and are used to mercantile pursuits.

Among the Jews, of the 3,978 employed in trade, 829 were peddlers, or over 20 percent; among the Germans only 64 out of 3,249, or only 2 percent; among the Britons the percentage of peddlers was even smaller—not more than 40 out of a total of 4,328 merchants, or barely one percent. If we take the top category of the gainfully employed—bankers and stock brokers—we find that 55 were Britons, 18 Germans, and only 13 were Jews.

Italians are also included in the table. They contributed the smallest percentage in trade and the largest percentage in domestic service. A striking fact is that the percentage of housemaids is relatively high among all ethnic groups, but is lowest

TABLE 16
OCCUPATIONAL STRUCTURE OF VARIOUS ETHNIC GROUPS IN BOSTON IN 1900 [18]

Occupation	Number	Russians and Poles (Jews) %	Britons %	Germans %	Italians %
Manufacturing	5,731	52.9	39.4	46.5	30.5
Trade	3,978	36.7	28.3	29.1	14.8
Professions	252	2.4	6.8	6.5	2.4
Domestic Service	758	7.0	20.9	15.2	50.0
Communications and Miscellaneous	115	1.0	4.6	2.7	2.3
Total	**10,834**	**100.0**	**100.0**	**100.0**	**100.0**

among the Jews: it is not only one-seventh of the Italian percentage, but one-third of the British, and one-half of the German. It has long been a well-known fact that Jewish girls tend to prefer other work, if at all possible.

Non-Jewish Poles in Boston must have been very few at that time, and non-Jewish Russians even fewer. Mass emigration of non-Jews from Russia, for the most part Ukrainians and White Russians, did not begin until after the abortive revolution of 1905. Previously they had migrated in very large numbers to distant places in Asiatic Russia, where they could get free land and, in addition, loans to help them establish themselves. The figures on the occupations of immigrant Russians up to 1900 therefore probably refer almost entirely to Jews.

TABLE 17
OCCUPATIONAL DISTRIBUTION OF "RUSSIANS" IN CITIES OF 250,000 INHABITANTS OR MORE, IN 1900 [19]

Occupation	Number	Percentage
Manufacturing	89,748	59.6
Trade	31,047	20.6
Domestic and Personal Service	12,138	8.0
Clerical and Public Service	10,492	7.0
Professions	3,958	2.6
Transportation and Communication	2,613	1.7
Agriculture, Fishing, Forestry, Mining	698	0.5
Total	150,694	100.0

Even assuming that a few of the "Russians" in the cities in question were non-Jews and the percentage of Jews in manufacturing was not more than 55, we still get a high proportion of Jews engaged in manual labor. At that time there were few large factories, and the work was done in small sweatshops, where the employers and the employees worked together. That the percentage of Jewish workers was quite large and kept increasing is beyond question. Neither is there any doubt that among the numerous "Columbus' tailors" (as they were jocularly referred to) there were a great many former yeshivah students, middle-class youths, *kestniks,* etc.

Thanks to the peculiar composition of the Jewish workers, the drift from the manual-labor occupations to trade and to the professions started very early, indeed soon after the influx of Jewish immigrants from Eastern Europe assumed a mass character. This is apparent from the occupational structure of the "Russians" in New York, according to the census of 1900. The number of "Russians" engaged in trade was 16,487. They were distributed by categories as follows:

TABLE 18
"RUSSIANS" ENGAGED IN NEW YORK CITY, 1900

Category	Number	Percentage
Retailers	9,016	54.7
Peddlers	4,215	25.6
Wholesalers	3,256	19.7
Total	16,487	100.0

The percentage of wholesalers among the "Russians" is quite high, considering that this was only about twenty years since the commencement of the mass immigration. Much more interesting and significant is the number of professional persons. In 1900 the "Russians" comprised the following professionals:

TABLE 19
PROFESSIONAL OCCUPATIONS OF "RUSSIANS IN" NEW YORK CITY, 1900

Teachers	658
Musicians (instrumentalists)	517
Physicians	305
Lawyers	217
Dentists	75
Actors	37
Total	1,809

These were exclusively Russian Jews: the Polish, Rumanian, Hungarian, and Bohemian Jews had arrived before the Russian Jews and no doubt comprised a larger number of professional persons. But it was almost a rule that the majority not only of the businessmen but also of the professionals first went through a period of working in a shop, usually in extremely difficult conditions. Yiddish literature abounds with description of the life of Jewish workers, who studied at night and eventually achieved professional and social success. An extremely interesting page of Jewish history, which would give us a more exact picture of the metamorphosis American Jewry went through before it worked its way up to the high position it occupies today, is yet to be written.

But the drift from factory work to trade and the professions was more than offset by the increasing arrival of new immigrants. After 1900 the influx of Jewish immigrants from the East European countries, and especially from Russia, grew enormously. With the growth of these immigrant masses, there was an enormous increase in the number of Jewish shopworkers, especially clothing workers. As was noted above, this was paralleled by the development in the East European countries generally and in Russia and Russian Poland in particular.

Proof of the foregoing is to be found in the records of the New York Jewish Community (Kehillah),[20] which was established in 1908 and existed until 1922. It was founded by J. L. Magnes and remained under his leadership until his departure for Palestine in 1922. In 1914 the Kehillah set up a Bureau of Industry, whose object was to protect Jewish workers against discrimination and exploitation. Magnes is quoted as having reported in 1916 that this was "the only Bureau of Industry that has the confidence of employers and employees, that knows the facts of Jews in industry." In the needle trades alone, we are told in the article from which we are quoting, "there were 300,000 Jewish workers: the relations between them and the employers were deplorable: strikes and lockouts were constant."

If we remember that in 1916, the year to which these data relate, there were not more than 1,300,000 Jews in New York City, this is an enormous number of Jewish workers in a single industry. And there were quite considerable numbers of Jewish workers in other industries, too. Even assuming that the figure of 300,000 workers

in the needle trades alone is an overstatement and that the real figure was 50,000 less, we still get a large number, amounting to nearly 40 percent of all gainfully employed Jews. Adding other Jewish manual workers, we find that there were at least 350,000 Jewish workers, apart from white-collar workers, which gives us a total of more than 50 percent of manual workers among all gainfully employed Jews.

About 1922 the membership of the Amalgamated Clothing Workers of America was 180,000 and of the International Ladies' Garment Workers' Union approximately 140,000,[21] the total for both unions being 320,000. At that time not all the workers by far were organized—not even in the needle trades. In 1922, though these unions were no longer exclusively Jewish, about 75 to 80 percent of the members were still Jewish. At the beginning of the Twenties therefore, hundreds of thousands of Jewish workers were in the needle trades. The proportion of Jewish workers in the mechanical trades had already increased considerably, and their number in the carpentering and painting trades also kept mounting.

We cannot enter here upon a more extensive study of the number of Jewish workers at that time. For our purpose, the figures just quoted are sufficient to warrant the conclusion that in the 1920's Jewish manual workers constituted a majority of all the gainfully employed Jews in America.

A change set in after 1925 and the introduction of immigration quotas. With the decline of Jewish mass immigration, there disappeared the reservoir which annually replenished with a great surplus the drain from manual labor to trade, whether as proprietors or as employees, and the professions. At the same time an American-born generation of Jews arose, which avoided the garment industries. Part of them took up other types of manual labor, but a much larger proportion turned to white-collar work and the professions.

Some idea of the tempo of the increase of Jews in the liberal professions may be gained from the number of Jewish graduates of medical schools in ten cities of the United States: New York, Chicago, Philadelphia, Los Angeles, Boston, Detroit, Cincinnati, Milwaukee, San Francisco, and New Orleans.

TABLE 20
JEWISH GRADUATES OF MEDICAL SCHOOLS IN TEN AMERICAN CITIES, 1876 TO 1935[22]

Years	Number of Graduates
1876-1880	7
1881-1885	25
1886-1890	67
1891-1895	153
1896-1900	277
1901-1905	460
1906-1910	716
1911-1915	977
1916-1920	1,273
1921-1925	1,786
1926-1930	2,069
1931-1935	3,213

From the first five-year period listed to the last such period of the 19th century the number of graduates from medical schools multiplied nearly fortyfold, whereas the Jewish population grew only fourfold. From the last five years of the 19th century to the last five years listed in the table the number of graduates multiplied nearly twelvefold, whereas the Jewish population increased barely fourfold.

Moreover, it should be borne in mind that from 1920 to 1935 a tacit *numerus clausus* prevailed in United States medical schools and that hundreds and often thousands of young Jews had to go to Europe in search of an opportunity to study medicine, something which not every family could afford. How effective these discriminations were is evident from the following figures: among the Jews who in 1936 passed the examination of the New York State Board of Medicine, there were graduates of 97 American medical schools, 77 European, and 9 Canadian.

From the 14,837 Jewish students enrolled in 106 of the most prominent institutions of higher learning in the United States in 1919,[23] the number increased to over 200,000 in 1952. While the Jewish population did not even double during this period, the number of Jewish college students increased nearly fifteenfold. Attendance by non-Jewish students evidently grew in the same proportion, for in 1920 Jews constituted 9.7 percent of all students in the institutions of higher learning, and today the percentage is the same. From this it can only be concluded that the educational progress of the Jewish population parallels the general progress of the country. From the percentage of the Jewish students, however, we cannot deduce their proportion in the liberal professions: it is generally understood that a larger proportion of Jewish than non-Jewish students complete their courses, and a larger percentage of Jews than non-Jews graduating from professional schools practice their professions.

We return to the number of Jewish workers, which is perhaps the best index of the social and economic status of the Jewish population.

The decline in the number of Jewish workers in the needle trades has been very striking. Some idea of the sharpness of the decline may be gained from the following figures on a single local of the International Ladies' Garment Workers' Union, which are doubtless representative of many other locals of both of the "Jewish unions."[24] In 1934, the percentage of Jews in Local 22 of the I.L.G.W.U. was 70.5; in 1953, 51.0. Even more interesting and significant are the absolute numbers: in 1933, the number of Jewish members of Local 22 was 21,400 and in 1953, 13,158. a *loss* of 8,242. The number of non-Jewish members, on the other hand, was as follows: in 1933, 8,900; in 1953, 12,642, a *gain* of 3,742. Will Herberg, from whom these figures are taken, gives even more significant data: in 1934, Jews comprised 65.5 percent of the newly enrolled members of the local and in 1948 only 24.2 percent.

So much for the trend, which is confirmed by all the leading figures in these unions. Herberg had a major article— "The Jewish Labor Movement in the

United States"—in *The American Jewish Year Book* for 1952. There he cited figures showing that the aggregate number of Jewish members of the four major unions in the needle trades (International Ladies Garment Workers' Union, Amalgamated Clothing Workers of America, United Hatters, Cap and Millinery Workers' Union, International Fur and Leather Workers' Union) was now 265,000. These figures were challenged by many authorities. At a Yiddish Encyclopedia conference the veteran officer of the Amalgamated, Abraham Miller, doubted that the Amalgamated had even 50,000 Jewish members, let alone 90,000, as estimated by Herberg. But even if we accept Herberg's figures, it should be remembered that the data derived from the New York Kehillah a generation earlier referred only to New York City, and that there were then many Jewish workers in other cities. Besides, the Jewish population of New York is now at least 900,000 more than in 1916.

We have quoted these figures not so much for their intrinsic value as for the illustration they afford of the intensity of the shift from manual labor to white-collar work and the professions. Herberg, who is director of research and education of the New York Dressmakers Union, Local 22, I.L.G.W.U., writes:

> But the main factor [in the decline of the Jewish workers in the needle trades], combined with the virtual cessation of the stream of immigration in the 1920's, was unquestionably the deep-seated reluctance of Jewish workers to have their children follow them into manual occupations instead of rising in the social scale to professional or white-collar status.[25]

And elsewhere in the same article he says:

> Almost from the beginning, observers had noted that the Jewish worker in America was typically a man of one generation: he was "neither the son nor the father" of a proletarian. In the "old country", his father, or he himself, had most probably been a petty merchant or artisan; in this

country, he had become a factory worker; his son and daughter, however, were not following him into the factory or trade, but were going into business, office work, or the professions.[26]

9. INTEGRATION OF THE JEWISH POPULATION INTO THE AMERICAN ECONOMY

By the middle of the Thirties the general features of the organic integration of the immigrant Jews into the American economy were already quite clear. We call this integration organic because it is in line with the age-old social and economic tradition of the Jews, and because it fully coincides with the developmental trends of the American economy. The particularity of the Jewish social and economic structure is not so glaring and sharp in America as it was in all the countries of Europe, even in those with a highly developed capitalist system, where the urban elements constituted the great majority not only among Jews but among the surrounding population as well. Yet even in America the Jewish group is different in structure from the general population, especially by virtue of the very small proportion of Jews in the lowest income brackets—i.e., among farmers and unskilled workers.

The exceptional character of the Jewish group is seen with particular sharpness and vividness in the small towns, where the whole Jewish population is engaged in trade and very often in particular lines of business, in which it constitutes the great majority. Frequently Jews representing a very small percentage of the total population control more than half of certain kinds of businesses. This becomes especially noticeable when the non-Jewish population consists of ethnic groups that have immigrated most recently and includes very few Yankees, Britons, Germans or Scandinavians.

Thus, in 1940 the population of New Haven, Conn., was approximately 162,000, of whom Anglo-Saxons (i.e., old Americans, or "Yankees", and those who came from the United Kingdom in more recent times) constituted about 12 or 13 percent of the inhabitants. The Italians were approximately one-third of the total population, and the Irish about 21 percent. The percentage of the Jews was about 15, or not much more than that of the British-Americans. We shall consider first the percentage of Jews among the owners, managers, and employees of the various types of business establishments in the central business district of New Haven.

TABLE 21

PROPORTION OF JEWS AMONG OWNERS, MANAGERS, AND EMPLOYEES OF VARIOUS TYPES OF BUSINESS ESTABLISHMENTS IN THE CENTRAL BUSINESS DISTRICT OF NEW HAVEN, 1940 [27]

Enterprise	*Percentage*	
	Employers or Managers	*Employees*
Shoes....................	90.4	47.8
Millinery................	89.9	55.6
Corset and Lingerie.......	85.7	45.0
Women's Clothing........	73.6	44.5
Men's Clothing..........	72.2	37.8
Department and Drygoods Stores.................	66.7	13.4
Liquor..................	62.5	33.3
Drugs and Confectionery..	60.0	17.3
Jewelry and Gifts.........	48.3	34.0
Flower Shops.............	20.0	22.7
Restaurants..............	15.0	1.9
Theatres.................	....	8.6
Banks...................	....	....
Miscellaneous............	13.3	7.4
Total.............	**54.9**	**20.1**

What is most striking is that the proportion of Jews in these firms is nearly four times their percentage in the population of the city. This, however, is true only of owners and managers, but not of employees. Among the latter the percentage of Jews is not much higher than among the city's inhabitants. In those businesses which are most frequented by the buying public and where it spends most of its earnings, the Jewish concerns constitute from 66.7 of the department stores to 90 or close to 90 percent of the shoe, millinery, and wear-

ing apparel shops. There are no Jews in the city's banks, either among the owners and managers or among the employees. In general, the percentage of Jewish employees is a little more than half the percentage of Jewish owners or managers.

Of great interest is the ethnic origin of the competitors of the Jews. In banking the Anglo-Saxons constitute 100 percent of the owners or managers, and 71.6 percent of the employees. Again, in jewelry and gifts, the Anglo-Saxons constitute 24.1 percent of the owners or managers and 30.4 percent of the employees. In flower stores, the same ethnic group comprises 80 percent of the owners or managers and 54.5 percent of the employees.

The Italians, who represent more than a third of the total population, make up 50 percent of the owners or managers only in the case of theatres and 15 percent in the case of restaurants. Among the total number of owners or managers, they constitute only 4.5 percent, or one-eighth of their proportion in the population. Among the employees they form 19.1 percent. All the other ethnic groups, who constitute more than a tenth of the city's inhabitants, comprise an insignificant percentage of the owners or managers in the central business district and two or three times as large a percentage of the employees in each type of enterprise.

The general impression is quite clear: The central business district is dominated by Jews and Anglo-Saxons, and mostly by the group that came later—the Jews. But the older group is dominant in a particularly decisive branch of the economy: banking.

When we turn to the small shopkeepers, the picture changes radically. Each group has its shops. This time the Italians lead with 41.6 percent of the owners; the Anglo-Saxons have 9.3 percent, less than their percentage in the population; all the others —Irish, Germans, Poles, etc.—are more or less represented. The Jews are the only group that constitutes also quite a large percentage of the small retailers—30.1, or double their proportion in the population.

So much for trade. The picture changes in favor of the Anglo-Saxons and the Irish in the liberal professions. Here the Jews constitute 19.3 percent, the Anglo-Saxons 38.2 percent, and the Irish 21.2 percent. The Jews are especially well represented among lawyers (33.6 percent) and physicians (22.1 percent). Among city employees Jews constitute 6.0 percent; among State employees, 3.3 percent; among post office employees, 3.7 percent.

The prominence of Jews in these lines of business which the buying public frequents most has been established by many studies. Here are a few figures on Stamford, Conn.: In 1938 Jews were 100 percent of the owners of large food markets and of children's and infants' wear shops; 93.8 percent of the dealers in men's clothing; 86.6 percent of the proprietors of jewelry shops; 80.0 percent of the owners of wholesale drug firms and cut-rate cosmetic stores; and 73.3 percent of the dealers in women's and misses' wear.[28]

The percentage of those employed in trade and commerce among the Jews of America varies inversely with the number of Jews in a given community: the sparser the Jewish population, the higher the percentage of those engaged in trade and commerce; the more compact the Jewish population, the lower the percentage of Jews employed in trade and commerce.

In the large cities the percentage of those employed in trade and commerce ranges between 50 and 55 percent of all gainfully employed Jews. In the middle cities the percentage fluctuates between 60 and 65 percent, and in the small towns it amounts to 80 percent. In the small towns business and the professions together account for virtually all the gainfully employed Jews. For the country as a whole it may be assumed that the percentage of those employed in trade and commerce among gainfully employed Jews is closer to 60 than to 55 percent.

Jews employed in manufacturing in the big cities are between 25 and 28 percent of all gainfully employed Jews, in the middle-size cities only 20 percent, and in the small towns only a few percent.

The percentage of Jews in the professional and public service amounts to 12 or 14 in the large cities, a little over 15 or 16 in the middle-size cities, and approximately the same in the small towns. In this connection it is worth noting that over three-fourths of all Jews who are included in this category are professional persons, while for non-Jews in this category the opposite is true: the majority are in the civil service.

10.   THE SOCIAL AND ECONOMIC PYRAMID OF AMERICAN JEWRY

The most characteristic feature of the social and economic pyramid of American Jewry consists in this, that on the one hand it has no base, namely, unskilled workers and farmers, who together comprise about 40 percent of the country's population and belong to the lowest income bracket; and on the other hand it has no apex, namely, the very wealthiest. Those with the greatest incomes, of course, are not necessarily the wealthiest. The richest persons in America stem from an earlier generation, before the income tax made subsequent massive personal capital accumulation impossible. And because Jews entered the category of those with extremely high incomes only in the last 20 or 25 years, it is natural that, although there are many Jews in the high income brackets, none of them is to be found among the richest men in America.

The noted sociologist Pitirim Sorokin published a study in 1925 on deceased and living American millionaires.[29] Among the 209 defunct millionaires of the second half of the 19th century, there were only 9 Jews, or 4.3 percent; the Germans had 19 millionaires, who constituted 13.9 percent of all the deceased millionaires. Next came data on living American millionaires in

1924. Among the 195 living in that year there were 30 Jews, or 15.4 percent, and the same number and percentage of Germans. The Jews thus had caught up with the Germans. The percentage of millionaires of English and Scotch-Irish stock was 71.8 among the deceased millionaires and only 57.9 among the living.

Of course, millionaires are not all alike: the possessor of one million is called a millionaire and so is the possessor of a hundred millions. And we know that Gustavus Myers, in his famous *History of the Great American Fortunes* (New York, 1936; first edition, Chicago, 1909) included only two Jewish individuals or families among the 30 richest persons in America: the Guggenheims (copper) and Julius Rosenwald (mail order business). Ferdinand Lundberg, in his *America's 60 Families* (New York, 1937), listed only 9 Jewish families (15 percent) among the sixty richest American families (Guggenheims, Lehmans, Warburgs, Otto Kahn, Mortimer Schiff, George Blumenthal, Michael Friedsam, Julius Rosenwald, and Bernard A. Baruch). One Rockefeller, or at the most the Rockefellers and the Duponts, are incomparably richer than all these nine Jewish families combined. The percentage of Jewish millionaires is now larger than it was in 1924. Among the more than 9,000 millionaires in America probably some 20 percent, or some 1,800, are Jews. But among the billionaires or semi-billionaires there are no Jews, nor can there be any today. It is in this sense that the Jewish economic pyramid is without an apex and will never have one.

In 1947 fifty American business executives were chosen as the country's foremost business leaders. The fifty were selected by a nationwide poll conducted by *Forbes Magazine of Business*. Three were Jews: David Sarnoff, President of Radio Corporation of America; Bernard F. Gimbel, President of Gimbel Brothers, Inc., and Samuel Goldwyn, the motion picture producer.

When we turn to the largest incomes, as opposed to the greatest wealth, we find that Jews are well represented in the highest brackets. In the years 1944 and 1945, first place on the list of those with the largest salaries, not necessarily the largest incomes, was held by Louis Mayer, the motion picture producer. (A native of Minsk, White Russia, he was brought at a very early age to Canada, where his father became a dealer in scrap metal and junk, and for a time the younger Mayer was a partner in the business.)

From the foregoing we got an idea of the upper reaches of the Jewish social and economic pyramid. As for the base, it is almost completely lacking. To be sure, we have some 30,000 farming families, who constitute about 1.5 percent of all gainfully employed Jews, or one-tenth of the ratio of farmers to the total population of the United States; but most of the Jewish farmers are concentrated in the vicinity of the big cities, which offer a large market for farm products, and they specialize mainly in the production of milk and eggs. They belong to the urban middle class rather than to the true farm population, the majority of which is engaged in raising grain and fibers. As for the urban unskilled workers, a survey made in New York in 1936 showed that the percentage of unskilled workers among Jews is one-tenth of the percentage among non-Jews: 3 percent among the former, and 30 percent among the latter. And in New York the percentage of wage earners among Jews is the highest in the country. In the rest of the country, especially in the very small towns, there are practically no Jewish unskilled workers. As a base for the pyramid, which should be broader than the higher strata of the gainfully employed, this group does not come into consideration.

The broadest stratum among the Jews of the United States is the lower and upper middle class. The percentage of owners and managers among American Jews is approximately twice as high as among the total population. Among the latter, these two groups constitute approximately 20 percent of all the gainfully employed, while among the Jews they represent at least 40 percent, and in small towns much more.

The income tax figures for the year 1951 show that of every 100 heads of families employed as managers, officials, and proprietors, 24 had an annual income of over $7,000, whereas only 6.6 of every 100 family heads employed as farmers had an annual income equally high.[30] Heads of families with an annual income under $1,000 constitute 28.5 percent of those employed as farmers, whereas of those employed as managers, officials, and proprietors in the cities they were only 6.0 percent. From this it may be inferred that the Jewish population, which comprises proportionately twice as many owners and managers as the non-Jewish, has a larger percentage of persons in the higher income brackets.

The Jewish population includes a larger proportion of another occupational group in the high income brackets than the non-Jewish. The percentage of professionals among American Jews is about twice as large as among non-Jews. And the percentage of those with the highest income—over $7,500 a year—among professionals is 24.5, whereas among public administrators it is only 8.4. The professional group must be analyzed further. Thus 52.4 percent of the self-employed professionals have an annual income of over $7,500, whereas only 18.1 percent of the salaried professionals have such an income. Jews have a large percentage of self-employed professionals. Owners and managers together with professionals constitute over 40 percent of all the gainfully employed among Jews; among non-Jews the percentage is less than half of this. We may consequently assume that among Jews there are many persons who, though not very rich, have a high enough income to save a good deal.

Since the Jews are concentrated in the large cities, where annual incomes are generally twice as high as in the rural areas and in the southern states, and since their prevailing occupations, trade and professions, yield an income above the average, it may be assumed that the annual income of the Jewish population is no less than 10 percent of the total national income, or approximately three times the percentage of Jews in the total population.

As for the Jewish working class, it is in one respect better off than the working class in general, since it includes few unskilled workers, who have the lowest incomes. On the other hand, it is worse off, in that it has a smaller percentage of highly skilled workers than is to be found in the working class as a whole. Among Jews semi-skilled workers constitute the highest percentage. This, however, is true only for manual workers. When it comes to white collar workers, the situation changes: the percentage of higher-placed and better paid specialists is larger among Jews than among non-Jews.

There are no exact, official data to confirm all our assertions. But the accumulated data of private researches and studies in general corroborate our conclusions. Most of these figures, unfortunately, pertain to the last years of the 1930's, but the development of the last 15 years has proceeded in the same direction, and has perhaps been intensified.

11. ECONOMIC ACTIVITY OF JEWS IN VARIOUS TOWNS

We have instructive data on some of the smaller cities. (See Table 22).

The basic difference between Jews and non-Jews is salient: among Jews the proportion of those employed in trade is more than twice as large as among the general population. The percentage of Jews in manufacturing, on the other hand, is slightly over one-third of the population as a whole. In the professions and public service the percentage of Jews is nearly twice that of the general population. The figures are antiquated and there is no doubt that today the percentage of Jews

TABLE 22

PERCENTAGE DISTRIBUTION OF GAINFULLY EMPLOYED MALES IN 47 SMALLER CITIES, 1930 and 1934 [31]

Occupation	General Population	Jews
	(1930) & (1934)	
Trade	25.6	57.4
Manufacturing	46.3	16.7
Professions and Public Service	8.4	16.6
Transportation and Communication	11.1	2.2
Miscellaneous	8.6	7.1
Total	**100.0**	**100.0**

in trade is larger than in 1934. It has also increased among non-Jews, though not at the same rate.

We have separate data for the native-born and for the foreign-born Jews in these 47 cities. The difference in the occupations of the two groups indicates the trend. Among the American-born Jews, those employed in the professions and the public service are 20.4 percent of all the gainfully employed; among the foreign-born they are only 7.1. In other words, the percentage of those employed in these two fields is approximately three times higher among American-born than foreign-born Jews. There is also a considerable difference in manufacturing: the native-born Jews in manufacturing constitute 11.9 percent and the immigrant Jews 18.3 percent of all the gainfully employed Jews. In 1934 there was a fairly high percentage of Jewish artisans in the smaller cities; in the last few years they have virtually disappeared, having transferred to more attractive occupations.

An interesting picture of the vocations of small-town Jewry is given by the B'nai B'rith Vocational Service Bureau's latest survey, conducted in 168 small communities in the United States and 53 communities in Canada, each with a Jewish population of 1,000 or under.

The percentage distribution of the gainfully employed Jews in various occupations was as follows: [32]

Occupation	Percentage
Owners and Managers	66.0
Professionals	20.0
Miscellaneous	14.0
Total	**100.0**

These figures speak for themselves: they indicate clearly the thoroughly middle-class character of the Jewish occupational distribution. If we take the older generation (51 years or over), the picture changes slightly at the expense of the percentage of professionals. The figures are then as follows: [33]

Occupation	Percentage
Owners and Managers	71.0
Professionals	11.0
Miscellaneous	18.0
Total	**100.0**

Eighty percent of the owners and managers are employed in the wholesale and retail fields, and the detailed listing of their occupations is typically Jewish: [34]

TABLE 23

Line of Business	Percentage
Clothing and shoes	31.0
Food, confectionery and beverages	10.0
Furniture and home furnishings	7.0
Scrap metal and junk	6.0
Jewelry	5.0
Department, variety & general merchandise	5.0
Automobile, accessories and parts	4.0
Drug stores	2.0
Hardware and building supplies	2.0
Other retail and wholesale fields	8.0
Total	**80.0**

Another 10 percent are employed in service fields, as follows: real estate and insurance, 2 percent; cleaning and laundering, 2 percent; hotels and restaurants, 2 percent; miscellaneous, 4 percent. And still another 10 percent are employed in manufacturing and construction: textiles and garments, 4 percent; metal products, 2 percent; building construction, 1 percent; miscellaneous, 3 percent. The author thus summarizes part of the findings:

> In summary, the small-town Jew in the United States is predominantly a retail business man or independent professional worker. About 9 out of 10 are self-employed. This indicates the strong urge among Jewish men to be their own bosses. [35]

The picture is clear: self-employment in business and professions is the main tendency of Jewish economic development. In the small towns it is realized in the largest measure. In the large cities, the process is slower, but the trend is the same.

On the basis of income, the Jews of the small towns surveyed may be included in the upper stratum of the middle class: half of all these small-town Jews who had gone through college reported income of over $7,500 a year in 1950. Professionals reported an annual income of about $7,000 in the same year.

Many studies have established that Jews stand on a higher rung of the income ladder than the non-Jews, with the exception of the Yankees. A poll taken among members of synagogues and churches of various denominations in 1945-1946 and analyzed by the Office of Public Opinion Research at Princeton yielded the following result (in percentage):[36]

TABLE 24
CLASS DISTRIBUTION OF RELIGIOUS GROUPS IN THE UNITED STATES, 1945-46

Religious Group	Upper Class	Middle Class	Lower Class
Jews...........	22	32	46
Protestants......	11	36	53
Catholics........	9	25	66

Although the Jews came later than other ethnic groups to the city which was given the fictitious name of "Yankee City," they rank in income immediately after the Yankees and ahead of all the other ethnic groups, some of which preceded the Jews by 50 years, like the Irish. A single quotation will suffice:

> Almost half of the Jewish families in Yankee City are of the middle classes. On the other hand, only one-fifth of the Armenian families, one-twelfth of the Greek families, one twenty-fifth of the Russian, and one-hundredth of the Polish families are middle class.[37]

Heretofore we have dealt with small towns. We shall glance now at larger communities.

TABLE 25
OCCUPATIONAL DISTRIBUTION OF GAINFULLY EMPLOYED JEWS, 15 YEARS OR OVER, DETROIT, 1935 [38]

Occupation	Number	Percentage
Trade and Finance...........	15,850	54.1
Manufacturing and Mechanical Industries..............	6,653	23.3
Professional and Public Service.	3,141	10.4
Transportation and Communication....................	627	2.2
Miscellaneous...............	3,028	10.0
Total.....................	29,299	100.0

Detroit is a distinctly industrial city, yet the Jews employed in trade constituted more than 54 percent of all gainfully employed Jews in 1935, and those employed in industry only slightly over 23 percent. There is little doubt that in the past 18 years the percentage of Jews in trade has risen still higher, and that there has been a particularly sharp increase in the percentage of those employed in professional and public service.

From the occupational distribution we turn to the social structure, using some figures on the Jews of Pittsburgh.

TABLE 26
SOCIAL STRUCTURE OF THE UNITED STATES AND OF THE JEWS IN DETROIT AND PITTSBURGH (IN %), 1930 TO 1938

Social Group	In the Whole Country 1930	Jews	
		Detroit 1935[39]	Pittsburgh 1938[40]
Owners and Managers.	9.3	26.8	22.3
Professional and Public Service......	10.4	10.4	12.8
Clerical and Kindred Workers...........	17.5	36.3	40.7
Manual Workers.....	62.8	26.5	24.2
Total...............	100.0	100.0	100.0

Considerable changes have taken place since then, but they have been in the same direction—a great increase, among both Jews and non-Jews, not only of professionals and public employees but of office workers as well. With respect to owners and managers, the increase among Jews is beyond question while it is doubtful for the non-Jewish population. Unfortunately, the returns of the last census are not yet available.

However, even figures for the 1930's are useful. The proportion of manual workers among non-Jews is more than twice as great as among Jews, whereas the proportion is reversed for owners and managers. The percentage of professionals is higher among Jews, while that of public officials is higher among non-Jews. The percentage of white-collar workers is twice as high among the Jewish population as among the non-Jewish.

We now turn our attention to differences among manual workers.

TABLE 27

PERCENTAGE DISTRIBUTION OF MANUAL WORKERS IN THE UNITED STATES AND AMONG JEWS, 1930 TO 1938

| Type of Worker | In the Whole Country 1930 | Among Jews | |
		Detroit 1935	San Francisco 1938
Skilled.......	16.2	8.9	5.6
Semi-skilled..	20.5	14.8	10.8
Unskilled.....	26.1	2.8	1.2
Total.......	62.8	26.5	17.6

There were few unskilled workers among the Jews of the United States, and in the years since then even this small percentage of Jewish unskilled workers has probably diminished. The proportion of skilled workers is lower among Jews than non-Jews. In this respect, too, it is safe to assume that a change has taken place in the last few years. The influx of Jewish workers into technical and mechanical trades must have increased the proportion of Jewish skilled workers.

In the space of some 50 years the Jewish working class has undergone a profound and revolutionary development. In the first place, the ratio of manual to white-

collar workers 50 years ago, and even 30 or 25 years ago, was two to one. Today the ratio is reversed. In the second place, only 25 years ago nearly all Jewish manual workers were employed in the production of consumers' goods, in the so-called "Jewish" trades (clothing, underwear, pocketbooks, millinery, furniture, and house painting). Of late there has been a considerable influx of Jews into the technical industries. Jews, however, tend to go not into big industry, but to small enterprises, where work goes hand in hand with business and where repairs are connected with the sale of new articles, such as radios, television sets and electric kitchen appliances. In these small shops it is easy to learn all about the business, in preparation for the time when the worker will want to go into business for himself. More recent data confirm these trends.

TABLE 28

OCCUPATIONAL CLASSIFICATION OF THE JEWISH LABOR FORCE IN LOS ANGELES, 1950 [41]

Social Group	Number	Percent
Proprietors and Managers....	40,600	31.1
Professional and Semi-Professional..............	22,000	16.9
White-Collar Workers.......	40,600	31.1
Manual Workers............	27,300	20.9
Total....................	130,500	100.0

Though Los Angeles is not a very typical community, it is not so unique as to make these data meaningless. The first two groups, having the highest incomes, constitute nearly one-half of all gainfully employed Jews, about 12 to 15 points higher than the percentage of these two groups in the 1930's in Detroit and Pittsburgh. The percentage of white-collar workers is somewhat smaller than it was in the 1930's in Detroit and Pittsburgh. This is natural: the higher the percentage of proprietors, the lower the percentage of workers. The percentage of manual workers is also slightly smaller than it was in Detroit and Pittsburgh in the 1930's.

In New York are concentrated those industries in which the largest number of Jewish workers have always been employed.

TABLE 29

OCCUPATIONAL DISTRIBUTION OF JEWS IN NEW YORK IN PERCENTAGES, 1933 [42]

Occupation	Percentage
Trade	44.9
Manufacturing and Mechanical Industries	37.8
Professional and Public Service	8.3
Transportation and Communication	3.7
Domestic and Personal Service	5.3
Total	**100.0**

The difference in the socio-economic structure is striking: the percentage of those employed in trade was smaller not only than in the small towns but than in the medium-sized cities as well. The percentage of those employed in manufacturing and the mechanical industries, on the other hand, was much larger. The percentage of those employed in professional and public service was rather low. But there is little doubt that substantial changes have taken place in the last 20 years, especially in the professions and public service. In 1933 the Jews in the public service constituted barely one percent of all gainfully employed Jews; today they probably represent several percent, the large influx of Jews into the public service, not only Federal but also State and city, having taken place in the last 20 years, beginning with the first administration of Franklin D. Roosevelt. Radical changes have also taken place with respect to those employed in trade and industry.

Up to this point we have dealt mainly with the socio-economic structure of the Jews as such. Let us now glance at the percentage of Jews in various branches of the economy as compared with the general population. (See Table 30).

It is striking that Jews constitute a smaller percentage of the employees than of the employers. The percentage of the latter is twice that of the Jews in the total population of New York City, and in two lines of trade it is three times as high.

However, the percentage of Jewish workers in trade is also considerably greater than the Jewish proportion in the total population. This is especially true in the retail trade, in which it is relatively easy to go into business for one's self.

TABLE 30[43]

PERCENTAGE OF JEWS IN CERTAIN LINES OF TRADE IN NEW YORK, 1937

Type of Business	Percent of All Employers	Percent of All Employees
Wholesale Trade	53.0	32.4
Retail Trade	68.7	42.3
Furniture Stores	87.3	53.0
Wearing Apparel Stores	86.8	78.5
Food Stores	72.5	46.6
Drug Stores	66.3	62.8
Hardware Stores	63.5	42.8
Drinking Places	23.7	19.8
Automotive Group	7.5	13.5

If we turn to industry, the picture is slightly different for Jewish employers and substantially different for Jewish workers.

TABLE 31[44]

PERCENTAGE OF JEWS IN CERTAIN INDUSTRIES IN NEW YORK, 1937

Industry	Percentage of Jews Among Employers	Percentage of Jews Among Employees
All Industry	61.2	33.5
Fur Industry	94.4	80.7
Apparel Industry	87.0	53.8
Textiles	57.5	13.7
Wood Products	61.5	35.1
Paper Products	56.5	21.8
Glass and Glass Products	50.8	36.5

In the years since 1937 considerable changes have no doubt taken place with respect to the participation of Jews in industry in New York, but only as regards the Jewish workers and certainly not in relation to the Jewish entrepreneurs. These figures are still useful, however, as illustrating the course of development. From 1889 to 1900 the labor element grew; from 1900 to 1937 the business element increased and labor decreased. And from 1937 on this shift from manual work to trade was even more marked than from 1900 to 1937, first, because of the general economic trend in America, and second, because there was an incomparably smaller immigration of Jewish workers from Europe.

Figures on the participation of Jews in the liberal professions do not reflect the present situation, but they do indicate a trend.

TABLE 32

PERCENTAGE OF JEWS IN THE PROFESSIONS IN NEW YORK, 1937

Professions	Percentage
Lawyers and Judges	65.7
Dentists	64.0
Musicians and Music Teachers	58.7
Physicians	55.7
Artists and Sculptors	50.8
Actors	43.1
Writers, Reporters, Editors	37.8
Architects	34.2
Teachers	29.4
Engineers	29.3
Chemists	28.6
Professors	11.1

Nearly all these figures are obsolete, particularly those on professors, teachers, and physicians. These are professions in which Jews have encountered marked discrimination either in gaining admission to an institution of higher learning or in obtaining a position there. And yet it is well known that the number of Jewish professors in the colleges and universities of New York, as of the country generally, has grown considerably in recent years. The same can be said of Jewish teachers in the public elementary and high schools. Of late the admission of Jews to medical schools has been less hampered by discrimination than formerly.

However, even the figures for 1937 show that in most of the liberal professions the percentage of Jews was higher than the Jewish percentage in the total population of New York.

Outside New York, the percentage of Jews in the liberal professions is in many cases three or four times the percentage of Jews in the total population. Here are some figures on the Jewish participation in 1938 in the professions in Greater Cleveland, where the Jews then constituted 7.7 of the population.[45]

Profession	Percentage
Pharmacists	26.1
Lawyers	23.1
Physicians	20.8
Dentists	17.8
Architects	5.0
Teachers	4.7
Engineers	2.2

Here, too, we should bear in mind the development of the last 10 to 15 years. The number of Jewish teachers and Jewish physicians has undoubtedly grown in recent years.

We have frequently referred to the typical desire of Jews for self-employment, so that a Jewish wage earner or salaried worker will prefer to work for a small enterprise, where it is easier to learn the business. This tendency is vividly illustrated by a few data on the Jews of New York.

Of each 100 persons engaged in trade as employers in New York in 1937, there were:

	Among Jews	Among non-Jews
Wholesalers	10.8	21.5
Retailers	89.2	78.5

The fact that the percentage of retailers among Jews is higher than among non-Jews, implies that a Jew with a small amount of capital will more readily open a small store than a non-Jew.

Here is another illustration.

TABLE 33

PERCENTAGE OF EMPLOYERS AND EMPLOYEES IN WHOLESALE AND RETAIL TRADES AMONG JEWS AND NON-JEWS NEW YORK, 1937

	In Wholesale Trade		In Retail Trade	
	Employers	Employees	Employers	Employees
Among Jews	10.3	89.7	36.8	63.2
Among non-Jews	4.7	95.3	18.0	82.0

Evidently, the class differentiation is much sharper among non-Jews than among Jews.

The same phenomenon—a larger percentage of employers and a smaller percentage of employees—is found in industry in New York. Of each 100 persons engaged in industry in New York in 1937, there were:

	Among Jews	Among non-Jews
Employers	7.5	1.4
Employees	92.5	98.6

For the Jewish milieu as such it is again evident that the ratio between employers and employees is lower among Jews than among non-Jews. The explanation is that Jews with a small amount of capital prefer more than non-Jews to go into business for themselves.

NOTES

[1] William S. Bernard, ed., *American Immigration Policy*, New York, 1950, pp. 299-300.

[2] Ibid., *passim*.

[3] *Census Bulletin*, Washington, D. C., No. 19, December 30, 1890, pp. 4-9.

[4] Julius Drachsler, *Democracy and Assimilation*, New York, 1920, pp. 124-128.

[5] Nathan Goldberg, "Jews in the Police Record of Los Angeles, 1933-1947", *Yivo Bleter* (Yiddish), New York, vol. XXXIV, pp. 129-156.

[6] Nathan Goldberg, "Jewish Juvenile Delinquency," *The Call*, New York, 1944.

[7] Frederick Lewis Allen, *The Big Change: America Transforms Itself*, 1900-1950, New York, 1952, p. 195.

[8] The figures in parentheses refer to Prussia without Posen.

[9] Rudolf Glanz, *History of the Jewish Labor Movement in the United States* (Yiddish), New York, 1943, p. 54.

[10] B. Hoffman, *Fifty Years of the Cloakmakers Union* (Yiddish), New York, 1936, p. 22.

[11] B. Weinstein, *Jewish Unions in America* (Yiddish), New York, 1929, p. 44.

[12] Maurice R. Davie, *Refugees in America*, New York, 1946, p. 41.

[13] Ibid.

[14] Jan Zieminski, *Problem Emigracji Zydowskiej*, Warsaw, 1937, p. 25.

[15] Isaac Markens, *The Hebrews in America*, New York, 1889, pp. 156-158.

[16] *Fortune*, February, 1936.

[17] Ernest O. O. Eisenberg, "93,000 Bankers; 0.6 percent are Jews!", *The National Jewish Monthly*, Washington, February, 1939, p. 190.

[18] The statistical data are derived from the census of 1900. The table includes only the foreign-born, the immigrants, because only these elements were singled out in the census returns and distributed by countries of origin. I have classed all "Russians and Poles" as Jews on the authority of a Boston scholar, Professor Frederick A. Bushee, who was quite familiar with the local situation, and who classed them so in his book, *Ethnic Factors in the Population of Boston*, 1903.

[19] Nathan Goldberg, "Occupational Patterns of American Jews," *The Jewish Review*, April, 1945, p. 11.

[20] Norman Bentwitch, "The Kehillah of New York, 1908-1922," *Mordecai M. Kaplan Jubilee Volume* (English section), New York, 1953, p. 81.

[21] George Cohen, *The Jews in the Making of America*, Boston, 1924, pp. 125-126.

[22] Jacob Goldberg, "Jews in U. S. Medicine," *Harofe Haivri* (Hebrew), New York, 1939, p. 42.

[23] "Professional Tendencies among Jewish Students in Colleges, Universities, and Professional Schools," *The American Jewish Year Book*, Vol. 22 (1920-1921), pp. 383-386.

[24] Will Herberg, "The Old-Timers and the New Members," *Zukunft* (Yiddish), October, 1953, pp. 408-409.

[25] Will Herberg, "The Jewish Labor Movement in the United States," *The American Jewish Year Book*. Vol. 53, 1952, p. 54.

[26] Ibid., p. 53.

[27] Samuel Koenig, "Ethnic Groups in Business, the Professions, and Civil Service in New Haven, Connecticut," *The Jewish Review*, July, 1945, p. 140.

[28] Samuel Koenig, "The Socio-economic Structure of an American Jewish Community," *Jews in a Gentile World*, ed. Graeber and Britt, New York, 1942. p. 200.

[29] Pitirim Sorokin, "American Millionaires and Multi-Millionaires," *Journal of Social Forces*, May, 1925. pp. 627-640.

[30] *Information Please Almanac*, 1953, p. 309.

[31] Nathan Goldberg, "Occupational Patterns of American Jews," *The Jewish Review*, October-December, 1945. Of the figures for the clerical category in the original table, we have added two-thirds to trade and one-third to manufacturing.

[32] Robert Shosteck, *Small-Town Jewry Tell Their Story*, Washington, B'nai B'rith Vocational Service Bureau, 1953, p. 14.

[33] Ibid.

[34] Ibid., p. 15.

[35] Ibid., p. 16.

[36] Liston Pope, "Religion and Class Structure," *The Annals of the American Academy of Political and Social Science,* March, 1948, p. 86.

[37] W. Lloyd Warner and Leo Srole, *The Social System of American Ethnic Groups,* New Haven, 1945, p. 112.

[38] *Patterns of Jewish Occupational Distribution in the United States and Canada,* New York, 1940, p. 14.

[39] Henry J. Meyer, "The Economic Structure of the Jewish Community in Detroit," *Jewish Social Studies,* April, 1940, pp. 131 and 139.

[40] Maurice Taylor, *The Jewish Community of Pittsburgh, December, 1938,* Pittsburgh, 1941, p. 122 (mimeographed).

[41] *American Jewish Year Book,* Vol. 54, 1953, p. 14.

[42] Maurice Karpf, *Jewish Community Organization in the United States,* New York, 1938, p. 14. Of the figures for the "clerical occupations," I have added two-thirds to trade and one-third to manufacturing and mechanical industries.

[43] Unpublished manuscript, Conference on Jewish Relations, New York.

[44] Unpublished manuscript, Conference on Jewish Relations, New York.

[45] Lee J. Levinger, "Jews in the Professions in Ohio," *Jewish Social Studies,* October, 1940, p. 406.

CURRENT MOVEMENTS IN THE
RELIGIOUS LIFE OF AMERICAN JEWRY

Jacob Agus

INTRODUCTION

Even as American civilization consists of a unique blend of the distinctive cultures of Europe, so the spiritual face of American Jewry taken as a whole is a novel and completely unparalleled expression of the immortal genius of the Jewish people. It appears that the mere act of physical translation transmutes a religious culture and effects a rearrangement within it of its constituent values and institutions. For while the message of religion is directed to the individual in the name of eternally valid truths, the language and symbolic structure of faith is inevitably affected by the ubiquitous pressures of the living cultures of the day. Accordingly, we propose to analyse the contemporary trends in American Judaism by describing first the prevailing winds of the American spiritual climate, tracing then in some detail the varied religio-cultural heritage of the Jewish community and outlining finally the massive processes of transformation to which the component institutions and trends appear to be subject.

Perhaps, the most fundamental factor in American society is the absolute separation of church and state. While in European countries this relegation of religion to the domain of private conscience had been achieved sometimes slowly, sometimes violently but always in a conscious opposition to a long and honorable national tradition, in America, the foundation of national life was laid out in accordance with the inviolability of this principle. Thus, as Americans return ever and anon to the basic principles of their heritage, they renew their contacts with the great liberal tradition of the eighteenth and nineteenth centuries. What has been a revolution and a protest to the older countries of Western civilization, was here a beginning, an axiom, the cornerstone of a brave new society. Organizationally, the impetus of liberalism makes for a progressive lessening of social pressure in behalf of any kind of conformity. Its basic implication is that any one religion is as good as another, their social validity varying in direct proportion to their tolerance of other faiths. As a consequence the liberal attitude in America has not resulted at any time in a wave of conversions to any form of the Christian faith. Reverence for religion, which is an intrinsic element of American liberalism, certainly includes reverence for our own inherited faith. As to the underworld of prejudice and social snobbery which scorns the Jew as a scion of a lesser breed, conversion to Christianity is likely to be of dubious efficacy in providing a safe escape. Thus, assimilation in the full and final sense of conversion was not ever and is not now a grave and massive threat to the existence of the Jewish community. From all appearances, the incidence of intermarriage is definitely on the increase, but most intermarried couples, especially in the middle and lower strata of society, choose to remain part of the Jewish community.

While American liberalism does not offer aid and comfort to the escapist elements in the Jewish community, it does definitely weaken the cohesive forces of the community. In fact, American Jewry is scarcely organized on the basis of community loyalty, which formed the basis of Jewish collective existence throughout all the centuries of life in the Diaspora. None of the forms of communal structure in European countries affords an exact parallel to the total lack of the communal base in American Jewry. While the Federations and Welfare Funds of some communities seek to embrace in their purview all the non-sectarian areas of service, they still remain mediating agencies, not basic units of identification. The substitution of the congregational unit of organization for that of the community is, of course,

an outgrowth of the liberal tradition of America and its emphasis upon the complete freedom of the individual. It is not at all taken for granted that the individual is to be regarded as part of any community, axiomatically and automatically. As the focus of all values, he is at liberty to choose out of the organic cluster of ideals and institutions that is Judaism whatsoever may appeal to him and reject the rest. In consequence, the American Jewish community is actually a loose association of organizations, ministering to one or another Jewish or general ideal.

Corresponding to the free individual is the congregation in its complete independence and virtual self-sufficiency. While the various national associations of synagogues along ideological lines endeavor to act respectively as Orthodox, Conservative and Reform "movements", they are actually free associations of more or less like-minded congregations, which can rarely be induced to follow any one policy. Nor do the lines of demarcation, dividing the ideological groups, follow the actual lines of congregational affiliation.

Individualism is believed by many observers to be the most distinctive basis of the American mentality. The source of all values and the goal of all ends is the living individual in his concrete particularity. All forms of group existence must be submitted to the test of the effectiveness with which they minister to the needs or respond to the ideals of the individual. On the organizational plane, which we discussed up to this point, the powerful impact of this emphasis was clear enough. But its implications for the future development of American Judaism are even more profound and enduring. For in the long run, this pervasive tendency is likely to undermine the purely ethnic loyalties of the Jew. Traditionally, Judaism consisted of a blend of religious and national loyalties, the proportion varying in accord with the temper of the individual thinker and the spiritual atmosphere of his day. In America there is little or no opposition to the cultivation of minority cultures, but the pervasive individualism of the dominant civilization tends to dissolve the loyalties of the individual immigrant to his specific culture.

The exaltation of the individual in American society is likely to affect the Jewish religion in itself, in addition to constricting the ethnic loyalties contained in it and clustering about it. With the living individual as the goal of all values, a religion is no longer "proven true" by arguments which demonstrate it to be congruent with the universal principles of logic and ethics. Religion must be approved not only in terms of abstract universals, but in the light of what it actually accomplishes for the anxiety-ridden, confused and groping individual worshipper. It is no longer consistency with Aristotle or with Darwin or with the impersonal majesty of science that is decisive, but suitability for the supreme goal of the individual's happiness, his "peace of mind" or his "peace of soul." The vague arts of psychiatry has come to occupy the center of the stage, serving as the final arbiter in all questions of truth and goodness. This popular emphasis may in time be redeemed through its blending with the Jewish ideal of the "perfect man" (shlemut). If the individual is to be the source of all values, then we must not take him as we find him, in all his empirical vulgarity, but in his quality of ideal perfection. However, concerned as we are with the forces playing upon the heritage of Judaism in American civilization, we must recognize American individualism for what it is presently, apart from what it might eventually become.

Another consequence of American individualism is its thoroughgoing pragmatism and its impatience with mere ideologies. It is scarcely possible to exaggerate the pervasiveness of this fundamental bias that it is not what ideas are that counts, but what they do. Since Judaism takes on the color of its intellectual environment, we may expect this earthy genius of prag-

matism to permeate the Jewish tradition which, in the pre-philosophical era, had many points of contact with it. As the Jewish movements of Russia, in all their variety ranging from revolutionary socialism to cultural Zionism were alike in being profound and impassioned, bursting with Messianic fervor, in keeping with the dark pathos of the Russian soul, and even as the Jews of Germany were meticulously orderly and systematic, guarding against the slightest "impurity" of ideological inconsistency, American Judaism is likely to unfold the happy insights of the pragmatic approach, which frequently scandalizes the philosophical purist, in its bold defiance of mere logic, its brave optimistic surge, and its determination to stay close to the realities and ideas of common sense. The issues which divide American Jewry are partly ideological and largely practical — such as, wearing of a hat, mixed pews, organ playing, etc. There is no attempt on the part of the Orthodox groups to discourage intermarriage with the Reform or Conservative wings. The lines of demarcation are inchoate, indecisive and ignored not infrequently. While strong opinions are held concerning practical questions, the ideologies of all these groups are kept flexible, open at the upper end, unrounded and unfinished. The characteristic ambition of German Jewish savants to tie their ideological boat securely to one or another anchorage in classic German thought is conspicuously absent in this country. The great founder of the American Conservative movement, Solomon Schechter, entitled his profound study of Talmudic thought, "Aspects of Rabbinic Theology", in the belief that a complete and rounded system was neither desirable nor possible. Contrast this attitude with the classic attempt of Moritz Lazarus to demonstrate that Jewish ethics is but an explication and systematization of Kant's ethics of "the pure will". Schechter's conception was as typically American as Lazarus' system was typically German. The place of Kant and Hegel in German Jewry is largely preempted here by the pragmatists and experimentalists, William James and John Dewey.

In describing the characteristic spiritual atmosphere of America, it remains but to add that the institutions of religion form a central focus of the cultural and social pattern of American life. Religion is not so much a set of convictions as a body of experience and aspiration. The quality of "moral optimism" which distinguishes the American temperament is easily projected into the infinite universe forming the buoyant mood of monotheistic faith "that underneath are the everlasting arms". With the impetus of individual initiative looming so large and important in our society, people are not disillusioned by the lack of absolute certainty in the sphere of religion, responding readily to the conception of faith as a brave and adventurous decision to live "as if" our noblest insights were rooted securely in the infinite reaches of the dark unknown. Philosophers cannot prove or disprove the theistic belief; hence, it is legitimate for the "will to believe" to tip the scales of doubt. This argument, which was developed by the most representative thinker of America, William James, articulates the living impact of its vibrant culture. This will to believe is so powerful an impulse in the national tradition and the character of the people as to be felt in every robust beat of the national pulse. Thus, American churches by and large are short on metaphysics and long on all forms of social service. Not mere dogma but the human equation in all its ponderous complexity is the theme of all liberal pulpits, and the church is the social center of the community, not merely an isolated refuge of comforting holiness. By the same token, the American synagogue is able to embrace under its wings every cultural and uplifting interest of the Jewish community, taking on quite naturally the role of a synagogue-center. The inclusion of a massive program of athletic and recreational activities within the budget of a synagogue is now a commonplace. The very conception of a synagogue-center, which makes room for social, recreational and all kinds of cultural activities within the walls of the same institution, is distinctly American. And the implications of this conception are far-reaching. For it reflects the belief that religion is not a static body of dogmas, but the upward surge of the human personality in all its fullness. Translated in Jewish terms, the message of the synagogue reads today, "nothing that is Jewish or human is alien to me".

These influences have been at work for many generations. But, since most American Jews have been until recently immigrants or sons of immigrants, the full effect of these factors is still to be felt. Manifestly, too, the Reform and Conservative groups have been permeated more deeply with the American spirit than the Orthodox communities, which still consist for the most part of recent immigrants. It does not follow from these circumstances, however, that the progressive Americanization of the Jewish community will lead to the emergence of a uniform type of American Judaism. For each group is sufficiently virile, thoughtful and tenacious to deal with the challenge of modern life in its own terms. In the spiritual atmosphere of America, the factors making for variety and growth are likely to prevail over the seductive appeals of unity and uniformity. The vistas of the future, so far as we can see them, reveal a number of confluent but not commingling streams flowing upon the wide bedrock of the same tradition.

I. THE ORTHODOX STREAM

American Orthodoxy has not yet matured to the point of assuming a definite cast of thought or pattern of practice. Consisting of many strands, which vary in the timber of their Orthodoxy and in the degree of their resistance to the modern temper, its fabric is still unfinished and

10706

uncertain. On the whole, it may be fairly stated that, apart from popular tracts and collections of sermons, Orthodoxy has not yet settled down to the task of rendering an account of itself in the American idiom of thought and culture. Among the thoughtful adherents, we may distinguish disciples of the three trends in Orthodox Judaism — the ethical-halakic emphasis *musar*, the mysticism of Hasidism and the transcendental rationalism of western neo-Orthodoxy.

Ethical-halakic supernaturalism continues to function as an effective, living faith largely in the form which it has taken in the *musar* movement. This movement especially influenced the teachers and students of the great Lithuanian *yeshivot*, so that it may be regarded as the philosophy of Orthodoxy's *élite*. Echoing the world-view of the thoughtful exponents of the movement, the *musar* ideology is vastly more important than the paucity of printed books which expound it would lead us to believe. In the domain of speculation, Orthodox rabbis were extremely reluctant to publish their reflections, contenting themselves with oral admonitions to their students. Thus Rabbi Hayim of Volozhin allowed his classic little volume *Nefesh ha-Hayim* to be published only after his death. The literary output of Rabbi Israel Lipkin of Salant is amazingly meager. In large measure, their disciples shared this characteristic reluctance to entrust to the printed page the delicate task of tracing a safe pathway through the danger-filled, forbidding domain of the "garden of metaphysical thought". Accordingly, we have to rely for the most part on secondary sources and on the published notes which the students took of the "conversations" (*sihoth*) of their masters.

As formulated by the unique genius of the aforementioned Rabbi Israel Lipkin, the *musar* movement was, in its early stages, thoroughly uninterested in metaphysics. Its principal concern was to deepen Jewish piety and to project the ideal of the perfect Jewish personality.

Unlike the Hasidic movement of Poland and the Ukraine, which directed its message to the masses of the people, the Lithuanian pietists appealed to the chosen few. The *musarists* aimed to develop great spiritual personalities, in the belief that the masses tend to follow blindly and to reflect in varying degrees the piety of their spiritual heroes. Rabbi Lipkin was wont to rebuke his disciples for the sins of the community, saying in effect: "if you had been careful not to take four steps without engaging in Torah-study, the people generally would not have been guilty of neglecting the Torah." Thus, the *musar* movement set its sights high, far above and beyond the fixed norms of the *Shulhan Aruk*. The Hasidim learned to serve God in joy, to sink their individuality with utter abandon in the total community of Israel, which is assured of salvation by the unbreakable word of the Covenant. In contrast, the *musar men* were asked to ponder in fearful anxiety over the fate of their own soul, to envisage the tremendous difficulty of meeting fully the demands of the Torah and to worry ceaselessly over the urgency of achieving the complete perfection of their souls, ere the curtain of death ended the possibility of growth. The keynote of *musar* was persistent and deeply anxious self-analysis and self-criticism. Before the bar of Divine judgment, the individual stands in total isolation, mindful only of his sins and failures, pleading tearfully and with anxious trembling for the undeserved boon of salvation.

The individualistic emphasis of the *musar* movement may be understood in the light of the powerful inroads which were made by the rise of *Haskalah*, the movement of humanistic and secularistic enlightenment. In the last decade of the nineteenth century, the Jewish community of Russia was no longer dominated intellectually and socially by pious believers, whose central concern it was to achieve the bliss of salvation in the hereafter. While the masses of Russian Jewry were still in the tenacious grip of old habits, the intelligentsia was swept along, for the most part, by the powerful storm-winds of the new liberal and revolutionary faiths. The rigid uniformity of naïve belief and practice which prevailed uninterruptedly for so many centuries was now broken up. Perforce, the Jewish individual became the center of attention since the empirical community was no longer identical with the ideal congregation of Israel (*Kneset Yisrael*) which is the counterpart of the Divine Presence.

The *musar* movement construed the challenge of *Haskalah* as a psychological, not a philosophical problem. They did not attempt to refute the arguments of the modernists, point by point, in the belief that dialectical fencing was only a subtle defense-mechanism. To the faithful, arguments are superfluous, and to the unbelievers, the most consummate apologetic will be of no avail. For faith dwells below the level of the conscious, in the domain of will and feeling, where the soul freely submits to its Master or rebelliously turns away from Him. Rabbi Lipkin would frequently offer the following illustration: We are bidden to love a student as much and more than a son. An observant Jew, in the full possession of his faculties, would save his pupil first in the event of a sudden conflagration. But, if he is in a sleepy condition, he is likely to save his son first and to reveal the unconscious rebelliousness of his inner nature. But, piety is only self-delusion if it does not penetrate into the innermost recesses of one's being. Hence, the problem of religious education is to reach down to "the unconscious feelings" of the people and to build up an impregnable foundation for the superstructure of faith (Dov Katz, *Tnuat ha-Musar*, I, p. 224).

In the subsequent development of the *musar* movement, two schools of thought emerged, which stressed respectively the two contrasting emphases in its teaching. The followers of Rabbi Yitzhok Blaser and of Rabbi Yoisel of Novarydok (Nowogrodek) devised a system of instruction and training, which aimed at the cultivation of the fear of God in all its gradations from the terrifying specters of "hell fire and brimstone" to the noble sense of awe and reverence of the philosopher. To the austere piety of these teachers, no man could ever grow beyond the level of fear-consciousness, so as to attain the assurance of Divine favor. Characteristic of this mood is the following episode told of Rabbi Yitzhok Blaser. Asked to address a group of yeshivah students, he narrated the allegory of a group of men who were lost in a forest. After days of wandering, they encountered an old man and implored him to show them the way out of the forest. But the old man replied to them — "You have been lost for only a few days. I have been lost for many years. How can I help you?" Applying the parable to himself, he concluded "You are young men and you feel perplexed for only a short time. I have been lost for a long, long time. Let us cry together. Perhaps, the Almighty will help us" (*Tnuat ha-Musar*, II, p. 250).

The awareness of perplexity is itself the way out, if it leads to fear and trepidation, for fear is the beginning of all wisdom and its end as well.

More influential in the long run, especially upon the American scene, was the trend of *musar* teaching which appealed to the sentiments of love and aspiration and set up the ideal of the perfect personality as the goal of piety. Growth toward ever nobler ends is the positive pole of all psychical impulses as fear and anxiety constitute their negative pole. Thus, Rabbi Simhah Zisel Ziv of Kelm and his disciples aimed to transform piety into an all-embracing ideal of perfection that would appeal to the healthy, outgoing instincts of Jewish youth, shunning no exercise or discipline that makes for growth of the spirit. While the other *musar* teachers, including the founder, Rabbi Israel Lipkin, opposed the introduction of secular studies into the curriculum of the yeshivot, for fear that the students might be influenced by the manifold errors of modern thought, Rabbi Simhah Zisel himself established the *Talmud Torah* of Grobin, a school where secular studies were taught with the aim of synthesizing Orthodoxy and modern culture so as to produce a new type of Jewish gentleman. His example was not followed by the heads of other yeshivot in Poland and Lithuania, but the founders of the great Yeshiva University, which constitutes today the educational cornerstone of American Orthodoxy, were certainly encouraged by his pioneering effort.

To Rabbi Simhah Zisel orderliness was the basic quality of the ideal personality, enabling the "pure and rational soul" to prevail over the body, "which is more ugly, repulsive and disgusting than the bodies of all other animals." Self-control can be effective only when it is habitual. Thus, he demanded of his pupils that they devote time to quiet reflection and self-examination day by day. "Not one day should be allowed to pass without habituation in the process of reflection for it is the key of wisdom, the focus of all the faculties, leading to the attainment of the noble man" (*Tnuat ha-Musar,* II, p. 161).

Since reflection is the key to perfection, man must strive to allay anxiety and to acquire the capacity to be calm, poised and unperturbed at all times. "In the quality of inner rest, all perfection is included." His disciples were asked to undertake a series of exercises so as to achieve the state of calm confidence, which is the necessary prerequisite for pious reflection on the nature of God and the destiny of the human soul. However, he cautioned, the goal of imperturbability must not be interpreted as implying disinterestedness in other people. On the contrary, the unquestioning and unreasoning love of our fellowmen is essential to the attainment of perfection. For the love of people serves to overcome our native selfishness, and it is also the one sure way to God (*Ibid.,* pp. 153, 154).

The emphasis on reflection in the Kelm branch of the *musar* movement was bound to reawaken the metaphysical interest, which was initially sidetracked. The *musar* teachers shunned the disciplines and methods of modern philosophy, seeking the authoritative answers to the baffling questions of faith in Jewish tradition and sacred literature. The following worldview is contained in a series of *musar* lectures (*Shiurei Daat,* New York, 1949) that were given in the European yeshivah of Telshe and later published by their disciples in America.

The authors present as a truth of revelation Plato's fundamental generalization that all the things and events which we encounter in this sensible universe are only shadows of ethereal essences that inhere in the upper realms of eternity. The more of value, beauty and goodness things possess, the closer they are in the chain of being to their counterparts in the domain of Emanation. "One range of existents is realized in all the worlds, and in every world the same thing assumes a different form in keeping with the nature of that world" (*Ibid.,* p. 11).

In this cosmic chain of being, the Torah fulfills at every level the function of soul to the body of the corresponding world, for the Torah too is not the same in all the realms. It constitutes a series of coarsening expressions of the Will of God, even as the universe represents a parallel descending series of His work. While the Kabbalists loved to contrast their "hidden wisdom" with the plain meaning of the Torah, the *musar* men saw the Kabbalah as an integral, organic phase of the revealed Torah, related to it in the same fashion as the Platonic essences are related to their earthly counterparts. "In the wisdom of the Torah and the reasons of the commandment, the revealed and hidden reasons are not unrelated. In reality, they form one reason, the hidden one being the root and soul of the revealed explanation. He who understands any motivation literally knows only the garment, but the Torah has a garment and a body, and a soul, and a soul to a soul, rising ad infinitum" (*Ibid.*, p. 13).

In the days of the Messiah, the higher expressions of the Torah will take the place of the ones we now possess.

"For the Torah which is given to us in this our world is of no account in comparison with the Torah which is going to be revealed in the days of the Messiah" (*Ibid.*, p. 66).

Because of this vertical and infinite dimension of the Torah, the faithful student senses the quality of endlessness and eternal truth in its study. "For the holy Torah is a long chain which reaches from this lowly earth to the loftiest heavens. When a person contemplates truly the reasons of the Torah, he moves this chain, so that he feels and hears a ring above which authenticates and certifies the truth" (*Ibid.*, p. 23).

The meaning of the Torah in this connection is, of course, the totality of Halakic and Agadic literature. As new discoveries in Torah-reasoning (*hiddushim*) are made, the nature of the universe is fixed accordingly. "For the act of voting and the establishment of the Halakah by the vote of the majority fixes the nature of creation" (*Ibid.*, p. 24). Naturally, this concession to the notion of growth in the Torah does not imply the possibility of modifying any Rabbinic enactment in accord with the needs of the times. "For whatever has been set into Halakah remains part of creation forever and is no longer subject to change."

As the sequence of events in nature is not one which could be deduced rationally but is only to be known by experience, so the reasoning of the Torah may frequently appear irrational. In reality, its seemingly absurd distinctions and superficially trivial niceties of ritual correspond to important "roots" in the higher worlds.

But if reason is powerless to comprehend the logic of the Torah, the student of Torah acquires after a while a "spiritual stature" (*shiur komah*), which enables him to discover new insights or to arrive at right decisions in new situations, with the aid

of the *Ruah ha-Kodesh,* or by the gift of prophecy. In a world of indifference and neglect, the remnant of the faithful "carries the burden which was designed for many others". It is for them to fulfill the purpose of all human life — to wit, "the uplifting of the low forces of matter in the human soul and in creation generally, bringing them back to their roots."

The most luminous representative of Orthodox mysticism was doubtless the late Chief Rabbi of Palestine, Abraham Issac Kook. While his visits to the United States were relatively brief, the influence of his personality and his writings was extensive. Through his work, the complex of ideas and sentiments in the Mizrachi interpretation of Zionism was articulated and dialectically justified. The moderate Orthodox elements that favor cooperation with non-Orthodox groups draw their inspiration from his life and thought.

Kook was primarily a mystic in the genuine, psychological sense of the term. Doubt and certainty were to him not opposing poles on the field of thought but overwhelming experiences by which his soul was tossed about as a helpless boat on a raging sea. He felt the onset of doubt as the ebb of his vital force, giving way again and again to the triumphant flow of Divine Grace, which infused his being with buoyancy, certainty and, as he felt, truth. Generalizing from his own mystical experience, he saw the world as presenting two faces to man — a happy, God-centered face, bearing the beneficient lineaments of the Torah and a melancholy, gray face of indifferent force, shadowed by doubts of the historicity of revelation and ringed about with the bitter, Satanic darkness of moral chaos, universal meaninglessness and total frustration. Thus, doubt was not an intellectual problem so much as a psychic letdown, appearing on the scene of consciousness along with multiple contradictions and deepening despair whenever God hides his face from man. When we are taken back into His favor and find ourselves carried on the crest of the current of love issuing from His being, we speedily behold the clouds of doubt vanish in the distance and we glimpse the truth, in all its infinite depth and healing power.

From his scattered and unsystematic writings, we gather the following description of the mystical experience of the "nearness of God". One is overwhelmed by an exquisite, consuming longing for the Divine Presence, "an intense thirst, pleasing in the extreme", which slowly deepens into "pure fear, the intensity of holy trembling". The mystic feels that he has been touched with a holy flame, wakening within him an unearthly yearning to break out of the confining bounds of the sensible universe and to sink his being into the Divine Reality, which extends beyond "the walls of deed, logic, ethics and laws". And in this heavenly yearning there is already a kind of fulfillment, so that the mystic wills to express to others his paradoxical delight and anguish, which remain stubbornly inconmmunicable.

"I am not one of God's elected heroes that found all the worlds within them and did not care if others their riches knew or not" (*Banner of Jerusalem*, p. 131).

Following this first pulsation of the Divine power, the mystic sinks back into the gray and tasteless world of conflict, contradiction and doubt. "Because of the narrow receptive faculty of man, one datum contradicts the other datum; one feeling combats the other feeling, and one image pushes out the other; but, in truth, one datum fortifies the other datum, different feelings vitalize each other, and the several images in one's mind complete each other. The more a man is uplifted, the wider his faculties expand, until he comes to find within himself the satisfying fullness of inner peace and the consequent consistency between all data, feelings and images" (*Ibid.*, p. 132).

Having once seen the veil of contradiction lifted so as to reveal the organic unity of all existence, the mystic looks forward to the reappearance of the vision, the dis-tinguishing mark of which is "the view of all things together".

> The gates are opened, the King of glory enters . . . The worlds are united, the hidden and the revealed are commingled, body and soul are merged, the 'lights' and the 'vessels' are linked together. And an exquisite sweetness, an inner, intense and highly exalted pleasure is uncovered in the source of the rejoicing soul. Then power and light from above appear unto thee with all the ornamentation of their many lights. Thou wilt recognize thy power and the intensity of thy exaltation; wilt know thy humbleness and thy unworthiness, the unworthiness of all creatures" (*Ibid.*, p. 135).

Thus, the alternation of faith and doubt in the human psyche is due to the continuous ebb and flow of the Divine current. The mystic, who has once sensed within himself the assurance of the divine reality, knows that holiness is the very core of being, and that truth is grasped to the extent to which one feels the "nearness" of the Supreme Being. Furthermore, the Jewish mystic finds that the Torah is the immediate channel of Divine light and grace. While the mystical vision does not contain precise and specific messages as did the stage of prophecy in the view of tradition, it does lead to the development of a taste for the quality of holiness. "Though we do not perceive articulate letters and distinct words, we regard our secular and Torah studies as intended solely for the purpose of obtaining as much as possible the clarity of words out of the exalted sounds which beat constantly in our inner ear, that we may present them to ourselves and to others in a form that leads to action and to properly ordered and systematized reflection" (*Ibid.*, p. 192).

While Kook achieved his mystical state through absorption in Kabbalah, he learned to correlate his intimate experiences with the concepts of general philosophy. The "lights of holiness", in his philosophy, played virtually the same role

BERNARD REVEL (1885-1940), NOTED SCHOLAR,
PRESIDENT OF THE YESHIVA COLLEGE,
NEW YORK CITY

as the *élan vital* in Bergson's last book, inspiring creative achievement in the arts and sciences as well as in the life of piety (*The Two Sources of Morality and Religion*). Thus the secular world was, in his view, the marginal manifestation on the surface of life of the pulsating current of holiness in the heart of things. The "light of the Messiah", which is the vibrant process of redemption, is manifested in the efforts of all "who labor for the perfection of the world" (*Shiklul ha-Olam*) and the ennobling of the human personality.

In the same integrating spirit, Kook saw the force of modern nationalism as a noble impulse, akin to religion, implanted by God for the sake of Messianic perfection. Jewish nationalism he regarded as a supremely holy movement, even if its exponents proclaimed from the housetops its total independence of religion. Every one who lends a hand to the upbuilding of the Jewish people in its homeland is working for the redemption of the *Shekinah*, since the national genius of

Israel is peculiarly suitable for the cultivation of true religion. And the physical health of Israel is a prerequisite for its spiritual growth. "The Holy Spirit and the light of God cannot come to Israel as long as a debilitating sense of fear continues to poison the Jewish soul. This sorry product of exile and persecution prevents the *Shekinah* from resting on the soul of Israel" (*Ibid.*, p. 204).

In Kook's view, the national genius of Israel was peculiarly organic and distinctly mystical, so that the atheistic pioneer and the Kabbalistic hermit constituted part of one organic society. The "physical exercises of Jewish youth . . . perfect the spiritual power of the esoteric saints . . ." (*Ibid.*, p. 210). For both activities constitute supplementary phases of the one process of redemption. "Mystical reflection is the freedom of Israel, in other words, the soul of Israel" (*Ibid.*).

With all his pietistic involvement in the idiom of Kabbalah, Kook became the saint and prophet of the liberal wing of Orthodoxy, which identified itself wholeheartedly with the Zionist enterprise, recognizing as their brothers in spirit and destiny the zealous nationalists who denied the sanctity of the Torah. In thought, Kook advanced at times to the Conservative position, as when he suggested that the cultural creations of Israel, produced as they were by the genius of Israel, constituted Torah. Thus, he declared, "And the congregation of Israel is itself Mosaic tradition from Sinai" (*Ibid.*, p. 211).

In summary, the mystical humanism and the spiritual nationalism of Kook reflected the vital currents of thought and sentiment of a considerable section of contemporary Orthodoxy. His writings are still read as guideposts, pointing the way toward a synthesis of the Orthodox tradition and the values of secular humanism.

Some of the noblest authorities in Judaism were neither philosophers, nor mystics, nor masters of the esoteric lore of Kabbalah. Dedicated to the arduous pursuit of

YESHIVA UNIVERSITY, NEW YORK CITY

religious truths, they found their satisfaction in study and action "within the four ells of Halakah". Does Judaism then contain a purely Halakic stream of thought that takes account of the fundamental questions of existence even while it skirts the pathways of philosophy and mysticism? — Historically, there is no question that many illustrious masters of Talmudic lore considered their learning to be utterly self-sufficient, with no legitimate room left either for the insidious doubts of speculation or for the excessive ardor of Hasidism. But, is this attitude tenable? Can Halakah get along with the one dogma of revelation, ruling out of consideration all that was not included in the peculiar structure of Jewish Law?

Joseph Baer Soloveichik, Professor of Talmud and Religious Philosophy at the Yeshiva University, champions the view that Halakah contains a characteristic structure of ideas and sentiments, which derive from a fundamental attitude of the human spirit. It articulates a psychic complex of ideas and values of its own and it does not stand in need of validation from any outside source. Founded on the solid data of Divine Revelation, Halakah has grown in continuous awareness of the tensions and paradoxes of human nature, which it sought to resolve and to integrate in its vision of ideal personality.

The "man of Halakah" is aware of the "tension" and the "crises" in the human personality. The passion for pure knowledge in our makeup finds satisfaction in the far-flung researches of science that are aimed at the dissolution of the novel and the mysterious elements of experience into a system of unvarying law. At the same time, our religious consciousness heightens our sense of wonder at the very quality of lawfulness that holds the entire range of existence in thrall. With masterful erudition, Soloveichik dwells on this dichotomy of the human spirit, ending with the assertion that Halakah provides the Divine answer to this human dilemma (*Talpioth*, 1944, New York, pp. 652-660).

The "man of Halakah" approaches the mystery of existence with "a priori concepts", with the aid of which he erects a satisfying image of the universe. Having received his principles and laws at Sinai, he comes armed with a "body of teaching which points out to him the way to the nature of being. There is no phenomenon, event or thing which a priori Halakah does not approach with its ideal measurements" (*Ibid.*, p. 661). While the religious consciousness centers round the awareness of

a noumenal realm supervening behind the realm of existence, the Halakist takes this circumstance for granted and proceeds to apply the principles deriving from the divine realm to the sanctification of this earthly dominion of existence. He can be intensely and wholeheartedly oriented toward the temporal world because he knows himself to be in full control of the channels which bend the realm of eternity into this temporal universe. The Halakist does not engage in a continuous battle against the "flesh", for the laws of the Torah are sober, life-affirming and altogether sufficient for a law-abiding citizen of God's world. Nor does the Halakist storm the heavenly heights of transcendental reality in his yearning to escape from the earthy and the temporal, for his "God-given *mitzvot*" enable him to build eternity within the earthly world — yes, the Halakist, in all his humility, figures out

THE OLDEST ORTHODOX SYNAGOGUE IN CHICAGO (PRESENT STRUCTURE BUILT IN 1950)

HEBREW THEOLOGICAL COLLEGE, CHICAGO—BETH HAMEDRASH LATORAH

norms and principles to which even the Lord Himself is subject, as it were.

The piety of the Halakist, then, is expressed in the construction of objective norms, or laws, which give shape and form to the amorphous and fluid, tempestuous and unpredictable "feelings" of religion.

> The Halakah which was given to us at Sinai is the objectification of religion in the shape of fixed and lucid molds, in clearly outlined laws and definite principles. It converts subjectivity into objectivity and into a fixed pattern of lawfulness (*Ibid.*, p. 688).

Thus, Soloveichik disapproves of the Hasidic emphasis on religious enthusiasm and feeling, citing the words of rebuke which his father addressed to a Hasid when the latter was overwhelmed by pious awe during the shofar-blowing ceremonies on Rosh ha-Shanah: "Do you tremble and cry on Sukkot, when you bless the *lulab*? Why then do you cry when the *shofar* is blown? —Aren't both observances equally commandments of the Lord?" (*Ibid.*, p. 689). It is interesting to observe that Rabbi Israel Lipkin was of the same opinion. "All my days", he is reported to have said, "I labored to acquire the same attitude toward all precepts" (*Tnuat ha-Musar*, I, p. 252).

Though the purpose of the *shofar* is to arouse the feelings of repentance and that of the *lulab* to express the feelings of gratitude for the ingathering of the harvest, the Halakist takes note predominantly not of the feelings involved but of the actual performance of the ceremony, in all its detailed exactitude. For the significance of the *mitzvah* is independent of the feelings it arouses or fails to arouse, consisting solely in its being a divine, immutable law. This legalistic emphasis does indeed subdue the stormy surge of religious feeling, but it compensates for this loss of inwardness and depth by the development of a joyous sense of dedication which accompanies the performance of *mitzvot*.

The Sages of Israel know nothing of the ceaseless battle against the Evil Desire, such as we read about in the lives of Christian saints . . . "While the faith of the Catholic fathers was won through a struggle and by an inner compulsion, the faith of our Sages was a free and serene growth of the spirit" (*Talpioth,* p. 692).

This sober restraint of the Halakist is by no means due to the modesty of his purpose. For in truth, the masters of the Law were animated by the dynamic ambition to be ceaselessly creative. In the domain of social life, the rabbis sought to bring about the realization of the Utopia of the Halakah, and, for the guidance of the chosen individual, they evolved the lofty goal of prophecy. The ideal personality is the prophet, his qualities of mind and heart having become perfected and balanced to the point where the Divine Presence actually dwells upon him. "Every person is called upon to renew his being in accord with the ideal pattern of the prophet and to engage in this creative process until he attains final consummation of prophetic achievement, the readiness for the reception of Divine Grace" (*Ibid.,* p. 729).

II. THE NEO-ORTHODOX

In the total complex of American Orthodoxy, the elements deriving from the thought and tradition of Western Europe are of particular interest. Designated on occasions as neo-Orthodox, the stream of romantic piety and inflexible zealotry which is associated with the name of Samson Raphael Hirsch is represented on the American scene by a very small number of congregations. However, its influence is likely to increase in both scope and depth, as the immigrant colonies are permeated ever more fully with the spirit of Western culture. Actually, the term neo-Orthodox does not betoken any essential departure in dogma or practice from the Orthodox pattern of faith. Yet, neo-Orthodoxy is distinctly and vividly a new interpretation of tradition, reflecting the genteel norms, universalist aspirations and this worldly emphasis of modern Western culture. Carried along by the passion for consistency, the exponents of this school are frequently more rigid and unyielding in practice than the unpretentious, unsystematic and altogether "natural" saints and sages of Eastern Europe.

The most recent and most thorough expression of West-European Orthodoxy may be found in Isaac Breuer's impressive volume, *Der neue Kusari.*

The author, trained in the German classical tradition, was painfully aware of the deep frustrations of modern man. As an idealistic philosopher, he regarded the realm of appearance which our senses convey to us as being a product of two entities, which are themselves outside the space-time world, transcending the iron laws of causality. The physical universe consists of influences and forces deriving from the "meta-physical" realm, and these are ordered and molded, fashioned and "willed" by the subconscious will of man, which is the same in all men and independent of the vagaries of thought and sentiment that supervene on the surface of consciousness. If we designate this unconscious will as the "meta-ethical" phase of the human personality, we recognize the physical universe as the fleeting surface of contact between the "meta-physical" and the "meta-ethical" worlds.

From this analysis it follows that truth is not to be discovered by the simple analysis of, and generalization from, the restless surge of phenomena on the surface of existence. Somehow, the inner will of man, dwelling in realms beyond our conscious reach and manifesting itself in the alternation of fearful anxiety and bold decision, must provide the answer.

To dramatize his solution, the author describes a young Jewish intellectual, who was launched on his way back to "Torah-true" Judaism by his persistent anxiety over the question, "how should I live my life?". Any sentimental or humanistic answer was to him unsatisfactory, for in his deadly earnestness, he needed detailed guidance for living, not remote ideals and vague generalities. Caught in the swirling currents of modern history, the young philosopher felt an inner certainty that the word of God was somehow conveyed by the unseen hand, writing on the broad canvas of human history. But history is the record of the struggle of the nations, and our hero could not but read this record from the standpoint of the Jewish people, "who live among the nations but are not one of them".

In Breuer's interpretation, the lesson of history is twofold — the inevitable frustration of all human efforts and the existence of the Jewish society as a kind of superhistorical or "meta-historical" people, which provides the answer to the dark, multifarious and infinite tragedy of mankind.

"Does not the history of the nations prove that people cannot liberate themselves by their own efforts from the power of evil?" (*Ibid.*, p. 154).

The author, writing in the late Thirties, as the devastating tide of nazism was gathering for the final burst of blind fury, saw the entire, timeless fate of Israel revealed in these stern predictions of Moses:

> And the Lord shall scatter thee among all the peoples, from the one end of the earth unto the other . . . And among these nations thou shalt find no ease, neither shall the sole of thy foot have rest; but the Lord shall give thee there a trembling

heart, and a failing of eyes, and a sorrow of mind . . . (Deuteronomy, XXVIII, 64-67). And upon them that are left alive of you, I will send a faintness into their hearts in the lands of their enemies; and the sound of a shaken leaf shall chase them (Leviticus, XXVI, 36).

In these and similar verses, the author saw proof of the divinity of the Torah and of the peculiar destiny of Israel.

It is through the Sinaitic covenant that *Kneset Yisrael,* the Congregation of Israel, was constituted. Hence, only those who are absolutely and meticulously loyal to the divinely fashioned community are truly Jews. The author is particularly incensed at the Zionists, whose ideology consists in a conscious rebellion against the "meta-historical" destiny of the Jew.

Yet, with all his impassioned exclusiveness *vis-à-vis* divergent interpretations of Judaism, the author reveals a powerful universalist trend of thought. The purpose of Jewish "meta-history" is to bring mankind to the goals of individual perfection and social harmony. In its role of "the people of peoples", Israel is "the herald of God's righteousness" and the symbol of the "meta-historical" goal of humanity. It was God's will that the Jews be scattered among the varying nations of the globe, in order "that the 'meta-historical' people learn to love and cherish the peculiar characteristics of each nation" (*Ibid.*, p. 159).

This entire world-view is founded like an inverted pyramid upon the one fulcrum of literal revelation at Sinai. But on what grounds is this dogma to be accepted? — The answer is that this dogma is "willed" by the one who identifies himself with *Kneset Yisrael,* utterly and without reservations. "The final truth cannot be grasped through thought, but only by the will, for in actuality to know and to will is one" (*Ibid.*, pp. 267-270). An event that happened only once in history cannot be proven, in the usual sense.

It remains but to add that some intellectuals have reverted to a species of Orthodoxy as a result of their disillusionment and despair. Thus, Ludwig Lewisohn embraces the Jewish faith by way of protest against the "idols" of "emancipation", "modernism" and "progress".

"We found, first, that the old emancipation of Jews is bankrupt.

"We found, finally, by the irrefutable facts of history that the Jewish people is different from *all* the other peoples by virtue of its endurance, acknowledged by all Christendom, both friend and foe, as an historic experience, as a matter of direct knowledge" (*The American Jew,* p. 88).

Continuing his reflections upon the unique miracle of Jewish survival, Ludwig Lewisohn arrives at the conclusion that the Sinaitic revelation must have been a real and true experience. Confessing his lack of the "power of faith" to accept the naïve interpretation of revelation, he nevertheless asserts,

> But, this much is certain: were two men to come to us, of whom one, a traditional Jew, asserted the exact veracity of the Biblical version, and the other, a modern man, were to assert that nothing happened at the foot of Sinai, that all these vast consequences pointed to a vacuum — one would have to say that, historically and philosophically, the traditional Jew was *within* the realm of truth and that the modern man was talking fantastic nonsense. Not "science" perhaps, of the kind we have examined, but reason and the evidence of history are on the side of the traditionalist (*Ibid.,* p. 109).

The account in the Bible and Jewish tradition is a rendering in the form of myth and legend of that unique experience, which cannot otherwise be told.

> What then, once more, was the character and content of that Sinaitic experience which made us into *this* people, with *this* character out of which sprang this forever recurrent destiny? — We cannot grasp it in intellectual terms. We are free to believe that God spoke to Israel through his

prophet. We know from the evidence of all history that we, that our fathers, were *there* and accepted or created the Law of our being which has been our Law and our life and the length of our days from that hour to this (*Ibid.,* p. 112).

Like Judah ha-Levi then, Lewisohn bases his faith upon what he construes to be the lesson of history. Endurance is the proof of the faith and survival is its goal. Accordingly, he recommends the upbuilding of firm forms of Jewish living, in accordance with the Law, so as to resist the corrosive effects of modern life.

"The Jew who has recovered his Jewish authenticity will spontaneously desire to practice the *mitzvot*. He will seek to reincarnate the Torah by what he is" (*Ibid.,* p. 114).

In sum, it is Jewish life that "proves" the Law, and it is the Law that assures the continuity of Jewish life.

Little known to the English reader is the work of the modest but profound thinker who composed his laborious and ponderous works in Yiddish. Reuben Agushewitz set out to prove the truth of the theistic position of Judaism by demonstrating the fallacies of the alternative conceptions of life. In his first work, he subjected to keen analysis the postulates of Hellenic philosophy (*Die Alt-Griechische Philosophie*). Then, he proceeded to argue that the idealistic interpretation of existence is alone adequate to account for the "unity" of experience. Finally, in his last work, *Emuneh un Apikorses* (New York, 1949), he analyzed the implications of atheism and materialism, arguing that the palace of faith remains undamaged by the attacks of philosophy. His meticulous analysis of the concepts of metaphysics leads him to leave room for "the unknown force", which escapes the mesh of our conceptual reasoning. At the same time, he refutes the standard arguments in behalf of determinism, leaving an area of freedom for the actions of the individual. Having projected these two postulates, he affirms

DAVID EINHORN (1809-1879), ONE OF THE
LEADERS OF THE REFORM MOVEMENT

the possibility of prophecy. In logic,
Agushewitz went no further than to demonstrate the *possibility* of a theistic faith.
In his sentiments, however, he was driven,
by the debacle of all "modern" ideals, to
embrace the faith of the Orthodox.

III. THE REFORM MOVEMENT

Unlike Orthodoxy, the Reform movement has by now acquired a definitely
American cast. At the turn of the century,
Reform was powerfully entrenched in all
the major communities of America, enjoy-
ing the overwhelming support of the German-Jewish population. While some few
German Jews remained staunchly Orthodox, the majority drifted into the Reform
camp, so that the differences of ideology
were added to the then existing chasm
between the Americanized German Jews

and their East European brethren. Except
in such big centers as New York, Philadelphia and Baltimore, the ideology of
Reform operated as a welcome barrier,
separating the immigrant Eastern Jews
from their happily situated and keenly
class-conscious German "co-religionists".
As the massive flow of immigration continued to build up the numerical strength
of the East European Jews, there developed
in almost every community two sets of religious and social institutions — the one serving the German Jews and their Czech and
Hungarian affiliates, the other serving
Polish and Russian Jewry. Through the
steady rise of Russian Jews to affluence and
influence and through occasional "mixed
marriages" with the children of the "Yahudim", the social line of demarcation is
being blurred steadily. Also, after the rise
of Hitler it became increasingly more difficult for German Jews to be inordinately
proud of the vaunted "Kultur" of their
Vaterland. As a matter of fact, at the
present time most Reform rabbis are
descendants of East European families, and
the membership of the temples too is constantly being replenished from these
sources.

Yet, even now it is impossible to understand the spiritual complexion of American Jewry without taking account of the
German background of the Reform movement. The fact that until recently the
German language was included in the curriculum of the Kneseth Israel Temple in
Philadelphia, while the study of Hebrew
was pointedly excluded, can scarcely be
understood apart from this tenacious
loyalty of German Jews to their cultural
heritage.

The founding fathers of American
Reform were the immediate disciples of
Abraham Geiger and Samuel Holdheim,
the architects of German Reform. Men like
David Einhorn, Max Lilienthal, Samuel
Hirsch, Kaufmann Kohler and Samuel
Adler came to these shores fresh from their
battles against Orthodoxy in Europe. Here
they found a fertile field for their philos-

ophy, principally because the restraining power of the overall community organization was lacking. While the Reform movement in Germany was in most cities compelled to effect an uneasy peace with the Conservative group, so as not to break up the central institutions of the community, the American Reformers were leaders of independent congregations, entirely free to translate their principles into action. Furthermore, insofar as Reform implied the negation of the value of ritual observances, the movement was aided by the general tendency of immigrants to drop all cultural impediments in their upward climb to material success. Manifestly, the ideologists limped pathetically behind the people, who were actually impelled by the harsh pressures of business to overlook some of the observances or to modify them. There was also the wish to achieve the blessing of inconspicuousness through the transformation of their distinctive heritage into a pattern that would not be distinguished from the prevailing mores in American life.

1. THE PITTSBURGH PLATFORM

The principles of the American Reform movement were first formulated in a brilliant and lucid manifesto that was drawn up by a conference in Pittsburgh in the year 1885. In the words of the historian of the movement, David Philipson, the Pittsburgh Platform, as this declaration came to be known, was "the utterance most expressive of the teachings of Reform Judaism".

Proceeding now to the analysis of the ideas and trends of thought that were reflected in this declaration of principles, we note first that the Reform movement did not tear itself away from the rest of the Jewish community to the point of becoming a separate and identifiable sect.

HEBREW UNION COLLEGE, CINCINNATI

The Pittsburgh Platform was not intended to be a "creed", but a set of guiding principles. The Reform ideologists looked upon themselves and their followers as the vanguard of the entire congregation of Israel, believing sincerely that their interpretations of the faith were likely to be universally accepted on the American scene. Their program was to become *minhag America,* the American form of Judaism. Thus, in 1899, at a banquet celebrating his eightieth birthday, Isaac M. Wise declared "Within twenty-five years, all the world will have accepted Reform Judaism" (Julian Morgenstern, *As a Mighty Stream,* p. 120). Nor was there ever in America a distinct line of demarcation, separating Reform from the traditionalists. The proponents of "radical" Reform, such as Rabbi Emil G. Hirsch of Chicago, pointed toward a possible exit from the Jewish community, while the right-wing of the movement shaded off gradually and imperceptibly into the Conservative camp. There was always a wide range of interpretation and practice within the movement, which was constituted by loyalty to some general principles rather than to a specific program of thought and action. The following may be considered the leading ideas of Reform:

A. *The Principle of Development*: The first principle of Reform is the assertion that Judaism is an evolutionary faith, which is capable of indefinite development and expression. Thus, in this Platform the authors speak of the "God-idea" as "being developed and spiritualized by the Jewish teachers, in accordance with the moral and philosophical progress of their respective ages".

This principle was variously interpreted within the movement itself. Geiger had emphasized the quality of *continuity* in the process of change, maintaining that the dynamic factor was contained in the very concept of tradition.

> Tradition is the developing power which continues in Judaism as an invisible creative agent, as a certain en-nobling essence that never obtains its full expression, but ever continues to work, transform and create. Tradition is the animating soul in Judaism, it is the daughter of Revelation and of equal rank with her . . . Tradition, like revelation, is a spiritual energy that ever continues to work, the higher power that does not proceed from man but is an emanation from the Divine Spirit, a power that works in the community, chooses its own ministers, manifests itself by its ever purer and riper fruits and thus preserves vitality and existence itself (*Judaism and Its History,* pp. 86, 87).

In this context, the term tradition stands for the authority vested in the scholars of every age to examine, organize and adapt the religious insights and values of the past. The power to legislate new *takkanot* for the "strengthening of the faith" made for a continuous progression "from precedent to precedent", ruling out any sudden or violent breaks with the past. Thus, Geiger favored the continued application of the methods of Halakah, modifying old laws, creating new forms, but maintaining the validity of the law.

Rabbi Isaac M. Wise, who did most to fashion the organizational structure of the movement, at one time favored only the kind of changes that were compatible with Halakah (Moshe Davis, *Ha-Yahadut ha-Amerikait be-Hitpathuto*).

In the Pittsburgh Platform, there is no mention either of Halakah or the modifying process of *takkanah*. Even the word Torah is rigorously avoided. The preservation of historical identity is urged, but not the continuity of the stream of tradition. The so-called *mitzvot maasiyot* (precepts of action) are designated as "Mosaic legislation", and put aside if they do not accord with the "views and habits of modern civilization". Not only are the dietary laws declared to be no longer "binding", but the observance of these laws is deplored and stigmatized as an unspiritual action — a deed "that is apt rather to obstruct than to further modern spiritual elevation". In the succeeding years, this tendency gained momentum. The requirement of circumcision was dropped for proselytes officially at the convention of the Central Conference in 1892. However, for children born within the faith, circumcision is ordained. As to the authority of Talmudic literature, the Conference in 1895 agreed that "the whole post-Biblical and patristic literature, including the Talmud, Casuistry, Responses and Commentaries is, and can be considered as nothing more or less than "religious literature."

The new ideas were reflected in successive revisions of the Prayer Book, with the result that the Union Prayer Book is now used in virtually all Reform temples. In its latest editions, it stresses social-mindedness and tolerance. Among the liturgical practices characteristic of Reform temples is the employment of an organ and mixed choir, from which Gentiles are not excluded, the disappearance of the daily *minyan* service, the abolition of the practice of calling to the Torah, the substitution of the Confirmation ceremony for the Bar Mitzvah, and the non-observance of the second day of Rosh ha-Shanah and the three festivals. The year 1885 marked therefore a radical break in the development of Reform Judaism.

The clean break with tradition, which the Pittsburgh Platform crystallized, was not only in part an extension and application of "the principle of development". In large part, too, it reflected the eagerness of Western Jews to "de-orientalize" the Jewish faith, so that it might be taken to be an integral element of Western civilization.

Speaking of the first generation of Reformers, Julian Morgenstern notes:

> A marked tendency to limit the functions of the *hazzan* and even to do away altogether with the cantillation of the services manifested itself. Not improbably, a prime consideration here was the feeling that this was purely an oriental mode of worship, and therefore offensive to modern oc-

cidental tastes . . . (*As a Mighty Stream*, p. 127).

Motivated by this aspiration to achieve complete at homeness on the American scene, the Pittsburgh Conference called for the inauguration of Sunday morning services to parallel those of Saturday, a step which led virtually to the abolition of the Saturday-Sabbath in many temples. Sinai Congregation of Chicago, a leading and radical Reform temple, discontinued Saturday services as early as 1882. Of revolutionary significance too was the call for participation in the solution of social problems on the basis of "justice and righteousness". No longer painfully self-conscious and preoccupied with internal problems, the American Jew was able to turn his attention to the problems of the community. Many Reform rabbis achieved great distinction in their valiant battles on behalf of humanitarian causes. Rabbi Stephen S. Wise of New York and Rabbi Henry Cohen of Galveston, Texas, may be mentioned as two contrasting types.

B. *The Enduring Essence*: If Judaism is an evolutionary faith, changing in accord with "the views and habits" of every age, what is its enduring core? Manifestly if there be in it no such core of permanent, time-transcending significance, there is no reason why the so-called "spirit of the age" should not be substituted for it altogether. In the Pittsburgh Platform, the "God-idea" is represented as the living essence of Judaism. Yet, not the "God-idea" as it is taught in the Bible, but this concept as it is formulated "in accord with the moral and philosophical program" of every age.

The choice of the term "God-idea" rather than the simpler designation of "the idea of God" reflects the vagueness of this conception in the minds of the Reformers. The term "God-idea" stands for a block of experience while the idea of God is an intellectual concept. Kaufmann Kohler thought of God in Kantian terms, as revealing His will in the "still small voice" of conscience. "God appears

JEWISH INSTITUTE
OF RELIGION,
NEW YORK CITY

actually to step into the sphere of human life as its moral ruler" (*Jewish Theology*, p. 36). There is no reason to assume any mystical experience or the possibility of miracles. "The whole cosmic order is one miracle", and all the wonder-tales of the Bible are illustrations of God's power and goodness. The principles of "ethical monotheism" may be summarized as follows — that God is one and ethical in essence, that mankind is one, that the human soul is immortal and that the perfect society of peace and justice will ultimately be founded.

But, are not these conceptions part and parcel of modern Western thought? Especially since the "God-idea" is formulated anew in every age in accord with the contemporary intellectual climate, what is there that is peculiarly Jewish about it? Geiger's answer was that the Reformers gloried in the complete identifi-

cation of Judaism with the modern spirit, maintaining that the impetus of Christian thought, its insistence on "original sin" and "salvation by faith", was essentially anti-modern and anti-liberal. The Pittsburgh Platform studiously avoids any invidious comparisons, terming both Christianity and Islam as allies in the advance toward the Messianic goal. Not all the thinkers of Reform concurred with Kohler's identification of the essence of Judaism with a set of true ideas. Geiger, it will be recalled, pointed to the psychological state of piety as the living essence of Judaism. "Religion is not a system of truth; it is the jubilation of the soul conscious of its eminence and at the same time its humble confession of its finiteness and limitations . . ." (*Judaism and Its History*, p. 21). This conception of religion as primarily an experience of the human personality is further elaborated and refined

in the latest exposition of Reform theology (Samuel Cohon, *Judaism — A Way of
Life*).

C. *Relevance of the "Spirit of the Age"*:
A potent factor within the Reform movement was doubtless the enthusiastic acceptance and even adulation of the "spirit
of the age". Children of the nineteenth
century, the Reformers were utterly persuaded of the inevitability of progress.
Since it was the liberal movement in European politics which brought about Jewish emancipation, they embraced the cultural philosophy of liberalism with complete abandon and even religious fervor.
Many were disciples of the Hegelian school
of thought, believing that they stood at
the "end of history" and that the spirit
of their age was achieving the consummation of all historical truth. Thus, the
Pittsburgh Platform speaks of "the modern era of universal culture of heart and
intellect" as approaching the realization
of the Messianic Kingdom. Similarly, the
protocols of the Reform conference in
Germany are filled with lavish encomiums
concerning the exalted "consciousness of
our age". As Gotthold Solomon put it,
"The age is also a Bible through which
God speaks to Israel". Even Julian Morgenstern, in an address, *the Achievements
of Reform Judaism*, given in 1924, betrays
this breathless rush to catch up with the
"spirit of the age", which was presumably
ahead of us even then.

"Whether we have completely closed the
breach which three hundred years of enforced standing still put between the world
and us, we cannot tell yet. Whether we
have caught up with the world entirely or
not . . ." (*As a Mighty Stream*, p. 159).

D. *The Antinomian or Antiritualistic
Tendency:* The brief reference in the
Pittsburgh Platform to the tendency of
dietary ceremonies "to obstruct rather than
to further modern spiritual elevation"
points to a powerful trend of thought
within the movement. The builders of Reform keenly sensed the Christian criticism
of Judaism as overly "ritualistic" and

"legalistic". In the abstract they were
compelled to recognize the inherent danger in the excessive employment of religious symbols, *i.e.,* the possibility that
the external rite might draw to itself the
devotional energy which properly belongs
to inner piety and actions. But, within
Judaism itself they found recurrent protest against the overemphasis of ritual,
protests which were voiced by the great
prophets in their battles against the sacer-
dotalism of the priests and the supersti-
tious fear of the people. "Prophetic Judaism", then, came to be the sign-post of the
Reformers in their anti-ritual emphasis.
Thus, Geiger wrote in 1840 "that the real
contrast is not between naturalism and
supernaturalism, but between religion and
legalism".

Holdheim was even more passionately
anti-legalistic. In his introduction to the
prayer-book of the Berlin Reform Temple,
he stated it to be the central purpose of
the movement . . . "to appreciate the kernel at full strength and to secure it by
breaking the shell" (quoted by Philipson, *The Reform Movement*, p. 253).

This conviction that the kernel is
strengthened when the shell is broken appears very frequently in the polemical
literature of Reform. We encounter again
and again references to the presumed contrast "between inner religiosity and outer
formalism" or between "the principle of
sincerity and empty formalism" (Philipson, *The Reform Movement*, p. 43). Kaufmann Kohler, doubtless the most influential exponent of Reform ideology in
America, held the spirit of legalism responsible "for the stifling of the ethical
and spiritual elements in Judaism" (*Jewish Theology*, p. 352). In the vehemence
of political passion, many Reform spokesmen came to take it for granted that "the
spirit of rabbinism" had indeed overcome
and "stifled the spirit of piety" in Judaism.

The opposition of the Reformers to
"legalism" and "formalism" was motivated
in part at least by the circumstance that
this aspect of the Jewish faith reflected

the motives of nationalism and communal exclusiveness. In the interpretation of Christian scholars, the universalism of the prophets was hampered and eventually negated by the racial arrogance of the Pharisees, who required complete amalgamation with the Jewish nation as a prerequisite to admission into the Jewish faith. And the rituals, from the circumcision to the dietary laws, were the national customs of the Jewish people. This utterly distorted view of the religion of the Pharisees and the Talmud was the vogue at the turn of the century. The Christians inferred it simply from the polemics of St. Paul, whom they interpreted with naïve anachronism as a crusading liberal theologian, and Jewish scholars found support for this view in the writings of Spinoza and Mendelssohn, who interpreted the ceremonial laws as "national legislation".

E. *The Questioning of Jewish Nationalism:* The express declaration in the Pittsburgh Platform, "we are no longer a nation, but a religious community", echoes one of the pivotal issues which the Reform movement brought to the fore. Since its creative period took place at a time when the Jews of Western Europe were struggling for the final consummation of complete emancipation, the movement absorbed the anti-nationalist bias in the very marrow of its bones. In Western Europe of the nineteenth century, the reactionaries, Jesuits and anti-Semites interpreted the history of Judaism in nationalistic terms. The Jewish religion in all its ritualistic complexity was nothing but a sublimation of intense ethnic pride. The Pharisaic insistence on the rites of Judaism, as against the early Christians, was due to the drive for self-isolation from the "impurity" of the Gentiles and the chauvinistic ambition to confine the glory of salvation to their own people. Thus, Jewish "nationalism" was in a class by itself, serving as a convenient weapon in the hands of reactionaries and anti-Semites.

In opposition to this exaggerated emphasis on Jewish ethnicism, the liberals maintained that the era of Jewish nationhood was ended long ago. Outside of a residual remnant of Orthodox die-hards, the repudiation of nationalism was virtually axiomatic among all Jewish groups in Western Europe down to the end of the nineteenth century. But the Reform movement endowed this principle with religious sanction and fervor.

In 1897, the Montreal Conference took note of the Zionist Congress in Basel with a resolution of "total disapproval" of the attempt to establish a Jewish State (*Yearbook* of the Central Conference of American Rabbis, IX, 12). In 1917, as the Zionist movement was building up toward the triumphant climax of the Balfour Declaration, the Conference resolved by a vote of sixty-eight to twenty, that "we look with disfavor upon the new doctrine of political Jewish nationalism, which finds the criterion of Jewish loyalty in anything other than loyalty to Israel's God and Israel's religious mission."

All through the turbulent Twenties, the impassioned opposition of the Reform rabbinate to the Zionist movement was broken only by the revolutionary stand of a few stalwart souls, such as Judah L. Magnes, Gustav Gottheil, Stephen S. Wise and Abba Hillel Silver. Gradually, the inexorable logic of events forced a modification of this anti-nationalist plank, which had constituted a chief pillar of the Reform edifice for nigh unto a century.

F. *The New Fervor and Dedication to a World-mission:* No survey of classical Reform in America dare ignore the undoubted fact that the movement brought about a renewed sense of dedication among its adherents. Released from the need of preaching on ritual niceties, the rabbinate was able to evoke fresh fervor in behalf of the central ideas of the Jewish faith. Knowing himself to be in the vanguard of the progressive advance of mankind, the Jew dared to look forward to the time when his faith will become the "universal religion" of humanity. The "deviation" of Christianity from the highway of theistic humanism was certain to be corrected with the progress of enlightenment, so that the Messianic Era, "when the Lord will be One and His Name One", seemed to be the natural terminus on the broad and bright road that led into the future. Kaufmann Kohler, for many years the outstanding theologian of the movement, struck a popular chord, when he dealt with this theme.

> Religion humanized and humanity religionized—that is the aim, the beginning and end of Judaism, as Reform understands and expounds it... Nowhere has Judaism better chances of becoming the pioneer of a humanitarian religion, nowhere can the Jewish faith venture to be the advocate of the broadest truth concerning God and man, and form the golden chain to embrace all religions and sacred books, and blend them into one religion of humanity than in this blessed new world (*Yearbook,* 1935, p. 194).

Thus, the Reform movement did not undercut by any means the Jew's feeling of being "chosen" for a sacred task. On the contrary, while the movement steered clear of nationalism in the sphere of politics, it stressed the unique ethnic qualities of the Jew. The Creator had implanted within the heart of the Jew a special "genius" for religion, as was made manifest by the glorious succession of prophets and rabbis, and by the endless martyrdom of the entire Jewish people. The Jew possessed "an instinct for religion", or a special bent for appreciation of the "purity" of ethics, or a unique predisposition for a "spiritual" philosophy of life. In their various ways, all these interpretations directed a ringing appeal to the Jew qua Jew—an approach which balanced somewhat the one-sided emphasis on the "idea" of Judaism.

Then, too, the American Reform Jew did not suffer from the malady of a split soul, so familiar to us in *Haskalah* literature, the poignant feeling of being rent apart by unresolved conflicts. Having achieved an inner synthesis between tradition, as he saw it, and modern values, he was not plagued by any guilt-feelings, arising from the contradiction between an inviolate code of religious demands and the actual pressure of life. He was relatively free of the danger against which M. Lazarus had warned.

> The decay of a religion, as well as of every spiritual society, must ensue if a large, yea a very large portion of its confessors no longer observe hundreds upon hundreds of its injunctions; no longer recognize their validity in their hearts, but nevertheless permit them to stand as injunctions of the faith . . . (Quoted in Philipson's *The Reform Movement,* p. 408).

To be sure, the Reform synthesis, which appeared to be a triumphant success at the turn of the century, developed signs of weakness, as the tide of liberalism began to recede. With the resurgence of Zionism, the consolidation of Orthodoxy and the rise of Conservatism, the Reform movement became a minority within the Jewish community. Its rigid rationalism and its "eternal verities" lost their appeal, as the years wore on, and its adherents were totally unprepared emotionally to withstand the shock of the rising tide of anti-Semitism in the Thirties. A revision of the original principles of the movement was now due so as to reckon with the deepened folk-consciousness of the people and the mentality of East European Jewry generally.

Thus, in 1937, American Reform adopted a new set of principles, which came to be known as the Columbus Platform.

G. *Criticism of the Pittsburgh Platform in the Thirties:* The Conference in 1935 brought to a climactic crescendo the tide of criticism that had been rising steadily within the movement. A number of factors combined to evoke this reaction—such as, the rise of Hitlerism and the awakened sense of Jewish unity, the rise of Conservatism and Reconstructionism and the emergence of a romantic nostalgia for mysticism, which might be called neo-Hasidism.

Thus, leading rabbis criticized classical Reform as being concerned more with the clichés of "the hour" than with the values of eternity. Religion, Samuel Cohon contended, was not an ideological essence so much as "the growing spiritual experience of a people" (*Yearbook*, 1935, p. 232). A complaint was registered against the architects of Reform, because "they forgot the sense of historic continuity of which the people is symbol and fact, and they created a gap between Jewish universalism and its particularism". A plea was heard for a renewed emphasis on the ethnic worth of the Jew. Calling for a return to Geiger's doctrine of the racial "genius" of the Jew, Felix Levy declared, "If I be permitted a generalization, the Jewish people had an instinct for God. That intuition can only be explained as the result of historic forces which the Jews would aver were set into motion by God Himself".

A new note of appreciation for the Halakic aspects of Judaism, as an excellent means of communal training in reverence for the Divine laws of the spirit, was heard in Samuel Schulman's summation, "Israel was chosen to teach the world the necessity of law in the lives of individuals and communities—the Law of God".

The spirit and accents of Ahad Haam were reflected in an address by Rabbi Abba Hillel Silver, who pointed to the unconscious, national "will to live" of the Jews as the source of all the spiritual values of Judaism. Even the "mission"-ideal arose "in response to a desperate national emergency, out of the indomitable will to live of the race . . ." It is in the blood of the nation that the dynamic source of creativity inheres as a dormant unconscious force, while ideas and ideals are nothing but the surface reflections of this irrational life-stream. Therefore, the primary sin in Judaism is the denial of national unity, and of this sin, classical Reform was guilty. To Silver, Reform participated in the error of St. Paul who sought to level the barriers "between Jews and Gentiles, Greeks and Barbarians".

"But, Paul, a product of the culturally diluted Hellenistic Diaspora entertained views which, centuries later, Reform rabbis in Germany and America were to entertain. The sense of belonging to a Jewish nation and the desire to preserve that nation and to establish the kingdom of Israel were hardly present with him" (*Ibid.*, p. 335).

Quite apart from this intemperate treatment of both Reform and St. Paul, this passage is a perfect example of the complete about-face that was now advocated within the movement in regard to nationalism. Having started out with the axiom that the essence of religion was the relationship of the individual to God, the movement now was told that the individual counts only insofar as he shares in the psyche of the nation, while even the idea of God is but a "projection" of the national "will to live". Rabbi Brickner put it thus:

> What is religion but the collective representation of a people throwing out a standard by which it measures the totality of life? As formal religion, based on revelation, begins to lose its hold, the Jewish people project a new ideal in which the whole of life is subsumed. We call it spiritual Zionism. In it, we have God, we have religion and all the values that religion participates in . . . (*Ibid.*, p. 352).

This central principle of Reconstructionism, placing the people rather than God in the vital center of Judaism, was now proposed as the basis for a new statement of guiding principles.

A more moderate and balanced critique of the Pittsburgh Platform was developed over the years by Julian Morgenstern, president of the Hebrew Union College. He thought that the framers of the Platform in 1885 sought to "transplant German Reform Judaism to America". Their ideology was too abstract and formal, not "American" enough. It dealt "with beliefs rather than with life and action". In fact, the name, America, occurs not once in the entire Platform. Also, it was too "universalistic", its framers believing that they were indeed living in the millennium. They had "little comprehension of the meanings and processes of history, or of what the full course and development of a historic religion must be; and Judaism is above all else a historic religion . . ." (*As a Mighty Stream*, pp. 424-440). The course of history had brought it about that a Jewish nation is now arising to take its place among the nations of the world. But, nationalism in itself remains a temporary, accidental phenomenon. The classical Reformers were wrong in speaking of Jewry as "a religious community", as the Zionists are wrong in their inability to think in terms other than those of a Jewish nation. Actually, Jewry is a *people*, or, more specifically, a "religious people". "Eternity for Israel lies only in the quality and consciousness of peoplehood, in being a people of destiny, in being a religious people". While nationhood is a political concept, peoplehood is taken to be a cultural-religious idea. The preponderance of power within the movement shifted steadily during the Thirties from the proponents of "ethical monotheism" as the vital core of Judaism to the aggressive preachers of an Ahad Haamist "spiritual zionism", with the result that the concept of "peoplehood", for all its ambiguity, appeared to be the only means of saving the unity of the movement. On the other hand, it conveyed a renewed appreciation of the historical quality of the Jewish faith, of the folk-elements in it, of the varied interests into which religion branches out, and finally of the "uniqueness" of the Jewish destiny. Thus, the impact of the "positive-historical" emphasis in Conservatism was felt in the new formulation of "Guiding Principles" that was adopted at Columbus, in 1937.

2.   THE COLUMBUS PLATFORM

The Columbus Platform of Guiding Principles is notable for its caution in avoiding a clash on the issue of nationalism. Its central emphasis consisted in its reformulation of the character of Jewry so as to embrace some elements of Zionism. The American Jew was not to consider Palestine as a place for personal settlement and self-fulfillment as a Jew, but as a hallowed country, affording the "promise of renewed life for many of our brethren". Unequivocally, it asserted, "We affirm the obligation of all Jewry to aid in its upbuilding as a Jewish homeland by endeavoring to make it not only a haven of refuge for the oppressed but also a center of Jewish culture and spiritual life" (*Yearbook*, vol. XLVII).

The other clear emphasis in this Platform is on the need of respecting the threads of historical continuity in the practice of the Jewish faith. Thus, it speaks of the obligation of each generation to "adapt the teachings of the Torah to its basic needs in consonance with the genius of Judaism". While the quality of this "genius" is not explained, the meaning of this phrase seems to imply a recognition of the need of respecting the historical precedents or at least reckoning with them.

In regard to the concept of Torah, the Conference asserted that the people of Israel achieved "unique insight in the realm of religious truth". The Torah, "both written and oral, enshrines Israel's ever-growing consciousness of God and the moral law." The positive implications of the Platform were emphasized in an address by the then president of the Conference, Felix Levy, who called for a return to Halakah. "Paulinianism is a real danger . . . It cannot be entirely met by a return to tradition unless we re-enthrone the Halakah as central to Jewish life" (*Yearbook*, XLVII, p. 184).

3. STANDARD REFORM PRACTICE

The attempt to rebuild the bridges with the past by linking up modern Reform practices with the medieval literature of Halakah has received marked encouragement from the Columbus Platform. Solomon Freehof's little volume, *Reform Jewish Practice and its Rabbinic Background,* describes the prevailing observances of Reform Jews from a distinctly traditional viewpoint, omitting altogether from consideration such negative enactments as the abolition of the dietary laws, the disregard of the ceremonies of *tallis* and *tefillin,* the virtually total neglect of Sabbath observance, etc. These and similar developments are deplored and described as due to the resistless current of popular sentiment. The following practices are described against the backdrop of an evolving tradition: the institution of one day observance for all festivals including Rosh ha-Shanah; the establishment of formal Sunday services, which fall into a semi-Sabbath category because the weekday service is no longer observed; the substitution of the Confirmation ceremony for the traditional observance of Bar Mitzvah, though permitting also the celebration of the traditional observance in a slightly modified form; the elimination of the custom of calling people up to the reading of the Torah *(aliyot),* though the honors of lifting up the Scroll of the Law and covering it are retained; also the institution of reading a portion of the Law at the Friday evening service in the temples where the attendance at the Sabbath morning service is very poor; the reading of the prophetic portion in English *(Haftorah);* the employment of an organ; a mixed choir; the worshippers are bare-headed and families worship together; elimination of the requirements of baptism and circumcision from the conversion ceremony for Gentiles, but circumcision is described as the universal practice, for those born in the faith; elimination of the *huppah* and the *ketubah* at weddings and the recognition of a civil divorce as being fully sufficient for remarriage; the recognition of the practice of cremation and the substitution of formal dress for the traditional shrouds *(takrikim).*

The marriage of a Jewish person to an unconverted Gentile is frowned upon by many Reform rabbis; nevertheless, the majority will officiate at such marirages, with or without the participation of a representative of the other faith. This practice, however, remains an open issue at meetings of the Conference. Affiliation with the Christian Science movement has been declared to be incompatible with loyalty to the Jewish faith. Nevertheless, this principle is not rigidly enforced, and a Christian Scientist of Jewish birth is accorded the right of burial in the Reform cemetery (Solomon Freehof, *Reform Jewish Practice,* p. 144).

4. SURVEY OF REFORM PRACTICE IN 1950

A report on the prevailing practices in Reform temples was presented at the 1950 convention of the Conference. Based on the information secured from 64% of its following, the survey may be taken as a fairly accurate record of the state of affairs in the Reform movement at the present time.

First, some statistical data:

1. As to the rite of circumcision, ninety percent use surgeons frequently, and of this number, ninety percent arrange to have the rabbi bless and name the child. About fifty percent of the temples use *mohels* generally.

   About seventy percent name the child at a Friday evening service, about fifty percent name the male child at a Sabbath morning service. Only twenty percent observe the ceremony of *pidyon ha-ben,* occasionally. (These statistics do not seem to mesh together, but so variegated is Reform practice at the moment that conflicting observances may well cohere in one congregation for a long time.)

2. While all but six of the temples prepare children for Confirmation, nine-tenths also conduct a Bar Mitzvah upon request, and of these temples sixty percent will observe the rite on Saturday morning and fifty percent on Friday night. Forty percent of the temples consenting to this ritual "permit the boys to wear *tallis*" and thirty percent "permit skull-caps". The age of Confirmation is generally fourteen.

3. Regarding marriage ceremonies, eighty percent of the reporting rabbis will "permit the use of a *huppah*" and will allow "the wedding party to wear hats", if these matters are insisted upon by the people concerned. Forty percent of the rabbis will permit the breaking of a glass at the end of the ceremony, though they object to the practice as a vestige of primitive magic. Only a few rabbis will conduct a wedding ceremony on the Sabbath. Only twenty percent would officiate at a marriage between a Jew and a Gentile, but thirty-three percent would do so, if the non-Jew, though unconverted, promised to raise the children as Jewish. On the other hand, thirty-three percent require even circumcision for conversion, and three percent require attendance in a *mikvah* (ritual bath).

4. As to a Jewish divorce, fifty percent of the rabbis will not marry the members of other congregations, if their own rabbi refused to officiate. All Reform rabbis marry a couple without a *get* (divorce), but the majority will help "to arrange for a *get* through an Orthodox rabbi, if requested to do so."

5. In reference to burial practices forty percent will permit the burial of a non-Jew in a Jewish cemetery and seventy percent will allow the burial of the unconverted non-Jewish spouse. A third of the congregations will exempt Christian Scientists from the general rule banning the burial of non-Jews.

Only a small percentage of congregations permit Christian ministers to officiate by themselves at a funeral, but nearly half will allow their rabbis to share funeral services with Christian ministers.

The seven-day period of mourning (*shivah*) is observed in full by twenty percent of the congregations, the rest observing one or three days only. Seventy percent will keep a memorial light during *shivah*. A similar percentage will observe *yortsait*, some remembering the Hebrew date. *Yizkor* services are held on the day of Atonement, the majority also conducting such services on Passover.

6. Within the synagogue the Friday night service is the rule in most synagogues, with only twelve temples reporting Sunday morning services. In twenty percent of the temples the rabbis wear skull-caps, and in forty percent they wear an adaptation of the *tallis*. The organist is Jewish in only thirty percent of the congregations but the members of the choir are Jewish in seventy percent of the temples.

Most temples kindle the Sabbath-light at the Friday evening service, though the time is long after dark, and recite the *kiddush*.

7. There is strong feeling among Reform rabbis in behalf of the reintroduction of home ceremonies. All urge their congregants to light the candles, recite the *kiddush* and say the blessing of *hamotzi* on the Sabbath. Fifty percent even urge daily morning and evening prayers.

Seventy percent urge the installing of a *mezuzah* on the door-post, and the majority urge the observance of some ceremony of dedication for a new home.

8. Though the dietary laws have been repudiated in the Pittsburgh Platform, remnants of them persist. Thirty percent of the rabbis reporting urge their congregants to refrain from eating pork, and some twenty percent plead for the observance of all dietary laws.

9. Regarding the High Holidays, some twelve percent observe Rosh ha-Shanah for two days, and most temples have reverted to the use of a *shofar,* but with a special metallic mouthpiece. Eighty percent of the rabbis urge their congregants to fast on Yom Kippur and fifty percent arrange for a continuous service on that day, with hardly a recess or none at all. Ninety-five percent of the temples have restored the singing of *Kol-Nidre* (All Vows) prayer for the eve of the Day of Atonement though in most cases only the melody is chanted.

Summarizing the results of their survey, the committee decided not to recommend the preparation of a firm code of practice, at least for the time being. It noted a country-wide trend, however, toward the reacceptance of religious disciplines and ceremonial observances.

"The early builders of our Movement failed to recognize that man cannot live by reason alone, that he needs to satisfy his emotional hunger for the poetry and beauty, for the mysticism and drama which are to be found in *meaningful* symbolism and ceremonialism. They were unaware of the role that ritualism plays in helping a Jew find identification with his group and self-fulfillment in his personal life.

"The old Biblical emphasis of world Messianism and daily social justice no longer seems to satisfy the home feeling, the folk feeling, the sense of Jewish personality . . ."

(Facts and quotes from the summary of the Berman report on *Prevailing Practices in Reform Congregation Today,* prepared by the office of the Union and dated November 1950.)

IV. THE AMERICAN COUNCIL FOR JUDAISM

While the majority of the Reform movement was thus caught up in the ground swell of nationalism and carried close to the Conservative position, a substantial minority resisted this trend for two decades defending the philosophy of classical Reform. This group is represented by the American Council of Judaism. At present the Council is preparing to enter the field of Jewish education for the purpose of resisting the surge of nationalistic sentiments within the Reform movement.

The basic thesis of the Council is that there is no such entity as a "Jewish people", only so many individuals, subscribing tenaciously to the Jewish faith and held together by the tradition of helping other Jews. "I cannot write about a Jewish people because there is none . . . There is no ancient, historic wrong to a 'Jewish people', for which this people 'is now demanding a collective retribution from the world'" (E. Berger, *The Jewish Dilemma,* p. 29).

Stated thus boldly, the thesis of the Council is obviously provocative, but its basic import is undeniably pertinent. In the course of the emancipation, the Jewish community, it is contended, agreed to demolish the "inner walls" of the ghetto in return for the removal of the outer barriers. In the modern world, there is no room for Jewish exclusiveness or for the ambition stemming from it of maintaining a separate "national" entity apart from or in addition to the religious faith and organizational structure. The "emancipation" has not failed, the Council spokesmen contend, urging that the dream of liberalism was hard-hit but not vanquished by the temporary triumph of Hitlerism. Hence, not only Zionism but all forms of organization "for the purpose

JEWISH THEOLOGICAL SEMINARY OF
AMERICA, NEW YORK CITY

In its official *Statement of Principles,* released in August, 1943, the Council disavowed any special relation to Palestine on the part of Jews, alleging that: "Palestine is a part of Israel's religious heritage, as it is a part of the heritage of two other religions of the world . . ." Americans whose religion is Judaism "envisage a world founded on the principle of individual human rights and religious freedom, and spurn with impassioned vehemence any residual, particularistic loyalties of Jewish people."

In the successful campaign of American Jews toward the establishment of the State of Israel, the American Council for Judaism has remained a small dissident group, but its influence within the Reform movement remains strong and deep. Drawing its inspiration from the classical literature of Reform, the Council may be expected

of creating Jewish communities, as such, are a vestige of medievalism and a detriment to integration and emancipation" (*Ibid.,* p. 48).

The Council clings to the Reform position as it was articulated by Isaac M. Wise in the same year when the first World Zionist Congress convened: "We denounce the whole question of a Jewish State as foreign to the spirit of the modern Jew of this land, who looks upon America as his Palestine and whose interests are centered here" (*Ibid.,* p. 240).

Jewish nationalism was rejected not only on the mundane grounds of providing ammunition for anti-Semites and hindering the process of "integration" of Jews into the American nation, but also for the reason that it "diverts our own attention from our historic role to live as a religious community wherever we may dwell" (From a statement by Rabbi Morris Lazaron. *Ibid.,* p. 243).

Courtesy Jewish Theological Seminary of America

SOLOMON SCHECHTER (1847-1915), **NOTED SCHOLAR, LEADER OF CONSERVATIVE MOVEMENT**

to continue as a potent factor on the American scene, whether or not it retains its present organizational structure.

V. THE CONSERVATIVE MOVEMENT

1. EMERGENCE OF THE MOVEMENT

In point of organization and official crystallization of ideology, the Conservative group is the most recent alignment on the American scene. While the Jewish Theological Seminary, the focal point of the movement, was first organized in 1886, largely as a protest against the adoption of the Pittsburgh Platform, the institution virtually ceased to function following the death of its founder and first president Sabato Morais. Later, as the massive tide of immigration from Central and Eastern Europe brought into being a large Jewish population that was not yet integrated into the pattern of American culture, the social gulf between the Reform and Orthodox communities became wide and impassable. In order to assist the East-European Jews to achieve their own synthesis of tradition and modernism, a group of public-spirited citizens headed by Jacob H. Schiff, invited in the year 1902, Solomon Schechter from England, to reorganize the Seminary, and to build around it an association of traditional synagogues. In fifty years, the movement has come to embrace some 450 rabbis and 500 synagogues, as well as an impressive number of central institutions.

It was the hope and conviction of Schechter that the United Synagogue would become the central rallying point of American Jewry. At the founding convention of the United Synagogue he declared:

> Indeed, what we intend to accomplish is not to create a new party, but to consolidate an old one, which has always existed in this country, but was never conscious of its own strength, nor perhaps realized the need of organization. I refer to the large number of Jews who, thoroughly American in habits of life and modes of thinking and, in many cases, imbued with the best culture of the day, have always maintained Conservative principles and remained aloof from the Reform movement which swept over the country. They are sometimes stigmatized as the neo-Orthodox. This is not correct. Their Orthodoxy is not new . . . A better knowledge of Jewish history would have taught them that culture combined with religion was the rule with the Jew . . . The "new" Orthodoxy represents therefore very little that is new. It was the normal state of the Jew in Spain . . . (*American Jewish Yearbook*, 1916, p. 62).

However, the logic of events brought the Conservative movement into being as an identifiable group, consciously formulating its own standards of piety. Today, Conservative synagogues are easily recognized by one or more of the following practices:

With rare exceptions, the women's gallery is abolished and families worship together. Worshippers wear the *tallis* at their morning prayers, and *tefillin* at the daily weekday services. The congregations sponsor an intensive program of Hebrew education and employ either the Orthodox prayer book or the one of the United Synagogue. The main changes in the United Synagogue Prayer Book consist in the elimination of a petition for the renewal of the sacrificial system (the prayers of the Musaf Service are retained, but the tense is changed, so that it becomes a recitation of what our ancestors did in the past) and in so phrasing the translation of *mehayeh ha-mesim* as to suggest God's creative power, not to teach the dogma of the resuscitation of the dead.

Prayers in English are included in the services. Many synagogues employ the organ to aid the cantor and choir, but the cantillation is in the musical tradition of the synagogue. Worshippers sit with covered heads. With the exception of one synagogue, two days of every festival are observed, and all synagogues celebrate the two days of Rosh ha-Shanah. All boys are prepared for the Bar Mitzvah ceremony; the *Bas* Mitzvah ceremony for girls is rapidly becoming a standard procedure, while the ceremony of Confirmation is also included in the total educational program. The dietary laws are observed in all public functions of the synagogue. The pattern of Sabbath observance among Conservative laymen includes permission to ride to the synagogue on the Sabbath, emphasizes the practices making for the hallowing of the day and distinguishes clearly between avoidable and unavoidable types of work. As of the present, Conservative rabbis do not perform marriages for divorcees without a Jewish bill of divorcement *(get)*.

2. TRENDS WITHIN THE MOVEMENT

In the past decade, thoughtful observers were frequently more impressed with the divisions inside the Conservative movement than with the overall character and ideology of the United Synagogue. Occupying the middle position between Orthodoxy and Reform, Conservatism may be understood either as a critique of the former or as a protest against the latter trend. Historically, the Conservative movement has arisen both in America and in Europe by way of secession from the camp of radical Reform. But, the congregations which constitute at present the United Synagogue had come largely into the Conservative camp from the ranks of Orthodoxy.

3. NON-LITERALISTIC CONCEPTION OF REVELATION

Along with Reform, the Conservative movement does not teach that every word in the Torah and every statement of the Oral Law were literally proclaimed at Mount Sinai. "The Torah speaks in the language of men", as the rabbis put it, but, as our understanding deepens, we must learn to disentangle the human, the conditioned and the temporary elements from the Divine, the absolute and eternal truths. To the Conservatives, then, the Torah *contains* the Word of God, especially when it is understood by way of a total self-identification with the historic experience of Israel, but the detailed precepts, phrases and words of the Holy Scriptures are not all, in their bare literalness, the Word of God. On the other hand, the Conservative view differs from the Reform position, as stated in the Pittsburgh Platform, which considered only the moral law as "binding". The Jewish tradition, in its entirety, including the Halakah, or the system of precepts and laws, is a steadily unfolding body of revelation, which is never wholly free from the manifold limitations of the human mind nor at any time entirely barren of the Divine spark of inspiration. The legalism of the rabbis was not a corruption of prophetic idealism but an inspired, collective endeavor to translate it into the realities of life. Tradition, in its entirety, not merely the moral law or the written letter of the Torah, is the source of Divine teaching.

There is, of course, ample precedent for this insistence that the Word of God is not simply the written letter of the Torah, but that it consists in the synthesis of the letter with the living spirit of interpretation, issuing out of the best scientific and philosophic knowledge of every age. Masters of the *Mishnah* like Rabbi Joshua ben Hananiah derived this principle from the verse, "it is not in heaven", and, in the Middle Ages, philosophical Judaism took this principle for granted all through its triumphant advance. Yet, the implications of a non-literal doctrine of revelation are more significant in our day because of the development of the scientific method in the study of history, especially since the rise of Biblical criticism.

For several decades, the Conservative movement shied away from the scientific study of the Holy Scriptures, principally because the science of "higher criticism", as it was developed by German scholars, was partly vitiated by a kind of "higher anti-Semitism", as Solomon Schechter aptly phrased it. Nevertheless, it was Schechter's first ambition, upon his arrival in the United States, to promote the scientific study of Scriptures by Jewish scholars, utilizing the rich treasures of our own commentaries as well as the discoveries and views of modern researchers and archaeologists.

The authority of Holy Scriptures for our day is twofold in origin—the truth of its central philosophy of monotheism and the interpretation that it enshrines, of the enduring bent of mind of the Jewish people. Monotheism is not so much a series of intellectual propositions as it is rather a fundamental attitude of the soul, which is validated by human experience generally. For us as Jews, monotheism is in addition, the soul of our historic heritage and the substance of our collective experience. It is through our complete identification with the life of our people, in the tragic travail of the past as in the living aspirations of the present, that we come to experience the vibrant reality of the monotheistic way of life. Judaism is not only philosophy; it is also a complex of psychic attitudes, a structure of loyalties and sentiments and a pattern of living.

4. THE "POSITIVE-HISTORICAL" VIEWPOINT

It was in the name of the "positive-historical" approach to the problems of Jewish theology that Zecharias Frankel, founder of the Conservative movement in Central Europe, seceded from the Frankfort Conference of Reform rabbis, in the year 1845. The issue in question was whether the use of Hebrew in the service was only "advisable", as the Conference contended, or whether it was absolutely essential. Trivial as this issue might appear to us today, it reflected the fundamental divergence that was to lead to the Conservative challenge to the rationalism of Reform. On any rational basis, wor-

shippers should pray in the language they know best, and the law of the *Mishnah* concurs in this proposition. But, in prayer, the individual must learn to merge his identity with that of the collective body of Israel, and the Hebrew language is the effective medium whereby the individual Jew is made to feel the unity, continuity and distinctiveness of Israel as the people of revelation. Insistence upon Hebrew was, therefore, in effect, tantamount to the negation of the basic Reform principle, that religion was strictly a relationship between the individual and God.

Essentially, the phrase, "positive-historical" implies, in the first place, an attitude of humility toward the great achievements of the past. In every age, it is well for man to remember that his ideals and judgments, self-evident as they may appear to him, might only be partial facets of the infinite mystery of reality, the inadequacy of which will be as obvious to future generations as are the certainties and absolutes of past generations to us. It is good to embrace "the spirit of the age" in wholehearted devotion, but our enthusiasm must be tempered by the realization that the "Weltanschauung" of our generation, as of all preceding epochs, is after all only a limited and partial view of that which can never wholly be known. Indeed, this fundamental humility is one of the essential functions of religion, in that it provides a perpetual counterbalance to the pride of reason and the inevitable acquisition of blind spots that accompany the perception of every new vista.

In the second place, the term "positive-historical" implies an attitude of reverence toward the *processes* whereby changes are effected in the religious life of a people. Frankel, Zunz and Schechter were fundamentally historians. They were not averse to any change in the pattern of worship or the regimen of prescribed rituals, provided that change was brought about organically, as a development of cumulative historical forces, not as an artificial fiat of

LOUIS GINZBERG (1873-1953), NOTED SCHOLAR

how the Law reflected the changing needs and aspirations of the people in the varying strata of its gradual formation. Thus, the Conservatives accept the entire structure of Jewish Law as valid for our time, save insofar as it was modified by the practice of the people, insisting however, that the Law arose as a human response to a divine call, and that it continue to be developed in such a manner as to respond to the deepest spiritual needs of our time. As to the application of this principle, the Conservative movement has been somewhat slow. Only in recent years has the attempt been made to systematize, clarify and apply in practice the implications of the Conservative interpretation of Jewish Law. These attempts will be described in a later chapter.

5. THE NATIONALISTIC MOTIF

From its beginnings the Conservative movement insisted on the indispensability of Hebrew and on the need of retaining the ideal of rebuilding the historic homeland. As Mannheimer, the leader of Aus-

a few men. As a living tradition, Judaism can and must continue to grow in accord with its inner genius, but it must not be tailored to suit an abstract geometric pattern, which may be theoretically more systematic and rational.

Continuing this line of reasoning, the Conservatives generally favor that interpretation of the Law which allows the living authorities of each age ample scope to enact such amendments as are needed for the "strengthening of the faith".

On this "positive-historical" view, Judaism is continuously being modified by the changing habits of the people and by the process of interpretation of Jewish law, which, too, is not meant to be abstract and self-contained, but pragmatic and life-centered. Conservative scholars like Louis Ginzberg, Louis Finkelstein, Chaim Tchernowitz and Saul Liberman demonstrated in a massive series of researches

CHAIM TCHERNOWITZ (1871-1949), NOTED SCHOLAR AND AUTHOR

trian Conservatism put it, "I am one of those who do not rationalize the Messianic belief; I believe in and defend the national interpretation of this dogma and hope for a national restoration . . . " (Philipson, *The Reform Movement*, p. 87).

In the Conservative view, the very existence and life of the Jewish people was a supreme religious ideal, for they could not envisage the Jewish faith as being separated even in the theory from the people that projected it upon the stage of history. Repudiating the anti-nationalism of the Reformers, Schechter wrote that they (especially Geiger) "saw in Israel a religious corporation, a sort of non-celibate monks, whose *raison d'être* was not in themselves, but outside of them . . . " (*Studies of Judaism*, vol. III, p. 69).

"We would have been spared all the terrible persecutions if we could ever have agreed to eliminate from it the national features and become a religious sect."

"It was just those things which distinguished us from our surroundings and separated us from the nations, such as devotion to the Pentateuch, the keeping of the Sabbath, the observance of the covenant of Abraham and the loyalty to the dietary laws, to which we clung for thousands of years with all our life and for which we brought numberless sacrifices. Is this now the time, when the thought of nationalism is universally accepted, to destroy it as far as Israel is concerned?" (*Ibid.*, p. 78).

If the inspiration of Reform was the bold rationalism of a Maimonides, the guiding light of Conservatism was Judah ha-Levi, who taught that Judaism was the living tradition of a divinely chosen and uniquely endowed people. Taken collectively, Jewry was a people of prophets, and anything that redounded to the benefit of the physical well-being of the people strengthened the foundation of the true faith. This organic unity of the particular people with the universal faith was articulated in the accents of contemporary thought by men like Samuel David Luzzatto, who saw the Jewish spirit as being arrayed against the secular spirit of Hellenism or "Atticism", as he put it, in all epochs and in every phase of culture, and Nachman Krochmal, who interpreted the entire sweep of Jewish history in terms of the unbreakable bond between the people of Israel and the Absolute Idea of God.

6. THE MOTIF OF ANTI-SECTARIANISM

The Conservative group was cast in the role of mediator and interpreter between the Orthodox and Reform conceptions of Judaism. While the Reformers concentrated their loving attention upon the *essence* of Judaism, the Conservatives sought to take account of the *totality* of the tradition, with the understanding that varying phases of the tradition might leap into the focus of significance at different times, while other phases temporarily move into the background. Thus, Schechter wrote:

> In other words, is it not time that theology should consist in the best that all the men of Israel, including Geiger, gave us, but should modify and qualify his views, dating from a rationalistic age, by the loyalty to the law of Rabbi Akiba Eger and Rabbi Mordecai Baneth, by the deep insight into Jewish history of a Zunz and a Krochmal, by the mysticism of a Baal Shem and some of his best followers, and by the love for Israel's nationality and its perpetuation of Herzl or Ahad Haam? (Essay on "Abraham Geiger" in *Studies in Judaism*, volume III).

The Conservatives stressed the fullness of the historic tradition, which included reverence for all that is genuinely Jewish and all that the cumulative knowledge of the age acknowledges to be true. The precepts of Halakah were not to be viewed in isolation, but against the historic background from which they emerged and in the light of the total tradition which they expressed. Thus, the validity of Halakah is reaffirmed, but only as one of the factors in the rich and varied tradition of Israel. And within the tradition, the source of authority is shifted from the written word to the living people, in all its confusion, variety and uncertainty. What is lost in definition and clearness is gained in vitality, relevance and comprehensiveness.

> Since then the interpretation of Scripture or the Secondary Meaning is mainly a product of changing historical influences, it follows that the center of authority is actually removed from the Bible and placed in some living body which, by reason of its being in touch with the ideal aspirations and the religious needs of the age, is best able to determine the nature of the Secondary Meaning. This living body, however, is not represented by any section of the nation, or any corporate priesthood, or Rabbinhood, but by the collective conscience of Catholic Israel as it is embodied in the Universal Synagogue (Introduction of *Studies in Judaism,* vol. I).

7. THE "HIGH SYNAGOGUE" MOTIF

An enduring emphasis in Conservatism is the high estimate of the importance of rituals and time-honored symbols in religious life. While Geiger maintained that, with the advance of culture, symbols become unnecessary, the Conservative movement in Europe and America insisted that religion was a total involvement of the soul and that its symbols and rites are directed to the vast reaches of the unconscious and the irrational. Thus, in Conservatism the prevailing tendency is not to abolish ceremonial practices, but as far as possible, to revitalize them and even to create new ritualistic channels for the flow of piety. Worship with covered heads and in *tallis* and *tefillin,* the dietary laws and the distinctive rites of each festival are cherished. The consecration ceremony for children entering the Hebrew School and the Bar Mitzvah observance, as well as the practice of blessing children on Sab-

bath nearest their birthdays are instances of the search for new vehicles of religious expression. The emphasis on the principle of creativity is particularly strong in the Reconstructionist version of the Conservative philosophy, which will be discussed presently.

8. THE FACTOR OF NEO-MYSTICISM

A renewed appreciation of the mystical element in religious experience is a potent factor in the formation of the Conservative ideology. While in the early days of Reform, the doctrines of Kabbalah and the institutions of Hasidism were derided as monstrous aberrations, the twentieth century saw the rise of a neo-Hasidic movement, which glorified the romantic and mystical trends in Jewish tradition. The works of Martin Buber, Yitzhok Leibush Peretz and Samuel Abba Horodezky exhibited the genuine beauty of mystical piety and its deep roots in the indigenous culture of the East-European Jews.

Thus, Solomon Schechter pleaded for the infusion of the mystical piety of the Baal Shem Tov into the life of the modern Jew.

"Rationalism could well appreciate all the virtues of manliness, but it could never value properly those qualities of obedience, submissiveness, meekness and self-denial which constitute a holy life."

The impact of mysticism is partly antinomian, since attention is directed away from legalistic correctness and toward the travail of the spirit. For this reason, the Lithuanian Mitnagdim, in their zealous passion for the Law, feared and fought the mass-movement of Hasidism. But the enduring pressure of mysticism is in the direction of a progressive intensification of loyalty to ancient practices and even in behalf of the proliferation of new customs and practices. It is in conformity with the established rituals and ceremonies that the mystical personality finds refuge from the blinding radiance of ecstatic piety. Also, in dwelling lovingly on the niceties of ritualism, the mystic forges a powerful bond with the religion of the masses and articulates a persistent protest against the pride of reason. While both rationalism and mysticism seek the spirit behind the Law, the former expects the ceremony to speak to the worshipper by the direct language of natural association, whereas the latter expects the worshipper to speak through the ceremony. The Conservative movement follows the guiding principle of Franz Rosenzweig, who, in a famous letter to a group of disciples, declared that it is not the objective character of the ceremony that is decisive, but whether or not we today can still bring ourselves to say through the rite or symbol, "Praised art Thou, O Lord, our God".

"Practice precedes theory for us", he wrote, "whereas, with the Reform movement the contrary was true" (Franz Rosenzweig, *Briefe*, p. 543). In the beginning, is the act of commitment to the Jewish faith and destiny—an act which is more volitional than rational, and for which virtually any rite may serve if it is part of the divinely designed synthesis of Torah and Israel. "Your Hasid too did not begin with *Kavvanah*. That will come one day, of course. But, to desire to begin with it as people tell us we must, is entirely un-Jewish" (*Ibid.*, p. 356).

To Rosenzweig, God is the creative principle of love, subsisting behind the universe. Flashes of His love penetrate the cosmic process from time to time, setting into motion the current of redemption which will one day sweep mankind to the blessed peaks of the Kingdom of God. It is of the nature of love to be selective. Hence, the recipients of the Divine ray of love inevitably feel themselves to be "chosen". The Jewish people was thus "chosen" by God, in a concrete and historical fashion, insofar as its collective consciousness is illuminated by this central religious experience of its prophets and saints. The individual Jew shares in this transforming experience, when he surrenders his individual identity to the collective consciousness of his people, which in turn is expressed in both thought and deed. Since the Law constituted the concrete expression of Jewish piety, obedience to the Law is an automatic articulation of the feeling of being the object of Divine love and of belonging to the "chosen" people.

Thus, while Rosenzweig placed the living people in the focus of attention, rather than the letter of the Law, he insisted that the worshippers must make every effort to address God through the approved channels of Halakah, discarding only the rites which have lost altogether the power to stir the religious consciousness. "I should not dare to declare any law as human, because it has not yet been permitted to me to say through it in proper fashion, 'praised art Thou." At the same time, he declared, "Judaism is not Law. It creates Law, but is not it. It is to be a Jew."

It is through symbols of action that the worshipper comes to feel, not as a disembodied "man in general", but as an integral part of the living body of Israel, that was made eternal by the Word of God. "People understand differently when they understand in doing. Every day in the year, Balaam's speaking ass may be a legend to me; on the Sabbath Balak, when it speaks to me out of the uplifted Torah, it is not."

Abraham J. Heschel is the exponent of neo-mysticism on the contemporary scene. Holiness is to him a dimension of existence, of which all men are aware in gradations varying from the sense of wonder and bafflement of the average person, to the overwhelming, lightning-like tremors of the saint in the blessed moments of ecstacy. Hence, piety is not a subjective attitude, but a "response" to the Divine call. "What gives rise to faith is not a sentiment, a state of mind, an aspiration, but an everlasting fact in the universe, something which is prior to and independent of human knowledge—*the holy dimen-*

sion of all existence" (*Man is not Alone*, p. 237).

God needs man even as man needs God, and in obedience to the Divine Law, man joins in the fulfillment of the Divine Will. "The pagan gods had selfish needs, while the God of Israel is only in need of man's integrity" (*Ibid.*, p. 245).

But, "man's integrity" includes his endless yearnings for the good life, yearnings which penetrate every aspect of life. Hence, the Law guiding our life must be regarded as an organic unity, not as a collection of precepts. "What constitutes the Jewish form of living is not so much the performance of single good deeds, the taking of a step now and then, as the pursuit of a way, being on the way; not so much the acts of fulfilling as the state of being committed to the task, of belonging to an order in which single deeds, aggregates of religious feeling, sporadic sentiments, moral episodes become parts of a complete pattern" (*Ibid.*, p. 270).

In illustration of this central purpose of building the dimension of holiness into life, Heschel describes the institution of the Sabbath as "a palace in time with a Kingdom for all".

Glancing away from any considerations regarding the origin of the Sabbath or the need of modifying some of its laws, the author devotes himself to the task of explicating the mood of the Sabbath as being the focus of time touched by eternity, spent in mystical wonder and contemplation in contrast to the space-oriented mood of work and civilization. As the approach of the mystic stands in polar opposition to the scientific and pragmatic attitude, so does the spirit of the Sabbath when time is lived with intimations of eternity, differ from the secular and mundane spirit. It follows that only from within is reform possible, issuing out of the organic growth of the spirit in the domain of holiness. Thus, mysticism as a living experience, a communicable mood and a popular attitude, functions as a potent brake upon the process of ritualistic reformation and modernization.

VI. THE EMERGENCE OF EXISTENTIALISM

The genius of Franz Rosenzweig is felt as a living influence in the intellectual circles that incline toward the impassioned decisiveness of existentialism. Starting out with the insistence that man cannot relate himself to God by the sheer process of objective thought, Rosenzweig declared that the human individual, in his inward being, continuously rebels against the abstractions of philosophy that deny the worth of individual existence. At the same time, our soul is unhappy when left alone in isolation from the universe. It finds the meaning of its life and destiny in the message of love that is directed to it from Him who dwells behind the veil of existence. Thereafter, the soul seeks to unfold the infinite implications of the assurance of Divine love that has come to it. True philosophy, then, begins with an act which is prior to thought, an act which occurs in the space-time world, between two ultimate beings, the individual and God.

In Rosenzweig's view, the Jewish people as a whole owes its character and destiny to such an act of Divine love—an act of revelation, which the collective consciousness of the Jewish people translated into a host of sacred books and a Law. It is through the Law that the Jewish people have been lifted out of the stream of history and removed from the ceaseless battle of nations for the goods of this world. The Law became for Israel a substitute for land, language, culture and government. Yet, Judaism is more than Law, consisting in that deposit of Divine energy that had been placed by God in the historic memory of the Jewish people.

Rosenzweig's philosophy was couched in the idiom of Hegelian thought—an idiom that is essentially foreign to American ways of thinking. Recently, Will Herberg essayed to expound the philosophy of existentialism in the dramatic and challenging language of an American journalist.

In *Judaism and Modern Man,* Will Herberg asserts first the utter meaninglessness and frustration of life when a man takes himself to be "the measure of all things". The individual cannot find meaning in his own existence, and, in his despair, he looks to a collective entity for the sustenance of the spirit. Thus, the proletariat, the nation, or the racial bloodstream becomes the false surrogate for God.

Since then man cannot live without faith in something, the only true alternative before us is the idolatry of our self, individual or collective, or the worship of God. A "leap of faith" is called for, whereby the self emerges out of the imaginary shell which encloses it and finds itself to be suspended from a Divine thread. But, so paradoxical is the nature of faith, that, when once acquired, it appears to have been inescapable. "We must dare the leap if the gulf is ever to be crossed; but once the decision of faith has been made, it is seen that the leap was possible only because the gulf had already been bridged for us from the other side" (*Ibid.,* p. 39).

In other words, faith is at once a human, subjective act and a Divine, objective fact. Thus, God is not the passive and hidden Ground of Being, but an active Spirit that is somehow akin to our deepest self. "The ascription of personality to God is thus an affirmation of the fact that in the encounter of faith God meets us as person to person" (*Ibid.,* p. 60).

It is the grace of God that makes human rightness possible not only in the act of faith, but in all the spheres of human life. "The weakness and evil in man operate out of the freedom of his own nature; his capacity for good, though grounded in his nature, needs the Grace of God for its realization" (*Ibid.,* p. 76).

Proceeding to the analysis of Jewish life and destiny, the author insists on the "uniqueness" of the phenomenon of the Jew, resulting from the covenant between God and Israel that had been effected by an enduring "existential" relationship.

Steering a middle course between fundamentalism and modernism, Herberg accepts the Holy Bible as Divine Revelation, in so far as it tells of the perennial encounter between God and man. Moreover, Scripture tells of the "self-disclosure of God in his dealings with the world". Revelation is an event in history, divine in substance but human in expression.

> The views of Abraham on the nature of things and even on the "nature" of the divine were presumably far more "primitive" than those of Isaiah so many centuries later, but their faith was the same, for they stood in the same crisis of confrontation with God, shared the same ultimate covenantal commitment, and recognized the same Lord and His absolute claim (*Ibid.,* p. 248).

Herberg maintains that "salvation is of the Jews", in conscious defiance of the entire sweep of modernity and the broad tolerance of liberalism. The very being of Israel is a mysterious anomaly, which cannot be understood in the mundane terms of sociology. We are a "unique" people, unclassifiable with other groups and incomprehensible by ordinary human standards. "It is a supernatural community, called into being by God to serve his eternal purposes in history. It is a community created by God's special act of covenant, first with Abraham, whom he 'called' out of the heathen world, and then supremely, with Israel corporately at Sinai" (*Ibid.,* p. 241).

This "super-historical" community is charged with the mission of bringing "salvation" to the world. The Jew lives his life "authentically" when he responds affirmatively to the demands and duties that are implied in "Jewish covenant-existence". It is through the laws of the Torah that the Jew takes his "authentic" place in the cosmic scheme of things. But,

Torah for the existentialist does not mean simply the rigid precepts of the *Shulhan Aruk*. Since it is upon the personal experience of faith that his piety is founded, the author insists on the need of taking account of the human and historical elements in the ritual of Judaism. As a blend of the historical and the "super-historical", the Torah must not be frozen into a rigid set of unvarying laws. "It is the historical belief and practice of the community of Israel—Kelal Yisroel—that provides us with the contents of Halakah" (*Ibid.*, p. 299).

In sum, Jewish existentialism begins with that double-faced experience, which is an act of Grace on the part of God and a "leap of faith" on the part of man at one and the same time. In the light of this total commitment of the soul, the Biblical-Rabbinic faith emerges as a satisfying exposition of the meaning of human life and Divine Imperative. The people of Israel emerged through a similar, collective "existential" experience, and its entire being is forever caught in the tension between the historical and the "super-historical". The "authentic" response of the individual to the Divine call is to live the life of holiness, and for the Jew, this authentic response implies the whole-hearted acceptance of the Law, insofar as it is a living reality to the conscience of "Catholic Israel".

VII. THE RECONSTRUCTIONIST MOVEMENT

The left wing of the Conservative movement consists of the disciples and followers of Mordecai M. Kaplan. For seventeen years now, this intra-Conservative group has been loosely organized in a Reconstructionist Fellowship, which has its headquarters in the Society for the Advancement of Judaism. *The Reconstructionist* (a bi-weekly publication) is the official organ of this group. In addition, a number of pamphlets and books have been published by the Reconstructionist Society in furtherance of its views.

In some of its projects, the Reconstructionist Fellowship transcends the lines of denominational differences, especially in its advocacy of varied programs for the Jewish community as a whole. Also, some Reform rabbis have joined the Fellowship, which remains however predominantly Conservative in orientation and practice.

In general, the Reconstructionist trend might be described as pragmatic in philosophy, liberal in theology and nationalistic in emphasis. The name chosen by the group reflects the central plank of its platform—to reconstruct the chaotic conglomeration that is contemporaneous American Jewry after the pattern of the "organic community". In place of the crazy-quilt jumble of organizations, the Reconstructionists contend, there should be formed in each city an all-inclusive communal organization that would provide for every legitimate need and ideal of its members. The rise of the Welfare Funds and Community Councils is a welcome development in this direction, but, even if this process is consummated in every city, the result will still fall short of the "goal of an organic community". For, while these communal agencies undertake to provide for the philanthropic and recreational needs of the people, they rarely assume full responsibility for the task of Jewish education and they do not ever undertake to minister to the religious needs of the community. In the "organic community", the synagogue community center and school would occupy the "nuclear" position, since religion constitutes the main expression of Jewish group life.

In effect, then, the Reconstructionists advocate that American Jewry give up the congregational form of organization, which is indigenous on the American scene, and revert instead to the *kehillah* pattern of Central and Eastern Europe. As to the difficulty of reconciling conflicting interpretations of Judaism, Mordecai M. Kaplan maintains that the Jewish community might well follow the example of any modern nation, which fosters the

MORDECAI KAPLAN—FOUNDER OF
RECONSTRUCTIONISM

national community and ultimately into a world-community that would take its place beside the great national states of the world. "World Jewry should unite as a people, and apply to the United Nations for recognition of its claim to peoplehood" (*The Future of the American Jew,* p. 80).

For Mordecai M. Kaplan, the "organic community" is an expression in organizational terms of the essential character of the Jewish people. In every phase of its organized life, American Jewry should express its character as an ethnic cultural group, its enduring "peoplehood", so as to articulate and keep alive the "we" feeling of the individual Jew. By his membership in the "organic community", the individual expresses his sense of belonging to the Jewish people, and it is this sense of sharing in the life and destiny of a people that is the matrix of all its cultural creations and values.

In the Reconstructionist ideology, the Conservative emphasis on the living people in the triad of people, God and Torah is carried to its outermost limit. Judaism is defined as the evolving religious civilization of the Jewish people. In his magnum opus, *Judaism as a Civilization,* Kaplan omitted the adjective "religious", which the Reconstructionist Fellowship now uses invariably. Even so, the factor of faith is conceived as only one of the elements of Jewish civilization, though historically the dominant one. It is conceivable that religion in the future might be expressed through forms of cooperative living that have nothing in common with the rites and even the ideas of traditional Judaism. Also, it is quite possible that the creative genius of the people will be unfolded in cultural directions other than those of faith and ethics—such as art, for example. The high esteem of creative expression among the Reconstructionists, leads them to accord to the domain of art a supreme rank among the shining constellations of the Jewish spirit.

principle of "unity in diversity". The "organic community" should not find it an insuperable task to work out an equitable arrangement whereby all interpretations of Judaism could be treated with equal consideration and its constituent members would attend the synagogues of their own choice.

In addition to its religious and educational functions, the community organization would provide, through designated committees, for Zionist work, public relations, philanthropic and recreational activities, so that there would be no need for any independent or supplementary organization. Also, those activities which are now neglected, such as, new creations in art and music, would be assiduously cultivated by the "organic community", which would envision Jewish life as a whole and lovingly care for its every phase and expression. The separate "organic communities" would be organized into a

The Reconstructionists do not minimize the role of religion in the "religious civilization" that is Judaism, especially for the Diaspora Jewry, but they maintain that religion itself derives its vital power from the "we"-feeling of the people. The Jewish religion lost its hold upon the masses of our people when the sense of ethnic loyalty was weakened by outside attractions and inner disorganization. The substitution in America of fragmentary congregational and denominational loyalties for the massive loyalty to the Jewish community as a whole served to weaken the purely religious sentiments of our people.

On this view, religion springs out of the life of the people, its social function being to hallow and to fortify the so-called "sancta"—the institutions, things, events and memories that the people require for their collective existence. Hence, a religion is woefully weakened when it is abstracted into a system of salvation and separated from the ethnic aspirations and concerns of the people among whom it has arisen.

It follows that the Jewish religion can only be regenerated if it is put back into the total complex of Jewish life, the individual congregation yielding to the all-inclusive community as the basic unit of identification, and the rites of religion surrendering their claim to the exclusive loyalty of the Jew in favor of all other forms of cultural expression. "Paradoxical as it may sound, the spiritual regeneration of the Jewish people demands that religion cease to be its sole preoccupation" (*Ibid.*, p. 345).

The will to live as a Jew is the fundamental source and motivation of Jewish existence, but, to be deserving of our highest loyalty, the life we seek must be conceived in the loftiest spiritual terms. Hence, the emphasis on the creation of new values and the construction of social instruments to serve the high ends of prophetic idealism. "All this effort at reconstruction and reinterpretation must come entirely from the urge of an inward creative life" (*The Meaning of Reconstructionism*, p. 25).

With this conception of religion, it follows that rituals and ceremonies cannot be accepted as literally revealed precepts, nor as expressions of fundamental truths, but as socially evolved aids to the good life, or, more technically, as "religious folkways". We cannot speak of "law" in Jewish religion, the Reconstructionists declare, since we have no sanctions for the enforcement of legal directives. Also, the Jewish community as a whole could legislate only in regard to those elements that are common to all the interpretations and trends that are current in Jewish life. Thus, it can formulate the rules that are to govern the relationship of committees and societies to the central community organization, and it can also deal with the domain of "public law", such as marriage and divorce. In the sphere of rituals, each denominational trend may formulate its own guiding principles and standards, imputing no guilt to those who prefer other "folkways" for self-expression. "The vocabulary of 'law', 'sin', 'pardon' is ideologically and pragmatically unjustified as applied to ritual."

Rites and ceremonies are forms of collective art, which spring ideally from the life of the people.

VIII. ISSUES AND PRACTICE IN THE CONSERVATIVE MOVEMENT

The ideology of Reconstructionism functions as one of the trends within the Conservative movement—fairly influential in some directions, but falling short of predominance. The movement, for the most part, insists on the unique historical position of Israel as the people of revelation, on the recognition of the totality of the tradition as the source of authority rather than the folkways of practices of the people and on the belief in the continued validity of Jewish Law or Halakah, when it is interpreted as part of a dynamic life-oriented tradition.

For many years, the Law Committee of the Rabbinical Assembly functioned in strict compliance with the letter and spirit of the *Shulhan Aruk*. Even the practice of mixed seating in the synagogue was not approved but only condoned in the spirit of the historian Zunz, who remarked that the spirit of peace and harmony in a community is more important than the harmony or disharmony of organ music. Thus, in practice, Conservative congregations deviated from Orthodoxy while, in theory, the Law was declared to be unchanged. At the Convention held in Chicago in 1948, a resolution purporting to bind the movement to strict compliance with the *Shulhan Aruk* was proposed and defeated. The Law Committee was then reorganized so as to reflect all trends within the movement. At its first meeting, it assumed the designation *Committee on Jewish Law and Standards,* in order to indicate that its scope is the application of the totality of the tradition to Jewish life and not merely the interpretation of the letter of the Law. Nor was the Committee to be confined to the task of writing responses to specific inquiries. Wherever new standards were to be set up, the Committee was to propose and to formulate resolutions for the movement. To the majority of its members, the process of legislating standards of ritual observance is a direct implication of the character of Jewish piety. In Judaism, man's response to the Divine challenge takes the form of a self-imposed "law" of action. While all men might concede the value of prayer and study, the religious Jew imposes upon himself the regular disciplines of prayer three times daily and the *mitzvah* of Torah-study at fixed times. This response of the individual is guided and molded by the collective "laws" of the people, so that the resolve of each Jew is reinforced and conditioned by the acceptance and the observance of the entire group. (See this writer's essay—J.Q.R., 1948, pp. 181-204, also articles on "Law" in *Conservative Judaism.*)

The relevance of this approach was demonstrated in the analysis of the problem of Sabbath observance. The Committee did not substitute for the Sabbath-Halakah a general principle, such as the obligation to hallow the day, nor did it proceed to interpret the Law in blithe disregard of existing conditions. Firstly, it set the problem in a positive frame by launching a campaign for the revitalization of the Sabbath, calling upon all congregants to pledge the acceptance of certain minimal standards of Sabbath-observance—to refrain from doing work on the Sabbath which is avoidable and which is not in keeping with the spirit of the day, and to hallow the Sabbath-day by positive practices. These general rules were to be spelled out in detail in the course of the campaign, which is even now in progress.

Secondly, the Committee affirmed the applicability of the principle of *takkanah*-legislation to our time and place. Jewish Law can be made and modified today in the same manner as it was made and modified in the past. Accordingly, the Committee called upon the Rabbinical Assembly to permit the practice of riding to the synagogue on the Sabbath, as a new *takkanah* designed to "strengthen the faith" —a *takkanah* made necessary by the peculiar circumstances of American life. When it is difficult or impossible to walk, the Committee declared it to be a *mitzvah* to make use of motor transportation for the sake of attending public worship.

At times, the Committee is stricter in the maintenance of religious standards than the bare letter of the Law. Thus, it makes use of its influence to prevent the holding of any business-meetings on the Sabbath, though traditionally Jewish problems were discussed on holy days in Medieval times, care being taken to avoid infringements of the ritualistic laws. Also, the Committee is even now combatting the suggestion to permit Gentile players on the Sabbath to play dance music for entertainment of dinner-guests at a Bar Mitzvah celebration in the vestry-hall of the synagogue. Ample precedent for this practice could be cited, from a strictly legalistic viewpoint, especially since the movement sanctions the employment of the organ at the services. Also, the Hasidim would dance on the Sabbath. But in the opinion of the Committee the consequences of this practice in the circumstances of American life would be deleterious to the dignity of the synagogue and the holiness of the Sabbath. Accordingly, the Committee called upon all Conservative synagogues to discountenance any such practice.

In the domain of Jewish Law, the main issue confronting the movement at this writing is the so-called *agunah* question, which really includes a number of problems relating to marriage and divorce. Suppose the husband refuses to give a *get* or *halitzah,* what recourse is left to the woman?—What if a *cohen* desires to marry a divorcee or a converted woman? What to do in the event of desertion when the woman obtains a divorce from the civil court and the whereabouts of the husband is unknown?—What to do with the many cases that are classified by the government first as "missing in action" and later declared to be dead without testimony by witness that is required by Jewish Law?

Already, in 1937, the late Rabbi J. L. Epstein proposed an elaborate plan involving the principle of conditioned marriage and making it possible for the woman to write her own *get,* under the direction of a Rabbinic court, in certain cases. Owing to the frantic protests of the Orthodox rabbis, this plan was never put into effect. The present plan of the Committee is all-embracing in scope and radical in approach. The principle of *takkanah*-legislation would be so employed as to solve the above-mentioned problem, without removing the rabbi, and the Jew-

ish faith which he symbolizes, from the realm of divorce and remarriage. The details of this plan are even now under discussion, but there is virtual agreement within the movement, that Jewish Law must be preserved through a dynamic process of interpretation and continuous legislation.

Having surveyed the varied theological currents in American Judaism, we may be permitted a speculative prognosis of the future. Are the three major trends drawing closer together, so that we may expect the emergence of a unitary American pattern, or are they stiffening their respective shells against one another?—Both tendencies are in evidence for the present and are likely to be operative in the foreseeable future. Organizationally, each trend is becoming steadily more effective, self-sufficient and self-conscious. Thus, in the past three years, the three Seminaries in New York launched three schools to train men for the cantorate, each movement insisting on training its own functionaries even in the seeming non-ideological field of Jewish music. The Jewish Theological Seminary even maintains a Jewish Museum of its own, insisting that its philosophy of Jewish life is expressed in this project, as well as in its national radio and television program and in its Institute for Religious and Social Studies, which is planned to supplement the education of Christian theological students.

On the other hand, the laity of the three groups is largely indifferent to the interdenominational boundary lines. The temptation to create hybrid syntheses is particularly strong in the new congregations in Long Island, New York, and Los Angeles, Cal. Certain it is that not one of the three trends is rigidly fixed and completely isolated. The history of American Judaism is just beginning.

BIBLIOGRAPHY

AGUS, JACOB B., *Banner of Jerusalem*. New York, 1946.

BREUER, ISAAK, *Der neue Kusari*. Frankfurt a. M., 1934.

BERGER, ELMER, *The Jewish Dilemma*. New York, 1945.

FREEHOF, SOLOMON, *Reform Jewish Practice and Its Rabbinic Background*, 2 vols. Cincinnati, 1944.

GEIGER, ABRAHAM, *Judaism and Its History*, 2 vols. New York, 1911.

GORDIS, ROBERT, *Conservative Judaism*. New York, 1945.

HERBERG, WILL, *Judaism and Modern Man*. Philadelphia, 1951.

HESCHEL, ABRAHAM JOSHUA, *Man Is Not Alone*. Philadelphia, 1951.

HIRSCH, EMIL G., *My Religion*. New York, 1925.

KAPLAN, MORDECAI M., *Judaism as a Civilization*. New York, 1934.

KAPLAN, MORDECAI M., *The Future of the American Jew*. New York, 1948.

KOHLER, KAUFMANN, *Jewish Theology*. New York, 1918.

KOHN, EUGENE, *Religion and Humanity*. New York, 1953.

LEWISOHN, LUDWIG, *The American Jew*. New York, 1950.

MORGENSTERN, JULIAN, *As a Mighty Stream*. Philadelphia, 1949.

PHILIPSON, DAVID, *The Reform Movement in Judaism*. New York, 1931.

SCHECHTER, SOLOMON, *Studies in Judaism*. First series, Philadelphia, 1896; second series, Philadelphia, 1908; third series, Philadelphia, 1924.

SCHECHTER, SOLOMON, *Some Aspects of Rabbinic Theology*. New York, 1909.

STEINBERG, MILTON, *Basic Judaism*. New York, 1947.

אגוז, יעקב, „איש המסתורין" תלפיות, 1948.

אגושעוויטש, ראובן, אמונה און אפיקורסות. ניו-יארק, 1949.

בלאך, יוסף יהודה ליב, שעורי דעת. ניו-יורק, תש"מ.

בלזר, יצחק, אור ישראל. ווילנא, תר"ס.

גלאצער, נחום, פראנץ ראזענצווייג, זיין לעבן און זיינע אירעעס. ניו-יארק, 1945.

דיינוים, משה, יהדות אמריקה בהתפתחותה. ניו-יורק, תשי"א.

חיים בר' יצחק מוואלאזין, נפש החיים, תקפ"ד.

כ"ץ, דוב, תנועת המוסר. תל אביב, תש"ו—תש"י.

קוק, אברהם יצחק הכהן, אורות הקדש. חלק ראשון, ירושלים תרצ"ח, חלק שני, ירושלים, תש"י.

POLITICAL AND SOCIAL MOVEMENTS AND ORGANIZATIONS

Philip Friedman

I. EARLY AMERICAN JEWRY

Conditions for the development of Jewish institutions and movements in America were far more favorable than for other ethnic minorities. To begin with, Jewish life was more concentrated geographically, in the larger cities, and economically, in a few major lines. The urban concentration of the Jewish population was accompanied by the concentration of Jewish movements in New York and a few other cities. Social and cultural institutions could grow rapidly.

It is estimated that there are approximately 90 ethnic groups in the United States, of which more than half originated in Europe. In 1954 there were 857 foreign-language publications in the country, including 46 in Yiddish and 17 in Hebrew. But of the 200 to 250 periodicals published by various minority groups in English, as many as 164 were Jewish (1952). Obviously, the number of publications cannot be taken as the sole gauge of the intensity of any social movement. Particularly characteristic of Jewish community activities in America are the many philanthropic and social institutions, with their large budgets and ramified fields of work, the various ideological groupings, and the cultural organizations.

During the earliest, Sephardic period of American Jewish history, the only Jewish social institution of any kind was the synagogue congregation. Each congregation led its own life, with no formal organizational ties to other congregations. One of the rare examples of united action was the letter of felicitation jointly addressed to George Washington in 1790 by the Jewish congregations of New York, Philadelphia, Newport and Richmond.

Much later than the congregation, and at a slower rate, there began to develop Jewish institutions unrelated to the synagogue. As far as can be established, the first Jewish secular institution in America was the Hebrew Club, founded in Newport, Rhode Island, in 1761, in imitation of the social clubs of non-Jewish society. Not until the end of the eighteenth and the beginning of the nineteenth centuries did there arise a few modest social groups like the Hebrew Benevolent Society in Charleston (1784) and New York (1822) and the first known Jewish women's organization, the Female Hebrew Benevolent Society, in Philadelphia (1819).

In the meantime the so-called German Jewish immigration was taking place. Actually these immigrants were not only German, but came from Austria, Bohemia, Galicia and Posen as well. The new immigrants soon outnumbered the Sephardic Jews and began to establish their own institutions, beginning with synagogues: Bnai Jeshurun in New York in 1825 and Anshe Chesed in 1828. The German Hebrew Benevolent Society in New York was founded in 1844.

German Jews were scattered throughout the United States. While, on the one hand, this dispersion hastened the process of adaptation to American life, on the other hand, it posed the danger of total assimilation and disappearance. Jewish communities began to think seriously of the need for a central organization, feeling that local institutions alone were inadequate. The first Jewish social movement of a national scope, B'nai B'rith, was founded in 1843.

II. RISE OF THE FRATERNAL ORDERS

Three basic reasons impelled the American Jewish community to establish a central organization. Foremost of these was the plight of Jews abroad, requiring material, moral and even political assistance from American Jewry. Not seldom have large Jewish organizations arisen in the United States for the sole purpose of helping Jews abroad.

The second factor was more local. The growth of the nativist, or "Know Nothing" movement in the years 1835 to 1860 greatly disturbed the Jews of America. These "hundred percent Americans" wanted to limit immigration in order to preserve the Anglo-Saxon Protestant majority. In 1855 there were several outbreaks against "aliens," the bloodiest being the Louisville riots against the Irish Catholics. Although the movement lost impetus soon afterwards, agitation against Catholic and Jewish immigration still continued. Even this purely "internal" impetus to the centralization of Jewish organizational life in the United States was related to a concern for European Jewry, through a desire to protect the existing policy of free immigration.

The third factor was entirely local. With the rapid growth of the Jewish community, the problem of helping the needy became more acute. Local Jewish organizations soon realized that they could not cope alone with the problem and that a central body was necessary. The cultural and spiritual needs of the community also required it. The intellectual leadership, for the most part rabbis and teachers, felt that only a central Jewish organization could preserve Judaism in the New World.

Thus, both external and internal factors played an important part in the creation of Jewish central bodies. With the ritual murder accusation in Damascus (1840), American Jews, for the first time in their history, organized public protest meetings "for the purpose of uniting in expression of sympathy for their brethren in Damascus, and of taking such steps as may be necessary to procure for them equal and impartial justice"—to quote from the resolution adopted at the protest meeting in New York in that year.

The demand for centralized organization came from two quarters. On the one hand were the religious leaders who had not ceased to importune American Jewry to unite in a central religious body (Isaac

Leeser's articles in 1841, 1845 and 1849; Rabbi Isaac Mayer Wise's in 1848); on the other hand were the well-to-do German Jews in New York who had founded the first secular Jewish organization in the country and had thus initiated the Jewish fraternal orders, which by 1913 had a membership of 500,000 to 600,000.

The early history of the fraternal orders was quite modest. On October 13, 1843, twelve German Jews met in a New York restaurant to discuss the regrettable situation of Jewish social life in America, the lack of unity, the internal conflicts and the discrimination against Jewish members in the Masonic Lodges and the Odd Fellows. At this meeting B'nai B'rith ("Sons of the Covenant") was born. The preamble to the constitution, which is still in force, reads as follows:

> B'nai B'rith has taken upon itself the mission of uniting Israelites in the work of promoting their highest interests and those of humanity; of developing and elevating the mental and moral character of the people of our faith; of inculcating the purest principles of philanthropy, honor and patriotism; of supporting science and art; alleviating the wants of the poor and needy; visiting and attending the sick; coming to the rescue of victims of persecution; providing for, protecting and assisting the widow and orphan on the broadest principles of humanity.

Eventually B'nai B'rith extended its organization beyond the borders of the United States. The first overseas lodges were founded in Germany (1882). By 1933 there were lodges and branches in more than thirty countries in Europe, Asia, Africa and Latin America.

The German cast of the organization was apparent in the society's original name, *Bundes-Brüder*, and in the use of German at meetings. The name was soon changed to the Independent Order B'nai B'rith and German gradually ceased to be used. In the first quarter-century of its existence

the order grew slowly. In 1857 it had fewer than 3,000 members and in 1869 20,000; but thereafter it grew steadily until by 1930 it had 85,000 members all over the world. (In 1940 the membership was 130,000 and fourteen years later about 375,000, including the women's and youth divisions.) B'nai B'rith was the only Jewish order that did not engage in insurance and mutual benefits for its members (which it dropped at the end of the nineteenth century). Its appeal was based not on benefits but on the opportunity to be of service. It is now no longer an exclusively German Jewish brotherhood but embraces all Jews. In 1920, after a prolonged struggle which had lasted since the 1890's, the secret ritual of the society was discarded.

The emphasis in the B'nai B'rith's program changed from philanthropy to educational and political activity. As early as 1851 it protested the discriminations against Jews in Switzerland. Toward the end of the 1860's Simon Wolf, the Washington representative of B'nai B'rith, began to be regarded as the semi-official "ambassador" of American Jewry, intervening with the authorities in various matters affecting his co-religionists. As a result of his influence, it is said, the President of the United States in 1870 appointed the Grand Sar of B'nai B'rith, Benjamin F. Peixotto, as American Consul to Bucharest—a gesture of no small significance for Rumanian Jews.

Political action was undertaken in the twentieth century in connection with the Kishinev pogrom of 1903, Palestine affairs, the persecutions and sufferings during both World Wars and the fight for the State of Israel in the Forties. Simultaneously, B'nai B'rith expanded its domestic political activity. Anti-Semitism in the country had long been the concern of American Jewish leaders. In 1913 the B'nai B'rith set up a body dedicated exclusively to combatting anti-Semitism, the Anti-Defamation League (ADL), which in the course of time became one of American Jewry's most effective instruments against anti-Semitism and discrimination.

The Hillel Foundations, established in 1923, are one of B'nai B'rith's important contributions in the field of education. Today, there are about 70 Hillel Foundations and 130 consultants at various American colleges and universities. Hillel has accomplished much in the dissemination of Jewish knowledge among American students.

The example established by B'nai B'rith was soon followed. In 1846, three years after B'nai B'rith was born, there arose the women's organization, United Order True Sisters, which, though professedly non-sectarian, had a 95% Jewish membership. In the 1940's it had 15,000 members.

In 1849 the Independent Order Free Sons of Israel was founded in New York. Its members were, for the greater part, of the German Jewish middle class and never exceeded 10,000 (at the beginning of the 1940's) in number. A far larger group was the Order Brith Abraham, founded in 1859. In 1887 dissension within the order resulted in the establishment of a separate body—the Independent Order Brith Abraham. The mother organization had over 70,000 members in 1913, but was dissolved in 1927. The Independent Order grew rapidly. Its membership, 5,000 in 1890, increased to 22,000 by 1895, to 182,000 in 1913 and to 206,000 in 1917. The members were mostly German, Hungarian, Polish, Russian and Rumanian Jews. At one time the Independent Order was numerically the largest fraternal order in the United States. It never managed to equal B'nai B'rith's importance in Jewish life and by the mid-40's its membership had dropped to 58,000.

Of lesser importance were the Independent Order Sons of Benjamin, founded in 1877 (15,000 members in 1901, dissolved in 1919) and the Ahabat Israel (founded in 1893, 21,000 members in 1913, disbanded a year later).

Altogether, in the course of the period between 1843 and 1953, more than thirty Jewish fraternal societies were organized. Only eleven of them survived into the 1940's and of these, only seven had a membership in excess of 10,000.

At the beginning of the twentieth century there arose a new type of fraternal order, with a special ideological orientation, the Zionist, the Labor-Zionist and the Labor orders.

Jewish membership in non-sectarian fraternal orders is quite common in the United States. It is not known just how many Jews there are in the Masonic Lodges (first established in America in 1733), with a membership of some 3,000,000. It is known, however, that from the very beginning of Masonry in this country Jews have belonged to it, even achieving high rank in the Masonic hierarchy.

The second largest American fraternal order, the Odd Fellows, which has 1,500,000 members, even has separate Jewish lodges. In 1949 the Odd Fellows had 35,000 members in New York and 225 lodges, of which many were Jewish. There is a similar situation in the Knights of Pythias, which has 290,000 members and an even larger percentage of Jews. Even the Elks have many Jewish members. Many of the Jewish lodges are active in the United Jewish Appeal, devote space in their publications to Jewish matters, such as holidays, Jewish literature, problems of Israel, etc.

III. FIRST NATIONAL REPRESENTATION OF AMERICAN JEWRY

Fraternal organizations, of course, did not represent all of the Jewish community. Their activities were mostly confined to mutual aid for their members and philanthropy. Any cultural or political work done was of a sporadic nature. At any rate, they had neither the power nor the desire to act as spokesmen for American Jewry.

The growing need for such a body gave rise to a conference in Baltimore in 1859 at which delegates from Charleston, Chicago, Cincinnati, St. Louis and Washington adopted a resolution of protest against discriminatory acts toward American Jews traveling in Switzerland. The resolution was officially submitted to President Buchanan by a delegation headed by Rabbi Isaac Mayer Wise. But the Baltimore conference, like other previous attempts (in Cleveland in 1840 and 1855), did not result in the establishment of any central Jewish organization.

Once again, persecutions abroad stimulated American Jewry to action. This was the ill-famed Mortara Case (Italy, 1858), which followed the conversion of a Jewish boy against his parents' will. This, as much as the tragic situation of Jews in the Near East, helped to bring about the creation of the Alliance Israélite Universelle in France and also impelled American Jews to do the same.

The Board of Deputies of British Jews served American Jewry as a model, both as to name and form. In November 1859 representatives of fourteen Jewish communities convened in New York and adopted a resolution to establish the Board of Delegates of American Israelites, with the following purposes:

1. the collection and arrangement of statistical information respecting the Israelites of America;

2. the promotion of Jewish education;

3. the adoption of measures for the redress of grievances under which Israelites at home and abroad might suffer for religion's sake;

4. the maintenance of friendly relations with similar Hebrew organizations throughout the world;

5. the establishment of a thorough union among all the Israelites of the United States.

The Board engaged in an energetic and, on the whole, successful campaign against anti-Jewish discrimination in the United States, particularly in Maryland and South Carolina. It also protested against anti-Semitic persecutions abroad (Morocco, Tripoli, Spain, Switzerland, Russia, Rumania, Serbia, Turkey, etc.) and extended material assistance to needy Jewish communities overseas. The Board sent its delegates to international Jewish conferences on emigration and maintained close contacts with such bodies as the Alliance, the Board of Deputies of British Jews and the Israelitische Allianz in Vienna. It failed, however, in its primary objective —to unite American Jewry and establish itself as a central body. Some historians have ascribed the Board's unpopularity to its failure to act vigorously on behalf of Jewish immigration to the United States.

The growing tendency among American Jewry to centralize about a religious organization brought about the creation of the Union of American Hebrew Congregations, which attracted a great number of organizations, including the Board itself. In 1878 the Board disappeared as such and was absorbed by the Union, which formed a committee—composed of its own representatives and those of the extinct Board—under the name of Board of Delegates on Civil and Religious Rights which, together with the B'nai B'rith, spoke for American Jewry in Washington. This committee was dissolved in 1925.

IV. ATTEMPTS TO ESTABLISH CENTRAL RELIGIOUS ORGANIZATIONS

In addition to the heterogeneity of American Jews in the nineteenth century (Sephardic, German, East European and, later, West European and Levantine groups) religious differences between the Orthodox, Conservative and Reform Jews also contributed to the cleavage in Jewish community life. The growth of these religious movements in the United States is dealt with elsewhere in this volume (see Current Movements in Religious Life of American Jewry). Here we are concerned primarily with their social aspects.

In an 1848 issue of the English-language Jewish periodical, *Occident,* Rabbi Isaac Mayer Wise called for an "association of Israelitish congregations in North America . . . to defend and maintain our sacred faith . . . to unite ourselves betimes to devise a practicable system for the ministry and religious education at large . . . to institute a reform in their synagogues." Rabbi Wise, one of the foremost leaders of the Reform movement in the United States, felt that American Jewry could achieve unity by embracing Reform Judaism. No immediate results came of his appeal and it was a full quarter of a century before his plan materialized.

In those intervening twenty-five years, Jewish life in America underwent a great change. Financial prosperity had followed in the wake of the Civil War, attracting to these shores streams of immigrants. The Jewish population rose from 50,000 in 1850 to 200,000 by 1880. Jewish community life received a new stimulus. New organizations sprang up, the most important being the Union of American Hebrew Congregations in 1873. Rabbi Wise's plan was realized, though only partially. The Union, despite its name, represented not all of the Jewish congregations in the country, but only the Reform congregations. It soon proved itself to be the most efficiently organized Jewish religious body in the United States. In 1873, 28 congregations were affiliated, and in 1943, 307. The Union succeeded in organizing the Reform rabbis in the Central Conference of American Rabbis (CCAR), with 30 members at the time of its founding in 1889 and 600 members in 1952. Other affiliates established by the Union are the National Federation of Temple Brotherhoods, the National Federation of Temple Sisterhoods and the National Federation of Temple Youth.

It was somewhat later that the Conservative elements began to organize around the Jewish Theological Seminary of America in New York (1886). The Con-servative movement began to flourish with the arrival in the United States of Solomon Schechter (1902). The United Synagogue of America, founded in 1913, included about 430 Conservative congregations in 1952. The Rabbinical Assembly of America, established in 1901, had 415 members by 1952.

The last to organize, and with the poorest results, were the Orthodox Jews. Despite the fact that a religious census showed 2,500 Orthodox congregations in the country in 1943, the Union of Orthodox Jewish Congregations, founded in 1898, embraces only 400 to 450 congregations, about 10 to 15% of all the Orthodox groups.

Although the religious Jewish organizations as a rule kept aloof from political activities, many of them took definite stands with regard to various political trends and movements.

V. NEW ATTEMPTS AT CEN-TRALIZATION OF NATIONAL ORGANIZATIONS

The large-scale Jewish immigration from Eastern Europe that began in the 80's completely changed the complexion of American Jewish life. From a population of 200,000, American Jewry increased to more than 2,000,000 in 1914 and to some 5,000,000 today. Jewish workers founded trade unions and innumerable labor groups. The middle class and Orthodox elements also had their separate organizations. In many communal institutions leadership remained in German Jewish hands. The East European newcomers established leadership in the Zionist and Socialist movements, in the unions and *landsmanshaften,* in the Yiddish press and cultural institutions, in Orthodox organizations, and the like.

One of the first attempts of the East European elements at centralization was the Alliance of All Institutions of Russian Jews in America (1890), among the founders being a number of members of the *Am Olam* (Eternal People) movement. They invited leaders of the Sephardic and German groups to join them in creating a Jewish Alliance of America "to unite Israelites in a common bond for the purpose of more effectually coping with the grave problems presented by enforced emigration." The Alliance was organized in Philadelphia in January 1891, but it was short-lived, apparently as a result of clashes between the German and East European elements.

One of the chief problems which faced the new immigrants was the question of "Americanization." This had never presented any particular difficulties for the comparatively small number of German Jewish immigrants, but for the East European Jews, concentrated into "ghettos" in the larger cities, adjustment to the American way of life was not easy. The very term "Americanization" had a different significance for each group. To the long-settled, assimilated resident it meant, simply, the adjustment of the new arrivals to the older habits of thought and behavior. But the nationalistic and labor-conscious elements among the new immigrants did not interpret adjustment to American democratic ideals as requiring imitation of the German Jews.

The promotion of Americanization became one of the primary objectives of the first large Jewish women's organization in the United States, the National Council of Jewish Women, founded in Chicago in 1893. The Council, active to this day, and with a membership of over 60,000 by 1942, set itself an ambitious program of education and social service. It has always stressed the "non-partisan character of the organization, which must be the platform of all Jewish women," regardless of differences in outlook and ideology. The Council does not believe in the solution of the Jewish problem through "national isolationism, which is both an impractical and an ungracious ideal." After the Hitler catastrophe, the president of the Council (Blanche Bauman-Goldman) said in a public statement that "because of . . . Hitler . . . Jewish people the world over have been inclined to develop an oversensitiveness about themselves, and have tended to desire to solve the problem of the Jews as it appears in the pathological light Hitler had focussed upon them. This is indeed a fallacy which must be exposed, for the Jewish problem is only a part of the whole abscess of prejudice and will be solved only when prejudice itself ceases to dominate thought."

Courtesy American Jewish Historical Society, New York

MEDAL ISSUED ON THE 250TH ANNIVERSARY OF THE JEWISH SETTLEMENT IN AMERICA

JACOB SCHIFF (1847-1920), A FOUNDER AND LEADER OF THE AMERICAN JEWISH COMMITTEE

VI. THE AMERICAN JEWISH COMMITTEE

The last decade of the nineteenth century and the first decade of the twentieth saw the rise of the Jewish nationalist and labor movements. Simultaneously, in the early 1900's, a new organization appeared, the American Jewish Committee, destined to become one of the most powerful and influential Jewish institutions unaffiliated with either of these movements. The Kishinev pogrom of 1903 was the immediate incentive for the creation of the American Jewish Committee. No other event had so outraged the Jews of America. More than 75 public protest meetings were held in 50 cities throughout the United States, among which the stirring demonstration in New York stands out. Campaigns were organized to raise funds for relief to the victims of the pogrom and for Jewish self-defense groups in Russia. B'nai B'rith submitted a peti-

tion to the President of the United States.

The abortive revolution of 1905 in Russia and the persisting pogroms roused American Jews to a state of high tension. More than ever they felt the need for a central body. As a temporary expedient, three prominent philanthropists, Oscar Straus, Jacob Schiff and Mayer Sulzberger, proposed a National Committee for the Relief of Sufferers of Russian Massacres. But there were other problems in addition to the tragic plight of Russian Jews, and from the nucleus provided by the temporary relief committee there emerged a permanent body.

In 1904 the 250th anniversary of the Jews in America was celebrated with great enthusiasm. Jewish devotion to the United States was intensified by the contrast between their own flourishing state and the misery of their brothers in Eastern Europe. The temporary relief committee participated actively in the anniversary cele-

LOUIS MARSHALL (1856-1929), A FOUNDER AND LEADER OF THE AMERICAN JEWISH COMMITTEE

MAYER SULZBERGER (1843-1923), A FOUNDER
AND LEADER OF THE AMERICAN JEWISH
COMMITTEE

brations. Soon thereafter, in January 1906, it sent a delegation to a General Jewish Conference in Brussels, Belgium, to discuss relief and migration problems. After the Brussels Conference, the leaders of the American relief committee resolved, in February 1906, "to consider the formation of a General Jewish Committee or other representative body of the Jews in the United States." In November 1906 the American Jewish Committee was established, with the following objectives:

> The objects of this corporation shall be, to prevent the infraction of the civil and religious rights of Jews, in any part of the world; to render all lawful assistance and to take appropriate remedial action in the event of threatened or actual invasion or restriction of such rights, or of unfavorable discrimination with respect thereto; to secure for Jews equality

of economic, social and educational opportunity; to alleviate the consequences of persecution and to afford relief from calamities affecting Jews, wherever they may occur; and to compass these ends to administer any relief fund which shall come into its possession or which may be received by it, in trust or otherwise, for any of the aforesaid objects or for purposes comprehended therein.

From the first the American Jewish Committee proved a powerful force in Jewish life, having at its disposal large funds and the active interest of prominent men. However, it was not unique in its field. B'nai B'rith and the Union of Hebrew Congregations were already in existence. Subsequently there arose various other influential organizations, some of which, especially the Zionist and labor groups, developed extensive political activities.

JULIUS ROSENWALD (1862-1932), A FOUNDER
AND LEADER OF THE AMERICAN JEWISH
COMMITTEE

In the space of its half-century of exist-ence the American Jewish Committee has achieved an impressive record, particularly in aid to Jews abroad. It undertook a number of successful interventions and organized demonstrations and relief cam-paigns on behalf of the victims of anti-Jewish laws and persecution in Tsarist Russia. The Committee made official rep-resentations in Washington regarding the blood-accusation against Mendel Beilis and the persecution of Jews by the Rus-sian military during World War I. Dur-ing the interbellum period and in the Hitler era it engaged in various political actions on behalf of Jews abroad. At the same time it was active on the home front in its fight against immigration restrictions and the spread of anti-Semitism.

In these endeavors the American Jew-ish Committee was obliged to cooperate with or seek the cooperation of other central Jewish organizations. Clashes arose over methodology and ideologies, particu-larly with reference to Zionism. The ex-clusiveness of the Committee was often stressed by its leadership. In an address in 1953, Dr. John Slawson, its Executive Vice-President, stated: "Ours has never been a mass organization and never will be." The Committee consisted of only a few hundred until about a decade ago; in 1948 it had 14,000 members and in 1952, 22,500. The first members were al-most exclusively German Jews but later the organization attracted increasing num-bers of the more Americanized and more affluent East European Jews. The Com-mittee's approach toward Zionism and, later, to the State of Israel, went through various phases. Though it voiced its sup-port of the Balfour Declaration, approved of the Jewish Agency and helped consider-ably in the struggle for Israel's independ-ence, it voiced criticism of the Biltmore Platform and subsequently of *halutziut* propaganda in the United States. A more detailed description of these points will be found further in this article.

VII. BIRTH OF THE ZIONIST MOVEMENT IN THE UNITED STATES

Zionism in the United States can be traced back to the end of the eighteenth century. Gershom Mendes Seixas, "reader" and spiritual leader of the Spanish and Portuguese synagogue, Shearith Israel, in New York, delivered a number of sermons (1789, 1798, 1799) in which he clearly formulated the Messianic hope and the dream of "a return to Zion."

Two years after the death of Seixas, Mordecai Manuel Noah delivered an ad-dress (April 1818) at the dedication of the congregation's new synagogue, in which he outlined a plan for a Jewish state in Palestine to be built with Jewish re-sources. In 1825 this colorful personality, —journalist, editor, lawyer, dramatist, New York politician and American Consul in Tunisia—appealed to Jews all over the world to settle on a quasi-autonomous territory which he had especially prepared for that purpose on Grand Island in the Niagara River. He called this spot, which was to serve as a "city of refuge for the Jews," Ararat. Nevertheless, Noah stressed the ultimate return to Zion:

> The Jews never should and never will relinquish the just hope of re-gaining possession of their ancient heritage, and events in the neighbor-hood of Palestine indicate an extra-ordinary change of affairs.

Noah aired his thoughts on this subject in his correspondence with two ex-Presi-dents of the United States, John Adams and Thomas Jefferson, both of whom re-plied in a friendly and encouraging tone. In an address before a Christian congrega-tion in Philadelphia in 1844, "Discourse on the Restoration of the Jews," he in-sisted that the return to Zion was the only solution for the Jewish problem.

Noah was not alone in his absorption with Palestine. In the 1840's Isaac Leeser, editor of *The Occident,* was writing fiery articles about assistance to the Jews in

Palestine. In 1853 a fund was set up for this purpose, to which Judah Touro, the well-known philanthropist of that day, contributed a large sum. Simultaneously, the walls of Temple Emanu-El—which was to become a stronghold of anti-Zionism—rang with the fervent appeals of the preacher Raphael De Cordova for a return to Zion. After several such harangues, Cordova was dismissed by the Temple's directors.

Zionism was gaining hold in many minds. There was the strange case of the proselyte Warder Cresson, a friend of Noah's. A wealthy Quaker from Philadelphia, Cresson made the acquaintance of Leeser and became interested in the Jewish religion. He was appointed the first American Consul to Jerusalem (1844-1848) and, after serving his term, chose to remain in Palestine, adopting Judaism and changing his name to Michael C. Boaz Israel. In 1853 he began to publish articles in *The Occident,* appealing to American Jews to come to Palestine and settle on the land. He propounded the theory that farming colonization would simultaneously help the Palestine economy and solve the Jewish problem. One such article bears the title "The Great Restoration and Consolidation of Israel in Palestine." It was his plan to establish the first colony in the Valley of Rephaim, close to Jerusalem. But his experiment collapsed because of lack of funds, the antagonism of the neighboring Arabs and climatic hardships.

By an interesting coincidence, a similar experiment was being sponsored by a group of American Christians. Clorinda S. Minor, a Philadelphian, had visited Palestine in 1849 and resolved that the Jewish youth must be taught farming. She returned to the United States where she interested a group of non-Jews in her project, and two years later, came back to Palestine with these enthusiasts. They purchased land in the area where Tel Aviv now stands and named their colony "Mount Hope." Wheat, vegetables and fruit were planted, but little flourished. Financial hardship assailed the group and the hostility of the Arabs was a constant menace. The death of the founder finally undermined the colony and in 1857 the experiment came to an end.

"The return to Zion" found adherents in diverse circles. Emma Lazarus of New York, of a thoroughly Americanized Sephardic family, knew little about Judaism until the 1880's. She was, by then, a recognized American poetess. About 1881 the poverty and distress of the new Jewish immigrants came to her attention and she began to write articles on Jewish problems. A fervid nationalist tone soon crept into her writing. In her "Epistles to the Hebrews," a series of articles which appeared in the *American Hebrew* in 1882 and 1883, she dwelt on the problems of the Jew, coming to the conclusion that only a free Jewish nation and repatriation in Palestine could bring any solution.

At about the same time, the first groups of Hovevei Zion (Lovers of Zion) were formed in New York and Baltimore. The maskil Joseph Isaac Bluestone founded the first Hibbat Zion circle in 1882 and launched the first Zionist periodical in the United States, *Hovevei Zion* (in Hebrew), as a supplement to the New York *Yiddishe Zeitung* (1885-1889) and, later, as a Yiddish weekly *Sulamit* (1890); Aaron Simcha Bernstein, chairman of one of the Hovevei Zion groups, edited a Hebrew periodical, *Ha-tsofeh ba-Aretz ha-Hadashah* (Observer in the New Land). All of these periodicals had brief and stormy lives. The lot of the Hibbat Zion groups was not better. Two groups in New York merged, in 1884, under the name of Hevrah Ohavei Zion.

An influx of young immigrants in 1888 gave new life to the Hovevei Zion group in Baltimore. The new arrivals formed the Isaac Ber Levinsohn Association. It was at the gatherings of this group that Henrietta Szold, daughter of the famous

Courtesy Zionist Organization of America

RICHARD GOTTHEIL (1862-1936), A FOUNDER
OF THE ZIONIST ORGANIZATION OF AMERICA

Hungarian scholar, Rabbi Benjamin Szold, had her initiation into Zionist activities. By 1893 the movement had acquired sufficient strength to expand into the more imposing Hevrat Zion. Simultaneously the movement began to gain ground in New York. About 1890 Joseph Isaac Bluestone, Rabbi Aaron Wise (father of Stephen S. Wise) and others founded the Shavey Zion, whose program was to settle its members in Palestine.

An interesting episode took place in Chicago during this time. In 1889 the Rev. William E. Blackstone, a small-town minister in Illinois, returned in an exalted mood from a visit to the Holy Land. Together with a group of friends, he arranged a conference of Christians and Jews in Chicago, March 1891. In the name of the conference Blackstone submitted a memorandum to President Benjamin Harrison, entitled "Why Should Palestine Not Be Restored to the Jews?" The petition was signed by a great num-

ber of prominent Americans from all walks of life—senators, congressmen, governors, men of the church, writers, businessmen, etc. It reached the President's desk, was politely acknowledged—and there the matter rested.

The appearance of Herzl's *Judenstaat* ("The Jewish State") and the convocation of the First Zionist Congress served as a stimulus to the Zionist movement in the United States. The period of isolated, scattered Hibbat Zion groups was coming to an end.

The first Zionist organization, as such, was established in Chicago. Two brothers, Bernard and Harris Horwich, together with a group of friends, formed the Chicago Zionist Organization Number 1 following their visit to Palestine. This group was the first Zionist body in the United States to delegate a member (the journalist, Leon Zolotkoff) to attend the First Zionist Congress in Basle (1897).

Other delegates and guests from the United States at the Congress were a representative of the New York Shavey Zion, a Conservative rabbi of Baltimore, a St. Louis journalist, a representative of the Hebrew National Association of Boston, and Professor Richard Gottheil and his wife. Richard Gottheil taught Semitic languages at Columbia University. The congress in Basle impressed him deeply and upon his return, together with Leon Zolotkoff and Rabbi Stephen S. Wise, he set about the preparation of a general Zionist conference in the United States. Meetings were arranged in Baltimore and New York (1897 and 1898). The New York gathering was attended by delegates from about 100 Zionist groups all over the country. Of that number, 36 were from New York and claimed a membership of about 5,000. Richard Gottheil was elected first president of the Federation of American Zionists and the 24-year old Stephen S. Wise its general-secretary. But the new organization did not live up to expectations. It was a loosely-knit body, composed

Courtesy Yiddish Scientific Institute, New York

JUDAH L. MAGNES (1877-1948), ZIONIST LEADER
AND PRESIDENT OF THE HEBREW UNIVERSITY
IN JERUSALEM

the United States. The split between the Federation and the Midwest group lasted even longer. In 1897 the Zionist groups of Chicago had founded a fraternal order called Knights of Zion, which had Gates of Zion chapters throughout the Midwest. These chapters subsequently united as the Federated Zionist Societies of the Middle West, with Judge Julian W. Mack as one of their guiding spirits. It was not until 1913 that the Federated Zionist Societies merged with the Federation, safeguarding themselves, however, by retaining an autonomous status in the organization.

In the hope of enlarging their memberships various groups throughout the country emulated the example of the Knights of Zion. But the attempts to form Zionist fraternal orders, such as the Progressive Order of the West (1896) and Bnai Zion (about 1910), had little success. Each of the orders had only 4,000 members by 1940. The Bnai Zion enjoyed a brief popularity when it was headed by some of the country's foremost Jews (the first *Nasi*, or Grand Master, was Judah L. Magnes).

of various groups not all of which even subscribed to the Basle program. Nor was it representative of all the Zionist groups throughout the country. The leaders were, for the most part, Americanized Jews and the proceedings were conducted almost exclusively in English. The membership itself, on the other hand, was composed mostly of Yiddish-speaking recent immigrants from Eastern Europe.

The older Hovevei Zion groups formed an opposition bloc and attached themselves to the religious Zionist groups (the Mizrachi had not yet been founded). Together, both elements left the Federation (1901) and formed their own organization —the United Zionists of America. It was a number of years before the rift was healed and the United Zionists returned to the Federation.

This, however, was not the only obstacle to a unified Zionist organization in

In general, the last years of the nineteenth century and the beginning of the twentieth were a critical period for the Zionist movement in America. In his memoirs, the veteran Zionist Louis Lipsky writes: "The protocols of our annual conventions reveal our provincial status—they must appear shockingly inadequate to our more experienced European parliamentarians. . . . Our system of taxation was curiously ineffective." During the years 1900 to 1910 almost all key positions in American Jewish life were held by non- or anti-Zionists. Behind the Zionists stood only a portion of the new immigrants, since most of the newcomers were under the influence either of labor movements or of Orthodoxy.

The first outside organization to express sympathy for the Zionist cause was the Union of Orthodox Jewish Congregations of America (founded in 1898) which stated in its Proclamation of Purposes: "The restoration of Zion is the legitimate aspiration of scattered Israel, in no way conflicting with our loyalty to the land in which we dwell or may dwell at any time." In general, American Orthodoxy expressed less opposition to Zionism in its initial stages than did the Orthodoxy of Europe. Conversely, the Reform elements sharply attacked the Zionist movement. As early as 1897 the Central Conference of American Rabbis adopted a resolution expressing:

> . . . total disapproval of any attempt for the establishment of a Jewish State. Such attempts show a misunderstanding of Israel's mission. . . . Such attempts do not benefit, but infinitely harm, our Jewish brethren where they are still persecuted, by confirming the assertion of their enemies that the Jews are foreigners in the countries in which they are at home and of which they are everywhere the most loyal and patriotic citizens.

In the course of discussing this resolution, the famous words of Gustavus Poznanski were recalled. Poznanski, Reform rabbi of Beth Elohim congregation in Charleston, South Carolina, had declared in 1841: "This synagogue is our temple, this city our Jerusalem, this happy land our Palestine."

Other Reform rabbis were even harsher in their condemnation, particularly Rabbi Isaac Mayer Wise.

The Hebrew Union College became such a stronghold of anti-Zionism that several pro-Zionist members of the faculty were forced to leave. Despite this, some Reform rabbis joined the Zionist ranks from the very beginning and gradually a strong pro-Zionist element developed within the Reform movement. Rabbi Stephen S. Wise was one of the most forceful figures among this group. He founded the Free Synagogue in New York in 1907, and in 1922 the Jewish Institute of Religion. In later years, the Reform

movement came increasingly to favor Zionism and the State of Israel.

Conservative Jewry was far more sympathetic from the beginning. It is true that in 1907 one of the chief trustees of the Jewish Theological Seminary, the well-known philanthropist Jacob Schiff, had accused the Zionists of "dual loyalties," but eleven years later his attitude had changed completely. Solomon Schechter. President of the Seminary (1902), was sympathetic to Zionist ideals, greatly helping to raise the prestige of the young movement by his sponsorship. He made a number of public appearances at Zionist functions, such as the National Zionist Convention in 1906. Louis Lipsky has stated that Solomon Schechter, "and later to some extent Professor Israel Friedlaender, made the Jewish Theological Seminary an institution for graduation not only of rabbis but also of Zionists. Its rabbis carried the message of Zionism into all parts of America."

Zionism found no adherents among the Jewish civic and fraternal organizations of that period (B'nai B'rith, American Jewish Committee), and the majority of Jewish labor organizations also had a negative attitude toward it. Under such conditions, the Zionist Federation had little influence in American Jewish life, and was weak both numerically and financially. At the Fourth Zionist Convention (1901) only $50 could be spared for the National Library in Jerusalem. In 1914 the Finance Committee proposed an annual budget of $12,000 for the Zionist Organization in America. At that time there were 14,860 registered shekel-holders in the organization.

The American Zionist organization played a small role in world Zionism in the early years, although 20 delegates attended the Eleventh World Zionist Congress in Vienna in 1913. One of the most serious concerns of the young movement was membership. Zevi Hirsh Masliansky, beloved "national preacher" and "wandering preacher of Zionism" did much to advance the cause. A man of unusual oratorical ability, he threw himself whole-heartedly into Zionist work soon after his immigration to America.

The Zionist press in the United States enlisted sympathizers for the movement. The first official monthly publication of the Zionist movement, *The Maccabean,* a bi-lingual (English and Yiddish) journal edited by Louis Lipsky, was founded in 1901. A Yiddish weekly—*Dos Yiddishe Folk* (The Jewish People)—first appeared in 1909. The first Zionist youth clubs were formed in Philadelphia (1901) and in New York where the young Abba Hillel Silver and Emanuel Neumann, together with several friends, formed the Dr. Herzl Zion Club (1904), while yet another group founded the Nordau Zion Club (1905). In 1909 all the youth groups convened in Atlantic City, where they created the national organization, Young Judaea. By 1914 this organization embraced 175 Zionist youth clubs and had its own monthly publication, *The Young Judaean.*

In 1912 several Zionist women's groups organized under the name of the Daughters of Zion, which later became Hadassah, with Henrietta Szold as its moving spirit.

The Kishinev pogrom had its effect on the Zionist movement. It impelled Zionists to emerge from the limited confines of party work and enter the scene of general Jewish politics. "That was a thrilling, a moving time," writes Louis Lipsky. "All this . . . made impossible the easy-going comfortable Jewish life of the past." The Zionist groups plunged into the work of arranging protest demonstrations, rousing public opinion and raising funds for the pogrom victims and, especially, for arms for Jewish self-defense groups in Russia. This work attracted new and forceful elements, and established a closer bond between the general Zionists and Poale-Zionists.

The World Zionist movement suddenly faced a serious crisis. The conflict over

Courtesy Hadassah, New York

HENRIETTA SZOLD (1860-1945), FOUNDER OF HADASSAH

Uganda, then suggested to Herzl by the British Government for Jewish colonization instead of Palestine, the death of Herzl and the departure of the Territorialists (a party advocating colonization in any territory suitable for Jews)—all created a difficult situation. The Territorialists had taken with them a significant number of Russian and British leaders, seriously depleting the ranks and striking a blow at the prestige of the organization. In addition to this crisis in world Zionism, the American organization was suffering defeat in its endeavor to create a "Unified Jewish Community" in New York City.

VIII. LABOR ZIONISM UP TO WORLD WAR I

After 1881 the immigrants who came to the United States were for the most part deeply rooted in Jewish tradition. They adjusted themselves to the new economic and social order, entering trade unions and creating their own Jewish unions. The union leaders were radicals and intellectuals who had become workers in America, while many of the members were Orthodox and deeply traditional Jews. The majority of the leaders had been trained in the conspiratorial atmosphere of the Russian revolutionary movement or in the school of German socialism. The religious leaders, on the other hand, had interested themselves very little in the social and political problems of immigrant Jewry. Thus, even the religious and traditional elements among the workers found themselves under the leadership of zealous socialist and anarchist intellectuals.

This was a period of sharp clashes between various socialist and anarchist factions, of passionate excoriation against religion, traditionalism and "bourgeois superstitions," of invective against "reactionary nationalist ideas," etc. The United Hebrew Trades (Fareinigte Yiddishe Geverkshaften) at that time went much further in its social radicalism than most non-Jewish labor organizations. In 1890 it proclaimed: "There can be no peace between labor and capital in the present social system." Its attitude toward Jewish religion and nationalism was equally uncompromising: "The world is our fatherland, and socialism is our religion."

In opposition to this cosmopolitan radicalism there began to develop a movement to effect a harmonious fusion between Zionism and Socialism. Among the immigrants coming to the United States during the first decade of the twentieth century there were not only experienced Bundist leaders, but also a large contingent of Poale Zionists. The latter were fewer in number than the Bundists because their movement was just emerging from its inception in Vienna, Berlin, Lwów (Lemberg) and the Russian underground. In the spring of 1903 five newly arrived Poale Zionists formed the National

Courtesy Yiddish Scientific Institute (YIVO), New York

NACHMAN SYRKIN (1867-1924), POALE ZION
LEADER AND WRITER

Radical Alliance Poale Zion in New York. One year later a similar group was formed in Philadelphia.

The party grew rapidly after it sponsored a protest meeting against the Kishinev pogrom—the first public undertaking of the Poale Zion in America. In May 1903, in a brochure entitled "Our Platform," it described its purpose as being "to create an organization in which both trends—the national and the labor—can unite and meet on common ground."

The tremendous upsurge of Jewish feeling evoked by the Kishinev pogrom attracted a number of socialist leaders and youth to the ranks of the Poale Zion. But regardless of its increasing membership, a central body was still lacking. The first effort to establish a permanent bond between the various labor Zionist groups was the creation of a Yiddish quarterly, *Die Naie Shtime* (The New Voice), in May 1904.

A serious ideological schism threatened the young party. A number of territorialists had come to the United States in 1905. The middle-class territorialists failed to develop their organization in the New World (although Israel Zangwill had made a special trip from England to help them), but Socialist Territorialists found fertile soil in America for their movement. In addition to the internationally known Chaim Zhitlowsky, who was then paying his first visit to the United States, the group had enlisted a number of labor leaders, among others Joseph Barondess, Moshe Katz, Baruch Zuckerman, Nachman Syrkin and Abraham Goldberg. The Poale Zionists therefore decided to hold a conference in Philadelphia (April, 1905) to enable territorialists and the advocates of Palestine to air their differences. At the conference it became apparent that the majority leaned toward territorialism. There were only six genuine Poale Zionists among the delegates and the threat of complete rupture hung in the air. To preserve the unity of the movement a resolution was adopted to maintain a neutral attitude toward the question of territorialism, pending the outcome of the Seventh Zionist Congress at which the Uganda question was due to be discussed.

That Congress concluded with the withdrawal of the territorialist faction and the creation of an independent Jewish Territorial Organization (JTO). Thereafter a formula was adopted by the Acting Committee in the United States for the preservation of unity in the Poale Zion-Socialist Territorialist movement in America. It remained one body, with two centers: a Palestinian (Zionist) and a territorial. This compromise proved most unsatisfactory for both sides. The first to rebel was a group of Poale Zionists who formed the Poale Zion Palestinian Society in New York and convoked the first Poale Zion convention in Baltimore (December 1905). At that convention the following program was adopted:

1. Endorsement of the Basle Zionist program;
2. Practical work in Palestine;
3. A liberal attitude toward the socialist movement, i.e., all members of the Poale Zion Alliance were free to affiliate themselves with whatever socialist group appealed to them;
4. Rejection of territorialism and insistence on Palestine as the goal of Zionism;
5. Acceptance of Hebrew as the national tongue, all other Jewish languages being Diaspora tongues.

It was also resolved to begin publication of a party journal, the *Yiddisher Kemfer*.

At the convention all ties with the Socialist Territorialists were broken. The Baltimore convention was attended by 18 delegates from 6 societies, the entire party having only 300 members. The Socialist Territorialists had five times that number.

The rift did not last long. In 1908 negotiations began for reuniting the Socialist Territorialists and the Poale Zion, and in August 1909 a convention for that purpose took place in Chicago. Two concessions were made to the territorialists: current work in the Diaspora and Yiddish as the language of the Jewish people were to be given full recognition. Although not all of the Socialist Territorialists joined—the Marxist faction held back—the Poale Zion gained vastly in prestige and membership. The influence of Chaim Zhitlowsky was no small factor in the campaign for unity, though he later became the severest critic of Poale Zion.

Another achievement of the Poale Zion was the creation of the Jewish National Workers' Alliance (later renamed Farband —Labor Zionist Order). The pioneer among Jewish fraternal orders in labor circles had been the Workmen's Circle, which proved a successful experiment. In 1908 Meyer Brown and a few associates took the initiative in proposing the creation of a similar fraternal order by the Poale Zion. The plan did not meet with the full approval of the party. There were conflicting opinions as to the advisability of establishing a separate order, some feeling that it was best to join Bnai Zion, and others that the Poale Zion should join the Workmen's Circle as a unit, establishing its own autonomous branches. Final victory went to the advocates of a separate order, and in 1908 the first National Radical Relief Society was formed. By 1950 the Farband had branches in 103 cities in the United States and Canada, and close to 30,000 members.

IX. THE Y'S AND THE JEWISH CENTERS

A most interesting and typically American feature of Jewish life in the United States is the Center. The earliest known institution of this type can be traced back to the 1840's, when Jewish literary and cultural societies were founded in various cities. The first Young Men's Hebrew Association (YMHA) was established in Baltimore in 1854, some years after the Young Men's Christian Association (YMCA), an "organization for social and religious work among young men." Both had similar programs: social and recreational activities for youth under wholesome and constructive auspices.

The Jewish Y's developed rapidly. By the end of 1874 there were 25 and in the six years that followed 50 more sprang up in various cities. By 1890 there were almost 100. In 1902 the first Young Women's Hebrew Association (YWHA) was organized in New York. In 1880 and 1890 attempts to federate all the Y's proved unsuccessful. The new wave of immigration after 1880 brought new problems to the Y's, whose leaders now envisaged their primary task as being to assist the newcomers on the road to Americanization.

In England, during the 1880's, various programs for improving slum areas were undertaken and groups were organized to work for social and housing betterment.

American philanthropists followed the British example, with certain modifications. "Settlement" and "Neighborhood" houses, staffed by professional and volunteer social workers, were established in the poorer urban neighborhoods. The first settlement house was opened in New York in 1886 and by 1910 there were 75 throughout the country. All were nonsectarian, having as their chief aim to further the brotherhood of man and help newcomers to become patriotic Americans.

The common purpose of the Y's and the Settlement-centers was the Americanization of the immigrant. To this end the Y's founded the Hebrew Institute of Jewish Education Alliance in New York (1891), which was later known as the Jewish Educational Alliance. Shortly thereafter similar institutions were founded in other cities.

It was not until the second decade of the present century that there arose a new type of Jewish Center, which showed greater appreciation and understanding of the cultural values of the immigrant himself. These Centers, with their essentially religious Jewish basis (they were frequently called "Synagogue Centers"), were inspired by the theories of Rabbi Mordecai M. Kaplan, the leading spirit of what was later to be known as the Reconstructionist movement. According to his ideas, the Center was to embrace all aspects of "Jewish religious civilization," and serve all Jews, regardless of ideology. As time went by, Hebrew schools became the nucleus for a certain type of Center. There also arose the Community Center which brought together under one roof all manner of previously separate activities.

By 1914 there was a great number of Y's, Centers and other institutions which presented a rich choice of social, cultural, religious and "non-sectarian" activities. Representatives of seventy such organizations convened in New York in 1913 to form the National Council of Young Men's Hebrew and Kindred Associations.

Following World War I, these institutions developed rapidly, particularly after the National Council joined the Jewish Welfare Board in 1921. Their development can be seen from the following chart:

| Year | Growth of Y's and Centers, 1926 to 1949 | | Annual Expenditures |
	Y's and Centers	Members and Visitors	
1926......	227	250,000	$ 2,500,000
1945......	288	427,000	7,100,000
1948......	317	468,000	10,000,000
1949......	325	483,000	11,535,000

Of the 325 Centers in 1949, 9 were in Canada, all the others being in the United States. In 1948 Professor Oscar Janowsky prepared an analysis of 301 Centers affiliated with the Jewish Welfare Board, which enumerated them as follows:

130 Y's, or 43% of all Centers,
112 Synagogue Centers, or 37%,
27 Settlement or Neighborhood Houses, or 9%,
32 Miscellaneous Centers, or 11%.

Fifty-five percent of the regular visitors to the Centers were youths under 21 years.

The Y and Center programs have undergone a radical change. Immigration no longer involves huge masses. The small number who do come are on the whole rapidly Americanized. It has become increasingly clear that the Y of yesterday was too limited in outlook and insufficiently Jewish in spirit. The Statement of Principles adopted by the Centers and the Jewish Welfare Board at their convention in Chicago in 1948 declared:

Jewish content is fundamental to the program of the Jewish Center. . . . The functions of the Jewish Center include:

A. Service as an agency of Jewish identification.

B. Service as a common meeting ground for all Jews. Membership is open to the entire Jewish community, no one to be excluded by reason of Jewish doctrine or ritual, or because of his political or social views.

C. Service as an agency of personality development. Jewish religion and tradition and the ideal of American democracy both emphasize the well-being of the individual.

Under the impact of the European Jewish catastrophe and the creation of the State of Israel, there was a general upsurge of Jewish feeling during the 1940's. Not all the Centers underwent the same change. As has been mentioned, only a small proportion of the non-sectarian Settlement Houses affiliated with the Council of the Y's and the Jewish Welfare Board. The majority have remained true to their non-sectarian ideology and are united under the National Federation of Settlements, which was organized in Chicago in 1911 and embraces 280 institutions.

X. THE LANDSMANSHAFTEN

Immigrants from the Old World created organizations inspired by labor or nationalist ideologies or by religious or philanthropic motives. They also founded countless groups appealing to people from the same town or region—the *landsmanshaften*.

The original motives for the organization of the *landsmanshaften* were economic or social. The difficulties of adjusting to new customs and a new language were greatly allayed by the help and guidance furnished to new immigrants by friends and relatives who had arrived in the United States earlier. They formed into societies of fellow-countrymen (landsmanshaften) which eventually became mutual aid societies, providing for their members in time of need, unemployment and sickness, and arranging for the burial of the dead. The landsmanshaften also met the social and cultural needs of the new arrivals, who were thus enabled to meet socially, attend lectures, establish houses of worship, etc.

JEWISH CENTER, HOUSTON, TEXAS

JEWISH CENTER, TOLEDO, OHIO

Each landsmanshaft had funds for assistance to its members and to families left behind in Europe. With expanded relief work, many of these groups appended the words "Benevolent" or "Relief Society" to their town-names. A number formed women's auxiliaries. Gradually the landsmanshaften enlarged their interest beyond their own members and began to help the large national Jewish relief organizations.

In the past three or four decades the landsmanshaften have contributed considerably to the campaigns of the Joint Distribution Committee, The United Jewish Appeal, the National Labor Committee for Israel (Geverkshaften Kampein), Israel Bonds, the Jewish Labor Committee, Yeshiva University, and the like. Many have units within the Workmen's Circle, the Farband—Labor Zionist Order, Brith Shalom, American Jewish Congress, etc. Landsmanshaften with memberships from the same country organized federations which, in addition to relief work, also made representations on behalf of their countrymen (e.g., the Federation of Polish Jews in America, the Federation of Hungarian Jews in America, the Federation of Lithuanian Jews, the United Rumanian Jews of America). The landsmanshaften flourished during the first 40 years of this century.

No complete investigation has yet been made of this important movement in American Jewish life. The earliest date we have for a landsmanshaft in the United States is 1859, when an organization of Dutch Jews was founded in New York. The first recorded Polish landsmanshaft dates dack to 1870. By 1880 there had begun a new development which eventually, in the early decades of our century, brought the number of landsmanshaften to several thousand. A study made in 1938 showed that in New York alone there were more than 1800 landsmanshaften, including women's auxiliaries (*The Jewish Landsmanshaften of New York*

[Yiddish], edited by Isaac E. Rontch, New York, 1938). In 1950 the United Jewish Appeal of New York had 2,000 landsmanshaften and 1,000 women's auxiliaries on its register. It must be remembered that countless smaller groups are not included in these statistics. It is difficult to estimate just how many of them are scattered throughout the United States.

The first federation of landsmanshaften was the United Galician Jews of America, founded in New York in 1904. Characteristically, it went through several periods of prosperity and decline. In 1932 it was dissolved, only to be revived four years later. In 1940 it had 260 affiliates. The Federation of Polish Jews (which changed its name to American Federation of Polish Jews in 1930) was founded in 1908. In 1930 it had 15,000 members and in 1945 the number had risen to 65,000. Since then, internal conflict has led to decline. The Federation of Rumanian Jews was organized in 1909; that of the Hungarian Jews, in 1919 (embracing 107 landsmanshaften by 1941), and a federation of Jews from Palestine in 1929. In the 30's and 40's the national-origin landsmanshaften federations mushroomed—Ukraine, Yugoslavia, Lithuania, France, Denmark, Austria, Czechoslovakia, Holland, Syria, Latvia, Bessarabia, Bukhara, Manchuria, etc.—but most were short-lived. In 1941 the thriving American Federation of Jews from Central Europe was founded, numbering 21 affiliated organizations in New York and another 16 throughout the United States in 1951.

The Sephardic Jews have their own landsmanshaften, the oldest being the Sephardic Brotherhood of America. The more recent immigrants organized the Union of Sephardic Congregations in 1929.

The landsmanshaft movement began to decline about 10 to 15 years ago, for a number of reasons:

a) The economic situation of the members had so far improved that mutual aid was no longer of great importance;

b) On the other hand, many of the landsmanshaften, because of inexperience in the handling of insurance funds, soon found that their obligations to their members exceeded their resources;

c) The landsmanshaften could not attract the youth. Although many had organized special young people's groups, the second and third generations were not interested;

d) With the cessation of large-scale immigration the primary *raison d'être* of the landsmanshaften was weakened. At the same time, Nazism destroyed the European Jewish communities that had been the recipients of their aid;

e) Internal political friction took its toll.

In recent years landsmanshaften have concentrated their work on three main objectives:

1. Aid to victims of Nazism and assistance in emigration to Israel or the United States;

2. Establishment and maintenance of institutions and colonies in Israel to commemorate the dead (Kiryat-Bialystok, Lodz Homes, etc.);

3. Publication of books to commemorate the lost Jewish communities of Europe. The number of these books, annals, records, brochures, etc., in the United States reaches into the hundreds.

It is interesting to note that in recent times the Family Circles have gained in popularity. The first known Family Circles (about 10) were formed in the period 1887 to 1916. In 1938 there were 76, and today the UJA of New York reports that about 1200, with an aggregate membership of 75,000, are on its roster. Few of them have clear-cut programs or definite objectives other than the social gathering of family members. There is no way of predicting whether this type of group will have any particular significance in American Jewish life, or in what direction it will eventually develop.

XI. WORLD WAR I AND THE JEWISH WELFARE BOARD

The impact of the First World War on American Jewry has been succinctly expressed by Prof. Salo W. Baron: ". . . during the years 1914-1918 the American Jewish Community grew into maturity." The war years established the leadership of American Jews. Eastern Europe, Palestine, the Balkans and certain areas in Western Europe were battle grounds. The large American Jewish community, untouched by the immediate dangers of war and endowed with a growing economic and political strength, accepted its financial and political responsibilities toward the less fortunate Jews in Europe and Asia.

By the time of World War I four distinct groupings had crystallized in American Jewish Life: the Zionists, the Orthodox, the non-Zionist and more or less well-to-do elements symbolized by the American Jewish Committee, and the socialist-oriented workers.

After the Joint Distribution Committee was organized, in the early months of World War I, the Jewish Welfare Board was created in 1917. This was an important step in the internal organization of the American Jewish community. Its direct purpose was to serve the Jewish man in the U. S. armed forces, but soon it expanded its program, enlisting the cooperation of the chief Jewish religious organizations throughout the country. It was supported by large subventions from the JDC, individual contributions, and subsidies from the United Service Organizations for National Defense, a body composed of seven large national organizations in which the JWB was the sole Jewish body. Altogether, the wartime budget of the Jewish Welfare Board was approximately $6,000,000.

After the war the Jewish Welfare Board decided to continue its work among Jewish veterans and extend it to Jewish youth. In 1921 it joined the Council of Y's.

During World War II the work of the Jewish Welfare Board increased greatly. In the First World War it had served Jewish soldiers through 182 local branches; it now required 626 branches. Jewish chaplains, recruited from all three wings of Judaism in America and assisted by the JWB, not only rendered outstanding service to the Jewish men and women in the armed forces, but also played an outstanding part in the rescue and rehabilitation of European Jewry.

Today the JWB is the central body for the Y's and Jewish Centers in the United States. One of its important arms is a Lecture Bureau which furnishes about 250 cities with lecturers and artistic programs on Jewish themes. The JWB also sponsors the Jewish Book Council of America and the Jewish Music Council, and at one time subsidized the American Jewish Historical Society.

XII. THE ZIONIST MOVEMENT IN AMERICA DURING WORLD WAR I

The outbreak of World War I threw the World Zionist Organization into a state of crisis. Almost all the members of its Executive were then living in Germany, the center of world Zionism. In order not to lose contact with the outside world, as well as to preserve the neutral character of the movement, the Central Bureau was transferred to the neutral city of Copenhagen. But even here it found itself suspected of anti-Russian and pro-German leanings and many Zionists residing in Allied countries (for instance, Chaim Weizmann in London) refused all contact with the Copenhagen bureau. For this, as well as other reasons, a *de facto* Executive was set up in London. It was this body (especially Chaim Weizmann and Nahum Sokolow) which later conducted Zionist negotiations with the British Government.

In the United States the need for a Zionist executive was also felt. The establishment of the English executive body had been juridically possible because of the residence in London of Nahum Sokolow, one of the veteran members of the World Zionist Executive. The chance presence in the United States of another member of the Executive, Shmaryahu Levin, made the same thing possible here. In August 1914 Levin and Louis Lipsky convoked an extraordinary conference of all Zionist groups. It was attended by 150 delegates from seven organizations: Bnai Zion, Young Judaea, Hadassah, Keren Kayemet (Jewish National Fund), Mizrachi, Poale Zion and the Federation of American Zionists. For the first time steps were taken to unite all Zionist forces in the United States under the common roof of a Provisional [Emergency] Executive Committee for General Zionist Affairs. The Provisional Committee immediately announced that it would establish a $100,000 emergency fund for Palestine (a large sum according to the standards of the day).

One of the greatest achievements of the American Zionist movement at this time was the enlistment of a number of outstanding personalities (Felix Frankfurter, Nathan Straus and others) and the election of Louis Dembitz Brandeis as head of the Provisional Committee. Coming from a background of assimilation, Brandeis was one of the leading liberals of his day, having risen to fame through his fight against monopolies in industry, transportation and finance. In 1912 he became interested in Zionism through Jacob de Haas, then secretary of the Zionist Federation of America, and Nahum Sokolow, who was on a visit to the United States. Brandeis' abrupt transition in middle-age (he was then 55) from assimilation to active, daily work in Zionism created a sensation.

The Zionist movement grew and by mid-1915 the Federation's 198 affiliated groups had increased to 270, with some 30,000 shekel-holders. The Mizrachi organized and consolidated its ranks. The income from the relief campaigns under- taken in August 1914 far exceeded all expectations—by the end of May 1915 almost $350,000 had been sent to Pales- tine. In that month the Zionist Actions Committee in Berlin acknowledged the Provisional Committee as an official body, as did the Zionist leadership in London.

Brandeis' administration was not univer- sally popular. He was criticized for cold- ness and lack of enthusiasm, as well as indifference to what might be called the mystique or pathos of Zionist doctrine. His reticence and reserve were ascribed to arrogance by his opponents. On the other hand, those who worked closely with him were his devout adherents. In his memoirs Stephen S. Wise summed up Brandeis' personality and administration thus:

> Brandeis' public leadership of the Zionist cause lasted for only two years. . . . But what enriching years they were and how inspiring to his col- leagues! . . . He was our leader in the most critical years of American Jewish history. . . . I can affirm . . . that since the days of Herzl Brandeis was indisputably and incomparably our greatest Jew. I think not of his gift as an economist, or even his genius as a statesman, least of all of his boundless personal generosity. Rather do I think of the spirit he brought to our cause that I can best describe by using the Hebrew term Kedusha—Holiness.

The movement faced a severe crisis when Brandeis, having been nominated by President Wilson, joined the Supreme Court in June 1916. Membership in the Supreme Court requires abstention from all political activity, to avoid partisan involvements. There was criticism in the Zionist leadership against Brandeis for having accepted a post, however distin- guished, which would automatically ex- clude him from Zionist work. Brandeis was also accused of being too negative or timid in his attitude toward the Ameri- can Jewish Congress movement. His reply

was to withdraw completely from the Congress.

Brandeis' retirement from Zionist ac- tivity, on the other hand, was only partial. He remained at the head of the Provi- sional Committee until 1918, gradually becoming a "silent leader" and communi- cating his decisions and opinions to the Executive through his devoted adjutants Stephen S. Wise and Julian Mack. (The latter had assumed the chairmanship of the Zionist Organization in 1918.) A num- ber of General Zionist and Poale Zion leaders decried this as undemocratic pro- cedure, one of them alleging that it made Brandeis into a kind of *Urim ave-Thum- mim* against whom any criticism was tantamount to high treason.

The entry of the United States into the war (April 1917) caused the second crisis in the Zionist movement in America. The Provisional Committee no longer sufficed; a permanent body was now needed. To that end a convention of all Zionist or- ganization was held in Baltimore in June 1917.

Zionism had gained strength in the United States since 1914. Both Mizrachi and the Poale Zion had acquired import- ance and stature. Each had its own world union and they now demanded propor- tionate representation in the executive bodies of the new Zionist Organization. The General Zionists would agree only to granting them seats on the Zionist Council. As a result, the Poale Zion and Mizrachi walked out of the Baltimore con- ference. The General Zionists then con- voked a new meeting in Pittsburgh (June 1918), at which they formed the Zionist Organization of America and adopted the following platform:

1. Political and civil equality in Pales- tine, irrespective of race, sex or faith;

2. Ownership and control of land and all natural resources and public utilities by the whole people;

3. Lease of land;

Courtesy Yiddish Scientific Institute (YIVO), New York

LOUIS DEMBITZ BRANDEIS (1856-1941)

4. Co-operative principle in agriculture, industry and commerce; and

5. Free public education.

Both Brandeis and Wise, who were close personal friends of President Woodrow Wilson, discussed Zionist and Palestinian questions with him. In the fall of 1914 Brandeis, Wise and Richard Gottheil presented a memorandum of Zionist demands to President Wilson and to the British and French ambassadors in Washington. Important contacts were established with Secretary of State Robert Lansing and with Col. Edward M. House, Wilson's close friend and adviser on foreign affairs. In the spring of 1916 the negotiations resulted in semi-official commitments by President Wilson and the British ambassador.

By the spring of 1917 Great Britain's interest in Palestine was common knowledge. England was trying to woo Jewish public opinion, particularly in the United States. In May 1917, a British diplomatic mission, headed by Lord Balfour, came to the United States. At the first official reception tendered to him in the White House, Lord Balfour met Brandeis and proposed a private meeting. His subsequent talks with Brandeis strengthened his favorable attitude toward the Zionist cause.

Both in England and the United States powerful anti-Zionist elements among the Jews were bitterly opposing the British intention to issue what subsequently became known as the Balfour Declaration. Brandeis, however, approached President Wilson, who sent a personal message to the British government, intimating his agreement with the idea of a pro-Zionist pronouncement. This message influenced the British government to ratify the Balfour Declaration.

The Balfour Declaration did not put an end to the debate on Palestine. A group of American anti-Zionists fought against United States approval of England's intentions concerning Palestine. (In 1919 a group of "prominent Jewish Americans" presented a memorandum opposing Zionist demands to the Peace Conference.) Since the United States was not officially at war with Turkey and was trying to wean her away from her Austro-German alliance, the wartime situation of the Zionists was most precarious. American Zionists had to be constantly on the alert to counteract all the inimical influences in government circles. President Wilson proved to be a wavering champion. On the one hand he asserted his own pro-Zionist sympathies (in his letter to Stephen S. Wise in October 1918 and in his reply to a Zionist delegation in March 1919), while on the other hand, he agreed to a mission to Palestine by observers obviously unsympathetic to Zionism, which subsequently came back with an unfavorable report and a recommendation that the plan for a Jewish Homeland in Palestine be abandoned. It was not until 1921 that the

United States Senate officially recognized the Balfour Declaration (confirmed in September 1922 by President Warren G. Harding).

There were other perils that the American Zionist organization had to watch out for. The British government was planning to establish the northern boundaries of Mandate Palestine according to a secret Anglo-French agreement (the so-called Sykes-Picot Agreement) with the Arabs, which would have cut off Upper Galilee from Palestine. The Zionist Organization alerted President Wilson who immediately sent a sharp cable to London. Lloyd George later wrote in his memoirs that Wilson's cable had a telling effect. Upper Galilee remained under British Mandate.

A less successful effort of the Zionist Organization was the attempt to gain Arab endorsement of the Balfour Declaration. Credit in this connection must go to Felix Frankfurter for his negotiations with Emir Feisal, which resulted in an agreement between Feisal and Chaim Weizmann, concluded in January 1919. Feisal subsequently sent Frankfurter a message of good will toward the Zionist cause. The agreement failed to eliminate Arab opposition or prevent the Arab riots of 1920 in Palestine.

The creation of the Jewish Legion must be credited to American Zionism. In June 1917, after lengthy negotiations and much procrastination, the British government finally agreed to attach three Jewish battalions to the Royal Fusiliers (rather than permit a separate Jewish unit). The first battalion, recruited in England, reached Egypt in February 1918 and was followed two months later by a second battalion, recruited in the United States. Both took part in the September 1918 battle which opened up the road to Transjordan. The formation of the American battalion involved several unique problems. Not only was the United States not at war with Turkey, but also the men recruited were mostly recent immigrants

Courtesy of the Jewish Institute of Religion, New York

STEPHEN S. WISE (1874-1949), ZIONIST LEADER AND PRESIDENT OF THE AMERICAN JEWISH CONGRESS

to America who, as non-citizens, were not subject to conscription. At first, only about 3,000 young men answered the call; later they were joined by several thousand more. The last group, however, never got further than basic military training.

As the war years advanced, so did the strength of the Zionist movement. In 1914 the annual budget of the ZOA had been $14,000, in 1919 it was $3,000,000. There were 20,000 shekel-holders in 1914, 30,000 in 1915, 150,000 in 1917 and 173,000 in 1920.

XIII. THE AMERICAN JEWISH CONGRESS

A dramatic episode during World War I was the American Jewish Congress movement in the United States. At the Zionist

Conference in August 1914 a proposal was made to convene a larger conference (or "Congress") which would embrace not only Zionists but all of American Jewry. Opinion on the suggestion was divided in the Provisional Zionist Council, but in 1915 the pro-"Congress" elements triumphed.

In order to achieve a Congress that would be fully representative of all American Jews it was essential to win the cooperation of various non-Zionist bodies, primarily the American Jewish Committee and the labor organizations.

The American Jewish Committee was alarmed at the possibility of being overwhelmed by a Zionist majority able to force through resolutions at variance with its philosophy. More generally, it disapproved of a Jewish "Congress," which by its very name, might imply that the Jews were a separate nation with its own national interest—which was in direct conflict with the basic ideology of the American Jewish Committee.

Another group which opposed the Congress movement was the National Workmen's Committee on Jewish Rights in the Countries at War and in Rumania. This Committee was composed of the United Hebrew Trades, Workmen's Circle, the Jewish Socialist Federation of America, Socialist Territorialists, Labor Zionists, Bundists and the Jewish National Workers' Alliance (Farband—Labor Zionist Order), whose aggregate membership totalled close to 350,000. The majority of the National Workmen's Committee opposed the plan primarily because they had little liking for close cooperation with representatives of the Jewish bourgeoisie and also because they feared that a Zionist majority would commit the Congress to a pro-Zionist line.

The Zionists (including Brandeis, who had become an ardent Congress advocate in 1915) launched an ambitious propaganda campaign and in September 1915 the National Workmen's Committee had a conference in New York, from which the pro-Congress factions emerged victorious. This paved the way for negotiations by the General Zionists and Poale Zion with the American Jewish Committee and the National Workmen's Committee.

The American Jewish Committee and its affiliated organizations wanted the "Congress" to be changed to a "Conference." They felt that it might otherwise become a permanent body, unlike a "conference," which is usually convened ad hoc and dissolved once its purpose has been accomplished. Also, they argued, a "conference" could avoid the partisan embroilments inevitable in a large massorganization such as a "congress."

After long negotiations, the name "congress" was accepted, but with the following limitations: it was to disband as soon as its mission had been accomplished; 75% of its members were to be elected directly and the remaining 25% were to be delegated to the Congress by various organizations.

The agreement raised a fresh storm, this time in the Zionist camp itself, the labor Zionists accusing the General Zionists of being too conciliatory toward the American Jewish Committee. After a bitter struggle a new agreement was made. Additional drama was provided when the National Workmen's Committee reversed its pro-Congress stand and, despite protracted negotiations, withdrew its support of the plan because it felt that the Russian Revolution (February-March, 1917) had now solved, in unequivocal fashion, all the problems of East European Jewry. At the last moment, just before the Congress was officially established, the National Workmen's Committee again reversed itself and rejoined the movement. The Congress thus became a representative body of all American Jews, except for the extreme assimilationist and religious elements.

The first Congress elections took place in June 1917, with 335,000 American Jews casting votes. Three hundred representatives were elected, and 100 delegates were appointed by 30 national Jewish organizations.

The opening session took place in Philadelphia, December 15-18, 1918. A list of basic Jewish demands was drawn up for presentation to the Peace Conference: full civil and political rights; the right of minorities to enjoy full communal, religious and cultural autonomy; recognition of the Jews' historic claim to Palestine and guarantee of a Jewish national home there, etc. The Congress appointed a delegation of nine to represent it at the Peace Conference in Paris.

The Congress convened again in May 1920 to hear the report brought back from Paris by the delegation. Immediately thereafter, in accordance with its commitment, the Congress dissolved.

But the Zionist delegates (including the Poale Zion and Mizrachi), who had been well represented at the Congress, refused to accept such an epilogue. Several minutes after the dissolution of the Congress these groups met and appointed a committee to draw up plans for a permanent American Jewish Congress. After lengthy preparations, the committee convened a conference in Philadelphia (1922), at which a new American Jewish Congress was born. This body was not a continuation of the first Congress. It included only Zionist groups and not until later did other pro-Zionist national organizations and landsmanshaften join.

The American Jewish Congress concerned itself with protecting the rights of Jewish minorities all over the world, aid in the struggle for a Jewish Palestine, protection of Jews against discrimination and prejudice in the United States and elsewhere, etc. It was also instrumental in the creation of the World Jewish Congress (Geneva, 1936), which was transferred during the early months of World War II (1940) to New York where it still has its central bureau.

XIV. ZIONISM FROM THE BALFOUR DECLARATION TO WORLD WAR II

1. THE ZIONIST ORGANIZATION OF AMERICA (ZOA)

With the rise of Zionism and the general changes taking place in American Jewish life after World War I, new impetus was given to the Zionist Organization of America. The years 1917 and 1918 brought a profound transformation in the entire Zionist movement. The loosely-knit Zionist Federation was no longer adequate for the changed tasks and objectives of the movement and the Provisional Council had also outlived its purpose. Both bodies were replaced by the Zionist Organization of America (ZOA) which embraced all the General Zionist groups in the country with the exception of Hadassah.

Soon afterward the ZOA found itself threatened by schism as a result of the so-called Brandeis conflict. Brandeis had differed with his American Zionist colleagues as early as 1916 but matters did not come to a head until he clashed with the greater part of the European Zionist leadership.

In June 1919 Brandeis visited Palestine for the first time and returned to the United States to announce the following conclusions: 1) that before an extensive immigration could be undertaken in Palestine, epidemic disease, and above all malaria, must first be eliminated; 2) that with the Balfour Declaration political Zionism had achieved its goal and there now remained for the movement only economic objectives and a program of constructive work; 3) that the economic activities of the Board of Delegates (Vaad ha-Tsirim), headed by Menachem Ussishkin, were amateurish and unsystematic. In place of idealistic romanticism, Brandeis said, the time had come for efficient work and the establishment of a healthy economy in Palestine, based on the principles of good management.

At the first post-war World Zionist Conference, which met in London in July 1920, the United States had a large delegation, headed by Brandeis. A number of vital questions were before the Conference: the Balfour Declaration, the Russian Revolution, and the minorities treaties stemming from the Paris Peace Conference. Further, the rise of a dozen new nations in Eastern and Central Europe and in the Near East required certain re-adjustments in Zionist policies and tactics.

The American delegation, unfamiliar with the complexities of European minority problems and inexperienced in world Zionist politics, had come to the London conference without any plans regarding these issues. Nevertheless it played an outstanding role at the sessions and Brandeis emerged as a central figure. Brandeis' appeal for a constructive economic policy was enthusiastically supported by a number of European Zionists. He outlined a three-year plan of economic and financial aid to Palestine, to be realized with the cooperation of Lord Melchett, Lord Reading and Lord Rothschild.

Brandeis' critics, both in Europe and in the United States, complained that he was totally indifferent to Zionist ideology. They insisted that political Zionism did not end with the Balfour Declaration and the British Mandate. They stressed the need for continuing and intensifying Zionist propaganda and educational work.

The ensuing conflict, referred to by some as "Pinsk versus Washington" (meaning Weizmann and Brandeis), went deeper than the relatively superficial difference between "economism" and "politics." Weizmann declared that this was not "a mere dissension over formal matters." The Brandeis group argued that the Zionist Organization should now become an exclusively economic instrumentality; since its political functions had been discharged with the Mandate, they did not see why non-Zionists devoted to the development of Palestine could not now become members of the Zionist Organization.

Weizmann's point of view was that the dispute concerned "much more than program and method; its source was a deeper divergence in what might be called folkways. It reached into social and historic as well as economic and political concepts; it was connected with the organic interpretation of Zionism." Others condemned Brandeis and his group for regarding Zionism only as a means of rendering financial and economic aid to settle needy Jews in Palestine and for disregarding those objectives of the movement which were concerned with a renascence of the Jewish people all over the world.

These disagreements had an economic repercussion. The resolution to establish the Keren Hayesod (Palestine Foundation Fund) did not receive the endorsement of the American delegation, which preferred to depend on private initiative and donations rather than on public or mass collections.

In the elections for a World Zionist Executive a compromise was suggested: that instead of a president, a triumvirate consisting of Weizmann, Brandeis and Sokolow be appointed. Brandeis refused and Weizmann was elected president, with Brandeis as honorary chairman, of the World Zionist Organization. He was the only American delegate elected to the Executive. After the delegation's return to the United States the rift widened between Brandeis and his opponents. Louis Lipsky, representing the opposition to Brandeis, resigned from the Executive Board of the ZOA.

In the meantime Palestine was experiencing a severe economic crisis and the Zionist Organization was forced to concentrate its efforts on the *aliyah* (immigration) program. The Keren Hayesod, of which much had been expected, accomplished very little because of the Brandeis administration's coolness to the National Funds (Keren Hayesod and Keren Kaye-

Courtesy Zionist Organization of America

MORRIS ROTHENBERG (1885-1950), **FORMER PRESIDENT OF ZOA**

met). The World Zionist Executive decided to step in and sent to America a delegation consisting of Chaim Weizmann, Shmaryahu Levin, Menachem Ussishkin, Professor Albert Einstein (to raise funds for the Hebrew University) and Ben-Zion Mossinson (to enlist support for elementary Hebrew schools).

The delegation was received with great enthusiasm by American Jewry when it arrived in New York at the beginning of April 1921. The American Zionist Executive, on the other hand, greeted it with a memorandum stating that national Zionist organizations were autonomous federations and that the only function of the World Zionist Organization was to serve as a coordinating body, without the power to intervene in the internal affairs of its constituent bodies. As to economic problems, the Brandeis administration was firm in its espousal of private initiative and individual enterprise.

Prolonged negotiations ensued between the administration and the delegation, with no tangible results. Chaim Weizmann, as president of the World Zionist Executive, demanded the formal establishment of the Keren Hayesod in the United States. At the ZOA convention in Cleveland (June 1921) an open contest developed between the Brandeis faction (including Julian W. Mack, Felix Frankfurter, Stephen S. Wise, and Abba Hillel Silver) and the opposition (Louis Lipsky, Emanuel Neumann, Morris Rothenberg, Abraham Goldberg, and others), with the latter group winning by a vote of 153 to 71. The Brandeis group promptly resigned their offices and formed a separate organization of a purely economic character. Louis Lipsky became chairman of the council and subsequently president of the ZOA, a post he held for a number of years.

Courtesy Zionist Organization of America

LOUIS LIPSKY, ZIONIST LEADER

The new administration soon achieved a great political victory when the Congress of the United States in 1921 ratified the British Mandate over Palestine. Another problem engaging its attention at this time was the resolution (January 1924) to establish a Jewish Agency for Palestine, to be composed of an equal number of Zionists and non-Zionists. Discussions on this project went on until August 1929, when final agreement was reached in Zürich, Switzerland. As the Jewish Agency was then envisaged, membership was evenly divided between Zionists and non-Zionists (112 each), with 44 of the non-Zionist seats reserved for America. The Jewish Agency suffered several severe set-backs right at the start. The first blow was the almost immediate death of Louis Marshall, for many years president of the American Jewish Committee and the leading non-Zionist in the Agency. The ranks of the non-Zionists abroad were also thinned by death and retirement, and gradually the Jewish Agency became an arm of the World Zionist Organization.

By the end of the 20's, the Zionist Organization of America again faced severe difficulties. The economic situation in Palestine and the bloody Arab outbreaks of 1929 had cast a pall on the entire movement.

The crisis brought about a rapprochement between the administration and the Brandeis group, although some of its leaders had already returned to the ZOA ranks (Abba Hillel Silver, Stephen S. Wise, Julian W. Mack). Peace was officially restored in 1930 at the convention in Cleveland, where a coalition administration was elected. Hadassah and its president, Henrietta Szold, deserve some of the credit for the reconciliation.

2. LABOR ZIONISM

As has been stated previously, Poale Zion gained ground and increased its membership during World War I. It played a primary role in the creation of the People's Relief Committee, in the American Jewish Congress movement and in recruitment for the Jewish Legion. From the first American Labor Zionists had maintained close contact with Palestine labor. This contact was strengthened when a number of labor leaders fled to the United States from Palestine, to avoid persecution by the Turkish authorities (David Ben Gurion, Isaac Ben Zevi, Pinchas Rutenberg, Solomon Kaplansky, Berl Locker and Leon Chasanovich; Ber Borochov came to the United States directly from Europe and returned to Russia in 1917). Their influence was particularly felt in the Jewish Legion movement, which was essentially the achievement of the Poale Zion in the United States.

No less important was the Poale Zion's share in launching the Hehalutz (pioneer) movement. In 1906 the first training group for practical work in Palestine was formed in the United States. (In Russia the same project was launched almost simultaneously.) A few years later Haikar Hatzair set up its first *Hachsharah* (training) farm in California. In 1915 and 1916 David Ben Gurion and Isaac Ben Zevi tried to inject new life into the Hehalutz movement in the United States but soon had to abandon this task in favor of recruiting for the Jewish Legion. After the war, when halutzism was adopted by other Zionist groups as well, the Poale Zion youth still remained in the vanguard of the movement.

Poale Zion was the first Jewish labor group to found Jewish schools with Yiddish and Hebrew as the language of instruction, and with a socialist and Zionist content. The first of these schools was organized in 1910. The Jewish Teachers Seminary was established in New York in 1917. Several years later the Farband and Poale Zion began to build summer camps for children and adults. A daily newspaper, *Di Tsait,* was launched in 1920 but survived only 16 months.

At the first world conference of the Poale Zion in Vienna (summer of 1920) catastrophe threatened with the withdrawal of a large segment of the Russian and Polish members, who then formed the Left Poale Zion. There was no immediate split in the ranks of the American Poale Zion, but at the end of 1920, when the party held its convention in Pittsburgh, a proposal was made by the left-wing group to join the Third International. The resolution was defeated, and the left wing walked out and formed its own party. Years later, when their ranks were increased by members of the Palestine Ahdut Haavodah then living in the United States (1947), they organized the United Labor Zionist Party—Ahdut Haavodah in the United States and Canada.

A membership increase compensated the Right Poale Zion for the losses suffered through the split. Most Socialist Territorialists had gradually been absorbed by Poale Zion and by 1938 only a small group remained, reorganized under the name of Freeland League.

An important achievement of the Poale Zion was the organization of the National Labor Committee for Palestine (Geverkshaften Kampein). During World War I the Poale Zion had tried to interest non-Zionist labor elements in the Jewish development of Palestine, convoking a labor assembly in New York (June 1918), in which a number of trade union leaders participated. Despite their issuing a statement hailing the development of a Jewish homeland in Palestine, these labor leaders were unable to effect harmony between Jewish labor and the Zionist movement. "In the early Twenties," writes the veteran labor leader and chairman of the Geverkshaften Kampein, Joseph Schlossberg, "anti-Palestine feeling was dominant among the Jewish laboring masses of America."

In the summer of 1923 the Histadrut ha-Obedim of Palestine (General Federation of Jewish Labor in Israel), which had been founded in 1920, appealed to American Zionist labor leaders and to the United Hebrew Trades for material and moral support. At a conference of Jewish labor unions and organizations it was resolved to launch a drive for the Histadrut. The resulting campaign was notable in that it finally bridged the gap between American Jewish labor and Palestine. The first Geverkshaften Kampein raised $51,000; the thirtieth (in 1953) $3,000,000. In the three decades since its inception, the Kampein has raised more than $35,000,000. It has also accomplished, under the leadership of Isaac Hemlin, much in the field of public opinion and in the mobilization of political assistance for Palestine, especially from the C.I.O. and the A.F. of L.

The League for Labor Palestine, another creation (1935) of the Poale Zion, merged with the party in 1946. Young Poale Zion (1920), after merging with the Zeirei Zion of the Gordonia group (1932), changed its name to Habonim. The women's group, Pioneer Women, was founded in 1925. In 1932 the American faction of the World Union of Hitachdut —Zeire Zion—Zionist-Socialists joined the Poale Zion.

3. MIZRACHI AND REVISIONISTS

A sector of Orthodox Jewry in the United States had adopted an affirmative stand toward Zionism from the very first (see pp. 154-5). In 1903, one year after the creation of Mizrachi in Europe, an American group was formed in New York, to be followed by similar groups in other cities in the United States—all of which joined the American Zionist Federation. On the whole the movement was weak until 1914, and the isolated groups in New York, St. Louis and Pittsburgh were rather inactive. At the close of 1913 Rabbi Meyer Berlin came to the United States following Mizrachi's decision to form a world union. At the first national convention of the American Mizrachi (1914) approximately 30 groups were represented.

During the war years the party grew rapidly and at its third national convention (1916) there were 101 participating groups. The Mizrachi Teachers Institute, which was founded in 1917 upon the initiative of Rabbi Meyer Berlin, became in 1921 the third department of the Yeshiva Rabbi Isaac Elchanan (now Yeshiva University).

The Mizrachi Hatzair, later changed to Hapoel Hamizrachi, was formed in 1921. It maintained close ties with its namesake in Palestine and evolved its own theories of religious socialism, rejecting the Marxist approach for Torah ve-Avodah (Torah and Labor). Although a number of Mizrachi leaders and eminent rabbis looked with favor upon the religious halutzism of Hapoel Hamizrachi, dissension broke out between the two groups and each formed its own world union—the Iggud ha-Olami of Mizrachi, and the Brit Olamit of Hapoel Hamizrachi. In theory both are united under the Merkaz Olami.

The ideological and organizational schism between the two largest Mizrachi organizations had its effect on the religious Zionist youth movement. The religious socialist youth organization Bnei Akiba (affiliated with Hashomer Hadati) was formed in the United States in 1939. It has its own halutz group. In 1940 Mizrachi decided to create a general Mizrachi youth organization, Hanoar Hamizrachi (Noam). In 1946 a branch was organized in the United States.

Shortly after the creation of the Revisionist World Union a branch of the organization was formed in the United States (1925), later calling itself the New Zionist Organization of America. The Revisionist youth organized as the Brith Trumpeldor (Betar). In the United States, following the European precedent, some of the Revisionists formed the Jewish State Party (1933). During World War II and the years of the struggle for the State of Israel, the Revisionists in the United States were extremely active.

XV. THE FIGHT AGAINST ANTI-SEMITISM AND NAZISM

Until 1920 the problem of anti-Semitism in the United States presented little cause for alarm to the Jewish organizations in the country. The American Jewish Committee, which since its creation in 1906 had sought to fight for Jewish rights and defend Jews against discrimination and prejudice, worked primarily on behalf of Jews abroad. When anti-Semitic incidents increased during the first decade of this century, B'nai B'rith formed a special committee, the Anti-Defamation League (ADL), which in 1913 became an autonomous body. In its four decades of service the ADL developed a great and vigorous activity in combating discrimination against ethnic, racial and religious minorities, in fighting the totalitarianisms of communism and fascism, and in promoting intercultural education and interreligious co-operation. The ADL works not only through its national offices but also through twenty-eight regional offices in key American cities, utilizing the mass media of communication as well as the direct approach of community and neighborhood relations.

After the war foreign anti-Semitic literature found its way to the United States, including the infamous *Protocols of the Elders of Zion,* which had appeared in English translation in 1920. From 1920 to 1927 *The Dearborn Independent,* published by Henry Ford, featured a series of anti-Semitic articles, a number of which later appeared in book form under the title *The International Jew.* The anti-Catholic, anti-Negro, anti-Jewish Ku Klux Klan flourished in the 1920's. In 1928 the Jews in a small town (Massena) in upper New York State were actually accused of ritual murder, but fortunately the incident passed without mishap and with an apology.

In 1927 Ford wrote an open letter to Louis Marshall retracting his vicious allegations and promising that he would not allow further distribution or reproduction of *The International Jew*. This followed a lawsuit and a sharp decline of Ford sales among Jews.

But it was with the rise of Hitler in 1933 that anti-Semitism began to loom as a real danger in the United States. Still, it was not so much the threat of domestic anti-Semitism as the brutal persecution of the Jews in Germany that aroused American Jewry. Mass protest meetings were held, public opinion was appealed to, and the United States and other governments were asked to apply pressure against Germany.

United though all Jewish organizations were in their desire to awaken the world to the menace of Nazism, there was nevertheless a divergence of opinion as to method. Both B'nai B'rith and the American Jewish Committee regarded it as a tactical error to convert the fight against Nazism into a purely Jewish concern instead of making it an issue of democracy versus terror and dictatorship. The American Jewish Congress, on the other hand, issued an appeal for public demonstrations and launched a boycott campaign in September 1933 against German goods. The Congress action was supported by the Jewish Labor Committee, founded in 1934 to help the victims of Nazism and Fascism. Later B'nai B'rith reversed its stand and joined in the boycott effort.

The Jewish organizations also strove to establish unity in the fight against domestic anti-Semitism. In 1933 B'nai B'rith, the American Jewish Committee and the American Jewish Congress formed a Joint Consultative Council for this purpose. The Council was short-lived but was revived in 1938, at which time the Jewish Labor Committee joined it. This second Council also had a brief career. It was not until 1944 that the more successful National Community Relations Advisory Council (NCRAC) was established.

Methods of combatting anti-Semitism and discrimination underwent a change in the decade between 1930 and 1940. Traditional apologetics and polemic were found to be ineffectual. Emphasis was increasingly placed on "inter-group relations"— the establishment of good relations with non-Jewish organizations and institutions and the common fight for democracy and against bigotry and totalitarianism. Local Jewish community relations committees were established in many cities throughout the country.

At the beginning of 1950 the NCRAC undertook a survey of the methods employed and the results achieved by its national and local affiliates. The task of compiling data and evaluating the material was assigned to Professor Robert McIver, a well-known non-Jewish sociologist of Columbia University. At the end of 1951 Professor McIver submitted his findings: lack of cooperation among the various member organizations; jurisdictional disputes due to overlapping; duplication of work; competition for funds. Professor McIver recommended that a standing committee be appointed to guard against these faults, and that specialized agencies be assigned responsibility in their particular areas, i.e., that investigation of discrimination in labor be assigned to the Jewish Labor Committee, relations with veterans to the Jewish War Veterans, relations with churches and religious groups to the synagogue unions, etc.

Heated controversy followed the McIver report. While the American Jewish Committee and the B'nai B'rith opposed the report as leading to an unacceptable central authority, the other members of the Council accepted it in principle with some individual reservations. The opponents of the McIver recommendations pointed out that the Council had, heretofore, been only an advisory body. If the McIver recommendations were to be accepted, the Council would be vested with greater power and authority.

The American Jewish Committee and B'nai B'rith finally withdrew from the NCRAC. It is too early to predict the consequences of this issue upon the future development and activities of the Jewish defense agencies.

XVI. WORLD WAR II

Even more than in World War I, the tragedy of European Jewry and the threat to Palestine spurred American Jewish organizations to seek closer cooperation. In 1939 an Emergency Committee for Zionist Affairs was formed. As an arm of the World Zionist Organization, the Committee made representations in connection with Palestine and the restrictions on Jewish immigration imposed by the British White Paper of May 1939.

The Extraordinary Zionist Conference of May 9-11, 1942, in the Hotel Biltmore, New York, resulted in the adoption of the historic document which has since become known as the Biltmore Platform. The convention condemned the White Paper, demanded approval for the formation of a Jewish army to fight under its own flag alongside other Allied forces, and appealed for unrestricted Jewish immigration to Palestine and the establishment of a Jewish state. Every Zionist organization in the United States subsequently endorsed the Biltmore Platform with the exception of Hashomer Hatzair and the Ihud Party, both of which favored a bi-national state.

For the better coordination of Zionist activities in America reorganization of the Emergency Committee was indicated. This was achieved in August 1943. The reorganized Zionist Council comprised the ZOA, Poale Zion, Hadassah and Mizrachi, and was later joined by Hapoel Hamizrachi, the Left Poale Zion, Hashomer Hatzair and the Revisionists. Rabbi Stephen S. Wise was elected chairman, and Rabbi Abba Hillel Silver vice-chairman.

Using all possible means to arouse public opinion—demonstrations, mass meetings, petitions to the Congress, articles and appeals in the press—the Jews of America demanded that steps be taken to end the Nazi murders. Neutral countries were urged to open their doors to Jewish refugees and save them from Hitler; Jewish writers and communal leaders protested the indifference of the Allies to the fate of Europe's Jews.

At the Anglo-American Conference in Bermuda (April 1943) to deal with the refugee question, three Jewish organizations presented memoranda on the problem. The Conference adopted no resolutions that could affect the issue and the British government announced its determination to keep the White Paper in effect.

For a time Rabbi Silver and his group were the driving force in the Zionist Council. The Silver policies led to dissatisfaction among other Zionists, coming to a head when the pro-Zionist resolution of Senators Robert Wagner and Robert Taft was again tabled by the Senate (December 1944). Dr. Stephen S. Wise and his group blamed Dr. Silver for this setback, attributing it to untactful relations with the State Department. Both Stephen Wise and Abba Hillel Silver resigned from the Council as a result of their clash. After reorganization, the Council elected Stephen Wise as sole chairman. But Zionist public opinion was mostly on the side of Silver and in July 1945 a reconciliation was effected and he returned to the Council as co-chairman.

While the fight for a Jewish state and unrestricted immigration to Palestine was being waged a no less energetic campaign for the establishment of a Jewish army was being fought. David Ben Gurion came to the United States in November 1941 for the special purpose of obtaining Jewish support for the project. In July 1942 a group of American Zionist leaders sent an urgent cable to Prime Minister Winston Churchill, urging the immediate mobilization for military training of all able-bodied Jews in Palestine. The Revisionists called a Conference to Save the Jewish People of Europe (New York, July 1943), an undertaking in which they had the support of a great many non-Jewish public figures. The Conference demanded unrestricted immigration to Palestine and the creation of a Jewish state. Later, the tactics of the Emergency Committee for the Rescue of European Jews caused a number of national Jewish organizations to disavow the organization.

The campaign of the Hebrew Committee of National Liberation took on an even more sensational form. It was led by Peter Bergson (Hillel Kook) who set up an "Embassy" of the "Hebrew People" in Washington, demanding a "co-belligerent status." After several years of tempestuous propaganda the committee closed its Washington office.

In 1939-1940 the Mizrachi and Agudat Israel jointly formed the Vaad Hatzalah to rescue Jews from Nazi-occupied Europe, arrange their emigration to other countries and help them to settle in their new homes. After the war the Vaad continued its work among the survivors, founding synagogues, schools and yeshivas, caring for orphans, aiding in emigration, providing for religious needs, etc. Hadassah dedicated itself to medical and social service work, especially in connection with the Youth Aliyah (immigration) to Palestine. The Labor Zionist organizations concentrated on helping the "illegal" immigration to Palestine, assistance to the Jewish underground defense (Haganah) and material aid to the workers in Palestine.

The most ambitious attempt by American Jews to establish a coordinating body for relief work and political representation at the future Peace Conference was the creation of the American Jewish Conference. The initiative came from B'nai B'rith, particularly its president, the late Henry Monsky. Early in 1943 representatives of 32 Jewish national bodies resolved to convoke an American Jewish Assembly, for the purpose of arriving at a common program for the peace negotiations and post-war problems. After long hesitation both the American Jewish Committee and Jewish Labor Committee agreed to join the Assembly on condition that it be called a conference and that it be disbanded as soon as it had accomplished its mission.

The first session of the American Jewish Conference took place from August 29 to September 2, 1943, with the participation of 502 delegates from local Jewish bodies and 123 from 65 national Jewish organizations. Almost every political and religious trend was represented. The Conference drew up a list of demands in connection with Nazi persecutions and the refugee problem:

1. Trial of the Nazi war-criminals;

2. Establishment of an international tribunal to try the cases of the war-criminals and issue a warning to the Nazis that their crimes would be severely punished;

3. Permission for "illegal" entrants to remain in Palestine;

4. Assistance to the victims of Nazism to emigrate to neutral countries;

5. Creation of a special international commission to arm and organize Jewish self-defense groups in Nazi-occupied territories.

The Conference also adopted, by an overwhelming majority, a Palestine resolution urging:

1. Establishment of a Jewish Commonwealth;

2. Abrogation of the British White Paper;

3. Vesting the Jewish Agency with the authority to regulate immigration to Palestine.

Two organizations abstained from voting on the resolution—the Jewish Labor Committee and the National Council of Jewish Women. The American Jewish Committee voted against the resolution and withdrew from the Conference, issuing a public statement (October 1943):

"We believe that the problems of world Jewry cannot be solved by a single political panacea [meaning by this the Zionist program] but only through concentrated efforts to obtain security for Jews all over the world." It is to be noted that the three organizations in question had all actively opposed the White Paper. Some of the members and affiliated organizations of the American Jewish Committee resigned in protest against the withdrawal.

The activity of Jewish organizations and the pressure of public opinion induced President Franklin D. Roosevelt, in January 1944, to establish the War Refugee Board and vest it with sufficient power to carry out various rescue programs. Bills urging the rescue of European Jews were presented in both Houses of Congress. Several Jewish groups drew up memoranda on post-war rehabilitation and an international Bill of Rights, which they submitted to the United States government in 1944 and 1945.

The date of the proposed United Nations Conference in San Francisco to discuss post-war plans was approaching. Jewish organizations in the United States made strenuous efforts to gain representation at the Conference. In April 1945 Secretary of State Edward R. Stettinius extended an invitation to 42 national organizations in the United States to send representatives to San Francisco as consultants to the American delegation. The Jewish organizations invited were the American Jewish Conference and the American Jewish Committee. The Jewish Agency, backed by the American Zionist Emergency Council, wished to attend the Conference as the representative of the Jewish people, but it was not invited.

The San Francisco Conference yielded meager benefits for the Jews. One of their chief demands, for an international Bill of Human Rights, was approved and the proposal was included in principle in the United Nations Charter, with a provision that a special Commission of Human Rights be instructed to study the matter and make recommendations for the implementation of such a Bill. The second demand, regarding Palestine, had been presented in the hope of forestalling any decisive action by the United Nations (among whom there were five Arab members) which might be inimical to the Jewish interest in that country. However, since it was decided that the British Mandate was to remain in effect, the question of a Jewish state was not even placed on the Conference agenda.

In February 1946 the question of making the American Jewish Conference a permanent body was raised. A number of the larger national organizations were strongly opposed to the suggestion, and the Conference was finally dissolved in January 1949.

XVII. THE ZIONIST MOVEMENT SINCE WORLD WAR II

The question of a Jewish state took precedence over all other problems on the Zionist agenda. Once this was achieved, there would be time to consider reciprocal relations between the State and the Zionist movement abroad, and the latter's adaptation to the changed conditions.

Rabbi Abba Hillel Silver had gained greatly in popularity after his return to the American Zionist Emergency Council in July 1945. Under his leadership a militant policy toward Washington was carried out. In November 1945 the ZOA elected him president. A year later the ZOA repudiated the British partition plan and reaffirmed its demand for all of Palestine as a Jewish state (the Biltmore Platform). This was an indirect criticism of the Jewish Agency, which had given its approval to the partition plan.

In May 1943, the Jewish Agency had established an American Section, with offices in Washington, under the direction of Nahum Goldmann. At the World Zionist Conference in London two years later

(August 1945) it was decided to reorganize the American Section. The Agency representation in the United States, which had formerly consisted only of Nahum Goldmann and Louis Lipsky, was increased to include Rabbi Abba Hillel Silver and Stephen S. Wise. The four large Zionist bodies (ZOA, Poale Zion, Mizrachi and Hadassah) were represented on the Jewish Agency Executive by Israel Goldstein, Hayim Greenberg, Leon Gellman and Mrs. Rose Halprin, respectively. In 1946 the World Zionist Congress appointed Rabbi Silver as chairman of the American Section of the Agency.

At the Twenty-second World Zionist Congress in Basle (December 1946)—the first since the outbreak of the war—the United States delegation represented half of all shekel-holders throughout the world. The Congress was faced with two grave problems: whether to accept or reject the partition plan, and whether to attend or boycott the London round-table conference on Palestine, sponsored by the British government. Most of the American delegation belonged to the Silver-Neumann group (the "activists") and were opposed both to the partition plan and to participation in the round-table negotiations. The "conservatives"—notably Chaim Weizmann, Nahum Goldmann and Stephen S. Wise—were defeated by the coalition led by Silver, Neumann, Ben Gurion, Moshe Sneh and Bernard Joseph.

The Americans elected to the new World Zionist Executive (from which Chaim Weizmann resigned) were Rabbi Silver, Emanuel Neumann, Hayim Greenberg, Mrs. Halprin and Rabbi Wolf Gold (Mizrachi). During the critical years between 1945 and 1949 the Silver-Neumann group dominated General Zionist policies in the United States.

The United States government had a vacillating policy on Palestine during that period. The strongly pro-Zionist resolution introduced in the House of Representatives by Joseph W. Martin, and in the

Courtesy Yiddish Scientific Institute (YIVO), New York

HAYIM GREENBERG (1889-1953), POALE ZION
LEADER AND WRITER

Senate by Robert Wagner and Robert Taft, was finally passed by a great majority in December 1945. But almost at the same time (October 1945), the correspondence between the late Franklin D. Roosevelt and King Ibn Saud was made public and revealed how eager the United States was for Arab good-will. Acting on behalf of the American Zionist Emergency Council, Rabbi Silver and Rabbi Wise protested vigorously to Secretary of State Byrnes.

Though the victory of the Labor Party in England (July 1945) was hailed with delight by the Zionists, disillusionment soon followed. The new British government offered the Jewish Agency a monthly immigration quota of 1,500, in accord with the terms of the White Paper. The anti-Zionist policy of the new Foreign Minister, Ernest Bevin, became increasingly apparent. The British government did not accept the recommendation of the Anglo-American Committee of Inquiry on Palestine (April 1946) that 100,000 Jewish refugees be admitted to Palestine. This was a further blow to the Zionists, who reacted with intense criticism. The intensity of anti-British feeling among American Zionists, and Jews generally, during this period was demonstrated during Bevin's visit to the United States in February 1949. Picket lines, letters of protest, and other demonstrations marked his stay.

In January 1947 Neumann stated that American Jews were prepared to contribute millions of dollars to finance illegal immigration to Palestine. Previously, in July 1946, the Zionist Council had announced that the Haganah resistance against the Mandatory authorities in Palestine had its fullest support. When the Palestine question was scheduled for discussion in the United Nations Special Committee on Palestine the Zionist organizations empowered the Jewish Agency to act as their representative. Rabbi Silver, as chairman of the Agency's American Section, delivered a historic speech before the United Nations in May 1947.

The uncertain policy of the United States demanded constant vigilance on the part of the Zionists. After the United States had agreed to the partition plan, its United Nations delegate, Warren R. Austin, issued a statement (March 1948) which indicated a complete reversal in American policy—back to a temporary Mandate. The American Zionist Council protested and proclaimed a day of mass demonstrations and prayer. A number of non-Zionist organizations joined the protest meetings as a gesture of solidarity with the Zionists: the Jewish War Veterans, the Union of Orthodox Rabbis, the Rabbinical Assembly of America and the Agudat Israel. In his memoirs, Weizmann paid tribute to the prominent Zionists and non-Zionists in the United States who helped the cause during this critical period through personal interventions with United Nations delegates and representatives of the United States Government.

It is still too early to assess how far—if at all—Jewish and Zionist influence affected President Harry S. Truman's historic decision to grant de facto recognition to the State of Israel, a matter of minutes after its declaration of independence on May 14, 1948. On January 31, 1949, Truman recognized Israel de jure, and the Export and Import Bank was authorized to extend credit to the new state in the amount of $100,000,000.

American Jews supported Israel's war of independence with money, materiel and man-power. The expert know-how contributed by American Jewish soldiers and technical specialists, and the political support of American Jewry, were invaluable assets.

Following the establishment of the State of Israel, the enthusiasm of American Jews receded slowly. After years of excitement and tension, there was a marked let-down in Zionist affairs. The old internal frictions again made themselves felt. Although Neumann had been re-elected president of the ZOA in 1948, it was evident that the opposition had gained strength. A Committee for Progressive Zionism, headed by Stephen S. Wise, Solomon Goldman, Louis Lipsky and Louis E. Levinthal, among others, criticized the administration, and Silver and Neumann both resigned from their Jewish Agency and ZOA posts.

In recent years there has been a trend toward compromise between the two camps. Rabbi Irving Miller was elected president of the ZOA in 1952 and again in 1953. The Miller administration, in which all ZOA factions are represented, has had as one of its chief aims the maintenance of peace within the ranks.

The establishment of the State of Israel has had the perhaps paradoxical result of creating serious problems for the Zionist movement.

The major goal of Zionism was the achievement of a Jewish National Home.

EMBASSY OF ISRAEL, WASHINGTON, D. C.

Now that this has been accomplished, Zionist bodies abroad must rethink their *raison d'être*. Financial and political support for Israel has passed out of the exclusively Zionist realm. Most of the money raised for Israel comes from non-Zionist sources and political aid has also ceased to be a Zionist monopoly. There is a school of thought that public relations and the promotion of halutziut (emigration of pioneers to Israel) should now constitute the chief work of the Zionist movement. Others feel that ideological reorientation and adaptation will come about naturally and automatically, and that there is consequently no need for immediate reorganization.

The organizational problem presents difficulties. If Israeli politics are the concern of the Israelis, and financial and public re-

lations work are the responsiblity of such organizations as the United Jewish Appeal, what activities are left for the World Zionist Organization? At its Twenty-third Congress (Jerusalem, August 1951) the World Zionist Organization asked for recognition by Israel as the official liaison between the State and the Diaspora Jewry, especially with regard to immigration and reconstruction work. Non-Zionist organizations, particularly the American Jewish Committee, objected to singling out one body to represent world Jewry. The Prime Minister of Israel, David Ben Gurion, announced that Israel would deal with all Jewish organizations offering cooperation.

There has been heated discussion of the question whether and how far Zionists abroad are entitled to influence in Israel's internal affairs. The question became most acute during the elections in Israel when the Silver-Neumann group gave active support to the Israeli General Zionists. Such men as Louis Lipsky disapproved, calling it unwarranted interference in the internal affairs of Israel. Hadassah also objected. The new ZOA administration's stand in the matter was summed up in Rabbi Miller's statement that the ZOA had nothing to do with the internal political affairs of Israel, which were the concern only of the citizenry of that country. Miller's statement was an indirect reply to the charges of dual allegiance which had been renewed against American Zionists since the creation of the State of Israel.

Another immediate problem was the need for reorganization of the Zionist movement and the Jewish Agency to avoid duplication of work.

A plan to consolidate all Zionist organizations within the framework of an alliance or federation, with each party retaining its own autonomy, was seriously considered. Many believed that the existing American Zionist Council could serve the purpose, provided that its jurisdiction and functions were extended. Others vehemently objected. There is also a plan under consideration to remodel the Jewish Agency along the lines initially mapped out for it, i.e., to admit prominent non-Zionists in addition to Zionists.

A reorganization of the Labor Zionist Party—Poale Zion took place in January 1946, when the old guard in the administration was charged with neglecting the English-speaking elements in the party. A new administration was elected and new plans were made for greater participation in Jewish life in the United States and the general politics of the country. The philosophy of the party was deepened, particularly by Hayim Greenberg, and the organization expanded under the leadership of Louis Segal who, after Greenberg's death, became a representative (along with B. Zuckerman) of LZOA in the Jewish Agency.

Labor Zionism also faced the need to reorganize and unify all four of its bodies: Poale Zion, Farband, Pioneer Women and Habonim. In 1949 each group appointed a commission to work out a reorganization plan along the lines of one of the following alternatives:

1. Amalgamation of all four organizations (with full autonomy retained by the insurance department of the Farband and by the Pioneer Women);

2. Creation of a central organization for financial affairs and relations with other organizations, otherwise leaving the four constituent bodies autonomous;

3. Creation of a Labor Zionist federation;

4. Coordination of the political and cultural activities of the four organizations.

In 1952 a plan was ratified to create a central council for all four organizations.

The situation within the American Mizrachi became critical after the creation of the State as a result of the organization's policy with regard to various problems of the religious bloc in Israel. It supported the Israeli Mizrachi and the American and Israeli Agudat Israel on the question of religious instruction in the *maabarot* (transition camps for new immigrants). It also protested against the prosecution of the religious extremists in Israel who were accused of trying to blow up the Knesset (Parliament) building in Jerusalem. But it disagreed with the Agudah's opposition to the unification of schools in Israel and the mobilization of Orthodox girls for national service, and severely criticized its protest demonstrations against the government. Mizrachi's decision to found the Bar-Ilan Unversity in Israel caused a new clash with the Agudah, which objected that the university would not be religious enough.

The Revisionist Organization (renamed the New Zionist Organization after 1935, and the United Zionist Revisionists of America in 1946) suffered a severe blow in the death of its founder and leader,

Vladimir Zhabotinsky, in 1940. During World War II and later, the Revisionist Party and its affiliate, the American League for a Free Palestine, advocated terrorist tactics against the Mandate authorities and were closely identified with the Irgun Zvai Leumi and the Herut movements. After the merger of the Jewish State Party with the Revisionist Organization, Meir Grossmann was elected president. Speaking in the name of his organizaton at the Twenty-second World Zionist Congress in Basle (1950), Grossmann urged militant action to obtain "a Jewish State within its ancient, historic boundaries." In 1953 Grossmann and a group of his followers abandoned the Revisionists for the General Zionist Party (he had settled in Palestine in the meantime), causing great consternation in the ranks of the Revisionists in the United States.

XVIII. NON-ZIONISM AFTER WORLD WAR II

During the struggle for Israel and the early years of the young State most of the larger Jewish organizations in the United States extended themselves to support it. When tension began to ease and enthusiasm to die down, Israel no longer dominated their activities.

The large numbers of Orthodox refugees from Eastern and Central Europe who came to the United States after the war gave new strength to the Agudah, and they gradually assumed important responsibilities in the organization. Even before the war some members of the Agudah in the U. S. had disapproved of the world organization's negative attitude toward Zionism and the creation of a secular Jewish State in Palestine, urging that it follow the example of the Mizrachi which had sponsored religious colonization in Palestine. After the war the American Agudah established the Hehalutz Haharedi to implement its own colonization

plans. It also formed a children's and youth organization (Pirhei Agudath Israel and Zeirei Agudath Israel), and a women's and girls' organization (Neshei Agudath Israel and Benot Agudath Israel). The women's and youth organizations are dedicated largely to relief work for Israel.

Although the Agudah opposed a secular Jewish state as contravening Messianic eschatology and was against the partition of Palestine for the same reason, public pressure and Jewish needs during the war and the immediate post-war years forced the organization to modify its attitude. Though it never helped politically in creating the State of Israel, once the state was established the Agudah faced the fact realistically. In Israel it joined in the coalition government, though it strongly opposed government policies on the question of religious instruction in the *maabarot*, the trial of the religious extremists for plotting against the Knesset, the clash with the Neturei Karta (the fanatical "Guardians of the City"), unification of the school system, and the mobilization of women for national service.

In 1918 the American Jewish Committee had hailed the Balfour Declaration and expressed the desire "to cooperate with those who, for historical or religious reasons, wish to create a center for Jewry in Palestine." In subsequent years the Committee endorsed the activities of the Jewish Agency without, however, engaging itself in any direct political work for Palestine. Its president, Joseph M. Proskauer, summed up the Committee's attitude in 1944:

> We endorsed the Balfour Declaration. . . . We have raised our voice for the abolition of the White Paper. . . . We do not believe that Palestine is the exclusive or the complete solution for the Jews in Europe. . . . The theory that regards the Jews of the world as constituting a "homeless people" living in "Exile" ignores the

JOSEPH M. PROSKAUER, LEADER OF THE
AMERICAN JEWISH COMMITTEE

is to betray a great concept and to create despair." In another address, in August 1953, the same speaker told his audience: "Israel as a new state is a blessed reality. I cannot and will not disassociate my religious and cultural interest from that piece of land and the people who inherited it. We are the descendants of those who made of Israel a holy place. To do this is to deny history. To do this is to cut myself adrift from my past and leave me only part of a person." Klutznick also stated the attitude of B'nai B'rith against assimilation and for Jewish survival: "Shall we be bystanders in this potent battle which may determine the characteristics of American Jewish life for generations to come, or shall we, with the vigor and intelligence of mature people who are deeply concerned with our heritage, assert our strength in one direction or another? The answers to you and to me are obvious."

stark yet happy reality that Jews are at home and should be at home in every country in which they live.

But when the dramatic struggle for the Jewish state began, the American Jewish Committee warmly supported the Zionist demands. Proskauer's successor as president, Jacob Blaustein, and a few of his colleagues, paid two visits to the young state (April 1949 and August 1950), after which Blaustein and Ben Gurion had a famous exchange of letters in which they attempted to define the extent to which loyal Jewish citizens of the United States could concern themselves with Israel.

Another great Jewish organization, B'nai B'rith, presented its views on these topics in the addresses of its president Philip M. Klutznick. "To preserve and strengthen Israel," said Klutznick in his address in June 1953, "is to sustain hope for all oppressed peoples—to permit anything else

JACOB BLAUSTEIN, LEADER OF THE
AMERICAN JEWISH COMMITTEE

It is evident that the trend in B'nai B'rith is toward a deeper commitment to Jewish culture and tradition without, however, committing itself to a nationalistic philosophy.

Reform Jewry had changed greatly in its attitude toward Zionism since the days of Rabbi Isaac Mayer Wise and the Pittsburgh Platform of 1885. In 1917 and 1918 the Central Conference of American Rabbis was still against "the new doctrine of political nationalism." In the 20's sympathy with the Zionist cause began to grow perceptibly. In 1924 the CCAR voted to participate in a non-Zionist preparatory conference for the creation of the Jewish Agency. After the creation of the Agency in 1929 the CCAR endorsed its program. In 1935, it ruled that its members individually were free to follow or reject the Zionist program. At the Convention of 1937, in Columbus, Ohio, a clearly pro-Zionist resolution was adopted: "We affirm the obligation of all Jewry to aid in its [Palestine's] upbuilding as a Jewish homeland by endeavoring to make it not only a haven of refuge for the oppressed but also a center of Jewish culture and spiritual life," and in the fight for the Jewish State it heartily endorsed the Zionist cause.

But not all Reform Jews favored this policy. In 1931, one of the leaders of the CCAR, Rabbi David Philipson, in his classic book on the Reform movement, wrote:

> This doctrine [of Zionism] the Reform Judaism rejects. It contends that the national existence of the Jews ceased when the Romans set the Temple aflame and destroyed Jerusalem. . . . Palestine is a precious memory of the past but it is not a hope of the future. With the dispersion of the Jews all over the world, the universal mission of Judaism began. The Jews are citizens and faithful sons of the land of their birth or adoption. They are a religious community, not a nation.

The advocates of a pro-Zionist orientation and the die-hard minority, who would have liked to return to the old Pittsburgh Platform, thrashed out the question at the CCAR Conference of 1942 in Atlantic City. When the CCAR adopted a resolution supporting the demand for a Jewish army in Palestine, a group of 95 rabbis publicly dissociated themselves from this policy. They were later joined by a number of lay anti-Zionists, especially by some members of the American Jewish Committee who objected to what they regarded as the Committee's excessive sympathy for Zionism. In December 1942, a new body, the American Council for Judaism, was formed and immediately set about the task of fighting the Zionist program. Its president was Lessing Rosenwald, and its executive director was Rabbi Elmer Berger. According to a statement issued by the Council in 1953, it then had a membership of 16,000. Lately it has begun to establish schools for Jewish children, with a curriculum "free from [Jewish] political propaganda, nationalism, chauvinism, racism, etatism, secularism, separatism and auto-segregation."

The Council's basic theme is determined opposition to Zionism and all other forms of nationalism and "separatism." To the Council, the Jews are a voluntary religious fellowship, and as such, should of course feel a warm bond with their coreligionists in other countries, Israel included, but as to the State of Israel itself, the attitude of the American Jew should be the same as to any other foreign country.

The Council regards all attempts to foster a bond between Israel and American Jewry as wrong and harmful, and considers Zionism to be fundamentally incompatible with good citizenship. When the State of Israel was proclaimed a split resulted in the Council. Arguing that there was now no need for the Council, Rabbi Louis Wolsey, one of its founders, proposed the dissolution of the organization. When the leadership rejected this suggestion, Wolsey resigned, taking with him a number of followers. In 1949-1950 the Council's anti-Zionist propaganda led to a clash with the National Community Relations Advisory Council, who charged that the Council's vituperation was discrediting all Jews in the eyes of the American public.

BIBLIOGRAPHY

American Jewish Year Book, Vols. 1-54.

BARON, SALO W., *Cultural Problems of American Jewry.* New York, 1939.

BARON, SALO W., *The Effect of the War on Jewish Community Life.* New York, 1942.

BERGER, ELMER, *Jewish Dilemma.* New York, 1945.

COHEN, ISRAEL, *The Zionist Movement.* New York, 1946.

DE HAAS, JACOB, *Louis D. Brandeis.* New York, 1929.

DUKER, ABRAHAM GORDON, *Jewish Community Relations.* An Analysis of the MacIver Report. New York, 1952.

EPSTEIN, MELECH, *Jewish Labor in U. S. A. (1914-1952).* New York, 1950-1953, 2 vols.

FELDMAN, A. J., SHULMAN, C. E., BLUMENFIELD, S. M., "Israel and the American Jew," *CCAR Yearbook,* Vol. LX, 1950.

First Fifty Years. History of the National Council of Jewish Women (1893-1943). New York, 1943.

FINK, REUVEN, *America and Palestine,* 2nd ed. New York, 1945.

JANOWSKY, OSCAR I., *The Jewish Welfare Board Survey.* New York, 1948.

Jewish Communal Register of New York City, 2nd ed. New York, 1918.

KAPLAN, M. M., *The Future of the American Jews.* New York, 1948.

LEAVITT, MOSES A., *The JDC Story 1914-1952.* New York, 1953.

LIPSKY, LOUIS, *Selected Works—Thirty Years of American Zionism,* Vol. I. New York, 1927.

MACIVER, ROBERT M., *Report on the Jewish Communities Relations Agencies,* section I. New York, 1951.

Mizrachi in America. New York, 1936.

POSTAL, BERNARD, "B'nai B'rith—A Century of Service," *American Jewish Year Book,* Vol. 45, 1943-1944.

Publications of The American Jewish Historical Society, XXIX, 1925.

RABINOWITZ, BENJAMIN, *The Young Men's Hebrew Associations (1854-1913).* New York, 1948.

ROSENBLATT, SAMUEL, *The History of the Mizrachi Movement.* New York, 1951.

WEIZMANN, CHAIM, *Trial and Error.* London, 1949.

WELT, MILDRED G., "The National Council of Jewish Women," *American Jewish Year Book,* Vol. 46, 1944-1945.

WISE, STEPHEN SAMUEL, *Challenging Years.* New York, 1949.

בראַון, מ. ל., „אַנשטײאונג און אַנטוויקלונג פון אידישן נאַציאָנאַלן אַרבעטער פאַרבאַנד". פאַרבאַנד זאַמלבוך, זז' 1—73.

דיווויס, משה, דרכי היהדות באמריקה. תל-אביב, תשי"ד.

דיווויס, משה, יהדות אמריקה בהתפתחותה. ניו-יורק, תשי"ד.

וואַהלינער, א., רעד., אידישער אַרבייטער יאָהר-בוך און אַלמאַנאַך. ניו-יאָרק, 1927.

לאָקער, ב., רעד., אידישער אַרבייטער יאָהר-בוך און אַלמאַנאַך. ניו-יאָרק, 1928.

סיגאַל, ל., „דער אידיש-נאַציאָנאַלער אַרבעטער פאַרבאַנד פון 1924 ביז 1945", פאַרבאַנד זאַמלבוך, זז' 263—338.

פאַט, עמנואל, יידן אין אַמעריקע — אָרגאַניזאַציעס, אינסטיטוציעס און פראָבלעמען. ניו-יאָרק, 1951.

פינסקי, דוד, סיגאַל, ל., שפיזמאַן, ל., רעד., אידיש נאַציאָנאַלער אַרבעטער פאַרבאַנד 1910—1946, זאַמלבוך. ניו-יאָרק, 1946.

צוקערמאַן ברוך, „די ראָלע פון דער ציוניסטיש סאָציאַליסטישער באַוועגונג אין אַמעריקאַנער יידנטום", פאַרבאַנד זאַמלבוך, זז' 74—140.

צינעמאַן, יעקב, די געשיכטע פון ציוניזם. ב' 2. פּאַריז, 1949.

שערמאַן, בצלאל, יידן און אַנדערע עטנישע גרופּעס אין די פאַראייניגקטע שטאַטן. ניו-יאָרק, 1948.

JEWISH COMMUNAL LIFE IN THE UNITED STATES

H. L. Lurie

I. THE AMERICAN SETTING

The evolution of Jewish communal life in the United States has been a unique event in Jewish history. In most of the past migrations resulting from persecution or expulsion, Jews came to an already settled nation, usually with an ingrained ethnic base and frequently with a state church antagonistic to religious variety. Migration to the New World was a totally different experience; an undeveloped continent was being settled by peoples of various national origins and religious and cultural backgrounds. Jews, like other people migrating to the New World during the colonial period, came to an unpopulated territory where cultural patterns were apt to be diverse and flexible.

By the time it was established as an independent nation, the United States, although predominantly Anglo-Saxon in population, was imbued with the revolutionary ideal of freedom and equality for all. To attain a population adequate for the exploitation of its undeveloped territories and its vast resources, America invited and welcomed immigrants from all lands. For most of the nineteenth century the United States received not only Anglo-Saxons but also people from Ireland, Germany and France, from Western, Central, Southern and Eastern Europe; not only Protestants but also Catholics, Jews and others. It tolerated radical experiments in community living such as those of the Oneida community, the Shakers, the Mennonites, and the Mormons, and developed new indigenous sects like Christian Science. Policies of restriction and exclusion on ethnic and racial grounds were yet to come. Though there were types of restriction and prejudices in colonial times as well as in the first century of the Republic, the general atmosphere was that of equalitarianism. During the colonial and early federal periods there was a limited immigration of Jews. The bulk of Jewish immigration arrived after 1870, when the spirit of liberalism was already beginning to ebb, although it was not until the 1920's that restriction of immigration of white people on an ethnic and national basis became the established policy of the United States. By that time Jewish communal life had established its basic character and direction.

The early settlements in the Western Hemisphere were made by people of European origin and background. The Atlantic seaboard in what is now the United States consisted of British colonies, though some regions were at first primarily Dutch, Swedish or German in population. After the American Revolution the federation of states was primarily Anglo-Saxon in language, culture and political institutions. The early settlers from Europe had come either as freemen or as indentured servants who became free after their period of service. African Negroes imported as slaves had a different status which took a Civil War to change.

Groups of people who settled in specific areas where they formed the majority population, such as the Germans in Pennsylvania (18th century) and the Swedes in Minnesota (19th c.), could, if they wished, maintain their separate language as well as their religious and cultural institutions. In the larger cities immigrants from the same country, living in close proximity, continued to use their old languages and practise the old customs while becoming adjusted to their new conditions, opportunities and responsibilities.

The perpetuation of distinctive ethnic communities was dependent upon a large number of environmental factors as well as upon the feelings and attitudes of the groups concerned. The immigrant settlements developed and continued to maintain communication in their own languages through the daily and periodical press and other forms of expression. In the early part of the 19th century, when the public school developed as the prevailing system of education, the English language became the natural medium of communication among the younger generation of the foreign-language groups. As the composition of ethnic groups began to include a larger proportion of native-born children, the English language and the related American cultural institutions tended to become dominant and to displace the language and the folkways of the immigrant sections.

The "Americanization" which confronted every immigrant was also affected by the time of his arrival, the number and character of the group with similar antecedents among whom he resided, the availability or unavailability of old-world cultural institutions in this country, whether in their original or in a modified form, the cultural milieu in which he earned his livelihood, and many other factors. Some immigrants, fleeing religious persecution, were determined to re-establish and maintain their institutions in the new land; others, disappointed with the economic and social conditions of the old country, were equally determined to throw off old habits, attitudes and associations as quickly as possible. The age of the individual immigrant was also a factor in determining how rapidly and how far the new language and culture would displace the old. The way in which the newcomers were received and the presence or absence of prejudice could check or accelerate the tempo of acculturation.

Recognition of the right of immigrants to maintain their own religious institutions and voluntary associations, coupled with the general open nature of American community life, acted favorably upon the development of social and religious institutions reflecting the needs and desires of the various immigrant groups. This was a cultural pluralism formed through cultural interaction, not a multiple group segregation. The net effect was the assimilation of new immigrants to the prevailing culture, with children assimilating more rapidly than their parents.

Shared experiences of people within a community may be transitory, ephemeral and highly impersonal, as among passengers in a subway train. The daily experience of an individual is filled with a large number of such interactions which take place by virtue of the fact that people living together in a geographical area participate in a complex of natural associations. But in addition to the relatively impersonal and transitory shared experiences, the daily life of every human being is also filled with a great number and variety of interrelationships and interactions which relate to more important personal needs and problems. Within the general community, of which every Jew is a part, both transitory and meaningful varieties of experience and interaction with many other members of the community arise in the course of work or play or civic activity.

There are, however, experiences and interactions which are limited to Jews as a group or involve relationships of Jews as such to other groups within the community. It is these more important shared experiences among Jews that we can consider as the concrete aspects of Jewish community life. These experiences are numerous, complex, and highly differentiated; Jewish communal life cannot be fitted into neat and simple categories. There are many different kinds of relationships between Jews and many varieties of Jewish communal experience, making for a patchwork quilt of association among people for whom the term "Jew" may be the only common denominator. Under the impact of the mingling and association of Americans, the term "Jew" is tending increasingly to suggest a connotation of diversity rather than uniformity for all those who may be so designated. For many Jews today it may not, as it did originally, involve a recognized pattern of religious beliefs or practices, a distinct area of residence or some concrete aspect of cultural affiliation or membership.

For a long time the New World, the land of opportunity for many people, organized its economic and social life on the basis of voluntary initiative. There existed only fragmentary or residual responsibility on the part of the state as a whole for individual welfare. The individual had political rights and civic responsibilities, but the state organized neither the economic interests nor the working life of the population. The state did not concern itself directly with the economic security of the individual, his health problems, his need for human association, or his leisure. As a result, not only did immigrant groups establish religious and cultural institutions, but they also had to maintain various instruments for dealing with the economic needs of members of their group and for their general health, welfare and social adjustment. Until the development of the public school and compulsory education even the education of the young was left primarily to the initiative of voluntary groups. In this atmosphere it was natural for any sizable group of immigrants upon arriving in this country to proceed as quickly as possible to organize not only their religious and cultural institutions, but also the numerous mutual aid, charitable and social associations growing out of their necessities and their interest.

Over the years there were various changes in the external factors influencing the character and extent of Jewish association in America. Gradually, in addition to the public school system, the nation developed other forms of general community-wide action to replace activities which had been originally within the domain of sectarian group effort—for example, large-scale commercial insurance in the twentieth century tended to displace the activities of the fraternal and mutual benefit associations of ethnic groups. Many of the new developments in social organization were the product of the New Deal of the

1930's, which came many years after the Jewish group had established a system of voluntary institutions. The substitution of state action for voluntary effort in charity, economic assistance, health programs and leisure-time activities is not complete, however, and there are still many areas in which voluntary rather than governmental action remains dominant. It will probably continue for some time as the socially sanctioned method of providing for many essential needs and services. Such group activities, however temporary in character, are a significant element in organized communal living.

From the beginning, Jewish communal life in the United States has not been an exact reproduction of the European communal organization. Immigration meant an abrupt uprooting of Jewish community life, which could never be fully transplanted or recreated in the New World. Jews from many different localities were now living together in large cities and no one European communal pattern could fit the needs of this diverse aggregation. Life in the large cities was bound to be different from the experience of the closely-knit small homogeneous communities from which the immigrants had come. Jewish immigrants, not being restricted to a ghetto or Pale of Settlement, were free to go to any area where there were prospects of earning a livelihood, although they were naturally inclined to settle in the larger urban centers of the Eastern seaboard. They were not restricted in their choice of occupation by other than economic conditions or the prejudices of employers or workers.

Given enough opportunities to share his cultural aims with a group, the immigrant could maintain the language of his forebears and set up schools for the transmission of that language to his children. Many of the groups could and did develop and maintain publications, theaters, and other cultural institutions in their own language and in accordance with their cultural backgrounds.

There were two specific obstacles hindering the perpetuation of patterns of European culture. The first was that immigrants could not establish a compulsory basis for adherence or financial support to the institutions which they founded. Unlike some European countries, the United States did not grant the right of taxation or police power to enforce adherence to any type of voluntary organization. This meant that group affiliation was completely dependent on individual consent, with no support from the body politic. A specific cultural group in a community might persuade the public school to serve as an auxiliary vehicle for cultural transmission in adding a foreign language to the curriculum, but only as secondary to the use of English. On this basis, the teaching of German or French or Hebrew has been added to the course of studies of the public schools of some cities where there is sufficient interest or demand for them.

But by far the more important obstacle to the perpetuation of a separate culture of an immigrant group in the United States was related to internal group attitudes rather than to outside pressures or restrictions. Immigrants could continue a unique style of dress or other cultural patterns but many preferred to abandon their distinctive cultural traits. The desire to be accepted, not to depart radically from the approved patterns of the surrounding population, exerted great influence on cultural change among immigrant groups. The forms if not the content of the prevailing culture began to be readily accepted as a model for the behavior of all immigrant groups.

In the first immigrant generation the feeling of being alien, which made it difficult to participate actively in the voluntary associations of other groups, the satisfaction of association with persons of similar background and cultural interests, and the high premium placed in this country upon adherence to one's religious faith worked strongly for the maintenance of group associations and group life. The history of Jewish communal life in this country, like the history of the communal life of other ethnic and national groups, is therefore the record of the establishment and maintenance of voluntary associations which continued old-world interests and traditions as adapted and modified to meet the conditions of American life.

II. THE BEGINNINGS OF JEWISH COMMUNAL LIFE

Since the primary purpose of this article is to present information covering Jewish communal activity in the United States during the 20th century, the nature of communal life in the previous 250 years of settlement will be touched upon briefly. At the present time it is estimated, on the basis of data which must be acknowledged as inexact, that there are about five million Jews in the United States. There were only about 3,000 Jews at the beginning of the 19th century, increasing through natural growth and immigration to about 50,000 by 1848 and 230,000 by 1880.

The earliest records of Jewish immigration, except for isolated individual instances, begin with the small group of Sephardic settlers who came to New Amsterdam in 1654 by way of Brazil. They were followed by others of Spanish and Portuguese origin from the early settlements in the Caribbean and South America and by immigrants from Britain and the European continent, with occasional immigrants from Eastern Europe and the Mediterranean area. In the 19th century natives of Germany and Central Europe constituted the largest segment of Jewish settlers until after the Civil War. About 1870 Jewish immigration in large numbers began to come from Eastern Europe—the Russian and Austro-Hungarian Empires and Rumania. By 1900 the estimated Jewish population had increased to approximately one million.

In the earlier period favorable pioneer conditions made for relatively easy absorption into the civic and economic life of the Eastern seaboard, and the opening up of the frontier made possible the beginning of small Jewish settlements in the midWest, the South and as far as California (by the 1850's). The earliest Jewish immigrants adjusted with relative ease to the culture and habits of the surrounding population, and the historical archives attest to the success achieved by some of them in the business, cultural and political life of the community as a whole. There were civil disabilities in some of the American colonies for Jews and for other minority religious sects, but these were gradually removed in the prevailing liberal and enlightened spirit of the time.

The early Jewish communities were relatively homogeneous in character. The immigrants of Ashkenazic origin who came to this country in the early years became members of the established Sephardic congregations, of which the first was Shearith Israel. There is no record of other than Sephardic synagogues before 1802, when the first Ashkenazic congregation, Rodeph Shalom, was organized in Philadelphia. In many areas the number of Jewish settlers was too small for a synagogue until after immigrants began to come in greater numbers from Central Europe in the 1830's and 1840's. There was a greater variety of organizations after that period, but the group was neither too large nor the diversity too great to prevent a large amount of cooperation. Sharp divisions and social stratification were aspects of communal living which did not become significant until the last decade of the 19th century.

Formal communal associations, besides those concentrated around the synagogue, developed gradually. At first charitable effort was largely individual and unorganized, with the more successful and charitable-minded assuming personal responsibility as leaders of their congregations. Individual and mutual aid continued for many years among immigrants who were tied by bonds of local origin, acquaintance or family relationship, but the growing numbers gradually led to formal organization to replace the uncertainties of individual help. These first formal activities were the forerunners of the charitable and relief societies which were established over the years as a matter of course in centers of growing Jewish population.

In addition to relief societies, specialized forms of care were gradually developed. The first orphan asylum was established in Charleston in 1801. Shearith Israel Congregation of New York City organized the first Jewish family welfare agency, the Hebrew Benevolent Society, in 1828; the first institution for medical care was established in Cincinnati in 1850; the first home for the aged in New York City was established in 1872. These were small and modest beginnings, increasing in numbers and in size as population grew and centers like Newport, Charleston and Savannah yielded to the larger Jewish populations settling in New York, Boston, Chicago and other cities.

In the development of the traditional welfare institutions Jews generally followed the methods and procedures of their Christian neighbors, but as Henrietta Szold pointed out in 1900, Jews met their group obligations as they expected of themselves and others expected of them. They responded vigorously to the new social welfare movements developing in the United States and were soon credited with operating "model" institutions. The settlement house is an example. It began in England with Toynbee Hall in 1885, but by 1889 the United States had the College Settlement in New York and Hull House in Chicago. Four years later Jews established the Maxwell Street Settlement in Chicago; New York followed with the Educational Alliance in the teeming East Side; other cities soon had similar educational projects, established by the older elements of the Jewish group for the benefit of the newcomers. Later, the educational and cultural differences between the older and the newer immigrant were to disappear and "community centers" were to replace the "settlement house."

Before the development of the public school system, private schools were established either as adjuncts to the synagogue or separately for the purpose of transmitting the religious and cultural heritage and for secular education. The growth of the public school system gradually led to the founding of religious schools on a supplementary basis. A few all-day schools, combining secular with religious instruction, continued or were established later. Talmud Torahs on a philanthropic basis were also an early development, created primarily for the growing numbers of immigrants who were settling in the larger cities and unable to afford Jewish education for their children.

In the early years cultural activities were largely local, partly informal and partly the natural result of association of people of like interests and inclinations. The first fraternal society, the Independent Order of B'nai B'rith, was founded in New York City in 1843 by twelve German Jews. There were then eight congregations operating in New York City with little formal interrelationships among their membership. This fraternal organization was destined later to become an important basis of communal association among a considerable part of the Jewish middle class.

For many years, reflecting the character of the Jewish population, B'nai B'rith remained largely German Jewish in membership, but before the turn of the century Jewish immigrants of other origins were being absorbed in the work of this fraternal organization. As a common meeting ground for the settled and adjusted middle class and with lodges throughout the country, B'nai B'rith was responsible for the creation of a considerable number of national or regional welfare institutions for the aged, the orphaned and for the sick; it also organized local participation in national resettlement, foreign aid and other programs.

Other national fraternal organizations, some with more limited functions, were established over the years—for instance,

Independent Order Free Sons of Israel in 1849, (beneficial) Order Brith Abraham in 1859, (beneficial) Order Kesher shel Barzel in 1860 (one of whose districts established the Montefiore Home for the Aged in Cleveland in 1889), and (beneficial) Independent Order Sons of Benjamin in 1877. Local fraternal societies, lodges, benefit organizations, *landsmanshaften* and *hevras* of every description and purpose followed in large numbers, reaching their greatest activity during the early 1900's and then declining in importance or going out of business with the growth of large-scale commercial insurance. Some have continued to flourish, but with changed functions, and new forms of organization and activity have replaced many of the old colorful immigrant group activities.

With the increase of the Jewish population and the dispersal of immigrants throughout the country the number of congregations increased. The first congregation of immigrants of Russo-Polish extraction was established in New York City in 1852, followed by other congregations in New York and elsewhere as immigration from Eastern Europe rose.* By 1873 there were enough Reform congregations and sufficient interest in religious association throughout the country for the incorporation of a national body, the Union of American Hebrew Congregations. This organization, which for some decades thereafter represented the majority of the established Jewish population, not only was active in developing its own religious institutions, including Hebrew Union College (founded in 1875), but also dealt with

* Moshe Davis, "Jewish Religious Life and Institutions in America," in *The Jews: Their History, Culture, and Religion* (ed. Louis Finkelstein), Vol. I, pp. 380, 381, estimates that as early as 1872 there were twenty-nine synagogues of the Orthodox Eastern European *minhag* in New York City, and fair-sized representations in "dozens of other cities as far west as California." Davis also states that "the census of 1870 reported a count of 189 Jewish religious organizations, 152 edifices, and 73,265 sittings, an increase from 77 synagogues with a total seating capacity of 34,412 as calculated in the 1860 census."

domestic and overseas problems through the Board of Delegates of American Israelites, the forerunner of such later bodies as the American Jewish Committee and the American Jewish Congress. In 1866 and for some time afterwards, the Alliance Israélite Universelle, which had been established in France to deal on an international basis with the conditions of Jews in various parts of the world, developed American chapters.

The large-scale immigration from Eastern Europe, beginning about 1870 and becoming increasingly numerous for the next fifty years, resulted in a parallel development of Russian, Polish, Hungarian, Rumanian and other congregational groups and national associations, local charitable societies, fraternal organizations and *landsmanshaften*. About the turn of the century, when there were about one million Jews in America, Charles Bernheimer in the 1900-1901 *American Jewish Year Book* reported that there were 791 congregations, 593 charitable societies, and 415 educational and fraternal organizations. The report for that year also lists 22 national Jewish associations, including fraternal groups with lodges in every section of the country.

Differences in date of immigration, cultural background, religious belief, and economic level not only made for a multiplicity of organizations but also stimulated considerable rivalry. The sociological term, "social distance", is particularly applicable to the relations between the various Jewish native and immigrant groups in this period. It would have been vain to expect such a heterogeneous group of people to achieve a unified communal life. Acute overseas problems, like the Russian pogroms in the 1880's, did serve to bring the varied groups together for transitory purposes; but lack of understanding among the various groups, amounting at times to open antagonism, was a distinct phenomenon of Jewish life in America for most of the latter part of the 19th and well into the 20th century.* Some remnants of those underlying attitudes persist to the present day.

The stratification was economic as well as religious and cultural. Unlike many of the earlier immigrants, who were members of the middle class when they came to seek their fortunes in the New World and were soon absorbed into the American middle class, a large part of the Jewish immigration from Eastern Europe belonged to the skilled and the unskilled laboring population. Others, with a middle class background, were forced down the economic scale and entered the labor market as wage earners in poorly paid occupations. Jews from Central Europe, who had established themselves earlier, were to some extent the employers of this new immigrant group. There was therefore an economic as well as cultural cleavage to be overcome. Many of the more prosperous group, though they maintained a charitable interest in helping, did not accept the new immigrants as social equals but looked upon them as beneficiaries and dependents, belonging to a lower order of culture. They were too far removed from the days of their own struggles as immigrants to be able fully to appreciate the problems which faced the newest immigrants. Fraternal societies and social clubs set up membership qualifications which were evidence of economic as well as cultural stratification. Many years were to pass before the Reform synagogues and more especially the social clubs were to welcome the children of the

* H. Szold, "The Year", in 1900-1901 *American Jewish Year Book*, page 32: "a development, distinctly marked, that has been going on for some years, and has now culminated in many of the larger cities. In Boston, in New York, in Baltimore, in Chicago, in Philadelphia, institutions have been or are about to be created that duplicate the hospitals, the orphan asylums, the homes for the aged, established a generation or two ago. What impels this parallel movement among Russian Jews is dubious—whether the older asylums are not conducted with due regard to religious feeling; whether the social division line between the two classes is as sharp as some maintain; or whether the desire to prove their mettle exists on the part of those currently regarded as beneficiaries *par excellence*. The movement may be ill-advised—though there may be two views on the subject—it certainly is not discreditable."

Orthodox immigrants into their ranks. Only after a period of adjustment to American life and improved economic status for some members of the new group did the barriers begin to break down. Marriage between the descendants of German and of Russian immigrants are now frequent but it was not so long ago that they were considered as undesirable on both sides.

Jewish communal life during the last two decades of the 19th century showed the concrete effects of cultural differentiation and social stratification. Newcomers settled in the congested low-rent areas which became the new "ghettos" of the large metropolitan centers. The older and better established immigrants moved out of these areas to the more prosperous districts of the city and there they established their synagogues and social and fraternal clubs. New responsibilities were imposed on the charitable organizations which had been established by the older immigrants for their own disadvantaged members. The services of the relief societies, settlement houses and charitable institutions were made available to the newcomers, but for many years a gap divided the givers from the receivers of help. The gap was cultural as well as economic.

Almost from the start the new immigrants began to develop their own agencies parallel to and in competition with the older institutions. Rivalry and clannishness were rampant, and duplication of agencies grew more and more excessive. To some observers the obstacles to cooperation seemed insurmountable. They did not recognize that the processes of economic and cultural assimilation which had affected the earlier immigrants would also affect the new groups and that only time was needed to bring about a greater degree of harmony. It was not generally foreseen that the forces of American acculturation would soon stamp a common pattern on all of them. The German immigrants of the early 19th century had absorbed the earlier Sephardic elements and it would not be long before the East European immigrants and their descendants absorbed their predecessors.

III. THE CURRENT SCENE: INTRODUCTION TO AN INVENTORY OF JEWISH ORGANIZATIONAL LIFE

From fragmentary studies it is estimated that more than two-thirds of the present Jewish population were born in the United States. They are the descendants of various immigrant strains reaching back to colonial days, but they are preponderately the children of the more recent East European migration. The remaining one-third of the Jewish population was born abroad and are the living survivors of the immigration of over two and a half million Jews to this country since 1870. It is calculated that fewer than half of the immigrants who have come since that year survive and that the number will decline rapidly.

The foreign-born fall into the age group in which communal activity is greatest. Local population studies in Passaic, New Jersey (1949), and Port Chester, New York (1950)—communities with a relatively recent history of Jewish settlement—show that there are very few foreign-born under the age of 30; the native-born from 30 to 45 years of age greatly outnumber the foreign-born. The condition is reversed for those of 45 years of age and over. In another ten years the native-born will outnumber the foreign-born through the 55 year age group, and in twenty years the foreign-born will be a very small fraction of the adult Jewish population. Increasingly, therefore, Jewish communal life will be determined by the culture of the American-born population. The foreign-born group under 45 consists mainly of immigrants who have been educated in American public schools and who are close to the native-born in their general outlook.

Because of the absence of statistics the national origins of the Jewish population today are uncertain. One may guess that less than 10 percent can trace their descent to German or early Sephardic settlers, or came here from Central Europe during and after the Hitler period. The rate of natural increase (excess of births over deaths) is also not known, and is looked upon as uncertain and unpredictable. During the 20th century the Jewish population trend was upward, more on account of immigration than natural increase. Jews in this country seem to have a fairly high longevity; the birth rate, which was low in comparison with the American average, has recently taken an upward turn as part of a general increase in the birth rate. There is now a considerable surplus of births over deaths. In the absence of detailed statistics, but judging from some local studies, we have the impression that there will be a limited increase in the Jewish population of the United States through natural causes at least for several more decades.

For the purpose of considering Jewish communal activities, the term "Jew" must be broadly defined. The number involved in Jewish group activities extends considerably beyond those who adhere to Judaism or are affiliated with a synagogue. There have been wide variations in religious practices not only among the American-born descendants of immigrants, but among immigrants as well. Many of those who came during the early part of the 20th century had modified or changed their religious practices before arrival or soon afterwards. A sizable proportion were not religiously affiliated and regarded themselves as freethinkers. We therefore cannot judge the number of Jews by those who attend religious services or who give formal Jewish education to their children. Many Jews unaffiliated with religious institutions consider themselves as Jews by religion and when there is a birth, a marriage, or a death, show a continued though tenuous adherence to religious institutions. There are many Jews whose affiliation with secular activities under Jewish auspices is their main tie to Jewish communal life.

Even where there are no such affiliations, there may still be a consciousness of being Jewish.

For these reasons we may assume that the communal life of Jews involves practically all of the estimated population of 5,000,000 Jews. Since the 1930's there have also been evidences of an intensified group consciousness and a greater readiness for affiliation. Even for the group who are not formally affiliated with one or more specific Jewish organizations there is a good deal of association on an informal basis with other Jews for social purposes.

There are no extensive statistics of intermarriage among Jews in the United States, but the figures for Canadian Jewry may be indicative. Statistics compiled by the Canadian government show that Jews married outside their group less than any other ethnic group; it reached a peak of 12.4% in 1944 and declined to 10.4% in 1946. A scholarly study of marriage records in New York City for the period 1908-1912 shows that intermarriage by Jews with non-Jews was only 1.17% of all Jewish marriages, the lowest intermarriage rate of the entire white population. The rate among Jewish immigrants was less than 1% but increased for the American-born generation to 4.51%. Statistics of intermarriage in Canada begin with a rate of 4.64% in 1926, when the foreign-born constituted two-thirds of Canada's Jewish population. Intermarriage in Canada is more apt to occur in areas where there is a sparse population of Jews; the rate was low in such cities as Montreal and very high in the Maritime provinces. It may perhaps be assumed that the rate of Jewish intermarriage in the United States may not have reached the rates reported for Canada because of the greater concentration of Jews in the United States. In any case, it is believed that a good part of the intermarried group remains associated with other Jews on a secular if not a religious basis. (A population study in New Orleans published in 1954 reports non-Jewish individuals in ten percent of Jewish households.) The close identification and association among Jews is also attested by residential studies, which show a large part of the Jewish population living in districts having a considerable proportion of Jewish residents.

Of the estimated 5,000,000 Jews in the United States, close to 45 percent live in New York City. Another 30 percent live in fourteen other large cities with Jewish population ranging from 30,000 to 325,000. The 1953 *American Jewish Year Book,* Volume 54, lists 801 other cities having from 100 to 26,000 Jews. It has also been estimated that from 100,000 to 200,000 Jews live in villages and rural areas. There is an estimated Jewish population of close to three million in the three States of New York, New Jersey and Connecticut.

The Jewish population, therefore, is concentrated in the metropolitan areas. The greatest concentration is on the Atlantic seaboard, the North Central states, and California. In other parts of the country the Jewish population is more sparsely distributed. The total is fairly stationary, with some of the smaller interior communities losing population to other regions, notably California and Florida. There is also believed to be a considerable movement from smaller interior towns to the larger cities and from the large cities proper to the surrounding suburban areas.

Jewish communal life in the United States is primarily by affiliation or participation in separate Jewish activities, religious and secular. Many Jews are affiliated with fraternal bodies, Zionist organizations, women's groups, congregations, social clubs and fraternities limited to Jews and "family circles," or they are identified as contributors to philanthropic appeals for domestic and overseas causes. It has been estimated that there are at least 1,300,000 contributors to federated funds, a very large proportion of Jewish adults.

The developing forms of central Jewish communal organization growing out of the structures of central fund raising are a new phase of communal organization. In a few

JEWISH COMMUNITY BUILDING, LOS ANGELES, CAL.

of the largest concentrations of Jewish population central communal machinery exists only for philanthropic fund raising and central philanthropic planning; other communities, however, have been developing central organization not only for fund raising but also for central welfare planning. These are being accepted increasingly as a means for communal planning and for activities appropriate to the broad range of needs and interests of the Jewish population.

It has been predicted that central communal organization for a variety of functions will in time become established in all sections of the country by a gradual enlargement of functions, especially the extension of the interest of Jewish federations, welfare funds, and councils to Jewish education, leisure-time activities and other cultural interests of the group as a whole. Organizing New York City with its huge Jewish population will be a complex and difficult task. But such developments as the Brooklyn Jewish Community Council (an association of Jewish organizations concerned with community relations and simi-

lar work) and the interest of the New York Federation in Jewish education, youth work, family counselling, hospital services and other programs which serve the independent as well as the dependent indicate that even in this metropolis there are potentials for central communal organization with comprehensive functions.

In several cities studies of the proportion of Jews affiliated with or participating in religious or secular organizations indicate that one-third or more of the adult population does not seem to be formally affiliated. The proportion may be greater in New York and in several other of the largest cities. But in all probability only a much smaller proportion is completely outside or on the extreme periphery of Jewish communal life. Many of the unaffiliated avail themselves upon occasion of the services of the religious institutions and the secular agencies. Some are intermittent contributors to Jewish philanthropic causes or otherwise indicate their feeling of belonging to the Jewish group. It is likely that those who would consider themselves as completely indifferent or antagonistic

UNIVERSITY OF JUDAISM, LOS ANGELES, CAL.

to Jewish communal life represent a relatively small fraction of the total Jewish population. In several cities Jewish censuses have led to the affiliation of some individuals not formerly participating in Jewish communal life. It was discovered that people often are not affiliated because they have never been invited; or else that while they considered themselves as belonging to the Jewish community their personal problems are too overwhelming to permit them much scope for group interest or activity.

Some understanding of organized Jewish communal life may be obtained by an examination of the varying types of formal associations. The list includes the religious institutions, the agencies for Jewish education, culture and recreation, the fraternal organizations and social clubs, the economic organizations among workers and professional groups, the large network of philanthropic health and welfare services, the agencies concerned with the problems of group relations and the civic and political status of Jews here and abroad, and Zionist and other ideological movements. Finally, an examination of the trend in the coordination of similar activities and the organization of fund raising will throw considerable light upon the status of Jewish communal organization.

IV. RELIGIOUS, EDUCATIONAL AND CULTURAL ORGANIZATION

The most important and most significant form of Jewish communal life continues to center around religious practices and the religious institutions. The 1900-1901 *American Jewish Year Book* reported that there were at that time 791 Jewish congregations, many of them "barely organized." Ninety-one were affiliated with the Union of American Hebrew Congregations (Reform) and fifty with the Union of Orthodox Jewish Congregations which had been but recently established (1898).

PETER M. KAHN MEMORIAL LIBRARY, LOS ANGELES, CAL.

It was assumed that the majority of the unaffiliated congregations were Orthodox. The Conservative movement had not yet become identified as a separate grouping.

It has been estimated that there are now over 4,000 Jewish congregations and that approximately 40 percent of the Jewish population are associated in worship with these congregations. The 1954 *American Jewish Year Book* reports 467 congregations affiliated with the Union of American Hebrew Congregations and 460 with the United Synagogue of America, which represents the Conservative movement. Sephardic congregations report 50 congregations which follow the Spanish rite. The Union of Orthodox Jewish Congregations reported a constituency of 720 congregations.

While the basic function of the synagogue is religious worship, this is not the only activity of congregational life. In many congregations members are organized in brotherhoods, sisterhoods, and youth groups. Reform, Conservative and Orthodox congregations are increasingly sponsoring leisure-time activities in the synagogue building or its adjuncts. These activities have produced a number of national associations affiliated with religious bodies, such as the National Federation of Temple Sisterhoods (1913) and the National Federation of Temple Brotherhoods (1923), both affiliated with the Union of American Hebrew Congregations, and the National Women's League of the United Synagogue of America (1918). There are others as well.

1. RELIGIOUS FAITH AND RELIGIOUS INSTITUTIONS

The religious faith and practices of American Jews reflect the 300-year history of American Jewry. The ritual of the Sephardic immigrants, that of the earlier and later Ashkenazim and the traditional Orthodoxy of East European immigrants since 1930—these and other currents of religious thinking and practice are represented in the religious life of American Jewry. Religious practices and institutions were changing in Europe both before and after the arrival of the later immigrants. Emancipation, Haskalah and Hasidism, the rise of international socialism and the Zionist, Yiddishist and nationalist movements—all had their effect on Jewish religious life in this country, both directly and through their impact on Jewish life in Europe.

These factors are reflected in the institutions for Rabbinical training and religious education. The Hebrew Union College (Cincinnati, 1875), which was recently merged with the Jewish Institute of Religion (New York, founded in 1922), was established by Reform Judaism. The Jewish Theological Seminary of America, first established in 1886 by those dissatisfied with Reform and reorganized in 1902, now represents the "Conservative" wing of Jewry. Immigration to the United States during and after the 1930's brought with it strains of European Jewish religious culture which had some influence on the related denominational groups in the United States. Orthodoxy was particularly affected by the arrival of large numbers of Orthodox rabbis and scholars uprooted by the Hitlerian catastrophe in Eastern Europe.

Of the Orthodox institutions for religious training the largest is Yeshiva University in New York City, founded in 1896 as the Rabbi Isaac Elchanan Theological Seminary. The Hebrew Theological College was founded in Chicago in 1921. Additional smaller institutions were established by Orthodox groups before the Hitler-influenced migration, such as the Yavne Hebrew Theological Seminary (1925) and the Rabbinical Seminary of America (1933). Others were the results of the 1930-1940 migration, such as the Ner Israel Rabbinical College of America (1934); Yeshivah Hakmei Lublin (1942); the Yeshiva Beth Joseph Rabbinical Seminary, an outgrowth of the Beth Joseph Yeshivah of Bialystok (1941); the Rabbin-

ical Academy of the Rabbi Chaim Berlin Yeshivah (1939); the Lubavitcher Yeshivoth, an outgrowth of the Habad Hasidic movement (1940); the Seminary of the Mesivta Tifereth Jerusalem; the Rabbinical College of Telshe (1941), a continuation of the former Yeshivah Etz Chaim of Lithuania, and the Torah Vodaath.

All these institutions are located in the New York area, with the exception of the Ner Israel Rabbinical College (Baltimore), Hakmei Lublin (Detroit), and the Rabbinical College of Telshe (Cleveland). A number of these Orthodox institutions not only prepare students for the Orthodox rabbinate but are also concerned with primary and secondary education both secular and religious. The three largest educational institutions, the Hebrew Union College-Jewish Institute of Religion (Cincinnati and New York), the Jewish Theological Seminary and the Yeshiva University (both in New York) provide not only Rabbinical training but also programs of higher Jewish education leading to academic degrees. Yeshiva University, which has a university charter, now includes an undergraduate college of liberal arts and sciences, a graduate school in education and community administration, and an Institute for Higher Mathematics. It is now (1954) establishing a medical school, to bear Albert Einstein's name.

Dropsie College was organized in 1905 as a non-sectarian institution under Jewish auspices devoted to higher Jewish and Semitic learning and offering only graduate degrees. Its chief purpose is to train scholars, Jews and non-Jews, to engage in research in branches of Jewish learning and to equip them for positions in Jewish and non-Jewish institutions of higher learning.

2. JEWISH EDUCATION

The Jewish education of youth, at one time dependent on private teaching, is now mostly undertaken by schools under congregational, communal or institutional auspices. The most frequent types are the part-time (3 to 5 day) schools, supplementing the education of children in the public schools; the Sunday and Sabbath School programs of congregations and other organizations, and Yiddishist schools developed by Jewish labor groups. Schools under congregational or group auspices reflect the religious denomination and cultural outlook of the sponsoring group.

The American Association for Jewish Education, established in 1939 to promote higher standards of Jewish education and to assist local communities with their Jewish educational programs, attempts to serve elementary and secondary Jewish schools. In 1952 the American Association of Jewish Education (AAJE) initiated a study of Jewish education in the United States for the purpose of gathering historical, cultural and statistical data, and for evaluating the effectiveness of Jewish schools.

In addition to the AAJE, which seeks to include all denominations and types of schools, there are a number of agencies primarily concerned with Jewish education under particular auspices. The Mizrachi National Educational Committee, representing the Orthodox wing of the Zionist movement, assists Orthodox all-day schools and Talmud Torahs in the United States; Torah Umesorah, established in 1944, sponsors the founding of Hebrew Day Schools in the United States, and the United Lubavitcher Yeshivoth, with branches in twelve communities in the United States provides elementary religious and secular education.

Some all-day schools have established national service agencies. Among these is the National Council of Beth Jacob Schools, established in 1943 to coordinate, advise and aid schools providing elementary religious and secular training for girls. Of the seventeen affiliated schools, twelve are located in New York City.

All-day schools combine Jewish and secular studies. Schools of this type—sometimes called "parochial schools" from their re-

DROPSIE COLLEGE, PHILADELPHIA

semblance to similar schools that have been developed by the Roman Catholic, Lutheran and other Christian churches—have been in existence for some time in New York City. Since 1930 their number has grown in other cities as well. A number of them are associated with the Orthodox theological seminaries and yeshivas. Others have been sponsored by groups with Conservative or Zionist orientations. They express the desire of some groups for an intensive Jewish education for their young.

According to the AAJE, enrollment in all types of Jewish elementary and secondary schools—including Sunday, weekday, all-day, Yiddish, and congregational schools, as well as classes held on released time from the public schools—increased from 239,000 in 1948 to 336,000 in 1952. What part of this increase is due to an increase in the number of Jewish children, longer stay in school, greater popularity of Jewish education, more inclusive statistical reporting or other possible causes, is not reported. There are no country-wide statistical data on the proportion of children attending Jewish

HEADQUARTERS OF THE YOUNG MEN'S AND YOUNG WOMEN'S HEBREW ASSOCIATION, NEW YORK

THE JEWISH MUSEUM, NEW YORK

schools during any one year, but local studies indicate that enrollment may vary in different cities from 25 to 65 percent of eligible children. Of the total Jewish-school population in 1952 it has been estimated that 47.6 percent are enrolled in weekday and all-day schools and 52.4 percent in Sunday schools. (For 1950 it was reported that eight percent of pupils were attending all-day schools.) In 140 communities for which statistics are available the report states that 63.4 percent were in Sunday schools and 36.6 percent in weekday schools. "The proportion enrolled under Orthodox congregational auspices was 17.1 percent, under Reform auspices 30.2 percent, under Conservative auspices 35.1 percent and under non-congregational auspices 16.6 percent;" most of the latter, however, were "Orthodox-oriented." A 1950 report indicates that fewer than four percent were enrolled in classes on the high school level.

JEWISH CENTER, COLUMBUS, OHIO

Jewish schools are financed by the congregations and other sponsoring groups, by tuition fees and by philanthropic support. A trend toward greater support of Jewish education by local federations and welfare funds has been noted. Part of this support is to supplement the income of the local Jewish school system, but more of it in the larger cities is devoted to the central bureaus of Jewish education, which provide a variety of services to the whole range of Jewish school systems in their communities.

Although bureaus of Jewish education have been established in most of the larger as well as in many of the middle-sized communities, no standard curriculum or program has been achieved. Schools continue to represent the religious and cultural objectives of their sponsoring groups, and there are many different kinds of Jewish schools.

3. INFORMAL EDUCATION AND LEISURE-TIME ACTIVITIES

Formal religious education in organized schools mostly reaches children of elementary-school age. Programs for informal education and other leisure-time activities are available in most communities for the youth and young adult population. A hundred years ago groups of young Jewish men and women began to associate with each other in various club activities. Since then there has evolved a considerable network of institutions, agencies and activities that play an important part in the social and cultural life of young American Jews.

The largest element in this organized program for leisure-time activities is represented by the Jewish centers, which have grown out of the Young Men's and Young Women's Hebrew Associations of an earlier day, and out of the settlement houses and the educational and cultural clubs established by Jews in all parts of the country. The National Jewish Welfare Board, organized in 1917 and amalgamated in 1921 with the Council of Young Men's Hebrew and Kindred Associations, serves the Jewish community centers and Y's and sponsors the Jewish Book Council of America and

JEWISH CENTER, DULUTH, MINN.

the National Jewish Music Council. It reports an affiliation for 1953 of 348 centers and other institutions, reaching an estimated total of 531,000 individuals. Of this membership, about 35 percent are under 14 years of age, and thus include many children enrolled in Jewish schools; about 40 percent are 25 years of age and over.

The programs of these centers are varied. They include health and physical education, nursery school and kindergarten education, Hebrew and Jewish history courses, arts and crafts, dramatics, music, dance, social activities, forums, discussions, holiday and festival celebrations, and civic projects. The scope and range of programs vary for different centers. Many activities are conducted by autonomous groups, including clubs and classes meeting under the aegis of the center. The activities conducted by Jewish centers provide for a variety of group associations. Sanford Solender in the 1953 *American Jewish Year Book* reports that the latest development has been "service to the very old and very

young"; there has been a growth in the number of nursery schools and in programs for the elderly—the latter frequently named Golden Age Clubs. The value of physical facilities in 1940 exceeded $40 million, and new building or expansion in the five years after 1948 cost $39 million. It also reported that the Jewish centers conducted 201 day camps and operated 36 country camps in 1951. There are 142 country camps under other Jewish communal auspices.

While practically all of the centers charge fees for membership and for most activities, they depend also upon continuing philanthropic support. In 1951, centers throughout the country received about 37 percent of their incomes from membership dues and program activities and 55 percent from philanthropic funds, mainly Jewish federations and community chests. The operating costs of Jewish centers in 1952 was estimated at $13,975,000.

An extensive survey and stocktaking of the Jewish Welfare Boards own program

JEWISH CENTER, HAMILTON, ONT.

and the program of the centers affiliated with it was made under the direction of Oscar Janowsky and a study commission headed by Salo Baron. Completed in 1947, the report recommended the inclusion of more Jewish cultural content in the activities of Jewish centers. It found that in too many instances what was Jewish about the program was solely the fact that Jews were engaging under Jewish auspices in activities which had no Jewish significance. This stress on more Jewish content induced considerable discussion, both favorable and unfavorable, but the thesis was generally accepted and the JWB agreed to expand its emphasis in this direction. There has not as yet been a follow-up study to determine to what extent the recommendation of the survey has found its way into actual practice in community centers.

A variety of youth groups are sponsored by national organizations, including the Intercollegiate Zionist Federation and other Zionist youth groups, the National Council of Young Israel, the B'nai B'rith Youth Organization, and the junior divisions of the National Council of Jewish Women, Hadassah, Workmen's Circle and other organizations. Solender estimates that these youth organizations have more than 3,600 local units with over 115,000 members.

Hillel Foundations, under the sponsorship of the B'nai B'rith, were established as a cultural program for college youth in 1923. Hillel operates 206 college units in the United States and Canada, serving 200,000 students. In addition, there are eleven national Jewish fraternities and sororities on college campuses and in high schools. Cultural programs and activities are also undertaken by a great variety of organizations primarily concerned with other functions.

Discussing the various organized youth groups, Solender says:

> The programs of these groups were varied. They involved social activities such as dances, parties, picnics, and bazaars. Health and physical educa-

JEWISH CENTER, TORONTO

tion activities were usually a part of programs including sports, tournaments, hiking, field days, festivals, and similar activities. Camping services were offered by some groups, and leadership training projects were common. Hobby groups, dramatics, folk dancing, music, art and crafts, and journalism were frequent activities. Cultural programs were conducted by each of these groups, including lectures, forums, seminars, book reviews, discussion groups, concerts, and institutes. Religious activities such as Sabbath programs, special holiday observance, and study groups were an important part of the programs of many groups. Particular stress was placed on programs related to Jewish events, with activities frequently related to Jewish holidays and festivals. Civic programs were featured in all of the organizations, including activities connected with civil rights and legislation, participation in local community welfare services, and support for fund-raising drives.

4.   RESEARCH AND CULTURAL ORGANIZATIONS

A number of scholarly and cultural organizations have been established. The American Jewish Historical Society was founded in 1892. The Menorah Association, organized in 1912 for the advancement of Jewish culture, has as its main activity today the publication of the *Menorah Journal.* The American Academy for Jewish Research, a membership organization established in 1920, sponsors scholarly research in Jewish history, religion and literature. *Bitzaron,* a membership organization created in 1939 to promote Hebrew culture, publishes a Hebrew monthly periodical of the same name. The Conference on Jewish Relations, established in 1935, engages in a limited number of Jewish social research projects and publishes a quarterly journal *Jewish Social Studies.* The Yiddish Scientific Institute (YIVO), founded in Wilno in 1925, transferred its main activities to the United States in 1940 and has been placing an increasing emphasis on research into American Jewish life; its findings are usually published in both Yiddish and English. The Histadrut Ivrit, established in 1922, promotes the Hebrew language and Hebrew culture in America. The Jewish Chautauqua Society, established in 1893, now operates under the sponsorship of the National Federation of Temple Brotherhoods, an affiliate of the Union of American Hebrew Congregations; its current activities are lectures on Jewish history, literature and philosophy to audiences in universities, colleges and summer camps. The Brandeis Youth Foundation (1941) initially supported by the American Zionist Youth Commission, is now an independently operated organization which conducts a summer camp offering young people a program of recreation and training as Jewish youth leaders. All of these cultural and research organizations depend primarily on membership and philanthropic support for their continued operations.

The Jewish Publication Society, founded as a non-profit body in 1888, publishes books of Jewish interest; it has a present membership of 8,500 who receive its publications, in addition to those who purchase its books in the general market, and it seeks philanthropic income to make up for a relatively small deficit. Sponsoring publications and providing cultural programs are also purposes that have been assumed by such organizations as the American Jewish Committee, the American Jewish Congress, and the Zionist Organization of America, among others.

5. FRATERNAL ORGANIZATIONS AND SOCIAL CLUBS

In addition to the educational and cultural activities which are sponsored by communities and other organized groups and which depend in part for their support on subsidies from their sponsors as well as on membership dues, there are many city and country clubs, fraternal organizations and similar groups which depend primarily on membership payments and are not supported by philanthropy. There is no systematic record of all these social activities, which have been established primarily to meet the recreational interests and to fulfill the desire of people to associate in their leisure-time with a congenial group. Some of the fraternal organizations and social clubs were founded initially for economic benefit and mutual aid; others from the beginning have also had in mind communal or cultural purposes as well as sociability. Family circles have been a growing social phenomenon in the last decade.

The pioneer Jewish fraternal organization in the United States is the Independent Order of B'nai B'rith. Beginning with a membership of twelve German Jews in 1843, as we have seen, B'nai B'rith by 1900 had 30,000 members in 315 local lodges; today it includes 200,000 men in 1,000 lodges, besides women's auxiliaries and youth groups. B'nai B'rith has undertaken a great variety of additional services and interests. The Hillel Foundations, the Anti-Defamation League, the B'nai B'rith Youth Organization, are some of the activities conducted under its auspices. In its earlier years, B'nai B'rith's focus of attention was on philanthropic and social welfare projects. It was responsible for organizing homes for the aged, children's institutions, and special hospitals such as one for tuberculous and one for arthritic patients. Several of these continue under its national or regional auspices. Increasingly the charitable activities first initiated by B'nai B'rith are becoming the responsibility of local communities or are being supported largely by national campaigns beyond B'nai B'rith's membership.

Over the course of the years a number of other fraternal and mutual benefit organizations were established, such as the *landsmanshaften* and *hevras* which represented the interest and organizing capacity of groups of immigrants brought together on the basis of common geographical origin in Europe or current association in this country. Among the most important of these is the Workmen's Circle, organized in 1892 for the Yiddish-speaking labor group; in 1927 this organization added an English-speaking division. The Workmen's Circle also has engaged in general welfare activities for its members, including a hospital for the tuberculous in Liberty, New York, educational programs, and many other cultural and humanitarian activities. The Farband—the Labor Zionist Order, established in 1912 and formerly known as the Jewish National Workers' Alliance, apart from its Zionism was also an outgrowth of the fraternal activities of labor and Yiddish groups. The National Council of Jewish Women was established in 1893 to stimulate the interest of women in community services, education, and other civic interests. The Jewish War Veterans of the United States, established in 1896, promotes patriotic and civic interests as well as fraternal relationships. The Jewish War Veterans has more recently become an organization handling veterans' claims and meeting other needs of veterans; it concerns itself actively with bettering community relations through its contacts with other organized veterans' groups.

Still in existence are some of the older fraternal organizations such as the Free Sons of Israel (1849), Independent Order of Brith Abraham (1887), the Progressive Order of the West (1896), and Brith Sholom (1905). Bnai Zion (a fraternal order of the Zionist Organization of America), organized in 1910, reported a membership of 5,400 with $3,600,000 of insurance in force. Growing out of the *landsmanshaften* and their interest are such organizations as the American Federation for Polish Jews (1908), the American Federation of Jews from Central Europe (1941), the Netherlands Jewish Society (1940), the Federation of Rumanian Jews of America (1909), and United Galician Jews (1937), among others.

6. COMMUNICATION

Many means are available for keeping the individual informed about Jewish communal activities and about what other Jews are doing, as well as for maintaining and promoting his interest in Jewish organizations. National, overseas and local agencies distribute a great deal of published information for fund-raising and related educational purposes. The radio has been extensively used and a beginning is being made in the use of television. The general American press carries a considerable amount of Jewish news; some items, considered to be of public interest, are secured by the press directly, while other items derive from the publicity releases of Jewish organizations. Since the general press, radio and television are addressed to a general audience, the amount of coverage given to Jewish affairs varies according to the size of the Jewish population. Because the *New York Times,* one of the great newspapers of the world, is published in a city in which Jews are estimated at more than 25 percent of the population, it includes a large amount of news about Jewish affairs. In smaller cities there may be less general Jewish news but considerable reporting of organizational events and social and personal items.

In addition to the Yiddish press, with several dailies and weeklies, there is a large number of weekly, monthly, quarterly and annual periodicals in the English language under commercial and organizational Jewish auspices, including the numerous "house organ" reports and special pieces of publicity. The *American Jewish Year Book* for 1953 lists 124 periodicals published in New York City and 94 published in other American cities. They represent practically every point of view and movement and are of widely varying literary and journalistic quality. A world-wide news service for the Yiddish and Anglo-Jewish press and Jewish organizations is the Jewish Telegraphic Agency, which is currently being subsidized by loans from the American Section of the Jewish Agency for Palestine. Two national radio broadcast programs for the general public are also maintained: "The Eternal Light" of the Jewish Theological Seminary, and the "Message of Israel," sponsored by the United Jewish Layman's Committee.

7. INDIVIDUAL USE OF RELIGIOUS AND CULTURAL OPPORTUNITIES

With this large network of religious and cultural programs and institutions, opportunities for individual participation are available in practically all sections of the country. In many cities there are multiple agencies reflecting the denominational and cultural differences among Jews. Only the very small aggregations of Jews living in areas of sparse Jewish population lack an accessible synagogue or social center. Even in very small towns, where opportunities for social intercourse among Jews are limited by the small number of families, a relationship to nationally organized activities is possible.

There is no national study of the extent to which Jews make use of religious and cultural opportunities. With the duplication of membership of religious, fraternal and cultural organizations, the total membership count would give us no indication of the proportion involved in such activities and of the proportion that has remained indifferent or unattached. Studies on the use of recreational and leisure-time activities in some communities indicate that from 20 to 40 percent of the eligible age-groups are members or participants in any given year in the Y's and centers under communal auspices. What additional proportion of the population avails itself of activities under congregational or other auspices is not recorded, but there are evidences of a great deal of participation by individual Jews in the large variety of membership activities that are generally available. Though much of this activity is social in character, a good deal of it seems to be related to philanthropic agencies with a communal objective.

One occasionally hears the cynical statement that while American Jews are building imposing synagogues and temples, these —unlike the social clubs—are used spar-

ingly, functioning in reality as monuments to a historical tradition rather than as centers of active worship. Most religious leaders, on the contrary, are convinced that the trend toward religious and cultural participation among Jews is increasing and not diminishing. Studies of Jewish centers report extensive use of facilities by younger age-groups of the community.

With the increasing proportion of Jews native-born and conditioned by the American environment, the question can be raised whether many of the organized communal services which were designed during the transitional period of adjustment from a European to an American background can continue adequately to serve the needs of the new generation. The entire history of American Jewish communal institutions has been one of adaptation and change. That programs develop to meet new conditions is indicated by the increasing variety of cultural groups and cultural organizations. To the extent to which established agencies adapt themselves to current sentiments and meet current needs they may expect to have an active continuing existence.

The problem of the need to adapt to conditions imposed by American life is most evident today in Yiddish culture and Yiddish-speaking organizations. Such organizations face the problem of survival as the numbers of foreign-born decline and the number of native-born increases. Similarly, attempts to develop the Hebrew language and literature in this country are meeting with only limited success.

Equally unknown is the use Jews make of cultural facilities not under Jewish auspices. The impression is that Jews participate actively in the general culture, read the general press, participate in the arts and sciences, etc., and that the leisure-time life of most Jews is primarily non-sectarian in nature. Like all other Americans they spend much time in commercial (and essentially passive) recreation and culture—baseball, football, movies, radio and TV; and also devote time to active recreation—to the theater, literature, and museums. It would seem, indeed, that the greater part of Jewish leisure-time is spent outside of the Jewish communal area. Nevertheless, a great deal of the leisure-time activities which have no specific Jewish cultural content is undertaken by Jews in the company of other Jews. It is also of interest to note that some aspects of Jewish culture have been finding their way into the stream of general American culture. Especially in New York and other large cities strains of Jewish culture and even a considerable number of Yiddish words have been incorporated into the general pattern of living.

V. COMMUNAL ASPECTS OF JEWISH ECONOMIC LIFE

During the decades of heavy immigration, from 1880 to 1925, the resources of the community were important for the economic adjustment of the individual Jew. Today, with only a sprinkling of new immigrants and the relatively stable economic position of the Jewish population, the economic significance of the community for the individual is diminishing. Help in finding a job and in meeting other difficulties of economic adjustment continues on a limited scale, for a small group of resident Jews who are not fully adjusted and for the few newcomers. Such economic matters as discrimination in employment continue to be of concern to communities and to various national agencies.

In the late 19th and early 20th centuries the prevailing economic philosophy in the United States left the problem of adjustment primarily to the individual, his family and his close associates. Many immigrants found it extremely difficult to gain a satisfactory foothold on this basis. There was a need, therefore, for a sustained communal interest in the economic problems of large sections of the Jewish population. Slum and sweatshop conditions, grinding poverty, chronic unemployment and under-employment, and low wages required not only relief and philanthropic assistance but also systematic and constructive group effort. There was a desperate need to raise the standard of living of large masses. This was the period which called forth the greatest degree of mutual aid on the part of the immigrants and stimulated vigorous labor activity for improving their unsatisfactory condition.

The initial economic problems were those involved in the first stages of arrival in the United States. Such organizations as the Hebrew Sheltering and Immigrant Aid Society (HIAS), made a great contribution to the reception and initial adjustment of immigrants. Much help of an informal character was given to the immigrant during this period by people from his own town who had arrived earlier. Today HIAS, the United Service for New Americans (formerly the National Refugee Service, organized in 1939, when refugees from Hitlerism began to arrive in considerable numbers), and the Department for the Foreign Born of the National Council of Jewish Women continue to receive immigrants and help them in the first phase of their adjustment. Merger of these services into a United-HIAS was announced early in 1954.

When so large a proportion of arriving immigrants were coming to New York and remaining in its crowded quarters, there was need not only for assistance in New York, but also for guidance and help in distributing them to other, less congested areas of the country. The most significant effort in that direction was the organization of the Industrial Removal Office of the Baron de Hirsch Fund, which for many years had been engaged in helping immigrants with relief and vocational training. After an initial vain effort in New York to obtain a decent livelihood a considerable number of immigrants were willing to settle in other parts of the country. The Industrial Removal Office at one time also tried to divert ships with arriving immigrants to Galveston, Texas, in the hope that by coming to a different port of arrival the immigrant might find opportunities in areas of the country which were not heavily populated. The Industrial Removal Office, from its inception in 1901 to its liquidation in 1922, sponsored the distribution of 79,000 Jews. Directly and indirectly this movement was responsible for a considerable part of the growth of Jewish population in the interior of the country. The National Refugee Service, organized in the 1930's, has continued the function of resettlement. It is estimated that over 40 percent of the refugee immigration settled outside of New York City, and others are gradually moving out of the city.

There have been continuing efforts to help the Jewish immigrant, primarily a town dweller, to become a farmer. A number of colonies were initiated and in several of them, such as an area in southeastern New Jersey, a considerable number of Jews are engaged in agriculture and other rural occupations. The Jewish Agricultural Society, established by the Baron de Hirsch Fund in 1900, continues to assist in the transfer of Jews from town to country and help the Jewish farmer with loans, technical advice and other services. At the present time the Jewish Agricultural Society reports about 100,000 Jews on farms and in rural occupations.

A related effort to encourage Jewish interest in agriculture was the establishment of the National Farm School in Pennsylvania in 1896. This school, now the National Agricultural College, is under nonsectarian auspices; it estimates that about 65 percent of its small student body is Jewish.

Philanthropic projects, important as they were, were still a minor factor in Jewish economic life compared with the Jewish trade union movement. The American trade union movement, which for most of the 19th century had to struggle to establish itself as an accepted part of the economic life of the country, appealed to Jewish immigrants who had been workers or became workers after arrival in this country. Beginning with the 1880's there were enough Jewish workers, their ranks increasing with continuing immigration, to create Jewish unions.

The parent institution of the Jewish labor movement in America was the United Hebrew Trades (Fareinigte Yiddishe Geverkshaften), established in 1888. The development of the trade unions,— the International Ladies Garment Workers' Union, the Amalgamated Clothing Workers Union and other unions in the textile and construction industries—included struggles for union organization, strikes, internal conflict and ideological change. Not only was the labor movement a major factor in the economic adjustment of Jews but it was also a creative element in their cultural expression, in their political thinking and organization, and in their general social advancement. In addition, the Jewish labor movement made a distinct contribution to trade unionism as a whole in the United States, to the development of social legislation and to the promotion of national concern with standards of living and conditions of employment.

Today the labor unions organized by Jewish workers are no longer primarily Jewish in membership. Will Herberg* notes that the labor unions originally established by Jewish workers had a total membership of 1,000,000 in 1951, of which only 385,000 were Jewish. However, the leadership to a considerable extent still consists of those who were instrumental in the establishment and development of these unions. In general, Herberg states that the aim of the Jewish labor union was not that of "obtaining special benefits for Jews. It was an idea that every responsible Jewish labor leader would have rejected with repugnance had it ever been suggested." He also notes "that the influence of Jewish labor was primarily the influence exerted by the Jewish unions and their leaders in the general labor movement."

* Will Herberg, "Jewish Labor Movement", in *American Jewish Year Book,* Volume 53, 1952.

There have been major occupational shifts among Jews, especially among the new generation, and an upward economic trend. A considerable proportion is now in white collar industries and other middle class occupations and enterprises, the newer immigrant groups having taken their places on the lower rungs of the economic ladder. Jewish workers who are moving into new occupations join the existing unions. The result is that there is no separate organization of Jewish labor except for the residual membership in the unions originally created by Jews and in a few associated activities.

The Jewish Labor Committee, established in 1934, seeks to bring to bear the influence of the American labor movement upon the solution of problems of group relationships. Its membership consists of representation from groups such as the International Ladies Garment Workers' Union, the Amalagamated Clothing Workers of America and other unions of the garment trades, the United Hebrew Trades, Workmen's Circle, the Jewish Daily Forward Association, the Jewish Socialist Verband and similar groups. It has no individual membership except for a recently organized Women's Division. Concerned originally with help to labor and Socialist groups suffering from the effects of Hitlerism abroad, it soon turned its attention also to the task of gaining co-operation of the American labor movement for overcoming discrimination, educating trade union members in the ideals of equality and fraternity among all racial and religious groups and work with and through organized labor for civil rights and civic standards.

The Jewish labor unions are considered by Herberg and other writers as a transitional phenomenon of great importance during the earlier years of immigration and until recently. While the Jewish labor movement will no doubt continue to exist for some time to come, Herberg believes:

that the long-term prospect is one of decline and ultimate dissolution.

It will have left an enduring contribution to our national labor and Jewish life in the United States. It is a contribution which is still being made in the everyday activity of the hundreds of thousands of men and women, leaders and rank-and-filers, who constitute the Jewish labor movement in the United States.

Aside from the Jewish labor movement only a few other Jewish groups are organized on an economic basis. In some of the larger cities there may be a Society of Jewish Physicians or Jewish Dentists. These are formed largely for social intercourse and occasionally for the furthering of professional interests. The Jewish Theatrical Guild of America, organized nationally in 1924, engages in non-sectarian theatrical charity. Its purpose was stated at one time as "perpetuating Judaism in the theatre," but it is no longer listed in that way in the *American Jewish Year Book*.

In cities with large Jewish populations the proportion of Jews finding employment with Jewish firms may be high, perhaps as much because of fortuitous reasons as because of discrimination and prejudice in hiring. On the other hand, there are Jewish-owned firms which may have only a small proportion of Jewish employees, such as department stores, laundries, and the like. Business is becoming more and more non-sectarian in character and the Fair Employment Practices Acts, in the states where they have been established, are helping to overcome prejudice in employment.

There are no associations of Jewish businessmen as such organized for economic objectives. Occasionally a local business association, as for example in the jewelry trade, may have a very high proportion of Jewish members. Jewish federations and welfare funds have helped to stimulate and to organize Jewish trade groups in the largest cities as a means for obtaining contributions from Jewish businessmen. After such groups have been established they may derive some additional satisfaction from their association on a social basis, but they exist primarily as conveniences to philanthropic fund-raising efforts. Such Jewish trade groups rarely consider themselves as organizations directly related to their professional or business functions; some of them in fact also include Christians sympathetic to Jewish fund-raising appeals.

It is not within the purview of this article to discuss the current economic status of American Jewry. There are surely many evidences of improvement as compared with the early days of immigration and labor struggle. In the larger centers of Jewish population many are employed as skilled and semi-skilled workers in diversified trades and occupations. Many Jews are in the distributive trades, merchandising, commercial recreation (including the theater and motion pictures) and other urban occupations, as well as in the professions. In the smaller Jewish communities there is apt to be a large proportion of Jews engaged in entrepreneurial and middle class occupations. While there remain evidences of discrimination and prejudice in some business and trade associations, the responsibility for the economic interests of business groups is assumed by non-sectarian trade bodies in the United States.

The economic improvement has also had its effect on the cultural creativity of American Jews. Where formerly the Jewish trade unions and socialist movements were closely associated with Jewish cultural activities, today most group activity must make its own way. The trade union movement stimulated and supported the Yiddish press and fostered the work of Yiddish writers and artists. Today communal support of cultural creativity is limited. The English-language Jewish press and the Yiddish press, when they are unable to support themselves commercially, may receive some help from Jewish organizations. In some cities an English-language Jewish press is developed under communal auspices or receives organized communal help. There is an occasional but limited family foundation as a source of help to Jewish writers in English, Yiddish and Hebrew, and more rarely to other creative artists. Creative art and culture are being fostered to a small extent by some of the religious, educational and other groups. The American Jewish Committee sponsors *Commentary,* and the American Jewish Congress *Congress Weekly* and *Judaism.* The creative artist who happens to be Jewish or who is concerned with Jewish culture must to a large extent find his place individually in the general American market. There are a few indications that the current rather feebly organized interest in the creative aspects of Jewish culture is growing.

VI. THE ROLE OF PHILANTHROPY IN JEWISH COMMUNAL LIFE

In addition to traditional religious activities, philanthropy is an equally broad and pervasive aspect of Jewish communal life and community organization. In the past, philanthropy, which was on a small scale and informal, represented the interests of special groups who devoted themselves to charitable causes. Today Jewish philanthropy has become highly organized. It is supported financially by nearly all sections of the Jewish community and enlists their direct participation. The spontaneous response to the overwhelming disaster which befell European Jewry, the opportunities for saving the survivors after the end of World War II, the creation of the State of Israel and the response to continuing calls for its financial and moral support have given philanthropy a major place in Jewish communal life. For many, including those whose religious ties have been weakening, philanthropy has become a dominant aspect of Jewish communal living. Since religious, cultural and social activities are organized as separate group interests, it is philanthropy that has become the common denominator of participation in the Jewish community. It seems no longer to involve, as it did in the past, major ideological controversies or group conflicts.

Reports covering most of the organized cities indicate that local Jewish hospitals, family service agencies, child care institutions and homes for the aged spent almost $106,000,000 in 1952. This was exclusive of funds spent locally for Jewish education and community centers, and expenditures by the national Jewish organizations and the overseas agencies. Of the sums spent by the local welfare institutions, $30,000,-000 represents income from philanthropic contributions, the balance coming from payments for service and from public funds. It is estimated that the yearly cost of maintaining Jewish education amounts to more than $20,000,000, of which from 20 to 30 percent is derived from contributions to supplement tuition payments. Community centers and Y's had operating costs totaling $13,975,000 in 1952 and of this more than half was met from philanthropic sources. In 1953 cultural agencies operating on a national basis reported expenditures of over $4,000,000; national religious agencies and institutions expenditures of close to $6,000,000; the community relations agencies expenditures of close to $6,000,000, and the national service agencies expenditures of $1,500,000. In 1952 American organizations raising funds for overseas work, including the United Jewish Appeal, reported receipts of approximately $90,000,000. There are additional local, national and overseas agencies which do not report their income and expenditures to the Council of Jewish Federations and Welfare Funds (CJFWF) so that these figures fall short of the true total perhaps by as much as 10 to 15 percent. Nor does it include the funds required by the operation of local synagogues and temples.

We can estimate with some confidence that in 1952 the organized sources of Jewish philanthropy raised about $125,000,000 in central fund-raising campaigns, and that an additional 30 to 35 million dollars were raised through separate appeals by non-federated agencies engaged in overseas, national and local work. This is a reduction from the high peak of fund raising attained in 1948, when over $250,-000,000 was received from Jewish contributors for the same Jewish philanthropic causes. The current level of fund raising, however, is considerably in advance of all previous records and compares with the total reached in the year 1946, when the end of the War greatly intensified interest in philanthropy, especially for overseas needs.

It is estimated that the bulk of philanthropic funds comes from a small proportion of all contributors. About 90 percent of the total raised comes from contributions of $100 or more by donors representing 20 percent of all contributors.

1. LOCAL PHILANTHROPY

Organized local welfare services have been a feature of Jewish life for generations and continue as an expression of communal responsibility. In about 230 cities with Jewish populations of 1,000 or over, in which close to 95 percent of all American Jews live, there is some form of central body for the welfare needs of the local Jewish population. Even in smaller communities there is likely to be some organized effort, such as a ladies' welfare society, on behalf of the occasional resident or transient person or family in need. Jewish educational, cultural or leisure-time programs are similarly available in many of the smaller as well as in the larger centers of Jewish population.

The larger cities have more elaborate programs designed to meet the health, welfare and cultural needs of the Jewish population. In about 125 of these cities, the scope of activities is large enough to require the employment of professional personnel. In cities with Jewish populations of less than 5,000 there may be only a federation director who functions both as fund raiser and community organizer and who directs the center activities and gives service to families with special problems. With larger populations more machinery and staff are needed, increasing in size to the comprehensive requirements of New York City, whose Federation includes scores of specialized health and social welfare agencies.

The improving economic conditions and the assumption of basic welfare responsibilities by governmental agencies have permitted Jewish agencies to broaden the scope of their services, and in some instances to make them available to other sections of the population. This is especially true of the hospitals under Jewish auspices, which have always accepted patients irrespective of religion or race. Requiring payment for service from those able to pay is not only the practice of all general hospitals but also an important factor in homes for the aged, in recreational centers, and to a lesser extent in the child care and family service agencies. Thus Jewish philanthropy is becoming increasingly a means of providing essential services not alone for the economically dependent families but for all economic classes.

There is a great variation in the extent to which the welfare services of the Jewish community are self-supporting through receipt of payments for service. Hospitals head the list, with an average of 72 percent of their costs derived from fees. Homes for the aged receive nearly 60 percent of their operating costs from their residents, and community centers 40 percent from membership dues and activities. A much smaller degree of self-support is registered by the child care agencies (9%). The family agencies, which in most cities are still looked upon as the source of material assistance, especially for recent immigrants, are also beginning to receive some income from clients who pay for the advice and counseling services which the agencies provide.

2. JEWISH HOSPITALS

There are 64 Jewish hospitals in the United States, with approximately 17,000 beds available for patients. Each of the sixteen cities with a Jewish population of 30,000 and over maintains a general hospital under Jewish auspices; in addition, five smaller communities maintain Jewish hospitals. There are also five national and four local hospitals primarily serving patients with tuberculosis and nine special hospitals for chronic illnesses, of which two specialize in the treatment of psychiatric ailments.

For 1952, 58 hospitals reported total admissions of over 420,000 patients. About one-half of all patients admitted to Jewish hospitals were Jews, but the proportion varied greatly among the hospitals.

In addition to caring for in-service patients, many of the institutions maintain out-patient clinics or departments. Forty-nine of these were reported in 1952 as serving over 260,000 different patients. In 1952 fewer than one-third of all patients in the out-service clinics of Jewish hospitals were Jews.

Despite variations among different sections of the country, there is an increasing development of public responsibility for patients in voluntary hospitals unable to pay for the care they receive. The amount of free care given by Jewish hospitals and not reimbursed from public funds has been diminishing over the years. For the general hospitals the proportion of patients receiving free care in 1952 was one out of five. Considerably more free care was made available by special hospitals for the tuberculous and for patients with chronic illnesses. Several of the national Jewish hospitals continue a policy of complete free care. The national as well as the local hospitals for the tuberculous, like the local general hospitals, are non-sectarian in their admission policies. Half of all admissions to Jewish hospitals for the tuberculous were non-Jews. Most hospitals for other long-term illnesses, however, serve predominantly Jewish patients.

MOUNT SINAI HOSPITAL, NEW YORK

The non-sectarian character of medical services has raised the question of the *raison d'être* for Jewish hospitals. The answer is partly that many voluntary hospitals in the United States are maintained by sectarian groups and that hospitals under Jewish auspices fit into this general pattern. The need of specific Jewish atmosphere and religious practices in hospitals for Jewish patients is considered as a secondary factor. While most Jewish hospitals maintain *kashrut,* it is reported that such policies are more the result of deference to the views of religious bodies than of the desire of the patients themselves. In recent years there has been an increasing insistence by Jewish religious bodies that Jewish hospitals conform with traditional Orthodox practice.

The proportion of Jews who use Jewish hospitals varies in different communities. A study in a large metropolitan center has indicated that not more than one third of Jewish patients use hospitals under Jewish auspices, the choice of the hospital to which a patient is sent being determined primarily by the affiliations of his physician.

One of the main motivations in recent years for the development and maintenance of Jewish hospitals has been discrimination against Jewish physicians by some hospitals in their selection of internes, resident doctors and affiliated and attending staff. Jewish hospitals therefore fill a vital need for Jews in the medical profession for training facilities. More recently, with the shortage of medical stu-

BETH ISRAEL HOSPITAL, NEW YORK

dents and graduates, some Jewish hospitals which do not measure up to the highest medical standards are finding it difficult to attract the best qualified practitioners. An urgent need is therefore felt by hospitals under Jewish auspices for improved standards, affiliations with medical schools, research opportunities and other ways of meeting the highest standards of hospital practice. Jewish hospitals are accepted today as a legitimate beneficiary of Jewish philanthropy in large cities and receive from 30 to 40 percent of all charitable funds spent for local Jewish welfare purposes. The continuation of Jewish hospitals as a part of Jewish communal organization of the future will be affected by the general organization of medical facilities in the United States. A complete system of public health or some radical form of compulsory health insurance which would shift hospital care more fully to government auspices (not likely to de-

velop soon) would alter this situation profoundly. Current governmental policies are reinforcing the continuation of voluntary hospitals by subsidies for new hospital construction and similar measures.

3. CARE OF THE AGED

Programs of care for the aged are of increasing importance on the welfare agenda. During the periods of heavy immigration America was a country of relatively young people, but with the stoppage of immigration and the passing of the years there has been a general aging of the population. Several decades ago local studies indicated that between three and four percent of the total Jewish population were 65 years and over. Today the ratio is closer to 8 percent.

To meet the needs of aged persons unable to care for themselves in their own homes or those of relatives, 80 homes for the Jewish aged have been established

CITY OF HOPE, LOS ANGELES

throughout the United States. At the present time, practically every city with a Jewish population of 5,000 or more has one or more homes for the aged, and there are eight homes for the aged in smaller communities. Several of the homes serve areas outside of the city in which they are located so that homes for the aged are available to practically all Jews in the United States. Sixty-six percent of these homes in 1952 reported having about 8750 beds with over 10,000 different individuals under care during the year.

The increasing number of aged has called for increased facilities. Several cities have already built new homes or enlarged existing institutions, and there are additional plans for expansion in about 20 cities, involving costs of over $12,000.000.

Homes for the aged are becoming increasingly responsive to the needs of older people unable to adjust in the community and are offering more than mere food and shelter. Many are developing comprehensive medical programs for chronic illness, which occurs more frequently in the later years. A number of these homes have achieved the status of medical institutions, and some of the medically qualified homes are beginning to make their facilities available to younger disabled persons. In 1952, homes for the aged reported that 10 percent or more of their residents were under 65.

Since the inauguration of the Old Age Assistance program by the Federal government the number and proportion of residents in Jewish homes for the aged receiving this form of public assistance have been rising. In 1952, nearly 60 percent of the residents in Jewish homes for the aged were recipients of public old age assistance, aid to the blind, and Old Age and Survivors Insurance. It is due to this reason, as well as to the improving economic conditions of the Jewish population,

WORKMEN'S CIRCLE HOME FOR THE AGED, NEW YORK

that Jewish homes for the aged are no longer exclusively homes for the poor but are also used by the self-maintaining members of the population for the special care available in such institutions.

Service to the aged is not limited to institutional care. Most communities assist the aged persons in their own homes and, where required, offer special services to a considerable number of Jewish aged living in their own homes who are recipients of Old Age Assistance and other forms of public aid. It is being recognized increasingly that the aged group of the population requires more than custodial care or pensions. Services are being made available to meet recreational needs, medical care and opportunities for work and other normal activities.

Unlike hospitals, whose services are largely of a non-sectarian character, homes for the aged and institutions offering long-time care for people with chronic illnesses are obviously required to provide the kind of religious and cultural atmosphere congenial to the needs of their residents. For this reason the appropriateness of homes for the aged under sectarian auspices is not questioned.

4. SERVICE TO FAMILIES AND CHILDREN

Family service agencies, an established form of Jewish communal service, were originally established for relief to the poor. Now, with public assistance available, they are largely engaged in offering skilled service on family and personal problems for the self-maintaining group as well as for those in economic need. There are 93 organized Jewish family agencies in the United States offering professional service. In 1952 these agencies reported serving over 45,000 families, of whom approximately 40 percent were recent immigrants (not including the New York Association for New Americans, which serves only the immigrant group). Jewish family agencies throughout the country gave approxi-

HOME FOR THE BLIND, YONKERS, N.Y.

mately $4 million for direct assistance to families in need, of which about 75 percent was for the recent immigrant families, the older resident families receiving assistance from the public agencies in most communities. NYANA, which in 1950 had expended $9,600,000 on relief and service to immigrants in New York City, reported $2,566,000 spent in 1952 ($1,500,000 for direct relief) and expected a further sharp drop for 1953.

Since the latter years of the 1930's the family service agencies have shown a consistent decline in expenditures for relief, but a corresponding increase in services for family problems. More service is being offered to people on a fee-charging basis; the practice of self-supporting people receiving service from the family agencies and paying for it is in its initial stages and is likely to grow.

In addition to serving families in their own homes, many of the family service agencies also serve children who require care outside of their family groups. More

than 30 of the family service agencies provide special care in foster homes for children. In addition to the family service agencies there are 24 agencies dealing exclusively with child care.

The trend in Jewish child care has been downward for more than 20 years. In 1930 there were 60 institutions for dependent and neglected children; by 1953 only 23 institutions for children were still in operation. In place of the institutions, foster care in families has been on the ascendant. In 1930 nearly 60 percent of the children under care were in institutions. By 1952, this figure had dropped to 30 percent, with 50 percent in family foster homes and the rest receiving care from special child serving agencies while living with their own parents or other close relatives. More than 60 percent of children in Jewish institutions are in the New York City "orphanages".

The total number of Jewish children under care in institutions and foster homes has been declining for nearly two decades, but the child-care agencies receive annually about the same volume of applications for care. The explanation is that since 1930 the problems which children present are capable of more rapid adjustment through the use of community resources for the economic maintenance of family life and through the professional services which help families to keep their homes intact. Economic improvement and public help available to dependent children in their own homes are additional factors. On the other hand, family breakdowns due to mental ill health, family separations and divorce continue to create need for the services of family and children's agencies.

Some child care agencies provide special services for the emotionally maladjusted child. A number of the agencies in New York, Chicago and Cleveland and elsewhere specialize in this form of service, which is needed by children of all economic groups. An increasing number of families are applying for this service; whether this is due to increasing strains and dislocations in Jewish family life or to other factors is not clear.

The rationale for Jewish services to families and children is self-evident. It is to be expected that care for Jewish children will be provided in Jewish homes and that the group as a whole will be concerned with providing services one of whose major purposes is the maintenance of Jewish family life. However, with the development of professional skills by medical and lay practitioners some individuals use services that are not under Jewish auspices, especially those which are available as a form of private fee-charging practice.

5. TRENDS IN WELFARE SERVICES

Depression, followed by wartime building restrictions, prevented the growth of welfare institutions and retarded modernization of buildings and equipment. After World War II, it was again possible to improve facilities for medical service and for the care of the aged and chronically ill and to provide more adequate facilities

for leisure and cultural activities. Many communities began to modernize their welfare and cultural institutions as well as to build new synagogues and to raise additional funds for these purposes. By 1953, most of the larger cities had either built or were planning to build additional facilities for the care of the aged, to improve or expand their hospital facilities and to provide more adequate facilities for youth activities and cultural work. There is no central record of the total costs involved, but it may be estimated that since 1945 perhaps as much as two hundred million dollars have been spent for these purposes in the Jewish communities of the United States.

Current trends in philanthropy reflect the changed economic and social conditions of the Jewish population and the increasing responsibiilty of government for meeting needs that formerly were met largely by church bodies and other voluntary organizations. Except for the depression years of the early 1930's, when an increased burden fell upon the voluntary agencies, during the last 30 years there has been a growing assumption of responsibility for economic assistance by federal, state and local governmental agencies. With the development of social security, unemployment insurance and public assistance for the aged, the blind and dependent children, and with state-supported local provisions for other types of assistance, there has been almost a complete transfer of responsibility from voluntary to governmental agencies for the basic underpinning of family income. Jewish welfare agencies are facing a long-time diminishing trend in the number of individuals and families requiring basic financial help, interrupted only temporarily by the need to help new immigrants.

Similarly, with the rising economic status of Jews, facilities such as hospitals and institutions for the aged are finding that a larger proportion of the costs can be borne directly by individual users of these agencies. In addition, government funds subsidize in part the costs of caring for the sick and aged in voluntary institutions. Group insurance for hospital and medical care, such as the Blue Cross and Blue Shield Plans, has further reduced the proportion of individuals unable to pay for necessary health services.

With the shift of responsibility for relief from private to governmental agencies, the Jewish community has been able to develop new services, to devote more funds for cultural services and to improve the welfare and health agencies. The increased knowledge available from psychiatry and psychoanalysis, supplemented by the experience of social work agencies, has been translated into an expanding program of counselling and other services to help individuals and families with such problems as relations between husband and wife or parent and child and disturbed behavior.

With these developments, the question of the Jewish community's responsibility is beginning to be related more to cultural and less to economic needs. All services, whether of Jewish education, use of leisure-time, medical care or family adjustment, are therefore seen as those which are generally applicable to all members of the Jewish community, not to the marginal economic group alone. For this reason there is a rapid transition in Jewish philanthropy from charity to communal services for the group as a whole.

6.   NON-SECTARIAN ASPECTS OF JEWISH PHILANTHROPY

Jewish philanthropy does not express itself exclusively through Jewish organizations. Jews as individuals, and occasionally as groups, are also contributors to institutions under other sectarian auspices and to non-sectarian causes such as the Community Chests (which also support Jewish agencies), the American Red Cross, the national health promotion agencies, universities and colleges, and hospitals and other welfare institutions. Jewish agencies

participate in community-wide planning through Councils of Social Agencies. Philanthropic foundations such as the Rosenwald Family Associates, the Guggenheim Fund, the Falk Foundation, as well as numerous other individual and family philanthropic foundations and trusts, have been established. Several of these philanthropic funds have been especially helpful to such general causes as the welfare of American Negroes, organization of general services, medical and social science research and other important undertakings which serve the total population. Other public-spirited Jews have for many years contributed funds for civic improvement and the general welfare. Individual lay and professional leaders have been active in welfare legislation and civic improvement.

A relatively recent special development has been the establishment of Brandeis University in 1947 as a non-sectarian institution of higher learning. Though it appeals primarily to Jewish contributors for its continued support, and though a large proportion of its Governing Board, students and faculty are Jews, Brandeis does not consider itself as a Jewish university; its avowed purpose is to enable Jews, like other denominational groups, to contribute to higher education in this country and to demonstrate the principle of non-discrimination in higher education. In 1950 Brandeis projected capital fund requirements amounting to over $13 million and had annual deficits of approximately $750,000 above its tuition income.

A project in medical education largely sponsored and supported by Jews is the Chicago Medical School. Established in 1912 under non-sectarian auspices, it has within the last ten years received increasing interest and support from Jews by reason of the fact that it maintained a non-discriminatory policy of student admission at a time when most medical schools were operating under a quota system. In 1947 the school affiliated with Mt. Sinai Hospital of Chicago and in 1948 it

AERIAL VIEW OF THE BRANDEIS CAMPUS, WALTHAM, MASS.

was accredited by the American Medical Association and the Association of American Medical Colleges. It reports that about 90 percent of its enrollment of 272 students in 1951 were Jews. Yeshiva University is now engaged in establishing a medical school in New York City which will be non-sectarian in its admission policy.

The scope and direction of Jewish philanthropy have been changing, as indicated, in response to changing social and economic forces. It will continue to change, expressing the recognition of important Jewish interests and sharing in the responsibility of all citizens for the needs of the American community.

VII. OVERSEAS AID

Help to Jews overseas, like other communal activities, had its origins in the continuing bonds of mutual interest which immigrants have maintained with their kin abroad. When small handfuls of Jewish settlers were attempting to develop their community life during the colonial period, fellow Jews in other lands helped immigrants on their way to America and assisted in the establishment of the first American religious institutions. It was not long before American Jews were able to reciprocate such help. *Shlihim* from European and Palestinian yeshivas and other organizations abroad visited the United States early in the 18th century to obtain help from American Jewry. Following persecutions and pogroms, funds were obtained to relieve the suffering of the affected groups and to assist in immigration. However, the chief organizations concerned with overseas aid were for many years centered in England and France, and later in Germany.

It was not until the First World War that the flow of American help to Jews abroad reached proportions requiring formal organization. The American Jewish Joint Distribution Committee (JDC) was organized in November of 1914 as a merger of two groups established earlier that year: the Central Relief Committee, organized by the Union of Orthodox, and the American Jewish Relief Committee, created by the American Jewish Committee. Some months later the People's Relief Committee, representing Jewish labor groups, became the third member of the new organization.

The JDC was active from 1914 through 1933 in assisting Jews in Eastern Europe and in helping the war-devastated and uprooted communities to re-establish themselves. In the 1920's the JDC contributed to the reconstruction of Jewish life in the Soviet Union through the work of the Agrojoint, which promoted agricultural colonization, and through other programs assisting Russian Jewry to adjust to the new economic conditions. By 1932, although sections of East European Jewry were still in economic distress, their own communal organizations were functioning actively and the work of the JDC was apparently nearing its end. With the rise of Hitlerism, which was to increase Jewish suffering everywhere in Europe, and as the spread of Nazism culminated in World War II, which inundated and practically destroyed the Jewish communities of Central and Eastern Europe, the JDC from 1934 again undertook an expanded program of help and rescue.

American Zionism dates from 1897. Within a few years the Federation of American Zionists was undertaking to raise money for the Jewish National Fund and for other organizations devoted to Palestine settlement. Though funds for Palestine increased over the years, sums raised before 1933 were relatively modest. Many of the immigrants to Palestine came with their own capital, and philanthropic funds available for land purchase and colonization were limited. From 1914 to 1932 the JDC had spent close to $100,000,000 for its work overseas, including several million dollars expended in Palestine. In 1932, because of the depression and other causes, JDC and Palestine fund-raising organiza-

tions in the United States each spent less than $400,000 abroad.

The persecution of Jews in Germany revived and intensified interest in overseas needs. Funds increased rapidly to help European Jews to escape the terrors of Hitlerism and to migrate to other countries, and to promote the development of Palestine. Since 1945 JDC expenditures alone have totalled nearly $350,000,000.

The United Palestine Appeal (which represented Keren Hayesod and Keren Kayemeth), the Joint Distribution Committee and the National Refugee Service, which assisted Jews who had succeeded in coming to the United States, required larger funds for their programs. In 1939 the United Jewish Appeal was organized as a more effective instrument in their behalf, and fund raising was accelerated and improved. The United Jewish Appeal (UJA) was able to secure more than $460 million for its three beneficiary agencies in the first ten years of its existence, and $350 million in the next four years. At first the largest share of its funds was channeled to the JDC for rescue abroad. As the work of rescuing the remnants of shattered Jewry and settling them in Israel and elsewhere reached its completion and with the creation of the State of Israel in 1948, most of the funds raised were channeled to Israel.

The JDC and the UPA (now called the United Israel Appeal), although they continued to be the major fund-raising instruments for overseas aid, were not alone in this field. HIAS continued its service to Jews abroad and assistance to immigrants arriving in the United States. In 1953, it spent close to $1,500,000 on its programs in Europe and America and on projects which it had undertaken in the State of Israel.

The American Federation of ORT (Organization for Rehabilitation Through Training), which was established in 1922 for organizing American support of ORT, continued to help its parent organization in its work of vocational training in Europe, Africa and Israel. To avoid a separate campaign ORT in recent years has been financed in this country by JDC. The Jewish Labor Committee also continues to assist labor unions and the work of democratic organizations abroad, but the extent of this help has been diminishing from the peak of over $700,000 spent in 1948 to approximately $250,000 at the present time. The JDC has also undertaken some projects in Israel.

In addition to the United Israel Appeal there are a number of organizations under Zionist and other auspices which campaign for funds independently. A number of them, such as the National Committee for Labor Israel (1923) and the Pioneer Women of America (Women's Labor Zionist Organization of America, 1925) are also concerned with other Zionist objectives. The largest of the independent Zionist fund-raising efforts is conducted by Hadassah, which in 1953 had income totaling approximately $9,600,000. (Organized primarily to secure the interest of women in the welfare needs of Israel and to obtain philanthropic funds for its overseas projects, Hadassah also conducts educational and other programs for its membership.) The Weizmann Institute, the Hebrew University, the Hebrew Institute for Technology in Haifa—the three institutions of higher learning in Israel—raise funds separately under the independent auspices of American committees set up for these purposes.

Other organizations raising funds for Israel include the Federated Council of Israel Institutions, which collects money from welfare funds in behalf of Israeli *yeshivot* and traditional welfare institutions, and which reports receipts of $217,-000 in 1953. The American Fund for Israel Institutions, organized in 1941 as the central fund-raising instrument for some of the leading cultural, educational and social welfare agencies in Israel, reported a total income of $1,060,000 in 1953.

In general, the funds raised for overseas programs, exclusive of other fund-raising efforts, in 1952 amounted to approximately $72,300,000 for the UJA and its subsidiaries and approximately $17,500,000 for the overseas agencies not included in the United Jewish Appeal.

The needs of Israel have called forth additional economic efforts, including the encouragement of American investments through the Palestine Economic Corporation, organized in 1926, and the American Palestine Trading Corporation, organized in 1942. In 1950 the State of Israel floated a $500,000,000 bond issue in the United States through the American Financial Development Corporation for Israel. The most recent report from the AFDCI (May 1954) is that from May 1951 the corporation sold or received payment for bonds totaling $145,000,000.

In addition to philanthropic and investment aid to Israel, American Jewry is also concerned with the help which the United States government has made available to the State of Israel. It has encouraged this policy and has endorsed the loans and grants which have been made. Since its organization in 1948, Israel has received a $135 million loan from the Export-Import Bank, almost the same total amount in grants-in-aid for the two fiscal years ending June 30, 1953, surplus goods in 1950 and 1951 estimated as being worth $24 million, and an appropriation for technical assistance amounting to $2,772,000. These combined grants and loans amount to a total of close to $300 million.

With the creation of the State, the gradual easing of conditions for Jews in Europe, and the Jewish depopulation of a number of countries from which the surviving Jews have emigrated, the center of American Jewish interest in overseas help has shifted to Israel. The condition of Jews in the countries in Eastern Europe is uncertain, and they are cut off from contacts and economic help from the West. Most of the Jews displaced by the war have either emigrated from Europe or have found some basis of adjustment in the countries of Western Europe where they

have remained. The costs and the programs outside of Israel are diminishing
while Israel continues to require considerable help to enable its population to
achieve economic stability. At the present
time, with Israel depending upon imports
for many essentials of living, and with the
relatively low rate of exports, the people
of Israel continue to rely largely on outside, principally American, help for the
maintenance and growth of their economy.
The only large area outside of Israel where
a large indigenous Jewish population is
living under low standards and is in desperate need of economic and social help
is North Africa.

Overseas help continues in the forefront
of American Jewish philanthropy in the
amount of funds it receives, the quality
of the public interest it arouses, the urgency of the problems it presents and the
vigor of the various fund-raising organizations involved. Nearly 70% of the funds
raised by central fund-raising bodies in
the United States goes for overseas philanthropy, but since 1949 there has been
a gradual decline both in the dollars raised
and the proportion going overseas.

Some organizations, such as Hadassah
and Pioneer Women, are membership as
well as fund-raising bodies. Other organizations, such as ORT and the American
Friends of the Hebrew University, also
have memberships which operate as an
auxiliary body paying nominal dues—a
policy acceptable to the welfare funds
which supply the major funds to these
organizations. Most of the major overseas
fund-raising organizations, however, do not
have an individual membership but are
operated by boards of relatively small size.
They rely upon the community welfare
funds and their 1,300,000 contributors,
who through their interest and continued
support are the underlying constituencies
of the overseas organizations. Thus, either
through the welfare funds or through direct membership affiliation, a large proportion of American Jewry relates itself to

overseas as well as to local philanthropic
activity.

VIII.   ANTI-SEMITISM

Concern with the problem of anti-Semitism and the need to improve group relations between Jews and other sections of the
American community was growing in the
early 1900's. During the preceding century
Jews achieved the full civil and political
rights inherent in the nature of American
democracy with only sporadic difficulties,
and occasional instances of overt anti-
Semitism against individual Jews could
be met by individual or informal group
reaction. The Board of Delegates of American Israelites, organized in 1859 "to bring
about the union of American Israelites
for their common welfare," had as one
of its stated objectives "to keep a watch-
ful eye on occurrences at home and abroad,
and see that the civil and religious rights
of Israelites are not encroached on, and
call attention of the proper authorities to
the fact should any such violation occur."
During its existence, it was largely concerned with the civic and political problems of Jews abroad.

In the last decades of the 19th century
the interest of individual American Jews,
local congregations, fraternal societies and
other groups had been secured for protests against pogroms and other forms of
anti-Semitism in Europe and North Africa.
Anti-alien and anti-Jewish attitudes were
perhaps never absent from the American
scene, but the character and extent of these
manifestations did not appear to press
heavily upon Jews and did not call forth
special organization to combat them.
When the American Jewish Committee
was organized in 1906, its major task was
the protection of the civil and political
rights of Jews, but for many years it, too,
was to concentrate its interest upon events
abroad rather than at home.

The early years of the 20th century
showed increasing evidences of strain and
conflict among American religious and
ethnic groups; though democracy and

equal political rights were inherent in law and social policy, the general environment was becoming less free from prejudice and discrimination. The prejudicial attitudes underlying the anti-alien movements and proposals for restriction of immigration led to expression of anti-Jewish feeling in the press and on the stage, especially after 1910 and with the upsurge of nationalist sentiment that began with World War I.

B'nai B'rith as an organization was interested in counteracting prejudice and unfavorable treatment of Jews and Jewish activities. In 1913 it established the Anti-Defamation League. Its methods were based upon an individual handling of specific situations through bringing to bear enlightenment and persuasion. In 1925 the scope of the Anti-Defamation League was expanded to include good-will efforts with Christian or non-sectarian groups, with the belief that discrimination could be more effectively combatted by intergroup cooperation than by exclusively Jewish efforts.

Individuals associated with Zionist groups in this country and sharing the Zionist point of view believed in the necessity of a permanent nation-wide Jewish body organized on a wide basis of popular participation and concerned with a wide range of problems, including those of group relationships. The present American Jewish Congress, which embodies these views, was convened in 1922 and became affiliated with the World Jewish Congress, which it helped to establish in 1936. The American Jewish Congress took for its arena of general purposes and activity the political rights of Jews in this country and overseas, and employment and other forms of discrimination in this country.

Although several organizations with a membership of Jewish labor elements were affiliated with the American Jewish Congress, none of the three Jewish protective agencies had obtained the direct participation of Jewish trade unions. The rise of Hitler and his attack upon organized labor in Germany led to an interest by Jewish labor leaders in a program through which organized labor in general and Jewish labor in particular might contribute to the solution of Jewish problems. Accordingly, in 1934 Jewish labor leaders established the Jewish Labor Committee, which sought to obtain the help of organized American labor against persecution developing in Europe.

The limited programs of defense work in the United States before 1933 involved few occasions for cooperation. With the acute phase of anti-Jewish manifestations after 1933, it was recognized that a more formal type of cooperation was required. A joint Consultative Council was established.

The growth of organized activity against anti-Semitism is indicated by the trend in its costs. Before 1933 the national organizations spent approximately $100,000 on all their programs, including a library of information, research work and other functions. In 1933 over $170,000 was spent; by 1938 the costs had reached $875,000; they have kept on expanding rapidly, with over $6 million spent by the four agencies in 1948. Fund raising having declined, the expenditures of the four major national agencies in this field came to approximately $5 million in 1953.

In addition to national organizations, the growing problems of anti-Semitism led to the establishment of local programs. Several of the national agencies had local chapters engaged in programs geared to the activities of their parent organizations. Some cities also developed local programs to deal with problems on a community-wide basis. By 1954 thirty cities and several regional areas had established permanent agencies with professional staffs, which have become members of the central coordinating body, the National Community Relations Advisory Council. In a number of other cities programs for improving intergroup relationships are undertaken by the central bodies through committees and other voluntary activities.

Efforts at coordination had succeeded in other fields of activity, such as overseas fund raising, and many believed that the tasks of counteracting anti-Semitism were particularly appropriate for coordination and joint action. In 1938 the national agencies organized the General Jewish Council, whose function was to serve as a common meeting ground for the major agencies engaged in civic defense work and to help them to arrive at agreement on principles and methods of fighting Nazism and anti-Semitism in this country. The American Jewish Congress withdrew from this Council following the failure of all of the constituent agencies to agree on a central fund-raising plan (and the establishment of the Joint Defense Appeal in behalf of the American Jewish Committee and the Anti-Defamation League). In 1944 the National Community Relations Advisory Council was established and added the local community relations councils to the national agency membership of its predecessor.

The National Community Relations Advisory Council (NCRAC) in 1944 adopted as its program the following objectives:

(1) To study, analyze and evaluate the policies and activities of the national and local agencies;

(2) to ascertain the problem areas from time to time;

(3) to ascertain the areas of activities of these organizations and to conduct a continuous inventory of their projects;

(4) to serve as a coordinating and clearance agency for projects and policies, to eliminate duplication and conflicts of activities and to recommend further projects to member agencies; and

(5) to seek agreement on and to formulate policies. After the formulation and adoption of policies, it was expected that the affiliated organizations would adhere to such policies and would not engage in any activities in contravention of such policies.

The record of the NCRAC includes agreement on a number of major policy issues. The member agencies were able to achieve unanimity on how to deal with some of the difficult problems in group-relations work. After six years of experience in the NCRAC a sentiment developed both among some of the national agencies and the local community members of NCRAC and among the welfare funds which contributed to the support of the defense agencies that a more vigorous coordination was essential. A general survey was agreed upon by the member agencies of NCRAC and Robert M. MacIver, Professor of Sociology at Columbia University, was selected to study the underlying problems and to make recommendations for improving coordination and central planning among the member agencies of NCRAC. The result of the study was a series of proposals which, after being interpreted or modified through various intermediary procedures, came before a Plenary Session of the NCRAC in September 1952. At this meeting the majority adopted recommendations for a more integrated form of cooperation among the national and local members of the NCRAC. The majority action was not acceptable to two of the major agencies, the American Jewish Committee and the Anti-Defamation League of the B'nai B'rith, which dissented from the action taken and subsequently withdrew. The NCRAC is continuing on the program adopted with a current membership of six national agencies, the Orthodox and Conservative congregational organizations joining with the (Reform) Union of American Hebrew Congregations, which had previously become a member of NCRAC, and thirty local community relations councils. The member agencies of NCRAC are engaging in joint planning of programs and joint assessment of their problems and the validity of the methods and techniques employed to deal with them.

The existence of separate national agencies for defense work is not due solely to fortuitous circumstances and represents more than a duplication of effort. It is highly probable that the organization of separate groups is related to the social and economic differences in the Jewish population. The American Jewish Committee represents in general the older and economically better established element of the Jewish population. The Congress is considered as having a middle class constituency, representative of the more recent immigrant elements. The Labor Committee, as its name implies, represents the organized Jewish labor elements, especially those with a close connection with the European background of the immigrants of the 20th century. The agencies representing the Jewish War Veterans and the religious groups are perhaps related more to specific interests outside of defense work rather than to a social or economic stratification directly related to ideological differences. The Anti-Defamation League of the B'nai B'rith largely represents an Americanized middle class constituency concerned with many different interests and functions.

The work undertaken by these various organizations in dealing with problems of group relations is to some extent colored by the character of their constituents. MacIver, however, found a great similarity in actual functioning among the agencies, indicating that perhaps a developing science of community relations work was emerging from the experience of these groups, resulting in programs not too strongly affected by the social philosophies of their constituents.

If we are to judge by the controversy raised over the 1952 NCRAC decisions, there is a considerable difference of opinion among the leaders of the agencies as to the nature of the Jewish community and the appropriate structure for its organizational life. There is the implied assumption that the difference in constituencies entails not only a difference in ideological orientation concerning the nature of Jewish communal life but also the need for distinctive programs based on these ideologies. The counter-argument for greater coordination is the belief that the problem of anti-Semitism cannot be divided in accordance with Jewish group beliefs but is an organic entity, and that the objectives and programs of these agencies need therefore to be functionally related.

The problem raised by the withdrawal of the American Jewish Committee and the Anti-Defamation League has not thus far been solved and continuing efforts are being made to find a basis of accommodation which will restore a cooperative relationship among all of the organizations in this field.

During the period under review there has been a considerable shift of understanding concerning the nature of anti-Semitism, the problems of group relations and the requirements for social action. Some of the ideas underlying the earlier work of the organizations are now considered as having been inadequate. At first primary attention was focused on acts of discrimination and defamation, and pressures and persuasion were employed as instruments for their solution, the hope being that an appeal to the decency of the better elements of the community would help to solve or alleviate the recurring incidents of prejudice, discrimination and defamation.

The next stage was marked by an interest in developing mass appeals through promoting the concepts of democracy in order to try to change the climate of opinion, with large use of the press, radio and other means of mass communication. This was later recognized as being of too wholesale a character, and it was followed by the technique of special educational efforts directed at special groups, such as the churches, labor and veterans.

Conscious of the limitations of programs and lack of exact knowledge concerning the nature of the problem and the effectiveness of methods for dealing with it, several of the national agencies, especially the American Jewish Committee and the American Jewish Congress, have fostered programs of social research. Most of the studies were made between 1945 and 1950, with a much smaller program of studies continued after that time. Since 1945, also, there has been a more intensive interest in law and social action, with the American Jewish Congress taking the lead but with the other agencies also accepting this as a valid area for defense work. Legal remedies for restrictions in housing, employment, admissions to educational institutions and other forms of discrimination based upon prejudices have been undertaken, sometimes by separate agencies or by groups of agencies, in cooperation with other religious or non-sectarian groups. Success in these programs has encouraged further efforts. The agencies properly have been interested not only in restrictions affecting Jews exclusively but in the civil rights of Negroes and other minority groups as well.

As in philanthropy, organized efforts to deal with problems of anti-Semitism enlist the membership not only of the specific agencies engaged in this work but also the members of other community organizations and the many contributors to the welfare funds which support the defense agencies. At one time or another practically all Jews have expressed a deep concern with these problems and many have engaged actively in the programs of the agencies attempting to deal with them.

IX.   ZIONISM AND OTHER IDEO-LOGICAL MOVEMENTS

The processes of adjustment to the American environment have given rise to individual and group attitudes resulting in a variety of types of American living. Though no human life can be wholly classified on the basis of sociological distinctions, many of the details of individual lives do conform to one or another category of experience. An individual may or may not be fully aware of the specific set of ideals which help to motivate his conduct. It is only in the expressions of individual living which are sufficiently prevalent to constitute some form of group behavior that we have a basis for identifying ideologies and for classifying individuals in accordance with some important aspect of group behavior. There are great variations in how people think and how they act even when they are affiliated with a distinctive ideological movement.

Some of the more prevalent patterns of behavior are expressed institutionally through the purposes and policies of organizations with which an individual becomes associated. While many do not select their Jewish associations by conscious design, the selection usually implies some theory of American Jewish living which presumably may be considered as the point of view to which the individual member gives direct or indirect allegiance, depending upon the meaning of the particular association to each individual concerned. The ideological pattern can be inferred from the quality of his participation in various religious institutions, his social status, his fraternal and social activities, his work associations and his recreational and leisure-time activities.

Some of the current ideologies which have arrived at group expression represent evolution and change in older forms of communal affiliation. For example, Reform Judaism, the Conservative movement, Reconstructionism and other recent developments in organized religion are forms of evolution from earlier religious practices.

Aside from changes in the forms of Jewish religion, the ideological movement which has had the greatest impact and the most profound effect upon contemporary American Jewry has been Zionism. It has aroused the most deep-seated loyalties and the sharpest controversies. Reinforcing the religious basis of group affiliation, Zionism promoted the theory of Jews as a nationality, a point of view which coincided with the rise of nationalism generally but which had not been dominant in the sentiments of most of the early immigrants.

When American Zionist organizations were established in the United States following the first World Zionist Congress in 1897 there was considerable opposition to Zionism, especially within Reform Judaism. Reflecting the views prevalent among Jews in Western Europe, many Americans rejected the goal of a national Jewish home not only for themselves but even as a solution for the problems of Jews overseas. The view held by many non- or anti-Zionists, who had welcomed the opportunities for civic integration in the United States and Western Europe, was that Jews everywhere should strive to become integrated into the national life of countries in which they lived. Other opposition came from those with a socialist orientation, who placed internationalism above nationalism as the proper goal.

Also at variance with the Zionist program, though on method rather than goal, was the program of the Territorialists—those who believed in setting up a homeland for Jews in some available section of the globe where they might constitute the dominant majority. The Territorialists believed that Palestine was either unavailable or unsuitable for Jewish colonization and that some other area would be better.

From its inception American Zionism proceeded to grow in strength. It was accepted increasingly by Jewish immigrants from Eastern Europe, where the program of Zionism met with more immediate and more widespread acceptance than in this country. Following the rise of Nazism, Zionism began to influence larger and larger sections of American Jewry. At the end of World War II, with the recognition of the catastrophe which had befallen European Jewry, acceptance of the goal of Zionism reached its highest

point, the climax coming in 1948 when the State of Israel was created.

Membership in Zionist organizations, reported as having reached large numbers before the creation of the State of Israel, has been declining. In Jewish education, in the stimulation of greater acceptance by American Jews of Hebrew as a language of cultural expression, and in other ways, the proponents of Zionism are attempting to find a basis for maintaining interest in the needs of Israel and supporting the State morally, politically and economically.

The major organized Zionist activities are primarily those concerned with help to Israel. Economic help is centered mainly in special fund-raising organizations, such as the United Israel Appeal which as a constituent of the United Jewish Appeal secures funds for the Jewish Agency. The National Board of the U.I.A., originally composed exclusively of Zionist agencies, now includes some members designated by welfare funds. The largest membership organization whose work is primarily help to Israel and selected welfare causes is Hadassah, the women's Zionist organization of America, which has enrolled a very large section of Jewish women for its aims. Active and vigorous Hadassah branches have been established in practically every community with a large enough Jewish population. While the main purpose of Hadassah continues to be assistance to Israel, it also fosters interest in American affairs and conducts other educational activities. Other organizations which combine fund raising with educational or political interests are the National Committee for Labor Israel, which besides raising funds for Histadrut engages in educational activities, and the American labor movement in behalf of Israel.

Beyond raising funds, stimulating investments in and trade with Israel, and engaging in educational activities, Zionist organizations also participate in movements designed to maintain the sympathetic interest of the American government, which had helped to establish the State of Israel. They are concerned with continuing government help and maintaining the good will of American people for the new State.

Support of Israel has for many years not been confined to Zionist groups. Many other sections of American Jewry, which previously considered themselves as non-Zionists, have a vigorous interest in aiding the State of Israel with philanthropic funds and through political sympathies. Their instruments are the welfare funds and community councils and the national community relations agencies, such as the American Jewish Committee and the Jewish Labor Committee. The most important fund-raising organization in behalf of Israel is the United Jewish Appeal—a non-ideological philanthropic organization which depends upon non-Zionist as well as Zionist supporters. The priority of non-Zionist bodies in raising funds for Israel is probably an additional reason why some of the Zionist organizations not primarily involved in fund raising have been losing members since 1948.

The organization with a point of view on the opposite extreme to Zionism is the American Council for Judaism (1942), which has as its purpose "to advance the universal principles of a Judaism free of nationalism and the national, civic, cultural and social integration of Americans of Jewish faith." The American Council for Judaism and the Zionist bodies have been in constant conflict with each other.

Their underlying philosophies and objectives are stated by some of the larger membership groups in the following terms: The American Jewish Committee "promotes a philosophy of Jewish integration by projecting a balanced view with respect to full participation in American life and retention of Jewish identity." The B'nai B'rith "seeks to unite Jews through cultural, social, civic, philanthropic and patriotic activities." The American Jewish Congress seeks "to promote the democratic organization of Jewish communal life in the United States; to foster the affirmation of Jewish religious, cultural and historic identity, and to contribute to the preservation and extension of the democratic way of life."

A number of organizations represent the affiliation of American Jews who have an orientation related primarily to labor or socialist interests as well as to Yiddish cultural activities. Such are the Workmen's Circle, the Jewish Labor Committee, some of the *Landsmanshaften,* and cultural agencies related to them by their membership or the outlook on Jewish life implicit in their work.

By affiliation with group activities which are considered as having an ideological orientation, American Jews select an ideology compatible with whatever theories of Jewish life they may hold. There have been few research studies that throw light on the ideological divisions or affiliations of American Jews. For many individuals the ideological distinctions of the organizations remain unclear. It is only through study of actual behavior rather than presumed attitudes that one could arrive at a clear understanding of group objectives among American Jews.

X. EFFORTS TOWARD COMMUNAL COORDINATION

1. LOCAL ASPECTS

The growing Jewish population and the diversity of groups and activities which developed with large-scale Jewish immigration in the 19th century brought about a complexity of Jewish communal life which has become more intensified with the years. In the earlier days the small size of the Jewish group and its greater homogeneity made for a simpler communal life. Diversified activities which involved the group as a whole were usually undertaken by a single agency. With the large-scale immigration of Jews having different backgrounds the bonds of common interest became more tenuous. There were tendencies toward isolation, and a fragmentized community gave rise to a large number of agencies duplicating and competing with each other.

The first efforts at coordination in the early 19th century were in philanthropy. Some of the first welfare organizations were created by the consolidation or merger of groups associated with synagogues representing largely the German immigrants and the Sephardic groups. With the rise in immigration from Eastern Europe separate agencies and activities were established and duplication and lack of unity were again an acute problem. By the end of the 19th century the duplications and conflicts in welfare activities began to receive increasing attention. Modern social work was developing in the United States and some of the better established Jewish welfare agencies were becoming acquainted with its views and programs.

The opportunity for coordination in Jewish communal service presented itself first in fund raising. Numerous welfare agencies were appealing to wider sections of the Jewish community on the logical assumption that charitable work, whatever its auspices, had a right to the interest and support of all Jews. The difficulties of fund raising during that period were many and in the larger cities the repetitious succession of bazaars, charity balls and individual solicitations became oppressive. When groups of the larger contributors got together to see whether they could pool their efforts to simplify the problem of fund raising and obtain more effective results, the Jewish federation movement was born. The first federations were established in Boston and Cincinnati in 1895. Although this movement for combining agencies for fund-raising purposes was new for the United States, its proponents were following a method developed abroad which was being publicized at that time. The name "Liverpool Plan" was applied to these early Jewish efforts even though

England had not been the scene of the first European effort at united fund raising. (Much greater progress in this direction was subsequently achieved in the United States than in Europe.) Jewish federations were soon developed in other large cities —Chicago and St. Louis (1900), Philadelphia (1901), Buffalo (1903), Cleveland (1904), Atlanta and Indianapolis (1905). On the Pacific Coast San Francisco federated in 1910 and Los Angeles in 1911. New York City established its federation in 1917.

At first the federation was primarily a method of unifying the solicitation of funds for the local Jewish welfare activities, mainly family relief, homes for the aged, orphanages, immigrant aid and hospitals. By 1925, about forty cities had some kind of Jewish federation of charities conducting annual campaigns for funds to meet the needs of its local beneficiary agencies. In several cities the federation movement at first was unable to combine under the same auspices the agencies representing both the newer and the older groups in the community. In Chicago a federation of Orthodox agencies, established in 1911, continued as a separate agency until it was merged in 1923 with the federation established by the Reform group.

The Community Chest movement, which applied the same idea of federated fund raising to the general community for agencies under Protestant, Catholic and non-sectarian as well as Jewish auspices, originated in Cleveland in 1913. Stimulated by war-time needs (1914-1918), the Community Chest became an established pattern for American communities. In many of the larger cities the Jewish federations joined these overall community chests and gave up their own fund-raising efforts, their beneficiary welfare societies becoming the constituents of the general chest. Under such arrangements the Jewish federations often retained responsibility for budgeting the funds made available by community chests for Jewish agencies, and gave greater attention also to central planning and coordination of welfare services. Community chests did not develop in New York and Chicago, where the Jewish federations continued their separate fund-raising activities. Limited chests were later developed in New York and Chicago, but they supply only a small fraction of the funds of the Jewish federations in these cities. In Baltimore the Catholic and Jewish agencies did not join the Community Chest and the Jewish federation has continued as an independent fund-raising instrument. In most other cities the original Jewish welfare agencies depend on the Community Chest for most of their philanthropic funds.

The transfer of responsibility from the Jewish federations to the Community Chests did not completely meet the financial needs of all Jewish agencies in the community. Most of the Community Chests did not accept a responsibility for sectarian activities such as Jewish education and in some communities for cultural work such as YMHA's. Almost in the beginning, therefore, the federations that were interested in Jewish education and culture found it necessary to continue some form of separate fund raising for these local agencies not eligible for inclusion in chests. In most cities, national and overseas relief agencies were not eligible for chest funds and continued to appeal directly to Jews for local support. As a result there developed first in Oakland and San Francisco, in 1925, another form of joint fund raising which usually goes by the name of the Welfare Fund and includes the national and overseas as well as selected local agencies. In Detroit it was referred to as the "double-barreled" Jewish Federation, with the federation doing general planning but not assuming financial responsibility for local services, and in addition conducting its separate campaigns for the non-Chest agencies. This became the standard pattern of organization for most of the larger cities. By the 1930's Jewish

welfare funds were developing in many other communities as a consequence of the increasing appeals of the numerous national and overseas agencies for help from local Jewry. By 1945, most Jewish communities with a large enough population had organized central fund-raising instruments to meet these needs and to discharge whatever else was required in the way of local responsibility for local welfare activities.

While the federations and welfare funds were primarily concerned with welfare problems and with fund raising, the 1930's also brought on a development known as Jewish Community Councils, which concern themselves with the relations of the various Jewish groups to each other and to the general community. A special feature of community councils is the fact that many of them are based on organizational rather than individual memberships. With a variety of synagogues, fraternal organizations, welfare agencies, Zionist groups and the like leading an independent existence, there began to be evolved a form of association which would recognize the common areas of interest of these separate groups and whose membership would consist of their representatives. In some cities federations and welfare funds stimulated the organization of community councils as a device for securing the interest and participation of segments of the Jewish population not formally represented through individual membership.

Rapid evolution has brought a high degree of coordination to many communities where one or more of such central instruments have been established. The terms "federation," "welfare fund" and "community council" are no longer mutually exclusive; communities as large as Cleveland and Newark discharge a variety of functions through one unified organization. In Cleveland, for example, the Federation, which is a constituent member of the Community Chest, raises funds in a single campaign to supplement the Community Chest allocations to its local beneficiaries, to finance additional agencies such as Jewish educational institutions, which are not in the Chest, and to respond to a variety of national and overseas appeals. The Community Council in Cleveland has been integrated with the Federation, and the enlarged Federation continues to perform its basic function of community and intra-group relations. In some of the other large cities, however, two organizations continue, one for the local federation and one for the welfare fund, or there may be a federation-fund, on the one hand, and a group relations program, on the other, separately organized. These agencies may have individual memberships, consisting of all contributors who give a minimum annual contribution, or a combination of individual and organizational memberships.

The current trend in central communal agencies is to assume interest and responsibility for more than fund raising or administration of the social welfare and educational programs. In some cities communal interests such as *kashrut* and a community newspaper—aspects of intra-group relations—are considered as legitimate functions for the central organization. The local associations representing separate interests or operating as branches of national organizations continue as autonomous groups while joining in the central federation or central council for coordination and planning. In general, the central organization depends for its effectiveness upon voluntary participation and the consent of individual and group members. A central council empowered by a majority vote to act or speak for all Jews on sharply controversial issues has not been attained in any city. Within the limits of voluntary cooperation, however, the central instruments perform a very important function in enabling representatives of various Jewish groups to come together for consideration of common problems and agree upon common action.

Studies of Jewish community organization made by the Council of Jewish Federations and Welfare Funds—including intensive pilot studies in Albany, New York; Camden, New Jersey; and New Britain, Connecticut, in 1952-1953—indicate that the idea of a voluntary central communal organization is generally accepted. Communal leaders accept the continuing autonomy of the separate groups but see the need for a central agency to achieve greater understanding of the mutuality of interest and relationships among the varied Jewish groups and to develop a more effective program of communal service than can be done by the individual groups separately.

Coordination of activities in Jewish communities is on a secular basis, limited to welfare and cultural activities. Coordination of religious efforts has not been achieved in most communities with varied congregational groups, although there may be formal or informal association among the rabbis and cooperation among the congregations on problems of common concern, such as Jewish education or cultural and leisure-time activities.

A basic question for federations and councils is the structural form which will be generally accepted as giving adequate representation to the various groups in the community. Effective administration of communal agencies demands a leadership of the most competent and most interested individuals, having the confidence and ability to secure the cooperation of all sections of the community. The large populations in the metropolitan areas, the many members and contributors to central funds, the different organized groups to be considered, the voluntary character of participation and the relatively small number that can function actively as an administrative body make this effective leadership and administration a difficult task. Because of the importance and the uncontroversial character of philanthropy, the federations and welfare funds have been able to enlist practically all sections of the population and have organized businessmen's groups, women's federations, youth councils and other bodies for cooperative participation in fund raising and administration for a wide variety of Jewish needs and services. Branches of national organizations find it possible to cooperate wholeheartedly with the local central organization without diminishing the intensity of their interest in their special activities. But methods of election and selection to administrative boards do not work spontaneously or impersonally. Though the results are rarely completely satisfactory to everyone concerned, they are pragmatic, and make Jewish central organization on the whole about as democratic as it can be under the circumstances. As in other human associations, the stresses and strains of imperfect relationships frequently generate their own remedies.

The problem of coordination in Jewish communal activities has been most difficult to solve in the largest centers of Jewish population, especially in New York City with its 2,000,000 Jews living in the five boroughs. A Federation of Jewish Philanthropies was first established in Brooklyn in 1909, and in Manhattan and the Bronx in 1917. These two federations combined their fund-raising campaigns in 1937 and were merged several years later into the Greater New York Federation for the whole metropolitan area.

The New York Federation includes among its beneficiaries most of the important Jewish health, welfare and cultural agencies. Some hospitals, children's institutions and other services have not as yet become members, though federations in most other cities include virtually all health and welfare agencies. In 1939 New York organized a local United Jewish Appeal which raises funds for the national UJA and a few national agencies. There is also a Jewish Community Council in Brooklyn, organized in 1939 for community relations programs and central planning of non-philanthropic matters. No central structure, resembling those in New-

ark or Cleveland, has been able to develop in New York, with its diversity of neighborhoods and suburbs and its thousands of Jewish organizations and associations. Occasionally for a specific welfare problem, such as help to immigrants, it has been possible to set up a single organization which assumes general communal responsibility.

2. NATIONAL COORDINATION

The degree of coordination achieved locally has not as yet been achieved on a national scale. In the local communities, where groups can meet together easily, there is a beginning of central communal association growing in importance and in function. The concept of a permanent national central body to represent Jewish organization in important matters of common interest has frequently been advanced as a desirable goal but has been achieved only for temporary periods and for limited functions.

The relatively more homogeneous Jewish population of the 19th century was able to coordinate a number of its activities. Thus, in 1859 there was organized the Board of Delegates of American Israelites, which for a time concerned itself with civic and political problems and with extending aid to Jews overseas.

The next most important development was the organization in 1899 of the National Conference of Jewish Charities, which was similar in purpose to the nonsectarian National Conference of Charities which had been founded in 1874. The National Conference of Jewish Charities (now the National Conference of Jewish Communal Service) was the first attempt nationally to bring together local Jewish organizations and individuals interested in social welfare. It held an annual conference for both the professional and lay leadership of the welfare societies of the country and its deliberations helped to set desirable standards and to promote local coordination. By agreement of its members the Conference developed policies on relationships among communities with respect to the care of transients. It was also instrumental in establishing a graduate school for professional training of Jewish social workers (1925 to 1941), and explored other areas of inter-city relationships and common interests. More recently this Conference has become primarily a forum for professional workers in Jewish welfare agencies, centers and educational institutions.

3. NATIONAL SERVICE AGENCIES

With the increasing gravity of domestic problems brought on by the depression of the 1930's, the growing number of Jewish federations and welfare funds took on added importance as instruments of communal welfare. In 1932 sixteen federations and welfare funds organized the Council of Jewish Federations and Welfare Funds (CJFWF) as a national service agency. The CJFWF, with 255 member agencies in the United States and Canada in 1954, acts as their research and consultative body and cooperative association for the federations, welfare funds and community councils. It assists in the development of communal organization, advises on welfare programs and represents its member agencies on many aspects of their relationships to the national and overseas agencies. Through the CJFWF the local federations and welfare funds come together to develop standards both for their own local functions and for their responsibilities toward national and overseas needs.

Other national organizations have been developed for service to specialized local agencies. Among these are the National Jewish Welfare Board for Jewish centers (organized 1917), the American Association for Jewish Education (1939), and the Jewish Occupational Council, organized in 1939 by a number of national bodies and local vocational service agencies.

There have been other efforts toward national coordination from time to time. In 1917, an American Jewish Congress was organized on a temporary basis to coordinate the activities of American Jewish national agencies and local communities with respect to problems arising from World War I, especially those which would be discussed at the peace conference following the end of the war. The American Jewish Congress represented a joining of all important sections of American Jewry, including Reform and Orthodox, Zionist and non-Zionist, labor, fraternal and other groups as well. It was concerned with the status of European Jewry and political and civil rights abroad. After the Peace Conference the Congress was disbanded, as had been agreed, but there were those who wanted a permanent central body for American Jewry. This sentiment led to the creation of the American Jewish Congress of today, organized in 1922 without the cooperation of many of the groups which had joined in the limited purposes of the first Congress.

The history of the American Jewish Conference closely parallels that of the American Jewish Congress. The problems growing out of the rise of Hitler in Germany and the ensuing war were much more devastating in extent and character than those of the First World War. Following the precedent of 1917, the American Jewish Conference was organized in 1943 as a temporary body with an elaborate structure of voting participation by national organizations and by local Jewish community councils. At the time of its inception 64 national membership organizations were represented, electing 123 of the 502 delegates who had attended the first conference. The remaining delegates were elected at community and regional electoral conferences called especially for the purpose.

From the outset the Conference confined itself to international political affairs and Jewish rights. Its stated purpose was to "bring about some agreement on the part of the American Jewish community" and "to voice the judgment of American Jews with respect to the post-war status of Jews and the upbuilding of Jewish Palestine." At the first session in 1943 the agenda covered the need for recommending action on the rights and status of Jews in the post-war world and the implementation "of the rights of the Jewish people with respect to Palestine." There was virtually complete agreement among the delegates on all proposals except the one relating to Palestine, which called for a Jewish Commonwealth and unlimited Jewish immigration under the Jewish Agency. This was a major controversial issue of the session but it was adopted with very few opposing votes. The American Jewish Committee voted against this resolution and withdrew from the Conference after the session. In 1944 the Jewish Labor Committee resigned in opposition to the admission to the Conference of the Jewish People's Fraternal Order, a left-oriented Jewish labor group.

At the end of World War II an attempt was made to continue the Conference on a permanent basis to speak authoritatively for the Jewish community—a hope which some had voiced at the first session of the Conference. An interim committee was established to explore the possibility of a permanent democratic representative Jewish body as a successor to the Conference. A plan of organization was drafted and presented to the Fourth Session of the American Jewish Conference in November 1947. Opinion was divided among important national agencies on the validity of such a structure for American Jewry and a number of the agencies were definitely in disagreement and refused to join. When the B'nai B'rith voted against joining on the ground that it "would not join a confederation where significant national Jewish organizations have failed as yet or refused to adhere", it became evident that the proposed body could not be established and the American Jewish Conference went out of existence.

As we have seen, machinery aiming at the coordination of the efforts of the American Jewish Committee, the Anti-Defamation League of B'nai B'rith, the American Jewish Congress and the Jewish Labor Committee and other agencies has been established at various times. The Joint Consultative Council, later the General Jewish Council, was organized in 1933, succeeded by the National Community Relations Advisory Council in 1944. Following sharp differences of opinion over recommendations of a survey adopted in 1952, the American Jewish Committee and the Anti-Defamation League withdrew from membership in the NCRAC. From time to time and on an ad hoc basis agencies meet for consultation and occasionally for action. One example of this form of coordination is the Conference on Jewish Material Claims against Germany, which was organized in 1951 for the specific purpose of obtaining redress and compensation from Germany and Austria. In this Conference the American Jewish Committee and the B'nai B'rith as well as the American Jewish Congress, Labor Committee and other organizations participate, together with the Jewish Agency and several European member agencies.

Similarly, while the religious denominations have accepted formal association only for limited purposes, the various national religious organizations frequently co-operate among themselves and with other bodies on additional objectives. The Synagogue Council of America, which includes Orthodox, Conservative and Reform Rabbinical and congregational groups, was organized in 1926. Its major aim is to "speak and act unitedly" for its affiliated Rabbinical and congregational associations and to further the religious interests which they have in common. Its limited financial support, with a total income of $22,000 in 1952, has restricted the scope of its activities. In 1953 the Conservative and Orthodox religious groups joined the NCRAC, of which the Union of American Hebrew Congregations was already a member. The participation of the religious bodies together with the national and local Jewish organizations concerned with group relations between Jews and non-Jews in the

American community may help further to foster the cooperative spirit among the religious organizations.

However, the outlook for a general national body concerned with a wide range of Jewish affairs or for a series of additional national councils concerned with various special interests is not now on the agenda of American Jewry or on the horizon. The Council of Jewish Federations and Welfare Funds for local central organizations, the NCRAC, the Synagogue Council—these are the existing vehicles for formal cooperation among organized Jewish groups. The reasons for failure to achieve a greater coordination of organized Jewish activities are to be found in the heterogeneity of American Jewry and in the vested interests of organizations. Perhaps an even more important reason is the attitude of some sections of American Jewry that are opposed to the concept of national coordination of Jewish interests. Such viewpoints derive from the diverse nature of American Jewish life, the varying rate of acculturation of the different elements, and their continuing economic and social diversity. American society, which fosters the integration of all its elements and bestows at best only a secondary role on religious and ethnic group divisions, increases the difficulties of evolving effective forms and structures for the association of sub-groups of the American population.

XI. THE INDIVIDUAL AND THE JEWISH COMMUNITY

An inventory of the organized forms which bring Jews into association with each other can give only an abstract notion of Jewish living. The trends and directions in personal experience and the relation of the individual to this complex of voluntary associations could only be known through personal histories. All that one can say without such knowledge is that there seems to be enough Jewish interest on the part of large sections of the Jewish population, perhaps the overwhelming majority, to warrant an expectation of continuing vigorous group existence. In practically every community there are religious associations, welfare agencies, and fraternal and social groups through which an individual can express his interest and solidarity with other Jews here and abroad.

During the 1920's fears were frequently expressed that interest and participation in Jewish association were diminishing. In the 1930's and 1940's the opposing point of view seemed closer to reality. World events and internal and external pressures had intensified group identification. Those who are concerned with the future of Jewish communal life are less worried about its disappearance than its deterioration. While there has been a gradual diminution in the number of adherents to traditional religious practices, old synagogues are expanding and new ones are being established in new centers of Jewish population. Still, the criticism is made that religious participation is increasingly becoming more conventional and perhaps superficial. Those concerned with Jewish cultural life sometimes feel that there is an attenuation of interest and a flattening of expression though centers multiply and membership increases. Cultural activities, it is said, may be more pervasive but they provide less deeply felt emotional experience. Whatever may be the merit of these opinions, they have not been substantiated in objective studies. On the surface, American Jewish life presents a wide panorama of interests and activities which are for the most part in a flourishing condition of membership and financial support. (Trends in specific associations vary, some of them losing in membership and others gaining. For example, there may be less participation in beneficial organizations and more in social clubs, fewer members of Zionist associations but an increasing number giving philanthropic support.)

The question which looms large when we consider the direction of Jewish communal life is the extent to which the recent upsurge in Jewish communal activity represents a reaction to external pressures and forces. How much of it is in fact in the nature of reflex action to Nazism and anti-Semitism? Is it likely to subside with the receding of that traumatic experience? How much of Jewish communal life is positively motivated by an acceptance of the value of continuing Jewish religious and cultural life and group association for their own sake?

American Jews are one of the many groups—in some ways a unique group—of the general American community. The differences between Jews and other groups are not merely differences of national origin or of religious denomination, but a combination of these and other factors. All immigrant groups in the American community are assimilating, but at different tempos and in different ways. Those with an English-speaking background lose their separate identification most rapidly and become merged into the undifferentiated American, white, Christian population. If the facts were known, the various components of the American population could be arranged in accordance with a scale of acculturation. What the record seems to show is that America assimilates all its national and ethnic groups no matter how slow the process appears to be at any given time for some specific group. It may therefore be said that while Jews remain as a distinctive group their separateness contains only few elements which differentiate them from the rest of the American people.

An important aspect of American assimilation is the differential rate of acculturation of the diverse segments within the same religious or ethnic group. Concerning the social relationships among the largely middle class Jewish leadership, a recent unpublished study of a Southern community contains the following pertinent comment on a local incident.

"Recently I had a party for a prominent visitor and about half of the guests were of East European ancestry and the remainder were German Jews. Such a combination would have been unheard of in our city a quarter of a century ago. Today many of the East European Jews are wealthier and better educated than the members of the German Jewish group. I believe that they may be more accepted by men than by women for the latter sometimes appear to place greater emphasis on social distinctions."

Social mobility and social acceptance are perhaps less fluid in the South than in other sections of the country, and there is an erasing of social differences based on the national origins of American Jews. This will become even more evident with time, as native-born Jews replace their foreign-born parents in Jewish communal life and leadership. The distinction of immigrant origin is losing its significance, even if social exclusiveness is still encountered in the synagogue and club life of the well-to-do.

No clear answer can be given to the question of the direction of Jewish communal life. Will the next half century resemble the period of emancipation and enlightenment, when assimilation was rapid, or will assimilation continue with the retarded tempo of the 1930's and the 1940's?

As has been indicated, there are a number of basic changes in the Jewish population of the United States which are now operating and of which the full effect will shortly be felt. In twenty years only a very small fraction of the population will consist of those born abroad or with any considerable European background. There are great differences in the Jewish training and religious education of the native-born youth. The proportion of those who have received an American college education, now estimated at one third, may be considerably higher then. Unless unforeseen economic factors reverse the trend, the shifts from manual work to white-collar occupations will have been increased. Religious life, be it on the Reform, Orthodox or Conservative pattern, may have lost still more of its original European cultural character, with the potential effect of Israel upon religious life in this country yet to be determined by the course of events.

On the other side of the picture there are these factors to be considered. The concentration of Jewish population in large cities will continue to facilitate natural group associations and will mean that most Jewish boys will continue to marry Jewish girls. The continuing lack of pressure for conformity in religious and cultural identification safeguards the maintenance of separate religious denominations, though there may be a continuing trend to conformity in matters of ritual and observance. A great deal depends also on the acceptance of group differences in American society and the degree of cordiality or hostility toward Jews and other minorities. Much will depend as well on the future character of American society. Will it be more liberal or more conservative? Will its economy expand or contract? Will democracy, as expressed in political institutions, gain or lose? All these conditions, largely unpredictable, will profoundly influence the future course of Jewish communal living, as they have influenced it in the past.

It is from the day-by-day trends of Jewish group and communal association that we can obtain an index to the nature of Jewish life and Jewish identification, and it is through the history of these associations that we can chart the progress or decadence of Jewish communal living. One can only assess the present as indicating a flourishing, vigorous and active condition of Jewish association in which the majority of Jews are involved.

BIBLIOGRAPHY

ABELES, HERBERT R., KANE, IRVING, BLAUSTEIN, JACOB, GOLDMAN, FRANK, "Jewish Community Relations in 1953", *General Assembly Papers,* November 1952.

American Jewish Year Book, "Review of the Year" which includes articles on social welfare, community organization, religious, educational, cultural activities, etc.

BERNHEIMER, CHARLES S., *The Russian Jew in the United States.* Philadelphia, 1905.

BOGEN, BORIS B., *Jewish Philanthrophy,* 1917.

Budget Digests (Annual Publications) : Overseas Agencies; Community Relations Agencies; National Service Agencies; Religious Agencies; Health and Welfare Agencies; Cultural Agencies.

Community Organization Studies: "Central Community Organization and Planning in Large Cities, 1949." "Central Community Organization and Planning in Intermediate Communities, 1950." "Central Jewish Community Organization and Planning in Small Communities, March 1952."

DUKER, ABRAHAM G., "The Religious Trends in American Jewish Life," YIVO, *Annual of Jewish Social Sciences,* Vol. IV.

EDIDIN, BEN M., *Jewish Community Life in America,* 1947.

GOLDBERG, NATHAN, "Jewish Population in the United States, *Jewish People—Past and Present,* Vol. 2, pp. 25-34.

GROSSMAN, MORDECAI, *Jewish Experience in America,* 1945.

GURIN, ARNOLD, "Financing of Jewish Communal Programs", *American Jewish Year Book,* Vol. 54, 1953, pp. 177-193.

HANDLIN, OSCAR and MARY F., "A Century of Jewish Immigration to the United States", *American Jewish Year Book,* Vol. 50, 1948-1949, pp. 1-84.

HERBERG, WILL, "Jewish Labor Movement in the United States", *American Jewish Year Book,* Vol. 53, 1952, pp. 3-74.

JANOWSKY, OSCAR I., ed., *The American Jew—A Composite Portrait.* New York, 1942.

KARPF, MAURICE J., *Jewish Community Organization in the United States,* 1938.

KOHS, SAMUEL C., "The Jewish Community", in *The Jews, Their History, Culture and Religion,* ed. Louis Finkelstein, Vol. I, pp. 1267-1324.

LOWENSTEIN, SOLOMON, "Discussion: Report on Jewish Communal Organization in America", *Proceedings of National Conference of Jewish Charities* (National Conference of Jewish Communal Service) , 1923.

LURIE, H. L., *Is Democracy Possible in Jewish Community Life?* March 1945, Mimeographed.

LURIE, H. L., *Norms for Jewish Communal Organization,* April 1950, Mimeographed.

MARCUS, JACOB R., *Early American Jewry,* Vol. I. Philadelphia, 1951.

MYERS, STANLEY C., "Jewish Community Organization in the Future", *General Assembly Papers,* November 1952.

"Platform Statement on Rights and Responsibility of Jewish Community Organization", *General Assembly Papers,* 1948.

Proceedings of National Conference of Jewish Charities (National Conference of Jewish Communal Service), 1902: "Federation of Charities", pp. 23-50; "Settlement Work Among Jews", pp. 269-275.

Proceedings of National Conference of Jewish Charities (National Conference of Jewish Communal Service), 1904: "Industrial Removal Work," pp. 138-162; "Federation of Charities," pp. 169-173.

SCHAPPES, MORRIS U., *A Documentary History of the Jews in the United States 1654-1875*. New York, 1950.

SEDER, SAMUEL, *The Problem of Leadership in the Jewish Community* (Presented at Central Atlantic Regional Assembly, March 1953).

SELIGMAN, BEN B., "American Jewish and Demographic Features", *American Jewish Year Book*, Vol. 51, 1950, pp. 3-52.

SELIGMAN, BEN B., "Recent Demographic Changes in Some Jewish Communities", *American Jewish Year Book*, Vol. 54, 1953, pp. 3-24.

SHERMAN, CHARLES B., "Jewish Communal Organization in the United States", *Jewish People—Past and Present*, Vol. 2, pp. 217-230.

WIERNIK, PETER, *History of the Jews in America*. New York, 1931.

WIRTH, LOUIS, *The Ghetto*. Chicago, 1927.

Year Book for Jewish Social Services, 1931-1953 (Annual Publication).

THE IMPACT OF AMERICAN JEWRY ON JEWISH LIFE ABROAD
PHILANTHROPIC AND POLITICAL ASPECTS

Mark Wischnitzer

INTRODUCTION

Every major Jewish community in history has made abiding contributions to the spiritual creativeness and way of life of the Jewish people. Just as we point with pride to the momentous achievements of the Jewish centers in Babylon, Spain, Poland, Germany and Russia, so the philanthropic and political aid rendered by North American Jewry to persecuted and needy Jews throughout the world will be treated by future historians as a significant and positive contribution. Never before in the long span of Jewish history, since the destruction of the Second Temple, has a single Jewish center so munificently responded to the economic, social and cultural needs of other Jewish settlements throughout the world, besides rendering them powerful political support.

Philanthropic and political activity by American Jews dates back two hundred years.

In the 18th century American Jews started to send aid to Palestine, directly and indirectly, through emissaries (*meshulahim*) and European relief organizations. Moses Malki, the first of many Palestine emissaries, arrived in 1759. In order to eliminate the cost of sending emissaries, who were not always trustworthy, the *Hebrah Terumat Hakodesh* (Society for Offerings of the Sanctuary) was founded in 1832 to collect funds for needy and oppressed Jews in Palestine. These funds were sent to the branches of the Hebrah in London and Amsterdam, which in turn forwarded them to Palestine. The Jews of New York worked out a method for distributing funds among the various communities in Palestine: at a meeting called by representatives of New York synagogues in 1850, it was decided to allot 38 percent of the funds collected to the Sephardim, 48 percent to the Polish and Russian Jews, and 14 percent to the German and Dutch Jews.

Eighteen hundred and forty was an outstanding year in modern Jewish history. The blood-libel trial in Damascus, capital of Syria, not only appalled world Jewry, but also affected Christian opinion, particularly in England. There was a storm of protest, and the Jewish community in North America (then numbering about

50,000) participated vigorously in the campaign to free the innocent Damascene Jews.

In August 1840 a committee of New York Jewish notables called a meeting in the Bnai Jeshurun Synagogue and resolved to send a petition to the President, requesting that the Government take the necessary diplomatic steps for a thorough investigation of the Damascus incident. Protest meetings were also held in Philadelphia, Cincinnati and Richmond. The State Department replied that the United States consul in Alexandria and the ambassador in Constantinople had received prior instructions to intervene, together with European diplomatic representatives, on behalf of the Damascene Jews.

After long months in prison, the Damascene Jews were released. This was the first instance of concrete political aid by American Jews on behalf of persecuted Jews overseas.

The next landmark was the Mortara case in 1858 and its aftermath in 1859. In 1852, a Jewish child, Edgar Mortara of Bologna (then under papal rule) was secretly baptized by his Catholic nurse. In 1858 the child was forcibly removed from the home of his anguished parents by the papal police and taken to Rome, where he was placed in a school for proselytes. Representatives of the Italian Jewish communities appealed to the Board of Deputies of British Jews in London and to the Consistoire Central in Paris to use their influence to have the boy released. When the news reached the United States, there was concerted protest in a number of cities. Many Protestants joined in the protest, but the Catholics sought to deny the validity of the case. Later, when the facts could no longer be doubted, the American Catholics took the side of the Catholic Church in Italy, and their stand was largely responsible for the refusal of the State Department to intervene with Pope Pius IX. Despite strong protests in both Europe and America, Mortara was not returned to his parents.

Courtesy American Jewish Historical Society

RABBI H. ZUNDER, MESHULAH (EMISSARY) FROM JERUSALEM (EARLY 19TH CENTURY)

The apprehensions attendant upon the Mortara affair, the civil disabilities of Jews in certain European countries, and the desperate situation of Jews in the Orient led American Jews to consider the formation of a central institution to aid oppressed world Jewry. In 1859 the Board of Delegates of American Israelites was founded to defend the rights of Jews in the United States and abroad and to maintain contact with similar organizations overseas. The dire straits of Rumanian Jewry occupied the Board up to the time of the Berlin Congress in 1878. Persecution of Jews in Morocco moved the Board to protest to the State Department, which then instructed its diplomatic representatives to intervene with the Moroccan authorities. Efforts by the Board to alleviate the situation of Jews in Russia were fruitless. With respect to Switzerland the Board petitioned Washington that Jewish citizens of the United States traveling in that country should not be discriminated against. This helped to bring about the Swiss Government's abrogation in 1866 of laws prohibiting the entry of Jews, and was also in part responsible for the emancipation of the Swiss Jews in 1874. The Board collected funds and sent aid to Morocco, Tunisia, Persia, Turkey, Palestine and other countries. It also lent financial support to the schools of the Alliance Israélite Universelle in the Near East.

In 1878 the Board ceased to exist as an independent organization. It amalgamated with the Union of American Hebrew Congregations, which then formed a Board of Delegates of Civil and Religious Rights.

I. BEGINNING OF MASS IMMIGRATION AND AID TO IMMIGRANTS

When mass Jewish immigration began in 1881, American Jewry was faced with the gigantic problem of helping the tens of thousands of new arrivals to establish themselves.

As soon as the terrible news of the Russian pogroms reached America in the summer of 1881, and the first boat-loads of refugees began to arrive, funds were collected and contacts made with committees in Europe. The initial reaction here was one of alarm, a fear of being flooded by a huge wave of refugees. But by the end of 1881 and the beginning of 1882 this attitude changed. The Hebrew Emigrant Aid Society was founded, which functioned until the beginning of 1883. Forty percent of its relief funds was supplied by the Mansion House Fund in London, the Alliance Israélite Universelle in Paris, and the Central Committee for the Russian Jewish Refugees in Berlin.

The year 1891 brought about a considerable increase in the number of immigrants from Russia. Consequently more aid was required for them. Besides fundraising committees, the following groups participated in the relief work: Board of Delegates of Civil and Religious Rights, the standing committee of the Union of

American Hebrew Congregations; B'nai B'rith; Baron de Hirsch Fund, founded in 1891 for constructive aid to immigrants; and the Jewish Alliance of America, which consisted chiefly of East European Jews. Leaders of the Alliance included members of the *Am Olam* (Eternal People) movement.

Rehabilitation of the new arrivals required such huge sums that the organizations were forced to call upon European groups for help. At a conference in Berlin in October 1891, which concerned itself with emigration problems, the two American delegates called for a contribution of $400,000 to enable American organizations to continue their relief work for another eighteen months. The conference approved the request.

Notwithstanding, the American delegates came away from the Berlin conference firmly convinced that if American Jewry was to receive and settle further masses of immigrants, it must intensify its relief activity. Thus, in 1891, was cemented the feeling of responsibility on the part of the American Jewish community for Russian and other East European Jews, whose prospects for the future were even worse than their dreadful present.

In the years 1880 to 1900 American Jewry underwent intensive training in social welfare, acquiring an experience which was to stand it in good stead in the 20th century.

News of the tragedy in Kishinev on April 6th and 7th, 1903, stunned American Jewry. A protest movement was begun, with the participation of Christians. B'nai B'rith handed President Theodore Roosevelt a petition for Tsar Nicolas II, signed by American citizens of all faiths. Obeying instructions by the State Department, the American ambassador in St. Petersburg delivered the petition to the Russian government. Though the Russians rejected the petition, they were made sharply aware of America's reaction to the pogrom.

ELLIS ISLAND, IMMIGRATION RECEPTION CENTER

Of equal importance was the drive to send financial aid to the victims. In a report issued in June, 1903, the Kishinev Central Aid Committee, to which funds were sent directly from the whole world, stated that American contributions constituted one quarter of the total. At that time American Jews comprised one tenth of world Jewry.

The last fifty years of American Jewish philanthropic and political assistance to Jews abroad can be divided into five periods:

The decade before the First World War: 1904-1914.

The First World War: 1914–1918.

The two decades between the two World Wars: 1919–1939.

The Second World War: 1939–1945.

Post-World War II: 1945–1953.

II. THE DECADE BEFORE THE FIRST WORLD WAR

The two largest relief campaigns of this period grew out of the Russian pogroms of 1905–1906 and the Balkan wars in 1912–1913.

The material losses sustained by Russian Jews were appraised as amounting to more than $54,000,000. Only one ninth of this sum, slightly more than $6,000,000, was allocated to the victims. All relief funds collected throughout the world were placed in a Central Relief Bank in London under the supervision of Lord Nathaniel Mayer Rothschild. American relief funds amounted to 51%, European funds to 49%. By 1906, therefore, American Jewry was in the forefront of relief for Jews in foreign lands.

Political activity on behalf of Jews in Russia, Rumania and the Near East was carried on from 1904 to 1913 by the Board of Delegates of Civil and Religious Rights of the Union of American Hebrew Congregations, the B'nai B'rith, and the American Jewish Committee, which was founded in 1906. The outstanding achievement of the Committee was its success in prevailing upon the American government to revoke the trade treaty of 1832 with Russia on the ground that the Russian government refused to recognize the passports of American Jewish citizens. The other organizations mentioned were also active in this connection, and Jacob H. Schiff, Louis Marshall and Simon Wolf must be singled out for special mention. In December 1911, the U.S. government announced that as a consequence of Russian discrimination against American citizens, the treaty would be abrogated as of January 1st, 1913.

Schiff wrote the following letter to Adolph S. Ochs, publisher of the *New York Times*:

> Our anxiety to see our government take action should not be misunderstood. It is not because the Jews of the United States lay stress upon the admittance into Russia of a few hundred of their number who may annually wish to go there, but because of the conviction that the moment Russia is compelled to live up to its treaties, and admit the foreign Jew into its dominion upon a basis of equality with other citizens of foreign countries, the Russian Government will not be able to maintain the pale of settlement against its own Jews. You see, it is a large question, involving the most sacred of human rights, in the solution of which the United States should be only too eager and proud to take the first leading step (Cyrus Adler, *Jacob H. Schiff, His Life and Letters,* New York, II, pp. 151–152).

The Jewish question in Rumania and other Balkan countries was of great concern also to the leaders of American Jewry. Thanks to their efforts, Presidents Theodore Roosevelt and Woodrow Wilson took steps on behalf of the Jews in those countries. In 1902 Secretary of State John Hay sent a note to the Rumanian government in Bucharest, which was not complying with the Treaty of Berlin of 1878 but continued to persecute Jews. The note brought no results. In 1913, during the peace conference in Bucharest after the Balkan wars, the Department of State instructed its representatives in the Balkan countries to inform the governments that America was interested in a guarantee of full civil and political rights for Jews. The United States ambassador in London likewise received instructions to make clear the position of his government to the conference of ambassadors of the European great powers in London, which was then occupied with the problems of a Balkan peace.

The decade before World War I had witnessed Jewish mass migration from Eastern Europe to the United States. To meet the needs of the immigrants, the Hebrew Immigrant Aid Society was founded in 1902; it amalgamated in 1909 with the Hebrew Sheltering House Association and became known as the Hebrew Sheltering and Immigrant Aid Society (HIAS).

III. THE FIRST WORLD WAR:
1914 — 1918

The First World War created new problems for world Jewry, and American Jewry had to stand ready to render increased aid. Half of the world's Jewish population was trapped in the military zone, severed from the neutral countries and from the sea. Overseas emigration from Europe came to a halt, and destitution among the isolated Jewish masses grew more intense from day to day. News of the cruel evacuation of hundreds of thousands of Jews from the western regions of Russia by command of the Russian military authorities was followed by reports of anti-Semitic excesses by the Polish population against Jews in military zones.

With the outbreak of the war in Europe, various Jewish groups in America started drives for relief funds. The Orthodox groups—Mizrachi, Agudas Yisroel, Agudas ha-Rabbonim—formed a Central Relief Committee. At a conference called by the American Jewish Committee in October 1914, thirty nine organizations representing 100,000 members resolved to form the American Jewish Relief Committee. At a joint conference of delegates of these two bodies, in November 27, 1914, it was decided that all funds to be raised should be administered by one organization to be created for that purpose, the American Jewish Joint Distribution Committee (JDC). Some months later, the People's Relief Committee, representing Jewish labor groups, became the third constituent member of the new organization.

The JDC (often called "the Joint") was regarded by its founders as a temporary, provisional agency, but it was to become one of the greatest central relief institutions in Jewish history. Though the JDC was organized to distribute relief funds raised by others, and continued to serve that purpose, by the end of December 1915 it began to organize independent fund-raising drives on its own. Its expenditures during the war years totalled about $15,000,000. The greatest part of this sum was expended on emergency aid, such as food, medicine, shelter for the homeless, and children's and old-age homes. In addition, it carried out a program of constructive aid such as credit to small businessmen and workmen and the subsidizing of vocational schools.

While the JDC and its cooperating groups were engaged in welfare work, the war introduced the urgent problem of guaranteeing the civil, religious, political and—a new question—national rights of Jews in Eastern and Central Europe after the war. The American Jewish Committee, considering plans for guaranteeing the rights of Jews in belligerent countries at a future peace conference, compiled information regarding war-time persecution of Russian Jews. This was disclosed to the American public in a publication called *Jews in the Eastern War Zone (1916)*. Zionist and labor groups maintained that

FELIX M. WARBURG (1871-1937), CHAIRMAN OF THE JOINT DISTRIBUTION COMMITTEE (1914-1932)

there must be widespread, public political activity on behalf of the East European Jews; that the question of insuring their civil and political rights must be negotiated, and that all of American Jewry must immediately state its demands concerning the future political status of East European Jewry.

In the first weeks of the war, Zionist and other nationalist groups called for an American Jewish Congress as a platform for broad and thorough discussions of the problem. In March 1915 a committee was formed to organize the convening of a Congress. Meanwhile, in September 1914, Jewish labor groups had formed the National Workmen's Committee on Jewish Rights in the belligerent nations and Rumania. This occurred at a convention of delegates, representing various labor organizations.

The convention instructed the National Workmen's Committee to inform the pub-

PAUL BAERWALD, HONORARY CHAIRMAN OF
THE JOINT DISTRIBUTION COMMITTEE

lic in America and Europe about the sufferings and desperate situation of Jews in belligerent nations; to appeal to the American government and the American people to protect the rights of European Jews at the post-war peace conference; and to establish contact with organizations of other Jewish groups in America to achieve these goals. After the Provisional Government of Prince Lvov proclaimed Jewish equality in Russia on April 4th, 1917, the Jewish National Workmen's Committee dissolved, regarding further activity as unnecessary.

The groups in and around the American Jewish Committee opposed the idea of a Jewish Congress, on the grounds that events themselves would disclose the proper moment to start political action. Months passed, spent in disputes and negotiations between the two camps. The National Workmen's Committee on Jewish Rights and the B'nai B'rith tried to mediate the controversy.

After the Congress Committee called a conference of its supporters in Philadelphia in March, 1916, and the American Jewish Committee called a conference of its sympathizers two months later, a basis for understanding was reached. Both parties agreed:

> That the Congress shall meet exclusively for the purpose of defining methods whereby, in cooperation with the Jews of the world, full rights may be secured for the Jews of all lands and all laws discriminating against them may be abrogated, it being understood that the phrase "full rights" is deemed to include: (a) civil, religious and political rights, and in addition thereto, (b) *wherever* the various peoples of any land are or may be recognized as having rights as such, the conferring upon the Jewish people of the land affected of like rights if desired by them, as determined and ascertained by the Congress, (c) the securing and protection of Jewish rights in Palestine.

Each faction selected seventy members for an Executive, which in June 1917 conducted democratic elections to the Congress, which was scheduled to meet in October 1917. Because of the collapse of the Tsarist regime and America's entry into the war, the date was postponed until the time when peace negotiations would begin.

The Congress convened on December 15, 1918, and appointed a delegation to the Peace Conference. In cooperation with Jewish delegations from other countries it carried out the program of the Congress, and together with the World Zionist Organization demanded that Jews be given the right to a homeland in Palestine.

IV. THE TWO DECADES BETWEEN THE WORLD WARS: 1919 - 1939

The twenty-year period of American Jewish rehabilitation work in Europe and the Near East can be divided as follows:

Post-war years: 1919 and 1920
Five years of rebuilding: 1921-1925

Rehabilitation during depression:
1925-1932
Aid during Nazi and Fascist terror:
1933-1939

The Versailles Peace Treaty brought calm to Central and Western Europe. Not so to Eastern Europe, where the aftermath of the war was revolution and civil strife. True, the Jews were not isolated in their sufferings—non-Jews were victimized as well. In addition, however, the Jews were stricken by a wave of pogroms in the Ukraine, White Russia, Poland and Hungary. Hundreds of thousands fled in panic.

In an appeal by the Alliance Israélite Universelle to the League of Nations on December 8, 1920, we read:

> From Odessa to Vilna a multitude of people, maddened by their sufferings, are appealing for help, and in despair, are preparing to abandon their homes. The countries on the other side of the Atlantic are watching with alarm the arrival of the first batches of emigrants . . . The problem is fundamentally an international one . . . Only the League of Nations can undertake this formidable task and all the problems it involves (Mark Wischnitzer, *To Dwell in Safety*, p. 143).

The League of Nations was flooded by petitions from all sides. Numerous meetings were held, countless resolutions adopted. But the Jewish organizations were forced to do their work alone.

1. POST-WAR YEARS: 1919-1920

During this period the American organizations, JDC and HIAS (Hebrew Sheltering and Immigrant Aid Society), were the two chief agencies rendering aid to East European Jewry. In these two years JDC's expenditures totalled about $23,000,000. The bulk of this sum went towards emergency aid, but much was done for rehabilitation also. Huge sums were forwarded to official and private institutions in various countries. Representatives of the Joint

JOHN L. BERNSTEIN (1873-1952), CO-FOUNDER AND LEADER OF HIAS

(JDC) visited Poland to investigate local needs and carry out specific projects. Two of its emissaries, Professor Israel Friedlaender and Rabbi Bernard Cantor were murdered by Ukranian bandits in January 1920. Its workers were occupied with medical and child welfare work in Poland and neighboring countries. Devastated hospitals, orphanages, old-age homes, public baths and the water-supply system were repaired; new buildings were erected. Elementary and trade schools, *yeshivas* and *heders,* were likewise re-established. Credit-cooperatives were re-opened. In Palestine, the Joint helped organize loan-banks.

HIAS concerned itself with the problem of the East European Jews who were waiting, sometimes for many years, to go to America and other countries overseas to rejoin their families. Its activity on behalf of Russian Jewish emigrants coming through Siberia, the Far East and Japan to the west coast of the United States started during the war. HIAS committees operated successfully in Harbin, Yokohama and other Far Eastern cities. In 1920

HIAS organized emigration bureaus in Danzig, Warsaw, Lwów and other European cities; they gave considerable help to East European Jewish emigrants.

2. FIVE YEARS OF REBUILDING: 1921 - 1925

In October 1920 Joint decided to initiate a systematic reconstruction program. Its work was divided into five parts: refugees, transients and repatriates; reconstruction of devastated Jewish homes and institutions, and credit aid; medical and sanitary help; child care and culture.

For the first time in modern Jewish history a large, strong Jewish community organized, carried out and financed systematic and constructive relief work in an impoverished, war-shattered area with a mass Jewish population.

A. *Aid for Refugees, Transients and Repatriates*: From July 1921 to April 1923, about 300,000 Jews wandered about on a vast stretch of land from the Baltic Republics to Rumania and Turkey, seeking to return to their homes and families. They needed food, clothing, medical aid, and transportation. JDC spent $1,750,000 to solve the refugee problem.

A special problem was that of a group of 8,000 Jews who held American immigration visas before July 1, 1924, the date when the new restrictive immigration law, passed in May of that year, went into effect. The 8,000 emigrants were stranded in various European ports. Over a period of several years some of them succeeded in getting to America, some went to other countries overseas, some were repatriated in their East European native lands, and the rest made their homes in other European countries.

B. *Reconstruction and Credit Aid*: Co-operative credit helped the mass of small businessmen, workers and farmers to return to their former occupation or to find new ones. This work was conducted in Poland, Lithuania, Latvia, Rumania and other East European countries, and in Palestine. Altogether, 404 cooperatives with 156,000 members were established

during the years 1921 to 1924. In Soviet Russia the Joint carried out the task of reconstruction in cooperation with the Jewish Colonization Association (ICA).

An important aspect of the reconstruction work was vocational training. Manual training schools and evening courses for craftsmen were organized and funds for their continued operation were assured. In this task the JDC worked closely with ORT and ICA, spending the sum of $5,400,000.

After 1924 the JDC, in conjunction with ICA, organized the American Joint Reconstruction Foundation, which functioned until February 1951. Funds totalled more than $5,000,000. The significance of the Foundation's achievements is illustrated by the following statistics: in 1938 the Foundation supported 687 credit cooperatives with 191,000 members. Credit was extended in the amount of $2,700,000. For the entire period from 1924 to November 1938, the cooperatives issued 5,052,000 loans, for a total of $581,000,000.

C. *Medical Aid*: In Poland alone the Joint established 216 public baths, 66 hospitals, a number of TB sanatoriums, etc., for a total of 498 institutions. The Society for the Protection of the Health of the Jews — OSE — and its Polish branch (known as TOZ) proved to be of inestimable value. For many years Joint financed the work of OSE and TOZ.

In Palestine this type of rehabilitation started after the First World War. It was conducted by the American Zionist Medical Unit until 1921 with the financial assistance of JDC, which also sponsored malaria research in 1921 - 1922.

During the years 1921 - 1925 the JDC spent a total of $1,908,000 on its work in public health.

D. *Child Care*: The estimated figure of war and pogrom orphans in Eastern Europe — excluding Soviet Russia — was 60,000. A large number received temporary help from JDC in connection with its general rehabilitation program; about

18,000 enjoyed full care and education until the age of maturity. Later the JDC took under its wing not only war orphans, but children of poverty-stricken parents as well. A wide network of institutions was established: elementary and trade schools, workshops for boys and girls, and summer camps.

In 1926 the child care institutions in Poland were taken over by CENTOS, a Polish Jewish central organization for child care. CENTOS received regular subsidies from the JDC. Similar support was rendered to the Palestine Orphans Committee. In the critical years 1921 to 1923 the JDC spent $3,240,000 for child care.

E. *Cultural Activity*: American Jewry, through JDC and other organizations and individuals, subsidized a vast number of schools, centers, publications, and other cultural projects. From 1921 to 1925 special attention was given to the rebuilding of East European schools, *yeshivas* and *heders*. During 1921 - 1925 American expenditures for this purpose totaled $1,342,000.

In Germany, defeat had brought about inflation and the collapse of the currency, and Jewish community institutions suffered greatly. Between 1920 and 1923 the JDC subsidized German Jewish institutions in the amount of $1,073,077. Although this was small in comparison with the efforts on behalf of the Jewish population of Eastern Europe, it nevertheless helped the German Jewish communities survive a period of financial crisis. In later years the JDC supported the Hochschule für die Wissenschaft des Judentums, and the rabbinical seminaries in Berlin and Breslau.

F. *Soviet Russia*: Emigration to these shores by Russian Jewry during the years 1881 to 1914 increased the size of the Jewish population and heightened its vigor. Despite mass emigration, Jews in Russia before the First World War numbered 6,000,000. After the war only half remained in Soviet Russia, the others living in the new republics — Poland,

JOSEPH ROSEN (1876-1949), AGRONOMIST AND EXPERT IN THE FIELD OF JEWISH COLONIZATION AND RESETTLEMENT (AGRO-JOINT)

Lithuania, Latvia and Estonia — in the western regions of the former Russian empire.

Aid for the Jews in Russia, which began during the war, afterwards continued in the form of widespread reconstruction. In 1920 and 1921 a network of credit cooperatives was established, as well as vocational and agricultural schools. In order to facilitate intensive and systematic execution of these plans, the Agro-Joint (American Jewish Joint Agricultural Corporation) was founded in 1924.

For fourteen years, from 1924 to 1938, the Agro-Joint functioned on behalf of Jews in Soviet Russia. The history of this institution marks an interesting chapter in American Jewish philanthropy. Space permits only a few statistics: Agro-Joint helped to build 215 agricultural colonies for 20,000 Jewish families; it subsidized 57 professional and technical schools, and 27 training courses. It also engaged in

JEWISH REFUGEES ARRIVING IN NEW YORK FROM NAZI GERMANY IN 1938

health and child care. In 1930 it supported 133 medical and health-care institutions, and 12 children's homes in 1931. Agro-Joint invested $16,000,000 in these projects. The sum total spent by Joint and Agro-Joint on rehabilitation work in Soviet Russia between 1917 and 1938 was $27,500,000.

3. REHABILITATION DURING DEPRESSION: 1925 - 1932

At the beginning of 1925 the directors of JDC proposed to liquidate its activity in view of the fact that its chief goals in Eastern Europe, excluding Russia, had been attained. But before 1925 ended, this plan was discarded. The chairman and several members visited Europe and returned with a pessimistic outlook concerning the economic future of European Jewry. At a conference called in Chicago in September 1925, it was decided that since there was good reason to fear that East European Jewry would collapse without strong American support, a United Jewish Campaign for $15,000,000 was nec-

essary. Later the amount was increased to $25,000,000.

The situation of East European Jewry continued to worsen. In Poland the depression paralyzed industry and trade, with half of all Jewish workers unemployed in 1926. In Bessarabia two years of bad crops resulted in famine. The depression also affected the credit cooperatives, and financial measures were needed to bolster them. The activity of ORT, TOZ and other institutions in Poland was also hard hit by the crisis and required American aid. In Poland there was the added problem of masses of Jewish small businessmen and artisans who were unable to join a cooperative, and were dependent on free loans. The initiative of Polish Jewish welfare workers and the financial aid of JDC made possible the establishment of free loan societies, which grew from 216 in 1926 to 826 in 1938. More than 1,350,000 loans, totalling 125,000,000 zlotys, were issued. In 1938 the capital of the loan societies amounted to 10 million zlotys, of which 5,200,000 came from JDC.

4. AID DURING NAZISM AND FASCISM: 1933-1939

At the beginning of the Thirties JDC's subsidies were reduced. In 1932 it spent only $340,815, the smallest annual total in its 38 years of activity, and once again it considered liquidation. But a year later Nazism triumphed in Germany and a fresh catastrophe struck the Jews of Europe. American Jewish philanthropy responded on a scale that surpassed all its previous achievements.

The events in Nazi Germany galvanized American Jewry and large numbers of American Christians. Protest meetings denounced the brutality of Hitler and his party. A Joint Consultative Council was formed, consisting of the American Jewish Congress, American Jewish Committee and B'nai B'rith. The policy of boycotting German goods was not supported by all the members of the Council, and in 1937 it was disbanded. In 1938 the General Jewish Council was organized, which included the American Jewish Congress, the American Jewish Committee, B'nai B'rith, and the Jewish Labor Committee. The General Council was regarded as the authoritative representative of American Jewry, which was prepared to conduct political work for all Jews. But a year later — in 1939 — the Second World War broke out and created a new situation.

Philanthropy now had even greater value. The inestimable importance of a central organization such as JDC, with its wealth of experience in international relief work, became clearer than ever.

The Nazi policy of discrimination resulted in a virtual pauperization of the German Jews, compelling one fourth of them to resort to charity in the years 1935 - 1936. In 1937 almost half of the 1,400 communities were dependent on subsidies. The middle class urgently needed cheap credit or loans without interest. Credit societies for low-interest loans and free loan societies were established by JDC and the American Joint Reconstruction Foundation. Another vital task was the retraining of thousands of young men and adults in farming, manual labor and technical work, to facilitate emigration to Palestine and other countries. This was done in cooperation with ORT, which was in part financed in America.

The Nazi regime thrust Jewish children out of the public schools. In 1933 there were 70 elementary schools, and there were 60,000 Jewish children between the ages 6 and 14 who needed Jewish schools. By 1939 the number of schools of all types increased from 70 to 139. Funds were needed to sustain educational and other Jewish cultural activity under the inimical conditions of Nazism. There was the added problem of subsidies for emigration and resettlement in countries of transmigration and immigration.

Close to 80,000 persons were helped to emigrate. Tens of thousands received support in one form or another in the countries bordering on Germany, to which they fled in panic in the first days of the Nazi regime, and later after the pogrom of November 10, 1938. Committees were formed in all these countries, giving aid with both local and JDC funds. *Hachsharah* camps and vocational training courses were established in England, Holland, Denmark, Sweden and other countries.

All these projects were financed in the main by American Jewry. From 1933 to 1939 the Joint Distribution Committee alone spent more than 17,000,000 dollars, mostly for aid to German Jews.

V. THE SECOND WORLD WAR: 1939 - 1945

German victories in Poland and Central and Western Europe, as well as in Russia, brought about a catastrophe unparalleled in Jewish history. A small portion of Jews managed to escape, but the majority were unable to save themselves in time. Almost all of them perished.

The Vaad ha-Hatzalah (Rehabilitation Committee), formed at the beginning of the Second World War (1939) by the Union of Orthodox Rabbis of the United States and Canada (Agudas ha-Rabbonim), started a drive to aid yeshivah refugees. Among the Jews who fled from western and central Poland to the eastern provinces and Lithuania, there were thousands of rabbis and yeshivah students. The yeshivas found temporary asylum in Lithuania, but when the Russians occupied that country, they left again. Yeshivah principals and students wandered through Russia and Siberia to Japan and China. They received considerable help from the *Vaad ha-Hatzalah*.

Following the invasion of Holland, Belgium and France in May 1940, the Jewish Labor Committee, which was founded in 1934, inaugurated a drive to rescue hundreds of socialist and democratic leaders and writers — Jews and non-Jews — from the Nazi menace. The Jewish Labor Committee prevailed upon the American government to permit the immediate entry of these people without the usual formalities. Rescue work by the JLC was intensified in the subsequent course of the war and after the war was over.

The chief war-time rescue work was conducted by the JDC. To the 25,000 Jews who fled from Poland to Wilno, which was occupied by the Lithuanians in October 1939, the Joint immediately supplied food and shelter. This was followed by widespread aid to Polish Jews who had found a haven in the Asiatic provinces of the Soviet Union. At the beginning of 1942 there were 600,000 Polish refugees in this territory. Through the Polish embassy in Kuibishev JDC sent food, medical and surgical supplies for Jewish and non-Jewish Polish refugees. In the fall of 1942 it organized a special program for Jewish refugees in Teheran, the capital of Iran. Ten thousand packages of food and clothing were sent every month via Teheran to various regions of Asia.

A third instance of intensive rescue work was the activity in Shanghai, to which German refugees began to arrive in 1938. Later the Japanese transferred further masses of Polish refugees to that city. From 1938 to 1944 JDC fed thousands of people there daily.

Not all Jews were able to flee Poland. Most of them remained imprisoned in the ghettos. The organizations which had been formed before the war, with American aid, now developed feverish activity, largely financed by the JDC. Before Pearl Harbor the New York office maintained contact with the ghettos, but later the welfare groups in the ghettos obtained funds from private persons who still had some means. Individuals loaned money, confident that the JDC would repay them after the war. Although information concerning this chapter of relief work is still incomplete, we do know that it was conducted in 400 localities. In 1940, 600,000 Jews were receiving daily support. More than 2,000 institutions, kitchens, medical clinics, children's homes and other centers were still functioning in 1941. On March 1, 1944, eight days before he was murdered by the Nazis, the historian E. Ringelblum wrote that the aid of the JDC had made possible the operation "of a wide network of secret charity organizations in Warsaw and throughout the land."

Despite the global war, there was active Jewish emigration to Palestine and to the Western Hemisphere. HIAS and JDC found ways and means to bring thousands of European Jews to these shores. At that time HIAS was an active factor in HICEM (a joint emigration association founded by HIAS, the Jewish Colonization Association and the United Committee for Jewish Emigration — Emigdirect).

In the first months of the war, before German occupation of Belgium and Holland in 1940, it was still possible to emigrate through these countries as well as through Italian ports. Later the only doors through which the refugees could leave Europe for America were Portugal and Spain, while Turkey was the transit center for emigrants to Palestine, especially after 1943. JDC and HICEM established European branches in Lisbon in the summer of 1941. HICEM, which was financed exclusively by HIAS during the war, carried out emigration programs in Vichy France, including Morocco.

During the Second World War — 1939 to 1945 — the expenditures of the Joint Distribution Committee totalled $52,285,-300 for all phases of its rescue work throughout the world. In addition, other American Jewish organizations collected and spent huge sums.

VI. POST-WAR PERIOD: 1945 - 1953

The disaster, as it was revealed in its full dimension after the war, confronted American Jewry with an unprecedented challenge. Above all, the *Sheerith ha-Pletah,* the survivors, had to be rescued.

From 1945 to 1952 the JDC alone spent three times as much as in the first thirty years of its activity.

In the midst of this rescue work, the State of Israel was proclaimed on May 14, 1948. This created new problems of transporting immigrants to Israel and settling them there. In this, the most recent and greatest achievement of Jewish philanthropy, American Jewry took the most prominent place.

The vast scope of rehabilitation work from 1945 to 1952 is brought into focus when compared with efforts of the past 30 years:

TABLE 1
THE EXPENDITURES OF JDC, 1914-1952

Years	Absolute Expenditures	Percent of Total Expenditures
1914–1918	$14,938,000	3.1
1919–1932	66,386,000	13.6
1933–1944	63,037,000	12.9
1945–1952*	343,885,000	70.4
	488,246,000	**100.0**

*For the year 1952 we included not expenditures, but appropriations for various projects.

The table indicates that of the nearly half a billion dollars spent by the JDC from 1914 to 1952, more than 70% was spent during the last seven years of that period.

When the war ended, there were 100,000 persons in the Nazi concentration camps of Germany, Austria and Italy, who had escaped the gas-chambers. In 1946 new streams of Polish refugees flowed into Germany and Austria. Many Jews had returned to Poland after the war, but the conditions they found, and particularly the Kielce pogrom of July 4, 1946, caused them to flee. About 100,000 Polish refugees came to Germany. In 1947 thousands of Jews fled from Rumania to Austria. Since not all of them were able to continue on to Palestine or the Western Hemisphere, a large number had to be supported for a shorter or longer period in the camps. In 1947 the JDC supplied 224,000 meals daily. At the end of 1947 it subsidized, in the American Zone of Germany alone, 47 kindergartens, 67 schools and 75 heders and Talmud Torahs. About 10,000 displaced persons were taught trades by JDC and ORT. Another important JDC project during those years was the printing and distribution of 500,000 copies of religious books for the displaced persons.

The establishment of the State of Israel alleviated this problem, the majority of D.P.'s going to Israel. There was also widespread emigration from the East European countries, North Africa and the Near East. JDC and HIAS substantially assisted in the emigration to Israel. JDC also gave emergency aid to about 80% of all new immigrants into the State of Israel. Almost the entire Jewish population of Yemen, besides a large number from Libya, was transported by the JDC to Israel, mostly by airplane.

In 1946, after some of the Jewish war refugees had returned to the six European countries listed below, and it appeared that an era of new Jewish life was beginning, the Jewish population picture was as follows:

TABLE 2

JEWISH POPULATION IN EASTERN EUROPE IN 1946

Country	Number of Jewish Population
Poland	220,000
Rumania	400,000
Hungary	180,000
Czechoslovakia	51,000
Bulgaria	49,000
Yugoslavia	15,000
Total	**915,000**

Although a great many Jews left Poland in the second half of 1946 and thousands fled from Rumania, about 750,000 Jews still remained in these countries until the beginning of 1947, trying to adapt themselves to altered political, social and economic conditions. The situation in some ways resembled the years following the First World War, but this time the Jewish aid program embraced emergency assistance over a longer period of time, and for larger groups of people — aged, infirm, invalids, unemployed, children; on a smaller scale it also undertook some long-range projects. In Poland alone 209 producers' cooperatives were established.

Altogether, JDC invested over 88 million dollars in its East European projects after the war. When, after 1949, one country after the other (except Yugoslavia) was blockaded behind the Iron Curtain, Joint, HIAS and ORT, which had begun operations there in 1946, were forced to terminate their activities.

Relief work was more successful in the western countries: France, Belgium, Holland, Luxembourg, etc., where about 350,000 Jews survived the Nazi occupation. Efforts by the JDC, the Jewish Labor Committee, and the Vaad ha-Hatzalah made possible the rehabilitation of the Jewish communities in these countries and the renascence of Jewish social and cultural life. Activity is still going on today, but to a steadily decreasing extent: from 65,450 persons who received JDC

help in 1946 the number dropped to 15,000 in 1952. This is explained by the fact that local philanthropic institutions and societies were increasingly drawn into welfare work. Following the American example, these countries are organizing drives for social and cultural needs. Thus, for example, the *Fonds Social Juif Unifié* in Paris is exercising ever stronger efforts to solve the question of Jewish welfare work in France.

New geographical territories — North Africa and the Near East — opened for American Jewish philanthropy during the post-war years. Before the Second World War, Jewish organizations in Europe, particularly the Alliance Israélite Universelle, tried to meet the social and cultural needs of hundreds of thousands of Jews in North Africa and the Near East. Because the Alliance was impoverished during the German invasion of 1940, the schools it supported in those countries would have closed down if the JDC had not taken over their support. After the war, the JDC continued to aid the Alliance schools, whose students numbered close to 60,000. In addition, the JDC supports the *Or ha-Torah* schools and subsidizes the ORT vocational schools in the Moslem countries.

Child care was of urgent importance. In these countries Jewish children were usually undernourished, and the JDC supplied them with daily meals. In 1952, 30,000 men, women and children enjoyed such aid. Another important task was health care. Trachoma, tuberculosis and other ailments endanger the lives of the local population, and are an obstacle for Jews desirous of emigrating. The JDC and OSE have worked intensively in this field.

In 1949 the Israeli government, the Jewish Agency for Palestine and the JDC formed a new welfare institution in Israel called MALBEN to help aged, infirm and invalid immigrants. In 1951 the JDC assumed full financial and administrative responsibility for MALBEN, which has processed a total of 24,000 immigrants in these categories and has provided many of them with loans to start a new life. Homes for the aged, hospitals, sanatoriums, cultural centers, workshops, etc., were established. Invalids and former tubercular patients are employed in the workshops under medical supervision. Kfar Uriel, a village for the blind, deserves special mention. A new hospital for the tuberculous, the largest of its kind in the Near East, was opened at the end of 1952 in Beer Yaakov. A village for the aged, with accommodations for 1,200 elderly men and women, was established north of Hedera. The value of American Jewish philanthropy becomes clear when we consider that 45,000 persons over the age of 60 have entered Israel since the proclamation of the State, and that at the present day one out of twelve new immigrants is 60 years old or more. It is also important to note that of the 25-million-dollar JDC budget for 1953, MALBEN received one half, or more than 12 million dollars.

In recent years, a number of social welfare projects in Israel have been initiated by HIAS, in cooperation with the Jewish Agency, Histadrut and other bodies, and under the direction of the HIAS Israel Committee. In 1953, HIAS operated in Israel 98 shelters for immigrants and needy persons with accommodations for about 3,000.

At first American Jewish philanthropy functioned through community organizations in the various countries, and also supported these organizations in carrying out their own projects. One such organization was ORT. The close cooperation with ORT dates back to the years after the First World War. In 1922 the American ORT was founded in New York to stimulate interest in ORT work in Europe and to collect funds in America. The funds collected by the American ORT, together with JDC subsidies, totaled $14,570,000 between 1920 and 1952. Before 1937, JDC subsidies amounted to about $1,500,000, but between 1942 and 1953 they climbed to $8,250,000.

Compared with the immense philanthropic assistance of American Jews, their political aid to European Jewry was meagre.

During the Second World War a Joint Emergency Committee for Jewish Affairs was formed in New York. It included eleven organizations, among them the American Jewish Committee, Jewish Labor Committee, B'nai B'rith, and a number of Zionist and Orthodox organizations. At the Anglo-American Conference held in Bermuda in April 1943, to consider the refugee problem, the Committee requested that negotiations be conducted with the Axis governments to free the Jews in their countries; it also asked the democracies to establish temporary havens for refugees. The Jewish petition to the Bermuda Conference brought no practical results. This was not the sole instance of the democracies' failure to take effective action on behalf of Hitler's victims.

In September 1943 the American Jewish Conference was formed in New York. It called on American Jewry to take immediate steps to save European Jewry from annihilation and to safeguard the rights of the Jewish people to Palestine. The American Jewish Conference did not become the central representative body of American Jewry, the American Jewish Committee and later the Jewish Labor Committee withdrawing from it. The Conference was dissolved at the end of 1948.

Among the Jewish organizations from all over the world which in 1946 worked out joint recommendations for peace treaties between the four great powers (France, Great Britain, the Soviet Union and the United States), on the one hand, and the former satellites of Nazi Germany (Bulgaria, Finland, Hungary, Italy and Rumania) on the other hand, there were two American organizations — the American Jewish Committee and the American Jewish Conference. Their chief demands were for protection of human rights and indemnification of material losses sustained by Jews; minority rights at this stage of history were out of the question. The treaties were signed in February 1947, but they had no practical significance. Bulgaria, Hungary and Rumania became Soviet satellites, and the situation of the Jews in these countries underwent a drastic change. American Jewish philanthropic organizations were forced to suspend activity there and efforts to preserve Jewish rights on the basis of the peace treaties would have been fruitless.

As we have previously pointed out, during the First World War Jewish labor groups in America participated strongly in aid for world Jewry. The Peoples' Relief, whose work constitutes one of the most impressive chapters in the history of social and cultural help, disbanded in 1924. Later, American Jewish workers cooperated with the National Labor Committee for Israel in its Palestine program. The Workmen's Circle and many trade unions sent help to other countries.

The Jewish Labor Committee was formed in 1934. Its initial aims were to combat Nazism and Fascism and to aid their victims; to strengthen the democratic underground in its struggle against totalitarian governments, and to support the labor movement in Poland. The outbreak of the Second World War led to an expansion of this program, its chief new task being to rescue, aid and resettle refugees. The Committee also subsidized Jewish labor groups in Poland.

When the war ended the JLC resumed contact with the displaced persons and sought to open the gates for immigration into the United States, Canada, Australia and the Scandinavian countries. The close contact it kept with American labor was very useful, especially in obtaining support for the creation of the State of Israel. Thanks to its close relationship with Social Democrats in Western Germany, the Jewish Labor Committee was able to make a significant contribution to the achievement of reparations for Jewish victims of Nazism.

The Labor Committee developed systematic social and cultural relief work in Western Europe and Israel. In Western Europe the program consisted of child care and cultural revival. In France and Belgium the Labor Committee supported more than twenty institutions, including children's homes, schools, summer camps, and a sanatorium. It established libraries and workers' clubs, as well as labor cooperatives; it also carried out a child adoption campaign. There are 2,500 children, orphaned and half-orphaned victims of the war, under the care of the Committee, living in children's homes or with private families.

In Israel the Jewish Labor Committee, together with the Workmen's Circle, cooperated with the Norwegian government in building 100 homes in a special Norwegian village in memory of Jewish refugee children who had perished in a plane crash in Norway. The Culture House in Tel-Aviv, named after the poet Abraham Liessin, was built by the Labor Committee and the Workmen's Circle. In addition, the Jewish Labor Committee erected in Tel-Aviv the People's House and Library in the name of Franz Kurski. In the Hebrew University in Jerusalem it endowed a department for research into the history of the Jewish labor movement.

VII. AMERICAN AID FOR RELIGIOUS AND CULTURAL INSTITUTIONS THROUGHOUT THE WORLD

1. ISRAEL

In order to regulate appeals for funds for religious institutions in Palestine, the Federated Council for Palestine Institutions was formed in 1940 on the initiative of the Central Relief Committee and the Union of Orthodox Rabbis of the United States and Canada (Agudas ha-Rabbonim). By agreement with the Vaad Leumi (National Council) in Jerusalem, the Council presented to the Jewish federations and welfare funds in America the needs of the yeshivas and religious charities in

PREPARING FOR LIFE IN THE STATE OF ISRAEL WITH THE AID
OF THE UNITED JEWISH APPEAL

Palestine. In 1942, 144 yeshivas and charitable institutions were subsidized by American welfare funds.

In 1940 there was established in New York a philanthropic organization for educational and cultural institutions in Palestine, the American Fund for Israel Institutions. The Fund supported seven Israel institutions in 1941 and 89 in 1950, but only 51 in 1953. Since 1944 it has also subsidized yeshivas and religious institutions.

JDC began to support religious institutions in Israel, chiefly yeshivas, in 1914. Between 1914 and 1952 it allotted the sum of $8,250,000 for this purpose.

In 1952 JDC supported 82 yeshivas and 8,500 yeshivah students and teachers, together with their families; refugee rabbis from Europe and widows and children of rabbis. It also gave help to teachers' seminaries and to fifty rabbis engaged in scholarly research. In addition, JDC made a one-time contribution for a food cooperative serving the yeshivas.

Another major contribution by American philanthropy was its support of secular educational institutions in Israel. Close to 80% of the sums of the American Fund for Israel Institutions went for this purpose.

Of even greater magnitude was the financial aid given by American Jews to the Hebrew University in Jerusalem, the Institute of Technology in Haifa, the Weizmann Institute in Rehovoth, and the projected Bar-Ilan University.

The Hebrew University was supported by American Jews even before its official opening in 1925, when the American Friends of the Hebrew University was founded to collect funds in the United States and Canada, stimulate interest in the University, and maintain contact between it and universities in America and Canada. By 1952 the American Friends

CHILDREN IN EAST EUROPE, SUPPORTED BY
THE UNITED JEWISH APPEAL

of the Hebrew University had collected a total of $7,678,000. The Friends obtained for the University endowment funds by private individuals amounting to $2,000,000. In addition, the University received financial aid from JDC, the United Jewish Appeal, Hadassah, and the American Jewish Medical Committee.

In 1940 the American Technion Society was founded in New York to raise funds and arouse the interest of technical and industrial groups in the Haifa Technical Institute, which trains technicians and engineers for Israel and bordering countries. The Institute was established in 1912 with the aid of large contributions by American, Russian and German Jews. From 1940 to 1953 the American Society collected $3,189,000. Its goal was a $10,000,000 fund to enlarge the Institute.

The American Committee for the Weizmann Institute for Scientific Research in Rehovoth, founded in New York in 1944, has raised substantial funds.

The Mizrachi organization in America collected one million dollars for the Bar-Ilan University, named after Rabbi Meyer

Berlin. The cornerstone of the building was laid in June 1953.

2.   EUROPEAN AND OTHER COUNTRIES

The First World War left Jewish communities impoverished and disorganized, Jewish education, both religious and secular, was at a standstill; school buildings were destroyed, and there were no funds to start anew. American Jews took it upon themselves to sustain elementary schools in Eastern Europe. Later, when the economic situation of the communities improved, the JDC withdrew its support of the elementary schools, though from time to time it granted funds for such special projects as pedagogical material and sanitary improvements. The JDC increased its support of institutions of higher learning, including yeshivas, teachers' seminaries, rabbinical schools and research institutions. In the period between the two World Wars approximately 1,800 institutions, ranging from elementary schools to academies, with a total of 225,000 students, were supported by JDC, and various other American institutions and individuals. After the Second World War cultural programs were revived in many countries.

In 1949 the JDC established the Paul Baerwald School near Paris to train Jewish social workers for Europe, the Moslem countries, and Israel.

VIII.   UNITED JEWISH APPEAL

In 1936 the United Palestine Appeal was founded. Combined appeals for funds had been undertaken by JDC and the Foundation Fund (Keren Hayesod) in 1930, 1934 and 1935. Experience having proved the superiority of unified fundraising, in 1939 the United Jewish Appeal was formed to collect funds for JDC, the United Palestine Appeal and the National Refugee Service (now the United Service for New Americans).

The United Jewish Appeal has become a powerful instrument in American philanthropy for Jews overseas. Its growth is evident from the following table:

TABLE 3

FUNDS COLLECTED BY UNITED JEWISH APPEAL AND RATE OF DISTRIBUTION, 1939-1952

Year	Amount		Received by			
	Collected	Distributed	JDC		United Palestine Appeal	
	(Dollars)	(Dollars)	(Dollars)	%	(Dollars)	%
1939	14,990,471	14,448,500	7,765,667	53.7	3,882,833	26.8
1940	8,944,121	8,454,500	3,705,000	43.8	1,795,000	21.2
1941	13,072,013	12,147,500	6,152,500	50.5	3,347,500	27.6
1942	13,678,978	13,442,571	6,747,547	50.2	3,920,024	29.2
1943	18,046,004	17,540,000	9,404,000	53.6	6,336,000	36.1
1944	25,673,105	25,080,000	13,872,558	55.3	10,127,442	40.4
1945	32,776,004	31,043,558	16,823,689	54.2	13,290,969	42.8
1946	77,814,541	75,313,356	41,409,589	55.0	31,254,116	41.5
1947	110,470,516	106,677,777	55,176,429	51.7	41,631,348	39.0
1948	147,305,405	142,723,659	66,914,058	46.9	64,958,682	45.5
1949	111,392,671	106,942,262	42,410,098	39.7	50,699,164	47.4
1950	89,008,993	86,805,662	30,581,776	35.2	44,345,580	51.1
1951	80,083,865	76,367,323	22,448,039	29.3	47,544,220	62.4
1952	69,752,705	65,818,137	19,244,780	29.2	43,469,062	66.2
Total	**813,009,392**	**782,804,805**	**342,635,730**	**43.8**	**366,601,940**	**46.8**

The figures show that the sums collected between 1939 and 1952 totaled $813,009,392. $782,804,805 was distributed among all the organizations. Of this latter sum, the JDC received $342,635,730, or 43.8%, and the United Palestine Appeal received $366,601,940, or 46.8%.

The table does not show the moneys allotted to organizations that are concerned with settling immigrants in the United States (United Service for New Americans), or the allotments given in 1947 and 1948 to the American ORT Federation and the American Friends of the Hebrew University in Jerusalem. It also excludes several smaller totals for various other organizations.

It is impossible to list all the American Jewish organizations which have sent money and help to Israel. In addition to those already discussed in some detail, Hadassah, the National Labor Committee for Israel and HIAS deserve special notice.

Hadassah, the major Zionist organization of women in the United States, was founded in 1912. It carries on activities in Israel relating to health, medical and social aid, child care and education. From January 1922 to September 1952, Hadassah raised $14,500,000 for its Israel program, including the Medical Center of Hadassah-Hebrew University and Youth *Aliyah*. Next to the Jewish Agency, Hadassah makes the largest contributions for bringing children to Israel and educating them there.

The National Committee for Labor in Israel collects funds for the Histadrut (General Federation of Jewish Labor in Israel) and helps settle and find employment for immigrants in Israel. From 1923 to 1953 it raised about $35,000,000. HIAS spent a total of $12,538,350 for overseas work—migration and projects in Israel—in the years 1940 - 1953 alone.

This account of American Jewish philanthropy on behalf of Jews throughout the world does not tell the whole story, but has dealt only with the most conspicuous activity. Not all financial contributions have been recorded, because not all organizations and committees that have helped Jews in one way or another have published regular reports. One thing is clear, however — the tremendous contribution of American Jewry to the survival of the Jewish people.

BIBLIOGRAPHY

Besides the annual reports of Joint and HIAS (1941-1953) and the budget bulletins of the Council of Federations for the last several years, the following works were made use of:

ADLER, CYRUS, *The Voice of America on Kishineff*. Philadelphia, 1904.

ADLER, CYRUS, *Jacob H. Schiff, His Life and Letters*, 2 vols. New York, 1929.

ADLER, CYRUS AND MARGALITH, AARON M., *With Firmness in the Right*. American Diplomatic Action Affecting the Jews, 1840-1945. New York, 1946.

DUKER, A. G. AND GOTTSCHALK, MAX, *Jews in the Post-War World*. New York, 1945.

FRIEDMAN, ELISHA M., *Inquiry of the United Jewish Appeal*. Report to the Allotment Committee of the United Jewish Appeal, 1940. (Mimeographed). New York, 1941.

GINZBERG, ELI, *Report to American Jews on Overseas Relief. Palestine and Refugees in the United States*. New York, 1942.

HYMAN, JOSEPH C., "Twenty Five Years of American Aid to Jews Overseas", *American Jewish Year Book*, vol. 41, 1939-1940, pp. 141-174.

JANOWSKY, OSCAR, *The Jews and the Rights of Minorities*. New York, 1933.

Jewish Distribution Committee, *Statistical Abstracts*. New York 1947-1953.

KOHLER, MAX J., "Jewish Rights at International Congresses", *American Jewish Year Book*, vol. 19, 1917-1918, pp. 106-160.

LEAVITT, MOSES A., *The J.D.C. Story 1914-1952*. New York, 1953.

LESTSCHINSKY, JACOB, *Crisis, Catastrophe and Survival. A Jewish Balance Sheet, 1914-1948*. New York, 1948.

POSTAL, BERNARD, "B'nai B'rith. A century of Service", *American Jewish Year Book*, vol. 45, 1943-1944, pp. 97-116.

RICHARDS, BERNARD G., "Organizing American Jewry", *Jewish Affairs*, II, No. 2, May 1, 1947.

SCHACHNER, NATHAN, *The Price of Liberty*. A History of the American Jewish Committee. New York, 1948.

SINGER, ISIDORE, *Russia at the Bar of the American People*. New York, 1904.

WISCHNITZER, MARK, *To Dwell in Safety*. The Story of Jewish Migration Since 1800. Philadelphia, 1949.

YIDDISH CULTURE

Samuel Niger

I. THE COLONIAL AND POST-REVOLUTIONARY ERA

The term "culture" in this article denotes all activities associated with creating, disseminating and acquiring spiritual values. It also includes those activities that aid in the preservation, transmission and enhancement of a group's heritage. Yiddish culture means the culture whose principal medium is Yiddish. We shall concentrate mainly upon its so-called secular values and institutions—the language itself and the literature, art and education associated with it.

Of course, we do not minimize the importance of religious content and form, nor do we imply that only in Yiddish did the Jews in America find spiritual fulfillment. This historical survey, however, is chiefly concerned with secular Yiddish culture.

We shall try to avoid repeating what has been said previously in *The Jewish People: Past and Present*. Special attention will be given to the beginnings of Yiddish culture in America, which date from a time prior to the Jewish mass immigration and which have suffered relative neglect at the hands of modern students.

1. BEFORE THE MASS JEWISH IMMIGRATION

Though Jewish cultural creativity in Yiddish began in America in the second half of the 19th century, Yiddish in America has a much longer history. It dates from long before the 1870's, when a Yiddish (and Hebrew) press first appeared in this country. Indeed, it goes back even before the 1840's and the large-scale immigration of German Jews, some of whom still spoke Yiddish.

The seeds of Yiddish were brought here as far back as the Colonial Period. At that time there were in America not only Spanish-Portuguese Jews, but also Ashkenazic, that is German, Dutch and even East European Jews. If it is at all valid to speak of the so-called Sephardic period in American Jewish history, that is only because the Iberian exiles, who came here by way of Brazil, the West Indies or Holland as early as the middle of the 17th century, set the religious and social tone in the first small Jewish communities. In numbers, however, as early as the first half of the 18th century, the German, Dutch and Polish Jews constituted a majority of the Jews in such cities as Philadelphia and Charleston.[1] In Georgia, too, there were German in addition to Sephardic Jews. In Shearith Israel, the oldest congregation in New York, as early as 1700 at least half of the members were Ashkenazim, that is, Yiddish-speaking Jews.[2] Professor Jacob Rader Marcus writes that in Charleston, about 1780, "there must have been enough Yiddish-speaking groups to form a little religious group of their own."[3] Among these Ashkenazim were East Europeans.

> The ritual of the first congregation [in Charleston] was, to be sure, *Sephardic* for almost a century, and so were members and leaders of the community; but others of the early community were *Ashkenazim* — Jews from Germany and Poland: seven of the eight men who laid the cornerstones of Beth Elohim's new synagogue in 1792 were German Jews . . . [4]

Similarly, Hyman B. Grinstein, the historian of the Jewish community in New York, states that "the Ashkenazim predominated also in other communities in America."[5]

This is a fact to which little attention has been paid hitherto. It is most surprising, however, that even historians of Yiddish literature in America have overlooked it.[6] Yet it is surely significant that even before the Revolution there were Yiddish-speaking Jews in America.

How did this come about?

Up to the beginning of the 19th century very few East European Jews "knew of the existence of America." So Abraham Ber Gotlober tells us in his memoirs,[7] in which he mentions Hayim Haykl Hurwitz's *Tsofnas Paaneyakh* (a free Yiddish translation of Campe's *Entdeckung von Amerika*), which appeared in Berditchev in 1817. To be sure, Gotlober's statement is slightly exaggerated. He himself says that Jews were already then curious to know how the New World had been discovered and what kind of world it was. "This book," he says, "was so popular that almost all read it." And he continues: "Needless to mention the women. They put aside the *Zeena u-Reena* [Yiddish paraphrase of the Bible with exegetical comments from the Talmud and Midrash, dating from the 17th century] and the devotional prayers and even the *Bovo-Buch* [a romance in *ottava rima* by Elijah Levita—Elijah Bohur, first published in 1541] and read nothing but Columbus."[8] Gotlober himself read it time and again, and "my imagination bore me together with Columbus to America." Imagination must have borne to America besides the Maskil Gotlober a number of other East European Jews. Scarcely six years after the publication and wide distribution of Hayim Haykl Hurwitz's *Tsofnas Paaneyakh* in the Ukraine, the well-known Lithuanian Maskil Mordecai Aaron Günzburg translated the same book into Hebrew (Wilno, 1823) and into a Germanized Yiddish (Wilno, 1824). Another Hebrew translation by David Zamość, *Metziat Amerika* (Discovery of America), was also published in Breslau in 1824. Günzburg's Hebrew translation, *Galut ha-Eretz ha-Hadashah* (The Discovery of the New World) did not have many readers. The translator, however, thought that the Yiddish version would find a ready market, not so much because America was then of practical interest to the Jews of Eastern Europe as because "they would find in it more edification, value and pleasure than in the tasteless lying stories of the Arabian Nights."[9] If the Jews did not stop reading the Arabian Nights, they at least added to these tales, which to them were tasteful rather than tasteless, the story of the discovery of America. Despite its Germanized Yiddish, Günzburg's translation of Campe's book was reprinted several times.[10] It might almost be said that the Jews in Eastern Europe had a presentiment of the great part that America was destined to play in the history of the Jewish people. It was not mere rhetoric when Hayim Haykl Hurwitz wrote in his introduction to *Tsofnas Paaneyakh* that "the whole history of America is a great book for our people." When they read this book, he continued, "they will see the blessings that the Lord, blessed be He, has conferred upon us through the discovery of the New World. We derive very many benefits from America."[11] What these "very many benefits" were he explained at length in his postscript. Among other things he mentioned the simple fact that "many millions of people have left these lands for America."[12]

He did not say whether there were any Jews among these many millions, but there is no doubt that there were already many individual Jews who went or, more correctly, escaped to America, particularly after 1827, when Russia began recruiting Jews for military service, and after the Polish Uprising of 1831.

Long before the beginning of the 19th century, however, some European Jews had left to seek their fortune in the "land of Columbus." Some of them made the long and very difficult journey directly, stopping over on the way wherever possible. Others were among those who had fled at the time of the Chmielnicki Massacres in 1648 and 1649. After settling in Germany or Holland, a number of these refugees, like some of the native Jews of those countries, "discovered" America and migrated there.

Like the East European Jews, the Jews of Germany and Holland spoke Yiddish in the 17th, 18th and a good part of the 19th centuries. After they had settled in some colony of the New World they continued to make use of their mother tongue (together with Hebrew) for the satisfaction of their Jewish cultural and practical business needs.

According to the testimony of W. C. J. Chrysander, there were Yiddish-speaking people in the first half of the 18th century "even in Jamaica and Barbados."[13] Such Yiddish-speaking Jews were also to be found on the North American continent as well.

2. DOCUMENTS AND LETTERS IN YIDDISH

The archives of the various local historical societies[14] and the collections of the American Jewish Historical Society, the Yiddish Scientific Institute—Yivo, and other institutions contain letters by Jews living in the colonies, many of which are in Yiddish. The American Jewish Archives in Cincinnati, Ohio, has in its files the entire document collection left by the well-known Gratz family. In this collection there are approximately one hundred letters written in Yiddish by Barnard and Michael Gratz in the second half of the 18th century. Not all of these letters have yet been published or studied, and some have been published only in English translation. Thus we find in Volume XXXIV of the *Publication of the American Jewish Historical Society* fully eleven Yiddish letters from the third quarter of the 18th century, almost all of them addressed to the German Jewish merchants Michael and Barnard Gratz of Philadelphia.[15] A Yiddish letter, dated July 28, 1776, written by the merchant Jonas Phillips, of Philadelphia, to his relative Gumpel Simson, a merchant in Holland, appeared in the *Publication* for 1917.[16] In the first series of the Sulzberger Collection, in the Archives of the American Jewish Historical Society, there are Yiddish letters from an even earlier period—1756 and 1759.[17]

In the Archives of the American Jewish Historical Society there is a note-book containing copies of business letters written by Uriah Hendricks, a member of the Dutch-Jewish Hendricks family which still resides in New York where it is quite active in Jewish affairs. Hendricks frequently inserts passages from the Bible and complete Yiddish sentences. Several are entirely in Yiddish. The letters were all sent from New York in 1759.

From a Hebrew letter, published by Yitzhok Rivkind and written in 1770 by Abraham Halevy, of Lissa (the Polish town in which Haym Salomon was born), to Aaron Lopez in Newport, we may conclude that even the Sephardic Jews in the colonies had acquired a little Yiddish from their Ashkenazic neighbors. Isolated words borrowed from Yiddish, such as *shul, yortsait* and *rebbe* (in the sense of teacher) are found in the minutes of Congregation Shearith Israel. Abraham Halevy's Hebrew letter is interspersed with Yiddish words and almost complete Yiddish sentences. He begins his letter with the Hebrew words: "I wish to inform you that I have arrived here safely, praised be the Lord and also . . ."; then he continues in Yiddish: "*zayn briv hob rikhtik opgigebin* [his letter I have promptly delivered]. *Ikh hobi da durkh mekabel toyve givezin* [I benefited thereby]." At the end of the letter he sends his regards to other Jews, including Sephardim, and again he uses some Yiddish words.[18]

The famous Haym Salomon corresponded with his parents in Lissa in Yiddish. Apparently he read Yiddish with greater ease than he wrote it, for his answers to his parents were written with the help of one Israel Meyers, who could write both Yiddish and Hebrew. Salomon occasionally flavors even his English letters with a Yiddish saying. Thus, for instance, he writes in an English letter to his uncle in London that in America there is *veinik yiddishkeit* (little Judaism).[19]

In the Yivo Archives there are photostats of B. Broches' collection of American letters. At least four of these letters, which are incidentally full of Anglicisms, date from 1824.

Other documents also indicate that just as the Sephardim used mainly Spanish and Portuguese, so the Ashkenazim of that early period employed Yiddish. There even appeared at that time the beginnings of *American* Yiddish. In one letter we find the word *gleikhn* ("*Di poyern bekan gleikhn es nit*"—The peasants here do not like it).[20] A receipt carries the legend in Yiddish: "*Resit fun kornel Bon far 10,000 agir lanit*"—Receipt from Colonel Bonne for 10,000 acres of land.[21]

Another Yiddish document that was preserved is an agreement to dissolve their partnership by the partners Cohen and Isaacs, which dates from 1792.[22]

Grinstein's claim (pp. 208-209) that all Jewish immigrants from Germany in the first half of the 19th century spoke German, the language that they are alleged to have brought from their old home, and not Yiddish, is unfounded. In the first half of the 19th century many Jews in Germany itself still spoke Yiddish. Moses Oppenheimer, a Jew born in Bavaria in 1845, writes in his memoirs that at home and among themselves the German Jews then spoke a dialect that varied greatly from that of the non-Jews in Germany. This Jewish-German was very similar to the Yiddish of the East European Jew.[23] From Moses Mendelssohn's Yiddish letters and from the Yiddish letters of the Lassalle family (*Historishe Shriftn*, Yivo, Vol. 1, 1929) we learn that in the middle of the 18th and the beginning of the 19th centuries many German Jews, especially in southern Germany, still spoke and wrote Yiddish. According to Max Weinreich, "Yiddish continued in northern Germany till the middle of the 19th century, in western and southern Germany even longer, in the district of Posen to the last quarter of the 19th century, in Switzerland and Holland to the 20th century."[24] After immigrating to America many, though not all, German and Polish Jews continued to read and speak Yiddish for some time. In 1849 a congregation of Polish Jews in Boston invited a Polish rabbi from New York to preach in Yiddish during the High Holidays.[25] As late as the 1860's Edward Bloch printed or reprinted in Berlin a series of Judeo-German booklets in Latin script for local sale and for the bookstore of Bloch and Company in Cincinnati, Ohio, which would constitute ample proof that both here and abroad there were still many Yiddish readers, particularly of humorous and satirical writings. Isaac Meir Dick's satirical and humorous stories, written in the Sixties, were popular not only in Eastern Europe but also here in America. According to Yitzhok Rivkind, librarian of the Jewish Theological Seminary, its Dick collection contains—like a voice of the past—a copy of one of Dick's smaller volumes (*The Marriage Without Matchmakers*). This book had belonged to the prominent collector Jacob License (1813-1877), who was also the public representative of the Shearith Israel congregation (Dick bibliography, *Yivo Bleter*, Volume XXXVI, page 204). As late as December 1871 the *American Israelite*, in arguing with the opponents of the Polish Jews and of their language, wrote that the discovery that their language is a jargon is no news. Hungarian, Moravian, Bavarian, Swabian, Hessian and Alsatian Jews also make use of a jargon.[26] There is all the more reason to assume that in the 18th century Yiddish was the language of the majority of immigrants from the East and West European Yiddish-speaking Jewries.

3. YIDDISH IN EDUCATION

If there were Jews who spoke Yiddish and conducted their correspondence in Yiddish, it stands to reason that Yiddish (together with Hebrew) was also the language of their children's Jewish education. Among the Sephardim the Jewish teacher had to know Spanish or Portuguese. We may assume that the teachers teaching Hebrew reading, Bible and other subjects to Ashkenazic children had to know and to use Yiddish. (As far back as 1825 Ashkenazic Jews in New York had their own Sabbath school, named Hebrah Hinuch Nearim.[27]) This is the conjecture of the historian Jacob R. Marcus. Though he stresses with particular satisfaction all developments testifying to the rapid Americanization and "integration" of the first immigrants, he surmises that while

there must have been among the sons and daughters of the second generation of immigrants in the 18th century some that had forgotten their mother tongue, other Yiddish-speaking Polish and German Jews in the colonies remained faithful to their mother tongue and "some even taught it to their children."[28] Benjamin Sheftall taught his son Mordecai, born in Georgia in 1735, the Yiddish language.[29]

4. YIDDISH BOOKS

It may be assumed that some whose vernacular was Yiddish had Hebrew religious books with parallel Yiddish translations and that later they had Judeo-German booklets. In Europe even German Jews, not to mention Dutch and East European Jews, had Hebrew religious books with Yiddish translations as late as the first half of the 19th century. Oppenheimer writes:

> There were few Hebrew books in my father's house, except prayer books and the like. Though both my parents could read Hebrew well, they understood little of it. They did have a number of books in Judeo-German, which they read regularly. . . . I particularly recall a folio edition of *Menorat ha-Maor*, bound in leather. This book occupied in our house the same prominent place that the family Bible occupied in Protestant homes. . . . During the week my father was very busy but on the Sabbath or holidays he would read at least one chapter, and thus repeat the reading year after year.[30]

What the *Menorat ha-Maor* was for Oppenheimer's father, the *Zeena u-Reena*, the *Kav ha-Yashar* and devotional prayers in Yiddish translation were for his mother and his older sister, after her marriage. The *Bovo-Buch* was also in the house, and when Oppenheimer was a boy he read it "with great delight."[31] When a family like theirs left for America it undoubtedly took along such precious family possessions as its Hebrew and Yiddish books.

In the library of the Jewish Theological Seminary of America there is a *Sefer*

Kinot, published in Germany, with an attached "dedication" in the form of a letter, written in 1853 in a Germanized Yiddish, to a friend for whom the book was bound as a gift prior to his departure for America, so that he should not forget the Fast of the Ninth of Ab, "although he is in America where there is no exile."[32] This was surely not the only book that the immigrant took with him or had sent to him before the beginning of Jewish book production in America.

Historians of the first Jewish settlements in the Colonial Period and post-Revolutionary times tell of the private libraries of some Jewish immigrants. These libraries included Hebrew and undoubtedly Judeo-German books. Prayer books, Bibles and the like, which were produced in America only later, were imported from Europe by way of London and Amsterdam. (The first Hebrew book published in America, *Avne Yehoshua,* a commentary on the *Ethics of the Fathers* by Joshua Falk ha-Cohen, was published in New York as late as 1860.) It is logical to assume that Hebrew books with Yiddish translation, and particularly such popular works as the women's prayer book *Korban Minhah, Zeena u-Reena,* the *Maaseh Buch* and the *Bovo-Buch* were also imported. Of one such book we know with certainty that it was among the possessions of a Jewish immigrant. Now in the library of the Jewish Theological Seminary of America, it is *ha-Maggid,* by Rabbi Jacob son of Isaac, a kind of sequel to his *Zeena u-Reena.* The copy in question bears an inscription by the New York *shohet,* Rabbi Benjamin Eliassy, dated 1720.[33]

5. A CULTURE OF CONSUMERS

The conclusion that we draw from these facts is that long before the mass immigration of East European Jews, Yiddish as a vernacular occupied a prominent place in the life of Ashkenazic immigrants, and that to a certain degree other forms of Yiddish culture, such as correspondence in Yiddish, Yiddish as the language of instruction in Jewish schools, or the reading of Hebrew books with parallel Yiddish translations and of stories in Yiddish, were also fairly common.

But the American Jews who used the Yiddish language were both quantitatively and qualitatively too poor to be culturally creative. The center of creativity was in the Old World. This should not surprise us. All American culture, especially literature, was in the beginning dependent upon Europe, and for many years the literary capital of New England was London.

Yet we can regard the first Ashkenazic groups of immigrants as pioneers of a Yiddish culture in America, if the two aspects of culture are borne in mind: in economic parlance, production and consumption. It is hard to imagine one factor without the other. No theater without dramatists or actors; but also no dramatists or actors without the theater. The culture of lands that were settled and developed by immigrants, like America, is in its early period inevitably a culture of *consumers,* with few *producers.* Importation from the old country takes the place of local production. Before the Puritans began to create their own literature here, their own American pattern of cultural life in general, they had been sustained by spiritual food imported from abroad. A considerable period of time elapsed before the Anglo-Saxons, the Dutch and other groups in America began gradually to adapt the cultural values and works of Europe to the circumstances and needs of the New World, and to weave new strands into the fabric of their Old World heritage.

So it was with the Jews in America. As late as the 1870's or 1880's, when Yiddish-speaking people wanted to read something in their mother tongue, or when Maskilim or scholars wished to read a Hebrew work, they had to import or reprint European publications. It was for this market that Bloch and Company, in Cincinnati, reprinted or imported an entire series of Yiddish booklets in Latin characters. The name of the series was *Gedichte und Scherze in Jüdischer Mundart* (Poems and Facetiae in Yiddish Dialect). It consisted of at least seventeen items. Number 8 was Isaac Euchel's famous Haskalah comedy, *Reb Henech Oder Vos Tut me Damit* (R. Enech or What Shall We Do with It?), written in 1792-93. (The title page of the Cincinnati edition, a reprint of a former Berlin edition, erroneously lists the author's name as Reb Shlomeh Euchel.[34]) The publisher makes it clear in a note that "the Hebrew and other passages unintelligible to the large public have been omitted." This edition was obviously meant for German Jews who had forgotten their Hebrew or had never known it, but could understand Yiddish in Latin characters. It was evident that the readers for whom this series was intended had a rather primitive sense of humor and were not too discriminating. This, however, does not alter the fact that in the middle of the 19th century, when there were as yet no Yiddish writers in America, there were Yiddish readers and possibly also lovers of the old traditional Purim plays.[35]

All kinds of announcements were published in Yiddish.[36] During the Civil War Yiddish placards were posted. If there were readers of secular works in Yiddish and not only of Hebrew works with parallel Yiddish translations, they were generally readers of a Yiddish that was no less mutilated and vulgarized than that of the *Gedichte und Scherze*.[37] Most of the Jewish immigrants, not to mention their children, were frightfully ignorant about things Jewish. Up to the second half of the 19th century, real scholars rarely left for America.

II. YIDDISH CULTURE IN THE 1870's

In the 1870's, among the East European Orthodox Jews in America many were far from ignorant. Judah David Eisenstein writes in a letter from New York in 1873:

It is a lie they tell in the cities of Poland that the Jews here do not observe their religion. . . . Inquire of people that were here and they will tell you, my friend, that whenever they come to the Bet ha-Midrash ha-Gadol, on 69 Ludlow Street, they find Jews engaged in study and that it has many books, as in the great Houses of Study in Poland. In the synagogue at 78 Allen Street an excellent preacher preaches daily between the afternoon and evening services.[38]

In a letter to *ha-Maggid* in 1871 we hear of teachers teaching the children the Pentateuch with Rashi's commentary as well as Talmud, with Yiddish as the language of instruction.[39]

New York in those days had a number, though small, of Maskilim—Judah David Eisenstein (born 1854), Henry Berenstein (1846-1907), Zevi Hirsh Gershuni (1844-97), Kasriel Zevi Sarasohn (1834-1905), Nahman Dov Etelson, Mordecai Jahlomstein (1835-79), Simon Berman, later the author of the travelogue *Masoes Shimen* (Cracow, 1879), and others. Some of them had arrived here in the 1860's, others, like Berman and Etelson, had come as early as the 1850's. They were the teachers and the religious functionaries; a little later they were also the printers, publishers and editors of Yiddish and Hebrew periodicals. Their cultural creativity was as yet only potential, and they had not succeeded in building new cultural institutions independent of religion as such. There was a Jewish printing firm in New York, but its output was limited to religious books. There were some readers of Haskalah books and magazines in Hebrew and Yiddish, imported from Europe. (One of the first Yiddish periodicals in 1871 announced the sale of the Hebrew publications *ha-Maggid*, *ha-Lebanon*, *Ivri Anokhi*, *Havatzelet* and Zederbaum's Yiddish weekly, the *Kol Mevasser* [Voice of the Messenger.[40]]) Yet even the Maskilim were still consumers, and not creators. Gustav Makman had to publish in Warsaw (in 1865) his long poem, *Di Gehaymnise fun Yener Welt oder der Tkias Kaf* (The Mysteries of the Other World or the Solemn Promise). In 1854 he had come to America, but like many others he did not remain.[41] He found no encouragement and little receptivity for his work here.

Samuel Hillel Isaacs (1825-1917), a scholar and Maskil, wrote books and pamphlets in Hebrew, Yiddish and English. Isaacs came from the Province of Suwalki to New York in 1847. At first he could not earn enough to go on with "traditional or modern studies." In the 1860's conditions improved a little "and the new Jewish immigrants could maintain a number of intellectuals." The Maskilim that "combined religion with enlightenment" and could speak German "became rabbis or preachers in the German Jewish congregations." Those who knew less German took to teaching. There were also some who were quickly Americanized, mastered the English language and began to write in the English-language Jewish press, subsequently leaving that for the field of American journalism. Others entered the universities and became physicians or lawyers.[42] In Yiddish and Hebrew circles there was no demand for their creative talents.

The demand appeared at the beginning of the 1870's, when the number of East European Jewish immigrants rose sharply. In New York alone there were 75,000 to 100,000 Jews, and in Chicago about 60,000.[43]

On Canal Street, in New York, Kantorovich's bookstore sold all kinds of books and magazines, including some in Yiddish, in the 1870's. M. Topolewski had his Jewish printing plant there.[44] Signs of secular cultural activity in Yiddish began to appear. J. K. Büchner announced at the beginning of 1872 a series of "humorous [?] lectures" in Cooper Union. His subjects were: "The Berlin Cantor," "Moses Mendelssohn," "Israel Baal Shem Tov" and "Israel Jacobsohn."[45] The same Büchner stated at the time of the establishment of his "Jewish-English Workers Institute" that American Jews must not only build synagogues, they must also "learn to aid one another."[46] These were words not heard before among East European Jewish immigrants. They marked, though weakly, the beginning of a secular Jewish cultural movement.

1. THE PRESS IN THE 1870'S

The first issues of the Yiddish press began to appear—*Di Yiddishe Zeitung* (lithographed), edited and published by J. K. Büchner,[47] on March 1, 1870, and *Di Post,* published by Zevi Hirsh (Henry) Berenstein and edited by Zevi Gershuni, in August 1871. The development was similar to what had taken place in the 1840's in the German-language Jewish press. Even those who had previously been publishing in English for the Americanized German Jews began to print German editions of their organs under the impact of the increased German immigration.[48] The favorable attitude of the German Jews to German continued to the end of the 19th century, or more precisely to the First World War.

Similarly, in the early 1870's an attempt was made to publish in Yiddish for the Yiddish-speaking groups. The motives were purely utilitarian and commercial. In the Hebrew editorial of the quadrilingual (Yiddish, Hebrew, German, and English) weekly, *Hebrew News,* which appeared April 5, 1871, we read:

> Hundreds and thousands of our brothers live here. Those arriving every day speak and understand no other language but the one spoken among our brothers in Russia and Poland. Despite their intelligence and civic spirit, these Jews cannot express their desires in matters of state, for they know no other language. For this reason and because they want to know what is going on in their old home, they need a newspaper in their own language. The publishers therefore plan to issue this paper in a clear and easy Hebrew, a simple Jewish-German and a lucid English.[49]

Further details about these and other Jewish periodical publications of the 1870's will be found in the *Algemeine Entsiclopedie, "Yidn* III", 1942. Here we merely wish to indicate a few general cultural traits of the Yiddish press and its precursors in the 1870's and the conditions under which it came into existence.

The Yiddish newspapers, despite their Germanized Yiddish, their purely utilitarian character and their expressed desire to cultivate not Yiddish, but Hebrew, were met with the contempt and hatred of the English-language Jewish press and all who advocated rapid Americanization and opposed Orthodoxy. They would have been against any publication for East European immigrants, even if it had not catered to the Orthodox, so long as its language was neither English nor German, but "the Jewish - Polish - German jargon." The *Jewish Times* said about Büchner's *Yiddishe Zeitung* that its content was just as ridiculous as its language. The *American Israelite* declared that the *Yiddishe Zeitung,* in the most corrupt Yiddish-Polish jargon, was a curiosity, although a disgrace to any community. It said about another Yiddish periodical, *Di Post,* under the editorship of Henry Berenstein, that this jargon amuses the masses and makes mock of Judaism. There are many writers of trash in this country and there is no need of this Babel of idioms to render us ridiculous.[50]

But these English-language Jewish papers were quick to encourage the first Hebrew periodical *ha-Tsofeh be-Eretz ha-Hadashah* (The Observer in the New Land), which began to appear on June 11, 1871, under the editorship of Henry Berenstein (who also published *Di Post,* the first printed Yiddish periodical in the United States). They respected Hebrew, the "tongue of the prophets," and some periodically published Hebrew poems in their English columns; but they could not tolerate the "jargon." The fact is that they were unfriendly not only to the language of the Jewish masses, but also to the

masses themselves. The increased Jewish immigration in the 1870's dismayed many of them. The beginning of the Yiddish press, weak though it was, was therefore also the beginning, though unconscious and unorganized, of the revolt against the material and cultural patronage of the English- or German-speaking "Yahudim."

The full results of this desire for emancipation from the tutelage of the richer and better established German Jews did not become manifest till later. Meanwhile, the hostile or indifferent environment in which the American Yiddish press was born was a handicap and did not lend prestige to it in the eyes of others or even in its own eyes.

This is the first point worth noting in considering the beginning of the printed Yiddish word in America.

A second very important point is the fact that the causes leading to the rise of the Yiddish press in America were purely external. One of them was related to the wars that broke out in the 1870's in various parts of Europe: the Franco-Prussian War in 1870 and the Russo-Turkish War in 1877, when the first Yiddish periodical in Chicago, *Israelitische Presse,* began to appear. The immigrants were very anxious to hear the news from the battle fronts in the old country. The growth of the Yiddish-speaking population and the possibilities of a considerable circulation were of course additional factors.

Among the negative traits of the first Yiddish organs were their Germanized Yiddish and the general negligence of their language and style. This was partly due to the fact that many of the readers, if not of the writers, were either German Jews or "Kalvarier" Germans, that is, Jews who came from regions bordering on Germany; partly it was due to the general tendency toward Germanizing, from which the Haskalah Yiddish press suffered in Eastern Europe as well, though less than in America. In addition, the editors and frequently also the contributors of the first Yiddish periodical publications were

Hebraists by inclination, as we can see from the fact that they introduced a Hebrew department in almost every periodical.

Culturally, most of the Yiddish press until the second half of the 1880's was favorable to religion and Haskalah; socially, it was mostly conservative.

On the credit side may be reckoned the fact that every publication had a section for belles-lettres, mainly stories, in translation, and for poetry, chiefly of the journalistic type.

Until 1885, when Kasriel Zevi Sarasohn's daily, *Yiddishes Tageblatt,* began to appear, the journals with very few exceptions had come out weekly or even monthly.

In the 1870's and a considerable part of the 1880's all these weeklies and monthlies had a small number of readers and led a precarious existence, although toward the end of the 1870's some 50,000 East European Jews were in the United States.[51]

There is some resemblance in style and outlook between the Yiddish press of the 1870's in New York and Chicago and the Yiddish press that Hebraist Maskilim published at the same time in London (*ha-Shofar,* 1874; *Londoner Israelit,* 1875, and others).[52]

These traits of the American Yiddish press in its first period throw light on the entire cultural situation of the Yiddish-speaking immigrants in those days. Although in such cities as New York and Chicago they were sufficiently numerous to include culturally creative individuals, their average intellectual and spiritual level was still rather low.[53]

The memoirs of that period furnish concrete and frequently graphic descriptions of immigrant life. Kasriel Zevi Sarasohn, enumerating the trials that his *Gazetten* had to undergo before they took root, said that "the religious Jew maintained that it is not permissible to read the *Gazetten* on the Sabbath; the time should rather be spent in reciting the Psalms or in the study of the Scriptures. The Maskilim who could decipher a telegram in the *Staatszeitung,* not to speak of those who could read *ha-Maggid,* were ashamed to take the *Gazetten* in their hands."[54] This is to say that both kinds of relatively learned immigrants, the pious and the religiously emancipated, had little use for Yiddish periodicals. The religious Jews were of the opinion that it was preferable to recite a chapter of the Psalms or to study a portion of the Bible than struggle through the paper, the language of which was more German than Yiddish. The Maskilim and semi-Maskilim were thrilled with the *Staatszeitung* or the *ha-Maggid,* although the "news" in the latter had become quite stale by the time the publication reached America. It was below the dignity of the Maskilim of that period to read a Jewish-German publication. (Later the Maskilim yielded and not only read the Yiddish press, but also wrote for it.) Reading Yiddish could be of interest only to the simple folk, but they first had to acquire the habit of reading a newspaper or a book. Unaccustomed to reading even their mother tongue, they could hardly be expected to read a heavily Germanized language. Abraham Cahan's memoirs include the following passage:

> Among the former Russian and Austrian immigrants there were very few or practically no intellectuals. Among the Suwalki immigrants there were a few Talmudists. In the peddlers' stores on East Broadway and Canal Street there were not infrequently discussions of a Talmudic passage or a Hebrew book. This was the spiritual aristocracy of the Jewish quarter. . . . It was under the spiritual rule of old-fashioned Jewishness, mingled with an uncultured Americanism.[55]

This was in 1882. According to Cahan's estimate, there were then in New York some 30,000 to 40,000 Jewish workers. But they were at least as backward as the middle-class elements.[56]

Similarly, B. Gorin writes:

> The ordinary Jewish workers among the immigrants were at that time [in the beginning of the 1880's] a very coarse element, the coarsest among the Jews. There were very many among them who could not even read Yiddish.[57]

And Ab. Cahan also has written:

> The Jewish artisan was even in the beginning of the 1890's an artisan in the old sense of the word. He spoke the artisan's dialect and hardly understood any other. Many of our workers could barely read unvocalized Yiddish texts. Not only did we have to teach them in our writings how to think, we also had to teach them how to read our writing.

And if this was true in the early 1890's, what could be expected of the 70's and 80's?

Ezekiel Sarasohn, K. Z. Sarasohn's son and partner, writes:

> Most Polish and Lithuanian Jews came from small towns. The older ones among them did not have the slightest need for a newspaper and its functions. They loved to hear the news, that is, from one who read aloud. To read for themselves, and every day at that, did not even enter their imagination. How can a Jew sit down to read a newspaper on an ordinary workday? The younger ones, those that had some education, read German newspapers, and gradually also English newspapers. The Maskilim were satisfied with ha-Maggid. The very young were ashamed of a newspaper with Hebrew characters.[58]

Ezekiel Sarasohn refers to the period when the Gazetten appeared daily, that is, the 1880's. In the 1870's the "very young," to the extent that there were any, were even more ashamed of the Hebrew characters. The Maskil was even more powerfully attracted to the ha-Maggid or to the Staatszeitung, and the ordinary folk loved even more to "hear the news" than to read it. Consequently, however much we allow for the small Jewish population, the number of Yiddish readers in the 1870's was extraordinarily small. Two newspapers could hardly exist at the same time.

The time was not yet ripe for a daily in Yiddish. Even in the first half of the 1880's Sarasohn's daily Gazetten could not exist. (Nor was there yet, even in the Old World, a daily Yiddish newspaper.)

But there were readers of Yiddish story books, and for them Yiddish literature had to be imported from overseas. The Yiddishe Gazetten of September 1, 1876, carried such an announcement: "Interesting Jewish story books, in the Jewish-German language, published in Warsaw and Wilno, may be had from the publishers of the Gazetten."

The American Yiddish periodicals reprinted stories and novels by Hebrew and Yiddish writers overseas. Even more popular were translations of the German Jewish writers (Bernstein's Fögele Maggid, Karl Emil Franzos' The Marranos, and others). Kasriel Zevi Sarasohn said that the Yiddishe Folkszeitung (1878) "filled two-thirds of its pages with novels and stories."

Poems, or more properly journalism in rhyme, no longer had to be imported as early as the second half of the 1870's. In 1876 Sarasohn's Yiddishe Gazetten, established in 1874, printed a number of poems, among them a long poem in three instalments, by a Hebrew writer recently arrived in the United States. This was the poem "Di Dray Printsipn der Toyre, oder Oylom Hatoyhu" (The Three Principles of the Torah, or The World of Confusion) by Jacob Zevi Sobol (1831-1913). In his early manhood Sobol, born of a Rabbinical family in Shavli (Siauliai), Lithuania, was a teacher in a yeshivah, a rabbi and a preacher in various towns in Lithuania. Later he became a Maskil and graduated from the Rabbinical School in Zhitomir, but did not take a position as a government rabbi. He settled in Odessa and became a student at the university, specializing in mathematics. He earned his livelihood by teaching, running a circulating library, and writing for the Hebrew press. Then came the pogrom of March 1871 and all that Sobol possessed, including his library and some of his writings, was plundered. The following year he published a Hebrew book in Odessa, *ha-Hozeh Hezyonot be-Arbaa Olamot* (The Seer of Visions in Four Worlds), written in the spirit of Mendele Mocher Seforim's *Takse* and other Yiddish and Hebrew radical writings of the 1870's. Sobol began to wander. In 1876 he came to America and within a few days completed his poem, which was published in the *Yiddishe Gazetten*.[59] It deserves at least brief consideration not merely because as far as we know it is the earliest or at least a very early more or less significant Yiddish literary production in America, but also because in a number of respects it is characteristic of the beginnings of all Yiddish literature in this country.

That the poem was printed in a periodical was no accident. The Yiddish press in America was the midwife of American Yiddish literature. If the Yiddish newspaper was a home (frequently, to be sure, an asylum) to the Yiddish writer, to the reader it was a *heder* (elementary school), if not a *yeshivah* (school of higher studies). It taught him to read an unvocalized text, it gave him a taste for reading stories and poems in addition to the news, it enlightened him, it told him what was going on in the world, and it gave him a certain degree of sophistication and an interest in secular literature.[60]

The title and the language of Sobol's poem are also characteristic. The language is Germanized Yiddish, as was the language of all of American Yiddish literature and the press in the 1870's and in the first half of the 1880's, and the title shows the usual blend of Haskalah and religion. The content referred primarily to the Old World, as did most of what was written here in Yiddish in the last quarter of the 19th century.[61] In the poem, which

Sobol had begun on the ocean, if not earlier, he describes the pogrom in Odessa and asks the recurrent question that haunted all Maskilim: "Who would have believed such things possible in the 19th century?"[62] Nevertheless he is ready to put his trust in the 19th century, on condition that the Jews unite, eschew fanaticism, eradicate pauperism and immigrate to America.[63] Though the poem has a certain vitality and even some literary merit, on the whole it is like most other Yiddish poems of the period—more journalistic and publicistic than artistic. It is replete with the standard social criticism that Haskalah made of Jews and their conduct:

> There are Reformers and Orthodox,
> Fighting among themselves like wild
>   oxen.
> Moderately, half and extremely Re-
>   formed;
> Moderately Orthodox, and bigoted.
> National sentiment is extinguished
>   among them,
> The magnificent [Hebrew] language
>   is worth a farthing . . .
> One small people—and yet so diverse.
> The Polish Jew hates the Russian,
> The cold German Jew hates them
>   both,
> The British Jew snubs them all,
> For he may come from Portugal.

To Sobol, America was a ray of hope. "Long live America! Long live Grant!" he is said to have exclaimed upon disembarking. On closer acquaintance, however, the Jews in America pleased him no more than other Jews. He asks: "Am I in the world of confusion or in paradise?" The "world of confusion" was the dissension among the various immigrants: Hasidim and Reformers, Lithuanian and German Jews. And there was the fact that "Jewish youth is without education, manners and virtue. . . ."

2. THE FIRST YIDDISH BOOK

For *Yiddishe Gazetten* and the other periodicals there was no dearth of verse.

(This too is characteristic of literary creativity in a community where everything is still in balance.) It is therefore not surprising that the first Yiddish book in America, published in New York in 1877, was in verse.[64] The first Yiddish book was by the same Sobol, a volume of Yiddish and Hebrew poems, manifesting greater attachment to Hebrew, the language of most of the Maskilim, than to the folk language.

Like almost all other Hebrew writers and journalists who arrived in America in the second half of the 19th century, Sobol became a Yiddish writer and journalist.[65] Like them, Sobol retained his Hebraist and Haskalah preferences. Although he himself began to write Yiddish and translated his Hebrew poems into "Jewish-German," he publicly announced on the title page of the "Golden Song" that

> The sacred tongue
> Is the only thing
> That wanders with us,
> When the language flourishes
> The Israelite knows
> He has courage, pride and fortitude.[66]

Had it been in the power of these Maskilim, they would have never written in Yiddish, only in Hebrew. Indeed, they made several attempts to publish Hebrew periodicals, of which the first, *ha-Tsofeh be-Eretz ha-Hadashah*, began to appear in 1871. But until the beginning of the 20th century the attempts were feeble and unsuccessful. There were Hebrew writers, but no Hebrew readers. As late as 1892 Hillel Malachovsky wrote to J. J. Weisberg: "Would you believe that not even one number of *ha-Melits* or *ha-Tsefirah* can be seen this year in Pittsburgh? So low has the Hebrew language fallen in America in general, and in Pittsburgh in particular."[67] Later, in 1898, Alexander Harkavy, who was a Hebrew writer himself, wrote: "The Hebrew language does not prevail here for the simple reason that it cannot prevail. To read Hebrew one must know it, and the number of people who know it is much smaller than the number of those who read Yiddish. The Hebraist himself reads Yiddish with greater ease . . ."[68] And so the Hebrew writers who did not become "teachers, clerks in stores . . . artisans, peddlers or merchants"[69] became Yiddish writers—in spite of themselves. It was these reluctant pioneers who imposed upon American Yiddish literature in its first period their cold and unloving stamp.

The Germanized language of *Yisroel der Alte*, like the Yiddish language in which everything was written in those days, has a considerable number of Anglicisms: *Jew, boy, supper, dinner, boss, gentlemen,* and the like.[70] But Yiddish writing in America was influenced by more than the new language, it was also influenced by the new conditions of life. In Sobol's collection at least one poem, *The Polish Jewish Scholar in America,* consisting of twelve twelve-line stanzas, was written under the impact of the new immigrant environment. This was the first Yiddish literary reaction to the total cultural situation of the new Jewish community and therefore, besides being the first book of Yiddish poetry produced in America, is of an especially direct significance for the history of Jewish culture in America.

Through the expanding Hebrew-Yiddish press and the growing number of Hebraist-Yiddish Maskilim, Yiddish culture in America was gradually acquiring its producers. Yet it still reflected the undecisiveness of a generation wandering between two worlds, an old and a new culture. No longer deeply rooted in the old Jewish culture, it had not yet succeeded in taking root in the new American culture. The scholar, the Maskil, felt very lonely. Like Sobol, he had come here with high hopes, and had found disappointment. Sobol writes:

> Here I am in the free land,
> Where equal rights prevail,
> The Jew is not put to shame,
> Where master and servant are alike,

Where there are no slaves,
No barons, no counts.
Now, thank God, I have succeeded in
    everything,
Meaningless aristocracy, "Your Excel-
    lency,"
Envy, hatred, arrogance, presumption,
Together with religious hatred the
    sea has swallowed.
Although I have no more than a
    penny,
Yet my son may possibly be Presi-
    dent. . . .

With this view of America, the Maskil lands upon the soil of the New World. He is sure that he will find freedom, equal rights, tolerance, unrestricted opportunity for his children. He believes that he will be rid of discrimination and hatred, from which he suffered so much overseas. The great internal shortcomings of Jewish life will be ended. Superstition will disappear and Jews will no longer engage in non-productive occupations:

I, a scholar from Poland—
There I have suffered much,
Here I shall recover and shall
Attain the golden goal.
Here I must strive
To live like a man,
To put an end to the wildness of the
    rebble.
An end to denunciations,
To petty rabbis, prohibitions,
An end to all swindle,
Here I am a Jew not by staring,
Work, honesty shall be my fortune.

When he speaks of work what he has in mind is farming, the dream of all Maskilim, beginning with Moshe Markuse in his *Ezer Yisrael*. Two sons will be farmers, two artisans, two professionals, and one, the youngest, a rabbi. What could be better? But this was the dream. The reality was peddling. "I see a burden on my back, I carry it with the last of my strength, there is nothing to sustain me. . . ." But like the German Jew the "Polish scholar" does not remain a peddler for long. He saves a little money and

works his way up. His is the road to success taken by hundreds of thousands of immigrants. The economic problem is solved, and other problems did not exist for the average immigrant. But for the scholar they exist. When his economic difficulties end his spiritual sufferings begin. His beautiful dreams have vanished. He had hoped to be rid of the "wild rebble" that had made life miserable for him in Poland, but in "the free land," just as in the Old World, people trample on each other for distinction in the synagogue. And outside the synagogue it is certainly not better; indeed it is worse, with coarseness, vulgarity and ignorance rampant. The "all-rightnick" boasts that he knows "how to handle fork and knife," that he speaks English, that his spouse is a "wife," that his "misis" has a golden tooth or "all new teeth." There are even Jews who go "on Sunday to tsorts [church]. . . ."Sobol is not pleased with the Jews of America.

Though he was exaggerating slightly, on the whole his unflattering picture of Jewish immigrant life in the 1870's is true to life. Until the mass immigration following the Russian pogroms of the early 1880's, Jewish life in New York (and undoubtedly also in other cities) was, in Abraham Cahan's words, "under the spiritual rule of old-fashioned Jewishness, combined with an uncultured Americanism."[71] Hebrew Maskilim felt superfluous. They had to adapt themselves to circumstances and to do what went against their grain, like writing in Yiddish rather than "in the sacred tongue," which "was the only thing that performed wonders for us," and the like. No significant achievement could be expected of these disillusioned and at times even despairing intellectuals. The only book that was published wholly or partly in Yiddish was Sobol's bilingual collection of poems.[72]

Yiddish journalism and literature were still in an embryonic state in the 1870's, and there was no trace of a Yiddish theater in any meaningful sense of the word.[73]

Undoubtedly some workers in the shops sang the songs and perhaps even repeated the scenes that they remembered from the theater in the old country, or scenes from Purim plays.[74] Amateurs may even have tried their mettle on such Purim plays. According to B. Gorin, the first historian of the Yiddish theater in America, attempts to play the traditional "Sale of Joseph" were made as far back as the end of the 1850's in New York. Gorin adds: "Who knows how many more such [Jewish workers] attempted to present such entertainment here in America and failed?"[75] More or less successful theatrical ventures begin only in the 1880's. Though Jews had a theatrical tradition in the 19th century it was not so strong as the literary tradition.

3. EDUCATION

The old custom of sending boys to *heder* was deeply rooted. The first congregations or synagogues in America maintained schools and teachers ("rebbes" as they were then called). Among the Sephardim the language of instruction was Spanish or Portuguese; among the German Jews, Jewish German or (later, until the close of the 19th century) German; and among the East European immigrants, Yiddish. Quite early, however, there appeared Jews (including some from Eastern Europe) whose language, or whose children's language, was English. These parents tended increasingly to send their children to the general schools.

The problem of Jewish education arose almost simultaneously with the establishment of the Jewish community and the more numerous and more deeply rooted the community grew, the more aggravated the problem became. It was not in vain that all responsible Jewish leaders and writers in the 19th century, beginning with Mordecai Manuel Noah, through Isaac Leeser, Bernard Felsenthal and Jacob Zevi Sobol, complained about the large number of Jewish children who received no Jewish education and were becoming progressively more alienated from Jews and Judaism. As late as the 1860's Rabbi Felsenthal, a spiritual leader of the German Jews in America, fought for Jewish schools giving instruction in both Jewish and secular studies. In 1865 he deplored the ignorance and crassness that pervaded American Jewry. "Respect for spiritual and moral superiority," he said, "is an unknown and uncultivated quality. Arrogance is supreme. Men who in Europe would be quite modest have the effrontery here to come forward and to offer opinions in matters that they do not understand at all."[76]

Maintaining that "education has become a burning problem," Rabbi Felsenthal advocated Jewish day schools, not merely the Sabbath or Sunday schools where the pupil was taught a smattering of religion. He argued that "the majority of the Israelites here are of German descent, and almost every Israelite father wishes and demands—and rightly so—that his children should acquire in school not only English but also German, thoroughly [not Pennsylvania Dutch or Jewish-German, he makes clear] and a little Hebrew."[77] He prepared a plan for a Jewish high school, in which besides English German would be studied thoroughly. The curriculum was also to include all of Jewish history and Hebrew. The plan did not materialize.[78]

Attempts were always being made to establish Jewish schools, in which Hebrew reading, Bible and other subjects would be taught more or less adequately. In addition there were private teachers who would come to the homes of the pupils and instruct them in Jewish studies for several hours during the week. About a hundred years ago New York had seven Jewish schools with 857 pupils and 35 teachers.[79] We do not know in how many of these religious and quasi-religious schools the language of instruction was Yiddish. There is no doubt, however, that long before Yiddish secular schools were established in this country in the 20th century, Jewish subjects were taught in

Talmud Torahs, *hadarim* or private homes in Yiddish. The correspondence in *ha-Maggid* of 1871, telling of teachers who taught the Bible with Rashi's commentary and the Talmud in Yiddish, has previously been cited.

> Yiddish as the language of Jewish studies, as well as the language in which Jews (not only East European, but German and Dutch also) spoke, wrote and read has a much older history in America than generally believed. (Longer and more intensive, of course, is the connection of Jewish education in America with Hebrew.)

With few exceptions, the *hadarim,* the Talmud Torahs and their teachers were on a very low level, as were Yiddish journalism and literature in the 1870's. Yiddish journalism and literature, however, began to show signs of improvement in the mid-1880's while the education of the *heder* and Talmud-Torah did not. Although Jewish education was transplanted to these shores long before Yiddish literature, it remained on the low level of its early beginnings much longer. The *hadarim* of the East European Jews and the teachers were on the whole less effective and less adapted to the circumstances of American immigrant life than the schools under the auspices of the German Jews. S. L. Marcus, co-editor of the *Israelitische Presse,* the first Yiddish periodical in Chicago, writes in his memoirs about two such schools, in which "the Bible with Mendelssohn's translation and Hebrew grammar" were taught[80] and the teachers had to pass an examination in German and in Hebrew grammar. The general language of instruction was undoubtedly Jewish-German or Germanized Yiddish, not German. According to Marcus, the schools were intended for the children of Lithuanian Jews, whose language was Yiddish. In most instances, however, when the German Jews organized or subsidized a Jewish school they introduced German as a subject of study and, wherever possible, as the language of instruction. Later on, when the German Jews became more Americanized, they demanded that English replace Yiddish."[81] When it was not English or German, it was quite frequently Germanized Yiddish that stood between the Talmud Torah and the parents of the children. Indeed, not infrequently the Talmud Torah, like Yiddish literature, became a victim of Germanized Yiddish. Zevi Hirsh Masliansky writes in his memoirs that when he came to America, as late as the second half of the 1890's, he found a principal of a New York Talmud Torah "who took great care that the translation of the Bible should be at least fifty percent in German."[82] This was a carry-over from the days when German Jews and "Kalvarier Germans" were the guardians of Jewish education.

In most *hadarim* and Talmud Torahs, however, language was not the major trouble, but rather the fact that both the teachers and the parents of the pupils were too busy, too preoccupied with making a living, too ignorant and uncouth.

Better Talmud Torahs began to appear in New York, Chicago, Pittsburgh and other cities in the 1880's. Nevertheless, most *hadarim* and Talmud Torahs, as well as the private instruction given by teachers of Hebrew or Bar-Mitzvah coaches, long remained as primitive as they had been in the 1870's and even earlier.

III. YIDDISH CULTURE IN THE 1880's

As we have indicated, in the 1880's Yiddish journalism and literature began to improve, and the foundation was laid for the Yiddish theater. It was especially in the second half of the decade that relatively new conditions arose for Jewish cultural life in America.

The number of immigrants whose language was Yiddish and who were in great need of Yiddish culture and its institutions was rapidly increasing. From 1871

ABRAHAM GOLDFADEN (1840-1908), PLAY-
WRIGHT AND FOUNDER OF THE
YIDDISH THEATER

still looked to Europe for its plays, such
as Goldfaden's *Koldunye* and *Shmendrik*.
But the plays were produced by actors
who had left Goldfaden's troupe in Europe in 1883 or earlier and had come to
America. Since there were no written or
printed texts of his plays, the parts were
reproduced from memory.[85] (These plays,
like the American Yiddish theater in
general, are discussed in the *Algemeine
Entsiclopedie*, "Yidn II.") Although the
Yiddish theater came into existence somewhat later than the Yiddish press, like
the press, it found more favorable circumstances here than overseas. In the
first place, it was not subject to police
pressure; in Russia the Yiddish theater
was altogether banned in 1883. Secondly,
economic conditions were better here.
"The Jews that immigrated to America
soon earned sums that they had hardly
dreamed of in the Old World,"[86] and
they could also afford the luxury of the
theater. Thirdly, they became less pious

to 1880, 70,000 East European Jews came
to America. After the Russian pogroms
of 1881 immigration rose so sharply that
between 1880 and 1900, 600,000 Yiddish-
speaking Jews[83] were added to the 100,000
that had come here previously. In the
1880's alone the Yiddish-speaking population increased by 142,000.[84] Nor was
this merely a quantitative development.
Among the new immigrants were many
scholars, Maskilim, intellectuals and talented people of all sorts. The growth
in demand for Yiddish cultural production was accompanied by a growing number of people capable of satisfying the
demand. Cultural dependence on the Old
World persisted, to be sure, but original
things were done both in the well cultivated field of literature and in the relatively new field of the theater.

1.   THE THEATER IN THE 1880's

The theater depends both on the play-
wright and on the actor. In the early
1880's the Yiddish theater in America

JACOB GORDIN (1853-1909), YIDDISH
DRAMATIST

JACOB ADLER (1855-1926) AS KING LEAR IN
JACOB GORDIN'S YIDDISH PLAY, *KING LEAR*

BERTHA KALICH (1870-1939) AS ETTIE IN
JACOB GORDIN'S *KREITSER SONATA*

BINA ABRAMOVITCH

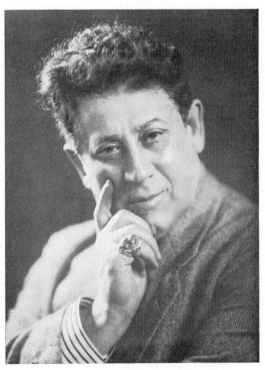

BORIS TOMASHEVSKY (1866-1939)

and less observant in America, more worldly and eager for amusements, so necessary to lonely immigrants separated from their families. And the means were now at hand to meet the need. There were actors who had come here after the ban on the Yiddish theater in Russia. There were also many amateurs, aspirants, former choir boys, and understudies in the Odessa or Jassy Yiddish theater.

The Yiddish theater encountered the same opposition as the press. The German Jews were greatly displeased with the transfer of the Yiddish theater from Eastern Europe to America, just as they looked askance at the Yiddish press. The first Yiddish theatrical performance in New York met with the antagonism of the German Jews, as had happened earlier in London.[87] They had a plausible excuse: the repertory, like the first Yiddish periodicals, was culturally not impressive. In addition, and perhaps more importantly, it was a dubious asset in the eyes of people who were always worried about what the anti-Semites would say. But the masses' thirst for relaxation and amusement was so intense that no opposition from without or interference from within could avail. The theater was established despite the fact that in its early years it was so short of talent that men had to play women's parts, as in the days of old. Later, however, young actors and actresses arose from the ranks of the immigrants themselves (such as Boris Tomashevsky's two daughters and son); more actors came from Europe; and gradually playwrights began to appear on the local scene. Even dramas of immigrant life were presented, although the largest part of the repertory, which consisted primarily of operettas, still derived from the Old World.

The Yiddish theater of the 1880's lacked intelligent leadership, although it had such distinguished actors as Sigmund Mogulescu, Jacob Adler, David Kessler, Leon Blank, Bina Abramovitch and Kenny Lipzin. Until the 1890's, when Jacob Gordin appeared, the Yiddish theater did not succeed in attracting the intellectuals whom the *Am-Olam* (Eternal People) movement brought here and who were such a boon to the Yiddish press.

2. THE PRESS AND LITERATURE IN THE 1880's

Even though the Yiddish press of the 1880's lacked the kind of creative forces that the Yiddish theater had in its actors and actresses, the press was in a superior position to the theater. In the second half of the decade it became the standard-bearer of enlightenment and social idealism, whereas the Yiddish theater of the pre-Gordin era was concerned only with entertainment. The press numbered among its contributors and readers many who were educated or sought education, actively interested in social and moral problems, whereas the theater had to cater to a primitive group, uprooted from its traditional cultural soil and not yet rooted in the soil of America. This, it seems to me, was the main reason why the press achieved as early as the 1880's what the theater was able to achieve only much later—cultural, social and moral leadership. A definite advantage that the American Yiddish press had over the East European was the greater political freedom of America.

As early as 1881 (and again in 1883) Sarasohn made an attempt to issue his paper daily instead of weekly. It was not until 1885 that the attempt succeeded with the establishment of the *Yiddishes Tageblatt,* which existed till 1928, when it merged with the *Morgn-Zhurnal.* (An extended treatment of the Yiddish press in the 1880's and the following years has been given in the *Algemeine Entsiclopedie,* "Yidn III".) Here we shall give only a brief summary of the relations between the growth of the Yiddish press and the rapid development of Yiddish culture as a whole in America.

The very fact that to the weekly periodicals, constantly increasing in number,

From Zalme Zylberzweig: *Album of the Yiddish Theatre*

L. to R.: IDA GROPER, SAM SCHNEIER, DAVID KESSLER, FANNIE LUBRITSKY
IN Z. LIBIN'S *MEN AND WOMEN*

there was also added a daily press in Yiddish was significant. Not only did it testify to the new opportunities for Yiddish journalism arising out of the sharp rise in the numbers of the Yiddish-speaking population, but it also was an expression of their intensified moral and intellectual needs and a proof that writers were emerging to satisfy those needs. Of these factors the most important was the immigrant's curiosity about developments in Europe and the world at large. In this respect the chief difference between the 1870's and the 1880's was simply that in the latter period there were more people eager to know what was going on in the world, hence more newspaper readers. Another difference was that in the 1880's the press was better in quality.

The Yiddish periodicals gradually began to free themselves from the German and Germanized Yiddish which had contaminated the American Yiddish press in its first period. Though they did not recover from this protracted disease very easily, the fear of "Yiddish Yiddish"

began to vanish. In 1886 Alexander Harkavy (1863-1939) argued in a revised version of a treatise first published in Hebrew that "Yiddish is a language like all other languages"; this thesis he set forth in Sarasohn's weekly and later in a pamphlet. But he was no longer alone in not being ashamed of "simple Yiddish." Indeed, others had stopped looking down on Yiddish even earlier. In 1882 Abraham Cahan (1860-1951) spoke "simple Yiddish" instead of English, Russian or Germanized Yiddish at meetings of Jewish workers. In 1886, when he began publishing, together with Charles Rayevsky, the socialist weekly *Di Naie Zeit*, he used "the simplest Yiddish imaginable."[88] Getzel Selikovitch (1863-1926) also wrote fairly straightforward rather than Germanized Yiddish in Sarasohn's *Yiddishes Vokhnblatt*, in Goldfaden's *New Yorker Yiddishe Ilustrirte Zeitung* (1889) and in the *Folks-Advokat* (1888). In one of his columns in the *Vokhnblatt* he declared:

We must speak to the reader in the language he understands best, the language in which lullabies were sung to him, the language in which he mumbled his first words before he was weaned, the language with which he took his first step into the everyday world, the language in which he conducts his daily affairs and in which he has sighed, flattered, mourned, rejoiced and loved.[89]

In this very passage, however, Selikovitch still used a rather Germanized Yiddish. Besides, he did not have any influence, nor did he try to have any, on the contributors to the *Vokhnblatt* and the other periodicals for which he wrote, and some of which he edited. Cahan did exert an influence upon his colleagues, and not only his *Naie Zeit,* but also the *New Yorker Yiddishe Folkszeitung* avoided Germanized Yiddish. To be sure, the latter did not give scrupulous attention to the simplicity and purity of its Yiddish as did Abraham Cahan. In an editorial the *Folkszeitung* declared:

> The Yiddish language is composed of words of various origin. It is without rules or grammar. We deem it inadvisable to have in our periodical only one type of Yiddish. Our readers need not be surprised, therefore, that different articles are written in different types of Yiddish. We only believe it important to eliminate all Russian words from our periodical.[90]

Still, it was freer of Germanisms than the *Yiddishe Gazetten* or *Yiddishes Tageblatt.* In closeness to the actual spoken language the *New Yorker Yiddishe Folkszeitung* followed in the footsteps of its socialist predecessor, *Naie Zeit.*

In another respect the *Folkszeitung* outstripped not only Sarasohn's conservative publications, but also Cahan's and Rayevsky's socialist weekly. These publications served only one group, either the Orthodox or the radicals. The *New Yorker Yiddishe Folkszeitung* wanted to be the spokesman for at least two trends in Jewish life in America: socialism, presented by one of the two editors, Braslawsky, and *Hibbat Zion* (Love of Zion), represented by Moses Mintz, the other editor. It was, in its own words, "socialist and Jewish."

Socially and culturally this was a new and bold step. In those days it was conceivable that socialists (or, as they were then called, social-democrats) and anarchists should "dwell together," after a fashion, in one periodical. But that socialists and *Hovevei Zion* should have a common organ was something new, particularly in view of the fact that it was not a mechanical amalgamation of two groups, but an attempt at a true synthesis of socialism and Jewish nationalism. After the pogroms of the early 1880's many Jews abandoned socialism and became Hovevei Zionists. Those, however, who remained socialists opposed Hibbat Zion. Moses Mintz was perhaps the only one who became a Jewish nationalist and an advocate of Palestine without ceasing to be a revolutionary. We may assume that he was the author of the "Program of the *New Yorker Yiddishe Folkszeitung,*" published in the first issue, June 25, 1886. This program asserted that the Jewish worker should feel united "with all the workers of the world," on the one hand, and with "the condition of the Jewish worker in the world in general and in America in particular," on the other. The program reads in part:

> On the battle-line he [the Jewish worker] has many comrades as a worker; as a Jew he has very few. The Jewish problem is very important and needs careful consideration for a proper solution. He will understand the solution only when he is familiar with Jewish history.

In those years similar declarations might be heard from Morris Vinchevsky, Chaim Zhitlowsky and several years later A. Walt-Liesin and Yitzhok Leibush Peretz, in Europe. In America Moses Mintz must have been a unique phenomenon, like the program of the *Folkszeitung.* Its aim was to shed light on "the labor problem, its development from the beginning to the present, and all the means that have been considered by the learned and outstanding representatives of the labor movement in order to solve that problem." It was equally to enlighten the Jewish worker "on the situation of the Jewish worker in the world and specially in America, as well as the Jewish problem in relation to the development of culture and civilization among various peoples." The *Folkszeitung* therefore promised to publish articles on "the general development of culture and civilization" and on "movements in Jewish history, written by the outstanding Jewish historians." This was the first step toward a broader approach to general problems as well as to problems of Jewish culture—but for the time being only a first step.

Another improvement in the character of the Yiddish press was its growing interest in literature. This change, too, was announced and promised by the *New Yorker Yiddishe Folkszeitung*. One point in its program spoke of "interesting original stories and good translations of the most recent writers."

To keep the promise of giving the reader original Yiddish stories or poems was in the 1880's at least as difficult as to be both socialist and Jewish. Except for Abraham Cahan, practically none of the Yiddish writers who were to lay the foundation of Yiddish fiction in America had yet arrived. Gordin, Libin, Kobrin, Gorin, Zevin, Levin—all the names ending in "in"—became known only in the 1890's. Of the more or less gifted Yiddish poets only the beginner Morris Rosenfeld, who had arrived in 1886, the year in which the *New Yorker Yiddishe Folkszeitung* began to appear, and the now half-forgotten David Goldstein, were then here. In these circumstances it was difficult to provide the readers of the *Folkszeitung* with interesting original stories or even with poems. Yet the *Folkszeitung* did everything possible to be a literary organ. Since even the anarchist *Freie Arbeter Shtime*

and the socialist *Arbeter-Zeitung* had hardly any original stories in the beginning and had to be content with poetry, and since these weeklies began to appear in 1890, it is little cause for surprise that the *Folkszeitung* could not accomplish much in the field of the short story. But there was no dearth of verse. From time to time there appeared genuine poems, not merely the rhymes which were then written by almost everyone who could hold a pen. Besides David Goldstein, who undoubtedly had a poetic spark, no less a figure than Morris Rosenfeld made his debut in the *Folkszeitung*. On December 31, 1886, in No. 26 of the *Folkszeitung*, Morris Rosenfeld published his first poem —a kind of a lament for the passing year. It embodied the old Haskalah motif, "Arise, my people!", but it was also animated by the revolutionary socialist spirit of Yiddish proletarian literature in England (Vinchevsky, Isaac Stone and others).[91]

The socialist and near-socialist press, which began to appear in the second half of the 1880's, was on the whole very important for the dissemination and fructification of Yiddish culture. Despite the fact that this press was not directly concerned with Jewish social or cultural problems, but with socialist (or anarchist) propaganda and enlightenment, it nevertheless stimulated Yiddish culture. Its socialist or anarchist mission was what linked it with Yiddish. It could not have found its way to the masses of Jewish workers and ordinary folk without using their language and striving by means of that language to arouse in them new cultural needs, and in part satisfying those needs. So that the rise of the radical Yiddish press in the middle of the 1880's was both the cause and the effect of profound changes in the character and purpose of Yiddish culture in America, one instance of which was the gradual abandonment of Germanized Yiddish that we have discussed here.

In the Yiddish press and in all of Yiddish culture the new progressive or even revolutionary tendency began to compete sharply with the conservative and Haskalah spirit, which had practically dominated American Jewish cultural life until that time. (The appearance of satirical and humorous publications toward the end of the 1880's may be related to this trend.[92])

The new militancy in the cultural life of the immigrant in the 1880's was a result of the disgraceful working conditions in the sweatshops. The populist intelligentsia of the new wave of immigration, the various Am Olam groups, with their ideals of labor and agriculture, and the growing number of radicals (anarchists or socialists) helped to create this militancy. Almost all of these immigrants were fairly well educated. Like the young men of the BILU movement, who were then going to Palestine to realize their dreams, there were also enthusiastic idealists in the Am Olam movement who had interrupted their studies in Russia in the hope of realizing their rather vague social and ethical program in America.[93] They did not succeed in realizing it, but many of them became increasingly active in Jewish communal life in America. Both in their bold attempts to establish farming cooperatives or communes and other organizations and in their new freethinking and radical publications they became a counterbalance to the old-fashioned forces of religion and Haskalah which had previously dominated Jewish life in America. The latter, in no mood to surrender, countered with their own aggressiveness.[94] Now they were confronted not merely with the old "external enemy," the American environment, but also with a new enemy, who sought to sap the foundation of Jewish tradition from within. The radicals, however, were able to strengthen their position. To the older immigrant institutions—the synagogue and the landsmanshaft—were added such new institutions as the labor union, the social club and the radical party.

In the 1870's and the early 1880's the institutions of East European Jewry in America had been almost exclusively religious and semi-religious. Now there began to appear a constantly growing number of secular or even anti-religious institutions, the radical intelligentsia and the radical press playing the major role in their establishment and maintenance. Their ideological and cultural effects continued to grow.

But the radicals were so engrossed in their propaganda activities and their internal ideological conflicts that they had little time or energy for such a problem as the education of the young. This left education under the control of the old-fashioned *hadarim* and Talmud Torahs. There were even some parents who did not send their children to public schools, being content to send them to institutions like the Yeshivah Etz Chaim (in New York), where a few hours a day were devoted to general studies. In 1887-88 Abraham Cahan taught English there. He noted that "children twelve and even fourteen years old could not read English properly," and that some of the trustees and Hebrew teachers regarded his subject as superfluous.[95] A very small number of children studied in slightly better Jewish schools and had more or less suitable teachers. Most children of Yiddish-speaking immigrants received their Jewish education—in so far as one may call it by that name—in institutions for which the memoirs of the period do not have a kind word.[96]

On the other hand, a growing number of adult immigrants were transformed under the influence of the radical enlightenment. They developed an interest in education, mainly in the natural and social sciences. Once ardently religious, they became ardently anti-religious.[97]

אונזער „צוקונפט".

אונזער פראגראם קענען מיר אייגענטליך אויס־
דריקען אין דריי ווערטער: מיר זיינען סאָציאַל־דעמאָ־
קראטען.

וואָס דאָס בעדייט, איז שוין ערקלערט גע־
וואָרען אין איינינע ארטיקלען אין דער „ארבייטער
צייטונג", און מיר וועלען עס נאָך גרינדליכער אי
אויספיהרליכער ערקלערען אין דער „צוקונפט" אויב
די טרייהייט און טהעטיגקייט פון אונזערע גענאָ־
סען און סימפאטיזירער וועלען אונז ג   עבען די מעג־
ליכקייט צו האָבען א צוקונפט....

מיר זאָגען דאָס גאנץ אָפען, מיר ווילען פון קיינעם
ניט בעהאַלטען דעם פאקט, דאָס מיר פאַננען אָן
ארויסצונעבען א וויסענשאַפטליכען זשורנאל אין
זשארגאָן:—א נייעם אין דער אָרימער זשארגאָנישער
ליטעראטור—נור אלס א   פ ר אָ ב ע. די אידישע
אַרבייטער בעוועגונג וואקסט זעהר שנעל און ענט־
וויקעלט אויך אזעלכע אַרבייטער, וואָס ווילען זעהר
גרינדליך לערנען: די סאָציאַלע פראַנע פון אונזער
צייט און איבערהויפט זיך אויספילדען; אָבער זיי
קענען דאָס לייערער ניט דערגרייכען, ווייל אויך
זשארגאָן האָט מען ביז די לעצטע צייט געשריבען
נור באַבע מעשיות און בדחנות, און אַנדערע שפרא־
בען קענען זיי ניט אָדער קענען אזוי ווייניג, אז זיי
זיינען נאָך ניט אין שטאַנד צו פאַרשטיין א בוך
אָדער אין ערנסטען ארטיקעל. פאר דיזע ערנסטע
ארבייטער וואָס נעהרען צו וויסען און צו ווערען גע־
בילדעטע מענשען, גיבען מיר ארוים די „צוקונפט";
און אויב זייער צאָהל איז ווירקליך אזוי גרוים, ווי
פילע נענאָסען בעהויפטען, וועט זיא עקזיסטירען און
ערפילען איהר ערציהונגס־אויפנאבע, און אויב ניט,

דאן וועלען מיר ווארטען אויף דיא צייט, ווען אונזער
פראָפּאַגאַנדע אויף פערזאַמלונגען און דורך דיא
„ארבייטער צייטונג" וועט ענטוויקלען אַזֹא צאָהל
ערנסטע ארבייטער, אז א וויסענשאַפטליכער זשור־
נאל זאל יא קענען עקזיסטירען. יעדענפאַלס מוזען
דיא גענאָסען טיכטיג ארבייטען, אז דיא „צוקונפט"
זאל בעקאַנט ווערען און קריגען א סך לעזער, דען אָהן
זייער היכפע וועלען מיר גלייך מוזען אַװעקקלייגען דיא
פעדער. מיר האָלטען פאר איבריג צו מאכען הייסע
און לאַנגע אויפרופען און מיר זאָגען איינפאַך: גענאָ־
סען! טוט אייער פּפליכט אלס ארבייטער און סאָ־
ציאליסטען—יעצט האָט יעדער פון אייך דיא מעגליכ־
קייט צו זיין ווירקליך טהעטיג, נעהמט זיך אַלֹא צו
דער ארבייט און זעהט, אז אונזער „צוקונפט" זאל
קענען האָבען א צוקונפט.

ווי דיא לעזער קענען זעהן פון דיא ארטיקלען,
וואָס ערשיינען אין דיזע נומער, איז דיא „צוקונפט"
ניט בלויז א סאָציאליסטישער אָרנאן אין ענגען זינען
פון דיזען וואָרט, נאָר אן אַלגעמיינער בילדונגס זשור־
נאל. מיר ווילען ניט נאָר, אז דער אידישער ארביי־
טער זאָל וויסען, ווי ער ווערט יעצט בעראויבט
עקאָנאָמיש און נעדריקט אום בעשווינדעלט פּאָליטיש
פון דיא קאפּיטאליסטישע קלאסע, און וואָס ער זאל
טאָן אום פון זיך אַראָפּצו־וואַרפען דעם קאפּיטאַלים־
טישען יאָך; זאָנדערן מיר ווילען אויך, אז ער זאל
גוט פ א ר ש ט י י ן, ווי דיא מענשהייט איז גע־
קומען צו איהר היינטיגע מדרנה, ווי אזוי זיא
האָט פרייהער געלעבט און ווי אזוי זיא האָט זיך
ענטוויקעלט. מיר ווילען, אז ער זאל אזוי גוט פער־
שטיין דאַרווין'ס לעהרע און וועגען קאמפף פיר עקזים־

IV. YIDDISH CULTURE IN THE 1890's

1. THE PRESS AND LITERATURE IN THE 1890's

The press was the main weapon in the battle for secularism and against piety, for revolution and against the existing order. The growth of radical journalism can be seen in the fact that in the early 1890's the newspapers and journals already mentioned and such weeklies as the *Varheit,* the first Jewish publication in America to be communally supported, no longer sufficed. A number of dailies appeared (of which the most important were the *Abend-Blatt,* 1894-1902, *Forward* [Forverts], 1897, and the Chicago *Yiddisher Kurier,* 1892-1944), as did serious monthlies. These publications were group and not private enterprises. In the 1890's the following began to be published:

Di Zukunft, a socialist monthly published by the Yiddish-speaking section of the Socialist Workers Party of North America, and edited by Philip Krantz, 1892-93 (it did not then appear regularly every month; by Abraham Cahan (1894-97), and by various other people until 1913 (with an interruption of five years, from 1898 to 1903). In 1913 the *Zukunft* was taken over by the Forward Association and A. Liesin became the editor. After Liesin's death the Central Yiddish Culture Organization (CYCO) took over the publication, which is now edited by a board of editors.

Di Freie Geselshaft, a monthly journal for advanced ideas[98], published from 1895 to 1902 by the Free Society Publishing Association under the editorship of M. Leontiev (L. Moisseiff) and M. Katz. In 1910 the *Freie Geselshaft* (with the slogan: "For literature and discussion of social problems") resumed publication under the editorship of S. Yanovski. It was, however, short-lived.

Di Naie Zeit, 1898-99, published by the Yiddish-speaking socialists who did not belong to the opposition that established

ALEXANDER HARKAVY (1863-1939), YIDDISH PHILOLOGIST

the *Forward* but remained loyal to the *Abend-Blatt.* It was first edited by B. Feigenbaum and later by Philip Krantz.

Der Naier Geist, 1897-98, a non-partisan "monthly for science, literature and art," edited by Alexander Harkavy.

Folkskalendar, 1895-1900, also edited and published by Harkavy.

At the same time the radicals continued in their attempts to launch weeklies: the socialist *Arbeter-Zeitung,* 1890-94; the anarchist *Freie Arbeter Shtime,* founded in 1890 and appearing with minor interruptions to date. After 1899, when the *Freie Arbeter Shtime* resumed publication under the editorship of S. Yanovski, it occupied a prominent place in Yiddish literature in America. Almost every Yiddish writer made his debut in its columns. Other publications were the *Morgnshtern,* 1890, and *Emes,* Boston, 1895-96.

The greatest immediate effect was of course exerted by the daily newspapers, but the influence of the weekly and especially the monthly publications was far more profound. Alongside the daily newspapers and as an important supplement to adult educational activity in the form of lectures and the like, the new publications helped to educate and raise the cultural level of the Jewish masses. This educational work was frequently one-sided and not thorough enough. However, if we consider the low cultural level of the average immigrant, particularly in secular matters, we must conclude that the slightest awakening of new social and intellectual interests, the most superficial information about the natural sciences, sociology, and political science, even a purely propagandistic call to solidarity, to union, to the struggle for better living conditions, social justice and freedom, was a cultural and moral achievement.

Attracting intellectuals previously alienated from the Jewish environment and the Yiddish language to Jewish cultural creativity was a substantial accomplishment. For this accomplishment we are indebted to the radical Yiddish press and the social ideas and ideals it propagated. Writers and speakers whose medium of expression had been Russian, Hebrew or German studied to become Yiddish writers and speakers. Where once there had been an intelligentsia without a people and a people without an intelligentsia, the Yiddish press and the social movement it represented gave the intelligentsia a people and the people an intellectual leadership. Both, the intellectuals and the people, benefited greatly. Creative individuals found an audience, and the spiritually thirsty masses found an opportunity to quench their thirst.

Following the 1880's, Yiddish progressed not only by eliminating Germanism but also by expanding the range of the subjects it could treat. Its vocabulary became richer and its style and syntax more flexible. From having been merely a workaday language, it became a medium for more ambitious ideas, including even scientific thought.

Popular science was the first field cultivated by the new Yiddish toward the end of the 19th century. This was a linguistic, cultural and literary achievement in one. The popularizers of the natural and social sciences—Abraham Cahan, B. Feigenbaum, M. Baranov, Abraham Kaspe, Philip Krantz, Isaac Hourwich, L. Budyanov (Budin), A. Frumkin, J. A. Merison, M. Leontiev, Isser Ginsburg, and many others —widened their readers' intellectual horizons and prepared them for reading journalism of a higher caliber, literary criticism and belles-lettres.

Increasingly, the daily, weekly and monthly press both originated and disseminated Yiddish literature in all its forms. More than half a century ago, I. Pfeffer pointed to the great difference between the Yiddish and non-Yiddish press in America. The latter had little relationship to literature, whereas the former prepared "an upper story" for literature from the beginning[99] and was in effect both "the upper story" and the foundation of Yiddish literary creativity in America. The Yiddish press taught the writer how to write and the reader how to read. In other languages journalism was at best a branch of literature; in Yiddish all literature stemmed from journalism. The newspapers and periodicals reprinted the works of European Yiddish writers, especially Mendele Mocher Seforim's stories and Peretz' stories and poems. They published the works of the new writers who made their debut in America. They were the meeting ground of the novelist, the poet, the critic, and the reader. In the first period of Yiddish literature in America practically every Yiddish short story, novel, poem, and critical essay appeared first in the press and only later, if at all, in a book.

There was no essential difference between the Yiddish journalism and the literature of the period. The only distinction was one of form, not of content. Yiddish literature at that time was not yet differentiated as to content, and there was little to demark one literary genre from another, or even prose from poetry. Both journalistic articles and scientific popularizations, on the one hand, and stories and poems, on the other, had only two aims: enlightenment, propaganda. Regardless of the form employed—journalism or belles-lettres, prose or poetry—the point of departure was not the creative need of the writer but the intellectual or moral need of the reader, not the writer's self-expression but the promotion of some doctrine or movement.

But the form in which the writer sought to affect the reader, to interest him in a cherished party or philosophy, was important. Frequently the form transcended the content. Without the volition of the writer and the knowledge of the reader form often had an esthetic and artistic and not merely a moral and intellectual effect. This was especially true of poetry. Those who read a poem and certainly those who sang it—and poems were frequently sung —enjoyed the very sound of the words, their assonance, rhythm and melody. Thus the readers and especially the singers of the poem enjoyed an artistic experience in addition to having been in a certain sense enlightened and guided. They became accustomed to poetic enjoyment, or at any rate prepared for it, although the poems themselves were far from poetic. Just as the writers could occasionally possess something of the poet, although their mission was to be enlighteners and propagandists rather than to sing "as sings the bird," so the reader or the singer of the poems could unconsciously have artistic needs and read or sing into the lines more than he wanted to, more than there was in them. The charm of the poetic sounds, weak and primitive though it was, sought and found a secret way to the reader and frequently had an artistic effect outstripping the non-artistic content of the poem.[100] Hence, in addition to true poets like Morris Rosenfeld, Yehoash, A. Liesin, A. M. Sharkanski, and Joseph Bovshover, such poet-propagandists as David Edelstadt are also of some significance for the creation of a literary climate and of literature itself. Similarly, together with true artists in prose like Z. Libin, Leon Kobrin, B. Gorin, I. Zevin (Tashrak), and Z. Levin, a propagandist and enlightener in prose like Jacob Gordin is of real significance.

Even in the 1890's, and particularly in the early years of that decade, journalism of propaganda and enlightenment, both in prose and in verse, was still dominant. American literature on the whole, although it was of a different character from Yiddish literature, was also permeated with a journalistic spirit. This was true of its typical representatives even in the early part of the 20th century. Henry Seidel Canby, the well-known literary critic, has written that it was not literature that appealed to them but the country. They were avid for news and their writings are essentially news, a kind of journalism, which is becoming an American art.[101]

Both American literature and immigrant Yiddish literature arrived by different roads at "the American art"—journalism.

The first representatives of Yiddish prose and poetry in America had a special reason for being journalistic and propagandistic. Practically all of them, with but a few exceptions, belonged to the social-revolutionary camp and had been factory workers or labor leaders. For them literature, whether in prose or poetry, was a weapon, a propaganda medium for socialism, anarchism, or (much more rarely) Jewish nationalism. Thus, in the last decades of the 19th century it became in America what it had been in mid-century in Europe, a literature of enlightenment.[102]

Book publishing was still in its infancy. In later years H. Alexandrov complained: "The masses provided thousands of readers of newspapers. . . . But for special editions of works, for books that cost more than 10 or 15 cents, there were no buyers."[103] In the 1870's only one or at the most two booklets were published. In the 1880's we have in book form *Di Gloke* (New York, 1888), the first collection of Morris Rosenfeld's poems; an anthology, *Kupletn un Yiddishe Teater-Lider* (1888); a textbook for the study of English, *Der Amerikaner*,[104] and several small socialist and anarchist propaganda brochures which were mostly parodies on the liturgy ("Devotional Prayer," "Haggadah, New Version," and the like). There were yet no Yiddish book publishing companies. Morris Rosenfeld could publish his *Di Gloke* only because "a relative, a wealthy butcher, guaranteed the payment of the costs" (J. A. Merison in *Pinkos* I, New York, p. 269). *Di Gloke* was published in 2,000 copies. Merison, who helped the young poet prepare his poems for publication, stated: "I doubt whether as many as a hundred copies were sold. The butcher took possession of the books and fed them to the mice in his cellar" *(Ibid.)*.

Though there were as yet no buyers of Yiddish books, the writers, particularly those who wrote for the press, no longer felt so forlorn. Some of them were now active communal leaders and not merely men of letters. In 1889 they even took the initiative in organizing their own writers' association (the first union of Yiddish writers in America). In the Germanized Yiddish in which the call of the initiators was issued, Yiddish was still referred to as "jargon", but note was also taken of "the constantly growing progress [of] the jargon literature," and all writers "to whom the interests of the jargon literature are dear" were called upon to join the association. Its aims were: "1. The improvement of the jargon literature in spiritual content and in form; 2. Mutual aid, both spiritual and material, of the jargon writers." The financial support of the association came from "weekly dues, public entertainments, lectures and other incomes." Among the founders and the first leaders of the association were Morris

MORRIS ROSENFELD (1862-1923), POET

Rosenfeld, Joseph J. Jaffe, D. Apoteker and Johann Paley.[105]

On the eve of the 1890's the number of writers was increasing, and Yiddish literature, education and culture in general were growing not only quantitatively but also qualitatively. Simultaneously the language was becoming more supple and powerful. This process began in America somewhat later than in the Old World, and the difference of American conditions led to a certain difference in content and form. In Europe the nationalist tendency was particularly strong, although there too the revolutionary Jewish labor movement contributed a very important chapter to the history of Yiddish literature; in America the radical spirit prevailed. In Europe this period was only one chapter in the history of Yiddish literature; in America (and before that in England) the radicals may be said to have laid the foundation of Yiddish literature, though new tendencies were to be revealed later. Overseas the socialists (Peretz, Pinski,

Gorin) were in the minority. Here it was the nationalist or folkist writers, such as Moses Mintz, Getzel Selikovitch, Dolitzki and Goldfaden, who were in the minority.

To most Yiddish writers in America the Yiddish language, Yiddish literature and Jewish culture in general were not yet values in themselves, but subordinate to cosmopolitan, socialist values. In the first number of *Zukunft* (January 1892) explicit mention was made of the growing number of Jewish workers who knew no language besides Yiddish and who "wanted to study thoroughly the social problems of our time and in general to educate themselves." It was for "these serious workers" that the publication of "the scientific-socialist monthly" was begun. Somewhat later, *Der Naier Geist*[106] and similar publications were launched for the same purpose. Though specifically Jewish cultural values did not yet figure in their ideologies, psychologically they had a certain effect upon the young Jewish intelligentsia in America. The major part of their enlightenment activity was still conducted in the anti-religious and anti-nationalist spirit of earlier years[107], but toward the end of the 1890's there began to appear in Yiddish purely cultural and literary values which were to compete strongly with radicalism and the striking of radical attitudes. The social ideology of a good many socialists and anarchists was no longer as opposed or even indifferent to nationalism as it had once been. The synthesis of socialism and Jewish nationalism, whose first harbinger in the 1880's had been the *New Yorker Yiddishe Folkszeitung,* could now count on a more favorable climate. The Dreyfus affair in France, on the one hand, and Zionism, on the other, had an indirect effect on some members of the Jewish intelligentsia in the second half of the 1890's. This effect was similar (in kind, if not in degree) to the direct effects of the pogroms on the Jewish intelligentsia in Europe in the first half of the 1880's, on the one hand,

and the Hovevei Zion movement, on the other.

Some Jewish intellectuals in America began to show a more intense interest in the Jewish problem in general and in the problems of Jewish nationalism and Zionism in particular. The heresy of nationalism was now to be heard in the camp of cosmopolitan radicalism.[108] In this way Yiddish literature, no longer satisfied to be only a medium of socialist or anarchist propaganda, gradually was emboldened to become Jewish literature.

B. Gorin, who had arrived here from Europe several years earlier and who was a disciple of Peretz, began to publish in 1897 his *Yiddish-Amerikanishe Folks-Bibliotek* in order to wage "open warfare against the yellow literature that flooded all Jewish homes in America and to clear a new path for a clean, decent literature" (quoted from the miscellany, *Tsu der Geshikhte fun der Yiddisher Prese in Amerike,* New York, 1923). Gorin did not abandon faith in the great significance "that such a thing [literature] has for the enlightenment of the people," but he also tried hard to make enlightenment significant for literature and help it achieve greater artistry. In the same year *Zukunft* added the following editorial note to Liesin's poem "Tsvey Tfilles" (Two Prayers): "We publish this poem on the strength of its poetic quality, although its tendency is somewhat foreign to us." This meant that there was such a thing as poetic quality that had to be taken into account, and it began to occupy a place, although not one of primacy, in literature. Gradually there even arose an interest in the theory of literary creation. As far back as 1894 *Zukunft* published such articles as Abraham Cahan's "Poetry, and How It Is Written," and K. Paulding's "A Few Words about the Development of Belles-lettres." Nearly all the Yiddish journals showed a deepened interest in literary criticism,[109]—a sign of deepened interest in literature as such.

In literary criticism, which Morris Vinchevsky and Morris Rosenfeld smuggled into their poems and Budyanov, Jacob Milch and others discussed in prose, there appeared the theory of "proletarian literature." Not all the members of the radical school were adherents of this theory. M. Leontief (Moisseiff), M. Katz, B. Gorin and, somewhat later, Y. Entin no longer maintained that "every poet of our times is a class poet" (L. Budyanov, *Der Naier Geist,* 1897, p. 104). In their eyes literature had artistic value independent of its social message.

The new sense of responsibility to art was most evident in the stories and, to a lesser extent, the poetry of the growing number of young writers and poets. Besides the well-known Morris Vinchevsky, Morris Rosenfeld, Yehoash, Liesin, David Edelstadt, Joseph Bovshover and the less known but highly gifted Sharkanski, there were nearly two dozen Yiddish poets, although some of them were quickly forgotten. Theirs was the period of transition from the time when the poem had to be a battle-hymn—the story could occasionally afford to be just a story—to the time when even the poem with a message was also intended as a work of art.[110]

Books were printed in a much larger number than heretofore. Novels, both as items in a series named *Heftn* and as separate books, mostly translations and adaptations, were published and sold in growing numbers.[111] According to Alexander Harkavy (writing under the pen-name "Americanus"), no fewer than sixty-five novels were published before 1898.[112] Though nearly all were of slight literary merit, they did broaden the reader's outlook and accustom him to read books in addition to newspapers.

The most flourishing branch of Yiddish literature in America was poetry. One of its distinguished representatives, Morris Rosenfeld, came to the attention of the general American reading public with a translation of his *Songs from the Ghetto* (1898) by Professor Leo Wiener, of Har-vard University, who also wrote an introduction to the book. The following year Wiener's *The History of Yiddish Literature in the Nineteenth Century* appeared, in which several chapters were devoted to Yiddish literature in America. Wiener did not believe that it had a future. Actually, it was only then beginning to flower.

2. THE THEATER IN THE 1890's

As early as the 1880's the theater occupied a prominent place in Jewish mass culture in America. Before there were many readers of Yiddish books the stage had already succeeded in attracting a considerable audience. This may explain why dramatic criticism preceded literary criticism. Even so, before the arrival of Jacob Gordin (1853-1909) Yiddish dramatic critics could write only about the actors and not the plays, for "most of the plays presented do not merit serious consideration."[113] Jacob Gordin made serious dramatic criticism possible and necessary. Gordin first began to exercise his function as reformer of the Yiddish stage in America in 1891, when his first play, *Siberia,* was presented by Jacob Adler. This and other major developments in the history of the Yiddish theater in America are discussed in the *Algemeine Entsiclopedie,* "Yidn II." Here we need only recall that his prime achievement was that plays now began to be presented which "merited serious consideration." Though they were not very impressive from a literary and artistic point of view, from a purely theatrical point of view they cleared the air because they were professional and competent. Gordin lacked the personal talent of many of the leading actors of the Yiddish theater, but he knew how to create unitary and relatively consistent parts that gave true artists an opportunity of demonstrating and developing their unusual abilities. Not only did Gordin educate the better Yiddish actors artistically, but by great effort he also had a profound cultural influence upon the

Yiddish theater audience. Gradually both actors and spectators learned to appreciate plays free of the claptrap of cheap operetta and primitive melodrama. In addition, Gordin tried to make his work serve as a vehicle of enlightenment.[114]

Thanks to him, some of the better educated radicals gradually began to take an interest in the Yiddish stage. In 1896 some of the socialist intellectuals established a theatrical association, "Di Freie Yiddishe Folksbine" (The Free Jewish People's Theater) for the purpose of "understanding, elevating and rendering more literary" the Yiddish theater,[115] and on Gordin's initiative there was also established an Educational League. Under his influence, too, other Yiddish writers (Leon Kobrin, Z. Libin) began writing for the theater. The Yiddish theater became less and less an institution of vulgar and cheap entertainment and more and more a cultural institution on a high plane. Yoel Entin and other dramatic critics aided greatly in this process. The "yellow" play and "yellow" acting did not disappear altogether from the Yiddish stage, but they no longer dominated it. There came into being a Yiddish theater worthy of the name, and when the Yiddish theater overseas awakened, the theater in America could exert a wholesome influence upon it. Contact was also established between the Yiddish and the general theater in America.

V. FROM THE TURN OF THE CENTURY TO AMERICA'S ENTRY INTO WORLD WAR I

1. THE BEGINNING OF THE TWENTIETH CENTURY

The interest in Yiddish cultural creation as a value in itself, and not merely as a medium of enlightenment or amusement, which had begun to be felt by some of the Jewish intellectuals in America as early as the 1890's, continued to grow in the early 20th century. Several causes can be singled out.

MORRIS VINCHEVSKY (1856-1933), POET

1. The gradual national and social awakening of the Jewish masses and the folk intelligentsia in Eastern Europe expressed itself in the rise of the Zionist movement, the establishment of the Jewish labor organization "Bund" in Lithuania, Poland and White Russia, Chaim Zhitlowsky's and Simon Dubnow's autonomism and spiritual nationalism, the less individualistic and more national and social character of the renewed enlightenment movement, the newly established organs of the Yiddish press, the intensified research in Jewish folk creation, and the new generation of young Yiddish writers. The effect of these and similar manifestations of new moods and tendencies in the Old World began to be felt in America as well, because of the ever-increasing numbers of new immigrants arriving here.

2. Among the immigrants themselves, particularly during and after the Russo-

Japanese war, there were many Maskilim of the newer, more nationalist school, including Socialist Zionists and Bundists. They generally had greater cultural desires than the earlier immigrants, their Jewish and general social and cultural interests were broader, and they had tasted of modern Jewish culture.

3. Men of this stamp found spokesmen present here: in poetry Yehoash, Morris Vinchevsky, A. Liesin and, of the later group, "The Young," I. Y. Schwartz and H. Rosenblatt; in journalism and literary criticism A. Litvin, K. Fornberg, Isser Ginsburg, Yoel Entin, F. Rosenblatt-Ben Yakir and H. Alexandrov.

4. Although the leadership in secular Jewish culture in America still belonged to the older cosmopolitan radicals, the position and influence of those who had a more positive attitude to Yiddish and to specifically Jewish culture were constantly strengthened.

In 1902, when the monthly *Zukunft* resumed publication after a five-year interruption, A. Liesin declared editorially that one of its tasks would be to open for the Yiddish reader "the entire radiant world of science and progress, as well as the intellectual world of art and esthetic enjoyment." Where formerly the goal of Yiddish literature had been "to combine the pleasant with the useful," it now included "art and esthetic enjoyment." The *Zukunft* and other periodicals began to publish Yehoash's national-romantic poems, in contrast to the previous decade in which he either wrote nothing or published nothing of what he had written. Even among radical readers there were now some who enjoyed such poems as "New Year of the Trees," "From an Old Minute-Book," and "A Chapter of Ezekiel." There was room now in the socialist press not only for Peretz' work, but also for the work of such "uncommitted" writers as Sholem Aleichem and Sholem Asch.

The new attitude to Jewish culture became more pronounced after the Kishinev

A. LIESIN (1872-1938), POET AND ESSAYIST

pogrom in 1903. Even more than the Dreyfus affair, ten years earlier, this brutal outbreak of anti-Semitism evoked nationalist sentiment among the radical intellectuals, and a new note began to be heard in the Yiddish socialist press.[116] A. Litvin proclaimed: "You, Mr. Feigenbaum, may say whatever you please; I am proud that I am not a descendant of the Hottentots or Chinese, but that I am a Jew."[117] In the 1880's and 1890's a publication like *Zukunft* would not have featured the nationalist Litvin. Now there was a different mood.

"At the open grave of the Kishinev victims" David Pinski conceived his drama, *Familie Zevi*, one of several new works that both crystallized and symbolized the change in the psychology and ideology of part of the Jewish intelligentsia in America. In *Familie Zevi* Pinski drew a contrast between representatives of the previous cosmopolitan or anti-nationalist generation of radicals and representatives of a more Jewish outlook: Reb Moshe

DAVID PINSKI, DRAMATIST AND NOVELIST

Zevi, the exalted symbol of old-fashioned Jewish piety, on the one hand, and his grandsons Lipman and Leon, the spokesmen for the new generation of national consciousness and aspiration, on the other. Leon says: "My way was the way of self-negation, while all around me Jews followed the way of self-liberation and self-affirmation—Jews full of strength, full of courage, of powerful will and gigantic faith." Leon's confession was the confession of a generation. It was clear evidence that Jewish life and culture in America were adding to the theme of struggle for education and social emancipation the new theme of national and cultural regeneration.[118]

What Pinski set forth in dramatic form Hillel Zolotarov (1865-1921), a leader of the Jewish anarchists, expressed shortly after the Kishinev pogrom journalistically (in his "Serious Problems"). He must be regarded as another pioneer of the nationalist cultural movement.[119]

5. European writers had a powerful effect, especially men like Y. L. Peretz (1852-1915) and Chaim Zhitlowsky (1865-1943). Though Peretz never left Europe and Zhitlowsky came to America only later, they wrote for Yiddish newspapers and periodicals in America. Their works, like the works of A. Liesin, Yehoash and others in this country, affected both the social and the nationalist cultural consciousness of their American readers. The older social and the newer nationalist themes gradually began to merge. In articles by Zhitlowsky (under the pen-name Ben Ehud), which were published in the *Forverts* as far back as 1900, he argued that it was in the interest both of socialism and of the Jewish people that the new Yiddish literature, which is "a link in the chain of Jewish literatures," should live and prosper. "With the publication of socialist works in Yiddish," he maintained, "a new chapter in the history of the Jewish people began." The importance of Yiddish, in other words, was at the same time socialist and Jewish. In 1904 he came to America for the first time, as a delegate of the Russian Social-Revolutionary party. Not content with an exclusively political mission, he spoke out vigorously, in articles and speeches, for a socialist-oriented Jewish nationalism and for Jewish culture.[120]

Zhitlowsky gave too much emphasis to the purely linguistic framework of culture and overestimated the possibilities of fashioning an America which would be the home of "the united peoples of the United States." On the whole, however, by means of his brilliant lectures, debates, literary treatises and new periodicals he contributed a great deal to the creation of a Jewish nationalist spiritual climate in the radical sector of Jewish leadership in America. He weakened its "historical association of ideas" between the Jewish people and the Jewish religion and also opposed the notion current among radicals that there was a conflict between nationalist and internationalist ideology. By such aphorisms as "the greater the man, the greater the Jew," and such slogans as "the national-poetic rebirth of the Jewish religion," he made Jewish nationalist thought and culture more acceptable to them. In sum, he prepared the ground ideologically for the Yiddish cultural movement in America, as Peretz, Yehoash, A. Liesin, Sholem Asch, Abraham Reisen and the writers of the younger generation who had recently made their debut prepared the ground artistically.

Growth and expansion were felt in all spheres of Jewish cultural life in the beginning of the 20th century—the press, literature, the theater, adult education, and trade-unionism, fraternal orders and *landsmanshaften.*

To the four dailies—the Orthodox *Tageblatt,* the left-wing socialist *Abend-Blatt,* the right-wing socialist *Forverts* and the non-partisan *Yiddisher Kurier,* in Chicago —two new dailies were added: the Orthodox *Morgen-Zhurnal,* in 1902, which took over the *Tageblatt* in 1928 and merged with the *Tog* in 1953, and the *Varheit,* in 1905, edited by Louis Miller (1866-1927), in the beginning socialist, later non-partisan but still fiery, which merged with the *Tog* in 1915.

The growth in the number of dailies was accompanied by growth in their circulation.[121] This was caused not only by the new wave of immigration, but also by the immigrants' increased cultural demands, the expanding labor movement, the renewed enlightenment activity, the rising Zionist movement, the growth of the *landsmanshaften,* and Jewish communal-mindedness in general.

The importance of the Yiddish newspaper, as the major expression of organized and unorganized Jewish life in America, continued to mount. Mostly on account of the intense competition, the Yiddish press sought to cater to the tastes of a mass readership by sensationalism and popular "literature." But the press was also affected by the demands of an increasing number of more cultivated readers and contributors, and therefore published an increasing number of essays, stories and poems of rather high quality. Another seeming paradox is that the Yiddish press helped to Americanize the Jewish immigrants by acquainting him with the major aspects and issues of his new country,[122] while it also constantly reminded him of Europe and European Jewish culture, deepening his consciousness of attachment and obligation to it. This is to say that the Yiddish press expressed the duality in unity of American Jewry, which is both a partner in the building of America and a part of the Jewish world people.

2. AFTERMATH OF THE RUSSIAN REVOLUTION OF 1905

The Yiddish press grew in cultural importance after the Russian Revolution of 1905. Many of the new immigrants had been in close touch with the new Jewish culture overseas, as well as with the new nationally oriented social movements, such as the Bund and Zionism. In the United States they "gave new vitality to Jewish life."[123] The arrival of these new elements was felt with particular force in cultural matters. They swelled the numbers of readers of Yiddish newspapers and books, attendants at lectures and the Yiddish theater, members in dramatic and other cultural associations. What is more, they introduced greater diversity into the ideological and cultural life of American Jewry.

Until the beginning of the 20th century the Yiddish periodical press had reflected the influence of two fundamental trends in sharp conflict with each other: the religiously Orthodox and socially conservative, which was dominant until the 1890's, and the radical (socialist or anarchist), which assumed the ascendancy thereafter. About 1905 or 1906 a new type of periodical emerged. In addition to these two ideologies it also represented various shadings of Zionist, socialist Zionist or "culturist" thought: *Dos Yiddishe Folk* (Zionist), established in 1909; *Der Arbeter* (Socialist and nationalist cultural), 1904;

PERETZ HIRSHBEIN (1880-1948), DRAMATIST
AND NOVELIST

For every ten newspapers sold in 1905 thirty-four were sold in 1916.[126] Yiddish newspapers in cities other than New York increased and trade-union periodicals began to appear.[127]

There was also improvement in quality. Any press could be proud of such publicists and writers as A. Liesin, Chaim Zhitlowsky, Isaac Hourwich (1860-1924), Isser Ginsburg (1872-1947), Nachman Syrkin (1867-1924), Zivyon (1874-1954), M. Baranov (1864-1924), Gedaliah Bublik (1875-1948), M. Olgin (1878-1939), L. Miller, S. Yanovski (1864-1939), and H. Alexandrov (1869-1909), Peter Wiernik (1865-1936), Ab. Goldberg (1883-1942), J. Fishman, K. Fornberg. The two chief monthlies, *Dos Naie Lebn* and *Zukunft*, became progressively more versatile and less partisan and propagandistic. They opened their columns more widely to poets, novelists, critics and essayists of every point of view. From the beginning,

Dos Folk (Territorialist), 1905; *Der Yiddisher Kemfer* (Socialist Zionist), 1906; Zhitlowsky's *Dos Naie Lebn,* 1908; Abraham Reisen's *Dos Naie Land,* 1911; *Der Yiddisher Sozialist* (later *Di Naie Welt*), 1913; and Abraham Reisen's *Literatur un Lebn,* 1915. *Unzer Shrift,* 1912, was an unsuccessful attempt to print Yiddish in the Latin alphabet.

In 1907 the Jewish Socialist Propaganda Bureau (after 1912 the Jewish Socialist Federation) was organized and engaged in a varied cultural and educational activity.[124] Earlier Zionist-socialist associations had been established which also engaged in cultural activities.[125] The Workmen's Circle, the first branches of which were organized in the 1890's, and the Jewish National Workers' Alliance, established in 1910, were also dedicated to the dissemination of culture and education among the Jewish masses.

Concomitantly the circulation of the Yiddish daily newspapers rose from about 191,000 in 1905 to some 646,000 in 1916.

MOSHE NADIR (1885-1943), POET AND
HUMORIST

DAVID IGNATOW (1885-1953), NOVELIST

The number of writers increased as well. East European writers and journalists contributed to the American Yiddish press more than ever. Several of them came here, first to visit and later to settle: J. Rolnik, L. Shapiro, B. Vladeck, B. Lapin, Sholem Asch, Abraham Reisen, Peretz Hirshbein and, toward the end of his days, Sholem Aleichem himself. Forerunners of the group later to be known as The Young—Joseph Rolnik, H. Rosenblatt, Yoel Slonim, H. Sackler, Moshe Nadir, I. J. Schwartz, M. J. Haimowitz— as well as The Young themselves—David Ignatow, J. Opatoshu (1887-1954), I. Raboy, Mane Leib (1883-1953), Reuben Eisland, Zisha Landau, Moshe Leib Halpern, A. M. Dillon, and, later, H. Leivick—had a progressively greater influence. They published miscellanies and journals of a kind new to Yiddish literature, and they introduced into it a fresher, more modern— sometimes *avant-garde*—tone, especially in poetry. Thus the increasing differentiation of Jewish social life was also seen in Yiddish literature. The personal emphases of

Zhitlowsky's *Dos Naie Lebn* had had a broadly nationalist cultural platform; *Zukunft,* under the editorship of A. Liesin and the financial support of the socialist-oriented Forward Association, became more nationalist in tone. Of the two, *Zukunft,* which is still in existence, was larger and much longer-lived than *Dos Naie Lebn.* It may be said that its evolution before World War I reflected and paralleled the evolution of all Yiddish literature in America in the last decade of the nineteenth century and the first fifteen years of the twentieth.[128]

Literature in its more conventional definition was also enriched. Publishing companies, whether owned by individuals or groups, were now established on a much larger scale—Max N. Maisel's Literarisher Farlag, the Hebrew Publishing Company, Evalenko's Internatsionale Bibliotek, Literarisher Farlag, Kropotkin Literatur Gezelshaft, and the like. The newspapers and the fraternal orders also published books from time to time on various subjects.

MANE LEIB (1883-1953), POET

MOSHE LEIB HALPERN (1886-1932), POET

the younger generation of writers were added to the social themes that had dominated Yiddish literature in America before 1903 and 1905, and to the nationalist themes of the period following the Kishinev pogrom.

The "uniformity," not to say monotony, of theme and style in Yiddish literature came to an end. The differences among the poets, with their diverse temperaments and preferences, was supplemented by the variety of groups and schools. On the whole, realism was still regnant in prose, but a powerful impressionistic or romantic tendency made itself felt more and more, especially in poetry. There was also a marked rapprochement between the American and the European branches of Yiddish literature.[129]

Chief among the literary achievements of the period was the modernization of the novel and even more of lyric poetry. In the last decade of the 19th century and in the first of the 20th Yiddish literature both in America and in Europe was not strong in the novel. About the year 1910 Sholem Asch and Leon Kobrin, among the older writers, and Opatoshu, Ignatow and Raboy, among the younger, gave a powerful impetus to the Yiddish novel. In verse the dexterity, the modern sensibility and the individuality of the "young" poets, as well as of older poets like Yehoash, Liesin, Rolnik and Rosenblatt, were a major contribution; these qualities also did much to refine and enrich the language. The poetic advance was consolidated when even the extreme individualists began to realize that not everything in the poet's thought and experience is a proper subject for lyric poetry, however personal. It was not until the years between the two World Wars that Yiddish poetry and literature in general experienced its finest flowering. (It was then also that America became the great center of Yiddish literary creativity, after Eastern Europe had been fragmented by the war and revolution.) The seeds of this flowering, however, were planted in the first fifteen years of our century.

In this creative period of Yiddish literature before World War I there began also the transition from popular science to real scholarship. (The highest stage in this transition was not reached before 1940, when the Yiddish Scientific Institute came to New York.) There were the beginnings of a philosophical literature. More and better translations appeared. In general, there was a striving for a widening of literary and cultural horizons as well as for a deepening and refinement of language and thought. The first steps toward children's literature and modern pedagogy were also taken in this period.

The development of the "literary" drama (Leon Kobrin, David Pinski and, somewhat later, Sholem Asch, Osip Dymov and H. Sackler) came in these years. The drama became progressively a work to be read

LIBRARY OF YIDDISH SCIENTIFIC INSTITUTE (YIVO), NEW YORK

and not merely to be presented in the theater, unlike Jacob Gordin's plays of the early 1890's. Gordin, however, remained a constructive force in the Yiddish theater. While those playwrights, actors and producers who gave the untutored audience what it wanted were still successful, there were more and more discriminating theater-goers and increasing opportunities for presenting better plays. In 1904 Gordin himself became a director of a theater for a short time and began to publish *Dramatishe Welt,* "a monthly for literature, criticism and drama, specially dedicated to the Yiddish theater." (In 1901 B. Gorin started to publish the short-lived *Teater-Zhurnal.*[130]) Gordin is a major figure in the history of the Yiddish theater, a number of his plays having remained to this day in the repertory both here and overseas (*Mirele Efros, Di Shehitah, Got, Mentch un Tayvl,* for instance), and some having been translated into English, Hebrew, Russian and other languages.[131] He

also influenced many Yiddish intellectuals by his Educational League, lectures, debates and written polemics. He had his opponents, but he also had friends and disciples, and when he died, on June 10, 1909, 250,000 Jews attended his funeral.[132] In 1953 his hundredth anniversary was celebrated.

Among his students in dramaturgy was one who from a literary point of view excelled him, Leon Kobrin (1872-1946). Kobrin's acquaintance with Jewish life was greater, his characterization more powerful, his dialogue more vivid and his Yiddish more natural and spontaneous than Gordin's. He affected the Yiddish theater powerfully by such plays as *Yankl Boyle* (The Village Youth). Such visitors from Europe as Sholem Aleichem, Sholem Asch and Osip Dymov and local dramatists like David Pinski were apparently too "literary" for the Yiddish stage in America. Only the amateur performances of various dramatic societies, especially the one directed by Yoel Entin, represented periodic attempts at merging the art of the stage with literature.

A new period in the Yiddish theater dates from World War I, when Maurice Schwartz began to present dramas like Peretz Hirshbein's *In a Forsaken Corner, The Smith's Daughters* and *Green Fields.* A public was now at hand for better theater.

The higher cultural level of many American Jews in America was also reflected on the eve of World War I in Jewish education. Lectures had for many years complemented the educational work of the Yiddish newspapers and books. Now education began to be conceived more broadly—not only as socialist or any other ideological propoganda, but also as knowledge of the social sciences, the natural sciences, literature and art. Besides the fraternal orders and the *landsmanshaften,* special literary and cultural associations arranged lectures, debates, concerts and readings for their members and the public at large.

The most characteristic development in the years just before the First World War was the gradual rise in concern with Jewish education for children. Until the early years of the 20th century all Jewish education was in the hands of individual teachers who conducted their own schools (or went to the homes of their pupils one or more times a week), or of congregations and philanthropic organizations. The language of instruction in the private schools was Yiddish. The scope of studies was very limited—mechanical reading of Hebrew, the prayer book, a smattering of the Pentateuch, preparation for Bar-Mitzvah. Even more inadequate was the method of instruction. In the better communal Talmud Torahs the program of studies was more inclusive, but there too the main subject was religion. The languages of instruction were Yiddish—frequently Germanized—, English and in rare instances (from the 1890's) Hebrew. Only religious Jews and to a lesser extent na-

tionalist Hebraists (from the 1880's on) were active in Jewish education.[133]

For radicals education meant indoctrinating youth in socialism. The Sunday schools organized by branches of the Workmen's Circle after 1906 had no trace of Jewish studies in their program. In the lower classes the curriculum included music and dancing, and in the advanced classes the history of culture, political economy, and biographies of heroes of social justice. Their purpose was "to accustom children from their early youth to radical thinking."[134]

While some radicals continued to want only a socialist education for their children, others, under the influence of Zhitlowsky, Entin, Liesin, Zivyon, and the nationalistically oriented socialists in Europe, began to worry about a specifically Jewish education for the younger generation. As early as 1908 an attempt was made to establish a secular Yiddish school in New York. This was a private undertaking. Only later was the establishment of modern Yiddish schools accepted as a responsibility of the Yiddish culture movement. The first founders of the secular Yiddish schools were the Socialist Zionists in the United States and Canada. Their aim was "to give Jewish children a truly Jewish and radical education, to bring them closer to their parents and people, to implant in their hearts a deep love of the Jewish people, Jewish ideals and aspirations for mankind, the humanitarian ideals of peace and freedom, international amity and fraternity."[135] In the first national-radical schools (as they were called) Yiddish and Hebrew were on an equal footing, but in later years Hebrew was taught only in the higher grades. The language of instruction was Yiddish and the slogan was "The Jewish child belongs to the Jewish people." In the beginning classes met only on Saturdays or Sundays, but later they met three or even five times a week. Attempts were also made to provide textbooks for the new schools.

OPENING SESSION OF THE FOUNDING CONVENTION OF THE CONGRESS
FOR JEWISH CULTURE (1948)

The non-Zionist socialists did not like this kind of education because they thought it both too nationalist and insufficiently radical. Such were many members of the Workmen's Circle and similar organizations. However, the influence of the new nationalist spirit was growing even there. Many of their newer members had belonged to the "Bund" in Europe, and for them the socialist Sunday school, conducted in English, was at the same time too propagandistic and not Jewish enough. A debate about education lasted for years and was only ended in the official approval of Yiddish schools by the Workmen's Circle as a whole in 1915 and 1916. In 1918, besides the national-radical and the Sholem Aleichem schools, there came into existence the Workmen's Circle schools, now called the Y.L. Peretz schools. To attract those parents who were more radical than nationalist, the slogan of the Workmen's Circle schools at first was "The Jewish worker's child belongs to the Jewish working class." As the schools became established and as nationalist feeling made its way, the class-struggle idea was increasingly subordinated and the differences between the various types of secular Yiddish schools gradually diminished.

This development, however, belongs to the period after World War I—actually, after World War II. Only then could the modern Yiddish school be seen in its full dimensions. As it became more national and less radical, it also became more American and less immigrant in character. (*The Jewish People: Past and Present*, V. II, is a good source of information about Yiddish education in America.[136])

Following this period there arose in all realms of Yiddish culture, particularly in the field of literature, new creative forces, just as the number of those faithful to the institutions of Yiddish culture, cherishing its high values, was constantly widening (particularly in the 1920's and 1930's).

From year to year these forces grew more promising and more varied. The theater not only attained a high level, but also drew into partnership representatives of the other arts, such as music, painting and dancing. Yiddish publishing houses created a place for illustrators. The Yiddish school, which could not do without teachers and teachers of teachers, together with Jewish communal movements created a need for scientific research in Yiddish, particularly in language, folklore and literature, history, psychology and pedagogy, economics and statistics. The growth of the East European Jewish community in America, its quantitative and qualitative enrichment in creative sources and forces, the expansion of its spiritual needs gave Yiddish culture an impetus toward expansion and a striving toward versatility, which until quite recently was still increasing. A brief survey cannot do justice to the cultural growth and cultural attainments of the period after World War I, when the center of Jewish life and Jewish creativity began to move to America. An entire book would be required for that purpose. We have therefore ended our account with the period of World War I. Brief summaries of the facts and the events in the realm of Yiddish and Yiddish culture in America for the past several decades are given in *The Jewish People—Past and Present*, Volumes II and III.

NOTES

[1] Jacob R. Marcus, *Early American Jewry*, Philadelphia, 1951, I, p. XII; II, p. 390; Oscar Handlin, "Our Unknown American Jewish Ancestors," *Commentary*, February 1948; W. Guenther, "Two Notes," *Hebrew Union College Annual*, 1937, pp. 575-576.

[2] Marcus, *op. cit.*, I, p. 82. According to the calculations of David de Sola Pool, *Portraits Etched in Stone*, New York, 1952, based upon inscriptions on tombstones, it was not until after 1775 that the Ashkenazim began to be a constantly growing majority in Shearith Israel. According to other calculations by the same author, by the first half of the 18th century there were already more Ashkenazim then Sephardim in that congregation.

[3] Marcus, *op. cit.*, II, p. 276.

[4] Charles Reznikoff, *The Jews of Charleston*, Philadelphia, 1950, p. IX.

[5] Hyman B. Grinstein, *The Rise of the Jewish Community of New York*, Philadelphia, 1947, p. 528.

[6] Kalman Marmor, in his *Der Onhoyb fun der Yiddisher Literatur in Amerike* (The Birth of Yiddish Literature in America), New York, 1944, p. 118, states that "Yiddish-speaking immigrants were in America as early as the 1840's." In reality they were here as early as the Colonial Period and came not only from Poland, as he indicates, but also from Germany and Holland.

[7] *Yiddishe Folks-Bibliotek* (ed. Scholem Aleichem), Kiev, 1888, I, p. 255.

[8] *Ibid.* A Hebrew translation of Campe's *Entdeckung von Amerika* (under the title *Metziat ha-Aretz ha-Hadashah*) was published as early as 1807. See I. Zinberg: *Geshikhte fun der Literatur bay Yidn*, New York, 1943, VII, p. 270.

[9] Quoted by Zalman Reisen, *Fun Mendelssohn biz Mendele*, Warsaw, 1923, p. 217.

[10] Z. Reisen, "Campe's Antdekung fun Amerike," *Yivo Bleter*, 1933, V, p. 38.

[11] Quoted by I. Zinberg, *op. cit.*, VII, p. 325.

[12] *Ibid.*, p. 327.

[13] Quoted by Max Weinreich in *Algemeine Entsiklopedie*, "Yidn II," p. 60.

[14] W. V. Byars, *B. and M. Gratz*, Jefferson City, Mo., 1916.

[15] *Publication of the American Jewish Historical Society (PAJHS)*, 1937, pp. 75-106. The Yiddish of the letters is full of Hebrew expressions, as was the style in those days. See also the long Yiddish letter of Solomon Bloch in London to his father Hirsh Bloch, written in 1763 and published in the *Festschrift zum siebzigsten Geburtstage Jakob Guttmanns*, Leipzig, 1915, pp. 245-53. This letter uses words taken from Dutch Yiddish, and it even has some early Americanisms.

[16] *PAJHS*, 1917, pp. 128-131.

[17] I am indebted to Rabbi Isidor S. Meyer, librarian of the American Jewish Historical Society, for the opportunity to examine some of these manuscripts.

[18] *PAJHS*, 1937, p. 72.

[19] Marcus, *op. cit.*, II, p. 154.

[20] According to Yudel Mark, in *Yorbukh fun Ampteil fun Yivo*, New York, I, 1938, the Germans in America also used the word *gleichen*, "to like."

[21] Marcus, *op. cit.*, II, p. 187.

[22] *Ibid.*, p. 182.

[23] *Zukunft*, April 1925, p. 222.

[24] *Algemeine Entsiklopedie*, "Yidn II," p. 63; *Yidishe Shprakh*, April-September 1953, pp. 36-47.

[25] Oscar Handlin, *Boston's Immigrants 1790-1865*, 1941, p. 57.

[26] *American Israelite*, December 1871.

[27] Grinstein, *op. cit.*, p. 231.

[28] Marcus, *op. cit.*, II, pp. 463 and 499.

[29] *Ibid.*, p. 342.

[30] *Zukunft*, April 1925, p. 223.

[31] *Loc. cit.*

[32] I. R., "A For Gezunt Nokh Amerike fun Yor 1853," *Pinkos*, New York, 1928, pp. 387-88.

[33] I. Rivkind, "Early American Hebrew Documents," *PAJHS*, 1937, p. 59.

[34] Zalman Reisen, "Di Manuskriptn . . . fun Reb Henech," *Arkhiv far der Geshikhte fun Yiddishn Teater un Drame*, Wilno—New York, 1930.

[35] B. Gorin, *Geshikhte fun Yiddishn Teater*, New York, 1918, II, p. 7.

[36] I. Shatzky, *Algemeine Entsiklopedie*, "Yidn III," p. 256.

[37] According to Dr. Rudolf Glanz, the stories in the "Jewish German" supplements to the German papers were also frequently of a humorous-derisive character. See *Geshikhte fun der Yiddisher Arbeter Bavegung* (ed. E. Tcherikower), New York, 1943, I, p. 55.

[38] *Otzar Zikhronothai* (Autobiography and Memoirs), New York, 1929, p. 11.

[39] Zevi Scharfstein, *Toldot ha-Hinnukh be-Yisrael*, New York, 1929, p. 174.

[40] Kalman Marmor in *Morgn Freiheit*, October 26, 1946.

[41] J. S., "Poilishe Yidn Reemigrantn fun Amerike," *Yivo Bleter*, New York. September-October, 1942, XX, p. 126.

[42] Kalman Marmor, *Der Onhoyb fun der Yiddisher Literatur in Amerike*, New York, 1944, p. 102.

[43] B. Steinberg, "Tsu der Geshikhte fun Yidn in Amerike (1823-1872)," *Yorbukh fun Ampteil fun Yivo*, New York, 1939, II, p. 160.

[44] Leo Wiener, *The History of Yiddish Literature*, New York, 1899, p. 216.

[45] B. Steinberg, *loc. cit.*, p. 168.

[46] *Ibid.*, p. 167.

[47] *Algemeine Entsiklopedie*, "Yidn III," p. 258. According to Kalman Marmor, in an article in the *Morgn Freheit*, May 16, 1943, Büchner's *Yiddishe Zeitung* did not appear until 1873, but in his book, *Der Onhoyb fun der Yiddisher Literatur in Amerike*, he states that the *Yiddishe Zeitung* appeared in 1870.

[48] B. Steinberg, *loc. cit.*, pp. 152 and 154.

[49] Cited by Kalman Marmor in the *Morgn Freiheit*, October 26, 1946.

[50] B. Steinberg, *loc. cit.*, pp. 170-72.

[51] E. Lifschutz, *Yivo Bleter*, December 1932, p. 315.

[52] See Kalman Marmor's articles in *Morgn Freiheit*, April 4 and 11, 1937; L. Schildkret, in *Yivo Bleter*, XI, p. 218.

[53] Zalman Reisen, "Briv fun Amerike tsum Greiditser Zaddik," *Yorbukh fun Ampteil*, 1939, II, pp. 190-218.

[54] M. Starkman, "Di Sarasohn Zikhroynes," *Yorbukh fun Ampteil*, 1938, I, p. 279.

[55] *Bletter fun Main Lebn*, New York, 1926, II, pp. 79-80.

[56] *Ibid.*, III, p. 198.

[57] M. Vinchevsky says the same about the Jewish immigrants in London: "Our reading public . . . is unfortunately a public that cannot read" (*Erinerungen*, Moscow, 1926, p. 199).

[58] *Yorbukh fun Amopteil*, 1938, I, pp. 289-90.

[59] Kalman Marmor, "Tsvey Yubileyen," *Pinkos*, 1928, pp. 38-52; also *Der Onhoyb fun der Yiddisher Literatur in Amerike*, p. 13.

[60] S. Niger, "Oyfn Shvel fun der Yiddisher Literatur in Amerike," *Zukunft*, January 1940, p. 11.

[61] S. Niger, "Mer Alt-Heymish vi Amerikanish," *Zukunft*, April 1940, pp. 212-16.

[62] Cited by Kalman Marmor, *Der Onhoyb fun der Yiddisher Literatur in Amerike*, p. 13.

[63] *Ibid.*, p. 13.

[64] According to Kalman Marmor, as early as 1850 a Yiddish book was published in America, a Judeo-German translation from Ben Sira (*Morgn Freiheit*, April 11, 1931), but this apparently was merely a reprint of a European edition or an accompanying text to a new Hebrew translation of the work. Essentially it was in German with Hebrew characters. (See Ephraim Deinard's *Kohelet Amerika*, St. Louis, 1926.)

[65] One of these Hebrew writers, M. M. Dolitzki, whom no less a poet than J. L. Gordon considered as his heir in Hebrew poetry, sarcastically expressed his regrets over his inability to be in America what he had been in the Old World:

> Let us deal wisely and become drawers of water,
> Load the peddler's pack and knock on the doors,
> Sit bent on the workbench,
> Bore with the awl or sew breeches—
> But of what avail is here the wisdom of Israel?

And again:

> Let us publish books and journals,
> In the corrupt language of Babylon, for maids and coachmen.
> Then we shall find many readers and buyers,
> But of what avail is here the wisdom of Israel?

Cited by M. Ribalow, *Ketavim u-Megillot*, New York, 1942, pp. 170-71.

[66] These and the following excerpts from Sobol's book are based upon the text, published by K. Marmor in the *Pinkos*, New York, 1928. Marmor errs when he takes Sobol's expression "one also has to study Jewish" to mean Yiddish, and not Hebrew. The Hebrew version of Sobol reads: "You will agree that it is necessary to study the Hebrew language [sefat Ever]," which last two words Sobol himself renders in Yiddish with the word "Jewish" [Yiddish], just as he renders the Hebrew words "Hebrew songs" [shire ha-Ivrim] with "the Jewish song" [dos Yiddishe lid]. See my article "Mer Alt-Heymish vi Amerikanish," *Zukunft*, April, 1940.

[67] *Kitve Hillel Malachovsky*, II, p. 66.

[68] *Der Naier Geist*, New York, March 1898, p. 352.

[69] Moses Weinberger, *Ha-Yehudim ve-ha-Yahadut be-New York*, New York, 1887, pp. 31-32.

[70] Rudolf Glanz has pointed out that "German spoken by the German Jews in America also left a good deal to be desired"; it was full of Americanisms, *Geshikhte fun der Yiddisher Arbeter Bavegung* (ed. E. Tcherikower), New York, 1943, I, p. 60.

[71] Abraham Cahan, *Bletter fun Main Lebn*, II, p. 80.

[72] According to K. Marmor (*Der Onhoyb fun der Yiddisher Literatur in Amerike*, p. 15), there appeared in 1877 A. Silberstein's *Dos Lebn und Tod fun Yeshua ha-Notsri Herausgenumen fun Sefer Toldos Yeshua ha-Notsri mit Tsugubn fun Sefer Tam u-Muad*. The Library of the Jewish Theological Seminary has a copy of this book, but it was published in London in 1874. The book, which according to Marmor was advertised in the *Yiddishe Gazetten*, was either a New York reprint of the London edition or an import sold by the *Yiddishe Gazetten*.

[73] Neither the sporadic performance in the German theater of plays dealing with Jewish life nor the choral and musical societies of the German Jews have any relation to Yiddish culture. It is possible, however, that they included some elements of Jewish German.

[74] B. Gorin, *op. cit.*, II, p. 11.

[75] *Ibid.*, p. 7.

[76] Bernard Felsenthal, *Jüdisches Schulwesen in Amerika*, Chicago, 1866.

[77] *Ibid.*

[78] S. Niger, *In Kamf far a Naier Dertsiung*, New York, 1940, p. 24.

[79] Zevi Scharfstein, *Toledot ha-Hinnukh be-Yisrael*, II, p. 163.

[80] Reprinted from *Dos Yiddishe Tageblatt*, March 20, 1910, in the miscellany, *Tsu der Geshikhte fun der Yiddisher Prese in Amerike* (ed. J. Shatzky), New York, 1934, p. 47.

[81] Zevi Scharfstein, *op. cit.*, II, p. 188.

[82] *Maslianskys Zykhroynes*, New York, 1924, p. 203; also Max Raisin, *Dappim mi-Pinkaso shel Rabbi*, New York, 1941, p. 178.

[83] Jacob Lestschinsky in *Geshikhte fun der Yiddisher Arbeter Bavegung*, I, p. 36. G. Leizarovitch, in *Yivo Bleter*, 1941, XVIII, p. 222, gives a slightly smaller estimate.

[84] S. Joseph, *Jewish Immigration to the United States from 1881 to 1910*, New York, 1914, p. 162.

[85] B. Weinstein, "Teater Zikhroynes," in *Arkhiv far Geshikhte fun Yiddishn Teater* (ed. J. Shatzky), Wilno, 1930, p. 250.

[86] B. Gorin, *op. cit.*, II, p. 6.

[87] *Ibid.*, pp. 18-20; see also "Fun Barondess Teater Zikhroynes," in *Arkhiv far Geshikhte fun Yiddishn Teater*, p. 436.

[88] Abraham Cahan, *Bletter fun Main Lebn*, II, p. 240.

[89] Quoted by A. R. Malachi, "Yiddishes Vokhnblat," in *Zamlbukh Lekoved dem 250-tn Yoyvl far der Yiddisher Prese* (ed. J. Shatzky), New York, 1937, p. 181.

[90] Quoted in *Tsu der Geshikhte fun der Yiddisher Prese*, p. 54.

[91] S. Niger, "Imigrantisher Amerikanizm," *Zukunft*, August, 1940.

[92] *75 Yor Yiddishe Prese in Amerike* (eds. J. Gladstone, S. Niger, H. Rogoff), New York, 1945, p. 36.

[93] Cahan, *op. cit.*, II, pp. 34-35; Alexander Harkavy, *Perakim mi-Hayyai*, New York, 1935, p. 35.

[94] *Geshikhte fun der Yiddisher Arbeter Bavegung*, I, p. 322.

[95] Cahan, *op. cit.*, II, p. 361.

[96] Zevi Scharfstein, *op. cit.*, II, chap. 3; *Geshikhte fun der Yiddisher Arbeter Bavegung in Amerike*, I, pp. 300 ff.

[97] N. Goldberg, "Di anti-Religieze Bavegung," *Geshikhte fun der Yiddisher Arbeter Bavegung*, 1945, II, pp. 418-457.

[98] In the third year the reading "most advanced ideas" of the sub-heading was replaced by "monthly journal for social science, literature and topics of the time."

[99] Quoted by Jacob Shatzky in *Tsu der Geshikhte fun der Yiddisher Prese in Amerike*, p. 10.

[100] S. Niger, "Zhurnalism in Ferzn," *Zukunft*, March 1942.

[101] *Saturday Review of Literature*, August 31, 1940.

[102] For a more comprehensive treatment of this subject see S. Niger, "Yiddishe Literatur in der Tsveyter Helft 19-tn Yorhundert," in *Algemeine Entsiklopedie*, "Yidn III," pp. 122-33; "Onhoyb fun der Proletarish-Yiddisher Literatur," *Zukunft*, September 1940.

[103] "Di Yiddishe Literatur in Amerike," *Dos Lebn*, St. Petersburg, February 1905, p. 37.

[104] M. Starkman, "Tsu der Geshikhte fun Yiddish in Amerike," *Yorbukh fun Amopteil*, 1939, II, p. 183. The textbook, *Der Amerikaner*, may have been the first American Yiddish publication to be sold in Europe as well (*Ibid.*, p. 90).

[105] M. Starkman, *Pinkos fun Amopteil fun Yivo*, 1928, pp. 388-89.

[106] See the statement by the editors, October 1897.

[107] S. Niger, "Onhoyb fun Proletarish-Yiddisher Literatur," *Zukunft*, September 1940; "Proletarishe Kritik," *Zukunft*, November and December 1940.

[108] *Idem*, "Di Sotsialistishe Oyfklerungs-Bavegung un di Natsionale Frage," *Zukunft*, December 1941.

[109] *Idem*, "Di Zukunft un di Yiddishe Literatur in Amerike," *Zukunft*, May-June 1942; also "Proletarishe Kritik," *Zukunft*, November 1940.

[110] *Idem*, "Di Yiddishe Literatur oyfn Shvel fun 20-tn Yorhundert," *Zukunft*, January 1951.

[111] E. Shulman, *Geshikhte fun der Yiddisher Literatur in Amerike*, New York, 1943, pp. 89-90.

[112] *Der Naier Geist*, March 1898, pp. 251-55.

[113] *Arbeter Zeitung*, 1890, No. 6.

[114] Jacob Gordin's bibliography may be found in Zylbercwaig's *Leksikon fun Yiddishn Teater*, I, pp. 459-61; Kalman Marmor, *Yaakov Gordin*, New York, 1953, pp. 227-41; J. Jeshurin in *Freie Arbeter Shtime*, May 22, 1953.

[115] Yoel Entin in his introduction to Leon Kobrin's *Dramatishe Shriftn*, New York, 1952, p. XIV.

[116] Cf. the articles by K. Fornberg, K. Frumin, A. Litvin, J. Milch and Philip Krantz in *Zukunft*, 1904.

[117] *Zukunft*, October 1904, p. 34.

[118] S. Niger, *Dertseilers un Romanistn*, New York, 1946, pp. 302-03.

[119] The profound effect of the Kishinev pogrom upon the minds and hearts of the radicals can be seen from the rancor with which Herz Burgin, one of those who remained true to their former extreme radicalism, speaks about it in his *Geshikhte fun der Yiddisher Arbeter Bavegung* (New York, 1915, p. 615). He writes: "This was a veritable nationalist epidemic. . . . The radicalism of the Jewish masses practically disappeared before the nationalist wave." It can also be seen in the memoirs of I. Kopelov, an anarchist of long standing. "The Kishinev pogrom upset me somewhat. . . . My previous cosmopolitanism, internationalism and similar ideologies vanished at one blow, like the contents of a barrel with the bottom knocked out. . . . " (*Amol in Amerike*, Warsaw, 1928, p. 458).

[120] S. Niger, *In Kamf far a Naier Dertsiung*, pp. 27-30. Similar activity was also undertaken by the Socialist Zionists, but with less vigor and success.

[121] The circulation of all Yiddish dailies toward the end of the 19th century was between 50,000 and 60,000. In 1901 it rose to 73,000, in 1903 to 98,000, and 1905 to over 190,000. See N. Goldberg, "Di Yiddishe Prese in di Fareinikte Shtatn 1900-1940," *Yivo Bleter*, 1941, XVIII, Table 1; also M. J. Shelubsky, *Yivo Bleter*, 1945, XXV, No. 2, pp. 290-94.

[122] Mordecai Soltes, *The Yiddish Press. . . ,* Philadelphia, 1924. Soltes deals only with the editorials and tends to over-emphasize the role of the Yiddish press as "an Americanizing agency."

[123] Herz Burgin, *op. cit.*, p. 668.

[124] *Ibid.*, pp. 682-83.

[125] *Ibid.*, p. 684.

[126] N. Goldberg, *Yivo Bleter*, XVIII, No. 2, p. 133.

[127] A. Goldberg "Yiddisher Fakh-Zhurnalism," *Zamlbukh Lekoved dem 250-yorikn Yubiley fun der Yiddisher Prese*, pp. 233-49.

[128] S. Niger, "Di Yiddishe Literatur in Amerike," *Zukunft*, May-June 1942.

[129] Cf. *Algemeine Entsiklopedie*, "Yidn III," pp. 148-50.

[130] Elizabeth Gorin in her biographical introduction to *B. Gorins Gezamelte Shriftn*, New York, 1927, I, p. 60.

[131] Kalman Marmor, *Yaakov Gordin*, New York, 1953, pp. 214-28.

[132] *Ibid.*, p. 208.

[133] Hebraists would occasionally employ Yiddish in their appeals to the parents. See J. Z. Frishberg, *Vos Iz Yiddishe Dertsiung*, published by the Histadrut Ivrit in New York in 1918.

[134] A. S. Sachs, "Unzer Yugnt un der Arbeter-Ring," *Fraind*, New York, May 1912.

[135] *Shulbukh*, Toronto, 1936, p. 103.

[136] See also S. Niger, *In Kamf far a Naier Dertsiung*; Zevi Scharfstein, *op. cit.*, II; Leibush Lehrer, *Di Moderne Shul*, New York, 1927; *Yivo Shriftn far Psikhologie un Pedagogik*, I and II; *Shul-Almanakh*, Philadelphia, 1935.

HEBREW LITERATURE IN THE UNITED STATES

J. K. Mikliszanski

I. BEGINNINGS OF HEBREW LITERATURE

The Hebrew language came to the New World together with the first handful of Jews about 1654. There had never been a Jewish community to which the sound of the Hebrew word was unknown. But for nearly two hundred years in America there was merely a passive culture of the Hebrew word. The first creative efforts in Hebrew appeared in this country only in the second half of the 19th century.

For purposes of orientation we shall divide our survey into two unequal periods: the first from 1871 to 1914 and the second from 1914 to the present time. In the first period Hebrew literary production is rather meager; it gains immensely in the second period both in scope and quality.

The modest achievement of Hebrew literature in America up to World War I can be described in several paragraphs.

In 1871 appeared the first Hebrew periodical on American soil—*ha-Tsofeh be-Eretz ha-Hadashah* (The Observer in the New Land), founded and edited by Zevi Hirsh Berenstein (1846-1907). It existed for only a short time. The number of Hebrew readers was very limited. Even those who had a need for the Hebrew word were too absorbed in the struggle for a livelihood to be in a position to satisfy their cultural demands. Nevertheless the pioneers did not give up hope. For them Hebrew was not a luxury, but a cultural and spiritual necessity.

It must, therefore, be noted that in the last thirty years of the past century there appeared in the United States some twenty Hebrew periodicals: about eight or nine weeklies and about a dozen monthlies. All of them were short-lived. Only the *ha-Ivri* (The Hebrew) succeeded in maintaining itself—with interruptions—for ten years (1892-1902). Of the monthlies, the *Ner Maaravi* (Light of the West) enjoyed the longest existence, one and a half years (1895-1896).*

The outstanding poets of the period were: Gershon Rosenzweig, Menahem Mendel Dolitzki, Naphtali Herz Imber and Isaac Rabinowitz.

Gershon Rosenzweig (1861-1914) was a prolific writer. He manifests originality mainly in his satires, which are keen, witty and disciplined. Linguistically, the author gives evidence of a thorough familiarity with the old and the new Hebrew literatures. For the first time there is reflected in Hebrew a critical approach to the pioneer settlement in this country, which in its eager pursuit of a livelihood neglected its spiritual heritage. In America, the

---

* See Meyer Waxman, *A History of Jewish Literature,* New York, 1941, Vol. IV, pp. 1048-1049. For further details about the Hebrew press of that period in America see *Algemeine Entsiklopedie* (in Yiddish), "Yidn" III, New York, 1942, pp. 340-342, and also the articles recently published by A. R. Malachi on *ha-Dror* (Freedom) and D. Persky on *ha-Toren* (The Mast), in the special issue, devoted to American Hebrew literature, of *Gilyonot* in Tel-Aviv, Israel, Vol. XXXI, 8-10, 1954.

HA-TSOFEH BE-ERETZ
HA-HADASHAH

FACSIMILE OF FIRST
PAGE OF FIRST HEBREW
PERIODICAL IN
AMERICA

Courtesy Moshe Davis

author concludes, "my people is altogether empty." In such poems as *Tofer Mahir* (The Nimble Sewer) one may detect the influence of Bialik. Like Bialik's *Matmid* in the yeshivah, the sewer wastes his strength over the sewing-machine.

Rosenzweig came from Russia to America at the age of 27. He was a contributor to all the short-lived publications of his generation, and edited the weekly *ha-Ivri,* established by Kasriel Zevi Sarasohn, and the monthlies *Kadimah* (Forward) and *ha-Devorah* (the Bee), which was the first humorous publication in Hebrew on American soil. His collected works are *Talmud Yankai* (Yankee Talmud, 1907), satires and parodies in talmudic style, and *Hamishah ve-Elef* (Thou-

sand and Five), one thousand and five epigrams in verse about various Jewish and general topics.

Menahem Mendel Dolitzki (1856-1931) was well known in Hebrew literary circles when he came to America in 1892. Here he contributed poetry and novels first to the Hebrew publications and later also to the Yiddish press. But the poet could not adjust to America. He felt as a stranger, not only among strangers, but also among his fellow immigrants. These Jews, who in the Old World were so close to him and served as a source of inspiration, were no longer the same people nor the same Jews. Dolitzki suffered because of this, and his suffering was transformed into resignation and helplessness. He no longer had

MENAHEM MENDEL DOLITZKI
(1856-1931), POET

faith in himself, in his readers or in his muse. He began to write Yiddish, for he gave up hope for the future of Hebrew.

Nevertheless there came from Dolitzki's pen a number of poems that still reflected the poet of former days and that occupied a prominent place in the Hebrew poetry of that generation. His main works are *Kol Shire Dolitzki* (Collected Poems of Dolitzki, 1895), *Shire Menahem* (The Poems of Menahem, 1900) and a novel *Milhemet ha-Tehiyah* (The Struggle for Revival).

Naphtali Herz Imber (1856-1909) is a tragic figure. His brief life was spent in wanderings, struggles, dreams, vacillations, physical and mental anguish. Whereas other poets find fulfillment in their works, Imber found no such fulfillment in his poetry. Nevertheless, Imber succeeded in writing several poems of a national character, one of which, the *Hatikvah* (Hope), was destined to become the Zionist and later the national hymn of the State of Israel. With that poem alone the author acquired an immortal name in modern Hebrew literature. Other songs of Imber are also sung in the State of Israel.

Imber was born in Galicia, Poland, and came to America in 1892. Here he married a proselyte. In 1905 his poems appeared in New York under the title *Barkai ha-Shlishi* (Third Morning Star). A special collection of his poems appeared in Israel on the occasion of the 75th anniversary of the publication of *Hatikvah*.

Isaac Rabinowitz (1846-1900), of Kovno, Lithuania, was a disciple of Abraham Mapu. When he came to America his poetical career was nearly over. He lived here only six years and these were a desperate struggle for a piece of bread, "under a strange sky and on a strange earth." He felt that "God had forsaken him and that also the muse would no longer accompany him." As in the case of his colleague Dolitzki, this disappointment forms the dominant note in the poetical works of Rabinowitz that were written in America. These were collected under the title *Al Nehar Kevar* (By the River Chebar, 1897) and *Pirhe Horef* (Winter Flowers, 1900).

Of the other poets mention should be made of Jacob Zevi Sobol (1831-1913), who described himself in a poem titled *Talmid Hakham Polani be-America* (A Jewish Scholar from Poland in America) and Moses Israel Garson (1861-1925), one of the very few writers who was well-to-do and thus in a position to act as a Maecenas to his friends.

The Hebrew prose of that period finds expression almost exclusively in the periodicals discussed above. These contain articles, essays, scholarly treatises, and the like. Belles-lettres are poorly represented. The leading writers are: Abraham Baer Dobsewitch (1848-1900), Ephraim Deinard (1846-1930), M. Jastrow (1829-1903), Moses Mielziner (1828-1903), Zev Wolf Schorr (1844-1910), M. D. Radkinson (1845-1904), Alexander Kohut (1842-1894),

Kaufmann Kohler (1843-1926), Judah David Eisenstein (b. 1854), Israel Davidson (1870-1939), Max Raisin (b. 1881) and a number of others.

As stated there are no definite boundaries between the periods and some of the above writers belong also to the second period.

II. DEVELOPMENT OF HEBREW LITERATURE

With the beginning of World War I a new period in Hebrew creativeness becomes manifest in America. After 1900 there was a new influx of Jewish immigrants from the Old World. In contrast to the earlier immigrant masses, among whom the cultured element was insignificant, the Jewish arrivals of the past fifty years include a considerable number of men and women dedicated to the advancement of the higher values of Judaism: rabbis, scholars, yeshivah students, teachers, professors, scientists, thinkers, public figures and others. But it took some time till the new immigration began to evince any creativity. These years were also the period of the triumph of the Zionist idea in general and of the modern Hebrew movement in particular. In Eastern Europe and in the newly built home in Palestine the old tongue of the Jews was revived and rapidly advanced both as the spoken and written medium. Even in the eyes of those who had long doubted it, the Hebrew language proved to be an integral part of Jewish reality and an unconditional factor in the national and political revival of the people. All these events must have had their effect upon the development of Hebrew creativity also in the large Jewish community in America. Here, too, in the different environment there grew up a Hebrew literature of considerable scope.

In our brief survey we shall employ the following divisions: poetry, short stories and novels, essays and publicistic writing and scholarship.

NAPHTALI HERZ IMBER (1856-1909), POET

1. POETRY

The hallmark of modern Hebrew literature in America is the absence of groups or schools, each poet goes his own way; there are no teachers and no disciples. Hebrew poetry in America is the creation of poets who have little contact with their surroundings, with every-day life. This is not said by way of disparaging the artistic value of their poetry. Since the number of Hebrew poets is comparatively small they can all be enumerated in the chronological order of their arrival in America.

Benjamin Nahum Silkiner (1882-1933) is considered the first modern Hebrew poet in America, that is, a poet who emancipated himself from the Maskilic rationalism of his predecessors. Hebrew poetry was to him no isolated universe. All this is true not only of Silkiner but of all Hebrew poets of the past generation in America. But Silkiner occupies in the modernization of Hebrew poetry a historical place, for, as stated, he was the first.

Silkiner writes as he feels. His poetry is one of mood and disposition. He never returns to his work and he cares little if something remains unfinished, if his poetry appears fragmentary, incomplete. From what he gave us it is evident that he could have offered much more, but he did not want to say all. Thus, his long epic poem *Mul Ohel Timmurah* (Before the Tent of Timmurah), could have become a great epic had the author taken the trouble and patience that this type of work requires. Its subject is neither Jewish nor American but American Indian. The action takes place at the time of the Spanish rule in America. It deals with the oppression and extermination of the original inhabitants of the New World, the Indians. The mere fact that a Hebrew poet sang and lamented the decline of a world that was so remote and so alien to the Jewish world and to contemporaneous events was startling. It may be said to have marked a revolution in the rigid attitude of the Hebrew poets. It dawned upon the people that one can speak and create in Hebrew—as well as in any other developed language—about any subject. Later on, several poets attempted the same themes, as will be seen below, but here, too, Silkiner remained the first.

Silkiner utilized a historical Jewish motive in another epic poem, *Manoah Franko,* dealing with Jewish life in Spain during the Inquisition. Another epic vision *u-Melekh en be-Moav* (And There Was no King in Moab) transports us to the distant past. His long poem, of legendary content, named *Agadat ha-Zelilim* (The Legend of the Sounds), remained unfinished. His sensitive poems, however, mostly lyrics and partly of national and folk character, are complete, polished and lucid.

Silkiner arrived in America in 1908. His poems appeared first in a number of publications and later, in 1927, in a separate collection, in Tel Aviv. He also translated *Macbeth* into Hebrew. In 1934 there appeared *Sefer Zikkaron le-B. N. Silkiner* (B. N. Silkiner Memorial Volume).

Abraham Samuel Schwartz (b. 1876, arrived in America in 1901), a physician, publishes from time to time poems in Hebrew publications, mainly in the *ha-Doar.* They excel in composition, apt forms of expression and keen observation. One senses in his poetry a desire to imitate the great Bialik, the master of all modern Jewish poets. The term *leshon kodesh*—the sacred tongue—fits his poetry better than the secular term Hebrew. His poems are invested with the sanctity of the old language both in word coinage and in theme. Here are some of the names of his poems: *Kedushah* (Sanctity, a description of a synagogue and its worshippers), *Kabbalat Shabbat* (Welcoming the Sabbath), *Ruth, Rabi Johanan ben Zakkai.* In his other poems the poet manifests a subtle sensibility for nature and its variegated nuances.

Ephraim E. Lisitzky (born 1885, arrived in America in 1901) attained his poetic maturity in this country. Unlike the other Hebrew writers he writes far from the tumult of New York—in New Orleans. But like most Hebrew poets he, too, earns his livelihood from teaching. From the point of view of output he leads all Hebrew poets in America. Others publish single poems or slender books, he publishes massive volumes. He employs all forms and writes about everything: short and long poems, lyrical and epical, realistic and legendary, dealing with historical as well as contemporary themes. His themes are love, hatred, God, man, the individual, the community, the people and the like. He includes everything and in every possible manner. Not because he belongs to those restless spirits who go everywhere in vain search of themselves, but—quite the contrary—because he is everywhere at home and knows how to master form and content. He is, in a manner of speaking, the virtuoso of Hebrew poetic creativity. One of his well-known poems is named *Naftule Elohim* (Mighty Wrestlings), a visionary drama constructed on a wide panorama of philosophical, theological and cosmogonic reflections. The scope is imposing, the structure impressive, the language remarkable. One gains the impression of an authentic poet, striving to raise Hebrew verse to new uncharted spheres.

Other important works of Lisitzky are: *Ele Toledot Adam* (These Are the Generations of Man), an autobiographical portrait; collected poems published in 1928 in Tel Aviv; *Adam al Adamot* (Man on Earth), collected poems published in 1947 in New York, and *Medurot Doakot* (Dying Campfires), an Indian epic based upon a rich legendary material about the tribes that inhabited the new American world before it was new and before it was America. The interest in Indian motives derives, as we have seen, from Silkiner. But in the hands of Lisitzky these motives came out richer, fuller and more profound in quantity, quality and linguistic form.

Lisitzky's recent collection of poems was published in Israel under the title *be-Ohole Kush* (In the Negro Tents, 1954). This volume of powerful verse and vivid portrayals was inspired by the debased condition of the life of the colored people in the midst of the free world of whites. For some explained and unexplained reasons, the Negro theme has been attracting a number of other Hebrew poets on American soil.

Israel Efros (b. 1891, arrived in America in 1904) has divided his talents almost equally between poetry and philosophy. These two realms, however, are strictly distinct in his writing: when he sings he is the poet throughout and when he philosophizes he is solely a thinker. To Efros poetry is a kind of relaxation from the disciplined strain, which his research requires. Hence his poetry is light, playful and unconcerned with issues. The poet does not want to boast of anything, to worry, to philosophize. All he wants is to observe and describe what he sees. He is a lyricist. He does not reproach, complain or grow angry. Not because everything in life is good and beautiful, not because life is an idyl, but precisely because life's current constantly hits upon all kinds of obstacles. "But without interfering rocks," he concludes in his song *be-Hayayh* (In My Life), "a stream has no resonance." To the poet life is a symphony of sounds, music—and indeed Efros' works were actually characterized by critics as a kind of music.

The above applies only to that part of Efros' poetry written before the Jewish catastrophe in Europe and the Jewish achievement in Israel. The poetry that he writes after these two historical events has a different character. It no longer possesses the tranquillity and the joy of song and play. There awakes in the poet not so much a sense of sympathy with the victims and hatred for the murderers, but a sense of mighty anger at the whole civilized world which regarded with passivity and indifference the cannibalistic bacchanal of the beast in the very center of progress and culture. Such an expression of Jewish and human reactions is the collection of poems *Anahnu ha-Dor* (We Are the Generation), which appeared in 1945. The book mourns over the destruction of European Jewry and condemns the nations for allowing this destruction. Written with dramatic pathos, Jewish pride and human faith, the language, the style and the flight of fancy manifest a high degree of creative character. Here the poet is no longer entirely separated from the thinker. The national and universal themes of the book require also intellectual reflections. And since the poet is also at home in these spheres his poems acquire a partly philosophic content.

Of special note among his works is the collection titled *Wigwamim Shotkim* (Silent Wigwams); its subject is a romantic love affair based upon Indian motives. *Zahav* (Gold), awarded the Louis Lamed Prize in 1943, is also noteworthy; it deals with the mass madness of the gold seekers in California a century ago. Despite the narrative half-epical character of the two books the aforementioned lyrical tendency of the author is very evident in them.

Aaron Domenitz (b. 1884, arrived in America in 1906), a dentist, was active in the Zionist movement in his early manhood in Russia and later in America. His first poem appeared in the *ha-Meorer* (The Awakener) and later poems in other Hebrew periodicals. In a short poem of eight lines, *Demi ha-Layil* (The Silence of the Night), he says that his heart is sustained by poetry and that between "one poetic work and the other his soul shrinks and is consumed by starvation." Domenitz also wrote a series of essays and stories, and edited a Zionist Yiddish weekly in Baltimore.

Reuben Grossman-Avinoam is one of the very rare Hebrew writers born in America (in 1905). His father, a Hebrew teacher and writer, spoke Hebrew to him in his childhood. At a very tender age, Grossman began writing poems, which were published in *Aviv* (Spring), a weekly for young people, and in *Shaharut* (Youth), a monthly for young people. When he was ten years old, his father published a small collection of his poetry titled *mi-Pi Olal* (Out of the Mouth of a Child), and when he was thirteen years old a second collection was published titled *Ibim* (Green Plants). From then on his poems, stories and articles appeared regularly in the *ha-Doar* (The Post), *ha-Tekufah* (The Season), *Sefer Touroff* (Touroff Jubilee Book) and others. Later, Grossman settled in Palestine where several collections of his poems appeared. Among these his translations of the following works occupy a prominent place: Israel Zangwill's *Dreamers of the Ghetto,* H. G. Wells' *The Outline of History,* Tennyson's *Enoch Arden,* Shakespeare's *King Lear* and other English works. As a poet Grossman is a man of moods. He is not at home in clear and definite circumstances. His muse does not thrive in the sun of day or in the hidden darkness of night, but midway between them, between light and darkness,

in twilight moods. Thus he confesses in his poem *Shaati* (My Time) . . .

Hyman Abraham Friedland (1891-1939) arrived in America in 1906. He made a name for himself in both literary and educational circles with his Hebrew poems and stories for children, published in the *ha-Toren* (The Mast) and the *ha-Doar*. The poems later appeared in the collections *Shiron* (Songster) and *Mizmor* (Psalms). In 1910 Friedland founded the National Hebrew School in New York and began to write modern Hebrew text books. He also engaged in literary criticism in Hebrew, Yiddish and English.

Toward the end of his life Friedland proved to be a poet and story-teller of considerable stature also for adults. He wrote several volumes of poems, sonnets and stories, which resound with the tragic note of one who is aware that his days are numbered. He does not weep and he does not mourn. On the contrary, in stoic verse he sings of life and death alike. Characteristic, in this respect, is the name of one of these poems, *Yesh Yofi la-Mavet* (Death Has Beauty) . . . Friedland's stories vividly reflect an aspect of American Jewish life. He was one of the first Hebrew writers to dwell upon such themes. In 1940 there appeared *Sefer Zikkaron le-H. A. Friedland* (H. A. Friedland Memorial Book), under the editorship of M. Ribalow.

Abraham Regelson was born in 1896, arrived in America in 1907, and left for Palestine in 1947. Since his experience is rich, he has a good deal to say. Yet he is not satisfied with merely saying or singing, but strives to say it in the most suitable form, in most apt words, and to create the keenest impression. He does not wield a facile pen. Writing is a struggle. His mission, however, is to write and he cannot renounce it. He regards himself the spokesman of unknown readers, who do not have the ability to express themselves in words. There is no embellishment in Regelson, no pose. It is no conceit in him when in one of his sketches, *Kabtzanim* (Paupers), in which he describes with humor reminiscent of Abraham ibn Ezra his own poetry, he says that he has an artistic soul, which he would not trade for anything in the world. It is not conceit; it is the truth.

Yet Regelson's muse is not always in a position to do justice to his enterprise. His *Cain ve-Hebel* (Cain and Abel, 1933) is a long narrative poem in which he attempts on a gigantic scale to weave into the Biblical episode of the first two brothers all the succeeding generations of man in the eternal struggle between the uncouth and primitive elements represented by Cain, and the advanced and civilized elements personified in Abel. The literary result is interesting, but far from perfect. It is an attractive poetic achievement, but does not attain more than an outline of the theme.

Regelson is also a gifted critic and essayist. His prose frequently possesses poetic cadences. Before his departure from America he published a collection of studies and essays titled *Melo ha-Tallit Alim* (A Cloakful of Leaves), which treats such diverse topics as "Kabbalah in the Poetry of Milton," "Henri Bergson," "Shakespeare's Sonnets," "The Song of Songs of Rashi" and "Tel Aviv Conversations." Regelson also writes Yiddish and English. Noteworthy are his numerous translations from Hebrew into English.

Simon Ginsburg (1891-1944, arrived in America in 1912) represents the romantic aspect of Hebrew poetry in America. He writes with feeling, simplicity and yearning. He yearns for his old home in the Ukraine, which he left at the age of 21, and for Palestine, where he hopes to settle. He yearns for the beauty of nature, love, kinship, friendship, dreams and fancies. He is an esthete. It is not hatred for or wrath at the murderers that one finds in his poems written in the years of World War I and soon thereafter, when his immediate family along with thousands of other Jews suffered indescribable agonies in the pogroms, but pain and loathing on the part of the degraded soul of man. Even

in *Pirhe Mavet* (Flowers of Death), written after the death of his young wife, the poet refrains from weeping and is content with perpetuating his sorrow in pathetic verses.

Ginsburg's romanticism is also evident in his descriptions of life in New York. In his long poem, *New York,* he sees the gigantic city as "a poem in prose, a divine and satanic poem, majestic and terrible, written in blank verse." The verses are the walls of the formless structure: here is a huge skyscraper like a long verse between two midget houses like two short verses. The poet seeks to find poetry everywhere, any kind, be it deformed, maimed, grown wild, materialistic, but poetry nevertheless. To the subtle ear of the artist the uproar of the tumultuous city comprising so many peoples is "a divine music that Wagner's ear could not conjure up" and to his romantic imagination the steel wires of the bridge spanning the Hudson River are strings of a magnificent harp. . . Ginsburg's *New York* belongs to the few works in Hebrew literature in America in which the rhythms of the surrounding environment resound vigorously. Also his *be-Har Bet Kolumbia* (Columbia University Hill) represents a colorful impression of the magnificent school, the poet's Alma Mater.

Of an entirely different character is Ginsburg's *Ahavat Hoshea* (The Love of Hosea), based upon an episode related in the first chapter of Hosea. A significant poetic work is his collection, *Shirim u-Poemot* (Songs and Poems, Tel Aviv, 1931). Considerable literary importance also attaches to his extensive studies about Moses Hayim Luzzatto. In 1945 part of his collected works appeared, titled *be-Maseket ha-Safrut* (In the Literary Web).

Hillel Bavli (b. 1893, arrived in America in 1912) is one of the most prolific Hebrew poets in America. "In Ginsburg," says Ribalow, "we hear the motive of family, in Bavli, on the other hand, vibrates the motive of the generations, 'an army of generations is embalmed and concealed in me like sealed wine-skins. . . ' And this outpouring is not accidental, for the consciousness of ancient generations is deeply engraved in his being" (*Antologiya shel ha-Shirah ha-Ivrit be-America*—Anthology of Hebrew Poetry in America, p. 22). As another parallel between them one may add that in both poets the motive of sorrow is evident. In Ginsburg this sorrow is depicted with a certain stoicism and objectivity. In Bavli it is a burden, too heavy to be borne. Ginsburg's poetry is not dolorous. Grief becomes purified, as it were, in the process of poetic creation and his poems written on sad themes are in reality not at all sad. With Bavli pain virtually inheres in the verses and words of the songs. One of his poems is titled *Tabaat Yagon* (Ring of Sorrow) and another, *Tseif Yegonim* (Veil of Sorrow). These names characterize his entire poetry—a ring of sorrow, a veil of sorrow.

The reasons for the poet's sorrow are manifold. In the first place there are the universal causes of the sorrow of all poets: the yearning for love, for beauty, for soulfulness, those lofty ideals that are like the peak of a high mountain, seen but never attainable (*Bavuot*—Reflections, *Al Saf ha-Sod*—On the Threshold of the Mystery, *Al Brekat George*—On Lake George, *Kevar Kaltah Marbit Yomi*—Most of My Day Is Gone, and others). But in addition to the factors of helplessness common to all poets, Bavli's poetry has other moments of sorrow. For Bavli bears the yoke of poetry not voluntarily, but like "a command, resounding with despotic voice in his blood." He attempts to revolt against "the yoke of laws and the chains of tradition," but he is too strongly linked with them for his opposition to last (*Avi*—My Father, *Tseva Dorot*—A Host of Generations, *Hafakim*—Contrasts, *be-Shaare ha-Netzah*—In the Gates of Eternity, and others).

Mention should also be made of the following poems of Bavli: "Mrs. Woods", an idyl, in which an old woman personifies a simple, natural and wholesome philosophy of life; "Eli", based upon the biblical story of Eli and Samuel; *Bivki Mimek Yatsati* (With Weeping I Departed From You), a farewell song upon leaving Palestine after a visit, which belongs to the most moving expressions in Hebrew literature in America on the subject of Palestine.

Bavli's poems appeared in a number of important publications. He is also a subtle essayist and literary critic. He translated Dickens' *Oliver Twist* into Hebrew (1924).

Pesah Ginzburg (1894-1948), who arrived in America in 1913, lived in this country only four years. He was a prolific poet, editor and translator. Of his American poetry mention should be made of the following: *Idiliot Amerikaiot* (American Idyls), narrative portraits of a local character, and *Shabbat be-Kefar* (Sabbath in the Village), short melodious verses in a popular style.

Moses Feinstein (b. 1896, arrived in America in 1914) began his literary career with a poem published in 1918 in *ha-Ivri*. From then on his poems have appeared regularly in Hebrew publications in America and Palestine. Since 1921 he has been dean of the Herzliah Hebrew Teachers' Institute in New York. Feinstein's poetry may be described as introspective. In his long poem *El Nafshi* (To My Soul), a monologue addressed to himself, he reveals his soul as a complex and his ego as fragmentized into countless generations and worlds, into dreams, prayers, passions, shouts, silences, humanity, barbarism, piety, heresy and many more contradictory manifestations. And who can tell where resides the true ego? If all of them together form the soul "how can I, the unfortunate," he asks, "find the right way among them all?"

In *Mevok ha-Dor* (The Perplexity of the Generation) Feinstein dwells upon the difficulty of finding the proper way between the consciousness of the individual and that of the group. "The human soul is hurled between the spheres of the ego and the group and it weeps because of the inability to grasp them both." Feinstein's vacillations between rational reflection and artistic description are evident in the very names of his poems: *Mayanay* (My Meditations), *Tsimtsum* (Concentration), *El Baruch Spinoza* (To Baruch Spinoza), *Abraham Abulafia, Sinay ve-Olimpus* (Sinai and Olympus), and many others. On the whole, Feinstein is better in his shorter poems and in his sonnets. His long poem *Halom ve-Goral* (Dream and Destiny), dwelling upon the disharmony between beautiful dreams and inexorable reality, is far more felicitous in individual passages than in the total structure.

Simon Halkin (b. 1899, arrived in America in 1914 and left for the State of Israel in 1949) introduces into the Hebrew poetry of the New World motives of old Jewish religiosity. This is not a religiosity of the emotions, but rather of the intellect, which may be said to be a *habadic* (intellectual-Hasidic) attitude toward the problem of God, faith, Jew, man and cosmos. In prose his reflections would become theological-philosophical treatises, in political form they emerge as prayers. When Halkin says in inspiring verse: "I have given up hope of finding God and I am weary of helpless wisdom" *(Al Hof Santa Barbara*—On the Shore of Santa Barbara)—it means that he is constantly finding God and that he never wearies of seeking for divine wisdom.

Had Halkin lived during the Middle Ages, in the days of the *payetanim* (liturgical poets), when Hebrew was truly the language of holiness, he would undoubtedly have written sacred songs in the traditional sense of the word, and possibly even *piyutim* (religious poems) and *selihot* (penitential prayers). Modern Hebrew poets no longer write sacred songs, but a good many of their secular songs are not too far removed from that language of holiness. Halkin wrote a trilogy, for which he found no more appropriate name than *Tefillot* (Prayers) and the three parts are named: *Shaharit* (Morning Prayer), *Minhah* (Afternoon Prayer) and *Arvit* (Eve-

ning Prayer). Here is the last verse in *Arvit:* "And my God, my God will rule, He alone. . . " In the poem *Lel Ahavah* (A Night of Love), in which the poet comes to the conclusion that the only truth in the world is love, the following refrain is constantly repeated: "I thank Thee God. . . " In general, in Halkin's poetry the words God, prayer, to pray, and similar expressions are frequently repeated.

The poet's religious philosophy may perhaps be summed up in the following quotation:

> Complete and whole was the work of the entire world on the day when God finished it, complete and whole in its majestic splendor that scintillates in the flesh of the creation like wine in a transparent goblet. Man, however, cannot grasp this cosmic completeness, for he alone is incomplete. His wholeness he can attain only by his eternal striving for the light of God, which is concealed among the crevices of his spirit like the sun among the clouds *(Baruch ben Neriyah*—Baruch the Son of Neriah). I have alienated myself from mankind, he concludes in *Tarshishah* (To Tarshish), therefore I am orphaned of God.

In addition to publishing collections of poetry and sonnets, Halkin is also prominent as a novelist, essayist and translator. His main works are *Yehiel ha-Hagri*, a novel in which the hero is a *habad* Hasid in New York; *Ad Mashber* (In Time of Crisis), a novel of Jewish life in America; *Arai ve-Keva* (The Transient and the Permanent), a collection of perceptive essays about Jewish and non-Jewish writers and problems of literature.

Isaac Silberschlag (b. 1903, arrived in America in 1918) is the most cosmopolitan of the Hebrew writers in America. In the first place, he is at home in the literatures of ancient and modern peoples. Secondly, the center of gravity of his cultural attitude is more within universal rather than national moments. Silberschlag writes almost exclusively short poems, and all he writes has charm, grace and elegance. His collection of poems *Ale Olam be-Shir* (Rise, O World, in Song) won the Louis Lamed Prize in 1946.

Silberschlag is also a fine critic. In his book *Tehiyah u-Tehiyah be-Shirah* (Revolt and Revival in Poetry) he discusses at length a number of figures in world literature that are close to his heart. His essays on many important modern Hebrew poets have appeared in various periodicals. He writes about all of them with a schooled pen and disciplined method.

Silberschlag won fame with his masterly translation of Greek dramas into Hebrew. His translation of the comedies of Aristophanes was awarded the Tchernichowsky Prize of the municipality of Tel Aviv in 1950. Occasionally he also publishes essays in English. Since 1948 Silberschlag has been dean of the Hebrew Teachers' College in Boston.

Baruch Katzenelson (b. 1900, arrived in America in 1922 and left for Palestine in 1934) published in America poems and essays in the *ha-Doar*. A collection of his poems titled *le-Or ha-Ner* (By the Light of the Candle) appeared in 1930. He also wrote poems and articles in Yiddish. The keynote of his poetry is simplicity and submissiveness. He has nothing in the world and lacks nothing. He demands nothing either of God, to whom he constantly confesses, or of man, whom he neither approaches nor shuns. A melancholy hovers over his verses, a melancholy of a sensitive soul, which feels itself a stranger not only in this land but everywhere. The short naïve confessions *le-Or ha-Ner, Ashre ha-Ish* (Happy Is the Man), *Eivel* (Mourning), *ba-Horef* (In the Winter), *Netzah* (Eternity), *Mavet* (Death), and others, are the saddest melodies in Hebrew on American soil.

Moses Brind (b. 1894) arrived in America in 1923 after having spent some time in Palestine. His poems were published in Hebrew periodicals here and in Palestine. They breathe a deliberate peacefulness of a delicate pen. "There are pleasant peaceful moments in the bitter life of men," he says in his poem that bears the significant name *Rige Osher* (Moments of Happiness). With these numbered moments of bliss the poet apparently attempts to be content.

Gabriel Preil (b. 1911, arrived in America in 1922) is the Benjamin of the Hebrew writers in America. Precisely he, the youngest, mourned fifteen years ago, "the decline of passed years, whose current beauty flows like a wound in my body . . . and a lament I shall lift over their death. . . . " *le-Yamim Ahavah* (Love for Days). Poetic yearning has really nothing to do with physical time or calendar years. One may yearn for a past that did not exist, for a future that is not yet or a present that is fleeting. Preil is a yearning soul. He yearns for his own self of yesterday, for a present that is hard to grasp. He yearns for the grave of his father in Lithuania. His yearning has no name and no object. He came to America as a young boy and is therefore one of the few "American" talents in Hebrew literature. He was undoubtedly influenced by the American environment and literature, yet American motives occupy a comparatively small place in his poetry. His poems have appeared in the *ha-Doar, Sefer ha-Shanah li-Yehude America* (Annual of American Jews), *Bitzaron* (Stronghold), *ha-Tekufah, Niv* (Expression), *Mabua* (Source), and others. His collection of poems *Nof Shemesh u-Kfor* (Landscape of Sun and Frost) was awarded the Louis Lamed Prize in 1945. His collected poems *Ner Mul Kokhavim* (A Candle Facing Stars), recently published in Israel (1954), have been very warmly received by Israeli readers and critics.

Abraham Solodar (1883-1937) arrived in America in 1925 after having spent 15 years in Palestine. Here he settled in Chicago, where he founded an illustrated Hebrew monthly *Dorenu* (Our Generation). He also edited children's publications and published a number of textbooks. His poems appeared in the *ha-Doar*, *ha-Olam* (The World), *ha-Aretz* (The Land) and other publications. The dominant note in his poetry is Palestine. He sings with pathos the splendor of that inspiring land for which he does not find enough superlatives *(li-Medurot Esh Homiyot*—To the Moaning Flames of Fire) and his remorse and pangs of conscience over his leaving the sacred soil *(Himnon*—A Hymn).

Aaron Zeitlin (b. 1898, arrived in America in 1939) is a fine illustration of the Talmudic adage that the son is the extension of his father. His work is a continuation of that of Hillel Zeitlin, particularly after the latter's tragic death in the Warsaw ghetto. He manifests an interest in the same subjects, a similar approach and almost similar conclusions. He even inherited his bilingualism from his father. He writes both Yiddish and Hebrew not casually, as is the case with other Yiddish and Hebrew writers, but thinks and publishes simultaneously and regularly in both languages. He belongs to that respectable group of artists, who acquired a permanent name in the creative advancement of both Hebrew and Yiddish.

Zeitlin's poetry and essays have appeared for the past fifteen years in the *ha-Doar*, *Bitzaron*, *Sefer ha-Shanah*, *Ahisefer*, *ha-Tekufah* and *Mabua*. The volumes of the *ha-Tekufah* that were published by the Stybel Publishing Company in New York were edited at first by Zeitlin and Isaac Silberschlag and later by Zeitlin himself. Zeitlin's poetry of the period is mystical, religious and philosophic in part. The poet delves into universal, Jewish and individual problems. He is a strongly emotional poet, but he conceals his feelings and clings as much as possible to reason. He wants to understand the creator and the creation, the true and profound meaning of life in general and of Jewish life in particular, the meaning of the Jewish mission and the Jewish tragedy, of diaspora and redemption. Zeitlin's is an artis-

tic soul deeply rooted in original Jewishness. His poetry contains fragments of Agada, Kabbalah and Hasidic literature. His prose contains many folk elements. He also translated into Hebrew some of the world's poetry. Whether in Hebrew or in Yiddish, in original creation or in translation, he remains what he is, within himself and with himself. All he writes excels in integrity of thought and wealth of feeling.

A. Z. Halevy (his collected poems appeared in 1948 under the characteristic title *Mitokh ha-Sugar*—From Within the Cage), M. S. Ben-Meir, David Kramer and I. J. Schwartz also belong to the family of Hebrew poets in America.

Zalman Shneour (b. 1887) spent several years in America. This country, however, cannot claim him; he belongs to the entire literary world of the Jewish people. His place is in the triumvirate (with Bialik and Tchernichowsky) that heads modern Hebrew letters. Nevertheless, while in America, Shneour contributed poems, novels, essays and articles to the Hebrew (as well as Yiddish) periodicals. His main works of that period are: *Luhot Genuzim* (Hidden Tablets), *la-Ivriya Tehilah* (Praise to Hebrew), *Al Rab Saadia Gaon* (On Rabbi Saadia Gaon), *Din Torah* (Religious Litigation), *Shir Hadash le-Reb Levi Yitzhok mi-Berditchev* (A New Song of R. Levi Yitzhok of Berditchev), and others. In prose: his own translation of his Yiddish works, *ha-Yehudim mi-Shklov* (Jews of Shklov), *ha-Kesar ve-ha-Rabi* (Emperor and Rabbi), *Noah Pandre,* and others.

But even these works are an integral part of Shneour's total creativity and their evolution does not belong in a study that deals exclusively with American Hebrew literature. For this reason none of the numerous Israeli writers contributing to Hebrew publications in the United States will be mentioned here.

2. SHORT STORIES AND NOVELS

In comparison with the poetic forces, the Hebrew prose writers in America occupy a less prominent position. There are few short story writers or novelists and few short stories or novels. Several sociological explanations for this condition have been offered. The real reason, however, seems to be the fact that the art of story telling requires considerable preparation, work and time, which only professional writers can afford. But in America, with the exception of a few journalists, there are no professional Hebrew writers. Hence the meagerness of prose production in Hebrew. This meagerness in quantity is to a certain extent compensated for by quality. The following is a brief survey of several prose writers and their works:

Abraham Shoar (1869-1939) is the only story writer of the first generation of Hebrew authors in America. He came here with a considerable equipment of knowledge and literary skill. Although he spent many decades in New York he came into limited contact with the New World. His thoughts, memories and entire mentality remained in the Old World, or rather in the ghetto of the Old World. Living in America he continued his existence there, seeking inspiration for his literary talent and actually finding his literary self-fulfilment there. He was aware of the fact that "that part was no more than a shadow, that he was set in a passing generation" (this is the name of his work in two volumes, *Dor Holekh*—a Generation that Passes). But he could not be reconciled to the present and all his life he felt at home in that small-townish past.

The *shtetl,* the keynote of the belletristic literature of the Jews in Eastern Europe, was also the hero of Shoar's *Dor Holekh.* This is a collection of stories of Jewish life in the small town of Tsarist days. There are several illustrative names: *Shloshah Kevarim* — Three Graves (the hero is Nahum, the baker, who was a close friend of the heretic of the town and demanded in his will that he should be buried next to the latter, who died first. Similarly, the rabbi of the town demanded he should be buried near the heretic); *Binjamin Pinhas* (deals with the life of the *cantonists*); *Yeno shel Eliyahu* — Elijah's Wine (also a story of the life of the *cantonists,* a group of them is being gathered at a *seder* arranged by some apostates, who remained Jews at heart); and *Ahat u-Shenayim*—One and Two (one woman and two men, one is her husband and the other her lover—the old triangle). Shoar's *Olam ha-Pelaot* (Wonder World), a collection of remarkable short stories, has enriched the children's literature in Hebrew in America.

Samuel Leib Blank (b. 1892) is the most prolific Hebrew prose writer in America. He, too, although he arrived in America in his youth, devoted the largest part of his creative efforts to the life he had left behind him. His roots, however, are not in the poverty-ridden and gloomy *shtetl* but in the broad and sun-flooded steppes and prosperous villages of Bessarabia. His creative pen brings him constantly back to those Jews who before World War I constituted a unique community in Russian Jewry. The Bessarabian Jews, who settled in the villages, worked on the land, lived with it and were intimately linked with it. They were Jewish peasants, radically different in their Jewish and human attitude from the Jews in the city and in the *shtetl.* Their Jewishness was somewhat removed from the stem and hence weak in external manifestations, but sound in its roots. Their humanity contained more primitiveness, passion, and rawness. This peasant quality penetrated the blood and the heart. The Americanized author could not free himself from that inner call. Thus came into being Blank's important stories and novels based upon village life in Bessarabia. They are written with a dynamic pen, artistic perception and mastery of the technique of narrative. The characters personify, on the one hand, the previously mentioned earthy elements: impulsive passions and wild instincts and, on the other hand, the basic values of the Jewish spirit, which remain unaffected even in a materialistic milieu. Suspense, which is the main factor in belles-lettres, is well maintained by Blank. The characters and the background appear vivid, the action quick and the language fluent. Blank is one of the most vigorous talents of modern Hebrew belles-lettres. The very names of his works have the fragrance of the village: *Tson*—Sheep, *Adamah*—Earth, *Moshavah* —Settlement, *Nahalah*—Patrimony, *ha-Aravah*—The Steppe, *bi-Sheat Herum*— In Time of Confusion, *Bat ha-Mayim*— The Naiad, *Havah*—Farm, *Al Admat Nekar* —On Foreign Soil, and others. *Maase ba-Hamishah Pelitim*—A Story of Five Refugees, *Soneim*—Enemies, *Tseliva*—Crucifixion, *Cain*, *Al ha-Gevul*—On the Boundary, are all descriptions of the pogroms in Bessarabia. American subjects are treated in *I ha-Demaot*—The Island of Tears, *Mister Kunis*, *Laylah Ehad*—One Night, *Yom ha-Menuhah*—Day of Rest, and others.

L. A. Arieli belongs to those writers who no longer sought inspiration in the memories of the old home but scrutinized the new milieu and attempted to describe it. One of his novels is entitled *New York,* and at first glance it describes life in America as an American would describe it. In reality, however, he looks upon the New World with the eyes of a Jew of the Old World, to whom everything appears peculiar, strange, empty and meaningless. The author had no desire or ability to see the manysided picture of American Jewry. He is content with a number of negative moments of Jewish existence on the American continent.

Nevertheless Arieli's novels indicate a certain fermentation in Hebrew belles-lettres of America. The very desire to describe the surrounding life means that the Hebrew writer here is not completely without a ground, that he at least attempts to express the new existence and is not entirely immured in an unreal world of the past.

A more concrete expression of alertness to the American milieu are the novels and stories of Reuben Wallenrod (b. 1901). He, too, describes New York in his work, *ba-Deyotah ha-Shelishit* (On the Third Floor), *be-Hug ha-Mishpahah* (In the Family Circle) and *Ben Homot New York* (Within the Walls of New York), but his descriptions are not, in a manner of speaking, of a moralistic character, but are drawn from a purely artistic point of view. He does not ridicule or look down. He, too, came from the Old World, but he is Americanized in the positive sense of the word. He sees the shortcomings and weak spots of American Jewry, but does not condemn. His task is to depict life as it is —the reader will decide what is good and what is bad. Hence Wallenrod's short and longer stories are interesting and afford literary pleasure. His most recent works are *Derakhim ve-Derekh* (Many Ways and one Way), travel impressions (1951), and *be-En Dor* (Without a Generation), a novel of the time of the First World War in Russia and its aftermath in the life of immigrants in America (1953).

Jochanan Twersky (b. 1904, left for Israel in 1948) has introduced original elements into Hebrew belles-lettres. His stories and novels are not altogether what is called fiction in America. Essentially, they are based upon actual events and real characters. They are historical-biographical novels. The author is in this respect to Hebrew literature what André Maurois is to French or Emil Ludwig to German literature. He chooses a historical character of the distant or near-Jewish past (sometimes also non-Jewish), which is close to his heart or mind, makes a thorough study of its period and milieu and on the basis of the gathered raw material, he limns a short or longer story, which contains naturally a goodly ingredient of imagination. The book possesses the same interest as fiction and has the advantage that the reader makes the acquaintance of real historical characters and events from an artistic point of view.

Twersky's writings are contributions both to Hebrew belles-lettres and to Hebrew historiography. Everything that comes from his pen bears the stamp of rich creativeness, stirring interest, honest thinking, a sensitive soul and an intensive inner life. His historical characters and events stand under the banner of this artistic versatility. Reading his book, *Uriel Acosta,* for example, one makes the acquaintance not only of the chief characters but also of the details of workaday life of Amsterdam Jewry at that time. A mere historian can never transmit such a vivid intimate portrayal of the past. To be sure, the author adds of his own imagination, but this addition does not alter the historical facts, but, on the contrary, brings them into sharper relief. Thus uniting historical documentation, artistic perception and creative language, the author has produced in the nearly twenty-five years that he lived in America the following biographies and essays: *Uriel Acosta, Ahad Haam, Rashi, Dreyfus, Mordecai Manuel Noah, Rathenau, Herzl, Bialik, Freud, me-Olam ve-Ad Olam* (Forever and Ever), and others. Besides stories and novels Twersky's works comprise articles, essays, sketches, encyclopedic articles, maxims, and the like. He never tires of constructing sentences, of weaving thoughts and creating literary values. His language is vigorous, original and a kind of specific Twerskian warmth pervades all his writings.

Harry Sackler (b. 1883) arrived in America some fifty years ago. His literary equipment identifies itself with the trilingualism of American Jewry. He writes in English, Yiddish and Hebrew. He has both dramatic and story-telling talents. His dramas appeared under the title *Sefer ha-Mahazot* (The Book of Plays, 1944). Leaving out minor attempts of other writers, these are the only dramas of Hebrew literature in America. His play *Rahav* was presented by the Habima in Israel.

In the field of belles-lettres Sackler published important novels and stories. His subjects are of a unique character. Sackler is first of all a thinker and afterward an artist. He surveys broadly the historical existence of the Jewish people and then dwells with greater attention upon those moments and episodes that must not be taken in their simple and factual meaning, but require deeper and broader interpretations. They must be placed not in the limited light of their time and place, but rather *sub specie aeternitatis,* in the light of the eternity of Israel. Here is an appraisal of Sackler by probably the best judge of Hebrew literary achievement in America:

> The realm of Sackler's art is the realm of the Agada, that is the realm of the historical midrashic traditions, as they were fashioned in the soul of the nation. His stories and dramas are based upon fragments of legends, snatches of popular accords and conversations. His heroes are remote historical characters or Agadic figures sprung up in popular imagination . . . and herein lies the strength of Sackler that he can bring back the Agadic world to its realistic basis and to invest the symbols with a vital and real content just as he is able to sublimate the real and the concrete to the level of the symbol. Thus he draws a bridge between the past and the present, between legend and reality, and the remote events come back and shine with a new and intelligible light (A. Epstein, *Sofrim Ivrim be-America*—Hebrew Writers in America, 1953, p. 294).

In other words, Sackler is the philosopher of Hebrew belles-lettres in America. He is more interested in the eternal problems of Judaism than in literary creativeness. Since, however, he is an artist, his reflections take shape in the form of first-rate literary achievements. Were not Sackler a dramatist and story-writer he would undoubtedly write historical treatises.

Sackler's stories appeared under the title *ha-Keshet be-Anan* (The Rainbow in the Clouds, 1948). Here are several characteristic names of his stories: *Hazut al Rosh Tsuk*—A Vision at the Head of a Cliff, *Honi ha-Meagel Hozer le-Maaglo*—Honi ha-Meagel Returns To His Circle, *ha-Tsur Tamim Poolo*—The Rock, His Work is Perfect. *Ari Ole le-Bavel* (A Lion Goes up to Babylonia) is a novel of the times of Rabbi Saadia Gaon. In *Kets ha-Pelaot* (Wonder End) the hero is the Baal Shem.

Isaac Dov Berkowitz (b. 1885), the son-in-law of Sholem Aleichem and his translator into Hebrew, spent some fifteen years in America. Unable to acclimate himself here, he left in 1929 for Palestine, where he has continued the literary activity which he began at a very early age in Lithuania. In America he was editor of *ha-Toren* (1916-1919) and *Miklat* (Refuge, 1920-1921). He was the final arbiter in all matters of literary taste, and not only the readers but also the Hebrew writers took his polished style as a model. He also published a number of stories and sketches of Jewish life in America. Like Arieli, he emphasized the grotesque and caricature aspects of American Jewry and the sense of alienation that possessed the immigrants with their memories of the Old World (for example, *Karet*—Extinction), his short comedies such as *Mi Navi ve-Yeda?* (Who Could Tell?) and *ba-Aratzot ha-Rehokot* (In Distant Lands). In America, too, appeared his Hebrew translations of Sholem Aleichem's autobiography, published by the Stybel Publishing Company in three volumes.

The contribution to Hebrew belles-lettres of the poets Simon Halkin, Hyman Abraham Friedland, Zalman Shneour, Ephraim Lisitzky were mentioned above. Other writers, who in addition to their regular articles and essays occasionally published stories, are: S. Kushtai, Zina Rabinowitz, Jacob Tarkov-Naamani, Shlomoh Damesek, M. G. Glen, B. Isaacs (his stories appeared under the titles *bi-Shne Olamot* (In Two Worlds) and *Amos Mokher Tapuzim* (Amos Sells Oranges), I. Osman, and others. During World War II Shlomoh Hillels enriched Hebrew literature in America with his novel *Tahat Sheme Bessarabia* (Under Bessarabian Skies) and *Artzah* (To the Land). After the war Hillels left for Israel. In recent years Jacob Churgin settled in America and has been publishing stories of a high caliber in the *ha-Doar, Bitzaron, Mabua,* and in other journals. He returned to Israel in 1954.

3. CRITICISM AND ESSAYS

In our survey of poetry and fiction we have pointed out that some poets and novelists have also extensively engaged in literary criticism (Halkin, Regelson, Ginsburg, Silberschlag, Wallenrod and others). Here we wish to dwell upon professional critics, that is, those who devote themselves exclusively to the literary works of others.

First and foremost is Abraham Epstein (1880-1952). He made it his task to study and interpret modern Hebrew belles-lettres, both poetry and prose. Endowed with an esthetic sense, psychological insight and talented pen, Epstein succeeded in fulfilling this task with great competence. Here are several of his conclusions about criticism:

"Essentially poetry is criticism—a criticism and concrete philosophical illumination of life. The genuine critic, the one of the highest integrity, is he who reaches the center of gravity of poetry—the poet himself. He who is able to present to the world an image of his own and of his fellow's soul, may be assumed to be able to penetrate the soul of his fellow's literary works. Hence we find that in the world's literature most poets and writers are also critics, just as the critics are also men of vision

MENAHEM RIBALOW (1899-1953), WRITER

and poetry" (Sofrim Ivrim be-America, p. 195).

Epstein is, indeed, a man of vision and poetry. The literary works of others were reflected in his sensitive soul with artistic splendor and expressed in fine interpretive prose. He devoted himself with special love to the Hebrew writers in America. Every Hebrew writer in the New World was dear to him, particularly the poets, the greater and the lesser. He deemed it his obligation to write about all of them, so that none should be forgotten.

Epstein's critical essays first appeared in the periodicals, mostly in the ha-Doar, and later appeared in book form under the title mi-Karov u-me-Rahok (From Near and Far), Sofrim (Writers), Sofrim Ivrim be-America, in two volumes.

The most prominent figure in the realm of Hebrew letters in America is Menahem Ribalow (1899-1953). For the past 30 years he was editor of the ha-Doar, the only

Hebrew weekly outside of Eretz Israel. (Before Ribalow, none of the twenty-odd Hebrew periodicals had lasted for any considerable length of time. The ha-Doar also appeared before Ribalow's editorship as a daily from 1921 to 1923.) He also founded and edited the Sefer ha-Shanah li-Yehude America and the quarterly Mabua. He was the moving spirit of the Histadrut Ivrit and the most prolific Hebrew writer in America. His editorials in the ha-Doar would fill volumes. They deal with a variety of subjects of a publicistic nature. They reflect practically all important events in Jewish life in this country and elsewhere and to a large degree also events in the world at large. They are written with enthusiasm, dynamism and that persistence which characterizes all of Ribalow's actions. He was one of those writers that are not static, but study and grow constantly.

Ribalow's critical essays embrace practically all of modern Hebrew literature. There is hardly a Hebrew writer in America about whom Ribalow had not written or spoken (he was a brilliant orator). Everyone receives his share—one a comprehensive discussion, another an essay and a third an article, none is overlooked. We have said that Epstein, too, is widely inclusive, he confines himself, however, to creative writers, whereas Ribalow includes translators, researchers, scholars, thinkers, public figures, educators and rabbis. He is, in a manner of speaking, the spiritual Maecenas of the Hebrew literary family. He encourages all and sees to it that every writer should feel that his work is properly evaluated. He stands guard and records all events in Hebrew letters in America. His ninety-page essay, for instance, on Hebrew literature in America in Ahisefer (a miscellany of 580 pages, published by the Louis Lamed Fund in 1944, under the editorship of S. Niger and M. Ribalow) is an apt summary of Hebrew letters from 1918 to 1943. Ribalow here furnishes a chapter of American Jewish history seen through the prism of the Hebrew language. Various categories of the written word are represented by 120 writers, such as publicistic writing, essays, bibliography, scholarship, poetry, the novel, criticism, and translation. Ribalow concludes with deep conviction:

> Hebrew literature became an integral part of the spiritual life of the Jewish community in America. Now there is no longer any doubt that so long as the Jewish community here will create national-cultural values—and there is no community without such values —the Hebrew language will remain the most faithful medium for such creation just as it had been in all the generations of our diaspora. A country whose Hebrew source has dried up and in which the voice of our literature has been silenced has from the national point of view returned to primordial chaos. This is the lesson of Jewish history (p. 181).

Ribalow's essays appeared in book form under the following titles: *Sefer ha-Masot* (The Book of Essays, 1928), *Sofrim ve-Ishim* (Writers and Personalities, 1936), *Ketavim u-Megillot* (Writings and Scrolls, 1942), *Im ha-Kad el ha-Mabua* (With the Pitcher to the Fountain, 1951) and so forth. Many other critical essays in the *ha-Doar*, *Sefer ha-Shanah* and *Mabua* are about to be published in book form. With the untimely death of Ribalow there passed away the most industrious builder of Hebrew literature in America.

His right hand in all his literary enterprises as Ribalow himself would express it was Misha Maisels, whose writings have appeared anonymously or under various pen names. Maisels is one of the most creative stylists in modern Hebrew philosophical and essayistic writing. He has been one of the literary pillars of the Hebrew periodical press in America for the past twenty years. Besides his eminent achievements in the field of editing, his brilliant articles and discussions in the *ha-Doar* alone would fill volumes of philo-

sophical criticism, publicistic dissertations and journalism. When his collected works appear it will be possible for the critic to evaluate properly the writer and his works. His *Mahshavah ve-Emet* (Thought and Truth), published under the pen name M. H. Amishai, will be discussed in the chapter on scholarship. With the death of Ribalow, Maisels has become the editor of *ha-Doar*.

Mention should be made also of the following critics: J. Ovsay, who writes in a polished style with subtle content about Hebrew writers and their works that are close to his heart; J. J. Wall, who dwells especially on foreign literatures; M. Steiner, who analyzes literary works and motifs in Hebrew literature in Israel and in America with a vigorous pen and professional competence; Isaiah Rabinowitz, who in his work *ha-Safrut be-Mashber ha-Dor* (Literature in the Crisis of the Generation, 1943) is not so much interested in literary works themselves and in their creators as in their meaning from the universal point of view.

Hebrew literature in America has also its meritorious essayists who invest it with a unique cultural flavor. In this respect S. B. Maximon and N. Touroff performed noteworthy service. The literary legacy of S. B. Maximon (1882-1933) is not great, but everyone speaks of it and of its author with special respect and reverence. One characterizes him as a worshipper of beauty, another as a stylist and a third designates him as the gentleman of Hebrew letters. All stress his modesty, humility, self-effacement, truthfulness and spiritual generosity towards all and especially towards the Hebrew writers.

Maximon was a man of a retiring disposition. All his life he dreamed of settling in Palestine (he named his daughter Zionah). He died at an early age. Maximon wrote only at the urgency of inner inspiration. Hence one feels inspired in reading his essays. A selection of these appeared under the title *Gevilin* (Parchments). They deal with outstanding personalities (among

NISSON TOUROFF (1877-1953), WRITER
AND EDUCATOR

them Ahad Haam, whom he mentions with
special reverence), philosophical, literary,
scholarly and timely topics. From 1927 to
1929 Maximon was editor of the pedagogic
publication *Shevile ha-Hinnukh* (Paths of
Education) in New York. A volume in his
memory titled *Sefer Maximon* (Maximon
Book) appeared under the editorship of
J. Twersky.

Of a similar high cultural caliber was
Nisson Touroff (1877-1953), the founder
of the *Shevile ha-Hinnukh*. He was not,
however, of a retiring disposition and his
pen was one of the most productive in
modern Hebrew literature. His literary
career began at the age of 12, in 1889, with
a correspondence in the *ha-Melits* (The
Interpreter) and continued in all the important Hebrew periodicals in the world.
It embraces stories, translations from and
into Hebrew, criticism, art, publicistic
writing, pedagogy and psychology. His
main achievements are in the realm of the

last two disciplines. He implemented his
pedagogical writings with practical work
first in Palestine and later in America. In
1938 appeared a miscellany in his honor,
Sefer Touroff (Touroff Book), under the
editorship of I. Silberschlag and J. Twersky.

Touroff resided in America for several
decades. Here he wrote his chief works on
psychology and education: *ha-Psikhologiya
Shel ha-Yahid* (The Psychology of the Individual), *ha-Psikhologiya Shel ha-Tsibur*
(The Psychology of the Community), *be-
Yodeim u-ve-Lo Yodeim* (The Conscious
and Unconscious), *Psikhologiya Shel Hi-
tabdut* (The Psychology of Suicide), *Haar-
akhot* (Evaluations; problems of general
and Jewish education) and a large number
of essays in various publications. He also
left some works in manuscript.

Another modest and profound essayist
and scholar is Samuel Isaac Feigin (1893-
1950), with his two books, *Mistere he-Avar*
(Mysteries of the Past) and *Anshe Sefer*
(Men of Letters).

Writings on education occupy a prominent place in Hebrew literature of
America. Zevi Scharfstein (b. 1884) is an
indefatigable author of textbooks, articles,
essays and studies about Jewish education
in America. Outstanding among his works
is his *Toledot ha-Hinnukh be-Yisrael* (A
History of Jewish Education), in three volumes. Kalman Whitman emphasizes the
religious moment in Jewish education; I. Z.
Frishberg is an expert in Hebrew textbooks; Elhanan Indelman specializes in
children's literature; Hayim Leaf is editor
of *Musaf la-Kore ha-Tsair* (Supplement
for the Young Reader), a supplement to
the *ha-Doar*.

Recently Simon Rawidowicz (b. 1897)
settled in America. He is a profound essayist and publicist and an original thinker
possessing an individual style, from whom
Hebrew literature in this country can expect much. In addition to numerous articles and essays, he has also edited the
Pinkas Chicago (Chicago Book, 1952) and

Sefer Dubnow (Dubnow Book, 1954). His *Bavel vi-Rushalaim* (Babylon and Jerusalem), a rich volume of essays on Jewish national and cultural problems in connection with the establishment of the State of Israel is about to appear.

The leitmotif of Rawidowicz's philosophy is the inner sameness and interdependence of Jewish communities the world over. Presently Rawidowicz is the head of the Semitic Department at Brandeis University. He is also editor of *Metzudah* (Fortress) and co-editor of *Bitzaron*.

Daniel Persky, the columnist of the *ha-Doar*, is also a Bialik expert. He occupies a special place in Hebrew literature. One of the most devoted builders of Hebrew literature in America, Persky excels as an essayist and columnist by virtue of his unique style. He is also a leading grammarian and historian of modern Hebrew literature. Persky writes with love and a gentle humor about writers, books and events in Jewish life. Special value is attached to his essays on the holidays. On the occasion of the twenty-fifth anniversary of his literary activity the *ha-Doar* published a special jubilee issue titled *Gileyon Daniel Persky* (The Daniel Persky Issue, Volume XIV, No. 29). Some of his writings have appeared in book form: *le-Elef Yedidim* (To a Thousand Friends), *Matamim la-Hag* (Tidbits for the Holiday), *Ivri Anokhi* (I Am a Hebrew), *Tsehok me-Eretz Yisrael* (Laughter from the Land of Israel), and others.

Another one of the literary builders of the *ha-Doar* and all other Hebrew periodicals in America of his time is A. R. Malachi (b. 1895) whose talents extend to many fields.

Other essayists, critics and publicists are: A. S. Orlans, E. Indelman, E. Ben Ezra, Reuben Brainin, Ab. Goldberg, I. Ginsburg, H. L. Gordon, Mordecai Halevi, Morris Halevi Levine, Yom Tov Helman, Hayim Weiner, Hillel Zeidman, Z. Werba, M. Hezkoni Shtarkman, M. Chochem, I. Jakobowitz, Chaim Tchernowitz, M. Katz,

REUBEN BRAININ (1862-1939), WRITER

M. Lipson (founder of the daily *ha-Doar*), J. K. Mikliszanski, S. M. Melamed, M. Prager, I. Z. Frishberg, Aaron Frankel, M. Komarovsky, M. Kosover, S. Kushtai, S. Rosenfeld, M. Z. Raisin, M. Rothblatt, Judah Rosenthal, Jacob Rosenthal and many others.

4. SCHOLARSHIP

The contribution of American Jewry to Jewish scholarship is significant and manifold. There are in America scholars and specialists in all branches of Jewish learning, first-rate institutions of higher learning, magnificent libraries and all facilities for study, thought and creation. Above all, there are a desire and a readiness to take over the legacy of European Jewry, and to continue the hallowed tradition of the people of the book. The axiom of previous generations that modern Jewish scholarship can appear only in a modern language continues also here. Important works continue to appear in English. In recent years, however, there is a tendency among scholars to write in Hebrew.

Even at present notable achievements on this score can be registered. In our brief survey we shall adhere to the following division: texts, Rabbinic novellae, monographs, historiography, philosophy, bibliography, miscellanies, translations, periodic publications.

Frequently the boundaries between one category and the other are indistinguishable. There are, for example, texts that are published in periodicals and there are philosophical works containing Rabbinic novellae and vice versa. Yet for purposes of orientation the above scheme is serviceable.

A. *Texts:*   These may be divided into two categories: a) new manuscripts discovered recently or in previous generations but never published; b) texts already in print, but requiring revision because of recent discoveries, modifications, new interpretations that have to be introduced into the text or its commentaries.

As an example of the first category we have the *Hilekot ha-Yerushalmi le-Rabenu Moshe Ben Maimon* (The Laws of the Palestinian Talmud of Rabbi Moses Maimonides), edited by Saul Lieberman, one of the leading authorities in all fields of the Halakah, and published by the Jewish Theological Seminary of America in 1948. The manuscript of this work was found in several folios without the name of the author. Considering the opinion of experts in the handwriting of Maimonides and his own proofs, Lieberman came to the conclusion that Maimonides is the author of these folios that were scattered in various libraries throughout the centuries. They are fragments of a longer work that has been lost and may yet be recovered. The introduction and the copious notes and explanations to the text determine the scholarly value of the work.

An example of books appearing for the first time on the basis of old manuscripts are the weighty tomes of Menahem bar Shlomoh ha-Meiri. These books are edited by various scholars and are published in Israel and America. The author was one of the leading codifiers of the Middle Ages.

To the second category—texts appearing anew—belongs the *Sefer ha-Mitzvot* (The Book of Precepts) of Maimonides, reissued in 1946 by one of the leading scholars, Rabbi Hayim Heller, on the basis of the Munich and London manuscripts "with corrections and emendations of the numerous errors and omissions that were in the previous editions," as indicated on the title page. The volume was published by the Rabbi Kook Institute in Jerusalem, but since the editor is a resident of America, Jewish scholarship in America may pride itself on his achievement.

An example of scholarly editions of old texts of a more specific character is the *Otsar ha-Baraitot* (Thesaurus of the Baraitot), published in New York in several volumes by Michael Higger, who is also known for his textual research in the *Masekhtot Ketanot* (Minor Tractates).

Mention should also be made of Philip Birnbaum's vocalized anthologic edition of Maimonides' *Mishneh Torah*. Such publications can bring the Hebrew reader closer to the Halakic sources that are inaccessible to him in the original.

B. *Rabbinic Novellae:*   Although this category embraces works in all branches of Torah, its main significance and activity are in the realm of Halakah. The Halakic literature occupies the outstanding place in Jewish letters after the Bible. It expresses the specific genius of Israel in its richest, most impressive and most creative manner. Every intellectual or literary achievement in the realm of Torah should be considered Jewish scholarship. Nevertheless some scholars maintain that the concept of Jewish scholarship be confined exclusively to the research work done in the modern schools of Jewish learning. The books that bear a traditional character are designated Rabbinic literature, a term that has no justification either in the Hebrew language or in the Hebrew tradition. The so-called Rabbinic literature is not necessarily by rabbis or for rabbis. It deals with Torah for the students of Torah.

No matter how they are classified, these writings occupy a prominent place in Hebrew letters in America both quantitatively and qualitatively. All Jewish immigrations, and especially since the Second World War, have brought numerous Torah scholars who continue their studies in this country in the yeshivah tradition. In the annual bibliographical study, *ha-Sefer ha-Ivri* (The Hebrew Book) for the year 5712 (1952), Daniel Persky pointed out that in the previous year fifty-two books in the field of Rabbinic literature appeared against thirty-six Hebrew books in other fields. Taking into consideration the fact that the thirty-six include also philosophical works that are close to Torah literature, the number of books in the category of Jewish scholarship will be even greater.

The result is that Hebrew literature in America consists in the main not of secular but of traditional material. Its general flavor is that of Torah and of Jewish scholarship.

To point out more concretely the connection between Torah and modern wisdom it need only be stressed that precisely from those circles that adhere to the traditional studies will arise the future scholars, just as the present scholars in the realm of Jewish learning have come from those circles and still derive their sustenance from those sources upon which they were brought up in the old yeshivot.

An illuminating illustration is *Perushim ve-Hiddushim bi-Rushalmi* (A Commentary on the Palestinian Talmud, 1941), a work in three volumes, by Louis Ginzberg, one of the most creative forces in Jewish scholarship of the past fifty years in America. In this work traditional Torah material is closely linked with modern research so that it is difficult to separate the new from the old, the "Rabbinic" from the scholarly-critical.

Moreover, the Torah literature is reinforced by a considerable oral expression of the same ideas. There are in America heads of yeshivot, lecturers and teachers who disseminate Torah and wisdom among wide circles of students. Thus the lectures in Halakah, Agada and philosophy of Rabbi Dov Ber Soloveichik in the Yeshiva University and outside the Yeshiva rank among the highest attainments of Jewish scholarship. Rabbi Soloveichik published very few of his numerous manuscripts, but the little that he did publish is of a high caliber. Thus, for example, his 85-page essay *Ish ha-Halakah* (The Man of Halakah, published in *Talpiyot,* Vol. I) is a masterly discussion of the essence of the Halakah and its bearers, informed with a classic profundity of thought and expression.

C. *Monographs:* This group is the most important from the creative point of view. We describe them as monographs, for each study in this category deals with a certain definitive theme. It embraces all works, large and small, on all aspects of the study of the Bible, Talmud, Midrash, medieval writings and many other subjects that come under the heading of Jewish knowledge. It employs the entire modern apparatus: determination of authenticity of manuscripts, comparison of various versions, archeological discoveries, linguistic examination, critical analysis of texts, paleography and so forth.

Much has been accomplished in this field in recent generations, and the share of American scholars—or better, of scholars who settled in America—in these accomplishments is considerable. The studies in the literary treasures of the *Genizah,* discovered at the beginning of our century in Egypt, were mostly done in America. The discoverer of the *Genizah,* Solomon Schechter (1847-1915), settled in America, where he reorganized the Jewish Theological Seminary of America and continued his scholarly activities.

It is impossible here to dwell upon individual scholars and their works. This is not a bibliographical account, but a general survey. We merely make use of certain illustrations. Thus recently Louis Finkelstein published a book titled *ha-Perushim ve-Anshe Kneset ha-Gedolah* (The Pharisees and the Men of the Great Synagogue). Although most of Finkelstein's works are in English, this work appeared in Hebrew, with a summary in English. This study is based upon a new analysis of Talmudic and Midrashic texts on problems about which other scholars have written at length. The author adopts new interpretations and comes to entirely new conclusions. Many conclusions of scholars in the field of Jewish learning are of a hypothetical character and even on fundamental subjects there are differences of opinion.

A variety of writings is now being published in this country in the field of interpreting, reviving and adapting ancient Hebrew Law to legislative requirements of the new State of Israel. Prominent in this respect are the many writings of Simon Federbush who is also very active in all Hebrew undertakings in post-war America.

One cannot disregard the important studies of American scholars in the field of medieval Hebrew literature. Mention must be made of the monumental work, *Otsar ha-Shirah ve-ha-Piyut* (Thesaurus of Poetry), of the late Israel Davidson, the numerous writings of Simon Bernstein, and the fine contributions of Joseph Marcus.

D. *Historiography:* In the field of Jewish historiography much was also accomplished in America. Here a prominent place must be assigned to *Toledot ha-Halakah* (A History of the Oral Law), in four volumes, and *Toledot ha-Poskim* (A History of the Codifiers), in two volumes, by Chaim Tchernowitz (1871-1949), published after the author had settled in America. These will remain classic works. It is to be regretted that they remained uncompleted. The millennium following the destruction of the Second Temple is not dealt with in these works.

In the field of general Jewish history Salo Baron published in several editions his comprehensive *Social and Religious History of the Jews* in English, and a number of studies in Hebrew.

Meyer Waxman, too, published his *A History of Jewish Literature,* which contains nearly 5,000 pages and has seen several editions, in English. He also published an anthology in Hebrew *Mishle Yisrael* (Jewish Proverbs), as well as many essays and monographs in periodical publications, some of which appeared under the title *Kitve Meyer Waxman* (The Works of Meyer Waxman, 1944). Of a local character is Moshe Davis' *Yahadut Amerika be-Hitpathutah* (The Shaping of American Judaism, 1951).

These are only a few examples of the wealth of historiographical works, general and local, cultural and sociological. They establish the fact that there is a will in American Jewry to study and to know our past, our spirit and our mission.

E. *Philosophy:* In the field of pure philosophy with its numerous ramifications the American contribution is also very considerable. The most prominent figure here is Harry Wolfson. It is due to his efforts that the famous Harvard University library is now a first-rate center of literature pertaining to Jews and Judaism in all languages, of all times and countries, including the most recent publications in the State of Israel and other countries. In the past twenty-five years, besides essays and monographs, Wolfson published three weighty tomes, which are considered part of the classic literature of world philosophy: *Crescas' Critique of Aristotle* (1929), the *Philosophy of Spinoza* (1934) and *Philo* (1947). They are in English and it would be highly desirable to have them translated into Hebrew.

A monumental philosophical work in Hebrew is *Mahshavah ve-Emet* (Thought and Truth, 1939) by M. H. Amishai, the pen name of Misha Maisels. The first volume (over 500 pages) deals with general philosophy, while the second (also nearly 500 pages) deals with "Judaism in its own boundaries and in the boundaries of the world." Let it be stated that Amishai's is a work of a great thinker and an ardent Jew, a remarkable synthesis of exalted thought and language. It will be among the classics of modern Hebrew prose.

F. *Bibliography:* In the field of bibliography the annual *ha-Sefer ha-Ivri* (The Hebrew Book), published by the Jewish Book Council of America in three languages: Hebrew, Yiddish and English, should be noted. It publishes complete lists and general evaluations of the literary achievements of the year in America and to a certain extent also in the State of Israel.

Boaz Cohen's *Kuntres ha-Teshuvot* (The Book of the Responsa), a bibliographical key to the Responsa literature, has considerable significance for a wide field that has not yet been properly studied. Cohen is also the author of other bibliographies and of important studies in Jewish jurisprudence.

Distinguished service to Jewish bibliography in America has been rendered by the following writers and scholars: A. R. Malachi, who specializes in Hebrew periodical literature; Yitzhok Rivkind, one of the builders of the famous library of the Jewish Theological Seminary of America; Joshua Bloch, chief of the Jewish Division, New York Public Library; Daniel Persky, a permanent contributor to the aforementioned *ha-Sefer ha-Ivri,* and others.

An example of bibliographies compiled by industrious librarians in the form of monographs is the brochure on the Gaon of Wilno, on the 150th anniversary of his death, by J. J. Dienstog, of the library of the Yeshiva University. The author is now preparing a comprehensive Maimonides bibliography.

G. *Miscellanies:* Under miscellanies are included collections containing works of various authors and various topics.

In the first place comes the *Otsar Yisrael,* an encyclopedia in ten volumes by Judah David Eisenstein, who also compiled several other anthologies. With all its shortcomings this work has remained the only complete encyclopedia in Hebrew to this day. However, work has recently begun in the State of Israel on Hebrew encyclopedias on a much larger scale. Essentially the *Otsar Yisrael* was a condensation of the *Jewish Encyclopedia,* which had been published in America and may be considered as the most valuable literary monument of Jewish scholarship in the New World.

In consonance with the above definition, the numerous jubilee volumes also belong in the category of miscellanies. They contain works of American and Israeli scholars. Such volumes as the *Sefer Touroff,* published by the Boston Hebrew Teachers College, *Sefer ha-Yovel li-Kvod Levi Ginzberg* (Jubilee Volume in Honor of Louis Ginzberg), *Sefer ha-Yovel li-Kvod Alexander Marx* (Jubilee Volume in Honor of Alexander Marx), *Sefer ha-Yovel li-Kvod Mordecai Kaplan* (Jubilee Volume in Honor of Mordecai Kaplan), published by the Jewish Theological Seminary of America, *Sefer ha-Yovel shel ha-Doar* (Jubilee Volume of the ha-Doar), and others.

H. *Translations*: We have in mind translations from Hebrew into English. Generally they appear with introductions, footnotes, sources, bibliographies and other apparatus. Mention must be made here of Maimonides' *Mishneh Torah,* published by Yale University as part of a large literary enterprise. Of a high literary and pedagogic merit are also the excellent translations of the prayers by Philip Birnbaum.

The multiform activities in the field of translation may be illustrated by the following: *Mekilta,* translated by Jacob Z. Lauterbach, Moses Hayim Luzzatto's *Mesillat Yesharim* (The Path of the Upright), translated by Mordecai M. Kaplan, Rabbi

Saadia's *Emunot ve-Deot* (Creeds and Opinions), translated by Samuel Rosenblatt.

The first attempt to translate the Palestinian Talmud into Hebrew was also made in America. The tractates *Berakot* (Benedictions) and *Peah* (Corner) were translated by Jacob Newman and published by the Hebrew Teachers College in Boston. The same institution also published the lectures and addresses of Z. Chajes, translated by Israel Lewin.

I. *Periodic Publications*: Many articles, essays and studies on all aspects of Jewish learning appear in various Hebrew and English publications. These periodicals are also organs of criticism and literary reviews. It must be admitted, however, that few competent scholars in America engage in evaluating the work of others, with the result that the field of criticism of Jewish scholarly works is neglected on the whole.

The organ of Jewish scholarship in America is the *Jewish Quarterly Review*. It is edited by Solomon Zeitlin, one of the most prolific scholars in America (who also writes Hebrew occasionally), and Abraham Neuman, president of Dropsie College in Philadelphia.

The American Academy for Jewish Research publishes its *Proceedings,* which contain the papers read at the annual meetings of the Academy. Studies on Jewish subjects are also published in non-Jewish publications, such as *Journal of Biblical Literature,* and others.

In Hebrew, scholarly studies are published in *Horev,* edited by Pinkhos Churgin; *Talpiyot,* edited by S. K. Mirsky; *Pardes* (Orchard), edited by S. A. Pardes, in the traditional manner of the novellae; *Bitzaron,* founded by Chaim Tchernowitz and now edited by a board of editors, which devotes considerable space to scholarly studies. Similarly, the several volumes of the *ha-Tekufah* that appeared in America under the editorship of Isaac Sil-

berschlag and Aaron Zeitlin contain a section devoted to scholarly studies. *Megillot* (Scrolls), founded by Hayim Greenberg, also publishes studies of scholarly interest. *Ha-Rofe ha-Ivri* (The Hebrew Physician), edited by M. Einhorn, although a professional journal, also publishes studies based upon Jewish classical sources.

Lastly, special mention must be made of the weekly *ha-Doar,* which recently lost its editor, Menahem Ribalow. This publication is dedicated to Hebrew culture in all its manifestations. Although primarily a literary weekly, it serves also as a platform for Jewish scholarship. There is hardly an issue that does not contain a study pertaining to Jewish learning. In the special and enlarged editions of the *ha-Doar* considerable sections are devoted to Jewish scholarship. This material, scattered over the pages of the *ha-Doar* in its thirty-three years of existence, could fill many volumes, and it is to be regretted that no complete bibliography thereof is available. Some of these studies, such as Simon Federbush's *Mishpat ha-Melukah be-Yisrael* (State and Government in Jewish Law) later appeared in book form.

The same may be said about the *Sefer ha-Shanah, Metzudah* and *Mabua.* All these stress clearly the unique place of Jewish scholarship in Hebrew literature and fulfil in this respect an important educational function for the Hebrew community in America. Without them important areas of Hebrew literature would remain entirely unknown to a large sector of that community.

Judging from the present conditions, the prospects of producing creative Hebrew writers, poets, novelists, dramatists, and the like in America are not too apparent. On the other hand, there are excellent prospects for Hebrew letters in America in the field of Jewish learning. The American Jewish scholar is here afforded favorable opportunities for creativity: institutions of learning, libraries, technical facilities, material compensation and the like. Therefore, it seems that in the future Jewish scholarship, which is gradually adopting Hebrew as its natural language here, will be a great blessing to Israel's spiritual existence in America and will enrich to a considerable degree the treasures of eternal Judaism.

BIBLIOGRAPHY

פרסקי, דניאל, „הספרות העברית באמריקה", לוח אחיעבר, 1918.

ריבולוב, מנחם, אנתולוגיה של השירה העברית באמריקה. ניו-יורק, 1938.

ריבולוב, מנחם, „הספרות העברית באמריקה", אחיספר, ניו-יורק, 1944.

ריידר, יוסף, „חכמת ישראל בארצות הברית", בצרון, 1940.

BLOCH, JOSHUA, "Hebrew Literature", *Universal Jewish Encyclopedia*, Vol. VII.

WAXMAN, MEYER, *A History of Jewish Literature*, Vol. IV. New York, 1941.

אפשטיין, אברהם, סופרים עברים באמריקה. תל-אביב, 1953.

ברגר, ישעיהו, „חכמת ישראל באמריקה", ספר השנה ליהודי אמריקה, תרצ"מ.

הספר העברי, קובץ שנתי.

זילברשלג, יצחק, „השירה העברית בעולם החדש", אחיספר. ניו-יורק, 1944.

מיקלישאנסקי, י. ק., „רב צעיר", צוקונפט, דעצעמבער 1945.

מלאכי, א. ר., „ראשית השירה העברית באמריקה", ספר השנה ליהודי אמריקה, תרצ"ה.

פייגין, שמואל, אנשי ספר. ניו-יורק, 1950.

THE JEWISH LABOR MOVEMENT

Abraham Menes

I. INTRODUCTION

1. THE SCOPE

The dramatic rise of labor organization among the Jewish immigrant workers in the United States, which began seventy-five years ago, cannot be described adequately by mere statistics of industrial conflicts or even by an account of the shifting patterns of labor-employer relations. Equally essential is a structural analysis of the clothing industry and its ancillary trades, in whose labor force, numbering more than a million, the Jews were the largest ethnic group as well as the most highly skilled workers. Nor can a recital of the new "way of life" created by the economic upheaval since the dawn of unionism among the makers of men's and women's garments in America be omitted from this epic story.

To encompass in full two generations of travail and achievement is beyond the ambition and frame of this article. What we shall try to do is to present briefly a balanced story of the economic, spiritual and social upsurge among the Jewish workers in the United States. While giving the basic facts, we shall emphasize the background and origins.

This upsurge was made possible by the freedoms and opportunities of the New World, but it also was due in no small measure to the incomparable fighting spirit of these once helpless and insecure immigrants; by their amazing capacity for genuine fraternity with their fellow workers of different origins in the shops; and, lastly, by an enduring attachment to their adopted land and its institutions, without an abrupt breach with their own past and their own cultural heritage.

2. THE OLD COUNTRY

When the early attempts to organize the Jewish workers were made in the United States in the 1870's no one could have foreseen that those feeble beginnings eventually would develop into a powerful and widely ramified movement, which would exert great influence on all Jewish life in this country. And it surely could not have been expected that the Jewish labor organizations would in many respects be the pioneers for the American labor movement as a whole.

It has often been pointed out that the Jewish labor movement in America had its roots in the old country. The first organizations of Jewish workers were often the outgrowths of artisan guilds. Jewish tailors, shoemakers, hatters and other artisans had not only their guilds but even their separate synagogues in many of the cities and townships of old Russia and Poland. We even hear of strikes by Jewish members of such guilds in some Russian cities during the Seventies of the last century.

It was in the Seventies, too, that the first efforts were made to organize Jewish workers in modern trade unions in what were then the two largest centers of Jewish immigration—London and New York. Equally significant is the fact that the emergence of Jewish socialism dates to approximately the same time. In the early 1870's a small group of Jewish socialists was formed in Wilno under the leadership of Aaron S. Lieberman and Aaron Zunde-

levich. Several years later Lieberman founded the first Jewish socialist organization, the Union of Jewish Socialists in London (*Agudat ha-Sozialistim ha-Ivrim be-London*).

To the Jewish socialists their early encounter with organized Jewish workers in the Seventies and even in the next decade came as a major discovery. For many Jewish intellectuals of that era the very existence of Jewish industrial workers was a dim and distant fact. The cities and towns of Lithuania, Poland and the Ukraine, it is true, teemed with Jewish workers, but the outside world took little notice of them. To that world the Jews were primarily a people of tradesmen and middlemen. These businessmen and traders were constantly in the public eye, in the markets and streets, while the poor artisans and laborers crowded the slums and side streets, curtained off, as it were, from the mainstream of their town's life.

In that outside world, besides, there were always to be found groups of anti-Semites, in whose eyes the Jews were not merely tradesmen and middlemen but also parasites, idlers and exploiters. Their anti-Semitic fulminations, ceaselessly repeated in a backward agricultural country such as Russia was at the time, and buttressed by the physiocratic theory that agriculture is the only "productive" occupation, could not have failed to leave some effect on the popular mind. A romantic picture of the peasant, of his "honest and simple life in the bosom of nature," became the central theme in the Russian revolutionary movement of that period. This was, in part, the Russian answer to the problems generated by the emergence of modern capitalism. The Russian intellectual youth, which had a feeling of guilt about the people, made a heroic attempt to "go to the people" and share the lot of the poor peasants.

The Jews had no peasant class. The Russified Jewish intellectuals, with few exceptions, lived quite apart from the Jewish milieu and had their eyes turned almost exclusively toward the Russian peasant.

They harbored the firm belief, moreover, that the realization of socialism would put an end to the Jewish problem and to the denial of civil rights to the Jews.

Nevertheless, the encounter with the Jewish workers aroused among some of the Jewish radical intellectuals a sense of guilt and remorse. The awakening came sharply with the outbreak of the pogroms in 1881. The tragic events in the Tsarist empire after the assassination of Alexander II on March 1, 1881, shook the entire Jewish world and particularly the Jewish intellectuals who had confidently sought an answer to the Jewish problem in Russia in legal emancipation and cultural assimilation. Their naive faith in the Russian peasant, in his goodness and uprightness, was shaken when they suddenly saw that the peasant could also be unjust, brutal and cruel. For the peasants had taken an active part in the attacks upon the Jews, and most of all upon the poorest Jewish workers.

In this atmosphere of despair, the only solution appeared to be emigration, a mass exodus from the Tsarist empire. But where were the Jews to go? Some felt that the answer was a return to the ancient, ancestral home. A second, larger group, turned its eyes westward, to the new, free world. The debates between the "Palestinians" and the "Americans" filled the pages of the Jewish press, and in every city in the Pale groups sprang up preparing to leave the country. An entire people seemed to have suddenly resolved to take its fate into its own hands and to find a haven of refuge.

II. BEGINNINGS OF THE JEWISH LABOR MOVEMENT

1. AM OLAM

The year 1881 thus marks the beginning of a new era in Jewish history: the beginning of mass emigration from Eastern Europe, and the first steps in the modern Jewish colonization of Eretz Yisrael. Though the great majority of Jewish emigrants streamed to America, the modest efforts of the Bilu pioneers in Eretz Yisrael

were destined to have equally epoch-making consequences. The ideology of the Bilu and the Hovevei Zion groups was given its classic formulation by the noted Zionist author, Leo Pinsker, who chose as the motto of his Auto-Emancipation the ancient Jewish proverb: "Who will help me if I do not help myself?" The Bilu pioneers laid the practical foundation for modern Zionism.

The great mass, however, preferred the New World. But not all of those who went to America had merely practical aims in mind. Some had wider ambitions, although they did not express them as cogently as the "Palestinians." The very name which some emigrant groups adopted—The Eternal People (Am Olam)—was symbolic. In free, democratic America, the adherents of Am Olam argued, the Jewish masses would find admirable conditions for building a new life. They thought of themselves as pioneers, whose historic mission it was to find and prepare a home for an entire people.

The Jewish emigration from Eastern Europe was different both in scope and in character from the Jewish emigration to this country which began in the 1840's and which consisted mainly of German and Austrian Jews. The Central Europeans had come in smaller numbers and had settled thinly all over the land, while the East European emigration had a mass character from the start. The immigrants from Western and Central Europe turned principally to trade and peddling, many of them eventually setting up their own businesses in various communities; the immigrants from Eastern Europe, on the other hand, were chiefly laborers and skilled workers, and even those among them who had been shopkeepers and middlemen took up manual work. While trading and peddling could not support any large number of the new arrivals, industry was capable of absorbing mass immigration of even such dimensions. Approximately three-quarters of all the newcomers went to work in shops and factories, mostly in the garment industry. But besides earning a living, this ever-growing Jewish working class also had to integrate itself in the life of the country.

The period between 1881 and 1887 was one of searching and experimentation for the *Am Olam*. This movement had set itself the goal of bringing about a social and economic renascence of Jewish life through the establishment of cooperative agricultural colonies. A revival of Jewish life, they believed, depended on a radical change in the entire social and economic order. The Jews, as they saw it, unfortunately occupied a particularly vulnerable place in the private-enterprise economy as tradesmen and middlemen. This must be ended, and a secure home for the entire Jewish people must be built in free America. Some of them even cherished the utopia of establishing an autonomous commonwealth in the United States. "Our slogan," one of their pronouncements read, "is agriculture, and our goal is the physical and spiritual regeneration of our people. . . . In free America, where different nationalities live peacefully side by side, we Jews shall also find a corner to rest our heads." The change to agriculture was also deemed to be the best answer to anti-Semitic slurs.

Altogether, six or seven *Am Olam* groups arrived in America in 1882. Among them were three socialist groups from Odessa, Kremenchug and Wilno; and though the others had no specific ideological commitments, they all dreamed of beginning a new life built on "just social foundations." Since they were unable at once to raise funds for colonization, some of the *Am Olam* members went to work on farms to learn American farming. Others found work in New York and formed "communes" there. Those who had gone to work outside New York sent part of their earnings to the collective treasury.

In September 1882 twelve members of the Kremenchug *Am Olam* founded a colony in South Dakota. These were the advance guard of a larger group who stayed behind on their jobs to accumulate funds for the colony. They named it Beth-lehem Judah and plunged into their labors with great enthusiasm. "At the sight of these courageous young people," a contemporary report on that colony reads, "one inevitably begins to feel that the great spirit of Israel is not yet extinguished, that the children of Israel have not yet lost their faith in their own powers. . . . This faith can work miracles."

The following excerpt from the constitution of the colony throws light on the spirit and the ultimate goals of the group:

> The colony Bethlehem Judah is founded by the first group of the Kremenchug *Bne Horin* (Free Men) to help the Jewish people in its emancipation from slavery and in its rehabilitation to a new truth, freedom and peace. . . .
>
> All members of the colony Bethlehem Judah must engage in farming. Only when all work on the farm is finished may they engage in other productive occupations. Commercial activity is absolutely forbidden. (This article may not be abolished or amended.)
>
> All members of the colony form one family enjoying the same rights and privileges. . . .
>
> The colony considers it its duty to continue the colonization of Russian Jews in America through the establishment of new colonies. . . .
>
> Women shall enjoy equal rights with men. . . .

The practical results of this ambitious experiment were, alas, not too happy. After eighteen months of cooperative farming the colony was disbanded. The colonists divided the common property, becoming individual farmers. A short time later the colony was liquidated entirely.

The New Odessa colony, in Oregon, fared little better, though it seemed to have had the best human material for such an enterprise. After the first few years, during which the project progressed rather well, there gradually began to appear signs of fatigue, spiritual as well as physical. The colony was far from Jewish centers, and the colonists felt isolated and abandoned. The spiritual depression led to personal friction. Abraham Cahan, who knew many of the New Odessa colonists, points out in his memoirs that their depressed moods and personal frictions were due largely to the lack of privacy. "Some of the members confused their socialism with the idea of eating from the same bowl and sleeping in the same bedroom." New Odessa, the most ambitious attempt at colonization by an *Am Olam* group, was finally liquidated in 1887, after having existed for five years. The members of the colony first moved to San Francisco but later went back to New York, where they attempted to carry on a "commune." They organized a cooperative laundry, which also was short-lived.

This ended the story of *Am Olam* as an organized movement, but the spirit and the idealism of its members had not been wasted. Many former *Am Olam* members later became leaders in the Jewish socialist movement in America. For many of its achievements in the years to come the Jewish labor movement owes these pioneers a debt of gratitude.

2.   LIFE ON THE OLD EAST SIDE

While "life on the farm," away from the profit-seeking spirit of the big cities may have beckoned to some idealistic young men and women immigrants in the early Eighties, the great majority of the new arrivals were total strangers to notions of colonization. Nearly all of them came here in steerage, without means of sustenance even for the first few weeks. Many had families to support, and since they had to look for work as soon as they landed, they were glad to accept any job that came along. And because of this desperate need of employment, there developed in the then young East Side Jewish community a peculiar "Jewish" economy, with "Jewish" trades, a Jewish mode of living, and special Jewish problems.

All the efforts of the Jewish relief agencies, which sprang up at that period to introduce some order into the chaotic stream of immigration brought no visible results. The choice of location and occupation available to the immigrants was limited, for a number of reasons. Religious traditions, customs, and eagerness for group life were the principal factors. To a great many the need to observe the Sabbath and the dietary laws was a compelling condition. Religious Jews—who were the great majority—could not think of leaving the city and hiring out as farm laborers or to seek employment in large plants where Saturday work was obligatory. More than any other immigrant group, the Jews had to look for work among their own people and to remain within the realm of the East Side.

Yet despite the helplessness of the immigrants, their ignorance of English, their lack of funds, and often even the lack of jobs, they were all imbued with a deep faith that in time they would succeed in gaining a firm foothold and building a secure home for themselves and their children. In this respect the immigrants of the last decades of the 19th century, most of them from Southern and Eastern Europe, were strikingly akin to those of the 17th and 18th centuries, who came largely from Great Britain and Western Europe. The new immigrants produced their own pioneers, men and women of courage, persistence and initiative; and their path was not easier than that of their predecessors.

There, however, the analogy ends. The immigrants of the colonial era had to fight against the wilderness and to endure the bitter struggles of a primitive existence. Their moral discipline and perseverance were important factors in the building of America, but they were fortunate in that they were not challenged in their culture, language and traditional system of values. Those pioneers had the great advantage of being able to transmit to their children not only their material but also their spiritual heritage.

The great mass of immigrants who began pouring into America toward the end of the 19th century and during the first quarter of the 20th, who in their culture and language differed decisively from the colonial settlers, did not share this good fortune. Their struggles and achievements have mostly remained unsung, and their lives were rarely caught in the full light of history. Quite often their own children failed to appreciate their parents' contribution to the building of our land. Nor did many of these children realize the extent of their indebtedness to their parents. The young generation often regarded their elders as "greenhorns," forgetting that it was only thanks to the parents' hard work, love and sacrifice that the children had been able to become what they were.

3. SEVENFOLD IN THIRTY-FIVE YEARS

The Jewish neighborhoods at the end of the last century were marked by poverty, wretched housing, and almost incredible overcrowding. Hundreds of thousands of immigrants had become concentrated on New York's East Side within the space of a dozen years. It is typical of all immigrant slum areas that crime goes side by side with poverty and overcrowding. In the slums it is easier to stay in the shadow and find safety from the hands of the law. No wonder, therefore, that most outside observers painted a picture of the New York East Side in the darkest possible colors. A balanced picture of the old East Side however, shows it to have been one of the most industrious and hard-working areas in the country. Serious observers were frequently astonished at the zeal, the ambition and the initiative shown by the freshly arrived immigrants. Thus, the well-known social worker, Mary K. Simkhovitch, wrote as follows about the life in the East Side tenements at the turn of the century:

> I spent 1898 at the College Settlement visiting these tenements and getting acquainted with the life on the East Side. What a deep chasm exists between publicity and facts! The word "slum" is used indiscriminately for poverty, disease and crime. These generalizations are not only inaccurate but misleading. For life in the tenement can and often does exhibit the loftiest character and the finest human relationships. But it is against great odds. . . . Cultural interests grew rapidly in this hotbed of energy, intelligence and freedom. The Yiddish theatre attracted many from other parts of New York as well as from the local population. Music, drama and poetry flowered in this scene of poverty and squalor (*Here is God's Plenty*, pp. 28, 30).

The congested housing and the almost unrestricted working hours in the sweatshops were also partly due to the immigrants' determination to extend help to their relatives as quickly as possible. Most of the new arrivals had left their families behind, and they confined their living budgets to the minimum, and frequently to less than that, in order to put aside what they could and to bring over the largest possible number of their kin within the shortest possible time. This feverish zeal and energy of the immigrants in pursuit of jobs and earnings, regardless of working conditions and wage rates, was one of the causes that helped to create the sweatshop. It is estimated that more than 80 percent of the over two million Jewish immigrants from Eastern Europe between the early 1880's and 1915 were brought over to America by relatives who had arrived here earlier.

At first the new arrivals would accept any job that offered itself. They worked under the most difficult conditions and at the lowest wages, on the docks, on railroads and at heavy manual labor in factories—wherever work could be found. Every immigrant went through a period of experimentation until he finally settled down, usually in some "Jewish" trade.

The concentration of Jews in certain trades was also characteristic of the Jewish cities and small towns in the old country. In America, however, this concentration became extreme. It is sufficient to point out that nearly two-thirds of Jewish wage-earners worked in the clothing trades, which became more and more Jewish after the 1880's.

EAST BROADWAY, CENTER OF THE OLD EAST SIDE

This was not accidental. Before the Eighties the Jewish immigrants from Germany and Austro-Hungary occupied a prominent place in the country's ready-to-wear clothing industry, as employers, workers, and retailers. Because the manufacture of ready-made garments was just beginning to expand at that time, it offered more opportunities to the new arrivals than custom tailoring. The rapid development of the ready-to-wear women's garment industry may be traced in the following table:

GROWTH OF THE WOMEN'S CLOTHING INDUSTRY IN THE UNITED STATES, 1879-1914

Year	Number of Enterprises	Number of Workers
1879	562	25,192
1889	1,224	39,149
1899	2,701	83,739
1904	3,351	115,705
1914	5,564	168,907

As we see, the number of workers increased sevenfold in this 35-year period. At the same time, however, the number of enterprises increased almost tenfold. In 1879 the average number of workers employed in an enterprise was just short of 50; in 1914 the average number was not more than 30. The development here was in a direction opposite to that of industry generally. While the ever-increasing concentration of industry was the most characteristic feature of the great industrial expansion which America was experiencing at the time, the needle trades were undergoing a process of fragmentation. As we shall see later, this exerted a potent influence on the entire subsequent development of the Jewish labor movement in this country.

4. "INSIDE" AND "OUTSIDE" SHOPS

In the needle trades mechanization never rendered small enterprises impractical. The sewing machine, like the later cutting and ironing machines, is a fairly simple and inexpensive tool, requiring no large investment of capital. Moreover, the organization and distribution of work in the garment workshops was also fairly simple. The small "enterpriser" could use his dwelling as his workshop, he paid smaller wages, and his working hours were longer. These factors led to the rise of the contractor, the middleman between the worker and the manufacturer, who is still an important figure in these trades.

The contractor received from the manufacturer or jobber, as the case might be, cut or uncut material, and his employees sewed it into garments. The contractor's income was the difference between what the manufacturer or jobber paid him and what he paid his workers. In the earlier years the small contractors would even work side by side with their employees. The dividing line between the contractor and the worker was not too sharp and it was not unknown for contractors to unite with workers in a strike against the manufacturers. As a rule, however, the contract system was encouraged by the manufacturers and jobbers because it lowered their costs and shifted responsibility for production upon the contractors, leaving manufacturer and jobber free to concentrate on finance and merchandising.

Thus there developed in the garment trades a triangle with complicated relations among the manufacturers, contractors and workers. The difference between the so-called "inside" shops, which belonged to the manufacturers, and the "outside" shops, operated by the contractors, tended further to sharpen these relations. The inside-shop workers were often regarded as "aristocrats of labor." They were usually more skilled and received better pay, while the workers in the contract shops, nicknamed "Columbus' tailors," had usually learned their part of the trade within a few weeks. The new immigrants went to work for a contractor for a variety of reasons: the environment of the inside shop was alien to them; in the inside shop it was necessary to work on Saturdays, and the inside-shop workers were often hostile to the new arrivals and refused to work with them.

INTERIOR OF AN IMPROVED SWEATSHOP

The working conditions in the contractors' shops were incomparably worse than those in the inside shops. The contractors were in a bitterly competitive business, they had hardly any capital, and their chief asset was their ability to hire the newly arrived immigrants for low wages. In those years the workers in the outside shops had to bring their own sewing machines and to pay for needles and thread. The standard features of the sweatshop—overcrowding, lack of sanitation, low wages and unrestricted hours of work—were often further aggravated by the contractor's irresponsibility. Irregularity in the payment of workers' wages was habitual, and contractors frequently held back as much as several weeks' pay. If a contractor went bankrupt, which happened quite often, the workers simply lost their wages.

To all this was added the seasonal character of the garment trades. During the busy seasons, when the shops were operating day and night, the workers would be driven practically to the point of exhaustion. When the slack period arrived, however, they would be without work for many long weeks. "The life of the 'green' immigrants in the Eighties was a veritable hell. . . . Today it is difficult even to imagine how people could exist in such conditions" (Bernard Weinstein, *Jewish Unions in America,* p. 51). Similar descriptions were given by other contemporary observers and their picture of the sweatshop is confirmed by the official reports of various investigating committees.

5. NO "RETURNEES"

Yet the life of the new arrivals was not quite so dark and hopeless as it is painted in the literature of the time. There were, indeed, many tragedies—older immigrants who could not adjust to manual work, and the sick who were unable to support their families. This was why the newcomers clung to one another, and this, too, was the reason for the formation of so many mutual-aid associations, *landsmanshaften* and free-loan societies. Intellectuals suffered greatly too. The very fact that they were compelled, if only for a brief time, to work in factories was a painful thing to them.

The great mass of the working people, however, did not feel that their lot was tragic. They were happy, to begin with, to live in a country "where there are no pogroms." Economically, too, the Jewish worker in America was even then in a far better position than he had been "at home." A wage of eight or ten dollars a week was, indeed, not very high by American standards; a worker with a family was just barely able to get along on it, especially in view of the frequent and long slack seasons, when earnings would cease. By the standards of the old home, however, quite a good deal could be done with eight or ten dollars. And the fact was that the ordinary immigrant was able to save a few dollars, send some money home, later bring the family over, and gradually establish himself. The Jews had the smallest percentage of re-emigrants of all immigrant groups. Even in times of severe crisis, few thought of going back. America became their home, and their hopes were bound up with this country. In moments of discouragement they might curse "Columbus," but they remained in "his country."

It is equally erroneous to speak of the low cultural level of the immigrants. This was the wholly subjective evaluation of the radical intellectuals, who perforce approached the Jewish worker with their own set of spiritual and moral values. It is important to note that nearly all the Jewish immigrants were able to read and write. Many of them had studied in *yeshivot* and had acquired by their own efforts a fairly extensive general education. Within a short period of time, there developed on the new soil a rich Yiddish literature, a Yiddish press, a Yiddish theater, and Jewish folk music. The worker found time to read books, to attend the theater, to come to meetings. Some even managed to continue their education, and eventually became lawyers, doctors, engineers or independent businessmen.

In one respect, however, the newer immigration was extremely backward. Unlike the immigrants from Germany of a few decades before, the arrivals from Poland and Russia did not manifest during the early period any talent for organization. It is true that they created *landsmanshaften,* congregations, and aid societies, but they formed few central organizations of larger scope. The only immigrants from Eastern Europe to have shown a capacity for organization on a wider scale from the very beginning were the radical intellectuals. Thus it was that the encounter between the socialist intelligentsia and the workers led to such extraordinary results.

6. THE KNIGHTS OF LABOR AND THE AMERICAN FEDERATION OF LABOR

During the Eighties industrial expansion was putting its stamp upon the entire development of America. The urban population increased with great rapidity, and the influx of immigrants from all parts of the world reached a high point. Hand in hand with industrialization went a concentration of capital to a degree heretofore unknown in this country. It was a period when great trusts and gigantic private fortunes were being created, an era of Grand Moguls in finance and industry.

The rapid growth of the cities and of urban industry, however, did not bring any prosperity to the great mass of the people, the workers and the farmers. On the contrary, the Seventies and Eighties were marked by long periods of depression. The prices of agricultural products declined steadily, and the pressure of large-scale immigration made itself felt on the labor market. Labor was also affected by the ever-growing mechanization. All this evoked recurrent moods of profound unrest and protest. Individualistic America was unwilling to accept the unrestrained power of "frenzied finance" and sought means to check its sway.

The struggle for reform centered mainly about three issues—free land, easier money and credit, and the fostering of cooperative enterprises. The anti-monopoly movement swept along, together with large numbers of farmers and urban workers, a section of the middle class and many intellectuals. But the leading place among the organized forces which opposed the power of the money lords was held at the time by the Knights of Labor, formed in 1869 as a secret order. In 1878 the Knights changed their constitution and became an open organization, which admitted everyone regardless of creed or race. The Knights accepted skilled and unskilled workers, farmers and artisans, small enterprisers and professionals. Entry was barred only to bankers, money-lenders, lawyers, gamblers and saloon-keepers.

Ideologically, the Knights looked back to an earlier America. They would not accept the irrevocable fact of the great industrial revolution and dreamed of rebuilding the economic life of the country on the basis of independent farms and cooperative enterprises. Their philosophy was *every man his own master.* Gradually the Knights were increasingly drawn into practical trade union work, including strikes. This attracted large numbers of workers, particularly during the years 1884-86, when the order attained a membership of more than 700,000. The year 1886 marked the high point in the history of the Knights. After that the order began to decline, and leadership in the labor movement was taken over by an organization that seemed better equipped to cope with the practical needs of the time.

This was the American Federation of Labor, which was organized in 1886 under the leadership of Samuel Gompers. The philosophy of the AFL was very different from that of the Knights. Gompers had a great belief in the ability of organized labor to achieve practical results by means of direct struggle in the factories. He did not believe that it was possible, or even desirable, to escape from capitalism. Regarding the ever-growing concentration of capital as a normal aspect of modern economic development, he felt that the struggle of the wage-earners must be waged primarily by the trade unions. He opposed the socialist leaders who sought to harness the trade union movement to politics. Gompers defined his philosophy as unionism, "pure and simple."

The AFL was built on the principle of craft unionism. Even within a single industry the workers were organized according to crafts, and the workers of one factory often belonged to several trade unions. Frequently one group would go on strike, while the others remained at work, and this often led to sharp conflicts within the ranks of the labor movement.

The AFL was, in effect, an organization of skilled workers only, and this may have been the greatest weakness of the American labor movement for nearly two generations. However, it must not be forgotten that it was at first extremely difficult to organize the unskilled workers, who came largely from the ranks of newly arrived immigrants. The breach in the AFL policy of craft unionism came in the first decade of this century with the affiliation of the miners, even though they were practically an industrial union and their skills hardly placed them among the "aristocracy" of labor.

Samuel Gompers had as much faith in the working class as many of his radical critics and opponents. His goal was to achieve for America's wage-earners the greatest possible immediate and practical gains. The workers, he felt, could not wait for the political leaders to bring about the promised reforms. They had to rely primarily on themselves and on their unions, which were the organizations "of, for, and by the working class."

A central point in the early struggles of the AFL was the demand for the eight-hour day. In 1888 the AFL adopted a resolution proclaiming May 1 as a labor holiday, to be marked by demonstrations for the eight-hour day. A similar resolution was passed a year later by the Socialist International, and in 1890 May 1 was celebrated for the first time as a labor holiday by organized labor in Europe and in America.

Basically, the AFL was a conservative organization and was suspicious of all forms of government intervention, including laws to protect labor. It was not until the New Deal that the AFL changed its position on this paramount question.

7. EARLY STRIKES AND UNIONS

In the early years of the labor movement in America there were sharp divisions on the role and importance of political activity. The differences were over the question whether socialism could be attained by democratic and parliamentary methods, or whether only revolutionary methods could be effective in the fight against capitalism. This controversy led in 1881 to a split in the Socialist Labor Party (SLP), which had been organized only four years earlier.

The meager results of political campaigns, the prevalence of municipal corruption in some of the larger cities, the brutal methods by which labor strikes were often suppressed—all these factors served to augment distrust of political activity by means of the ballot. A convention held by the SLP opposition in 1881, consisting of anarchists and syndicalists, passed a resolution opposing political campaigns. Two years later, at a second convention held in Pittsburgh, this group, led by Johann Most, whose influence on the German workers and on some of the Jewish radicals was extremely strong, adopted an outspokenly anarchist program. The Pittsburgh convention rejected every form of political campaigning or parliamentary activity and declared that

our "sole purpose must be to prepare the workers for revolutionary struggle." The program likewise expressed disbelief in the possibility of practical achievement through trade union work. With the syndicalists the anarchists held that the unions should primarily be "an instrument of revolutionary propaganda."

It is difficult to guess more than a half century later what political influence the anarchist ideology might have exercised on the general labor movement if it had not been for the Haymarket tragedy in 1886. It is well to bear in mind that, like the early socialist movement in America, anarchism was also chiefly a movement of German workers. Its center was Chicago, where it published a daily paper in German, *Arbeiter Zeitung*.

As has been noted, 1886 was a crucial year in the American labor movement. In New York the United Labor Party came into being and in a number of cities there were parades in favor of the eight-hour day.

On May 4, 1886, several thousand workers met in Haymarket Square in Chicago. The meeting was almost over, and some of those assembled had already left. Suddenly the police began to disperse the remaining crowd. At that moment a bomb exploded and shots rang out; ten persons, including seven policemen, were killed, and a number of others were wounded. It was never discovered who threw the bomb. Nevertheless, seven of the most prominent anarchist leaders were sentenced to death. Despite hundreds of appeals, the Governor of Illinois refused to spare the lives of the condemned men. Only two of the death sentences were commuted to life imprisonment; one of the condemned committed suicide before the execution, and the others were hanged on November 11, 1887.

Although the Haymarket tragedy aroused a great wave of sympathy for the condemned, anarchism as a political movement lost all its influence. Simultaneously the influence of the moderates increased both in the socialist movement and in the trade unions. The end of 1886 also saw the formation of the American Federation of Labor, which has since become the most important factor in the life of American labor.

Among the Jewish workers sympathy for the unjustly condemned men led to a certain strengthening of anarchist feeling. On October 23, 1886, soon after the Chicago trial, the Jewish anarchists formed their own organization, *The Pioneers of Freedom*. A Jewish anarchist movement gradually developed, exercising a substantial influence upon Jewish labor in the Eighties and the early Nineties.

The development of trade unionism among Jews was unique in several respects from the beginning. There was no sharp dividing line between the skilled and unskilled, since most Jewish workers were semi-skilled, as could be expected of men employed in the needle trades. There were, of course, minor exceptions. The sample makers and the cutters, for instance, often regarded themselves as "aristocrats" and looked down upon the ordinary workers. This attitude, however, was not typical of the general atmosphere in the garment shops. Narrow craft unionism held no appeal to the leaders or the rank and file of the Jewish unions.

The first Jewish labor organizations in America appeared as early as the 70's, even before the beginning of the Jewish mass immigration. By then a number of Jewish artisans had arrived from Germany and Austro-Hungary, and a smaller number from Russia as well. Some of these workers joined labor unions. There were also some attempts to form Jewish labor organizations not for ideological reasons but simply for practical considerations. In 1874 there was a strike of capmakers in New York, reported to be "mostly Jews." But it was the beginning of the mass immigration that led to the creation of "Jewish" trades, and consequently of Jewish trade unions.

The needle trades, with the sweatshop system, the small factories and the triangle of manufacturer, contractor and worker, had created special conditions for the Jewish unionists. The Jewish labor movement, for instance, did not share in the general mood of protest against the growth of capital concentration and of large industrial units. On the contrary, the leaders of the Jewish workers complained about the disadvantages of the small shops. One of the principal demands of the Jewish socialists, in fact, was the abolition of the contracting system, which meant, in effect, the abolition of the small enterprise. Graduation into a big factory was the dream of many Jewish workers. Frequently the Jewish unions were on better terms with the big factory owners than with the small contractors. We shall see later how this special situation affected the Jewish unions in their relation to the problems of technological progress and the rights and duties of the worker in the shop.

The first "immigrants' strike" which aroused public interest was the strike of ladies' tailors in the inside shops in 1883. Altogether 750 workers went out on strike for fifteen dollars a week and a working day from 8 A.M. to 6 P.M. Half of the strikers were women. The Knights of Labor helped in leading the strike, and also promised material assistance. The following is a newspaper description of this remarkable strike of Jewish workers in the early Eighties.

> The members of the new Cloak and Dress Makers Association have never before been on a strike, and had never before taken part in labor movements. Nevertheless, the men and women who compose the union have realized all the hopes of the leaders in standing by the Association. . . .
>
> There were fears that the great poverty of many of them . . . might induce these poor people to return to their daily toil for the pittance they were receiving, but the weak ones were encouraged, and now they all

seem determined to stand out until their wages are raised (quoted by Louis Levine, *The Women's Garment Workers,* p. 33).

Two years later there was a strike of 1,500 workers in both the inside and outside shops. The workers complained that the piece-work rates were so low that they had to work from 6 o'clock A.M. till 8 P.M. to earn enough to live on. They were willing to work from 7 to 6 and demanded that the rates of pay be revised to enable a skilled worker to earn from twelve to fifteen dollars a week. Another important demand was for better treatment of the workers: "They will also demand that in the future they be treated with politeness and consideration. It is alleged that they have been roughly treated by their employers in the past" (*Ibid.,* p. 37).

We are told in the memoirs of Abraham Rosenberg, who was president of the International Ladies' Garment Workers' Union from 1908 to 1914, that a large strike of ladies' tailors broke out in the spring of 1885 because an employer had struck a worker in the face. According to Rosenberg, a group of former students in Russia helped in the conduct of the strike. After a second strike, which took place in the summer of that year, the Knights of Labor took over the leadership, and the ladies' tailors became a local of the Knights.

The men's tailors began to organize in 1883, the initiative being taken by a number of workers in inside shops, mostly immigrants from Hungary and Galicia. Special mention must be made of Jacob Shein, a Hungarian immigrant and a former *yeshivah* student. In America he became an active socialist and contributed much to the organization of Jewish workers. Another leading figure was one Maybaum, who was subsequently elected Master Workman of the Operators' Local of the Men's Tailors. Still another active leader of the tailors' union was Louis Smith, who had a long history of activity in the labor movement. A native of Poland, he had gone to France, where he took part in the

uprising of the Paris Commune in 1871, and later to London, where he became one of the founders of the first Jewish tailors' union in 1874 before coming to the United States.

In 1884 a union of men's tailors working in outside shops was organized in New York, and a speaker from the ranks of the intelligentsia was invited to one of the initial meetings to inspire the workers and to raise their morale. He was the young Abraham Cahan, who had come to the United States only two years earlier, with one of the *Am Olam* groups. In his *Pages from My Life* Cahan has an interesting description of that meeting. It took place on the evening after Yom Kippur in a hall, in which "prayers had gone on all day." The workers assembled "an hour or so after the last prayer of Yom Kippur." This represented the transition between the old guild, which had been so closely linked with the synagogue, and the secular Jewish labor movement, which often fought bitterly against religious traditions.

Soon afterward the mens' tailors in the outside shops stopped work. Their strike lasted six weeks and ended in victory.

Attempts to organize Jewish workers were also made during the Eighties in Boston, Philadelphia, Baltimore and Chicago. In the spring of 1886 there was a spontaneous strike in the outside shops of Chicago which involved a considerable number of workers. The strike failed but it led to the founding of the first union of Jewish cloakmakers in Chicago.

All the unions that sprang up in the Eighties were short-lived. Most of them arose in the heat of struggle, and soon after the strike was over the workers forgot about the union. Toward the end of the Eighties strikes became frequent in the needle trades. Though Jewish workers acquired the reputation of good strikers, they were reproached for failure to maintain their unions.

This character of the Jewish labor movement at that time is explained, in part, by the seasonal nature of the work in the needle trades. Every work season was opened with bargaining over rates. The pay was on a piece-work basis, and every new style required a separate determination of rates. When agreement was not reached, which was fairly often, the workers would leave the shop almost spontaneously. The employer knew where to find them. He would go to them, bargain some more, and in the end both sides would agree on a price. At the end of the season, when work began to be scarce and the contractors felt more confident, they would again begin to reduce wages. Seasonal strikes and seasonal unions became the vogue in the needle trades of that era.

Sometimes, of course, even the first stages of bargaining would not be amicable. The employers, contractors or manufacturers, would resolve "to teach the workers a lesson." Strikes would follow inevitably, causing great hardships to the workers. As a rule, the strikers had no savings and the unions, such as they were, had no strike funds. Privation naturally led to unrest and insecurity among the strikers. In such cases the intellectuals would be brought in to encourage the doubters with speeches and to introduce some order and planning into the conduct of the strike. A professional, experienced union leadership did not yet exist.

There was still another reason for the fitful character of the Jewish unions—the unsettled status of the Jewish workers, which was discussed earlier. Work in the shops was to a great many of the people engaged in it merely temporary employment. Some went into business for themselves, others changed their trade, and still others sought an education. And these were the most active elements, with the greatest initiative and resistance. Their ranks were being constantly depleted, and it was not easy to find replacements.

This was not only a Jewish phenomenon, for in many of the basic industries the labor force was constantly changing in those years. At the beginning of the 20th century, most of the workers in the coal mines and the steel mills, for instance, were recent immigrants. This made the organization of unions so difficult.

8. WORKERS AND INTELLECTUALS

Political and social thinking among the Jewish immigrants was quite different from what it was in America generally. To begin with, the immigrants brought with them a spiritual heritage which was quite complex in itself. When they came to America they were further influenced by the ideas and strivings they encountered here. This resulted in a mixture of political, social and religio-ethical doctrines in which it was difficult to discern any system or order. It was only in time that more or less definite trends became crystallized. The East Side of those days seethed with discussions about everything—politics, science and, above all, socialism.

In those years socialists ardently believed that knowledge and scientific progress were the best and surest way to the solution of all social, political and economic problems. Their major goal, therefore, was to educate themselves and others. Hence their ambition for learning, which has always been widespread among the Jews. What is more, study was a way to forget the hard and monotonous life in the shop, and perhaps even to leave it behind altogether. Morris Hillquit, who had come to the United States in the late Eighties, gives us a vivid picture of the state of mind of the Jewish intellectuals on the East Side in that period:

> They had not been trained for work at any trade and were impelled by economic necessity to engage in unskilled and unattractive occupations at which they earned a meager living. They felt unhappy and forlorn in their workshops, but at night on the roofs they again lived in a congenial atmosphere. Once more they were students among students, forgetting the miseries of their hard and toilsome lives and enjoying the pleasures of freedom and companionship with the abandon

and enthusiasm of youth. . . . Most of their evenings were spent in discussion. And what discussion! There was not a mooted question in science, philosophy or politics that was not aired on the roofs in ardent, impassionate and tumultuous debate. Politics was the favorite subject (*Loose Leaves From a Busy Life,* p. 2).

Most of the Jewish socialist intellectuals of the period were cosmopolitan in outlook, with no specially Jewish aspirations. Nevertheless, the tragic events in Russia and the anti-Semitism spreading over Central Europe tended in time to strengthen their sense of Jewish responsibility. They came to regard the struggle against anti-Semitism, especially among workers, as their historic mission. And it must be said that their accomplishments in this respect were quite substantial.

Their task was, indeed, extremely important. To begin with, they felt that it was necessary to create an atmosphere of understanding, sympathy and respect for the Jewish worker through a Jewish labor movement. The mass immigration of the Eighties and Nineties, which had brought so many new elements from Southern and Eastern Europe, aroused anxiety and animosity among many Americans. Proposals to limit immigration were popular. And the organized workers were prominent in the opposition to immigration. The unions often felt that there was little use in fighting for better labor conditions as long as hundreds of thousands of immigrants, who had to sell their labor power at any price, came pouring into the country without restriction year after year. One of the labor leaders formulated the question in the following words:

> Our living is gauged by immigration; our wages are based on immigration; the condition of our family is gauged by immigration. (Cf. Allan Nevins and Henry Steele Commager, *America, the Story of a Free People,* Ch. 14.)

The harsh conditions in the sweatshops, the low wages and the long hours had naturally aggravated the feelings against the immigrants generally and against Jewish workers specifically. "Greenhorns" were excluded from many unions. In some trades this exclusion was the reason why Jewish workers — painters, backers, etc. — had to form unions of their own.

The threat of serious conflict between the new Jewish immigrants and the organized workers became apparent in the first months of the mass immigration. Very characteristic is the story of the attempt in June 1882, to trick some new Jewish immigrants into becoming strikebreakers. Approximately 5,000 longshoremen were on strike in New York and several hundred Jewish immigrants accepted jobs loading and unloading the ships without the slightest suspicion that they were taking the places of striking workers. After a few days some of the immigrants were severely beaten by the strikers. By chance this group of Jewish workers included several intellectuals of the *Am Olam* movement. They learned what had happened and the immigrants joined the strike.

The clash with the striking longshoremen on the docks, incidentally, led to the founding of the first Jewish socialist group in America. July 7, 1882, was the date of the first meeting of the Propaganda Society, dedicated to popularizing the ideas of socialism among the Jews. The speeches at that meeting were delivered in German and Russian, its organizers apparently not suspecting that Jewish workers might be addressed in Yiddish. The speakers included Abraham Cahan, who was later to become the famous editor of the *Jewish Daily Forward (Forverts).* Sensing that many of the listeners had not understood either the German or Russian speeches, Cahan suggested that Jewish workers should be addressed in Yiddish. He volunteered to make a speech in Yiddish himself, and the experiment was made six weeks later. That first socialist speech in Yiddish, according to a participant in the meeting, Bernard Weinstein, "kindled a flame of excitement

and enthusiasm . . . as if the mute had begun to speak and the deaf had begun to
hear. . . ."

The Propaganda Society ceased to exist
in less than a year. Some of the society's
leaders were unrealistically ambitious for
it, and others, especially members of the
Am Olam, gradually drifted away to other
cities.

In June 1884 another attempt to organize Jewish socialists was made in the
form of a Russian Workers' Union, whose
members were in reality neither Russians nor workers, but Jewish intellectuals
who spoke Russian. Somewhat later the
Russian Labor Lyceum came into existence.
Both organizations were short-lived.

A new chapter began early in 1885. As it
gradually became clear that the mass of the
new Jewish immigrants would remain in
the cities, Jewish workers began to organize, and the importance of Yiddish became
ever more obvious; the Russian-Jewish
Workers' Union, organized in February
1885, conducted most of its lectures in Yiddish. Two months later it united with an
organized group of Hungarian and Galician workers and socialists under the simple
name of Jewish Workers' Union.

The Jewish Workers' Union was the first
systematic effort of the Jewish intellectuals
to organize the workers. In the few years
of its existence the Union accomplished a
good deal both in propaganda and in organization. On its initiative, the Anti-
Sweating League was organized in 1886,
with a membership of union leaders and
social reformers. From the first the Jewish
Workers' Union tried to link Jewish labor
with the general labor movement.

The Union's attempt to raise funds for
the publication of a labor weekly failed. On
June 25, 1886, however, there appeared a
newspaper of socialist orientation—the *New
Yorker Yiddishe Folkszeitung* — which,
though privately owned, was recognized as
deserving the full support of labor.

III. THE FORMATIVE YEARS
(1887-1900)

1. THE UNITED HEBREW TRADES

It took some time before the Jewish
workers and the Jewish socialist intelligentsia found themselves and their social
and political thinking became more or less
crystallized. The era of experimentation
and searching was far from over, debate
was still intense, and there were as many
failures as successes. But there was one important difference in comparison with the
early years: the period between 1887 and
1900 witnessed the formation of the most
important Jewish labor organizations,
which exist to this day and which have left
their special mark on the entire course of
Jewish life in America.

This began with the founding of the
United Hebrew Trades in 1888. Only a
year later the Jewish socialists sent a delegate to the first congress of the Second Socialist International. The first socialist and
anarchist periodicals—the *Varheit,* the *Arbeter Zeitung* and the *Freie Arbeter Shtime*
—appeared in 1889-90, and in 1892 the first
Jewish socialist monthly, the *Zukunft,*
came out. The Workmen's Circle *(Arbeter
Ring)* was founded in the same year. The
publication of the first socialist daily in
Yiddish — the *Abend-Blatt* — was begun in
1894. Three years later the *Jewish Daily
Forward (Forverts)* began to appear. The
United Garment Workers came into being
in 1891, and the International Ladies' Garment Workers' Union in 1900.

Simultaneously there was a flowering of
Jewish socialist literature, another evidence
of the special conditions attending the development of the Jewish labor movement
in America. The most important Jewish
poets and prose writers of the time—Morris
Vinchevsky, Morris Rosenfeld, Joseph Bovshover, David Edelstadt, Abraham Cahan,
Jacob Gordin, Abraham Liesin, Leon Kobrin, and many others—dedicated their talents to the labor movement. Some of the
most gifted Jewish writers knew what a
sweatshop was from personal experience.

The most important event in the life of Jewish labor in the late Eighties was the founding of the United Hebrew Trades. As we have seen, conditions in the needle trades were not very favorable for the building of strong unions. The immigrants lacked the experience to maintain stable unions, to conduct negotiations with employers, and to preserve the necessary discipline among the workers. It was also impossible to maintain a paid union staff. The Jewish socialists therefore realized that it was necessary to start "at the top," to quote J. Magidov, the initiator of the plan. It was decided that a central organization should be established to stimulate the creation of a network of unions in the Jewish trades. The United Hebrew Trades was formed with the initial participation of three unions having a combined membership of fewer than eighty persons. Six months later the UHT comprised eleven unions with a total membership of some 1,200. By 1890 the number had risen to 22 unions with a membership of close to 6,000.

DAVID EDELSTADT (1866-1892)

2. THE JEWISH QUESTION AND THE SOCIALIST INTERNATIONAL

The United Hebrew Trades was founded by socialists, and this was clearly reflected in its character and activities for many years to come. Morris Hillquit, a young shirtmaker and a former student from Riga, who later rose to eminence as a labor lawyer and socialist theoretician, was its first corresponding secretary. Inevitably the new body was drawn into the ideological conflicts that were to have such a divisive effect on the Jewish trade union movement in the Nineties.

Although the Jewish socialists of that period did not consider it necessary to formulate their attitude toward Jewish problems, they were unable to ignore the fact of the special position of the Jews in the world. The mere fact of their helping to

form separate Jewish labor organizations had provoked discussions at the very outset, both among Jewish leaders and in the general movement. Samuel Gompers had also expressed his doubt about the desirability of creating separate foreign-language trade unions. Experience, however, had shown that the founders of the United Hebrew Trades, who could cite the example of the United German Trades, were on the right track.

The Jewish socialist press and socialist literature developed *pari passu* with the trade union movement. In February 1889 the anarchist *Varheit* was launched to close down five months later. On March 7, 1890, there appeared the first issue of the *Arbeter Zeitung*, the beginning of what was later the widespread Jewish socialist press in the United States. Three months later the anarchist *Freie Arbeter Shtime* began to appear and has been in existence since then as an influential libertarian and literary publication. In 1890 an attempt was

MORRIS HILLQUIT (1870-1933)

dlers, that none of them earns an honest living—at such a time it is more important than ever to show the world that the Jews have not only workers, but also a labor movement, and a progressive and strong one at that. The United Hebrew Trades of New York has thoroughly understood the need and utility of sending a representative of the Jewish labor movement to the Congress of the International in Brussels, in order to show the world what Jewish workers can accomplish in a country where they have the same rights as everyone else.

In Brussels, Abraham Cahan, the delegate of the United Hebrew Trades, introduced the following question for discussion: "What must be the attitude of the organized workers of all countries toward the Jewish problem?" In order to clarify his question, Cahan published a pamphlet containing information on the Jewish labor movement in America, and on the persecution of Jews in various countries. As Cahan writes in his memoirs, the very fact

also made to establish a central organization, uniting Jewish workers throughout the country (the United Hebrew Trades representing only the Jewish workers in New York). The convention of Jewish labor organizations in the United States and Canada, which opened on Saturday, October 4, 1890, was attended by 87 delegates from 36 organizations, with a combined membership of fourteen thousand. However, the efforts to create a permanent organization did not succeed.

In 1891 the United Hebrew Trades once more decided to send a delegate to the Congress of the Socialist International in Brussels. An appeal "To All the Jewish Unions and Labor Organizations in America" was published in the *Arbeter Zeitung* on June 26, 1891. It read, in part, as follows:

> At a time when the Jew is everywhere regarded and treated as a savage beast, hounded and persecuted at every step, when the anti-Semites are shouting in unison that all Jews are only bloodsuckers, thieves, robbers and swin-

S. JANOVSKI (1864-1939), FOR MANY YEARS EDITOR OF THE *FREIE ARBETER SHTIME*

of the existence of Jewish workers was a "pleasant surprise" to many of the delegates who had believed that "all Jews are bankers." On the other hand, such prominent socialist leaders as Paul Singer and Victor Adler were extremely displeased that the Jewish question had been placed on the agenda, and tried to induce Cahan to withdraw his motion. They were afraid that the anti-Semites would argue that the Socialist International was taking Jewish capitalists under its protection. Cahan, however, persisted in his motion, and introduced a resolution condemning the anti-Semitic persecutions. In the debate two French delegates opposed Cahan's resolution on the ground that there were not only anti-Semitic but also "philo-Semitic" persecutions. Finally, the Congress adopted an absurd compromise resolution, condemning both anti-Semitism and "philo-Semitism."

Although this resolution could not, of course, satisfy the Jewish socialists, Cahan's attempt was of historic significance. It showed that even the socialists in Europe had no conception whatever of Jewish problems and were still not free of certain anti-Semitic prejudices. That this changed as time went on was partly due to the fact that the question had been raised. To be sure, the Dreyfus affair and the work of men like Emile Zola and Jean Jaurès were very important; the beginning, however, was made by the courageous resolution of the delegate of the United Hebrew Trades in 1891.

3. YIDDISH PRESS AND LITERATURE

Meantime, the Yiddish press and literature, which we have touched on earlier, continued to make impressive gains. In a relatively short time the *Arbeter Zeitung* attained a circulation of some 8,000. The socialist monthly *Zukunft* had the ambitious goal of dealing with the theory and problems of social science. The *Arbeter Zeitung,* the *Freie Arbeter Shtime,* like the daily *Abend-Blatt,* also treated political and

ABRAHAM CAHAN (1860-1951)

social problems very seriously. The best Jewish writers published their work in the socialist press. Yiddish newspapers, magazines and books became a major educational factor on the East Side and among Jews in America generally. An independent thinker of the caliber of Morris R. Cohen has given the following characterization of the Jewish socialist press in the last years of the nineteenth century:

> . . . What chiefly helped me in attaining an understanding of the ways of my adopted country was the Jewish press, principally the old *Arbeiter Zeitung,* which Abraham Cahan, Benjamin Feigenbaum and Philip Krantz edited and to which the old grandfather of the Jewish Socialist movement, Morris Vinchevsky, frequently sent letters from England. I owe a good deal of my education to the Yiddish press. It taught me to look at world news from a cosmopolitan instead of a local or provincial point of view, and it taught me to interpret politics realistically, instead of being misled by empty phrases.

As I look back on the Yiddish and the English press in the last decade of the nineteenth century, I cannot help feeling that the former did more for the education of its readers than the latter. Having no army of reporters to dig up sensational news, the Yiddish press necessarily paid more attention to things of permanent interest. It tried to give its readers something of enduring and substantial value. . . . The Yiddish press has prepared millions of Jewish people to take a worthy part in American civilization while also promoting the natural self-respect to which Jews are entitled because of their character and history (*A Dreamer's Journey*, p. 219).

4. STRUGGLE FOR RECOGNITION AND HUMAN DIGNITY

Upon coming to America the immigrants clustered together and tried to recreate the *shtetl* in the guise of the *landsmanshaft*. The Jewish immigrants from Russia felt little sympathy for the oppressive Tsarist empire, but they longed for their families and were nostalgic about their native towns.

The *landsmanshaft*, however, could not substitute for the *shtetl*. In the turmoil of the great city the immigrant felt isolated and forlorn, with the alienation of one who has been uprooted from his old home and who has not yet struck roots in new soil. Economic adaptation was achieved most quickly, while cultural and social integration proceeded at a much more laborious pace.

Because in his first years in America the immigrant had little time for anything except material survival, it is not surprising that economic success became his chief ambition, and that its attainment also paved the way to social recognition. Material success became the yardstick with which all values were measured, and this, in turn, engendered indifference for spiritual values, particularly the cultural traditions of the old home. The "allrightnick" was not content with his place in economic life but asserted a claim also to the position of spiritual leadership.

For many immigrants financial success was synonymous with Americanization — a fallacious conception based on partial truth. America was built by pioneers confident in their strength and luck. Faith in the individual contributed greatly to the fantastic growth of America. In a land of unlimited opportunities consistent effort nearly always paid off in the end, at least as long as America was a land of independent farmers and reasonably small business enterprises. Out of this experience had grown the cult of the self-made man, which was sanctioned by the prevailing religious philosophy in Colonial America. The Calvinist Puritan ethic elevated man's economic activities to the level of a religious commandment: work is an important way to serve God; every man must therefore work hard and respect his calling; labor, commerce, even finance are basic elements of the divine scheme for man.

Material success is therefore a visible token of grace, and it is only natural that the successful should be well satisfied with themselves. In his book *Puritanism and Democracy* Ralph Barton Perry writes:

> According to this philosophy, if a man is rich he has himself to thank; if he is destitute he has himself to blame. The rich man is an object of commendation, and not merely of envy; to be a pauper is not a misfortune, but a disgrace (p. 302).

From this it follows, as a matter of principle, that there is no room for radical social reforms. Since God chose to create the poor, we must not interfere with his plan:

> Poverty being a sign of spiritual weakness, the Puritan cure would be found in reprobation. Poverty is to be condemned rather than pitied or relieved (*Ibid.*, p. 304).

This theory was made to order for the pioneers of capitalism. It spared them many sleepless nights and relieved their conscience of the nagging doubt: Why do

I deserve such good fortune, and what sin has my brother committed that he must live in need? The philosophy of success left no room for the type of problem which faced the Biblical Job.

The Jewish historical experience, however, had been of a different kind, and Jewish thought was preoccupied with those who failed despite all efforts. Job's problem and the Jewish problem were basically alike, and to the question posed by the existence of suffering in the world, the Jews counterposed the old answer of faith in the coming of a new world at the end of time. This old, yet ever-new, Jewish solution to the problem of suffering was now propounded by the tailors and cloakmakers of the East Side.

It is impossible to account for the unique response of the East Side to socialist propaganda without taking into consideration the messianic tradition in Judaism. To the Jewish masses socialism was infinitely more than the program of a political party, even more than the dream of a beautiful future. For the workers of the East Side socialism was a new faith which helped them endure the great hardships and disappointments of everyday life. What is more, socialism bolstered their faith in themselves; it saved them from despair and from loss of respect for themselves and for their fellows in need.

For the East Side workers dignity was not less important than bread. In the *shtetl* everyone was recognized as a distinctive personality, everyone had a recognized status, even if on the lower rungs of the social ladder. In the metropolis, on the other hand, individuality was threatened. Of what account is an individual among millions of his fellows?

Much of the unrest of our time is the result of society's pressure for depersonalization. The *mass man* refuses to become reconciled to his fate. He resents having to remain a mass man all his life. He wants recognition as an individual. The conflict between rich and poor is becoming overshadowed by the conflict between those who count, the class of *somebodies,* and the great and nameless mass lost in the turmoil of modern life, the class of *nobodies*. The East Side fought with special vigor against this trend toward depersonalization.

Today we can scarcely grasp what the teaching of the socialist propagandists, who stressed the unimportance of individual success and the insignificance of money as a yardstick for social values, meant for the poor workers of the East Side. If the poor were indeed the righteous ones, and if the workers were the true creators of wealth for society, then the poor laborers need not be ashamed of their status. Socialism restored their sense of worth, aroused their individual pride, and gave them a confident hope in the future.

The pioneers of the Jewish labor movement, besides giving the Jewish worker a sense of his own dignity, also contributed to the respect with which the East Side came to be regarded in the non-Jewish world. Above all, they won for the Jewish worker the respect of the general labor movement. The conditions prevailing in the sweatshops of the East Side were not of a kind to win the sympathy of organized labor. But this attitude changed almost overnight when a series of bitter strikes in the garment industry aroused public opinion, and the world became aware that the Jewish workers knew how to defend their rights and their human dignity.

5. INTERNAL STRIFE

The bitter factional and partisan conflict which marked the Nineties had a particularly bad effect on the development of the Jewish trade unions. The United Hebrew Trades, for instance, entered the Nineties with thirty-three member unions, and emerged with barely three. If the political propaganda of the various groups was of great help in building many trade union organizations, the constant internal friction destroyed even more. However, one extremely important result was achieved. The existence of the unions in the needle trades, as a decisive factor in regulating

JOSEPH BARONDESS (1867-1928)

and off, for nearly a decade, he took an active part in the cloak strikes of the Nineties. In later years Barondess drifted out of labor and socialist affiliations, though he always displayed warm sympathy for the cause of the cloakmakers, if not for all their leaders. He also acted as arbitrator in many union-employer conflicts in a number of garment trades at the request of both parties.

The 1890 strike started a series of bitter conflicts in the cloak industry, breaking out every work season for a number of years. The situation became more complicated as a result of factional clashes between the anarchists and the socialists in the cloak union. In this seemingly endless friction, personal ambitions made themselves felt on both sides.

To all this was added the bane of "dual unionism," which did so much to poison the atmosphere in the needle trades during the Nineties. The fratricidal struggle between rival unions was not confined to the Jewish unions alone, those being the years when rivalry between the Knights of Labor and the American Federation of Labor was at its height. Dual unions had been formed in many trades, and the struggle between the two large labor organizations could not help affecting the Jewish unions as well.

As a result of party conflicts and personal quarrels, leadership in some of the unions came into the hands of unscrupulous men and groups, who often exploited the resources and the prestige of the labor organizations for their private ends. Many capable and idealistic leaders, it is true, were already active in the Jewish labor movement at the time. However, as the union expanded, it became necessary to recruit subordinate leaders. There were enough generals, but there appeared to be a shortage of other officers for the intermediate and lower posts. This situation first began to change a decade later, with the immigration of thousands of workers who had already been trained in the socialist and labor movement in Tsarist Russia.

working conditions, was now recognized both by the workers and by an increasing number of the employers, as well as by public opinion. The workday was shortened and conditions in the shop were improved.

The struggle for union recognition during that decade began with the great strike of the cloakmakers in 1890. The strike broke out spontaneously, but soon the workers appealed to the United Hebrew Trades for leadership. The UHT accepted the invitation and tried to introduce some order into the conduct of the strike and the distribution of assistance to the needy. The strike was led by Joseph Barondess, who very soon won the complete confidence of the workers.

Barondess, a colorful figure with a great personal following, especially among the cloakmakers, was not a hard-working organizer, but he exerted tremendous influence over worker audiences by his oratory. On

But the gravest crisis in the Jewish labor movement came as a result of the conflicts in the ranks of the socialist movement itself. The leadership of the Socialist Labor Party had launched a systematic campaign for hegemony in the labor movement, and in 1890 open conflict broke out. The question at issue was whether branches of the SLP could join a central city body of the American Federation of Labor. The problem arose in New York, where the New York branch of the SLP wanted to join the Central Labor Federation of New York. The socialists argued that the SLP was not only a political party, but also a worker's organization. In this dispute the opposite point of view, voiced by Samuel Gompers, prevailed and SLP branches were not permitted to join the AFL.

Open warfare followed between the SLP and the AFL, the SLP urging its followers and the unions under its influence to join the Knights of Labor. This caused a great deal of disturbance in the Jewish unions, since these were predominantly under SLP influence.

But the situation involved more than a fight between the Socialists and the AFL. In 1892 Daniel De Leon became the editor of *The People,* the organ of the SLP. De Leon was a man of ascetic and fanatical temperament. He admitted of no compromise and fought all his opponents as hard as he could, not hesitating to resort to calumny and slander. It must be said, however, that, though he had little regard for parliamentary methods in the fights with his opponents, the SLP leader never repudiated the democratic idea.

De Leon's attempts to seize control of the Knights of Labor failed, although he came close to his goal. The failure aggravated De Leon's bitterness even further, and he decided that the only way to attain leadership of the labor movement was through an uncompromising fight with the existing labor organizations and the establishment of outspokenly socialist unions. Accordingly, at the end of 1895 the Socialist Trade and Labor Alliance was set up by the SLP as a rival organization challenging the existing unions.

The United Hebrew Trades was among the first organizations to join the Alliance. In the Jewish labor movement generally, however, De Leon's policies evoked great dissatisfaction, for he resorted to the same methods in fighting his opponents within the party that he used in fighting those outside. It therefore required great courage to criticize the SLP leadership. Nevertheless, we find sharp criticism of De Leon's methods in the *Arbeter Zeitung* of November 1895. Commenting on his struggle against both large labor organizations, the *Arbeter Zeitung* said:

> We must say candidly that we are not in the least pleased with Comrade De Leon's "victory" and his entire "struggle," particularly in both national labor organizations. Comrade De Leon goes much too far in his accusations and attacks against the "pure and simple" unionists and the "labor fakers," and it seems to be his mania to attack and fight them on every suitable and unsuitable occasion. . . . These quarrelsome and intolerant tactics are a misfortune to our party and have created enemies among friends of socialism.

Opposition to De Leon's intransigeance grew, while within the Jewish movement additional grounds for friction were accumulating. Some of the intellectuals, who had begun as workers in the shops, in time acquired academic education and became professional people, but they remained in the movement, in which they held leading positions. This development only served to intensify personal rivalries among some of the leaders.

By early 1893 there were clear indications of conflict in the Jewish socialist movement. The opposition was headed by the most prominent orators and writers: Abraham Cahan, Louis Miller and, later, Morris Vinchevsky. Control of the *Arbeter Zeitung* (and, after 1894, of the *Abend-Blatt* as well) was in the hands of the

LOUIS MILLER (1866-1927)

Arbeter Zeitung Publishing Association, which was accused by the opposition of having become a closed group, admitting no new members. Cahan and Miller demanded that control of the party press be placed directly in the hands of a board consisting of representatives of socialist and labor organizations. The organizations in a number of smaller cities were also dissatisfied. The sharpest criticism came from Boston, where the opposition published its own organ, *Emes* (Truth), under the editorship of Morris Vinchevsky, at that time the most eminent Jewish socialist writer, who had come to the United States from London at the end of 1894.

The struggle was directed mainly against the SLP and De Leon's tactics. The point of highest tension was reached after the founding of the Socialist Trade and Labor Alliance. The political and ideological nature of the struggle against De Leonism had now become clear to the rank and file as well. De Leon's politics were the politics of a sect, while socialism in the Jewish neighborhoods of New York and other cities was already a popular movement. The party strife had thus become a fight for the independence of the Jewish labor movement.

6. FOUNDING OF THE *Forverts*

The atmosphere became more and more charged until finally, on January 7, 1897, an open split occurred. The opposition left the Arbeter Zeitung Publishing Association and created its own press fund for the publication of another newspaper. The appeal of the opposition found a strong response among the workers. In a relatively short time the necessary sum was raised, and the first issue of the *Forverts* appeared on April 22, 1897. Bernard Weinstein, one of the most active members of the opposition, provides the following picture of the mood of the workers at the fund-raising meetings:

> Remarkable scenes of enthusiasm and sacrifice took place at these meetings. Men and women workers gave more than they could. Instead of money, many of them took off their rings and watches and flung them into the hats which were passed around the hall by the committees (*Jewish Unions in America,* p. 183).

The founding of the *Forverts* was as significant a turning point in the history of Jewish life in America as the organization of the Bund, some six months later, was in Jewish life in Russia. The same year also witnessed the first Zionist congress in Basel, a historic event in the Jewish life of our time. And although there is no direct connection among the three events, they were all an expression of radical changes in the Jewish world. The Jew had come to have greater faith in his capacity to determine his own destiny.

While the *Abend-Blatt* was bound by De Leon's policies, the *Forverts* was much more free, and the opposition, which soon left the SLP, was now able to pay greater heed to the readers and to give more attention to the needs and interests of the masses. This was expressed most clearly in the attitude toward the Dreyfus case, which deeply stirred the Jewish people at that time. While the *Abend-Blatt* held that the Dreyfus affair was a squabble among capitalists that had no particular significance to the working class, the *Forverts* unequivocally took the side of Dreyfus. A similar situation developed with the outbreak of the Spanish-American War. Here, too, the *Forverts* was closer to the feelings of the Jewish masses, who were unable to forget the Spanish Inquisition and who regarded the United States as a land of freedom for themselves and their children.

At the same time the *Forverts* group created the Federated Hebrew Trades as a rival to the United Hebrew Trades, which went along with De Leon's Socialist Trade and Labor Alliance. A number of unions avoided both central organizations. The consequence was the practical disintegration of the United Hebrew Trades.

In the SLP, meanwhile, the internal crisis was becoming more acute. Though in the elections of 1898 De Leon's party achieved its greatest success, this was the last occasion on which the SLP still represented the American socialist movement. The hardest blow to the SLP came with the split of 1899, when a group of prominent leaders, headed by Morris Hillquit, left the party. At first the dissident group declared that *it* was the party, and that it had the right to the name and property of the SLP. There were even fist fights for the possession of the party offices. In the end De Leon succeeded, with the aid of the "capitalist" courts, in retaining the name and the property of the party for his group.

The followers of De Leon also managed to retain control of the *Abend-Blatt,* although the editor, Philip Krantz, and some of its leading contributors sympathized with the so-called "kangaroos," as De Leon called those who had split off.

The Jewish segment of the "kangaroos" at first had no intention of joining the *Forverts* group. For a time they even tried to

BERNARD WEINSTEIN (1866-1946)

publish their own Yiddish newspaper (*Folkszeitung*). But there was not enough room for three Yiddish-language socialist newspapers, and after six months it closed down.

The split of 1899 had finally made possible a thorough reorganization of the socialist forces in the country generally, and of the Jewish socialist movement particularly. It was not easy to create a new united socialist party, but by the time of the 1900 Presidential campaign an understanding had been reached. Eugene V. Debs, the renowned leader of the great Pullman strike of 1894, was the unanimous choice of the non-SLP Socialists for President. In that election Debs polled almost 100,000 votes, compared with the approximately 33,000 votes of the SLP. In the summer of 1901, in Indianapolis, the most important socialist organizations finally united and formed the Socialist Party of the United States, under the leadership of Eugene V. Debs, Morris Hillquit, Victor L. Berger, and others.

Early in 1899 the United Hebrew Trades also left De Leon's Alliance. This made possible the reunification of the Jewish trade union movement, and the two central Jewish labor bodies reunited in 1899 under the old name of United Hebrew Trades.

Symptomatic of the new atmosphere that had now developed was the formation, in June 1900, of the International Ladies' Garment Workers' Union, the first nationwide labor union with a distinctive Jewish character. In 1900 another important event took place as the Workmen's Circle Association, which had been a local organization, became the Workmen's Circle Order. The Workmen's Circle was now able to establish branches all over the country. Indeed, in a very short time it became the most important and stable Jewish labor organization in the United States.

Thus the foundation was laid for the "golden age" of the Jewish labor movement in America. As the first great wave of Jewish immigration was about to approach its end, new vistas, with a brighter economic and political outlook, were opening up for the Jews of the New World.

IV. THE "GOLDEN AGE" (1901-1918)

1. A TURNING POINT IN SOCIALIST THINKING

The 20th century began in an atmosphere of high optimism. Economic conditions in Europe were improving and the stream of immigrants from the industrialized countries in Western and Central Europe had slowed down to a trickle. In politics, the democratic and progressive forces were making important gains. This progress had a marked effect on socialist thinking everywhere. The extremist wings were weakened, while the reformist wing, which now had its theoretical spokesman in the person of Eduard Bernstein, became stronger. While officially the opponents of orthodox revolutionary Marxist ideology remained almost everywhere in the minority, in practice the movement in most of Europe and America favored evolutionary socialism.

In Russia, however, where the denial of human rights continued to intensify the revolutionary mood among the workers and other major sections of the population, the profound unrest that precedes revolution prevailed. The Jews of Russia had become more hopeful. Some of them vaguely hoped that the impending revolution would bring about a general improvement of Jewish life in Russia, and even the less optimistic were far from despair, for beyond the borders of Russia there was a free and open world. Above all, the doors of America were open.

This openness of the world's frontiers was clearly reflected in the statistics. Jewish emigration from Eastern Europe now reached its highest point. In the course of the fourteen years from the beginning of the century until the outbreak of the First World War, an average of 100,000 Jews emigrated to America every year. As a result of this immigration, as well as of natural increase, the Jewish community in America almost tripled in size. And the number of Jewish wage-earners in the big cities increased in about the same proportion.

2. THE "SECOND WAVE"

This second wave of Jewish mass immigration included a large number of politically mature people. In Russia there had arisen an independent Jewish labor movement, which evoked the admiration of Jews and socialists for its discipline and heroism. This movement consisted primarily of the General Jewish Worker's Union (the Bund) which has contributed a glorious chapter to the Jewish history of our time.

The conditions in which the Jewish socialist movement developed in Russia were quite different from those in America. In Russia normal political and trade union work was quite impossible. Socialist activity was carried on underground, and involved constant risks. Nor was it legal even to wage the purely economic struggle. The general political oppression was further aggravated for the Jews by their lack of elementary civil rights and the difficult economic life in the Jewish Pale of Settlement. All this created an atmosphere of idealism and heroic romanticism around the socialist movement in Russia generally. And with the emergence of the Bund revolutionary enthusiasm among the Jewish socialists in Russia and America rose even higher.

It was an event of the greatest historical importance when, after generations without political rights, the Jews in Russia now suddenly felt that they could fight for their rights and that they were not alone in their struggle. The Bund had thus undertaken a great national mission, that of fighting for the rights and honor of the Jewish people against the oppression and tyranny of Tsarism.

It was no wonder, therefore, that the new immigrants were unable at first to adapt themselves to the conditions of the legal, democratic, and consequently more prosaic life in America, which lacked the romantic aura of underground struggle and heroism. This often caused clashes and misunderstandings between the "old" and the "new" immigrants. In time, however, the new arrivals were able to adjust themselves and to cooperate in full measure in the organizations established by the earlier immigrants.

At the same time the general American labor movement was also making substantial progress. The old Knights of Labor gradually lost influence, and the AFL assumed unchallenged leadership. Within a relatively short time the number of workers in the AFL reached almost two million. A similar development took place in the socialist movement. The SLP lost more and more of its influence and was reduced to the state of an insignificant sect, while the Socialist Party (SP) came to be generally recognized as the party representing socialism in America. Socialist sentiment continued to grow and was becoming a force in the general life of the country, although electoral victories were few. Throughout this period the socialists man-

aged to elect only two representatives to Congress: Victor Berger from Milwaukee and Meyer London from New York's East Side.

Even more pronounced was the growth of the Jewish labor movement. The circulation of the *Forverts* rose from seven or eight thousand at the beginning of this period to 200,000 in 1916, and the Workmen's Circle grew from a small group of a few hundred at the turn of the century to more than 60,000 in 1917.

3. INTERNAL MUTATIONS

The entire structure of the Jewish labor movement was now different from what it had been in the Nineties, and also very different, internally and externally, from the Jewish labor movement in Russia. While the socialist ideology had not lost its influence over the Jewish workers, a change was beginning to manifest itself toward socialism as a political party movement. Since most workers had become weary of internal political quarrels and had lost some of their faith in the political leadership, there was little room for the kind of rigid centralization symbolized by the old SLP. The ranks of the faithful followers of De Leon among the Jewish workers had shrunk to the vanishing point, and April 13, 1902, marked the last appearance of the *Abend-Blatt* — the first socialist daily to be published in Yiddish. There was left only the weekly *Arbeter Zeitung*. Seven months later even this modest weekly ceased to appear.

The Jewish labor movement had become more independent as the socialist energies of many Jewish workers were increasingly centered around the *Forverts* and the Workmen's Circle. A major reason for this shift was that the Jewish worker was beginning to demand more of socialism than political discussions and even political campaigns. He felt a greater need for a daily newspaper and an intimate group of friends sharing his outlook on life, such as he found in the Workmen's Circle.

The *Forverts,* the Jewish trade unions and the Workmen's Circle all supported the Socialist Party, but at the same time they were careful to preserve their complete freedom and the Socialist Party, for its part, was adapting itself gradually to the conditions of American life. It was growing more American in its membership, and it did not seek to interfere in the internal affairs of its allied labor organizations or to issue orders in the SLP manner.

Simultaneously the Jewish workers' groups were becoming more Jewish. The influx of new immigrants strengthened interest in the fate of the Jews in Russia and in Jewish problems generally. The new immigrants saw it as their duty to help their comrades who had remained at home to carry on revolutionary work. All the points of view within the Russian socialist movement and, above all, the Bund were now represented in America. A branch of the Bund was formed in New York as early as 1900, several branches were later organized in a number of cities, and in 1904 some fifty Bund branches were united in the Central Union of Bund Organizations. The Central Union devoted itself principally to providing material assistance to the Bund in Russia. Similar groups were also created by followers of other Jewish and general socialist trends in Russia.

The Bundist immigration brought a stream of Jewish national energy. In Russia the Bund had assumed leadership in the struggle for Jewish rights. But very soon it became necessary to understand what was meant by Jewish rights. Did they consist only of civil and political rights, or did they include national rights as well — the right of the Jews to lead their own lives and to preserve their own culture. Conditions in Russia and the ideological struggle with Zionist tendencies compelled the Bund to ponder the problem of Jewish existence as a people. The greater the movement grew in influence and prestige, the more it felt its responsibility for the fate of the entire people.

After long and searching discussions, the Bund adopted its program of national autonomy. It was not easy for the Bund to combat the assimilationist prejudices which were so widespread among socialists. The Russian Social Democrats and a large number of prominent Jewish socialists looked upon the Bund program of national autonomy as a nationalist heresy. It was difficult for them to accept the idea that the Jews should be regarded as a separate national group with its own cultural life. On the other hand, some Jewish socialists felt that the Bund did not go far enough. National autonomy in *galut,* they thought, could not assure the existence of the Jews as a people. Furthermore, the Jewish socialists who had Zionist leanings did not share the Bund's optimism concerning the safety of the Jews in a democratic world. Thus there developed a Socialist-Zionist school of thought which attempted to combine Marxist socialism with the old Jewish dream of a return to Zion.

Under the influence of developments in Russia, some notable socialist writers in America urged the need for a separate Jewish socialist party like the Bund. The first to raise this question was Morris Vinchevsky in 1902. The discussion continued for some time without tangible results. But the debate concerning socialism and the Jewish fate turned in a different direction in 1903, with the news of the pogrom in Kishinev. To us today, after the frightful Hitler massacres, it is hard to believe that the Kishinev pogrom shook the Jewish world so deeply. At that period, however, people still sincerely believed in the sacredness of human life and the world could still be stirred by the fate of a few innocent victims.

The shock was so profound that some of the socialist and anarchist leaders of the older generation, who had for years simply ignored the very existence of the Jewish problem, were now overcome by a sense of guilt. "In our enthusiasm for the socialist dream," some of them declared, "we have forgotten the tragic needs of our own brothers." Such prominent and active anarchist leaders as Hillel Zolotarov and Moshe Katz now found their way "back to the people." And the way back to the people led them to Zionist-Socialism.

The bulk of the movement did not go so far, some socialists even becoming alarmed at the "nationalist epidemic." But the re-awakened nationalist mood served to pre-pare the ground for the emergence of more nationally-conscious trends among Jewish radical groups. In 1903 there was formed in New York the National Radical Union of Poale Zion. There had also come into existence, in addition to the large number of Bundist groups, several Jewish groups directly connected with the Socialist Party. In 1907, at a convention in Rochester, N. Y., there was organized the Jewish Agi-tation Bureau of the United States and Canada. This Agitation Bureau, however, had few achievements to record. It was dissolved in 1912, giving way to the Jew-ish Socialist Federation, which set itself broader goals.

The intensified national feelings among Jewish workers had not lessened their in-terest in the general problems of American labor. This was clearly evidenced at the time of the kidnapping and trial of the leaders of the Western Federation of Min-ers, Charles H. Moyer, Bill Heywood and George Pettibone, in 1906. This trial, a brazen violation of the most elementary rules of justice, outraged the feelings of organized labor and liberals and gave rise to a campaign of protests and appeals, in which the Jewish workers were among the most active participants. Moyer-Heywood-Pettibone Defense Conferences were or-ganized in New York, Philadelphia, Chi-cago and other cities, and there were many demonstrations on the East Side.

In a purely organizational sense, the Jewish socialist movement could not claim any significant achievements during the first decade of this century. Election results were also disappointing. It was not until 1906 that election campaigns met with sub-

HILLEL ZOLOTAROV (1865-1921)

stantial moral success on the East Side, at any rate.

4. "WORKERS" OR "TRADESMEN?"

Developments in the trade union field were not much better. In 1900-01 a wave of strikes spread through the Jewish trades, the most noteworthy of which was the great strike of thirty thousand men's tailors in New York in the summer of 1901, ending in partial success. A year later another gen-eral strike broke out among the New York men's tailors, this time unsuccessfully. The industry still suffered from the old malady of seasonal strikes and seasonal unions. The complaint that the Jewish workers were good strikers but poor union members still seemed valid. Many people regarded this as virtually a national trait, rooted in the Jewish character and tradition. Thus, Pro-fessor John R. Commons, the noted labor historian, in a special study of labor con-ditions on the East Side wrote:

The Jew's conception of a labor or-ganization is that of a tradesman rather than that of a workman. In the manufacture of clothing, whenever any real abuse arises among the Jewish workmen, they all come together and form a giant union and at once engage in a strike. They bring in ninety-five percent of the trade. They are energetic and determined. . . . They stay out a long time, even under the greatest of suffering. During a strike, large numbers are to be found with almost nothing to live upon and their families suffering, still insisting, on the streets and in the halls, that their great cause must be won.

But when once the strike is settled, either in favor of or against the cause, they are contented, and that usually ends the union, since they do not see any practical use for a union when there is no cause to fight for. The Jew joins the union when it offers a bargain and drops it when he gets, or fails to get, the bargain. The Jew is also exceedingly abstract and metaphysical and greatly interested in general principles. His union is always, therefore, except in time of a strike, a forum for the discussion of socialism and the philosophy of the labor movement (*Report of the U.S. Industrial Commission*, Vol. XV, pp. 319-352).

Professor Commons appears to be utterly baffled by the workers of the old East Side. On the one hand, he marvels at their fighting spirit and endurance, and perceives that the Jewish workers regard their union not merely as the defender of their economic interests but as a forum for the discussion of socialism and the philosophy of the labor movement. On the other hand, Commons asserts that the approach of the Jewish worker toward his union is that of a "tradesman." For an outside observer, even a penetrating and friendly observer like Commons, it was very hard to assess the true mentality of the Jewish workers of that period.

The greater wonder, of course, lies in the fact that, all difficulties notwithstanding, the East Side workers did succeed in achiev-

ing as much as they did during those hard years. Such a close observer of the old East Side as Hillel Rogoff has written:

When the Jewish workers of the East Side began organizing unions they had all the odds against them. By all the accepted standards of the American labor movement the attempt to organize Jewish workers into unions should have proved a miserable failure. Firstly, it was an attempt to organize immigrants, strangers in a new land, at a time when fresh immigrant waves were pouring into the country uninterruptedly. The newcomers appeared ready to invade the shops where the older immigrants were employed and seeking to improve their work conditions.

Secondly, the East Side of that era was under the heel of the most corrupt Tammany machine in New York's annals. The workers, striving to build unions, had to wage battles not only against the employers and "green" strikebreakers but also against the police, the courts, and the entire organized power of the municipality.

Thirdly, there was the grim, bitter poverty of that period. The workers literally had to work every day to have enough to live on. Their trades were seasonal. During the brief work seasons day-and-night toil was the rule, in order to accumulate some savings for the coming "slack" months. The loss of even a part of a season's labor in a strike, therefore, spelled lean and hungry days during the slack time. . . .

Yet the Jewish workers of those early times succeeded in achieving the miracle which other immigrants and groups in other trades and industries were unable to achieve (*Der Wecker*, July 1, 1953).

There was still another factor in these years which distinguished the Jewish workers from American labor in general. At the turn of the century the American unions embraced no more than ten percent of the industrial labor force, and these were chiefly the skilled and better-paid workers.

They were proud of their skills and derived considerable satisfaction from their work, in accordance with their religious, ethical and social values.

The philosophy of craft unionism and pride of trade found little response among the Jewish immigrants, many of whom had come here with totally different outlooks and traditions. The Jewish immigrant, as a rule, was not very happy at his work. He was in most instances, a "Columbus tailor," and was not overly proud of the fact. He did possess an idealized sense of labor's place in society, a concept reinforced by the prevailing socialist thinking, but this had no relation to crafts or special skills.

Perhaps that was why the East Side workers, who showed such enthusiasm for discussing the "philosophy of labor," were attracted in large numbers to organizations like the Workmen's Circle, or the "literary societies" of those days. There were even union leaders who voiced complaints that the Workmen's Circle "diverted the best elements to itself" and "left the trade unions short of intelligent forces." There is no need, however, to prove that the Workmen's Circle, which in numbers alone profited so greatly from the mass influx of Jewish immigrants in the first two decades of the new century, made a major contribution to the building of a stable labor movement, particularly in the needle trades.

5. YEARS OF TRIAL

The deeper reasons for the lag in the development of the Jewish labor movement were altogether different.

It took considerable time for even the most active among the new arrivals to link their destinies firmly to America. During the first years of the century — the years which marked the defeat of the Tsarist armies by Japan, and the outburst of the 1904-1905 revolution inside Russia—many still clung to the hope that the victory of democracy in Russia was in the offing, and that they might be able to return to a free Russia. Furthermore, the American labor movement had little appeal for many of the new immigrants. Only after it had become obvious that the revolutionary upheaval in Russia was defeated did many of the former Bundists and Social Democrats realize that America was their home and that it was time to face the realities of life in this country. Slowly they were preparing themselves for participation in the gigantic mass strikes of 1909-13, which shook Jewish labor.

How deep was the change wrought by the huge conflicts which began in 1909 may be inferred from the upsurge of the clothing unions and the United Hebrew Trades. The International Ladies' Garment Worker's Union (ILGWU), which as we have seen was founded in 1900, made substantial gains during its first few years, its membership growing from 2,310 in 1900 to almost 9,000 in 1903. But the depression of 1903 halted this growth. Another retarding factor was the "open shop" campaign launched by the new National Manufacturers' Association. The International, like the other new unions, obviously was not yet strong enough to fight back effectively. When signs of economic improvement appeared a few years later, several thousand reefer makers struck in New York and won important concessions. But this was soon followed by another severe crisis, which wiped out the hard-won gains. The resulting pessimism was painfully evident at the ninth convention of the ILGWU in Philadelphia, in June 1908. The convention even debated a resolution to liquidate the union and to merge with the United Garment Workers, at that time the union of the men's tailors.

> In every other way, the Philadelphia convention was a sad affair. . . . The thirty-eight delegates who answered the roll call, represented a very small membership. Of these delegates four men came from Boston and two women from Peekskill. All the others were from New York and from Philadelphia. There were no delegates from Chicago, Baltimore, Cleveland, or any

of the other cities represented at the previous conventions. Some of the New York delegates could not pay the railroad fare and walked most of the way to the convention city, using interurban trolley cars part of the way. The reports to the convention were one melancholy tale of disorganization and discouragement (Louis Levine, *The Women's Garment Workers,* p. 139).

It was the darkest period in the history of the Jewish trade union movement. However, as Levine correctly pointed out, it was "the darkness before dawn"; in the course of a few years, there had accumulated in the Jewish districts of New York, Chicago and other cities a vast reserve of spiritual and moral energy which expressed itself in a series of path-blazing demonstrations of labor solidarity.

6. WAISTMAKERS IN THE VAN

The wave of the great strikes began with the "uprising of the twenty thousand." It came unexpectedly. No one would have predicted that young and helpless women workers in the shirtwaist factories of New York would evince so much courage, stubborness and moral discipline in a heroic struggle that would electrify American public opinion.

The general strike of the shirtwaist makers broke out at the end of November 1909. Some eighty percent of the workers were women, and of these by far the largest proportion were girls between the ages of 16 and 25. The New York shirtwaist industry (shirtwaists are now generally called blouses) had in the first decade of the 1900's come to be the second largest women's garment industry, employing more than 25,000 production workers in the metropolitan area. Working conditions in the shirtwaist shops were no better, and in part were even worse, than in the other needle trades. Hours were long, wages were low, the shops were unsafe and unsanitary, and the workers were treated callously. The contractors, all of them men who worked themselves, each employed from three to ten girl apprentices at a wage of three or four dollars a week. The entire trade was practically unorganized, the Waistmakers Union, Local 25 of the ILGWU, having a total membership of a few hundred. Organizing the girls into a union was further complicated by the fact that most of them regarded their work as a temporary interlude before marriage.

Despite these obstacles, the union's leaders launched an intensive campaign in the summer of 1909 and shortly succeeded in carrying out a successful strike of 200 workers employed by the firm of Rosen Bros. The outcome of this strike raised the spirits of the workers in the entire trade and encouraged the leaders of Local 25 to call out on strike the workers employed in two of the largest shirtwaist factories in the industry — the Leiserson and the Triangle firms. It soon became evident, however, that the resources of Local 25 and of the financially weak ILGWU could not overcome the resistance of these large firms. In this emergency the leaders of the strike, among them John A. Dyche, Abraham Baroff and Samuel Schindler, began to think of broadening the fight and calling out the entire trade. This daring plan at first frightened even its initiators, but as it became all too evident that failure of the strike in the Leiserson and Triangle plants would mean the collapse of everything, it was decided to leave the matter to the shirtwaist makers themselves.

A meeting of all the workers in the trade was called for November 22 at Cooper Union. The hall was filled to overflowing, and a thousand workers were sent to neighboring meeting halls. The speakers included Samuel Gompers, Mary E. Dreier (chairman of the Women's Trade Union League), Benjamin Feigenbaum and Meyer London. For two hours the assembled workers listened attentively and in silence. Then a girl rose from the audience and asked for the floor. She was Clara Lemlich, a striker from the Leiserson factory. She ascended the platform and addressed the assembly in Yiddish:

I am a working girl, one of those who are on strike against intolerable conditions. I am tired of listening to speakers who talk in general terms. What we are here for is to decide whether we shall or shall not strike. I offer a resolution that a general strike be declared, now.

A storm of applause broke out. When the crowd had calmed down a little, the chairman called for support of the motion. The entire assembly rose.

The general strike of the waistmakers was on. It was the first large strike of women workers in America. The entire Jewish labor and socialist movement was drawn into the battle. The splendid fighting spirit of the working girls aroused great public sympathy, particularly in the women's suffrage movement. Especially valuable was the help given by the Women's Trade Union League.

The heaviest burden, however, fell upon the strikers themselves. They made up most of the picket lines on the cold winter mornings, and it was mostly they who were arrested and fined. Many of the girls refused to accept the modest aid distributed among the strikers, though in great need of it. Seven hundred and twenty-three women pickets were arrested by December 25, 1909, and nineteen were sentenced to workhouse terms. The attitude of the police and the judges aroused public protest. One of the judges said to a girl picket as he pronounced sentence: "You are on strike against God and nature, whose firm law is that man shall earn his bread in the sweat of his brow. You are on strike against God."

All this persecution failed to intimidate the strikers. A social worker gave the following eloquent description of the typical striker:

Into the foreground of this great moving picture comes the figure of one girl after another as her services are needed. With extraordinary simplicity and eloquence, she will tell before any kind of audience, without any

BENJAMIN FEIGENBAUM (1860-1932)

false shame and without self-glorification, the conditions of her work, her wages, and the pinching poverty of her home and the homes of her comrades. Then she withdraws into the background to undertake quietly the danger and humiliation of picket duty (Louis Levine, *op. cit.*, p. 157).

A committee of society women, including Mrs. Oliver H. P. Belmont, Miss Anne Morgan and Miss Elizabeth Marbury, organized a meeting in the aristocratic Colony Club with the object of presenting to New York society a full picture of the bitter fight of the shirtwaist makers. The meeting was attended by some 150 women, many of them, press reports said, "with fortunes in the seven figures." The meeting collected $1,300 for the strike fund.

The strike lasted a little less than three months. (On December 20, the waistmakers of Philadelphia also struck.) Some individual firms, however, settled with their workers earlier. And although the strikers did not win all their demands, the valiant struggle of the girls added a glorious chapter to the history of the Jewish union movement. The waistmakers paved the way for further labor victories, and the strike also won for the East Side the respect of the more enlightened elements of the community.

The "uprising of the twenty thousand" presented the Jewish labor world with a new question. How was it, many asked themselves, that rich women and the daughters of wealthy families had taken the side of the working girls in the shirtwaist strike? The *Forverts* commented that the help given by the upper-class advocates of women's rights to the waistmakers on strike was "incalculable." Later, however, in an editorial published while the strike was still going on, the *Forverts* warned the Jewish workers "not to allow themselves to be misled by the illusion that the daughters of American millionaires, who are acting in this instance contrary to their social status and economic interests, have become their true allies." Their attitude toward the strike, the editorial went on to say, might be quite different if the interests of their own families were affected. In the final analysis, the strike was to them only a contest between immigrant employers and immigrant workers.

There undoubtedly was a kernel of reality in the *Forverts'* interpretation. Yet the Jewish labor leaders appeared to have realized even then the value of winning the support of public opinion in labor's struggles.

When the waistmakers' strike began, Local 25, as we have seen, had only a tiny membership; at the end of the strike, it numbered more than 10,000 members. Still more important, however, was the fact that the mass of Jewish workers suddenly understood that they were not alone in their fight. Less than five months after the waistmakers returned to work, the even greater strike of the New York cloakmakers was about to begin.

7. THE GREAT REVOLT

Like "the uprising of the twenty thousand," the "Great Revolt" of the cloakmakers, involving nearly 60,000 workers, also made labor history. However, while the waistmakers strike had erupted suddenly, the cloakmakers had more time and opportunity to prepare for their struggle. For a number of years past, the cloakmakers union had not been able to do much to improve conditions in the industry. The employers had complete power over wages and work hours, while the workers were a great mass of unhappy, dissatisfied people. Because in their case the system of subcontracting was a major grievance, the union could not confine its demands to higher wages or shorter hours. This meant a hard and bitter fight.

In December 1909, at the height of the waistmakers' strike, the New York cloakmakers taxed themselves two dollars each to build up a strike fund. An intensive preparatory drive in the shops and through the *Forverts* was launched, and the question of a general strike became the chief topic of discussion in every workshop. In April 1910 the Joint Board of the Cloakmaker's Union began to publish the *Naie Post,* to keep its members in touch with the progress of the campaign. By June the Joint Board locals already numbered 10,000 members, and hundreds of workers daily beleaguered its offices demanding the speedy calling of a general strike before the work season got under way. During the same month the tenth convention of the ILGWU meeting in Boston, adopted a resolution "to make all necessary preparations for a general strike in the cloak industry in New York."

There seemed to be in the air, however, more than routine preparations for a strike, leaders and rank and file workers obviously feeling that they were on the threshold of a great event. The accumulated protest of tens of thousands of men and women against penury and degradation was bursting forth and seeking an outlet.

The mass meeting of the Joint Board on June 28 in Madison Square Garden was phenomenally successful, the greatest labor meeting ever seen in New York until then. AFL President Samuel Gompers and several other top labor leaders spoke. A few days later in a secret ballot 18,771 voted for a general strike, and 615 against. The strike was called for July 7, at two in the afternoon. At the designated hour streams of people began flowing from all sides toward Fifth Avenue.

> Every minute the crowds grew larger, and all moved in the same direction. . . . In many of the streets, cars and trucks had to be stopped because of the crowds. . . . Many of our most devoted members cried for joy, at the idea that their lifelong labors had at last been crowned with success. . . . In my mind I could only picture to myself such a scene taking place when the Jews were led out of Egypt (Abraham Rosenberg, *Memoirs of a Cloakmaker*, p. 208) .

The enthusiasm and the discipline of the first day prevailed throughout the strike, despite all obstacles and provocations. "It is not a strike, it is a popular movement," wrote one of the older socialist leaders. The fact that it had been possible to halt work in the entire trade had galvanized the morale of the strikers, who now became aware of their strength and of their importance to their industry. The well-known poet Abraham Liesin wrote: "The sixty thousand nobodies now became sixty thousand fighters. . . ." The East Side worker, no longer content with a passive role in the factory, had gone on strike for full recognition as a human being and a citizen.

The union's principal demand was that the workers be given a voice in the affairs of the shop in so far as they affected them as workers — abolition of the subcontracting system and adequate sanitation. Next came a series of demands for higher wages and shorter hours.

The greatest resistance of the manufacturers and their association was to the demand for the closed shop. Early efforts to arbitrate were unsuccessful. Louis D. Brandeis, later to become a celebrated Supreme Court Justice, proposed to satisfy both parties by offering as a compromise the "preferential union shop," that is, a shop in which union members would have priority in obtaining jobs, but his plan found no favor at first. The strike dragged on, and as the need among the strikers grew more acute the unions and the *Forverts* launched a campaign for help. Finally, at the initiative of Jacob Schiff and Louis Marshall, a solution was reached. On September 2, the union and the association signed an agreement which became known in industrial history as the Protocol of Peace.

8. PROTOCOL OF PEACE

The Protocol granted the workers a fifty-hour working week, a rise in wages, and abolition of a number of unfair practices, including subcontracting inside the factory. Especially important, however, was the establishment of certain principles. The Protocol created an institution that was entirely new in the history of the industry — the Joint Board of Sanitary Control. Secondly, it established the system of the "preferential" shop, which soon led to the acceptance of the union shop. Thirdly, it introduced a system of settling conflicts and grievances through special committees. A Board of Arbitration was set up to forestall serious conflicts, and was to consist of "one nominee of the manufacturers, one nominee of the unions, and one representative of the public."

As soon as it became known that the strike was over, tens of thousands of ecstatically joyful people began to stream to the *Forverts*. "The scene defied description. . . . It cannot be imagined — it had to be seen," one observer commented.

The philosophy of the Protocol was basically in sharp contrast to the prevailing policies of the Jewish unions. The chief intention of Brandeis and the other initiators of the Protocol method was to prevent economic conflicts, in so far as pos-sible, by negotiation and arbitration with the aid of an impartial third party. Was it possible, however, to achieve peaceful settlements of the conflicts between capital and labor? Many Jewish socialists were more than doubtful on this score in 1910. On the other hand, it was conceded, the Protocol immeasurably strengthened the position of the union in the shops. The union's agents were officially recognized, and they sat as equals with the employers on the various committees set up under the Protocol. This gave the workers a perma-nent stake in the union, thus tending to win them away from the evils of seasonal unionism. The union, in brief, acquired a recognized and firm status.

Still labor opinion was sharply divided between those who favored the Protocol as a permanent institution and those who op-posed it, and this led to conflicts and squab-bles in the union leadership during the early years. The oppositionists under Isaac Hourwich, who became the Joint Board's chief clerk (enforcement supervisor) in 1913, led a spirited fight on this issue in the Cloak Joint Board and among its affili-ated locals. Among the employers, too, opinion was divided. Some manufacturers were interested in strengthening the union's position in order to eliminate the competition of the non-union shops. A larger number, however, were displeased with what they felt was the excessive inter-ference of the workers in their business. There was much cause for friction all around.

The Protocol system was also adopted in other branches of the garment trades. In 1913 a second general strike of waistmakers was followed by an agreement similar to that of the cloakmakers, and a joint board of sanitary control and an arbitration board headed by an impartial chairman were also introduced by the fur workers. The chair-man of the furriers' arbitration board was the late Judah L. Magnes.

The Protocol of Peace was regarded by its initiators not merely as a temporary agreement, but as a kind of timeless consti-tution for the amicable solution of all con-flicts between employers and workers. The agreement therefore had no time-limit and did not provide for any renewal date. It soon became apparent, however, that the Protocol was by no means strife-proof. The employers continued to smart over the growing influence of the union in the shops, hence a serious conflict broke out in 1916 and 25,000 workers were locked out of the factories. The union replied by call-ing a general strike. This marked the end of the Protocol period, and the new agree-ment ,which introduced certain changes in the conditions of work, was concluded for a specified period. The other unions which had copied the cloakmakers' Protocol con-tract shortly followed the new example by introducing time-limits into their collec-tive contracts.

9. NEW WAYS AND NEW ACHIEVEMENTS

As the first decade of the new century was drawing to an end, the men's tailors also began to stir. The leadership of the United Garment Workers, with which the men's tailors were affiliated, appeared to have little interest in the Jewish trades. It was interested mainly in the overall workers, most of whom were women of native stock, and relied largely on the union label, with its strong appeal to users of overalls, nearly all of them workers. The union label, however, carried no weight in the merchandising of ready-to-wear men's clothing. Moreover, the leaders of the United Garment Workers seemed to have nothing in common with the men's tailors, looking down upon them as radical immi-grants "always ready to strike."

The tailors thus virtually remained with-out a national leadership, and the initia-tive for any activity to improve economic conditions in the big and growing men's clothing industry had to come from below. Chicago led the way. On September 22, 1910, the 6,000 workers employed by the firm of Hart, Schaffner and Marx, the largest men's clothing factory in the country, went out on strike. The movement spread rapidly, and in the course of three weeks 38,000 tailors in Chicago left their shops.

This spontaneous mass movement put pressure on the local leadership of the UGW to agree to declare a general strike. The strike of the Chicago tailors quickly won wide public sympathy. Moral and material support came from a number of groups and individuals in Chicago and from Jewish labor organizations outside the city. The Women's Trade Union League and the settlement workers from Chicago's famous Hull House, headed by Jane Addams, were active in behalf of the strikers.

The leadership of the UGW, however, remained cool toward the strike. A few weeks later this became clear to all when President Thomas A. Rickert of the UGW accepted a compromise proposal from Hart, Schaffner & Marx without consulting the strike committee. To the embarrassment of Rickert, however, the workers promptly rejected the proposal because the firm refused to recognize the union. In this critical juncture a special strike committee, headed by John Fitzpatrick, the stalwart president of the Chicago Federation of Labor, stepped into the situation. After hectic negotiations an agreement with the firm was finally reached on January 14, 1911, providing for partial recognition of the union and establishment of an arbitration committee.

The other clothing manufacturers, however, persisted in rejecting the workers' demands, and the position of the strikers became more and more difficult. On February 3, Rickert called off the strike on his own responsibility. Disappointed and weary, the workers returned to their jobs. The great strike of the men's tailors in Chicago was practically lost.

Still the partial success with Hart, Schaffner & Marx had won the union an important beachhead in the Chicago market. Furthermore, the arbitration machinery set up under that agreement functioned to the satisfaction of both sides. The Hart, Schaffner & Marx pact gradually set the pattern for the entire industry throughout the country.

In New York City the Brotherhood of Tailors in 1911 was busy with preparatory organizing activity. The tragic fire in the Triangle Waist Company firetrap plant, in which 146 women waistmakers lost their lives in the spring of that year, deeply shocked the Jewish community and stunned public opinion all over America. Union activity in all the needle trade unions was stepped up, and although no large strikes developed, union sentiment in a number of shops which had previously barely been touched by trade unionism was greatly intensified.

As in the case of the cloakmakers and waistmakers a year or two earlier, there were many people in the movement who questioned the feasibility of organizing the tailors. The answer was not long in coming. After several months of high-tempo propaganda, carried on by a squad of field organizers, through the columns of the *Forverts* and at numerous meetings, the tailors began to stream into the union's offices.

The final decision was left to a referendum of the members. More than 35,000 voted for a general strike and fewer than 3,000 against. On December 30 the general strike was declared.

It was a historical moment for the New York tailors, as the active members and the leaders of the strike fully realized. "On the night of the 30th we did not go to bed," one of them wrote, "everyone was asking himself: will the tailors respond and leave the shops tomorrow morning? . . . ."

The strike call reflected the mood of the day. Some of its passages read:

> This is a historic day for the labor movement. A golden chapter is being added to its annals. Fathers will tell about it to their sons and daughters, and mothers will sing about it over the cradles of their babies. . . .
> The tailors have waited long for this moment. They were weary with wait-

SCENE OF THE TRIANGLE FIRE OF 1911

ing. The workers of other trades have waited long for this day. The great day has come. . . . Brothers and sisters, slaves of the clothing industry! Let your employers today feel your strength, let them see your unity! . . .

In the course of a week some 70,000 left their shops. The offices of the *Forverts* were converted into strike headquarters, and its entire staff was placed at the service of the strike. The Cloakmakers' Union donated $22,000 to the strike fund, and the *Forverts* and the Workmen's Circle also raised substantial sums. The United Hebrew Trades, the East Side branches of the Socialist Party, and a number of settlement workers volunteered aid. Several free kitchens and two grocery supply stores were set up to distribute food among the strikers' families. The Jewish bakers' union supplied wagonloads of bread daily to the relief centers and the free kitchens.

The chief demands of the strikers were for a 48-hour work-week, a twenty percent wage rise, and the abolition of subcontracting. Daily clashes between strikers and the police took place before the struck factories, and once again the courage and solidarity which had marked the earlier great strikes of the waistmakers and the cloakmakers were displayed on the tailors' picket lines. Responding to an injunction restricting the right to picket, some 25,000 striking tailors paraded in the main streets of the clothing center with banners and placards.

As in Chicago, so in New York the leadership of the United Garment Workers showed little understanding of the special problems of the tailors. As the strike progressed, many of the smaller firms began to settle with the union, but the wealthiest firms, headed by the Alfred Benjamin concern, stubbornly held out. Then, on February 28, 1913, without the knowledge of the leaders of the strike, Rickert accepted a compromise agreement with the association representing the larger employers. When the strikers learned about Rickert's action, their bitterness and anger were boundless. A committee of representatives of the entire movement, among whom were John A. Dyche, general-secretary of the ILGWU, Jacob Panken, Meyer London, and Fiorello LaGuardia (who at that time was the attorney for the Italian local of the tailors), was formed to speak up for the

strikers. The negotiations with the association were reopened and a compromise agreement was reached, providing for some improvements over the Rickert proposal. The workers won a rise in wages, *de facto*, though not official, recognition of the union, and a 53-hour week, which was to be reduced to 52 hours after the first year.

Even more important than the immediate gains won in the strike, however, was its moral effect. Like the cloakmakers earlier, the tailors gained confidence in themselves. The strikes in Chicago and in New York had also brought to the fore a number of young leaders. Especially conspicuous was the contribution made by a young cutter from Chicago, Sidney Hillman (of whom more later), employed by Hart, Schaffner and Marx. The younger men who distinguished themselves in New York included, among others, Joseph Schlossberg, Isaac Goldstein, Louis Hollander and Abraham Miller. It was now clear to the tailors that they could no longer rely on the leadership of the UGW, and that their union needed a basic reorganization.

This now appeared possible, since the New York and Chicago strikes had proved beyond doubt that the national offices of the UGW represented only the minority of the membership. The tailors' unions expanded greatly as a result of the strikes, and this sharply altered the power relationships in the UGW. A struggle for control of the union was inevitable and both sides began to prepare for the UGW convention, which was called for October 1914 in Nashville, Tenn.

The national officers of the UGW controlled the machine, and they made good use of it. When the convention opened, 105 delegates from the tailors' locals, representing the majority of the membership, were denied admission by Rickert's credentials committee. The attempt to open the proceedings without the "Jewish radicals from New York" elicited sharp protest from a small number of delegates from some Chicago locals who had been admitted to the convention. After a stormy

debate the small opposition group, among them Frank Rosenblum, Sam Rissman and S. Pass, all of Chicago, left the hall, denouncing the convention as illegal. Together with the 105 delegates who had not been seated, they met at the Duncan Hotel and declared themselves the legitimate convention. The 28-year-old Sidney Hillman was elected president, and Joseph Schlossberg was chosen general secretary.

At the convention of the American Federation of Labor several weeks later, two delegations from the United Garment Workers presented themselves. The AFL convention recognized the Rickert group and rejected the proposal of the ILGWU that the opposition group be heard. The rejected group thereupon found only one course open to it: to constitute itself an independent union. This took place on December 26, 1914, when the Amalgamated Clothing Workers of America came into being at a special convention held in New York.

Now outside the AFL, the Amalgamated leaders were faced with difficult problems. The UGW stubbornly refused to give up control over the locals in the tailoring industry. This raised the question of dual unionism, and the danger that the Amalgamated might find itself completely isolated from the rest of the labor movement. The employers, too, looked askance at the new and more militant union which had come into existence under such stormy circumstances. On the other hand, the Amalgamated had the full support of the Jewish labor organizations. The *Forverts,* the Workmen's Circle, and all the Jewish unions unreservedly took the side of the tailors, and this support helped the new union to overcome the stresses and trials of its early years.

And its trials were not long in coming. In January 1915 a group of manufacturers in New York declared a lockout. They would take back, they declared, only those workers who joined the UGW. The hostile alliance of the old union and the employers met with the unanimous resistance of the tailors. After a strike of several weeks the fight ended with full recognition of the Amalgamated by the employers. Similar struggles against UGW collusion with the employers had to be waged by the Amalgamated in other cities, and these conflicts did not always end in Amalgamated victories. In a relatively short time, however, the Amalgamated succeeded in establishing itself as the recognized union of the men's clothing workers. The prestige of the new union increased steadily, and by the end of World War I it had won a prominent place in the labor movement.

One of the factors that contributed to this development was the prosperity of the war years, which the leadership was skillful enough to turn to the advantage of the workers. The Amalgamated, the ILGWU, and other Jewish unions now concentrated their efforts on a reduction of hours of work. The unions had barely achieved the 48-hour week when they proclaimed the goal of a 44-hour week. In men's clothing Toronto led the field with the establishment of the 44-hour week in 1917. As soon as the war ended, the Amalgamated declared a general strike in New York, which resulted in the introduction of the 44-hour week throughout the trade. Before long the 44-hour week was standard in the men's clothing industry all over the country. In January 1919 there was a series of strikes to establish the 44-hour week in ladies' garments, and the goal was achieved almost everywhere. In the other needle trades, too, such as the cap and the fur industries, the 44-hour work-week was introduced in 1919. A thoroughgoing revolution had thus been carried out, in ten short years, in trades so notorious at the turn of the century for their frightful sweatshop conditions. The 44-hour week, besides giving the workers an opportunity for leisure and a better life, also added stature and prestige to the garment workers and their unions.

But post war prosperity did not last. The depression that began in the latter half of 1920 was used by the employers throughout the country to take back from the workers and their unions some of the gains they had won in the previous years. On December 8, 1920, the manufacturers of men's clothing in New York locked out 50,000 workers, to start one of the bitterest struggles in the history of the needle trades. The workers fought back with fierce vigor, and the Amalgamated succeeded in raising a fund of $2,000,000 to assist the jobless and to carry on the strike. After six months the conflict ended in a compromise. Though the union was compelled to yield on certain points, it succeeded in keeping the 44-hour week and the union shop. The long struggle proved the strength of the Amalgamated and the discipline of the tailors.

Several months later the organized cloak employers in New York launched a concentrated attack on the ILGWU. In October 1921 the chief employers' association in the New York market notified the union that in the following month every worker in the industry would be placed on piecework and that other working conditions, such as hours and rates, would be reconsidered by the leadership of the association. This was a flagrant violation of the contract, which still had some time to run. The ILGWU insisted that the employers must abide by the terms of the contract, and 55,000 workers went out on strike. A short time later strikes followed in Chicago and Philadelphia. In the end the employers' association in New York was roundly defeated after the ILGWU obtained an injunction ordering the association to take back the workers under the old conditions. The Chicago and Philadelphia strikes also ended in favor of the union. Despite concessions here and there, the garment unions, thanks to the loyalty of the workers, succeeded in keeping gains achieved in the years during and immediately following the war.

10. CULTURAL RENAISSANCE AND
JEWISH SURVIVAL

Jewish socialists of the last two decades of the 19th century displayed little interest in the problem of the existence of the Jewish people as such. The attitude in radical circles towards religion likewise was generally negative, and their feelings about the specifically Jewish way of life, which is permeated by religious traditions and values, were equally reserved. The same was true of the attitude of the Jewish radicals toward Zionism and the Hebrew language. Even Yiddish, the language of the people, they regarded as nothing more than an instrument of propaganda and popular education. The possibility of total assimilation, therefore, did not dismay the pioneers of the Jewish labor movement in America. To them socialism also meant cosmopolitanism. They were seriously disturbed by every expression of national aspirations, although paradoxically their own intensive cultural work in Yiddish did much to strengthen respect and affection for Jewish life and culture among the Jewish masses.

Socialism and science — these were the faith of the radicals of that time, who were profoundly convinced that the combination of socialist organization and scientific method was the answer to all the problems and anxieties that beset mankind. While the anarchist groups distinguished themselves for their militant anti-religious propaganda, the socialists did not go quite as far. Formally they maintained the principle that religion was a private affair. But this was a matter of tactics, of expediency; they did not want to alienate the religious workers, and trusted that education and the scientific spirit would gradually eliminate religious influence.

In this respect the Jewish socialists differed from the general socialist movement in America. The Jewish socialists were almost wholly under the influence of the socialist movements of Russia, Germany and France, where the dominant church practically always supported the reactionaries. Conditions were quite different in the Anglo-Saxon countries, where religion and socialism were not regarded as incompatible. No one thought it strange to see religious persons and even organized religious groups participating in the general socialist movement in America, but such a situation would have been unthinkable in the Jewish socialist movement.

Gradually, however, a change could be observed in the approach of the socialists to Jewish life. The influence of the Jewish labor organizations on the Jewish community was steadily increasing, the socialist press was growing in importance, and there was coming to the fore a modern Yiddish literature strongly influenced by socialist ideas. The Jewish worker began to participate more actively in the life of the Jewish community, and a great many Jewish socialists naturally began to think about their share of responsibility for continued Jewish existence.

This ideological shift began in Russia in the last years of the Nineties. The growth of Jewish secularism gave rise to a demand for a secular and "realistic" answer to the Jewish problem. The people were no longer satisfied with religious Messianism; they had waited too long, "and there was no more strength to wait." That was one reason why political Zionism, as formulated by Theodor Herzl, found such a ready response. Zionism, however, did not provide a complete answer for the problems of the Jews who expected to remain in *galut*. Was complete assimilation, some people asked themselves, indeed the inevitable fate of all the Jewish communities outside Israel?

The well-known Zionist thinker Ahad Haam, who sharply opposed Herzl's political Zionism, suggested as his answer the theory of spiritual Zionism. He argued that a spiritual center in Israel was needed to maintain the Jewish communities in the Diaspora. In spiritual Zionism Ahad Haam saw the force that was to counteract the trend toward assimilation and to meet the spiritual needs of modern Jews.

CHAIM ZHITLOWSKY (1865-1943)

At the same time, while Ahad Haam was formulating his theory of spiritual Zionism, the historian Simon Dubnow developed for the first time a systematic exposition of the philosophy of Jewish cultural nationalism. All of Jewish history in *galut*, Dubnow maintained, has been marked by the struggle for national autonomy. Modern Jewish cultural nationalism is therefore also an organic stage in the development of the Jewish tradition, adapted to the demands of our time.

The socialist variant of Jewish cultural nationalism was developed and formulated by Chaim Zhitlowsky, the theoretician of Yiddishism, and Vladimir Kosovsky, the Bund theoretician. The socialist theoreticians laid particular stress on the importance of Yiddish, the language of the people, in the effort to modernize Jewish cultural life. The phenomenal development of the Yiddish press and Yiddish literature in the early years of the twentieth century did much to endow Yiddish with cultural pres-

tige, and the striving for significant cultural creativity in this language of the people found a particularly warm response among Jewish socialists.

In America there was a similar development, with such eminent socialist writers as Morris Vinchevsky, Abraham Liesin, Yoel Entin and A. Litvin persistently stressing the need for a thoroughgoing change in the socialist approach to the problems of Jewish culture and education. The strongest influence, however, was exerted by the mass influx of new immigrants, a great many of whom were followers of the Bund in Russia.

Among those who were carried to America by the mighty immigrant stream were a goodly number of intellectuals. These included such personalities as Chaim Zhitlowsky, Nachman Syrkin, Ben Zion Hofman (Zivyon) and B. Charney Vladeck. Ideologically Zhitlowsky was the most influential member of this group. He was a brilliant speaker and an excellent stylist. His prominence in the Socialist-Revolutionary Party in Russia and his great personal prestige helped him to win substantial support among the socialist intellectuals for the ideas of Jewish cultural nationalism.

The new aspirations made themselves felt first of all in creative literature, with poets, novelists, dramatists and essayists constantly setting higher standards for themselves. Jewish cultural nationalism had a vision of the language of the people as the language of the Jewish future, and therefore the language in which the children must be educated. The creation of a modern Yiddish school system thus became an aim of those who hoped and worked for a renaissance of Jewish culture, rooted in the Yiddish language.

The creation of Yiddish schools was enormously difficult. There were no teachers and no textbooks, and few had faith that it could be done. A number of attempts were made, many of them ending in failure, until the way was shown by the Poale

B. CHARNEY VLADECK (1886-1938)

adopted to levy a special assessment on the members to secure the needed funds for the schools. Thus the material basis was created for the widely ramified educational work of the Workmen's Circle. The resolution of the 18th convention of the Workmen's Circle was also of great moral significance: the small number of Yiddishist pioneers no longer felt isolated. They now had behind them the great fraternal organization created by the Jewish labor movement, as well as a large majority of Jewish workers. It was not long before the Yiddish schools became most important centers of Jewish socialist cultural activity both in New York and throughout the country.

Party activity did not occupy a central place in the Jewish labor movement in America, as it did in Europe. As we have seen, the Jewish Socialist Agitation Bureau was dissolved in 1912, after a few unimpressive years. Its place was taken by the Jewish Socialist Federation, which had more ambitious aims. The founders of the

Zion. In October 1910, at a convention in Montreal, the Poale Zion adopted a resolution to set up modern "national radical" schools with instruction in Yiddish. Six weeks later the first such school was opened in New York. It had two aims: 1) to give the children a Yiddish education that would make them aware of their bond with the Jewish people; 2) to give the younger generation an understanding, in the socialist spirit, of the great social problems of the day.

In 1910 the question of providing children with a Yiddish education had also been raised in the Workmen's Circle. After years of debate a resolution was finally adopted (in 1916), requesting the branches and the members of the Workmen's Circle "to join the work of the socialist Jewish schools where such schools are already in existence, and to help in building new schools where there are none at the time."

Two years later, at the 18th convention of the Workmen's Circle, a resolution was

ZIVYON (BEN ZION HOFMAN, 1874-1954)

Federation — J. B. Salutsky-Hardman, Zivyon, B. Charney Vladeck, M. Terman, among others — were all products of the Bund, and their ambition was to build in America a Jewish socialist movement which would have the dominant position in the life of the Jewish workers in this country that the Bund had in Russia and Poland. From a membership of scarcely 1,000 in 1912 the Federation went to 5,000 by 1917. This was a fairly good record, yet far short of what was necessary to win for the Federation the importance to which it aspired. The Federation never was able to arrive at a clear formulation of the goals of a Jewish socialist movement in America. Nor was any other group of Jewish socialists able to do so. The reason was simple enough: the program of the Bund, like that of other Jewish socialist movements, presupposed the existence of an intensive Jewish community life. The demand for national cultural autonomy could have little meaning otherwise. In America there was no Jewish community like those of Eastern Europe, and the nature of American society made it unlikely that such a system of community organization would develop.

Nevertheless, the Socialist Federation brought into the Jewish labor movement new zeal and enthusiasm. The Federation represented the more militant trend in the socialist movement, and this won it a number of enemies. But the differences between the "old" and the "young" in the movement were an expression of normal and healthy disagreement, and both elements worked side by side, especially in the struggle against the corrupt rule of the Tammany machine on the East Side.

Indeed, in the election campaigns on the East Side the unique character of the Jewish labor movement could be seen with particular clarity. This district had been under the complete control of Tammany for nearly a century. Protected by the Tammany machine, the underworld had entrenched itself comfortably, and the East Side became notorious all over the country. Its unsavory reputation constantly evoked protests in the Jewish socialist press. These feelings of pain and protest were expressed in a classical manner by the socialist poet and publicist, Abraham Liesin.

> No district in New York is so permeated with the honest sweat of labor as the 12th District. And it is precisely this district that became known to the outside Christian world as a nest of rogues, murderers and criminals.

Inevitably, therefore, every election campaign was transformed into a fight for decent government and against cynical corruption and lawlessness. The Jewish socialists and the unions which supplied both the manpower and the financial sinews of the campaigns were fighting for the honor of the hard-working Jewish immigrants, and trying to show the world the true face of the despised East Side.

Small wonder, therefore, that the election campaigns on the old East Side were conducted with so much passion and zeal. But it was not easy to break the Tammany machine. During the campaigns enthusiasm in the socialist ranks would reach a high pitch. Disappointment with the election returns, which were often manipulated quite brazenly by Tammany's henchmen, was therefore all the more bitter.

The congressional elections of November 1914 finally brought the long-awaited results. Meyer London, the socialist candidate, was elected to Congress from the 12th N. Y. District. The result electrified the East Side and heartened the labor movement as a whole. Tammany had been beaten at last, by an alliance of the socialists and the Jewish trade unions. (The election campaigns on the East Side are graphically described by Hillel Rogoff in his *An East Side Epic*, published in 1930.)

11. WORLD WAR I DAYS

The outbreak of the First World War put the socialist movement in Europe to a severe test. For decades the socialists had preached international solidarity and conducted the most active propaganda against militarism. Would the individual socialist parties meet their moral obligation?

The test was too severe. Events developed with a speed no one could have foreseen, and the socialist parties were plunged into utter confusion. The result was the bankruptcy of the Socialist International.

The conditions faced by the American socialists were somewhat more favorable. The St. Louis convention of April 1917, several days after America's entry into the war, adopted a resolution which sharply protested the war policy of the government and solemnly reasserted the unshakable faith of the party in the principles of socialist internationalism. However, the Socialist Party remained isolated in its opposition to the war, and events proved more potent than the party had been able to foresee. The unions, under the leadership of Gompers, had from the very start supported President Wilson's policies, and a number of socialist intellectuals left the party during this period. This was the beginning of a profound crisis in the socialist movement that was to become acute a few years later, with the emergence of communism.

American Jewry was particularly alarmed over the European events. Most of the Jews in this country were fairly recent immigrants, and therefore had ties to the old country, where they had left families and friends. East European Jewry was largely concentrated in the border areas of Russia and Austria, a major battle ground from the outset of the war. Alarm over the fate of friends and relatives, already exacerbated by the deliberate anti-Semitic course of the reactionary Tsarist regime in the years before the war and in the first months of the war (expulsion of great numbers of Jews from the border territories, pogroms in Eastern Galicia), helped to intensify anti-Russian feeling among the Jews in the United States.

The plight of East European Jewry, meanwhile, was growing worse daily. Immediate material and moral help was needed, and in the early years of the war

MEYER LONDON (1871-1926)

America was the only large neutral country from which such help could come. All sectors of the American Jewish community devoted themselves unstintingly to the task of bringing relief to the harrassed Jews of Eastern Europe.

The American Jewish Joint Distribution Committee, which was organized in November 1914, did not entirely satisfy the labor groups. Moreover, the Jewish workers wanted to take an active part in the common task. In 1915, therefore, they formed the People's Relief Committee, in which all the Jewish labor organizations and a number of well-known individuals close to the labor movement were represented. The People's Relief Committee conducted vigorous fund-raising campaigns, and its work was carried out in close collaboration with the JDC.

From the moment when the American Jewish community assumed leadership in the Jewish world, all the problems of Jewish life confronted it with special urgency.

Thus there arose the question about the advisability of a Jewish Congress as an instrument for presenting Jewish needs and the Jewish demands to the victorious powers. The major Jewish organizations were also compelled to take a stand on the question of Zionism after the Balfour Declaration in 1917. As might be expected, Jewish workers were divided on these problems.

On the whole, the influence of the Poale Zion increased substantially during the war years. This was partly due to the fact that the most prominent leaders of the Poale Zion movement, including Ber Borochov, David Ben Gurion, Isaac Ben Zevi, Nachman Syrkin and Pinchas Rutenberg were then in America. The Jewish National Workers' Alliance (now called Farband — Labor Zionist Order) also grew considerably in numbers and influence during the war years. As in the case of the Workmen's Circle, the initiative for the labor Zionist fraternal order came from a small group of younger people. In 1908 a unit for mutual aid in Philadelphia was formed, with but eleven members from a Poale Zion group in that area. The order was officially launched at a convention of the labor Zionists in Rochester, N. Y., in 1910.

The growth of the Farband has mirrored the rise of pro-Zionist sentiments over the years. Its membership had doubled by 1917, the year of the Balfour Declaration, and its most rapid gains have come since the middle of the 30's.

Zionism and Jewish culture have been the Farband's central objectives from its very formation. Its members have raised many millions of dollars for the institutions and settlements of the Histadrut. The *Yiddisher Kemfer,* organ of the Poale Zionists, is also the organ of the fraternal order. The *Kemfer* was edited for many years by Hayim Greenberg (1889-1953), one of the most imposing figures in labor Zionism. (Labor Zionism is dealt with extensively by Philip Friedman in the article *Political and Social Movements and Organizations* in this volume.)

V. IDEOLOGICAL CRISIS, PROSPERITY AND DEPRESSION

1. THE BOLSHEVIK REVOLUTION AND THE SPLIT IN THE SOCIALIST MOVEMENT

The socialist world responded to the Bolshevik Revolution in Russia with mixed feelings. On the one hand, the brutal terror launched by the communists provoked a storm of protest in all democratic circles. On the other hand, some socialists justified the excesses on the ground that they were inevitable in the extraordinary conditions under which the communists captured power. There were some socialists and others who tried to reassure themselves that the reign of terror was only a temporary phase, and that as soon as the bolsheviks began to feel more secure they would return to democracy.

The most uncompromising enemies of communism were to be found among the Jewish socialists who understood Russian conditions. Characteristically, when the Socialist Party split in 1919, the majority went with the Communists, while in the Jewish Socialist Federation the majority remained with the SP. The splits, however, had a catastrophic effect on morale. Factional strife caused so much revulsion and disillusionment among the majority of the workers that within a very short time all socialist groups — whether "Left" or "Right" — lost the greater part of their members.

During 1920-21 the revolutionary wave in Europe began to subside, and in the socialist parties anti-communist tendencies everywhere gained the ascendancy. This development created a complicated situation for the Jewish Socialist Federation. A large majority of the Jewish socialists took a position midway between right and left, still hoping for a reunification of the divided labor movement. The leaders of the Federation therefore tried to create a third force which could, perhaps, in time rally the majority of the socialist workers.

A minority did not believe in the feasibility of a third force. This minority felt

Jewish National
Workers Alliance
אידישער נאצ. ארב. פערב.
April 22-26. 1914.

SECOND CONVENTION (1914) OF THE JEWISH NATIONAL WORKERS' ALLIANCE
(FARBAND—LABOR ZIONIST ORDER)

that the weakening of the Socialist Party through more splits would strengthen communist influence still further. The debate over the question whether the Federation should or should not remain in the SP became ever more heated. At its convention in September 1921 the Federation decided by a majority of 41 to 33 to leave the SP. The majority hoped to create "an independent Jewish socialist movement . . . until a more favorable time, when it will be possible to build a united socialist movement in this country."

There were no winners at that convention, however. It was clear that the opposing trends had to separate, since their views diverged so sharply. But everyone was deeply moved when Nathan Chanin, spokesman for the minority, declared:

> We are now leaving the convention. Tomorrow we shall confront each other as bitter political opponents. We do it with regret, with sorrow. But it cannot be helped. We stand in defense of our Party. We are fulfilling our duty as we see it.

The minority had judged the situation accurately. There was no room for a third force. The majority, for its part, was constrained to cooperate with the communists in an effort to unite all militant socialists. After long negotiations the leaders of the Federation agreed to make an attempt, together with the Jewish communists, to form the Jewish Federation of the Workers' Party. In April 1922 the first issue of the *Freiheit* was published.

The marriage was not a happy one. From the first the communists had no intention of collaborating faithfully with the socialists. It did not take long before the most prominent leaders of the former Socialist Federation left the *Freiheit* and severed their connections with the Workers' Party. Most of their followers, however, who had also joined the Jewish Federation of the Workers' Party, remained with the communists.

2. PRO-SOVIET ILLUSIONS

Pro-Soviet sentiment rose considerably during the years 1919-25 among the Jews in the United States. The terrible pogroms in the Ukraine and the excesses committed upon the Jewish communities by the White Armies during the Civil War aroused Jewish public opinion in this country. Increasing anti-Semitism in Poland, in contrast to the official outlawing of anti-Jewish propaganda by the Soviets, could not fail to impress American Jews.

But the roots of the illusions about the Soviet dictatorship, which prevailed at that time among many radical and socialist-minded people in this country, went deeper. Thousands of young men and women had been raised in the climate of Russian revolutionary aspirations. The emotional ties which still bound them to the dreams of their youth inclined them to the wishful acceptance of the Bolshevik upheaval as a real victory for the socialist ideal. This illusion, it should be noted, affected not only many American Jews. It was noticeable in many European countries among radicals of all shades of thought. Among American Jews it was widespread because so many of them had come from Russia.

The difficult and unpleasant task of stemming the pro-communist tide was un-dertaken by the minority of the Jewish socialists when they left the convention of the Federation in 1921. "We immediately hired another hall in the *Forverts* building, and we organized the Jewish Socialist Verband," Nathan Chanin tells us (*Tsen Yor Sotsialistishe Arbet*, p. 17). It was also decided to publish a weekly newspaper, under the traditional Bundist name *Der Wecker*. During the next dozen years the *Verband* concentrated its entire energy on the work of reassembling the shattered and confused Jewish socialist units everywhere in the country. It organized tours of lecturers — American and foreign — who criss-crossed the land scores of times, preaching social democracy as opposed to communism, on one hand, and helping to combat communist efforts to subvert the Jewish trade unions and the Workmen's Circle, on the other. Among the lecture tours which proved of lasting value were those organized by the *Verband* in 1924-25 and later in 1929 for Raphael Abramovitch, a prominent leader of the Russian Bund and spokesman for the Menshevik fraction of the Russian Social Democratic Party; A. Litvak, a leading Jewish journalist and socialist lecturer; and Henryk Erlich and Victor Alter, principal leaders of the Polish Bund, who visited America in the common interests of their own organization and of the Verband. (Erlich and Alter were treacherously murdered by the Soviet government in 1941.) Among the other notable lecture tours organized during those years were those of Noah (Portnoy), one of the venerable founders of the Bund, and David Einhorn, a well-known poet and journalist, who has since settled in this country.

The Verband started as a small group, with but scant intellectual support, and it was obliged to swim against the prevailing currents a good deal of the time, but its founders had one significant advantage: they had a clearly defined political position, and they knew what they wanted. In time, it gained considerable strength, and its ideological influence made itself increasingly felt in the Jewish labor movement. The writings of many leading American and European socialists have appeared in the columns of its weekly publication, *Der Wecker,* over the years.

The Socialist Verband today has a history of more than thirty years. These years held many troubled and agonized moments in the life of the Jewish workers in this country. The Verband not only helped to combat the mirage of Russian communism, but it played an equally important role in preserving the best traditions and the prestige of democratic socialism.

3. YEARS OF INTERNECINE STRUGGLE

The economic upswing of 1922-1929 brought about a significant change for the better in the general labor market, including higher earnings. It is remarkable, however, that the American trade union movement, instead of gaining members, lost them during those prosperous years, as can be seen from the following figures:

Year	Union Membership
1920	5,047,800
1922	4,027,400
1925	3,519,400
1929	3,442,600

This decline, in a time of rising employment, was especially marked in the needle trades, owing to the internal struggles that raged in the Jewish unions. Bitter strife, instigated by communists, came close to destroying everything the Jewish workers had built at the cost of so much sacrifice and devotion over the decades.

Opposition groups had existed in the garment unions for some time. The growing influence of administrative routine upon the life of the unions — an inevitable result of growth and maturity — had dimmed some of the idealism of the pioneering years. In many cases, too, the legitimate complaints of the rank and file were ignored, and this bred dissatisfaction. Furthermore, while the unions increasingly had to adapt themselves to the practical needs of their daily work, a substantial proportion of the workers in New York and in other cities grew more and more radical. Unfortunately, however, the dissatisfactions of many garment workers, while in themselves far from sinister, were demagogically exploited in the Twenties.

It was among the Jewish socialists that communist propaganda encountered particularly strong resistance. In fact, the general socialist movement in America suffered far more as a result of the struggle between the "Right" and the "Left" than did its Jewish section. Both the *Forverts* and the Workmen's Circle remained consistently steadfast bastions of democratic socialism. And thanks in no small degree to this sturdy resistance, the most savage onslaughts of the communists upon the Jewish unions were in the end successfully repelled.

On the other hand, sympathy toward Russia naturally tended to be strong among Jewish workers, with their personal memories of Tsarist oppression and their old enthusiasm for a Russian revolution. So, while there were never many active and organized communists among the Jewish workers, the myth of a revolutionary and supposedly free Russia helped the communists greatly in influencing a considerably larger number of the vacillating and discontented.

The communist battle for control of the unions and the Workmen's Circle was fought with every stratagem known to demagogy, in particular personal vilification. The struggle went on for years. Especially critical for a time was the situation in the ILGWU, where the communists succeeded in capturing control of the most important New York locals. At the 1925 convention of the ILGWU the 109 pro-communist delegates claimed to represent the majority of the workers, although they constituted not more than about 40 per cent of the delegates. The leadership managed to retain control of the General Executive Board.

The turning point in the struggle came in 1926. The reckless 1926 general strike in the cloak industry, which the communists called in order to entrench themselves still further in the unions and the industry, actually demonstrated how little they cared for the true interests of the workers. The strike dragged on for months, and the communist leaders of the New York Joint Board, obedient to party orders, prevented its settlement on favorable terms. As a result the ILGWU and the Joint Board sank into a morass of debts. On December 13 the union's General Office finally took over the conduct of the strike. A reorganization was carried out in a number of locals and in the Joint Board. On January 12, 1927, the unfortunate strike was over.

Years of internecine struggle and the unhappy cloak strike, which had burdened the ILGWU with a debt of more than a million dollars, left the Ladies' Garment Workers' Union shaken to its foundations, and the next few years were the most critical in its history. But the revelation of the moral bankruptcy of the communists paved the way for rehabilitation. With material and moral aid from other Jewish labor unions, and especially from the *Forverts*, the ILGWU's leadership managed in a relatively short time to put the union back on its feet.

It would be hard, in this limited space, to give a full account of the services of the many leaders who distinguished themselves in the touch-and-go struggle that saved the ILGWU from capture by the communists. The officers who gained the gratitude of the Jewish trade unions for this major repulse of communism were Morris Sigman, president from 1923 to 1928, David Dubinsky, who later was to acquire renown as president of the union, and Benjamin Schlesinger, three times president, whose tireless energy and initiative were largely responsible during this final term of office, 1928-32, for putting the union morally and financially back on its feet, after so long and bitter a siege.

4. THE AFTERMATH

Just as the communists' attempt to seize control of the ILGWU failed, so their efforts to gain control of other Jewish unions also ended in failure. After their crushing defeat in the ladies' garment trades, the communists' assault on the Amalgamated, never carried on with as much vigor as on the ILGWU, was turned back without too much trouble. Only in the Fur Workers' Union did the communists manage to entrench themselves, and in time to take over the leadership. In 1929 the communists, in conformity with a revamped party line, tried to create a dual organization — The Needle Trades Workers' Industrial Union — to include workers from all the needle trades. This attempt met with no appreciable success and came to an end a few years later.

Finally, at the end of 1929, the communists made another desperate attempt, this time to split the Workmen's Circle. Its results were negligible, by far the greatest number of the members remaining loyal. In March 1930 the communists launched the International Workers' Order, its Jewish section adopting the name of Jewish People's Fraternal Order.

During 1928-29 the condition of the unions gradually began to improve. There were a number of successful strikes and organizational campaigns, and some of the lost ground was recovered. Prosperity, however, was drawing to an end. The fall of 1929 brought with it the most severe economic depression in the history of America, and many of the most valuable gains of organized labor were almost entirely wiped out. Sweatshops reappeared in the needle trades, and the power of the unions declined steadily. Efforts to retain hard-won positions by desperate strikes were of little avail, and the memberships of most unions declined as unemployment mounted. Unable to fight and on the verge of bankruptcy, many unions were reduced to a state of almost total ineffectiveness, some of them becoming mere shadows of their former selves.

Not all sections of the Jewish labor movement, however, suffered in equal measure from the economic catastrophe. The *For-

verts and the Workmen's Circle were more or less successful in holding their own during those years of crisis. Their relative strength also made it easier for some of the unions to weather the storm and wait for better times.

VI. THE NEW DEAL

1. THE BEGINNING OF A NEW ERA

The depression that began in 1929 shook the entire economy of the country to its foundations. As it continued to affect more and more people adversely, the conviction grew that America could no longer rely on the free play of economic forces, and that energetic government intervention was needed to save the country from total collapse. The presidential election of 1932 reflected this radical change of attitude and resulted in a new Administration in Washington.

The New Deal marked the beginning of a new era, with a new approach to the problems of labor and capital. The new policy called for more democracy in industrial relations and greater responsibility by government and society for the welfare of the individual. The idea of "constitutionalism in industry" found a classical expression in the National Industrial Recovery Act of June 1933.

Under the NIRA a system of "codes," under the supervision of the government and with the participation of employers and organized labor in each industry, was to determine maximum hours and minimum wages. The law protected the workers' right to collective bargaining through their own chosen representatives. This was a radical departure from the tradition of "rugged individualism" which had dominated the economic development of the country since the industrial revolution. For the first time in the history of America, the organized workers could expect fair play from the government and greater acceptance by society as a whole. The unions were presented with an opportunity to attract many new members, since they now had concrete

BENJAMIN SCHLESINGER (1876-1932)

advantages to offer the workers. The unions in the needle trades were especially successful in using the opportunities provided by the New Deal. The fact that internal conflicts had subsided by this time also helped. In 1929, as we have seen, the communists had abandoned the policy of "boring from within" and attempted to organize a separate union of garment workers. This dual union, however, only served to split the opposition, and many of the most active workers left it to return to their old unions.

There was another reason why opposition to communism had grown among the Jewish workers. At the time of the Arab attacks upon the Jewish colonists in Palestine in 1929, Jewish communists, following orders from Moscow, came out squarely in favor of the Arab aggressors. To that part of the radical Jewish intelligentsia which had naively believed in the sincerity of communist propaganda, this was a heavy blow. A number of prominent writers who had even written for the *Freiheit,* although they had never belonged to the CP, protested sharply and completely severed their connections with the left wing groups.

The leadership in the garment unions was now able to concentrate on rebuilding the weakened unions and signing up the tens of thousands of workers who had either fallen out of the ranks during the years of crisis or who had never belonged. They met with amazing success. Thus, for instance, the membership of the ILGWU rose from less than 50,000 in early 1933 to over 200,000 a year later. The Amalgamated, which was in a relatively better situation at the beginning of the New Deal, also succeeded in substantially increasing its membership and strengthening its organization all over the country. The same was true of the Cap and Millinery Workers' Union, and of many smaller unions with large Jewish memberships.

To the Jewish workers the New Deal policies were not entirely new or unfamiliar. Elements of "constitutionalism in industry" were already, in fact, contained in the Protocol of Peace of 1910. Nor were the Jewish workers strangers to the idea that the government has a duty to help wage earners in times of unemployment and depression. The Jewish unions had strongly supported unemployment insurance, old-age benefits and similar welfare measures long before the general labor movement came out in their favor.

The unions in the needle trades, by and large, were able to retain the gains secured through the NIRA even after the act was declared unconstitutional by the Supreme Court in 1935. In the short period of the NIRA's existence these unions had succeeded in winning the confidence of many thousands of new members. This difficult task was accomplished despite the fact that the greater part of this new membership had but little in common with the older generation of garment workers who had built up the garment unions several decades earlier.

2. SOLIDARITY UNAFFECTED

As early as the great strikes of 1909-13 it had become apparent that the number of non-Jewish workers in the needle trades was steadily rising, and even then the leadership had to exercise great tact and understanding to hold the diverse groups of workers together.

After the early Twenties, when the stream of Jewish immigration from Eastern Europe was practically shut off by the new immigration laws, the numerical strength of Jewish labor in the needle trades declined greatly. The children of the Jewish garment workers seldom entered their parents' trades. This was of course a standard feature of the economic and social mobility that had characterized American life from the start, but it was especially marked among the Jewish immigrants. The vacant places in the garment shops gradually came to be occupied by other groups, both immigrant and native. The Jews were still the most active element in the membership, but by the early Thirties they had become a minority among the workers.

It now became the task of this active minority to draw the large mass of the still unorganized into the unions, and the leadership of these unions met the challenge. There were moments, it is true, when cooperation between the new and the old groups ran into difficulties. In the 1930's, when the wave of Nazism and Fascism in Europe was at its height, there was occasional tension in the garment shops. The Italians, for instance, constituted the majority in many shops, and some of them felt the need to defend the Mussolini regime — not because they liked Fascism, but because of their ties to the old homeland, Italy. Influential Catholic circles — and many workers in the garment shops are Catholic — lent moral support to the Franco regime in Spain. The Jewish workers, on the other hand, took an active part in the fight against Nazism and Fascism, and the Jewish leaders of these unions were also leaders in the anti-Fascist movement.

Nevertheless, the influence of the Jewish leadership in the garment unions has not been affected by these difficulties. The Jewish workers learned much from their own experience, and this was helpful in achieving the necessary cooperation with other groups. Selig Perlman, an outstanding authority on the American labor movement, justly points out the role of the Jewish leadership in the garment unions:

> As members of the ethnic group with the longest record of persecution and adverse discrimination, they cannot but feel great pride in their own clear record on the minorities issue as when judged by the test of deed ("Jewish Unionism and American Labor", in *Publications of the American Jewish Historical Society,* Vol. XLI, p. 337).

3. ACROSS THE ROUND TABLE

The stronger the garment unions became, and the more prestige they acquired, the more they were able to safeguard the interests of their members without having to resort to strikes. During the past two decades the garment unions have made industrial history by settling practically all their major economic clashes with their employers at the conference table.

The needle trades unions, so strongly influenced by socialism since their formative days, have paradoxically become the most consistent practitioners of labor-management cooperation in order to avoid costly strikes. In large measure this may be explained by the fact that while in former years industry-wide strikes in the needle trades were not merely struggles for economic betterment but also protests against the inferior status ascribed to labor by employers and the general community, this social factor is far less important now. Labor has come a long way, and its recognition by industry and the community is beyond question now.

The special conditions in the needle trades and the constant threat of competition from low-wage areas have in recent years often induced the garment unions to

help manufacturers to reorganize their plants. The garment unions are vitally interested, above all, in preserving the competitive capacity of the larger cities, where labor conditions are most favorable. Sometimes the unions have even buttressed the employers' credit in order to preserve the jobs of their workers. The ILGWU and the Amalgamated have also set up engineering departments to deal with the technical problems of production and to give employers information and advice — all to maintain employment in the union shops.

The Jewish labor leaders, as Perlman correctly points out, had no feeling of inferiority in relation to the employers in their industry. "The garment unions' leaders," he says, "indeed felt themselves at least the equals of the employers with whom they dealt as regards technical proficiency" (*Ibid.,* p. 315). Consequently they had no insecure fears of cooperation, and they were able to accept the introduction of new methods in the shops. From their own experience the Jewish workers knew the advantage to the worker of the progressive factory, efficiently organized and equipped with the best and most modern machines.

Developments in the Thirties gradually brought the Jewish unions and the general labor movement into closer contact and understanding. While Jewish unions learned a great deal from the experiences of other labor organizations, they also gave to other unions out of their own experience and tradition. The Americanization of Jewish labor was a matter of give and take, of influencing and being influenced.

In 1933 an understanding finally was reached between the Amalgamated and the United Garment Workers, which made it possible for the Amalgamated to join the American Federation of Labor. In 1934 there was a merger between the United Hatters and the Cap and Millinery Workers International Union, which had been feuding for more than a quarter of a century. But the Amalgamated did not long remain in the AFL. The great upsurge of organized labor in the Thirties led also to a reawakening of the old strife between craft and industrial unionism. In the garment unions this problem had long been solved, which was one reason why they were able to attract great masses of hitherto unorganized workers. In 1935, when the conflict between the advocates and opponents of industrial unionism in the AFL emerged into the open, Sidney Hillman, David Dubinsky, and Max Zaritsky were among the founders of the Committee for Industrial Organization. The Jewish unions also contributed very substantial sums for the extensive and phenomenally successful organizing campaigns of that Committee. In 1938 the Committee for Industrial Organization constituted itself as a separate national body under the name of Congress of Industrial Organizations (CIO). Among the largest Jewish unions the Amalgamated, under the leadership of Sidney Hillman, was the only one to remain with the CIO.

4. SOCIAL WELFARE AND CULTURAL ACTIVITIES

During World War II and the immediate post war years, the various branches of the needle trades experienced substantial prosperity. Wage rises, shorter hours, and other gains kept the union's morale high. Soon, however, the major garment unions became acutely aware of a problem which was increasingly concerning their membership, the problem of security. The fear of illness or unemployment, permanent or temporary, has always prevailed in the needle trades because of their seasonal nature. Among the workers in some of these trades, many of whom were past middle age, the sense of insecurity was especially intense. The attention of the leadership was now turned to a search for solutions.

Since the New Deal most of the garment unions, and many unions in other industries, had succeeded in winning paid vacations and health benefits for their members. The ILGWU set out in 1946 to win old-age retirement pensions, first for the New York cloakmakers and later for the industry as a whole. Like the other "fringe" benefits, the old-age pensions were to be financed from a percentage of the weekly payroll of every employer in the industry. By 1954 the ILGWU had established this welfare program for a majority of its membership in many garment markets. The Amalgamated, which pioneered in unemployment insurance for its members, subsequently converted these funds into life and health insurance and organized its own state-chartered companies for this purpose. In 1947 the Amalgamated began to distribute retirement pensions to its members 65 years of age. The ILGWU's imposing medical service system for its members, with 18 health centers throughout the country, has been paralleled in recent years by the Amalgamated's comprehensive medical program for its members in New York and other cities.

From their earliest years the women's garment unions gave much attention to cultural and educational activities. Lectures, courses in English and American history, theatricals and concerts were organized by the locals, or through the initiative of the national offices. The presence of a large number of young women members in the women's wear unions undoubtedly strengthened this type of activity. In 1934, when a great many new members were entering the union, most of them women, the ILGWU further expanded the scope of its educational and cultural programs. Its educational department has since 1936 been directed by Max Starr, with Fannia M. Cohn as secretary. The systematic educational work of the ILGWU, carried on all over the country, with summer schools for members, leadership training courses, and its Officers Training Institute in New York City, is rated highly by the adult education profession.

The Amalgamated also developed intensive cultural activity. In 1921 J.B.S. Hardman was appointed as educational director, and in 1938 a Department of Cultural Activities was formally established. The Amalgamated also pioneered in cooperative housing, having promoted two large housing developments, one in the upper Bronx and the other on the lower East Side, in New York City. (At this writing, the ILGWU is building a $20,000,000 cooperative apartment project on the lower end of the East River Drive, with nearly 1,000 units.)

In 1922 the Amalgamated opened a bank in Chicago, and later in New York City. Both institutions have prospered and have helped to strengthen the position of the union. The beginning of the Twenties saw the first attempts of the Amalgamated (in Chicago) and the ILGWU (in Cleveland) to set up unemployment insurance for their members. When unemployment insurance became a government function during the New Deal, these projects were given up.

A few figures will best illustrate the scope of the social and welfare activities of the two largest garment unions. In 1953 the ILGWU, with a membership of nearly 440,-000, paid out more than $34,000,000 in benefits, and early in 1954 its welfare and retirement funds had total assets of $130,-000,000. The Amalgamated's present membership is nearly 400,000. It controls two insurance companies of its own, as well as eight insurance funds, with reserves of more than $108,000,000. In the beginning of 1954 the three large garment unions — the ILGWU, the Amalgamated and the Hatters — controlled an aggregate capital of over a quarter of a billion dollars.

The general labor movement in America has not succeeded in attracting the intellectuals. In part this was an intentional estrangement. Samuel Gompers had no confidence in the socialist intellectuals. His distrust was well founded. The ideological conflicts among the various political trends in the Eighties and Nineties caused no little harm to the labor movement. The political wrangling and the bitter polemics that engaged the various party groups were also not without effect on the East Side, but here labor and the intellectuals never parted ways. The dividing line between workers and intellectuals was not sharply drawn on the East Side. Nearly all Jewish immigrant intellectuals began by working in shops, and many workers came to America with a considerable education. Moreover, the two elements needed each other too urgently. The intellectuals needed the workers of the East Side as an audience. In turn, the labor movement was a powerful influence in Jewish cultural life and Jewish literature. Gradually the spheres of influence were marked out. The unions, the Workmen's Circle and the Farband (Labor Zionist Order) were dominated by workers — more correctly, by a group of leaders who came from the shops. At the same time the Jewish labor movement created a mighty press which the intellectuals dominated and through which they exerted their influence on the entire movement. The purely political organizations, on the other hand, lost much influence and prestige. The "nonpartisan" socialists assumed the moral leadership.

The Workmen's Circle and the Farband effectively fulfilled the role of a socialist party on the practical level, though they did not conduct political campaigns. In this respect, too, the East Side blazed a new trail, and students of modern social movements can learn much from the experience of the Jewish labor organizations in America.

BIBLIOGRAPHY

BUDISH, J. M. AND SOULE, GEORGE, *The New Unionism in the Clothing Industry*. New York, 1920.

COMMONS, JOHN R. AND ASSOCIATES, *History of Labor in the United States,* 4 vols. New York, 1918-1935.

EPSTEIN, MELECH, *Jewish Labor in U. S. A.,* 2 vols. New York, 1950-1953.

FINE, NATHAN, *Labor and Farmer Parties in the United States*. New York, 1928.

HARDY, JACK, *The Clothing Workers*. New York, 1935.

HERBERG, WILL, "The Jewish Labor Movement in the United States," *American Jewish Year Book,* Vol. 53, 1952, pp. 3-74.

HILLQUIT, MORRIS, *Loose Leaves from a Busy Life*. New York, 1934.

HOURWICH, ISAAC A., *Immigration and Labor*. New York, 1912.

LEVINE, LOUIS, *The Women's Garment Workers*. New York, 1924.

PERLMAN, SELIG, *A History of Trade Unionism in the United States*. New York, 1922.

RICH, J. C., "The Jewish Labor Movement in the United States," *The Jewish People—Past and Present,* Vol. II, pp. 399-430. New York, 1948.

ROBINSON, DONALD B., *Spotlight on a Union*. New York, 1948.

ROGOFF, HILLEL, *An East Side Epic*. New York, 1930.

SEIDMAN, JOEL, *The Needle Trades*. New York, 1942.

Socialism and American Life (eds.: DONALD DREW EGBERT AND STOW PARSONS), 2 vols. Princeton, 1952.

STOLBERG, BENJAMIN, *Tailor's Progress*. New York, 1944.

STRONG, EARL D., *The Amalgamated Clothing Workers of America*. 1940.

ZARETZ, CHAS. E., *The Amalgamated Clothing Workers of America*. New York, 1934.

אַשעראָוויטש, מ., „די געשיכטע פון פאַרווערטס" (געדרוקט אין די זונטאָגדיקע נומערן פון פאַרווערטס: 25-סטן מאַי 1947 — 13-טן יוני 1948).

בודיש, י. מ., געשיכטע פון קלאָט, העט, קעפ און מילינערי אַרבעטער. ניו-יאָרק, 1926.

בורגין, הערץ, די געשיכטע פון דער יידישער אַרבעטער-באַוועגונג אין אַמעריקע, רוסלאַנד און ענגלאַנד. ניו-יאָרק, 1915.

הערץ, י .ש., 50 יאָר אַרבעטער-רינג אין יידישן לעבן. ניו-יאָרק, 1950.

הערץ, י. ש., די יידישע סאָציאַליסטישע באַוועגונג אין אַמעריקע. ניו-יאָרק, 1954.

ווינשטיין, ב., פערציק יאָר אין דער יידישער אַרבעטער-באַוועגונג. ניו-יאָרק, 1924.

ווינשטיין, ב., די יידישע יוניאָנס אין אַמעריקע. ניו-יאָרק, 1929.

זאקס, א. ש., די געשיכטע פון אַרבעטער-רינג, ב' I — II. ניו-יאָרק, 1925.

משעריקאָװער, א. (רעד'), געשיכטע פון דער יידישער אַרבעטער-באַוועגונג אין די פאַראייניקטע שטאַטן, ב' I — II. ניו-יאָרק, 1943 — 1945.

יאָנאָווסקי, ש., ערשטע יאָרן פון יידישן פרייהייטלעכן סאָציאַליזם. ניו-יאָרק, 1948.

לאנג, ה. און פיינסטאָן, מ. (רעד'), געווערקשאַפטן — זאַמלבוך צו פופציק יאָר לעבן פון די פאַראייניקטע יידישע געווערקשאַפטן. ניו-יאָרק, 1938.

צען יאָר סאָציאַליסטישע אַרבעט, 1921 — 1931 (אויסגאַבע פון יידישן סאָציאַליסטישן פאַרבאַנד). ניו-יאָרק, 1931.

קאהאן, אב., בלעטער פון מיין לעבן, ב' 1 — 5. ניו-יאָרק, 1926 — 1931.

ראָזענבערג, אברהם, ערינערונגען פון די קלאָוקמאַכער און זייערע יוניאָנס. ניו-יאָרק, 1920.

THE JEWISH LABOR MOVEMENT

FACTS AND PROSPECTS

Max D. Danish

I. INTRODUCTION

There is a belief, sometimes amounting to dogma, that each generation begins its career by a rupture with the past. This is not true of that unique American phenomenon, the Jewish labor movement, nor is it true of what has been known as the Jewish trades. There has always been continuity, a constant merging of the new and the old—from the early gropings at the beginning of the mass Jewish immigration of the last decades of the nineteenth century to the achievement of security and the sense of being at home in a free and hospitable society.

The Jewish unions have not attempted to set themselves apart from the general labor movement; nor have the Jewish unions ever seriously thought of building a national federation of Jewish trade unions. The Jewish workers have organized themselves and have functioned in much the same way as their fellow workers in the whole range of American industry, and they have affiliated themselves with the central bodies of American labor as a whole—the Knights of Labor, the American Federation of Labor, and the Congress of Industrial Organizations.

The synthesis of the new and the old within the Jewish labor movement has created a heritage of permanent value to the organized Jewish workers, as citizens and members of the social and industrial communities of America. This heritage includes these elements:

a) a sense of having achieved a fair degree of economic security; b) a comfortable and uncoerced identification with all that is best in the American tradition; c) pride in the knowledge that their own unions have made great and tangible contributions to American labor as a whole and to the larger American society as well; d) pride in their decisive influence in making the garment industries pioneers in industrial democracy and responsibility, almost as much as the garment unions have been pioneers in labor; and e) complete acceptance of the full integration of the Jewish labor movement in American labor as a whole.

The Jewish labor movement, which has affirmatively demonstrated the capacity and responsibility of immigrant workers, men and women, as devoted members of good unions, is a major contribution, of an institutional and group character, to American life.

Nearly all of the order and stability in the garment trades, the principal field of Jewish labor unionism, is due to the unions. Collective agreements in these trades have often embodied programs of industrial reform in addition to provisions governing wages and hours.

On the other hand, collective agreements, by their nature, cannot be one-way streets. By virtue of the responsibilities imposed upon them by their contracts, trade unions become less unilateral in thought and action and acquire a sense of having a stake in the industry. The leaders and members learn that labor unions cannot prosper in a sick industry.

This change from belligerency to an acceptance of a working agreement involving reciprocal obligations has not weakened the status of labor. The progress of the needle trades unions in the past twenty years proves that the workers are pleased with the "industrial citizenship" they have acquired.

II. THE "BIG THREE"

A survey of the range of accomplishments of the "big three" in the needle trades labor movement, the International Ladies' Garment Workers' Union (ILGWU), the Amalgamated Clothing Workers of America and the United Hatters, Cap and Millinery Workers, provides a graphic lesson in the meaning of labor's industrial citizenship.

1. THE INTERNATIONAL LADIES' GARMENT WORKERS' UNION

Few people realize the magnitude of the women's wear industry: the size of its labor force, its annual product, and its rank in American industry as a whole. Twenty years ago it employed about 275,000 workers in a little more than 6,000 shops, and its total volume of business was slightly over one billion dollars. Today women's clothes are produced in nearly 15,000 plants employing more than half a million workers, of whom nearly 450,000 belong to the ILGWU. The annual value of the industry's production exceeds five billion dollars. A century ago most of the workers were women; later most were men; and for several decades now the women have again been in the majority.

At the celebration of the ILGWU's fiftieth anniversary, in 1950, the delegates heard a report by their president, David Dubinsky, on the major achievements of the union during that period. These included: the "preferential" union shop, which later evolved into the union shop; the first market-wide collective bargaining and arbitration mechanisms in the needle trades; the attainment of the 40-hour work week, and later the 35-hour week, which is now standard in more than 80 per cent of the ladies' garment industry; the introduction of the principle of "guaranteed employment" in the industry's main markets; the establishment of the labor movement's first full-time workers' education program; the first trade union health center in America; the first union vacation resort; a research department; a management-engineering department; an international labor relations department to coordinate the unions' far-flung activities, a political department to promote the union's program of independent political action.

Some of the ILGWU's other pioneering enterprises included: a union-administered system of health and vacation funds, maintained by industry-contributed money, covering the union's entire membership; a retirement fund for workers reaching 65 years, covering more than half of the membership of whom nearly 14,000 have already retired on union pensions. The ILGWU was also the first international union to publish complete annual financial reports for its national and local offices. Some years ago it created the ILGWU Training Institute, a full-time school to train future union officers and to develop leadership material from among the younger members.

Photo from the collection of Harry Rubenstein

INTERNATIONAL LADIES' GARMENT WORKERS' UNION—40TH ANNIVERSARY, 1940

The ILGWU's far-flung program of industrial citizenship extended beyond the strictly trade union field into larger political and communal activities. Thus, its long and successful experience in defeating communist infiltration in the 1920's enabled it to serve as an example of effective anti-communism to other trade unions and civic groups, and this experience prepared it to assume leadership in combatting the communist-dominated World Federation of Trade Unions after 1945 and in helping to form in 1951 the International Confederation of Free Trade Unions, which subsequently encompassed more than 55 million free workers throughout the world. The ILGWU also took the initiative, in conjunction with other independent liberal persons and groups, in forming the Liberal Party in New York, and it continues to render aid to other anti-communist liberal political forces. Finally, the ILGWU and

its affiliates have, during the past 35 years, contributed some $25,000,000 to various international, communal, and labor causes and institutions.

For more than twenty years the name of David Dubinsky has been synonymous with the ILGWU. Dubinsky was preceded in the presidency of the ILGWU by Benjamin Schlesinger, three times its chief executive since 1903, and by Morris Sigman, who was president from 1923 until 1928. Among the other chief leaders of the ILGWU were John A. Dyche, Abraham Rosenberg and Abraham Baroff. Israel Feinberg, an ILGWU vice-president for a great many years who passed away in 1952, was one of the cloakmakers' "immortals," a far-visioned and constructive leader.

Among those who currently stand out in President Dubinsky's "cabinet" are: Luigi Antonini, general secretary of the Italian Dressmakers' Union; Isidore Nagler, gen-

SIDNEY HILLMAN (1887-1946)

eral manager of the Cloak Joint Board; Julius Hochman, for many years head of the
Dress Joint Board; Joseph Breslaw, veteran
leader of the Cloak Pressers; Charles S.
Zimmerman, manager of the Dressmakers'
Union, Local 22; Louis Stulberg, manager
of the undergarment workers' organization
in New York City; Morris Bialis, ILGWU
director in Chicago and the Midwest;
Harry Greenberg, director of the children's
wear trades; Charles Kreindler, director of
the Blousemakers' Union and of the
ILGWU Upper South areas; Louis Nelson,
leader of the Knitwear Workers; Samuel
Otto, director West Coast region; David
Gingold, director of the Northeast territory; Meyer Perlstein, George Rubin,
Israel Horowitz, Philip Kramer, Ben Kaplan, and Bernard Shane, head of the
ILGWU organizations in Canada.

Also Mark Starr, director, and Fannia M.
Cohn, secretary, Educational Department;
Moe Falikman, manager Cutters Union,
Local 10; Rubin Zuckerman, chairman
New York Cloak Joint Board; Nathaniel

M. Minkoff, secretary New York Dress
Joint Board; Zachary L. Freedman, director Embroidery Workers Union, Local 66.

2. THE AMALGAMATED CLOTHING WORKERS OF AMERICA

The history of the Amalgamated and its
achievements is inextricably interwoven
with the career of Sidney Hillman, its first
president, who died in 1946. In 1954 the
delegates to the Amalgamated's Fortieth
Anniversary Convention heard a report
from Hillman's successor, Jacob S. Potofsky, on the union's "Forty Years of Progress." This report of "tailors' progress"
offers a resume of the union's economic
struggles, from the 1910 Chicago strike, in
which Sidney Hillman, then a cutter in the
Hart, Schaffner & Marx plant, first appeared as a leader of the clothing workers,
to 1937, when national industry-wide collective bargaining became a reality. (See
a full account of the rise and growth of
the Amalgamated in a preceding article in
this volume by A. Menes.) This forty-year
report, however, lays even greater emphasis on measures the Amalgamated had
sponsored and attained for the greater
security of its members—life and health insurance, pensions, medical care and union
banking and housing.

Concern with the problem of seasonal
unemployment led the Amalgamated to
initiate in 1923 unemployment insurance
funds in New York, Chicago and Rochester.
And when in 1936 a federal system of unemployment compensation made continued
union activity of this character unnecessary,
the Amalgamated turned to more comprehensive social insurance. It chartered the
Amalgamated Life and Health Insurance
Company to operate a system of sick and
health benefits in all the union branches.
Later a network of retirement funds was
established in the clothing industry, maintained by employers' contributions of three
percent of their payrolls; the first eligible
members were able to retire in 1947. Four
years later the Sidney Hillman Center was
opened in New York to provide medical

THE AMALGAMATED CLOTHING WORKERS OF AMERICA—FIRST CONVENTION, 1914

services for the city's 40,000 men's clothing workers; in addition, the union maintains a medical center in Philadelphia, and medical centers for the New York laundry workers and for Chicago members were under construction in 1954.

The Amalgamated pioneered in two other social welfare ventures for its membership: labor banking and cooperative housing. In 1920 the union founded the Amalgamated Trust and Savings Bank in Chicago, and in 1921 the Amalgamated Bank of New York. Among their valuable features, these banks initiated a program of small loans services to protect low-income customers from loan sharks. The critical housing shortage after World War I induced the Amalgamated to undertake a cooperative housing program in the Bronx and on the East Side of New York. Expanded after World War II, these projects now house more than 2,500 families.

Along with the rest of American labor, the Amalgamated thrived during and after the New Deal period. In 1933 it settled its long-standing jurisdictional dispute with the United Garment Workers and entered the AFL for a brief stay. Shortly thereafter it joined with other unions, such as the United Mine Workers, the ILGWU, and the Hatters and Millinery Union, in forming the Committee for Industrial Organization to spur the organization of workers in mass production industries in industrial unions. This Committee, having broken with the AFL, became the Congress of Industrial Organizations (CIO) in 1938; the Amalgamated remained in the CIO thereafter.

During this same period the Amalgamated expanded its membership rolls to include thousands of laundry, cleaning and dyeing, and glove workers, and salesmen in retail stores. At the same time, as a result of the amicable labor-management relations that prevailed under the NRA, the basis was laid for industry-wide collective bargaining, which was achieved in 1937; and the machinery for industrial peace in

the clothing industry, always a dominant concern of the union leadership, was perfected. Since 1952 a standard national men's clothing contract has prevailed in the industry. The men's clothing industry and its affiliated trades accounted in 1953 for over 3.5 billion dollars in production volume. At this convention the Amalgamated reached a peak membership of 385,000.

Like the ILGWU, the Amalgamated has taken a leading role in labor's political action, chiefly through the CIO Political Action Committee. Its president, Sidney Hillman, was appointed a member of the National Defense Advisory Committee in 1940, and Associate Director of the Office of Production Management during the subsequent war years. In the postwar years the Amalgamated contributed heavily to a variety of communal activities, foreign aid, and international labor unity, affiliating first with the World Federation of Trade Unions, and later, satisfied that the WFTU was a communist front, with the International Confederation of Free Trade Unions.

Until his death Hillman was the unchallenged leader of the Amalgamated. In his memory the union established the Sidney Hillman Foundation for scientific, educational and charitable purposes. It has actively promoted the welfare of labor and the public.

Among Hillman's most capable associates, many of whom are still directing the destinies of the Amalgamated today are: Jacob S. Potofsky, upon whose shoulders Hillman's mantle has fallen since the latter's death; Frank Rosenblum, General Secretary-Treasurer; Louis Hollander, New York leader of the Amalgamated, who is also N. Y. State chairman of the CIO; Hyman Blumberg, executive vice-president of the union; Jack Kroll, of Cincinnati, for many years director of the CIO's Political Action Committee; Gladys Dickason, director of the Southern Organization department; Abraham Miller, veteran secretary of the N. Y. Joint Board; Murray Weinstein, leader of the Amalgamated powerful cutters' union; Abraham Chatman, Rochester, N. Y., Amalgamated leader; Samuel Levin, Amalgamated's lifelong Chicago leader; Bessie Abramowich Hillman, the late president's widow, who has been an active Amalgamated officer for many years; and Elias Rabkin, editorial board, *Advance*.

3. THE UNITED HATTERS, CAP AND MILLINERY WORKERS

The 40,000 members of the United Hatters, Cap and Millinery Workers' International Union represent some 90 percent of the capmakers, 80 percent of the millinery workers, and 70 percent of the employees in the men's hat industry. Their work standards are among the best in the needle trades: the members enjoy job security, health benefits, paid vacations and similar welfare benefits.

During its first decades the union was plagued by all the ills common to the early history of the other needle trades unions: the sweatshop, homework, short work seasons, internecine strife, inability to hold members between strikes.

The capmakers formed their first union in 1873 in New York; it soon disintegrated and was not resuscitated until 1895, when Local 2 waged a partially successful strike against 12 New York firms. During the ensuing years the efforts of the capmakers to gain a foothold in their trade were handicapped not only by the opposition of the employers but also by the persistent and divisive campaign of Daniel De Leon to subordinate the Jewish unions to the political control of the Socialist Labor Party.

In 1901 the capmakers formed a national organization, the United Cloth Hat and Capmakers Union, which received a charter from the AFL in 1902.

The threat of dual unionism was revived in 1906 when the Industrial Workers of the World invaded New York and, abetted by De Leon's languishing Socialist Trade and Labor Alliance, formed an opposition capmakers' local. For the next few years

the union was compelled to conduct a two-front battle, against the opposition union and against the employers. By 1911 the capmakers had overcome the internal threat and, having attained a membership of 3,000, were prepared to continue the struggle for the improvement of working conditions. They successfully fended off efforts to cut wages during periods of economic depression and to abolish week-work. And in 1936, after several decades of attempts to curtail the evils of the jobber system, the union won an agreement by which the jobbers confined their purchases to union contractors and divided their work assignments equitably among these contractors.

Meanwhile the capmakers had begun a campaign to organize the rapidly growing millinery trade. The AFL had granted jurisdiction over the millinery trade to the capmakers' union in 1903; the union chartered its first millinery local, Local 24, in 1910, and subsequently this local became the major vehicle for organizing the New York millinery workers. In 1915 the first collective bargaining agreement was signed with the Ladies' Hat Manufacturers Association; by 1917 work hours in the millinery shops were reduced to 45; and by 1918, as a result of a successful general strike, the union's position in the industry was firmly established. Nevertheless, for several decades after its inception, the capmakers' union was engaged in a fluctuating jurisdictional dispute with the United Hatters of America, the union of workers in the men's hat industry. The conflict was finally resolved in 1934, when, as a result of their cooperation under the NRA Code Authority of 1933-34, the two unions amalgamated under the aegis of the AFL.

For a decade after 1922 a unique situation prevailed in the millinery industry: unable to reach a contract agreement with the employers and desirous of avoiding a strike, the union proceeded without a collective contract to become the sole enforcer of union conditions in the shops. A collective pact for the trade was finally renewed in 1934, stimulated by the NRA

Code Authority for the industry. The union was able to use the Code to enforce the observance of the union label and to secure a 35-hour work-week.

During that decade the union contended with two disruptive forces: the communists and the racketeers. The communists used their standard tactics, and it was only after several years of bitter in-fighting, as in the other needle trades, that the communist infiltration was defeated. A similar success was won against the racketeers who had begun to infest the millinery shops after 1930. Following the renewal of the collective agreement for the industry, the union called a "reorganization strike," chiefly for the purpose of cleaning out the racketeers.

During the past decade the union has maintained a record of stable management-labor relations and has demonstrated its capacity for industrial citizenship. Thus, it participates as a partner with the New York millinery manufacturers in a year-around campaign to stimulate the sales of women's hats; it shares responsibility in production problems with the men's hat manufacturers, and it sponsors its own campaign to revive the popularity of men's hats.

In 1953 and 1954 the Hatters' and Milliners' International Union provided two vivid illustrations of the principle that its self-interest coincided with that of the industry and of the community at large. The first instance was the ten-month strike of the 1,400 men and women employed in the plants of the American Hat Corporation of Norwalk, Conn. The firm had opened a new plant in a low-wage area of Tennessee, to which it had transferred its straw-hat division, and it envisioned the eventual removal of its entire production to other southern areas.

The immediate issue was "job security." But also at stake was the threatened uprooting of an industry that for nearly a century had provided the city with a substantial proportion of its payroll and purchasing power. The strike cost the union more than two million dollars in strike benefits, raised through weekly assessments on all the union's members and loans and gifts from other unions including AFL and CIO. The strike was ultimately settled in a manner that assured the city's retention of the industry and the jobs for the duration of a three-year contract.

The second instance of industrial citizenship was the union's loan to the Cartiganer Millinery Corporation of West Upton, Mass., which operates three plants in several small New England towns. Despite the drain on its treasury by the Norwalk strike, the union raised a loan of $250,000 for the Cartiganer firm, enabling it to overcome its difficulties and salvaging both the 700 workers' jobs and the community's industry.

Among the leaders who piloted the Cap and Millinery International through the last five decades were the late Max Zuckerman, who became its secretary-treasurer at the turn of the century; Max Zaritsky, first president of the international union, a post created in 1919, who had been a union officer for 40 years, retiring in 1950 upon reaching the age of 65; Alex Rose, who succeeded Zaritsky in 1950, and who had previously served as secretary of Millinery Local 24 for more than a quarter of a century; Abraham Mendelowitz and Nathaniel Spector, managers of Local 24 and of the Millinery Joint Board, respectively; I. H. Goldberg, a vice-president of the old United Cloth Hat and Millinery Workers since 1921; the late vice-president Lucy Oppenheim; and Rose Schneiderman, a leader in the famous capmakers' strike in 1904, and today still honorary vice-president of the United Hatters and Millinery International Union.

III. THE SMALLER "JEWISH" TRADES

Aside from the "Big Three," there are tens of thousands of Jewish workers in a variety of smaller trades—handbag and luggage, custom jewelry, bakeries, butcher shops, house painting. Many of these workers are immigrants who arrived in the United States as skilled artisans.

1. HANDBAG AND LUGGAGE INDUSTRY

The development of trade unions in the handbag and luggage industry paralleled that of the apparel unions, with the qualification that work in this industry required greater skill and preliminary training. In addition to the usual handicaps of short seasons, the caprices of fashion, inadequate capitalization by the manufacturers, and the recurrent inability to maintain union continuity following short-lived victories, this union was also plagued by nearly continuous factionalism, internal strife and unstable leadership.

Following the complete failure of a general strike by leather goods workers in 1911, union activity remained virtually dormant until the war years, when the pocketbook workers undertook intensive organization that led to the acceptance by a large group of the Fancy Leather Goods Association of the union's demands, including a 48-hour week, elimination of homework, equal pay for women and men, arbitration machinery and limitation of the contractor system.

During the decade and a half following the First World War, the union underwent a series of power struggles and other internal crises, aggravated by the communist thrust for domination. This culminated in the disastrous strike of 1934, in which 12,000 workers were involved, and which was called to secure a 36-hour week to replace the 40-hour week established by the NRA industry code. As a result of this failure, working conditions deteriorated and some of the larger firms left New York. This development frightened all the factions into forming a "united front" administration and organizing, in 1936, the International Handbag, Luggage, Belt and Novelty Workers Union. The "united front" soon disintegrated and factionalism and communist intrigue reasserted themselves. In 1939 the Pocketbook Workers withdrew from the parent body and became the only important element in this trade to succeed in enforcing union conditions in the shops.

In 1951 a unity convention was held and succeeded in introducing a measure of stability into the international union. One of the measures instituted for this purpose was the banning of communists from holding union offices. The revitalized organization is estimated to have more than 40,000 members, of whom some forty percent are Jews. Most of the union's leaders are also Jews, many of whom have been active in the labor movement for a generation.

Heading the list of these officers is Ossip Walinsky, president, who has been with the handbag workers since 1916 and who was manager of the Bonnaz Embroidery Workers' Union of the ILGWU prior to that. The 1951 convention also reelected Norman Zukowsky secretary-treasurer, and Morris Fuchs became executive vice-president. Philip Lubliner and Benjamin Feldman, leading officials of the Pocketbook Workers, were also elected vice-presidents.

2. JEWISH PAINTERS

From the earliest years of this century, organized groups of Jewish immigrant painters tried often and vainly to join existing locals of the Brotherhood of Painters and Paperhangers. They were rebuffed by the union's officers on the pretext that they were only re-painters, not craftsmen. The Jewish painters were allowed only one local, the Alteration Painters Union, restricted to activity on the East Side. Even efforts by AFL President Samuel Gompers failed to move the Brotherhood to more favorable action until the Jewish painters' local won a strike in 1914, gaining thereby a wage advantage over Brotherhood members. Thereafter the Brotherhood agreed to admit more than 5,000 Jewish painters, though without the right to hold office. This disability was removed in 1916, and within a year the Jewish members became a dominant element in seven of the thirteen painters' locals in the Greater New York area.

The next few years witnessed a grueling struggle between a reformist element of newcomers, headed by Philip Zausner, and the entrenched leadership and the District Council, which was associated with racketeering interests. In 1916 the reformers succeeded in electing their slate of business agents in a campaign to abolish the "kickback," but that system was too deeply ingrown to be liquidated quickly. The reform leadership conducted a successful strike against the powerful Master Builders' Association in 1918, winning the battle against squads of gunmen, and gaining a 25 percent wage increase and the closed shop. A year later the District Council won a nine-week strike for the five-day week. But a nine-month strike called in 1920 to gain a $10 a day minimum wage involved the Council in a bitter fight against Robert Brindell, a racketeer and powerful figure in the Brotherhood of Carpenters, who had been hired by the master painters to break the strike by forming a fake rival union. Brindell subsequently was jailed for his racketeering activities.

For the next six years Zausner built a powerful machine and achieved complete control of the District Council, despite growing opposition, until he was deposed in 1926 in the aftermath of the discovery of the looting of the union treasury by one of his subordinates. He returned to the industry in 1929 as a working painter and by 1933 had regained his old power. He was finally deposed and permanently ousted in 1935 as a result of widely credited reports that a strike he led and won in 1934 had been conducted in collaboration with an underworld gang.

The elimination in 1935 of the racketeering element from the New York District Council left a vacuum that was quickly filled by the communists, who had begun to gain influence in the early 1930's by exploiting rank-and-file discontent with the Zausner machine. A loyal communist agent, Louis Weinstock, became Council secretary and during his regime the Painters' Council became a pliant tool of the Communist Party, contributing large sums to communist causes. The communists were not ousted until 1947, and Weinstock himself was expelled from the union in 1950.

The painters' craft in New York is now solidly organized, numbering some 10,000 members, about half of them Jews, in Manhattan and the Bronx. They have established a union welfare fund and a retirement insurance fund, maintained by a 7 percent weekly payroll contribution by employers. They enjoy the high average hourly wage of $2.83, but their work-seasons have been steadily shrinking in recent years.

Smaller Jewish painters' locals are to be found in Brooklyn, Chicago, and Los Angeles. The three locals of the Brooklyn District Council, which at one time numbered several thousand Jewish painters, now have only a little more than 1,000 members. The loss of membership, as well as prestige, is the result of the consistent misrule and racketeering of the District leadership, involving kickbacks to employers, frequent membership taxes, and a rule of near-terror. In Chicago's Painters' Local 552 there are only some 600 members. The rest of the city's 4,000 Jewish painters belong to other locals. Local 348 in Los Angeles, with more than 1,000 members, is largely Jewish. Its eight-member delegation to the National Brotherhood convention in 1951 was refused recognition on the ground that they were communists. Cleveland also has a substantial number of Jewish painters, but there is no specifically Jewish local.

3. THE FUR WORKERS

The first Jewish fur workers' union was organized with the aid of the United Hebrew Trades in 1892. The crisis of 1893, however, wiped out this union and it took eleven years before a new fur workers organization was formed. Unstable and brief work-seasons and wretched sanitary conditions which literally mowed down fur workers with tuberculosis and asthmatic ailments made union advance a slow and uphill process.

By the summer of 1912, however, heartened by the gains made in the other needle trades, 9,000 fur workers, about 7,000 of them Jews, left the shops. After ten weeks of striking, the fur workers won substantial wage and work-hour improvements and a joint board of sanitary control to police health standards in the fur factories. In 1913, the fur workers formed an international union and joined the AFL.

During World War I years the fur shops were busy, but the postwar period found nearly all fur workers idle. Despite the severe slump, the militant group which was gaining ascendancy among the furriers and was led by young Ben Gold put forward new demands and called a general strike in the spring of 1920. This walkout proved to be the longest in the history of Jewish labor. It lasted eight months, and was finally settled on the terms of the old contract.

The next half-dozen years witnessed bitter clashes between right and left elements in the fur union. In 1926, the communists, now in practical control, maneuvered the fur industry into another general strike, which lasted seventeen weeks and was marked by extreme violence, beatings and arrests. The union won only one of its main demands, a 40-hour work-week. After the strike was over, the AFL's Executive Council appointed a committee to investigate the conduct of the strike, and this committee found, among other things, that the strike leaders had mismanaged huge sums of union money, had brutally suppressed members who dared to criticize their conduct, and had bribed police and court officials. The AFL thereupon expelled the Fur Workers International Union and attempted to reorganize the furriers in the New York market. This effort failed, however, largely because the communists had succeeded in disrupting the opposition through ruthless control of jobs in the shops, on the one hand, and by granting surreptitious concessions to many employers whenever it suited their purpose to keep them in line, on the other.

The past dozen years have seen employment and work terms in the fur industry dip to tragic levels. Literally thousands of furriers have left the trade and hundreds of others have been crowding daily the "fur streets" in New York and other markets with barely a hope of getting permanent work. As before, the better-paid and more stable jobs are doled out by the communist job-controllers to safe henchmen.

The Fur Workers International, which joined the CIO some years after it was expelled by the AFL, was also expelled from the CIO in 1951 for serving the Communist Party. Ben Gold, its president, two years later was indicted by a Federal jury on charges of having lied in an NLRB affidavit that "he is no more a communist." Gold was tried and convicted to a prison term and a monetary fine, a verdict currently on appeal before the Supreme Court. At the union's convention in 1954, Ben Gold resigned as president, turning over his post to Abe Feinglass. A few months later, however, he turned up again as a consultant of the New York Furriers' Joint Board.

IV. THE UNITED HEBREW TRADES

The United Hebrew Trades was established in 1888 in New York City for the purpose of popularizing trade unionism among the masses of new Jewish immigrants that were streaming into New York. The UHT's goal was to overcome the prevailing tendency of Jewish unions to disintegrate following a strike, and to secure permanent existence of the union movement. At the time there were only two "permanent" Jewish unions on the East Side, the typographers and the theatrical choristers. Thus the leaders of the UHT undertook, as one of them put it, to "build a house from the roof down." Among the UHT's first leaders were Bernard Weinstein and Morris Hillquit. Hillquit subsequently became a dominant figure in the socialist movement in the United States.

The UHT's early activity consisted of distribution of leaflets, calling meetings, and a sustained effort to overcome the timidity and fear of the immigrant workers in the face of an antagonistic public opinion and police violence. During those early decades the United Hebrew Trades was closely associated with every step that led to the formation of Jewish unions in New York. Its financial and moral support were key factors in the successful drive to organize the Jewish trades. Always a delegate body, its member unions came to include virtually every large and small Jewish union — all the garment unions, teamsters, cabinet makers, waiters, textile workers, theatrical employees, printers, musicians, jewelry workers, clerks, painters, bakers, cigarette makers, furriers, pocketbook workers, motion picture operators. It has always been essentially a central trade union body.

The UHT has from the beginning been deeply involved in all the inner struggles of the Jewish labor movement. It weathered the disruptive tactics of the De Leon and the IWW groups and gradually drew closer to the AFL, whose views on trade union policies and tactics it came to share. Thus, most of its affiliates joined the AFL, chiefly through their own international organizations, and these fraternal relations have remained strong despite periodic crises.

During the 1920's the UHT took an active part in the struggle against the communist infiltration and subversion of the labor movement by forming its own Committee for the Preservation of Trade Unions. And it successfully repulsed the communist effort to set up a "united front" of labor during the critical years of the depression after 1929.

With the formation of the Committee for Industrial Organization in 1935, the UHT faced the internal danger of dual unionism that threatened to disrupt the whole American labor movement, since some of its affiliates remained loyal to the AFL while others joined the Committee. But as the CIO became firmly established

after 1938 and the early turmoil subsided, the initial fears faded out, and the UHT continued to function uninterruptedly within the scope of its original program.

The UHT also performed valuable services in helping to link the Jewish trade union movement with the larger American labor movement and with Jewish communal and humanitarian programs. Thus it cooperated closely with the Hebrew Immigrant Aid Society (HIAS), the People's Relief Committee and the Joint Distribution Committee during and after World War I in programs of refugee assistance here and abroad. It has also been instrumental in initiating and conducting large-scale programs of aid for the Histadrut, the Jewish Federation of Palestine, through the *Gewerkschaften* campaigns and sponsorship of the National Labor Committee for Palestine.

The UHT, through its patient and persistent efforts and close collaboration with the AFL and its top leadership, aided in the integration of Jewish labor into the American labor community by helping to overcome the initial antagonism and suspicions against the immigrants.

Among the men who stood at the cradle of the UHT and shaped its future were Morris Hillquit, its first corresponding secretary in 1888; Bernard Weinstein, the "daddy of them all" in Jewish unionism; M. Wolpert, an octogenarian and today still an active trade unionist; Max Pine, a near-legendary figure in Jewish organized labor; A. J. Shiplacoff, a socialist legislator who served the UHT in many critical occasions, and Morris S. Feinstone, whose tenure as secretary with the UHT began in 1915 and came to an end with his death in 1943. William Wolpert, son of M. G. Wolpert, has been secretary of the UHT for the past eleven years.

V.   JEWISH LABOR COMMITTEE

The Jewish labor movement played an important and effective role in alerting the American labor community to the evils and dangers of Hitlerism after 1933. In the fall

JEWISH LABOR COMMITTEE—NATIONAL CONVENTION, 1947

of that year a provisional Jewish Labor Committee was established, under the leadership of the late B. Charney Vladeck, to speak for the organized Jewish workers in the fight against Nazism, and in 1934 the Committee was officially launched at a conference in New York City representing many unions, Workmen's Circle branches, the *Forverts,* and a number of socialist groups. From its inception the JLC was able to elicit the strong support of the AFL, and later the CIO, in its effort to expose the menace of Nazism and to engage in a vigorous defense effort against the Nazis' anti-Semitic onslaught.

After the outbreak of World War II the JLC successfully undertook, against extraordinary odds, a historic rescue mission. As a result of its efforts and the personal intervention of the late AFL President William Green, the U. S. State Department issued a substantial number of visitors' visas to European political refugees and intellectuals, facilitating the escape of more than

1,000 distinguished European personalities, Jewish and non-Jewish alike, at the critical point when Hitler's armies had overrun and occupied most of France. In addition, the JLC's successful action enabled a large number of Jewish socialists, labor leaders, and liberals to escape from the Soviet-occupied territories of Poland and Lithuania to the United States and a few neutral European countries.

The JLC did not confine its endeavors to rescue work. By expanding its sponsorship of cultural activities, it helped the refugee intellectuals to continue their work in this country. And after the war's end the JLC greatly expanded its relief program for the surviving Jews of Europe and the displaced Jews who migrated to the United States. In all of these activities it succeeded in creating an awareness of these specifically Jewish problems and support for their solution in the larger American labor movement.

During the postwar period, the JLC has also expanded its educational activity in improving race relations and in pressing Jewish labor's viewpoint on this question within the American labor movement. Its role in this enterprise has been fully accepted and supported by the other Jewish organizations engaged in similar activities.

When Vladeck died in 1938 Adolph Held became chairman of the JLC. The general secretary of the JLC was at first Isaiah Minkoff, and then Jacob Pat. David Dubinsky is treasurer of the JLC.

VI. THE *FORVERTS* TODAY

Even the briefest story of Jewish labor in America could not afford to omit reference to the *Forverts* — known to the non-Yiddish speaking world as the *Jewish Daily Forward*. In the 57 years of its existence the *Forverts,* born in a burst of popular protest and anger against dictatorial party dogmatism which shackled freedom of opinion within the socialist milieu at the end of the past century, has clung tenaciously to the doctrine of democratic socialism and trade unionism. The *Forverts* has run the full gamut of Jewish labor history during these hectic decades. There has not been a single major event in Jewish life in which the *Forverts* did not take part as inspirer, definitive partisan or antagonist.

The *Forverts,* from the day of its founding, has stood out as the champion of the budding Jewish labor unions in their pathetic labors to find a firm foothold in the shifting sands of their trades. One wonders, indeed, if the great early strikes which had launched the mighty unions in the needle trades and in the smaller Jewish industries would have brought the results they did, were it not for the all-out support the *Forverts* had given them. It is equally as difficult to speculate whether the over-all counterattack launched by the Jewish unions and the Workmen's Circle against communist infiltration and sabotage in the 20's and 30's would have been consummated with such excellent results had it not

been for the day-in-and-day-out dedicated cooperation of the *Forverts* and its staff.

During its first 50 years, it was the personality of its great editor, Ab. Cahan, which spelled out the driving force, the content and the ideology of the *Forverts.* With the death of Cahan in 1951 at the age of 91, the last of a heroic period passed away. Ab. Cahan came to this country on the wings of a European utopia (*Am Olam*) and marched on from there toward newer frontiers rooted in American realities. His logical successor to the post of editor-in-chief in 1951 became the veteran managing editor of the *Forverts,* Hillel (Harry) Rogoff. Rogoff, with the assistance of Leon Fogelman, has continued the policy of full allegiance to the free trade union movement. Its support of Israel and of its Mapai (moderate socialist) government is as strong as ever, though not uncritical on occasion.

Among the journalists and writers whose contributions helped to shape and clarify opinion in the Jewish labor movement during recent years, the following names should be mentioned: B. Hofman or Zivyon whose column "Jewish Interests" became quite an institution by itself (he died recently at the age of 80); Raphael Abramovitch with his widely read column "Men and Politics"; David Shub, expert on Russian and international communism; Harry Lang, former labor editor of the *Forverts;* David Einhorn, poet and essayist; Jacob Rich, Mendel Osherowitch, Jacob Lestschinsky, Mark Khinoy and many others.

Among the newsmen who had rendered genuine service to organized Jewish labor belong also the late Louis Stark, for more than 35 years labor editor of the *New York Times,* and Joseph Shaplen, for many years labor editor of the *New York Herald Tribune* and later also on the labor staff of the *Times.* Both these men helped, because of inner conviction and unalloyed sympathy for the Jewish workers, to present to vast audiences the epochal picture of the struggles of the Jewish masses to win "a place in the sun" for themselves and for their industries.

VII.   THE WORKMEN'S CIRCLE

Well up in the sixth decade of its existence, the Workmen's Circle, the oldest and largest fraternal aid organization in Jewish labor, is currently facing up to a number of problems of a vital and compelling nature.

While its chief functions through the early years have been to provide sick benefits, life insurance, and free burial the Circle has also made its goal mass education on the basis of socialism and cooperation with the Jewish trade union and the socialist movement. Thus the Workmen's Circle from the outset became an organic part of the militant Jewish labor movement. As such it became indirectly involved in the internal ideological and political strife in the labor movement.

As time passed by, the educational activities of the Workmen's Circle grew less political and more cultural. In the years after World War I, a network of Yiddish afternoon schools was created to provide education for the American-born children of its members in the Yiddish language, Yiddish literature, Jewish history, and the history of the labor movement in order to prevent the estrangement between immigrant parents and their English-speaking children. In the 30's and 40's the educational trend became more national, with more emphasis on Jewish history and Jewish motives. (See *Jewish People — Past and Present*, Vol. II, "Jewish Education in the United States.")

With the years, however, the Workmen's Circle began to face what every other fraternal aid order is bound to face, namely, the spectre of membership decline caused chiefly by the aging of its members. And like every other fraternal order it had only one source of member replenishment to turn to — the native-born children of their own members. The leadership of the Circle had recognized the dire need of such a step

when it launched its youth movement in 1929. In the subsequent years it began organizing Youth and English-speaking branches in a special division under expert leadership with a pattern of social and cultural life of their own.

By 1951 the W. C. had some 100 of these English branches with a membership of nearly 9,000 out of a total of about 71,000 in the whole organization. It would seem, on the face of these facts, that the W. C. is gradually though slowly assuming the outline of a two-generation body similar, in fact, to the rapidly changing memberships of many, if not most, labor unions and other social groups which have stepped across their half-century marks. This fact, however, imposes upon it an ever greater urgency to redouble the efforts in tapping the reservoir of younger elements within its reach.

The trend toward the younger generation found its expression at the last convention of the Workmen's Circle in the election of Jacob Zukerman, a relatively young native-born lawyer, as president. This was the first time in the history of the organization that a representative of the younger generation was chosen for the highest post in the order. In former years only very prominent members of the "Old Guard," such as Reuben Guskin, Joseph Weinberg, Ephim Jeshurin, Leon Arkin, Ezekiel Eberil, could aspire for the W. C. presidency. After the death of Joseph Baskin in 1952, the post of General Secretary went to Nathan Chanin, who for sixteen years directed W. C. educational activities. Benjamin Gebiner is assistant secretary of the order.

VIII.   AMERICAN LABOR AND THE JEWISH UNIONS

Except for some early instances of discrimination with regard to admission of Jewish workers into some of the older high-standard trade unions, mostly in the construction trades, the record of the general American labor movement and of its leader-

WORKMEN'S CIRCLE—21st ANNUAL CONVENTION IN BOSTON, 1921

SAMUEL GOMPERS (1850-1924)

ship throughout the past half-century toward organized Jewish labor is unimpeachably fine.

The American Federation of Labor has had three presidents since it came into existence in the mid-8o's, and all three have manifested, time without number, their unqualified acceptance of the Jewish trade union movement and a warm relationship towards it. Long before the big strikes of 1909 and 1910, Samuel Gompers addressed garment workers' meetings and concerned himself with the fate of the needle trades' unions. It was Gompers who had presided over the negotiations which ended the great cloakmakers' strike in 1910. The prestige of his name and of the AFL became a factor in every struggle these unions had to wage as long as he lived. And William Green, who took over the presidency of the AFL in 1924, continued this close relationship and friendly attitude towards the Jewish unions. Green's tenure as AFL president — from 1924 to 1952 — covered one of the most tragic periods of Jewish history. But it encompassed also the birth of the State

of Israel. Green did everything within his power to arouse the American people to the menace of Nazism and of its consequences to world democracy, and he ceaselessly called on the American community, and in the first place on organized labor, to support the new Jewish commonwealth and its labor federation, the Histadrut.

George Meany, who succeeded William Green, has already proved convincingly his progressive outlook on domestic and world affairs. Meany's admiration for the pioneering attainments of the Jewish trade unions in the areas of welfare and "fringe" benefits and their alert progressivism is frank and outspoken.

No less open-minded and sympathetic toward the Jewish trade unions has been the CIO. Sidney Hillman, David Dubinsky and Max Zaritsky stood at the cradle of the Committee for Industrial Organization and contributed abundantly toward its progress during its formative years. From the beginning the CIO's top command, and that includes John L. Lewis, has never per-

WILLIAM GREEN (1873-1952)

mitted intolerance in any shape or form to enter the portals of their unions. Both the late Philip Murray and his successor, Walter Reuther, have consistently demonstrated their appreciation of the role of organized Jewish labor in the American trade union community.

IX.   A NEW CLIMATE EMERGES

The tragic events of recent European Jewish history and the inspiring events associated with the establishment of the State of Israel have not failed to have a profound impact on the Jewish labor movement in the United States. The problem of Jewish survival as a people has become a predominant concern of this movement as of all other Jewish communal bodies. The events of the past decade have impelled many Jewish socialists to re-think their relations to the Jewish spiritual heritage and to the role of the Jewish people in the world. A new climate of understanding and respect for the traditional Jewish heritage has been created. Differences of opinion naturally remain — about the role of Yiddish and Hebrew in the Jewish labor movement's educational systems in the United States, about the role of Yiddish in Israel, about ideological relations to Zionism, about religious Orthodoxy and secularism. But to a large extent these differences have lost their sharpness, and the various elements in the movement have come to find it easier to meet on common ground, to find greater mutual understanding, and to increase the areas of joint action on cultural and other communal problems.

This new climate is reflected clearly in three great areas: relations with Israel, reorientation of the Bund's philosophy and program, and communal philanthropy. The development of ever-closer relations with Israel, and especially with the Histadrut, has been mentioned earlier. The UHT and many of the individual Jewish unions have forged increasingly closer links with the Israeli labor organization, despite the fact that they have not themselves generally accepted the Zionist ideological orientation. Virtually all Jewish labor unions are actively assisting in the building up of the State of Israel.

In 1939, on the eve of World War II, a delegation of the Polish Bund arrived in this country to spur activity in behalf of the Bund. The outbreak of the war stranded them here, and they gradually became absorbed not only in rescue work abroad but also in promoting cultural and educational activity in the United States. During the war it became evident that the Bundist group in America would have to shoulder the responsibility of furthering the Bund's tradition and articulating its philosophy. This reorientation, stemming from the practical realization that the Bund could no longer restrict its activity to the East European Jewish community, which had been martyred by the Nazi murderers, led to two practical results: the creation of a monthly Yiddish organ in the United States, *Unser Tsait,* and the establishment of a coordinating committee in 1947 to unite all Bundist groups throughout the world and to guide Bund activity in the years ahead.

In no activity has the Jewish labor movement evinced its close ties to Jewish communal traditions more graphically than in its continuing adherence to the ancient Jewish tradition of philanthropy. This has been true of the unions, of the Workmen's Circle, of the *Jewish Daily Forward,* and of the Jewish socialist groups. They have ever been ready to come to the aid of their fellow Jews, of other non-Jewish labor groups, and of humanitarian American and world causes, and their generosity through the decades has been striking. These Jewish labor institutions have been responsible for the collection and contribution of many millions of dollars to a great variety of labor, communal and Jewish causes.

Despite many differences within Jewish labor, the movement is wholly united on the fundamental issues of Jewish survival and on the importance of encouraging the growth of a free Jewish cultural life within the framework of the democratic world community.

X. ASPECTS AND OUTLOOK

It is much more difficult today than it was a few decades ago to answer the questions: what *is* the Jewish labor movement and what does the future hold in store for it? A few prospects in sight may be cited with reasonable certainty, nevertheless.

The garment and clothing industries in which the Jewish trade unions largely function will continue to remain under Jewish ownership regardless of the ethnic complexion of their working staffs. Most of these needle trades will continue to operate in their present locations despite a trend to run away from the major production areas, either in search of low-wage areas or in order to escape union work controls.

The needle industries will continue to be plagued by uncertain and short work-seasons, changing styles and vacillating consumer tastes. Still, annual take-home pay may equal and, in many instances, exceed total per-year earnings in many other trades. The younger folks, children of the first-generation Jewish immigrants, will continue to shy away from the garment trades as permanent vocations. There is, however, a growing recognition that a skilled dressmaker, millinery worker or handbag operator earns more money and in less work hours than a stenographer, a filing clerk, a salesman or saleswoman, in addition to being protected on the job by strong and responsible unions.

The gradual substitution of non-Jewish for Jewish workers may in the course of years bring about some structural changes and administrative mutations in the needle trades unions. The foreseeable future, however, does not offer any sharp outlines of such developments. The leadership of these unions, predominantly Jewish, seems deeply rooted, and it is an attestation to the high morale prevailing in these organizations that no racial, color or ideological cleavages are visible either on the surface or in the practical "co-existence" of these various groups.

* * *

The entire movement has undergone vast economic, social, and political changes, particularly in the past two decades. The old Jewish ghettos in the major urban centers have all but disappeared; the East Side as a great center of Jewish population is virtually a memory today. Nor is it any longer relevant to speak of Jewish trades and Jewish unions in the old sense. There remain hardly any unions in which Yiddish is the "official" language. Most of the unions that were built largely by Jewish workers today have non-Jewish majorities. And since the American Jewish population is today far more widely distributed economically, the relative weight of the Jewish workers in what used to be "Jewish" trades has been materially reduced, even where plant ownership and management remain in Jewish hands. Socialism, at least domestically, is no longer a force in the Jewish labor movement. With the decline of the Socialist Party as a factor in American politics generally, the socialism of the older generation of the Jewish labor movement expresses itself primarily in support for democratic socialist and labor forces abroad.

Nevertheless, despite these overwhelming changes, there remain certain inescapable ways in which one may still speak of a Jewish labor movement. To begin with, there is what might be called a "historical political consciousness." Despite the ideological and political decline of socialism, Jewish labor remains keenly aware of the enormous contribution made to American society as a result of the decades-long struggle for social and labor welfare conducted by the coalition of Jewish socialists and the Jewish trade unions. This played a key role in the subsequent enactment of the whole body of progressive labor legislation that is now part and parcel of the American social and economic scene.

* * *

With the decline of the Socialist Party in the mid-1930's, and the consequent elimination of this base of independent labor political action, the leadership of the Jewish unions moved to form the American Labor Party, with the immediate objective of enabling their members and other adherents of the New Deal to vote for President Roosevelt in 1936 without having to cast their ballots for the Democratic Party. Its ultimate aim was to establish an independent and permanent party through which labor and all other liberal forces could make their political influence felt. The ALP mustered 275,000 votes for Roosevelt in 1936.

It soon became clear, however, that the ALP was rapidly being infiltrated by communists, without effective resistance. Within a few years the trade union and liberal leadership found itself in the minority, and in 1943, after the communist wing had manipulated a victory in all New York counties except the Bronx, the party split and most of the democratic, anti-communist forces left the ALP. Within a few years, the remaining democratic labor unions, such as the Amalgamated, the Transport Workers and the National Maritime Union also left the ALP, leaving the communists without the protective coloration of democratic trade unionism. Today the ALP is moribund, with but a tiny fraction of its former following.

In 1944 the same labor leadership that had formed the ALP created the Liberal Party to support the fourth-term candidacy of Franklin D. Roosevelt and to enhance his chances of winning New York State. The Liberal Party, which offers the voters "no blueprints for a utopian future, but a balanced program to meet current issues and to solve fundamental problems," has grown steadily and has gained increasing acceptance among the unions and other liberal groups.

Today the Liberal Party embraces the full strength of the ILGWU, of most of the other Jewish unions, and of many non-Jewish unions in the Greater New York area. It has become a decisive factor in New York City elections and aspires to become the balance of power in New York State. And while the Liberal Party has generally endorsed and helped to elect liberal and pro-labor candidates of other parties, notably of the Democratic Party, its successes have given concrete meaning to the notion of independent labor political action. The Liberal Party has become the "political home" that the Jewish labor movement has consistently striven to build.

BIBLIOGRAPHY

Documentary History of the Amalgamated Clothing Workers. New York, 1954.

EPSTEIN, MELECH, *Jewish Labor in U.S.*, 2 vols. New York, 1950-1953.

GREEN, CHARLES H., *The Headwear Workers*. New York, 1944.

HARDY, JACK, *The Clothing Workers*. New York, 1935.

HARRIS, HERBERT, *Labor's Civil War*. New York, 1940.

HURWITZ, M., *The Workmen's Circle*. New York, 1936.

ILGWU—News History (1900-1950). New York, 1950.

LEVINE, LOUIS, *The Women's Garment Workers*. New York, 1924.

LIEBERMAN, ELIAS, *Unions Before the Bar*. New York, 1950.

ROBINSON, DONALD B., *Spotlight on a Union*. New York, 1948.

SEIDMAN, JOEL, *The Needle Trades*. New York, 1942.

STOLBERG, BENJAMIN, *Tailor's Progress*. New York, 1944.

YELLEN, SAMUEL, *American Labor Struggles*. New York, 1936.

ZARETZ, CHAS. E., *The Amalgamated Clothing Workers of America*. New York, 1934.

האפמאן, ב. (צבּיון), פופציק יאר קלאוקמאבער יוניאן (1886 — 1936). ניו-יארק, 1936.

וויינשטיין, ב., די יידישע יוניאנס אין אמעריקע. ניו-יארק, 1929.

לאנג, ה. און פיינסטמאן, מ. (רעד'), געווערקשאפטן — זאמל-בוך צו פופציק יאר לעבן פון די פאראייניקטע יידישע געווערקשאפטן. ניו-יארק, 1938.

ראזענבערג, אברהם, ערינערונגען פון די קלאוקמאבער און זייערע יוניאנס. ניו-יארק, 1920.

AMERICAN JEWISH SCHOLARSHIP*

Joshua Trachtenberg

I. INTRODUCTION

1. GENERAL EVALUATION

A survey of Jewish scholarship on the occasion of the three-hundredth anniversary of Jewish settlement in America may not seem very pertinent. The date 1654 has no bearing on the history of Jewish academic interests and pursuits. Not until two centuries later can we detect the first dim spark of that love of learning which has always characterized Jewish life, and not until this very century did it burst into flame bright and steady enough to light up the record of accomplishment set down here. Yet this survey is not without meaning at this juncture in the story of American Jewry. It is already a cruel commonplace that the destruction of European Jewry has thrust our community into the forefront of Jewish life, into a position of world Jewish leadership. Jewish history is bound to ask concerning us, as it has of other Jewries, what we contributed to the sum total of Jewish life. And since learn-

* I have not attempted here to compile an exhaustive bibliography of American Jewish scholarship, but rather to assemble a comprehensive, if selective, picture of fields of interest and research which have occupied Jewish students. It is with pleasure and gratitude that I record my dependence on the counsel and opinion of many authorities who graciously responded to my request for aid. While I have pursued my own judgment and assume sole responsibility for the views expressed here, I am deeply indebted for the advice and information proffered by William F. Albright, Salo W. Baron, Israel Bettan, Boaz Cohen, Samuel S. Cohon, Solomon B. Freehof, Cyrus H. Gordon, Abraham S. Halkin, Henry E. Kagan, Bertram W. Korn, Franz Landsberger, Jacob R. Marcus, Ralph Marcus, Leon Nemoy, Raphael Patai, Joseph Reider, Ellis Rivkin, Cecil Roth, Samuel Sandmel, Eric Werner, Rachel Wischnitzer, and the librarians and officers of a number of institutions. I extend to them my hearty thanks.

ing is the heart of traditional Jewish values, and the extinction of Europe's great centers of Jewish culture leaves a void where once were springs of life-giving waters, the question is more pointed still: Do we possess the capacity to fill the role history has imposed upon us? Can we be the new center to share with the new Israel the historic function of preserving and enriching Jewish culture in and for our day and the morrow as did the great centers of the diaspora in the past?

The generation of the great names has virtually passed. What of the new generation, the younger scholars who today bear the mantles of yesterday's greats with honor and distinction? Are they products of America? Not yet. Most of them are still imports, if not actual refugees in their adult years from the Hitler terror in Germany and Poland, then refugees in reverse, who having been born or reared here spent their mature years abroad receiving the specialized graduate training America could not offer them.

The predominant characteristic of American Jewish learning is that it has been and still remains almost entirely an importation from abroad. Only a tiny minority of the men and women whose works are reported in this survey received all of their education, Jewish and secular, undergraduate and graduate, in the United States. But this minority must now burgeon into the whole, lest Jewish scholarship have little indeed to add to these pages a century hence. The Jewries of Europe are no longer extant to bequeath us their best intellects; the *yeshivot* are in ashes; many of the scholars have perished. Jewish America must finally produce its own men of learning.

Can it? The most dismaying aspect of Jewish scholarship in America today is its appalling mortality rate. A generation of young American-born and trained students is arising, but how few of these young people have followed up their promising first work? They publish one volume, usu-

ally an excellent academic thesis, and never produce anything else in the fields of their specialized training. The fault is not theirs. The community offers so little reward in appreciation and more tangible return that unless a young man has independent means along with a strong sense of dedication, or succeeds in obtaining a position in one of the very few Jewish institutions of higher learning, he is obliged to immerse himself in the prosaic business of earning a living (in the Rabbinate, teaching, social work, etc.), which leaves little time or energy for creative study, or turns to other fields of research with better academic status or promise.

Professional possibilities are severely restricted. There are too few Jewish academic institutions to provide posts in any field for more than a dozen scholars at the most at any one time—indeed, in one generation; and Jewish studies are pursued in only a very few general universities. Communal agencies have begun to employ trained researchers on their staffs, but here, too, the number of available positions is very limited. Thus scholarship on a professional level, which may be expected to be most active and productive, is confined to a select few.

The responsibility is twofold: the scholar has functioned in a social vacuum; and the dynamics of Jewish life have displaced the scholar as the preeminent symbol of its value system.

Scholarship breathes and lives in the written word. Yet the end-product of learning is surely not books, but knowledge and understanding. However much precious information is enshrined in weighty tomes, it is inert until it is translated into the informed opinion out of which intelligent judgments and wise decisions grow. But Jewish scholarship in America has concentrated on producing books, many of them, and not a few of outstanding worth, without regard to the needs and interests of the community, and with little if any concern for their digestibility or the means whereby they might be absorbed into its thinking. Scholarship, by definition, must not be "practical"; and yet it dare not be so esoteric as to isolate itself from life and lose all relation to it. If Jewish learning has ceased to be "popular" in America, in both senses, as it has always striven to be, the sin must be ascribed at least partly to the scholars.

What has brought this about? We must attribute it mainly to the German orientation of Jewish studies, which persisted until quite recently. This is not to single out Germany as the source of all evil, for before Hitler destroyed its academic integrity it led the world in its standards and accomplishments. But the rabbis and scholars trained in German methods brought to these shores a detachment from everyday interests and a dedication to learning as a sort of sacred abstraction which kept them aloof from the turbulently expanding community of American Jews. Thus, along with German academic emphasis on philology, wide erudition and proficiency in classical and Semitic languages, American Jewish learning tended to be "idealistic," minimizing if not excluding altogether social and economic forces; it was also apologetic, with a strong assimilationist tinge, in the interests of emancipation and integration in western society, and respectably middle class in so far as it had any social orientation whatever.

To some extent a change has slowly manifested itself. The arrival of students from Eastern Europe sensitive to contemporary currents, caught up in the political ideologies of dissent and revolution, disillusioned with the messianic promise of western-style emancipation, attracted to socialist or nationalist modes of thought, has forced the cold draft of modernity into Jewish studies. They represent a new approach, acknowledging the reality of socioeconomic forces and of the national and secular aspects of Jewish experience. Their outlook is less blandly optimistic and more inclusive than that of their conservative,

respectable academic predecessors. They are deeply interested in Zionism and socialism and the communal aspects of Jewish life. Thus they are closer to the people and more directly attuned in their scholarly interests to those of the community. That they have turned their attention increasingly to the American scene, and have engaged in valuable pioneer explorations of its recent history and current problems, is a significant token of their ability to penetrate the living tissue and assimilate to its needs and processes.

Moreover, native-born and native-trained young Jewish students, no longer affected by European academicism and responsive to the trend in American scholarship at large, may be expected to follow its lead, and that of the East Europeans, in introducing the broader sociological approach, the contemporary mood and interest, and the literary standards which characterize it, into Jewish learning. Signs of this revolution are already apparent. Jewish scholarship is approaching the actualities of Jewish life and may yet infiltrate the literate consciousness of the American Jew. As this comes about we may be able to point to Jewish learning as an American product, not only in the limited sense that its practitioners are native, but that its products too are indigenous in content and conception and style.

American Jewry has the capacity and the potentiality to assert its inherited urge to pry and to understand, to squeeze meaning out of life, or to force meaning into it. Whether it will impress its resources into the realization of that potentiality, and whether in so doing it will resurrect and revivify the Jewish tradition, making learning the key to understanding, and knowledge the spur of meaning, deepening and expanding the spiritual and intellectual insights of the Jewish search for truth as an American Jewish contribution to the totality of human wisdom, all this is a question for the next century to answer. But that it is a fascinating and intriguing and important question no one can doubt. And this is why a survey of Jewish scholarship in America has pertinence just at this juncture—even if it cannot boast a history of 300 years.

2. THE HISTORICAL BACKGROUND

The first Hebrew book printed on this side of the ocean was a grammar, *Dikduk Leshon ha-Kodesh* (1734), by a convert to Christianity, Judah Monis, who served for a time as instructor in Hebrew at Harvard College. This unoriginal volume, based on the works of earlier grammarians, was intended not for Jewish use but for students at Harvard.

Thereafter, until the mid-nineteenth century, with the gradual increase in population there accumulated slowly a tiny library of publications intended for popular instruction and use, consisting mostly of English translations of the ritual, addresses and sermons delivered on special occasions, and of a few Hebrew texts for children, but also of some works of a more scholarly nature. Among the latter were such works as Joseph Aaron's *Mafteach el Leshon Ivri ve-Hokmat ha-Dikduk* (A Key to the Hebrew Language and the Science of Grammar, 1834); *A Critical Grammar of the Hebrew Language* (2 vols., 1838-1841) by Isaac Nordheimer, professor of Semitic languages at the University of the City of New York; *Imre Shefer* (1838), by M. Henry, a dictionary of Hebrew and Aramaic roots found in the Bible; and a German translation of Judah ben Zeev's Hebrew version of Ben Sira together with the Hebrew text, *Sefer Hokmat Yehoshua ben Sira* (1850), by Isaac Mayer.

This last work points to the opening of a new era in American Jewish history. The author was a "forty-eighter," a Rabbinic refugee from the abortive revolution in Germany, contributing his mature learning and talents to the edification of the new community sprouting in the new land. Two men in particular embody most strik-

ingly the spirit of this age and the scholarly impetus they brought to its unfoldment: Isaac Leeser (1806-1868) and Isaac Mayer Wise (1819-1900). Uncompromising opponents, champions of diverse camps, they more than any others set the tone and created the media for the Americanization of Judaism and the Jewish community.

Leeser was without intensive Jewish or academic training; he was essentially self-educated. But he early saw the need to raise the cultural level of American Jewry, and he set his indefatigable energies and incomparable dedication to this purpose. His most notable contributions to Jewish learning were his translation of the Bible, the first Jewish version in English, and his monthly periodical, the *Occident,* which he edited from 1843 until his death, and which provided a forum for discussion of religious and social issues and a medium for publication of many scholarly essays. Among his many organizational projects was the first American-Jewish academic institute, Maimonides College in Philadelphia. It existed only a short while (1867-1873), but it was the harbinger of the permanent institutions which succeeded it.

Wise's impact was even more telling. Almost from the day of his arrival from his native Bohemia he threw himself into the struggle for an American Reform movement, and quickly assumed its leadership. A prolific and versatile writer, he poured forth an unending stream of sermons, addresses, articles, short stories, novels, and scholarly essays on every Jewish theme, not only in the columns of his papers *The American Israelite* (founded in 1854) and *Die Deborah* (1855-1900), which he edited, but in every other periodical which would print him. Besides this he composed a dozen volumes which inaugurated Jewish scholarly activity in the fields of history, Bible, religion, and Jewish-Christian relations. When after long and bitter factional dispute he succeeded in establishing the Union of American Hebrew Congregations in 1873, one of its express aims was "to establish and support a scholastic institute, and the library appertaining thereto, for the education of rabbis, preachers and teachers of religion." Learning was the chief cornerstone of Wise's vision of the new Jewish center in America. Two years later the Hebrew Union College came into existence.

The last decades of the century also witnessed several related developments. In 1887 the Jewish Theological Seminary of America was founded in New York by Sabato Morais, previously associated with Leeser's short-lived Maimonides College, to train rabbis for traditionally inclined congregations. By the 1890's the Jewish Publication Society and the American Jewish Historical Society were functioning. Jewish studies were introduced into American universities, and Richard J. H. Gottheil, Cyrus Adler, Morris Jastrow, Jr., Emil G. Hirsch and William Rosenau began to teach at such great institutions as Columbia, Pennsylvania, Chicago, and Johns Hopkins. Jewish learning was acquiring respectability. A seminal half century was drawing to a close. In 1902 the JTS was re-organized under the leadership of Solomon Schechter, who assembled a brilliant faculty. The HUC responded to this challenge by calling to its presidency Kaufmann Kohler, and surrounding him with an equally gifted staff. Simultaneously the *Jewish Encyclopedia* was produced, the first great fruit of Jewish learning in America. In 1907 the Dropsie College opened its doors, the first non-theological Jewish institute of graduate studies and the source of much valuable research. In 1915 Rabbi Isaac Elchanan Theological Seminary, later to become the great Yeshiva University, a peculiarly American amalgam of secular and Orthodox learning, was launched.

The new era in scholarship, in opportunities for productive study and research, was in full swing. When the Hitler persecution uprooted the Jewish scholarly world of Central Europe, American Jewish institutions were ready to absorb many of the learned refugees and thereby to enrich Jewish learning here. When later the Second World War extinguished the Jewries of Eastern Europe many of those fortunate enough to escape found their way to these shores and poured their rich fund of learning and experience into the channel of American Jewish scholarship.

Here we stand today. Ours has been an immigrant scholarship, fostered and created by refugees in and for an immigrant community. Viewed in the perspective of American Jewish history, however, it has not been tardy in its emergence.

3. COLLEGES AND INSTITUTES

The dominant feature of American Jewish institutions of higher learning is that, but for the Dropsie College, all the major schools are representative of a distinct trend or religious ideology. This tends to color their outlook and academic interests, so that students must align themselves with one or another branch of American Judaism before embarking on their studies, and teachers are usually expected to subscribe to a specific doctrinal position. However, the level of instruction is uniformly high, and research methods are objective and critical on a plane comparable to that of the general academic community. The Hebrew Union College, Cincinnati, the oldest Rabbinical seminary in the United States, was founded in 1875 by Isaac Mayer Wise to train rabbis for Reform congregations. Rigidly adherent for a long time to the "classic" pattern of early Reform, and representing the middle-class ideology of the German Jewish community, it has since the 1930's absorbed and responded to the influence of the newer East European community in its curriculum and outlook. It has pioneered in developing a department of social studies and human relations, and in courses in American Jewish history and pastoral psychology. Its graduate school now offers the Ph.D. degree. In 1950 it merged with the Jewish Institute of Religion. The presidents of the College have been: Isaac M. Wise (1875-1900), Moses Mielziner (1900-1903), Gotthard Deutsch (1903), Kaufmann Kohler (1903-1921), Julian Morgenstern (1921-1947), and since 1948 Nelson Glueck.

The Jewish Theological Seminary of America, New York, was founded in 1887 by Sabato Morais and S. Pereira Mendes to train rabbis for what have become known as Conservative congregations. Its major emphasis has been on Rabbinic studies. It pioneered in the establishment of a Teachers' Institute and of interfaith projects on an academic level. Sabato Morais (1887-1897) was succeeded as president by Solomon Schechter (1902-1915), Cyrus Adler (1915-1940) and Louis Finkelstein since 1940.

The Dropsie College for Hebrew and Cognate Learning, Philadelphia, was established in 1907 as a result of a bequest by Moses Aaron Dropsie; it was the first non-sectarian graduate institute for Jewish studies in the world, whose sole purpose has been scientific research and learning in all fields of Jewish interest. The first president, Cyrus Adler (1907-1940), was succeeded by Abraham A. Neuman.

The Yeshiva University, New York, is the result of a merger in 1915 of the Etz Chaim Yeshiva (founded 1886) and Rabbi Isaac Elchanan Yeshiva (founded in 1897) to form the Rabbi Isaac Elchanan Theological Seminary, which in 1928 inaugurated Yeshiva College. This was the first college of liberal arts and sciences under Jewish auspices in the United States, and the first union of a traditional Talmudic academy with a modern academic college in Jewish history. In 1945 this institution became a university, with a total of twelve academic divisions today, including a graduate institute of Jewish studies. This school, which remains staunchly Orthodox in its philosophy, has particularly emphasized Talmudic and Rabbinic learning. Bernard Revel served as president from 1915-1941, and Samuel Belkin has occupied that post since 1943.

The Jewish Institute of Religion, New York, was founded in 1922 by Stephen S. Wise to train liberal rabbis uncommitted to any one interpretation of Judaism. Wise was president from 1922 to 1947, and in 1948 Nelson Glueck was elected to succeed him. When the Institute merged with the Hebrew Union College in 1950, Glueck continued as head of the united College-Institute.

There are a number of Orthodox *ye-shivot* in several cities, of which the Hebrew Theological College at Chicago is the largest and most progressive. Teachers' training institutes have developed extensive undergraduate programs, and have also sponsored some graduate seminars under the guidance of the competent scholars of their faculties. Among the leading schools in this category are the Baltimore Hebrew College, the Boston Hebrew Teachers' College, the College of Jewish Studies in Chicago, Gratz College at Philadelphia, the Hebrew Union School of Education and Sacred Music, New York, the Teachers' Institute of the Jewish Theological Seminary, and the Jewish Teachers' Seminary and People's University, New York. The rapid growth of the Jewish community in Los Angeles has prompted the recent establishment there of two such schools, the College of Jewish Studies and the University of Judaism, sponsored respectively by the Hebrew Union College and the Jewish Theological Seminary.

The newly established Brandeis University, which includes Judaic studies in its curriculum, has attracted to its faculty a considerable number of Jewish scholars. Indeed, more than 200 universities and colleges offer undergraduate and graduate courses in Hebrew and in general Jewish subjects.

Research in Jewish affairs is also fostered by several academic societies. The American Jewish Historical Society was founded in 1892 to collect and publish material bearing on the history of the Jews in America;

it has engaged primarily in building up an excellent specialized library and archive, and in publishing studies and documents.

The American Academy for Jewish Research was organized in 1920 but did not become active until several years later; it serves primarily as an agency for research projects and publication.

The Conference on Jewish Relations was organized in 1933, mainly at the instance of the late Morris R. Cohen, to apply the social sciences to the study of Jewish life. Besides its publications and conferences on economic and social problems, the Conference organized the Commission on European Jewish Cultural Reconstruction which investigated the cultural assets of the communities destroyed by the Nazis. It later stimulated the establishment of the Jewish Cultural Reconstruction, Inc., which salvaged and redistributed more than 400,000 books, some 10,000 artistic and ceremonial objects, and some 1,200 Torah Scrolls, about one-third of these going to American institutions.

The Yiddish Scientific Institute—YIVO was founded in Wilno in 1925 for the study of Jewish life and history the world over, but particularly in Eastern Europe. This organization speedily became through its training, research and publication programs, a focal point of Jewish intellectual activity. When the war broke out and put an end to its flourishing center in Wilno, the headquarters was transferred to New York, to which some of its leading scholars managed to make their way with sections of its library and archives. Since then YIVO has continued its active program here, turning its attention increasingly to the study of Jewish life in America, and beginning the issuance of some publications in English.

Some of the communal agencies employ specialists and sponsor research projects, usually limited to their own needs or to some restricted area of interest, but often productive none the less of good and stimulating results. Thus the American Jewish Committee is responsible for excellent studies in the psychology of anti-Semitism; the American Jewish Congress has delved into the problems of relations between church and state; B'nai B'rith has closely followed the ups and downs of anti-Semitism in the United States; the Council of Jewish Federations and Welfare Funds has made useful demographic and social service studies; and the various Zionist organizations have produced much good material on the development of Palestine and Israel.

Before we go on to consider the contributions of individual Jewish scholars, mention must be made of an extraordinary accomplishment in the field of Jewish learning—*The Jewish Encyclopedia*. This epoch-making work was the cooperative product of a number of men and still stands unsurpassed as the greatest single achievement of American Jewish scholarship. It was unprecedented in Jewish literary history, entailing a vast labor of condensation and systematization, and of pioneer research in completely new areas. Isidore Singer, whose dream it was and who ultimately was able to make it a reality, succeeded in obtaining as sponsor a non-Jewish publisher, Isaac Funk, of Funk and Wagnalls. The principal American contributors were Cyrus Adler, Gotthard Deutsch, Judah D. Eisenstein, Louis Ginzberg, Richard Gottheil, Emil G. Hirsch, Joseph Jacobs, Kaufmann Kohler, Jacob Z. Lauterbach, and Solomon Schechter. Of these Ginzberg and Lauterbach, as well as William Popper among others, made their first significant appearance as researchers and systematizers in its pages, so that it was a testing ground for new talent, as well as a proving ground for talents already well tried.

II. BIBLICAL LITERATURE AND HISTORY

1. SEMITICS AND ARCHAEOLOGY

The importance of a knowledge of the languages, literatures and histories of the peoples of the Near East for a better understanding of the Bible text has long been recognized, but never before so widely exploited as during the past few decades. The discovery of ancient Near Eastern literary treasures and the unravelling of unknown tongues have shed bright light upon many obscurities in the text and upon its general background. It is now considered a matter of course that a Biblical scholar should be an expert not only in Hebrew but also in cognate languages and literatures. It should be borne in mind, moreover, that the Semitic languages are an important adjunct to the fields of Rabbinics, Jewish philosophy, and literature, so that authorities in these disciplines are usually outstanding Semitists as well. Max L. Margolis, whose specialty was the Septuagint, was one of the greatest Semitic philologists on American soil; Louis Ginzberg, Isaac Husik and Harry Wolfson must be included among the leading scholars of Hebrew, Aramaic and Arabic, as well as of their respective specialties.

The pioneer among Jews in this field was Richard J. H. Gottheil (1862-1936), whose best contributions were perhaps in Syriac, though he was productive also in Hebrew and Arabic. Morris Jastrow, Jr. (1861-1921), was for years a leading world authority on Mesopotamian religion, and was well known as a general all-around Semitic and Biblical scholar. His *Hebrew and Babylonian Traditions* (1914) was an early study of the influence on the Bible of Babylonian mythology and literature.

Among contemporary Semitists H. L. Ginsberg, the foremost Jewish Biblical philologist, is probably unexcelled anywhere in the field of Biblical Hebrew language. Besides having contributed extensively to Biblical exegesis, he has distinguished himself as an expert in Ugaritic studies, a field opened up by the recent discovery of a large collection of documents closely allied to the Canaanite tradition, among the ruins of ancient Ugarit at Ras Shamrah in North Syria. Cyrus H. Gordon has also won renown as an Ugaritic expert with his edition and translation of *The Loves and Wars of Baal and Anat and Other Poems from Ugarit* (1943), and his *Ugaritic Handbook* (1947) among his other writings in this field. Another Jewish specialist in Ugaritic is Theodore H. Gaster, whose studies have appeared in a number of journals. The literature and language of these documents are so intimately related to the antecedents of the Bible text as to open up new avenues of comprehension of the utmost significance.

One of the leading authorities in the world on the history and languages of the ancient Near East is Ephraim A. Speiser. B. Landsberger, perhaps the greatest living Assyriologist, settled in the United States as recently as 1948. Samuel Noah Kramer has performed a prodigious task in reconstructing and elucidating a large segment of the Sumerian language and thus making available a large part of the world's oldest literature, dating from the fourth and third millennia B.C.E. Another eminent scholar who has contributed to our knowledge of Assyrian-Babylonian mythology and literature is Julius Lewy, who has published a number of essays on various Semitic subjects in relation to Jewish history and religion. I. J. Gelb, head of the great Assyrian Dictionary project, and A. L. Oppenheim are to be included among the leading Assyriologists in the United States.

Among Arabists William Popper, whose edition of many volumes of the great work of Ibn Taghri Birdi is one of the best such publications ever issued, ranks at the very top. He has also worked in the field of Biblical studies. Julian Obermann, another leading specialist in Arabic studies, has published material also on ancient Semitic languages; in *The Archaic Inscriptions from Lachish* (1938), for example, he pointed out that the Northern Semites employed other alphabetic systems than the Phoenician or even Ugaritic for purposes of writing.

The publication of Abraham S. Yahuda's (1877-1953) *The Language of the Pentateuch in Its Relation to Egyptian* (1933; published in German in 1929) caused a considerable stir among Bible scholars at the time, but its argument for a predominantly Egyptian rather than Mesopotamian influence on the Bible and for the accuracy of the Pentateuchal chronology has since been largely discounted.

Nelson Glueck, a leading Biblical archaeologist, conducted a series of explorations in Transjordan and the Negev. The results were reported in detail in *Exploration in Eastern Palestine* (5 vols., 1935-1951), and won the acclaim of scholars. His two books *The Other Side of the Jordan* (1940) and *The River Jordan* (1946) are among the best popular works in Biblical archaeology. In these volumes, and in his numerous articles, he describes in detail the progress and results of the most extensive topographical survey of the area ever undertaken, and of his excavations at many ancient sites, including Solomon's famous seaport of Ezion-geber on the Gulf of Akaba. Among his conclusions are that parts of this area, including the Negev and the upper half of the Jordan Valley, were rather thickly inhabited in ancient times; that there has been no important change in climate during historic times; and that the breaks in sedentary civilization were due to political conditions rather than the weather, as had been surmised. It may be noted that Glueck's findings—he is now engaged in an intensive exploration of the Negev—have had considerable practical value in promoting the search for natural resources in the State of Israel.

2. EXEGESIS

Bible studies have been notoriously neglected by Jewish scholarship, a situation all the more glaring in the face of the exceptional interest and progress in this field during the past century. The development of the school of "higher criticism," which demolished the unity of the Pentateuch and challenged its integrity, was not calculated to attract Jewish scholars, most of whom rejected its methods and conclusions. It should be noted, however, that the trend of Bible study nowadays is decidedly less radical than it was half a century ago, while the methodology of higher criticism has won such wide acceptance that we may expect a considerably increased activity in this field on the part of Jewish scholars.

The only scholarly student of the Bible in this country (aside from I. Leeser and I. M. Wise) before the twentieth century was Benjamin Szold (1827-1902). His *Hebrew Commentary on Job* (1886), generally conservative in its exegesis, dated this enigmatic and compelling book from the Babylonian Exile, and rejecting the popular view that it offers a solution to the problem of suffering, propounded the thesis that Job's refusal to deny God was intended as an object lesson on how the righteous should withstand adversity. The change in viewpoint introduced by the modern critical approach is ably reflected in Morris Jastrow's *The Book of Job* (1920). Here the famous Semitist, who also cultivated Biblical studies, discarded the traditional Jewish conception completely, considering *Job* to have been originally the bitter outpouring of a skeptic who discounted God's providence because of the sufferings of the righteous, which later generations rendered "respectable" by the addition of more orthodox sentiments.

Moses Buttenwieser (1862-1939), an enthusiastic exponent of higher criticism, also contributed a volume to the perennial debate on Job. In *The Book of Job* (1925), in which he pursued with zeal the game of emending the admittedly difficult text, he proposed the view that this book was meant to refute the prevailing notion of religion as a way to win God's favor and reward, voiced by Job's friends, and to substitute for this the prophetic spiritual conception. Buttenwieser had already published, in *The Prophets of Israel* (1914), a provocative exposition of the Graf-Wellhausen hypothesis. His last book, *The Psalms* (1938), contains a new translation and a minutely detailed commentary, with a great deal of illuminating exegetical and philological discussion. However, his attempt to date each of the psalms and then to utilize them as a source for the political history of Israel often leads to questionable conclusions. There may be mentioned too in this connection the striking "restoration" of *The Book of Job as a Greek Tragedy* (1918) by the noted social philosopher Horace M. Kallen, which possesses literary rather than exegetical interest.

In recent years a lively controversy has centered around the question of the original language of Ecclesiastes. Frank Zimmerman, whose field of specialization is Biblical Aramaic, and who has written a number of excellent studies on Biblical philology, first entered the lists with several telling arguments for the Aramaic provenance of Kohelet. One of his opponents, the noted philologist H. L. Ginsberg, at first took strong exception to this view, but has finally come to agree in his little volume, *Studies in Koheleth* (1950), that the obscurities in that book are to be traced to a translator who often failed to understand the original Aramaic text. Robert Gordis, however, has refused to alter his conviction that what we have now is essentially the text as it was originally composed. In a number of essays dealing with various aspects of the problems posed by the wisdom literature generally, and by Ecclesiastes in particular, and finally in *Koheleth: The Man and his World* (1951) he elaborated his position most effectively. His conclusion is that the Aramaisms of the extant text are due to the author's free use of the vernacular language, Aramaic. Nor does he accept the frequently advanced contention that this book is a composite work. A novel suggestion made by Gordis is that the supposed glosses, which have presented so much difficulty to interpreters, are actually quotations of popular sayings, with comments by the original author. Gordis has most recently turned his attention to *The Song of Songs* (1954), in which he provides an equally perceptive introduction and commentary to, as well as a new translation of, this most secular book of the Bible.

Interesting and, in some respects, important contributions to the exegesis of the Bible have been made by several scholars, especially trained in Semitic languages, who have utilized this background particularly for the elucidation of the Biblical text. Arnold B. Ehrlich (1849-1919) published two noteworthy works, *Mikra ki-Peshuto* (The Bible in its Plain Meaning, 3 vols., 1899-1901) and *Randglossen zur hebräischen Bibel* (Marginal Notes to the Hebrew Bible, 7 vols., 1908-1914), the second book a revision and enlargement of the first, in which he made an original and valuable contribution to Jewish exegesis marked by ingenuity of interpretation (sometimes overdrawn) and linguistic insight.

A staunch champion of the accuracy of the extant Masoretic text was Israel Eitan (1885-1936), who argued in *A Contribution to Biblical Lexicography* (1924), that the text only appears to present difficulties because the variant connotations which many Hebrew words originally had have been lost or neglected. Eitan also published exegetical notes to Isaiah and the Minor Prophets and essays on Semitic and Hebrew philology in learned periodicals.

Samuel I. Feigin (1893-1950), a noted Assyriologist, issued a collection of his studies *Mi-Sitre he-Avar* (Secrets of the Past, 1943), dealing with Hebrew philology and Bible exegesis and history in relation to Mesopotamian sources and parallels. His exceptional knowledge of the language and literature of this region, as well as of Hebrew, enabled him to cast fresh light on many difficulties in the Biblical text.

3. BIBLE STUDIES AND HISTORY

Among Jewish Bible scholars in America the name of Julian Morgenstern stands out from all the rest as the most consistent and constructive representative of higher criticism. He has written many essays in various Biblical fields, but his principal work has been on the calendar, the legal codes, and the folklore of the Bible. Basic to many of his studies is his view that three different calendars were used successively in ancient Israel. Out of the harmonization and adjustment of these calendars, which is reflected in conflicting Pentateuchal accounts, according to his conception, developed many of the characteristic institutions and practices of ancient Israel. Morgenstern's *Amos Studies* (1941) comprises the first half of a most detailed critical analysis of the Biblical book and its historical background, resulting in the conclusion that the prophet delivered only a single address, at the Israelite sanctuary of Bethel, "one of the most logically and artistically perfect and oratorically effective and inspiring addresses in all literature."

Sheldon Blank, a pupil of Buttenwieser and Morgenstern, has written a few excellent studies on exilic and post-exilic writing, using the critical approach effectively.

In a brief study, *The Hebrew Scriptures in the Making* (1922), Max Margolis provided a comprehensive popular account of the development of Biblical literature, following a moderate course in his judicious evaluation of the traditional and the "untraditional" views.

Production has been meager in the field of Bible history. Harry M. Orlinsky, a Septuagint specialist who has written essays on Biblical and Talmudic philology, recently published a popular but authoritative little textbook *Ancient Israel* (1954), on the history of the Bible period, in which he takes a middle road between the conservative and radical positions. Jacob Hoschander's *The Priests and Prophets* (1938) offered a social interpretation of pre-exilic history which adhered to a conservative interpretation and analysis of the Biblical text. Also dealing conservatively with the early period from the Judges until the institution of the monarchy, Joseph Zuckerbram's *Yesodot ha-Ahdut be-Yisrael* (The Bases of Unity in Israel, 1919) sought to establish the cultural and social forces which eventually unified the Israelites.

Several writers have focussed their attention on social and legal conditions. Among them Max Radin (1880-1950), whose primary field was general jurisprudence, wrote an interesting little book *The Life of the People in Biblical Times* (1929). Much valuable information is contained in Isaac Mendelsohn's *Slavery in the Ancient Near East* (1949). On a closely related theme, *The Status of Labor in Ancient Israel* (1923), we revert to a figure associated with the very beginnings of creative Jewish scholarship in America—the distinguished jurist, patron of learning, and amateur Bible student, Mayer Sulzberger (1843-1923). In this book and his other studies— *The Am ha-Arez* (1909), *The Polity of the Ancient Hebrews* (1912), and *The Ancient Hebrew Law of Homicide* (1915)—he developed a theory that the struggle between the local town councils, adopted from the Canaanite city-state system, and the centralized federal government which eventually superseded them, determined the evolution of juridical and institutional patterns during the formative period of ancient Israel.

4. ANCIENT VERSIONS

Max L. Margolis, a product of the old *bet ha-midrash* and of Columbia University's Semitics Department, won his greatest renown in the field of Septuagint research. His *Book of Joshua in Greek* (1931) is one of the most exhaustive editions of any book of the Septuagint ever published. Harry M. Orlinsky has to a considerable extent carried on Margolis' work in his many essays on the text and method of the Septuagint. Several monographs on the Septuagint text and its relation to other Biblical versions have been published by Alexander Sperber, who has also worked in the field of Hebrew philology.

In 1916 Joseph Reider published his *Prolegomena to a Greek-Hebrew and Hebrew-Greek Index to Aquila,* an introductory essay to a contemplated larger work on the Greek terms used in Aquila's translation, with Hebrew equivalents. In this volume Reider discussed Aquila's method and exegesis, and the Hebrew text with which he worked, which differed in some respects from the Masoretic text.

The Targum Jonathan to the Prophets (1927), ascribed to Jonathan ben Uziel, a pupil of Hillel, was critically examined by Pinkhos Churgin, who concluded that it is a composite of official Aramaic translations used during synagogue services, which in time assumed unified form. Churgin, whose studies on Targum texts and on the period of the Second Commonwealth have appeared in various journals, enters here upon a detailed discussion of the characteristics of the exegetical method of Jonathan and of its deviations from the Masoretic text.

III.   THE HELLENISTIC-ROMAN PERIOD

1.   HISTORY

The period of the Second Commonwealth, a time of profound political, social and doctrinal dissension and change, presents a host of trying problems for the historian. For the sources, though in a sense abundant, are peculiarly abstruse and oblique, veiling more than they disclose, and their dating and interpretation have given rise to lively controversies.

The moot question of the origin of the Sadducees and Pharisees and of the nature of the differences which so sharply divided them has received a good deal of attention.

A significant contribution in this area, which has had much influence, was made by the noted Talmudic scholar Jacob Z. Lauterbach (1873-1942), three of whose illuminating papers on the subject were recently reprinted in a collection of his *Rabbinic Essays* (1951). He ascribes the emergence of these parties to a conflict between the priestly and lay leaderships (which came to a head during the period of Greek rule as a result of changing political conditions) over the authority to introduce legal and religious innovations, and the method of interpreting the Torah so as to validate such changes.

Louis Finkelstein provided a fresh and stimulating approach in his discussion of *The Pharisees* (2 vols., 1938), and in his more recent volume *Ha-Perushim ve-Anshe Kneset ha-Gedolah* (The Pharisees and the Men of the Great Synagogue, 1950), in which he laid much more stress on the socio-economic background of this portentous conflict. To him, it was a phase of the perennial struggle between patricians and plebeians, which expressed itself in terms of legal and ceremonial differences but did not succeed in hiding its class-conflict roots.

A leading specialist in the Second Commonwealth and a man of profound Talmudic erudition is Solomon Zeitlin. His *History of the Second Jewish Commonwealth* (1933) deals primarily with the political and economic aspects of the era of Greek rule (about 300-150 B.C.E.), which includes the rise of the Pharisaic and Sadducean parties. His *Megillat Ta-anit* (1922) is a scholarly and original study of this early historical chronicle as a source for the chronology and history of the Hellenistic-Roman period. In his essay, *The Jews: Race, Nation or Religion* (1937), he analyzed the attitude of Palestinian Jews toward the Jews of the Diaspora during the Second Commonwealth, and concluded that in their view the Jews constituted a religious-cultural entity. In *A Historical Study of the Canonization of the*

Hebrew Scriptures (1933) he advanced a novel interpretation of the Mishnaic criterion that a canonical book "defiles the hands."

Sidney B. Hoenig's volume *The Great Sanhedrin* (1953) is a competent investigation of the origin, development, composition and functions of the *Bet Din ha-Gadol* during this period. Several studies on the Maccabean revolt have been published by Elias J. Bickerman. A good study—*The Jews Among the Greeks and Romans* (until 70 C. E.) — was written by Max Radin (1880-1950). It deals with the cultural, social and legal status of the Jews during that period. Harry J. Leon is the author of several essays on the catacomb and other inscriptions which provide evidence for the life and history of Jews in Rome and other Italian cities. In a number of articles and monographs the late Eugen Tauebler illuminated phases of Jewish history in Palestine and the Diaspora in the Hellenistic-Roman era.

Of especial value have been the volumes by Saul Lieberman, the ablest Talmudic expert in America today. These are *Greek in Jewish Palestine* (1942) and *Hellenism in Jewish Palestine* (1951), describing the influence of Hellenistic culture on the life and thought of Jews. Luitpold Wallach has also written articles on the relation between Palestinian and Greek literature and culture, and on early Jewish gnosticism.

2. LITERATURE

The earliest serious Jewish student of the Apocrypha on American soil was Kaufmann Kohler, whose *Origins of Synagogue and Church* (1929) reflects his lasting interest in the so-called "inter-testamental" period. The most notable recent development has been the inauguration of the Dropsie College editions of Jewish Apocryphal literature, of which four have thus far appeared: *The First Book of Maccabees* (1950, Zeitlin and Sidney Tedesche), *Aristeas to Philocrates* (1951, Moses Hadas),

The Second Book of Maccabees (1954, Zeitlin and Tedesche) and *The Third and Fourth Books of Maccabees* (1954, Hadas).

Among studies in this field the most noteworthy is Ralph Marcus' *Law in the Apocrypha* (1927), which includes also a discussion of various theological questions, and thus constitutes an important contribution to the history of Jewish thought. Marcus has published many articles on the religion and literature of this period, in which he has specialized. Articles on Enoch and Jubilees and on the Sadducees have been written by Chaim Caplan; on the original language of such books as Judith and Enoch by Frank Zimmerman; and on the Jewish literature of the period by Moses Hadas, a prominent student of classical Greek and Roman literature. Joshua Bloch, who has issued several studies on Biblical and Apocryphal literature, contends in his book *On the Apocalyptic in Judaism* (1952) that the Apocalyptical element in Jewish literature is based on essentially Jewish ideas, though it gives them a unique interpretation. One of Solomon Zeitlin's more important contributions in this field is his study, *The Book of Jubilees* (1939), characteristically original in its conclusions as to the character and significance of this book.

The only important monograph on Philo (aside, of course, from the massive work by Wolfson, which is concerned more with that writer's philosophy than his religious views and will be discussed later) is Samuel Belkin's *Philo and the Oral Law* (1940), which establishes Philo's close relation to the Halakah and exegesis of Palestine.

The most exciting and important development in modern scholarship is the emergence to light of the so-called Dead Sea Scrolls. Since 1947, when the first group of manuscripts of Biblical and non-Biblical texts was discovered by Arabs, more have been turning up in a steady stream, in the original Khirbet Qumran area, and latterly also some distance away, from the Wadi

Murabbaat. These documents are of great variety, even including letters purportedly written by Simeon Bar Kochba, the leader of the revolt against Hadrian. Although only a very few of these documents have been published in facsimile and transcription, the world of scholarship, almost without exception, has been in a great rush to acclaim them as genuine, to date them from a very early period ranging from the second century B.C.E. to the second century C.E., and to ascribe the non-Biblical texts to various sectarian groups of the time.

Against the overpowering weight of universal scholarly opinion and of the archaeological evidence Solomon Zeitlin, virtually alone, has had the temerity to challenge the scholarly world for its haste in embracing these documents, has denied their authenticity and their value for the history of Judaism, and on the basis of paleographic, stylistic and linguistic characteristics (by no means conclusive) has ascribed them to the Middle Ages, probably from Karaite sources. His position is presented in a series of vigorous articles and in his introduction to *The Zadokite Fragments* (1952).

IV. TALMUDICS AND RABBINICS

1. EDITIONS

The task of editing the classic Talmudic and Midrashic texts, essential to the understanding of this basic literature and of its full bearing on the development of Judaism, has proceeded slowly primarily because of the difficulties involved and the high degree of specialization required. An outstanding work of this sort in Talmudics is by Henry Malter (1864-1925), *The Treatise Taanit* (1928), an exemplary critical edition and English translation, with exegetical and historical notes. Malter also prepared a scholarly edition in Hebrew, with introduction, extensive notes and

critical apparatus, which was published in 1930. Abraham Schreiber has just issued his edition of the treatise *Shekalim* (1954), based on a unique manuscript in the Bodleian Library, with explanatory notes and references, and including two commentaries by thirteenth-century rabbis. A diligent laborer in this field was Michael Higger (1898-1953), who turned out a series of editions of minor Talmudic texts, aiming to establish correct readings. He also compiled the *Otzar ha-Baraitot,* a useful collection of Tannaitic dicta excluded from the canon of the Mishnah, but recorded in considerable numbers in the Tosefta and Halakic Midrashim, as well as in the two Talmuds.

Solomon Schechter, who was responsible for editions of late Midrashim, including the *Midrash ha-Gadol on Genesis* (1902), originating in Yemen, and the *Agadat Shir ha-Shirim* (1896), both previously unknown, also published a text of the *Mekilta di-Rabbi Shimeon,* a Halakic Midrash on Exodus. His edition of *Abot di-Rabbi Nathan* (1887), an Agadic commentary on the Mishnaic tractate *Pirke Abot,* included along with the standard text a second version, hitherto unpublished, from a Vatican manuscript. Jacob Lauterbach, in preparing his edition and translation of the *Mekilta di Rabbi Ishmael* (3 vols., 1933-5), came to the conclusion that this Tannaitic Halakic Midrash on Exodus underwent many redactions before it assumed its final form in late Amoraic times. The Halakic Midrash to Numbers and Deuteronomy, known as *Sifre,* has been edited by Louis Finkelstein.

One of the foremost Talmudic philologists of today is Saul Lieberman. His *Yerushalmi ki-Peshuto* (1938), an edition of three tractates, with critical notes, and *Hilkot ha-Yerushalmi* (1947), the laws of the Palestinian Talmud utilized by Maimonides, are representative of his works in this field.

2. LEXICOGRAPHY AND GRAMMAR

Two of the most valuable works of Jewish scholarship produced in America stem
from the era before its twentieth-century
flowering and reflect the exceptional ability
and training of many of the German rabbis. Marcus Jastrow (1829-1903) devoted
twenty-five years to the composition of a
*Dictionary of the Targumim, the Talmud
Babli and Yerushalmi, and the Midrashic
Literature* (2 vols., 1886-1903), the first
such work in the English language. Drawing upon its predecessors in other tongues,
it is nonetheless an original contribution
of the first magnitude. Of equal importance is the monumental edition of the
Aruk ha-Shalem (Aruk Completum, 8
vols., reprinted 1926) by Alexander Kohut
(1842-1894). Kohut devoted a quarter of a
century to the preparation of this tenth-
century lexicon by Nathan ben Yehiel of
Rome, adding notes and cross-references,
so that it has become the basis of all modern Talmudic lexicography.

Max L. Margolis, whose earliest graduate studies were in the field of Talmudic
textual criticism, wrote a brief *Manual of
the Aramaic Language of the Babylonian
Talmud* (1910), which also appeared in
German. A comprehensive study in great
detail ,*Dikduk Aramit Bablit* (A Grammar
of the Aramaic of the Babylonian Talmud,
1930) was prepared by Caspar Levias, a
talented Semitist whose publications were
few but of considerable value.

3. STUDIES IN TALMUD AND MIDRASH

Moses Mielziner (1828-1903) wrote the
earliest work in this field, *Introduction to
the Talmud* (1894), primarily as an aid to
students who lacked basic texts in English.
The usefulness of this popular survey is
indicated by the fact that it was reprinted
three times, the last (1924) in a revision
by Joshua Bloch and Louis Finkelstein.
Also dealing generally with the Talmud,
but on an entirely different level, is *The
Redaction of the Babylonian Talmud*

(1933), in which Julius Kaplan (1885-1939)
concluded, after investigating closely its
literary structure, that the Talmud was
given its present form by the Saboraim on
the basis of the Gemara collection of Rab
Ashi, and hence Rab Ashi is not the redactor of the Talmud, as has been generally
assumed. Arriving at a similar conclusion
in his *Hithavut ha-Talmud bi-Shlemuto*
(The Babylonian Talmud as a Literary
Unit, Its Place of Origin, Development and
Final Redaction, 1943), Abraham Weiss
showed that the Talmud developed in lay-
ers at various schools, multiplying gradually until, by the beginning of the sixth
century, when conditions in Babylonia put
an end to this process, it reached its ultimate form. Thus he concluded that the
Talmud had no redaction and no redactor,
again defying the accepted tradition that
it was edited by Rab Ashi.

The greatest name in American Jewish
scholarship is undoubtedly that of Louis
Ginzberg (1873-1953), whose encyclopedic
knowledge of the Rabbinic and related
literatures, linguistic skill, and acute critical faculty enabled him to make signal contributions in the fields of Agada, liturgy,
Gaonica and Yerushalmi. Indeed, his impress can be discerned in virtually every
area of Jewish learning, for not only did
he range over them all in his voluminous
studies, but he also influenced and guided
almost the entire current generation of
students by his own work and by his interest and aid in their work.

His first love was the Agada. As early as
Die Haggadah bei den Kirchenvaetern
(The Agada in the Writings of the Church
Fathers, 2 vols., 1899-1900) he had marked
out the direction his studies were to take.
Here he was able to show the early date
of a great deal of Agadic material incorporated in later Midrashim by pointing out
its use by early Christian commentators on
the Bible. *The Legends of the Jews* (7 vols.,
1909-1938, the last an index volume prepared by Boaz Cohen) is a massive and

masterly collection of the enormous Agadic material relating to the characters and events of the Bible. The two volumes of notes, citing sources and parallels and ranging often in fairly long essays over the entire literature and the problems it poses, illumine obscure regions in every field, and are an inexhaustible source of information.

Major contributions in Gaonica and liturgy are contained in two other publications by Ginzberg. *Geonica* (1909) contains a survey of Gaonic literature and of the development of the liturgy, essays on the history of the period, and Gaonic Responsa from the Genizah. In *Ginzei Schechter* (Genizah Studies in Memory of Solomon Schechter, 2 vols., 1928-1929) he published many fragments of Midrashic collections and of Karaite Halakic works, Gaonic Responsa, and essays dealing with Agada, Halakah, *Piyut,* ritual and custom.

The first part of Ginzberg's uncompleted major work, *Perushim ve-Hiddushim bi-Yerushalmi* (A Commentary on the Palestinian Talmud, 3 vols., 1941) displays his unique scholarship superbly. Formally a commentary on the first four chapters of the Tractate *Berakot* of the Yerushalmi, the commentary proper is almost incidental to the large number of essays, some almost of book length, on a wide variety of problems in Halakah and Agada and in the broader field of Jewish theology, history and culture.

Jacob Z. Lauterbach (1873-1942), another leading Talmudist, made notable contributions in his studies of Halakah and Agada, several of which are reproduced in his collected *Rabbinic Essays* (1951). His *Midrash and Mishnah* (1916), following his theory of the evolution of Pharisaism, ascribed the change from the Midrash form, giving the law and its derivation, to that of Mishnah, which states the law only, to the lay teachers who sought thus to accredit popular practices on a par with those emanating from the Written Law and to supplant the priestly leaders as effective legislators.

Louis Finkelstein, an outstanding student of Rabbinic literature, has written extensively on the theology, liturgy and Halakah of the pre-Talmudic and Talmudic periods. His *Akiba* (1936) projects the biography and the views of one of the founders of Rabbinic Judaism, based on the scant data scattered through the vast Talmudic literature, somewhat tenuously, but skillfully, against the background of social and economic tension which he described in *The Pharisees.* His more recent work, *Mabo li-Mesektot Abot di-Rabbi Nathan* (Introduction to the Treatises Abot of Rabbi Nathan, 1950), is an analysis of the texts of these treatises and the literary problems they pose.

Comprehension of the Tosefta has been advanced by Boaz Cohen's critical comparative analysis of the Mishnah and Tosefta of the Tractate *Shabbat,* in his *Mishnah and Tosefta* (1935), and by Alexander Guttmann's studies in the literary structure of the Tosefta.

Also of value in this field has been Alexander Marx' critical edition of *Kelale ha-Talmud* by the sixteenth-century authority Bezalel Ashkenazi, which deals with Talmudic methodology.

The distinguished historian and Rabbinic scholar Jacob Mann (1888-1940) published one volume of an uncompleted major work, *The Bible as Read and Preached in The Old Synagogue* (1940), which has an important bearing on our understanding of the structure and evolution of the Midrashic homilies.

An invaluable reference work still in process is the vast *Torah Shelemah* by Menahem M. Kasher, a complete collection of comments and notes on the Biblical text culled from the entire Rabbinic literature until the Gaonic period, a veritable Rabbinic encyclopedia of the Pentateuch. Kasher is not only a compiler but an editor as well; he includes much manuscript material, and his notes and appendices contain useful critical comments. In 1953 an abridged English version of this work, *Encyclopedica of Biblical Interpretation,* began to make its appearance.

Among monographs a number may be selected as illustrating the areas of interest. Ben Zion Bokser, in *Pharisaism in Transition* (1937), analyzed the recorded dicta on religious matters of Eliezer ben Hyrcanus to show how these reflect the social conservatism of their author in a time of social and economic change. The Rabbinic attitude toward proselytism has been ably treated in two books: *Proselytism in the Talmudic Period* (1939) by Bernard J. Bamberger, and *Jewish Proselyting in the First Five Centuries of the Common Era* (1940) by William G. Braude. Samuel K. Mirsky, who has written essays on later Rabbinic literature, and a good study of the Halakah in the Agada, published in *Bein Shekiah li-Zerihah* (Between Dusk and Dawn, 1951) a study of the evolution from Sanhedrin to the later Babylonian Academy. Paul Romanoff's (1898-1943) *Onomasticon of Palestine* (1937) is an exhaustive work on post-Biblical topography, listing all references to Palestinian sites in the Rabbinic literature until the thirteenth century, including all those in Biblical, archaeological and Greek and Latin sources. Samuel Rosenblatt explored the Mishnaic exegetical methods and lexicographical and grammatical understanding of the Biblical text to show in his *The Interpretation of the Bible in the Mishnah* (1935) that they are critically sound.

4. LAW AND CODES

The earliest American monograph on Jewish Law was the work of Moses Mielziner, *The Jewish Law of Marriage and Divorce* (1884). Louis M. Epstein made the field of family law his special province and published several valuable books on its historical and legal aspects—*The Jewish Marriage Contract* (1927), *Marriage Laws in the Bible and the Talmud* (1942), *Sex Laws and Customs in Judaism* (1948), dealing with the Jewish standard of sex conduct outside of marriage, and a Hebrew work on the *Agunah* problem. *The Protection of the Weak in the Talmud* (1925) by Mordecai Katz explores the laws regulating the status and rights of slaves, minors, women, debtors, tenants and the poor, reflecting the lively concern of the rabbis for the welfare of the weak which often prompted them to modify Biblical law. Samuel Atlas has written several essays on Talmudic law, including *Rights of Private Property and Private Profit* (1944). *The Jewish Law of Theft* (1929) by Moses Jung, includes comparative references to Roman and English law, as does Samuel Mendelssohn's (1850-1922) *The Criminal Jurisprudence of the Ancient Hebrews* (1891).

Contributions of fundamental importance to the history of Jewish law were made by one of the truly great figures in modern Rabbinic scholarship, Chaim Tchernowitz (1871-1949). His unique contribution to the history of the Halakah, in the four volumes of *Toledot ha-Halakah* (History of the Oral Law, 1934-1943) is that he treats it in accordance with modern methodology, bringing out the role and scope of custom, precedent, judicial decision and academic opinions as sources of Jewish law, and he uncovers underlying concepts such as the "social contract" and the "discovery" of the law by judges and jurists. His historical reconstruction traces the development of the Halakah from its origin in a threefold source—kings, prophets and priests, or law, equity and ritual—through the early period of the Second Commonwealth, when the schism between urban and rural priests determined its subsequent course.

Le-Toledot ha-Shulhan Aruk ve-Hitpashtuto (The History of the Shulhan Aruk and its Acceptance, 1897-98) was an early essay on the history of codification. Tchernowitz' interest in this subject culminated in another epochal work, *Toledot ha-Poskim*

(3 vols., 1945-47), the first comprehensive summary, analysis and evaluation of the history of codification of Jewish law, from the Gaonic period to the Shulhan Aruk and its commentaries, a masterful feat of organization on the basis of underlying principles. The analysis of the individual works covers in each instance the historical background, the author's methods and personal predilections, and the aim of the work, with copious quotations to illustrate the argument, so that an exceptional insight is provided into every aspect of the development of codification.

The greatest of all codes, the *Mishne Torah* of Maimonides, is being presented for the first time in English translation by the Yale Judaica series (sponsored by the Louis M. Rabinowitz Foundation). Of the five volumes which have so far appeared, three have been prepared by American Jewish scholars: *The Book of Civil Laws* (1949) by Jacob J. Rabinowitz; *The Book of Judges* (1949) by Abraham M. Hershman; and *The Book of Acquisition* (1951) by Isaac Klein. The task of translating the fourteen books of the *Code* is stupendous, requiring a profound and thorough knowledge of Talmudic literature, an understanding of the historical development of Talmudic law, and a mastery of legal English.

5. RESPONSA

A renewed interest in the vast Responsa literature has been evinced of late, but much of it is primarily concerned with the incidental information there disclosed concerning social and historical developments and will therefore be mentioned in the section on history below. Considerably less attention is being focussed on the purpose of the *Sheelot u-Teshubot*, the adjudication of legal and ritual issues. However, a number of excellent editions have appeared, with introductory essays discussing the major implications of their contents, and explanatory notes, thus adding materially to the sources available for the study of law and religion, as well as of Jewish history and life. Among these may be mentioned Boaz Cohen's *Kuntres ha-Teshubot* (1930); K. L. Mishkin's *Teshubot Rabbenu Gershom* (1951); Israel Elfenbein's *Teshubot Rashi* (1943); and Irving A. Agus' *Teshubot baale ha-Tosafot* (1954). From the last author we have also an analysis and translation of almost eight hundred Responsa by *Rabbi Meir of Rothenburg* (2 vols., 1947). *The Responsa of Solomon Luria* (1938) by Simon Hurwitz offers a digest of this sixteenth-century authority's *Teshubot* arranged according to subject matter, without any comment on the Halakic or historic significance of the contents.

Pertinent here, too, is the compilation of *Responsa* (1954) by Jacob D. Schwarz from the *Yearbooks* of the Central Conference of American Rabbis. This volume, arranged according to subject matter, contains all the replies by the leading scholars in the Reform movement to the religious and ritual questions posed from 1890 to 1953, and reflects the legal reasoning and social and religious considerations which prompted and justified many of the innovations during this period.

Solomon B. Freehof, a well-informed student in this field, has just published *The Responsa Literature* (1954), a popular but soundly-based survey of the origin, characteristics, development and influence of this literature, which should contribute to a wider interest in it.

V. PHILOSOPHY

1. HISTORY OF JEWISH PHILOSOPHY

Among the best products of American Jewish scholarship are the writings of three academicians of the highest distinction on the history of medieval Jewish philosophy: David Neumark (1866-1924), Isaac Husik (1876-1939), and Harry A. Wolfson.

Neumark, an original thinker and a Hebrew stylist of a high order, set out to construct a massive history of Jewish philosophy in ten volumes which was to deal comprehensively with its central concepts and problems in relation to contemporary non-Jewish philosophical currents. His aim was not exclusively academic, for he sought to expound the thought of the past in order to derive from it a modern philosophy of Judaism, "to present a systematic exposition of the principles of Judaism based on a modern philosophic view of life," as he put it. Unfortunately, he was able to publish only two volumes and part of a third in German, *Die Geschichte der jüdischen Philosophie des Mittelalters* (1907), which appeared later (1921-29) in a revised Hebrew edition, *Toledot ha-Pilosofiah be-Yisrael,* and another Hebrew work on dogmas, *Toledot ha-Ikkarim be-Yisrael* (2 vols., 1913-19), intended to be the tenth in his series. As it is, these constitute an important contribution to the subject, for his introductory volume provides a concise summary of the development of Jewish thought from the Biblical period to the end of the Middle Ages, and in the others he discusses the problem of matter and form, the attributes of God, and dogmatics in a manner which reflects his complete mastery of the material and his creative critical approach. His many essays in German, Hebrew and English contain valuable insights into the central issues dealt with in Jewish philosophy.

Isaac Husik was a profound student of Jewish philosophy who developed no Jewish philosophy of his own, and expressed none. His *History of Jewish Philosophy* (1916, 2nd edition 1930) is a sober, methodical account of the development of Jewish thought from the tenth to the fifteenth centuries, including Karaite as well as Rabbinic writers. Except for the introductory chapter, in which he outlines the principal doctrines of Aristotelian and Arab philosophy and the main problems considered by Jewish philosophers, his treatment follows a chronological pattern, analyzing the major works of the period and the problems they discuss.

Harry A. Wolfson has not written a formal history of Jewish philosophy, but in his three massive works on Crescas, Spinoza and Philo he has treated virtually the entire field of medieval philosophy—Aristotelian, Arab and Jewish—both historically and problematically, with consummate mastery. His method may be described as *pilpulistic-dialectical* in the best sense of the term, aiming to ferret out the thought processes which produced the concise, concentrated, often enigmatic prose in which these writers expressed themselves: weighing their words judiciously, critically analyzing their technical terminology, exploring the historic antecedents of their ideas and the literary and contemporary influences which they reflect. In his first book, *Crescas' Critique of Aristotle* (1929), Wolfson coupled his examination of the problems treated in Crescas' *Or Adonai* with an analysis of the presentation of these same problems in Aristotle's *Physics* and *De Caelo,* and their subsequent treatment in the Arab and Jewish tradition.

In his second work, *The Philosophy of Spinoza* (2 vols., 1934), Wolfson used the same method to analyze the *Ethics,* tracing between its lines the philosopher's critique of the Hebrew and Latin traditions, and relating his thought, in the dual role of last of the medievals and first of the moderns, to the philosophical background, particularly the Jewish. His trilogy was completed with *Philo: Foundations of Religious Philosophy in Judaism, Christianity and Islam* (2 vols., 1947), which presents Philo as a great and original thinker, whose conception of philosophy dominated European thought until Spinoza turned its course into its modern channel. Although this opinion is obviously controversial, there can be no doubt that Wolfson has constructed an original, consistent theory of the development of philosophy until

Solomon Schechter made a signal contribution in *Some Aspects of Rabbinic Theology* (1923) which, as the title indicates, comprised essays on some central theological themes in Rabbinic literature, post-Talmudic as well as Talmudic, such as God and man, God and Israel, the Kingdom of God, Sin and Repentance, etc. His three volumes, *Studies in Judaism* (1896-1924), containing persuasive and informative essays on a wide range of subjects, include some on theological themes: Dogmas in Judaism, the Doctrine of Retribution in Rabbinic Literature, etc.

David Neumark's *Toledot ha-Ikkarim be-Yisrael* (The History of Dogmas in Israel, 2 vols., 1913-19) is the standard work on the content, history and formulation of creeds, a painstakingly critical and comprehensive analysis of the subject.

An original and controversial conception of the nature of Rabbinic theology has been elaborated by Max Kadushin in three provocative volumes: *The Theology of the Seder Eliyahu* (1932); *Organic Thinking* (1938); *The Rabbinic Mind* (1952). His thesis is that Rabbinic thought is not essentially logical but what he terms "organismic," that is, characterized by an inner organic relationship between fundamental concepts and the entire current of thought in which they merge.

Two aspects of theology have received extended treatment. The one is the concept of the Messiah. Julius Greenstone wrote a general, extensive survey in *The Messiah Idea in Jewish History* (1906), which Joseph Sarachek followed with an intensive study titled *The Doctrine of the Messiah in Medieval Jewish Literature* (1932). Abba Hillel Silver finally produced a close study in his *The History of Messianic Speculation in Israel* (1927). The subject of fallen angels has also proved intriguing, both in its folkloristic and theological aspects. Leo Jung's *Fallen Angels in Jewish, Christian and Mohammedan Literature* (1926) is essentially a comparative study,

as its title indicates. Bernard J. Bamberger's *Fallen Angels* (1952) offers a more comprehensive survey of the Jewish literature, with Christian and Islamic parallels, as a basis for illuminating their respective attitudes to the problem of evil.

Karaite studies in this country have been almost entirely textual. Solomon Schechter published in Part II of his *Documents of Jewish Sectaries* (1910) a large portion of the hitherto unknown *Book of Precepts* by Anan ben David. Two valuable contributions were made by Solomon Skoss (1884-1953), a leading Arabist, who edited Ali ibn Sulaiman's *Commentary on Genesis* (1928), and of supreme interest, the monumental *Hebrew-Arabic Dictionary of the Bible* (2 vols., 1936-1945) of David ben Abraham al-Fasi. Israel Davidson used his expert knowledge of *Piyut* to edit the complete text of Salmon ben Yeruchim's *Wars of the Lord* (1934). *The Arabic Commentary of Yefet ben Ali the Karaite on the Book of Hosea* (1942) has been ably edited by Philip Birnbaum. Of major importance also has been the work of Leon Nemoy, a distinguished expert in Judaeo-Arabic, who has published many articles in this field, and whose studies of one of the most important literary documents of early Karaism, Al Kirkisani's *Book of Lights and Watch-Towers*, culminated in the massive edition and translation of this work, *Kitab al Anwar wal-Maraqib* (5 vols., 1939-1943). Nemoy has also produced the first *Karaite Anthology* (1952) in any language, depicting the evolution of this sect during its first seven centuries, until 1500, through a selection of excerpts from the writings of its spokesmen. Probably the most useful contribution, in the breadth and variety of information disclosed, was made by Jacob Mann, who published in the second volume of his *Texts and Studies* (1935) a large number of hitherto unknown Karaite documents, mostly of the modern period (after 1500), revealing a mass of new data on the intellectual, religious, social and economic life of Karaite settlements in Palestine, Byzantium and Eastern Europe.

Bernard Revel's (1885-1940) uncompleted work *The Karaite Halakah* (1913) indicated that the Karaites tended to adopt the Pharisaic position in legal issues, rather than the Sadducean, as had been generally supposed; Zevi Cahn makes the same point in *The Rise of the Karaite Sect* (1937), holding that there is little divergence between Karaite and Rabbinic law. A materialist interpretation of Karaism as a disguised revolt of the poor and oppressed against the political and social order is advanced by Raphael Mahler in his Yiddish volume *Karaimer* (Karaites, 1947).

Although there has been a marked revival of interest in the Hasidic movement during recent decades, this has remained largely on a sentimental level on this side of the Atlantic and has elicited insufficient academic attention. Illustrative of the popular approach is Jacob S. Minkin's *The Romance of Hasidism* (1935), the sole attempt to provide a full account of the lives and ideas of its principal figures, from the Besht to Nahman of Bratslav, including a rapid introductory survey of Jewish mysticism, and a final chapter on the opposition to Hasidism and its contributions to Judaism. *The Hasidic Anthology* (1934) by Louis I. Newman and Samuel Spitz, a topical compilation of brief philosophical- theological comments, anecdotes and aphorisms culled from Hasidic literature, contains a useful introductory section on the history, literature and doctrines of the Hasidim. A few serious studies have been contributed by Abraham Heschel in the periodicals. Raphael Mahler's *Der Kamf Zvishn Haskalah un Hasidus in Galitsie* (The Struggle Between Haskalah and Hasidism in Galicia in the First Half of the Nineteenth Century, 1942) advances the social-economic thesis that Hasidism expressed the opposition of the poorer class to the emerging Jewish bourgeoisie and intelligentsia who constituted the Maskilim. A considerable number of studies on Hasi-

dism also appeared in various periodicals, mainly in Hebrew and Yiddish. (For the recent trends in Jewish religious thought see Jacob Agus' "Current Movements in the Religious Life of American Jewry" in this volume.)

2. LITURGY AND RITUAL

Although a number of translations of the ritual into English appeared earlier in the nineteenth century, the first good analytical and historical account, *Jewish Services in Synagogue and Home,* came out only in 1898; it was prepared by a learned amateur, Lewis Naphtali Dembitz (1833-1907). William Rosenau's (1865-1943) *Jewish Ceremonial Institutions and Customs* (1903) is a brief but useful survey of ritual and ceremonies. The standard work in English is *Jewish Liturgy* (1932) by the well-known musicologist Abraham Z. Idelsohn (1882-1938). It is a comprehensive, detailed and scholarly treatment of the subject in all its aspects.

Important contributions to the history of the liturgy have been made by quite a few Rabbinic students, most outstanding being those of Louis Ginzberg, Jacob Z. Lauterbach, Louis Finkelstein, Solomon B. Freehof and Leon Liebreich in various journals. David de Sola Pool's study, *The Kaddish* (1909), covers the history, language, date, and the use in the synagogue of this doxology.

Specific ritual and ceremonial institutions have received some close attention. The first work to deal exhaustively with the methods and effects of Jewish ritual slaughter and its history is *Shehitah* (1941) by Jeremiah J. Berman. Following up this study, Berman prepared, in conjunction with Isaac Lewin and Michael L. Munk, the volume *Religious Freedom: The Right to Practice Shehitah* (1946), a history of anti-*shehitah* legislation as a form of religious discrimination. An interesting project was carried out by S. I. Levin and Edward A. Boyden in *The Kosher Code of the Orthodox Jew* (1940), the former furnishing a literal translation of *Hilkot Terefot,* dealing with defects which render animals unfit for food, from the *Shulhan Aruk,* and the latter, a professor of anatomy, appending a scientific commentary on Talmudic knowledge of and contributions to anatomy, physiology, embryology and pathology.

A pioneer study of the popular institution of Bar Mitzvah is to be found in *Le-Ot ul-Zikkaron* (1942) by Isaac Rivkind, a noted bibliographer and student of Jewish culture. *The Lifetime of a Jew* (1950) by Hayim Schauss (1884-1953) is a popular account with a sound scholarly background of the evolution and variations in practice of the rites and ceremonies associated with the life cycle and the home.

Schauss also produced a useful volume on *The Jewish Festivals* (1938), combining a popular approach with much learning. Theodore H. Gaster, an outstanding Semitist and a student of ancient folklore and ritual, has written two felicitous little books, *Passover: Its History and Traditions* (1949) and *Purim and Hanukkah* (1950), as well as a study titled *The Festivals of the Jewish Year* (1953) incorporating the latest knowledge of their origins and early significance, the traditional observances associated with them, and a modern interpretation.

Reform appears to have become somewhat self-conscious about its deviations from traditional ritual and ceremonial, if we may judge from Solomon B. Freehof's *Reform Jewish Practice and its Rabbinic Background* (2 vols., 1944-1952), which embodies a good deal of research. This cites the Halakic references to current Reform usage only to indicate in many instances that Reform practice is not consonant with the Halakah.

VII. LITERATURE AND LANGUAGE

1. HEBREW

Meyer Waxman's encyclopedic *History of Jewish Literature* (4 vols., 2nd ed., 1938-1941) is the standard reference work in English on this vast subject. It is a running account, arranged topically in four major chronological divisions, of the entire corpus of Jewish literature since the close of the Bible until 1940, not only in Hebrew, but in all languages. Its special value lies in its excellent detailed summation of the contents of virtually every work of any importance produced during these two millennia and its skilful surveys of the intellectual trends that characterize the various periods and areas under discussion.

The outstanding authority on medieval literature was Israel Davidson (1870-1939) whose many studies in the field are of basic importance. *The Otzar ha-Shirah ve-ha-Piyut* (Thesaurus of Medieval Hebrew Poetry, 4 vols., 1924-33, and 2 supplements) is his master-work, a record of more than 35,000 Hebrew poems written between the fifth and twentieth centuries, with identifying data as to source, authorship and form. Besides his editions and studies of poetic works, he also edited a number of prose works of the period, including the *Sefer Shaashuim* (The Book of Delight, 1914) by Joseph ibn Zabara, an interesting and historically important collection of fables, proverbs and anecdotes. In *Parody in Jewish Literature* (1907) he provided a history and analysis of this popular literary form, which had been generally neglected by earlier literary historians, and listed and in many instances reproduced the texts of over 500 works in Hebrew and Yiddish satirizing many aspects of Jewish life in styles parodying the sacred religious writings.

Another student of Hebrew poetry who has brought to light much material from manuscript sources is Simon Bernstein. He has published many valuable finds in the scholarly journals and ably edited the works of Leon de Modena (1932) and Emanuel Frances (1932), two Italian-Jewish poets of the seventeenth century, and of Meshullam da Piera (1946), a thirteenth-century Spanish writer.

A prolific and tireless anthologist, the centenarian Judah D. Eisenstein, has contributed to Jewish scholarship not only through the ten-volume encyclopedia *Otzar Yisrael,* which he edited, but also through his many collections of Hebrew writings in special areas, which he thus made readily available to students. Among these are his *Otzar Midrashim* (1915), containing the texts of 200 smaller Midrashic works; *Otzar Massaot* (1926), reports of Jewish travellers from the Middle Ages to the nineteenth century; *Otzar Vikuhim* (1928), apologetic and polemical writings; *Otzar Derashot* (1919), an anthology of sermons, and *Otzar Zikronothai* (1929), a yearly chronicle of data of Jewish interest from 1872, when he arrived in the United States. His works also include topical compilations of Biblical and Talmudic maxims, *Otzar Maamare Tanak* (1925) and *Otzar Maamare Hazal* (1922), and a handy compendium of Rabbinic laws and customs, *Otzar Dinim u-Minhagim* (1917).

Modern Hebrew literature has received a good deal of attention, but works of sound scholarship and esthetic judgment are few indeed in this field. Two biographical studies are deserving of mention, Simon Ginzburg's careful investigation, *The Life and Works of Moses Hayim Luzzatto* (1931), and *Leon Gordon* (1910) by Abraham B. Rhine (1876-1941), a competent account of the literary activity of the late nineteenth-century Hebrew poet.

Simon Halkin's *Modern Hebrew Literature* (1950) offers a penetrating analysis of the literary trends and values which reflect socio-historical forces in Jewish life during the past two centuries. A good survey of the renaissance of the Hebrew language and literature during this period *is Hebrew Reborn* (1930) by Shalom Spiegel, a series of enthusiastic and informative essays on the life and writings of representative figures. Abraham S. Waldstein's *Modern Hebrew Literature* (1916) is a somewhat more critical and academic study of the important writers of the second half of the nineteenth century.

One of the very few important contributions to the literature of Hebrew philology is William Chomsky's edition of *David Kimchi's Hebrew Grammar Mikhlol* (1952). The product of twenty years of devoted labor, this systematically presented and critically annotated edition includes an especially valuable analysis of the basic contributions of the medieval Spanish grammarians summed up in this classic work. Henry Englander (1877-1950) wrote a number of excellent essays on the grammatical knowledge and terminology of Rashi and his successors, the Tosaphists.

The most notable lexicographical contribution to modern Hebrew is the *English-Hebrew Dictionary* (2nd ed., 1938) compiled by Israel Efros, Judah Kaufman and Benjamin Silk.

An offshoot of Hebrew philological studies is the special field developed by David S. Blondheim (1884-1934). A brilliant student of Romance languages, he pursued an interest in the influences exerted upon each other by Hebrew and these languages, and published in *Les Parlers judéo-romans et la vetus latina* (1925) a pioneer study of the vernacular linguistic tradition of the Jews of medieval Europe reaching back without interruption to antiquity. Thereafter he devoted himself to an analysis of the *loazim,* the French glosses in Hebrew script used by Rashi in his commentaries. Together with Arsène Darmesteter he issued a work on this subject, *Les Gloses françaises dans les commentaires talmudiques de Raschi* (1929), and his second volume, subtitled *Etudes lexicographiques,* appeared posthumously in 1937. His pupil Raphael Levy continued these fruitful researches in *Recherches lexicographiques sur d'anciens textes français d'origine juive* (1932). In collaboration with Francisco Cantera, Levy then edited and translated both the original Hebrew and a thirteenth-century French version of *The Beginning of Wisdom* (1939), an astrological treatise by Abraham ibn Ezra, which has value not only for the study of old French, but also for the history of ideas and the Hebrew astrological terminology.

2. YIDDISH

When L. Wiener wrote his pioneer study *The History of Yiddish Literature in the Nineteenth Century* (1899) he held forth little hope that Yiddish could long survive as a spoken language in the United States. The mass influence of Yiddish-speaking immigrants before and immediately after World War I, the arrival here of some of the leading creative literary spirits from Eastern Europe in the postwar years, and the transfer to the United States during World War II of the vastly productive scholarly energies and initiative of the Yiddish Scientific Institute (YIVO) have belied his pessimism. Yiddish is still a vital spoken and literary tongue, and interest in its literature and linguistic history has quickened and flourished. An important group of scholars has devoted itself to the study of old and modern Yiddish and has produced many significant contributions to all phases of Jewish learning in that language.

The need for a full-length history in English of this area of Jewish literary creativity still remains unfulfilled. The excellent surveys in *The Jewish People: Past and Present* (Vol. III, 1952) by N. B. Minkoff, Judah A. Joffe and Samuel Niger, all three of whom have published valuable studies in Yiddish in this field, must for the present suffice as the best available. A. A. Roback's *The Story of Yiddish Literature* (1940), while containing much information, is unfortunately too sketchy. A useful volume, *The Yiddish Press* (1925), dealing with the history of the Yiddish press in America and its influence as an Americanizing agency was published by Mordecai Soltes and recently (1950) reissued with a foreword summarizing and analyzing developments in the intervening quarter-century. B. Gorin's *Di Geshikhte fun Yiddishn Teater* (The History of the

Yiddish Theater, 2 vols., 1918) is a standard work in this field, which has since been supplemented by archival and other materials by Jacob Shatzky and others.

Besides those mentioned above, Yiddish writers who have contributed valuable studies on the history of Yiddish literature include Jacob Shatzky, Isaac Rivkind, author of *The Fight against Gambling among Jews* (1946), an interesting study of Yiddish poetry and cultural history, and Shlomoh Noble, author of *Khumesh-Taitsh* (1943), a study dealing with the archaic Yiddish of the *heder*.

Samuel Niger, the outstanding Yiddish literary historian and critic, has published a number of significant works in America on various phases of Yiddish literature. Among these mention should be made of his books on Sholem Aleichem, Mendele Mocher Seforim, Yitzhok Leibush Peretz, and H. Leivick as well as a volume on some of the most important Yiddish novelists and story-tellers. He has also written a volume entitled *Di Zweishprakhikeit fun Unzer Literatur* (The Bilingualism of Our Literature, 1941), an intriguing historical study, with special reference to the recent period.

Max Weinreich, outstanding Yiddish philologist and literary historian, has also done considerable work in various other fields of Jewish learning. Among his studies, mention should be made of his *Hitler's Professors* (1946) and the excellent essay "Yiddishkayt and Yiddish" in the *Mordecai M. Kaplan Jubilee Volume* (1953).

Translations of recent Yiddish belles-lettres have been appearing with increasing frequency. The older literature still remains inaccessible to non-Yiddish readers. All the more valuable, therefore, is Marvin Lowenthal's felicitous edition and translation of the classic *Memoirs of Glückel of Hameln* (1932), the fascinating personal record of a remarkable early eighteenth-century matron. Worthy of note, too, are Maurice Samuel's captivating syntheses of the genius of two of the greatest figures in Yiddish literature and the life they depicted, *The World of Sholem Aleichem* (1943), and *Prince of the Ghetto* (1948), on Y. L. Peretz. Solomon Liptzin has also contributed a warm biographical study of the famous *badhan, Eliakum Zunser* (1950), one of the founding fathers of modern Yiddish literature, who as poet, composer and singer reflected the life of his people during his long and colorful career.

Not content merely with historical and critical investigations, most of the students of Yiddish literature have also contributed notably to linguistic research.

Judah A. Joffe, eminent philologist, one of the outstanding authorities on old Yiddish literature and author of notable studies in the field of Yiddish, has recently published an academic edition of Elijah Bohur's *Bovo-Buch* (1949) with an explanatory introduction. Yudel Mark, besides his many articles on literature and education, has worked intensively in this special field, and has fostered its development as editor of *Yidishe Shprakh*. A valuable lexicographical contribution has been made by Alexander Harkavy (1863-1939). Not himself a trained philologian, but gifted with a fine linguistic sensitivity, and an assiduous laborer, he began to issue, in 1895, his series of pioneer English-Yiddish, Yiddish-English, and Yiddish-English-Hebrew dictionaries. Another signal contribution to Yiddish lexicography was made by Nahum Stutchkoff in his *Thesaurus of the Yiddish Language* (1950). This major achievement is a comprehensive work, the first of its kind in Yiddish, and represents a solid basis for future efforts in this field.

3. OTHER LANGUAGES

Many of the great works which shed such lustre on the "Golden Age" in North Africa and Spain were written in Judaeo-Arabic, which is, therefore, an area of particular importance in the study of Jewish literary history. The high degree of technical specialization required to achieve scholarly proficiency in this area has undoubtedly militated against its popularity. Although the number of scholars who have entered it remains small, their output has by no means been inconsiderable. Some of the more important contributions in philosophy and theology, and particularly in Karaism, referred to above, are due to their efforts. In the main, the work has been limited to edition of texts, with relatively little in the way of critical study, except for such evaluations as are included in introductions. Nor has there been any systematic selection of material for editing, which has usually been confined through the personal choice of the editors to religious texts.

Among the earliest works in Judaeo-Arabic by American scholars are Alexander Kohut's edition of Midrashic texts in *Studies in Yemenite Hebrew Literature* (2 vols., 1892-94); Stephen S. Wise's (1874-1949) edition of Solomon ibn Gabirol's *Improvement of Moral Qualities* (1901); and David Levine's *Bustan al Uqul* of *Nathanael ibn al Fayyumi* (1908). Richard Gottheil did some textual work in this field. Israel Friedlander, whose tragic early death cut short a career that might well have made him the foremost American specialist, published only articles in a number of journals, but they are highly valuable. Henry Malter and Ben Zion Halper (1884-1924) were among the first to become actively interested in this literature, and to devote themselves to it as well as to foster an interest in it among students. Both published useful studies; Halper's work includes an edition of Hefez ben Yazliah's *Book of Precepts* (1915), the first code in which decisions are grouped according to subject matter, and a catalogue of the Genizah fragments in the Dropsie College Library (1924). Julian Obermann's *Studies in Islam and Judaism* (1933) comprises an edition of the Arabic original of *Ibn Shahin's Book of Comfort* by Nissim B. Jacob of Kairawan, an eleventh-century anthology of Midrashic stories, the earliest work of its kind. The work of Solomon Skoss, Samuel Rosenblatt and Abraham S. Halkin has already been mentioned. These editors have not only elucidated, in their introductions and notes, the life of their authors and the content of their works, but have also seized the opportunity to explore the linguistic characteristics of the Arabic dialects employed, so that a considerable body of philological information is gradually accumulating.

The only scholar working actively in the field of Samaritan literature and thought is Abraham S. Halkin, who has published several valuable studies and has prompted some of his students to work on Samaritan texts. A product of his efforts is *The Joseph Cycle (Genesis 37-45) in the Samaritan-Arabic Commentary of Meshalma ibn Murjan* (1951) by Gladys Levine Rosen.

The first specialist in the United States in Falasha literature and life is Wolf Leslau, who has done considerable work in Judaeo-Arabic dialects and documents. Having made first-hand studies of the black Jews of Ethiopia during his recent field trips in that country, he published some excellent articles on their language, life and religion and the first *Falasha Anthology* (1951) in English, containing translations of texts dating from medieval or earlier times. Simon D. Messing, who is at present in Ethiopia, is also concentrating in this field.

Still another area which has received virtually no scholarly attention is that of the archaic written idiom (Ladino) which the Sephardim took with them into exile from Spain, and the interesting literature to be found in it. Aside from a few random articles in modern language publications, the only serious studies of note are on the vernacular variants known as Judezmo by Max A. Luria, *A Study of the Monastir Dialect of Judeo-Spanish* (1930), based on oral material collected in Yugoslavia, and *Judeo-Spanish Dialects in New York City* (1930-31).

So various in content, language and provenance is "Jewish literature" that it often requires abrupt transitions, but surely none more precipitous than that from the exotic areas just discussed to the modern western languages and culture. The emergence of Jewish litterateurs in Europe and America, addressing themselves primarily to a non-Jewish public, is of course, a recent phenomenon, and what relation this has to Jewish letters is still a moot question which touches on subtle cultural and psychological issues. Several pioneer studies have been made by Solomon Liptzin, whose penetrating and sensitive analyses have done much to clarify the Jewish characteristics and elements in the writing and thought of such outstanding German men of letters as *Arthur Schnitzler* (1932) and *Richard Beer-Hofmann* (1936). A particularly interesting and enlightening volume is *Germany's Stepchildren* (1944). Here Liptzin examines critically the lives and works of outstanding German, Austrian and Czech Jewish writers who exemplify varied responses to the "tragic duality" imposed by the assimilatory pressures of European culture.

Judaic Lore in Heine (1948) by Israel Tabak is an analysis of the Jewish elements in his writings, with the conclusion that he acquired his Jewish learning in his childhood home and *heder*. However, this contention has been questioned. Among modern writers whose Jewish backgrounds and attitudes have been the subject of recent critical attention, none has elicited as much interest and discussion as Franz Kafka, on whom a small library of studies has already appeared.

A few studies have been published of Jews in the role of subjects as well as of authors with, of course, important sociological and cultural, as well as literary implications. But this is a field that has barely been entered upon. *Russian Literature and the Jew* (1929), by Joshua Kunitz, is an outstanding example of this type of study. Dorothy Lasher-Schlitt's analysis of *Grill-*

parzer's *Attitude Toward the Jews* (1936) provides a penetrating view of the inconsistencies of the leading Austrian dramatist of the nineteenth century. David Philipson (1862-1949) produced an initial study of *The Jew in English Fiction* as early as 1889, which was followed by Edward N. Calisch's (1865-1946) *The Jews in English Literature* (1909). Joseph Mersand incorporated a series of interesting critical essays on Jewish writers and the Jew as portrayed by non-Jewish writers in *Traditions in American Literature* (1939), which also includes several useful bibliographies. *The World of Emma Lazarus* (1949) by H. E. Jacob is a competent and sensitive biography of an American-Jewish poetess.

VIII. HISTORY

1. GENERAL

Although its development is uneven, historiography has come to the fore in the past century as the most favored branch of Jewish scholarship in America. Whereas formerly it was but an adjunct to other studies, today all other departments are contributory to it. Embracing the evolution of Jewish religion, philosophy, literature and culture it has latterly expanded, in keeping with the trend in general scholarship, to include analysis and evaluation of political, social and economic forces, operating within and upon the Jewish community, and the *mores* and conditions of daily existence of the Jewish masses. It has thus become the broadest of the scholarly disciplines, capable of utilizing the most diverse data from every source. Hence virtually every scholar working in any field is to a greater or lesser degree a historian as well; in fact, most Jewish scholars of note have consciously exploited the historical implications of the materials with which they deal in their specialties. We must therefore not overlook the significant contributions that have been made in special areas, already discussed, in our

consideration of Jewish historiography. As in other fields, here too it was Isaac Mayer Wise who was the real pioneer. He projected a *History of the Israelitish Nation from Abraham to the Present Time,* of which the first volume, covering the period until the destruction of the First Temple, appeared in 1854. His *History of the Hebrews' Second Commonwealth* came out in 1880. Beyond this he did not get. Nor is his work of critical scholarly importance today. But it marked a beginning, and a by no means unworthy one for his day.

Gotthard Deutsch (1859-1921), who joined the HUC faculty in 1891, was the first general Jewish historian of distinction in America. But he wrote little, and was so fond of the anecdotal approach that he was sometimes gently chided as a *Professor der Geschichten* rather than *Geschichte.* Alexander Marx occupied the chair of history at the JTS from 1903 until his death in 1953, but like his mentor Moritz Steinschneider he was primarily a bibliographer. He was productive in many areas besides that over which he presided in his official capacity. These two men inaugurated the formal study of Jewish history on a scholarly level in this country, and exerted their greatest influence as teachers.

In general it must be said that Jewish historiography in the United States is just about emerging into its own. The apologetic note remains strong, as is probably inevitable in view of the continuing insecurity of Jewish life, though there is evidence of a more objective trend. The new disciplines of the social sciences have, it is true, been finally recognized as having validity in historical research and reconstruction, but are not yet being applied with a thorough appreciation of their import. On the whole the standards of Jewish historiography still lag behind the quality of work being produced by general American historians. Yet, if we take into account the brief period of its development, the vast and complex area it embraces, and the limited personnel and resources devoted to it, we must acknowledge that it may boast no mean achievement and has established itself as one of the more creative branches of Jewish scholarship.

The most eminent contemporary Jewish historian is Salo W. Baron. The sober objectivity of his approach, his rejection of the popular martyrological conception of Jewish history, and his attempts at broad generalization soundly grounded in the literature, stamp him as a modern historian in the grand manner. As Professor of Jewish History and Institutions at Columbia University for more than two decades, and leading figure in several organizations dedicated to the furtherance of Jewish historiography, his influence has been widespread and salutary. Though his expert competence in one or another special area has at times been challenged, his work displays an encyclopedic knowledge of the sources and of the vast monographic literature which commands unqualified respect. His *A Social and Religious History of the Jews* (3 vols., 1937; 2nd ed., 2 vols., *Ancient Times,* 1952) is not a chronological account, but an effort to probe the dynamic factors in Jewish history. Baron's basic concept is that the Jewish religion "has been from the very beginning and in the progress of time has increasingly become a historical religion, in permanent contrast to all natural religions." Time rather than territory or state and social rather than natural forces have conditioned the development of Judaism and the history of the Jewish nation, which has thus been enabled to persist beyond the ordinary confines of geography and politics in pursuit of its historical messianism. His companion work, *The Jewish Community* (3 vols., 1942), the first study of this kind, contains an exhaustive historical and sociological analysis of the forms the Jewish community has assumed from the pre-exilic period until the age of Emancipation. Treating his subject both chronologically and topically Baron shows that by accommodating itself flexibly to shifting social and political conditions while preserving its inner patterns the Jewish community has remained essentially the same under the varied forms it has assumed in the course of time.

It must be added that the final volumes of both works, devoted to notes and bibliographies, contain probably the most intensive critical surveys of the scholarly literature. Besides these major works, Baron has written a host of essays on historical and literary themes in German and Hebrew as well as in English, and has contributed notably to the field of modern Jewish history, including the volume—*Modern Nationalism and Religion* (1947).

The Rise of the Jew in the Western World (1944) by Uriah Zevi Engelman is a pioneer attempt to survey Jewish history from the Roman period to the First World War from an economic and social angle with special reference to demographic factors. While it contains much valuable material, a large part of its contents is too conjectural in the present state of historical knowledge.

Joseph Jacobs (1854-1916) undertook to present a historical survey in *Jewish Contributions to Civilization* (1919), a work he was not enabled to complete in accordance with his projected plan. Although its usefulness is impaired by its avowedly apologetic aim, the book includes interesting information on various aspects of the contacts between Jewish life and thought and western civilization.

A gifted and exceptionally erudite scholar, Isaiah Sonne, whose essays range over virtually the entire area of Jewish learning, including bibliography, Rabbinics, the religion and literature of the Hellenistic-Roman period, the Dead Sea Scrolls, Italian Jewry, the art of the Dura Synagogue, and even the philosophy and theory of music in Judaeo-Arabic literature (with Eric Werner), has also made important contributions to the philosophy and methodology of Jewish history in several of his articles.

2. THE MIDDLE AGES

A number of excellent studies have appeared illuminating the inner life and organization of various medieval Jewries, as well as the political, social and economic conditions which shaped their fates. Jacob Mann, a pre-eminent literary historian, whose *Studies and Texts* exploited so successfully for historical purposes Genizah materials bearing on the Gaonic age and on Karaism, published in *The Jews in Egypt and Palestine under the Fatimid Caliphs* (2 vols., 1920-22) a large number of such documents from which he elicited important information about the intellectual interests and organizational structures of these communities, and, to a lesser extent, about their political and economic status. He was able to show that Palestinian Jewry, although politically dependent upon the more powerful and prosperous neighboring Egyptian community, exerted the greater moral and intellectual influence.

The tragic death of Joshua Starr (1907-1949) cut short a fruitful interest in the Balkan Jewries. *The Jews in the Byzantine Empire, 641-1204,* which he published in 1939, contains a good deal of interesting material on persecutions and legal discriminations to which these communities were subjected, their economic and demographic status, communal and social life. *Romania: The Jewries of the Levant after the Fourth Crusade* (1949) is a study of the available data on the history of the Jews in medieval Greece. Starr also wrote a number of excellent essays on the medieval and modern history of Jews in Italy, Rumania and Greece. Supplementing Starr's work is a study titled *Jewish Life in Turkey in the XVIth Century* (1952) by Morris S. Goodblatt.

The early history of the Jews at the opposite extremity of Europe was treated by Solomon Katz in *The Jews in the Visi-gothic and Frankish Kingdoms of Spain and Gaul* (1937). Abraham A. Neuman's *The Jews in Spain* (2 vols., 1942) is an excellent study of their social, political and cultural life during the thirteenth and fourteenth centuries in the areas under Christian rule. This work describes not only the inner life of the community but also its relationship to the Spanish crown and church. Neuman has published several essays in the field of history, and also on the literary and historical background and contents of the *Josippon*. A more limited view of the period is provided in *Rabbi Isaac ben Sheshet Perfet and his Times* (1943) by Abraham M. Hershman.

Guido Kisch's profound knowledge of German legal history enabled him to open up a virtually unexplored approach to medieval Jewish history so novel that he had to create a new term to identify it: Jewry-law, that is non-Jewish legislation pertaining to Jews, as distinguished from Jewish law, representing the Jewish tradition. In a number of outstanding essays he explored various institutions in medieval Germany which illustrated the effects of Jewry-law on Jewish life. *Jewry-Law in Medieval Germany* (1949) contains the texts of laws and court decisions concerning Jews on the basis of which Kisch prepared his excellent work *The Jews in Medieval Germany* (1949). As a result of this penetrating study Jewry-law emerges as a prime determining factor in the objective situation of the Jews in the later Middle Ages.

Two notable volumes have utilized medieval Responsa and other Rabbinic sources to elucidate important phases of Jewish communal organization and life. Louis Finkelstein's *Jewish Self-Government in the Middle Ages* (1924) contains an analysis of the ordinances (here published and translated) issued by Rabbinic synods from the tenth to the sixteenth centuries in Western and Southern Europe as they affected Jewish personal, family and communal life. *The Jewish Court in the Middle Ages* (1931) by David Shohet is a detailed account of the authority, procedure and jurisdiction of these courts in medieval Germany.

The relations between the Church and the Jews are the subject of three excellent monographs. Solomon Grayzel examined official policy as revealed in the Papal Letters and the Conciliar Decrees of 1198-1254 in his work *The Church and the Jews in the XIIIth Century* (1933). *The Devil and the Jews* (1943) by Joshua Trachtenberg explores the medieval popular conception of the "demonic" Jew and its relation to modern anti-Semitism, though it fails to develop the latter half of this theme adequately. Baruch Braunstein's *The Chuetas of Majorca* (1936) is an account of the origin of the Inquisition, and of the effects of its policy on the fate and ritual of the Majorcan converts and their descendants who are still obliged to lead a separate existence although they have been for centuries observant Catholics.

An important aspect of Jewish-Christian relations is discussed in the essays on medieval Jewish physicians published by Harry Friedenwald in *The Jews and Medicine* (2 vols., 1944), which includes much valuable material on the history and literature of Jewish medical practice. Solomon Gandz and Jekuthiel Ginsburg have made valuable contributions to the history of Jewish scientific interests, particularly in mathematics and astronomy, in the Middle Ages and earlier.

3. THE MODERN PERIOD

Of general works on the recent period mention should be made of Abram L. Sachar's lively *Sufferance is the Badge* (1939), an account of events between the World Wars, and of Ismar Elbogen's (1874-1943) *A Century of Jewish Life* (1944). Jewish affairs in various countries since the close of the Middle Ages have been treated in a number of special studies and monographs. Mordecai Wilensky's articles include studies of the Sabbatai Zevi movement, and of re-admission of Jews to England in the seventeenth century. A very capable study is Herbert L. Bloom's *Economic Activities of the Jews of Amsterdam in the Seventeenth and Eighteenth Centuries* (1937). It also deals with the relations of the Amsterdam Jews and the widely scattered Jewish communities with which they traded.

On the history and sociology of the Jews in France we have an excellent collection of essays, edited by Elias Tcherikover (1881-1943), *Yidn in Frankreich* (2 vols., 1942), based largely on archival material, and dealing mainly with the nineteenth century. Zosa Szajkowski has devoted himself with great diligence to the study of French Jewish life and history, producing many valuable essays on the political, economic, social and communal affairs of this Jewry both before and after the Revolution. Italian Jewry has had the attention of Moses A. Shulvass, whose articles have explored various phases of its life since the Renaissance.

A study of a seventeenth-century figure whose colorful career lights up the life of Italian Jewry, *Yehuda Arye de Modena* (1901) by M. S. Liebowitz, is mainly concerned with refuting the charge of heresy levelled against him by modern historians. Preparatory to a full-length biography, Ellis Rivkin has published an essay on the same theme, *Leon da Modena and the Kol Sakhal* (1952), which contains material on the cultural environment. Another interesting figure of the same period, the physician and Rabbinic scholar Tobias Cohen has been treated by Abraham Levinson in *Tubia ha-Rofe* (1924).

An outstanding example of well-written and yet generally sound popular history is Marvin Lowenthal's *The Jews of Germany* (1936), which is perhaps over-zealous in its condemnation of the assimilationist tendencies of the past century. Selma Stern's scholarly account of the history and functions of that unique phenomenon *The Court Jew* (1950) against the background of general European history, is based on exhaustive research in almost all of Germany's many state and municipal archives. A more limited area, the organization of charity and welfare services between 1500-1800, has been expertly treated by Jacob R. Marcus in *Communal Sick-Care in the German Ghetto* (1947), which contains a mass of interesting information on the *hevrah kadisha* and other communal agencies dealing with such matters, and thus provides a valuable insight into ghetto life. Shedding light on its intellectual and cultural life is Mortimer J. Cohen's stimulating biography of the eighteenth-century rabbi *Jacob Emden* (1937). In view of the absence of sufficient pertinent data Cohen's socio-psychological interpretation of Emdens' motivation in his notorious controversy with Jonathan Eibeschuetz seems overdrawn and hypothetical, but his approach is nonetheless novel and provocative. A number of excellent contributions to our understanding of Jewish life in Germany in modern times have been made by Adolf Kober, whose articles have appeared in various periodicals.

The development of the *yishuv* in Palestine in recent decades has, of course, received a great deal of attention, most of it journalistic and propagandist in nature, but some of it quite sound. Without attempting to survey this literature *in extenso,* we may select a few works which deserve special mention. The first history of *Zionism* (1914) in English was written by Richard Gottheil; although long since superseded it is still a good succinct account of the early period. A most thorough study in English is *The Life of Theodor Herzl* (2 vols., 1927), and at the same time an informal history of the Zionist organization during its formative years, is by Jacob de Haas (1872-1937), who was able to weave into his work the intimate knowledge derived from his close personal asso-

ciation with both. Another pioneer work in English is de Haas' *History of Palestine* (1934) from the Roman conquest until 1922; although not based on independent research the book is crammed with detail from a thorough study of the extensive literature. The best general survey, both detailed and comprehensive, of the history of Jewish immigration and settlement and of every phase of Jewish life and organization in Palestine before the establishment of the state, is *Jews in Palestine* (3rd ed., 1945) by Abraham Revusky (1889-1946).

Walter J. Fischel, who has made a specialty of studying the Jewish communities of Asia, has published a number of excellent and informative essays and monographs on the history of the Jews of Kurdistan, Persia, Khorasan, India and other oriental places. The history of the Jews in China has been treated in several papers by Rudolph Loewenthal, who has also written on other communities, such as the Judaeo-Tats in the Caucasus.

An important source of information for the history of Jews in many European, Asian and North African states is to be found in the selections from U. S. government archives published by Cyrus Adler (1863-1940) and Aaron M. Margalith, *American Intercession on Behalf of Jews in the Diplomatic Correspondence of the United States, 1840-1938 (PAJHS,* XXXVI, 1943), which incorporates and amplifies the material published earlier in the *PAJHS* by Adler (XV, 1906) and by Max J. Kohler and Simon Wolf (XXIV, 1916).

4. EASTERN EUROPE

Although the bulk of American Jewry derives from Eastern Europe, very little attention was paid to this teeming and creative center of Jewish life until the past decade. This neglect reflects the attitude of the German-oriented school of Jewish historians which tended to look down upon the "primitive" communities of the East and preferred to focus its light on the past or on the more "advanced" western Jewries. The barbaric extinction of the East European community cast a lurid gleam on its role in world Jewish history and gave it a poignant respectability it had formerly been denied in American Jewish scholarship. The death of the parent forced upon its offspring a sudden awareness of a heritage it had not until then appreciated and acknowledged. The decisive role in this new scholarly interest has been taken by recent immigrants from that region who had already produced important studies before their arrival, and who continue to write in Yiddish; but a number of useful English volumes testify to the re-orientation of American Jewish historiography.

An outstanding specialist in this area is Jacob Shatzky who, besides his contribution to the history of Yiddish literature, has written many valuable essays and monographs on the history of the Jews in Poland. His monumental *Geschikhte fun Yidn in Varshe* (3 vols., 1947-1953), which carries the story from the fifteenth century to 1896 and is planned to continue until the present contains an exhaustive description of every phase of Jewish life, its inner organization and social divisions, its religious and intellectual ideologies, its economic, social and political vicissitudes during the entire existence of this largest Jewish community in modern Europe.

Di Yidn in Poilen fun di Eltste Zeitn bis tsu der Tsveiter Veltmilkhomeh (The Jews in Poland from Earliest Times to the Second World War, 1946), a broad synthesis of Polish Jewish history, includes studies by Raphael Mahler, Abraham Menes, Jacob Shatzky and Victor Shulman. A comprehensive account of Jewish life in Eastern Europe is presented in the *Algemeine Entsiklopedie* (Yiddish), Vol. *Yidn D.* (1950), with articles by Jacob Lestschinsky, Raphael Abramovitch, Joseph Kissman, Jacob Shatzky and Abraham Menes. Another work of great significance is the large collective volume *Lite* (1951), compiled and edited by Mendel Sudarsky, Uriah Katzene-

lenbogen and J. Kissin. This is an outstanding work in its range and scope, covering many phases of Jewish life in Lithuania.

Jews in the Province of Posen (1939) is a study of the communal records of several Jewish communities of the eighteenth and nineteenth centuries, by Michael M. Zarchin. Several excellent articles on nineteenth-century Polish Jewish history have been published by Abraham G. Duker. Koppel S. Pinson has also written some valuable articles on ideological and social trends. Raphael Mahler's studies have been directed mainly to social and economic aspects of Polish Jewish history and to the social implications of the Haskalah or Enlightenment movement.

The Haskalah is the subject of what is probably the first American scholarly work in this area, *The Haskalah Movement in Russia* (1913), by Jacob S. Raisin (1877-1946). However, this theme is actually subordinated in the book to a survey of the background of the movement, including a good sketch of Russian Jewish history and of the life and problems of the community. Israel Friedlander's *The Jews of Russia and Poland* (1915) is no more than it claims to be, a "bird's eye view" of their history and culture, but it is a good popular summary of Dubnow's *History of the Jews in Russia and Poland* (3 vols., 1916-20), which he had translated into English.

The Jews in Russia (2 vols., 1944-51) by Louis Greenberg (1894-1946), is an account of the struggle for emancipation, from 1881 to 1917, which adds nothing new to the story, but contains many interesting biographical sketches of leading Jewish figures and worthwhile chapters on the origins of Zionism in Russia and the role of Jews in the revolutionary movement. An excellent study of the records of *hevrot* — associations for study, burial, sick-care, charity, of craftsmen, and the like—in Russia, Congress Poland and Galicia by Isaac Levitats in *The Jewish Community in Russia 1772-1844* (1943), provides useful insights into daily life and community organization. Mark Wischnitzer, a student of East European Jewish history and institutions, has published several articles on the history of Jewish crafts and guilds, and has prepared a volume on the subject.

Zevi Scharfstein's pioneer works *Ha-Heder be-Hayye Amenu* (The Heder in the Life of the Jewish People, 1943) and *Toledot ha-Hinnuk be-Yisrael be-Dorot ha-Aharonim* (History of Jewish Education in Modern Times, 3 vols., 1945-49), although not restricted to Eastern Europe, contain a thorough and comprehensive account of the development and institutions of its extensive educational system. Other studies on this theme, of limited scope, are Bernard D. Weinryb's *Jewish Vocational Education* (1948), and Miriam Eisenstein's *Jewish Schools in Poland, 1919-39* (1950).

Jacob Lestschinsky is a leading Jewish specialist on economic and demographic developments in Eastern Europe, on which he has written many valuable articles and monographs. He is one of the few scholars who have made an intensive study of Jewish life under Soviet rule, and produced one of the first detailed accounts of the political, economic and cultural changes through which Russian Jewry passed after 1917 in *Dos Sovetishe Yiddntum* (Jewry in Soviet Russia, Past and Present, 1941). Since the appearance of this work he has continued to survey developments in Russia. Avrahm Yarmolinsky's *The Jews and Other National Minorities under the Soviets* (1928) was written before Soviet policy toward Jews was fully unfolded and therefore presents a picture which subsequent developments have rendered obsolete. The latest and most reliable work is *The Jews in the Soviet Union* (1951) by Solomon M. Schwarz ,a sound scholarly account of the reversal of the early policy of recognition of the Jews as a distinct nationality, and of the corresponding shift in attitude toward anti-Semitism.

The difficulty of obtaining and assessing information on the situation of Jews be-hind the "iron curtain" has not prevented the authors of *The Jews in the Soviet Satellites* (1953) from producing an excellent survey; Czechoslovakia and Bulgaria are covered by Peter Meyer, Poland by Bernard D. Weinryb, Hungary by Eugene Duschinsky, and Rumania by Nicholas Sylvain.

The catastrophe which overwhelmed and extinguished the historic Jewries of Central and Eastern Europe a decade ago has produced a special literature of its own which is growing rapidly and is still difficult to assess. One department comprises the memorial volumes seeking to recapture the feel of Jewish life in individual communities, and to record for posterity their histories and the distinctive features of their communal patterns and activities. Many such works have appeared in Yiddish, memorializing various Polish and Lithuanian communities. These contain mainly a conglomeration of essays and vignettes, biographical sketches, serious historical studies, reproductions of documents, and the like, of varying scholarly value.

Another phase of this literature comprises the records of personal experiences and observations in the ghettos and concentration camps. Still another is the result of systematic studies of the development of the Nazi program of extermination, its application in different areas, the organization of ghetto communities, the social and psychological conditions which characterized the ghettos and camps, the attitude of local non-Jewish populations, resistance to the Nazis, etc.

The problems of recording the full extent and meaning of these catastrophic events have already given rise to a special department of Jewish historiography. Two volumes of the *Yivo Bleter* (XXX, 1947, and XXXVII, 1953) and vol. VIII of the *Yivo Annual of Jewish Social Science* (1953) have been devoted entirely to essays and documents dealing with this period. *Jewish Social Studies* (XII, 1950) contains a series of papers on "Problems of Research in the

Study of the Jewish Catastrophe." Philip Friedman, a distinguished historian and educator, is today probably the leading specialist in America on the history of the Jewish tragedy. He has compiled an exhaustive bibliography of the literature which is scheduled to appear shortly.

5. THE UNITED STATES

It must seem odd that the history of the largest Jewish community in the world should have been so grossly neglected, even by historians in its midst, that we may speak of a mature American Jewish historiography as the product only of the most recent years. Nevertheless, it would not do to undervalue the pioneer work of such men as Max Kohler (1871-1934), Samuel Oppenheim (1859-1928), A. S. W. Rosenbach (1876-1952), Leon Hühner and George Alexander Kohut (1874-1933), who made notable contributions to early American Jewish history and bibliography in the *Publications* of the AJHS, which contain a great deal of useful information.

The growing self-consciousness of the Jewish community as it matured and acquired stability, and the harsh impact of the Hitler campaign which thrust American Jewry into the forefront of world Jewish affairs (as America was reluctantly being propelled into world leadership) were the stimuli which prompted the development of a serious program of research and study at the beginning of the 1940's. The pioneer steps in this direction were apparently taken by Jacob R. Marcus, the leading authority today in this field, who was responsible for the establishment in 1940 of a department of American Jewish manuscript archives in the HUC Library, which by 1947 had matured into the independent American Jewish Archives, the largest repository of such archival materials in the country.

Although not many students are as yet doing concentrated work on this subject, the change in philosophical and methodological approach is making itself rapidly felt. The apologetic, "filio-pietistic" motivation is gradually being abandoned, cultural and socio-economic developments are being analyzed, the fixation on the colonial period is giving way to a broad concern with the entire panorama of Jewish experience in America. The Tercentenary commemoration appears likely to provide impetus for an increased interest and activity. In December 1953 the JTS established an American Jewish History Center, primarily an advisory institute to encourage and assist writers in the field and to help publish their writings. A ten-volume *Documentary History of American Jews* is under consideration by the Tercentenary Committee, as well as a *Biographical Dictionary of American Jews* under the auspices of the AJHS. YIVO and the American Jewish Archives are planning several publications, and considerable individual activity on local histories and other projects is in evidence. The Tercentenary then, may provide the fillip which will project this field into full growth as a major department of American Jewish scholarship.

Specialists agree that insufficient basic data and analytical studies of specific areas are as yet available for the preparation of a connected history of American Jewry. However, several attempts have been made to produce one, with results that appear to confirm this view. The first work which attempted to present a coherent history of American Jewry was Isaac Markens' (1848-1928) *The Hebrews in America* (published in 1888). It consists of a series of historical and biographical sketches, not always accurate and without documentation, but in view of the scant information then accessible it contains a good deal of useful material. Simon Wolf's (1836-1923) *The American Jew as Patriot, Soldier and Citizen* (1895) is also sketchy, and as its title indicates is quite limited in its approach. *The History of the Jews in America* (2nd ed., 1931) by the well-known Yiddish journalist Peter Wiernik (1865-1936), is especially good in its treatment of the period from 1880 to 1920, to which it devotes more than half its space, and contains much information on cultural and communal developments, but fails to consider economic and social trends. The materialist approach is introduced by Philip Foner in *The Jews in American History 1654-1865* (1946). An effort to present a complete and detailed account is to be found in *Pilgrim People* (1951) by Anita L. Lebeson. Two volumes have appeared in 1954: Oscar Handlin's *Adventure in Freedom* is concerned with general trends rather than with detailed information and is more appreciative of the integration of Jews in American life than of the special characteristics which distinguish the community; Rufus Learsi's *The Jews in America* is a broader and more comprehensive survey, as good a work as can be produced in the present state of American Jewish historiography.

A very useful work, the first comprehensive collection of documents, pertaining particularly to the political and economic aspects of Jewish life in America, is Morris U. Schappes' *Documentary History of the Jews in the United States, 1654-1875* (1950). Each entry is provided with an informative introduction and is carefully annotated; the editor's comments, however, are marked by a pronounced materialist interpretation.

The Colonial period has been most assiduously explored by researchers. The volumes of the AJHS *Publications* are particularly rich in useful material, even though it is often uncritically presented, and historians have mined this source with great success. One of the outstanding amateur historians, Lee M. Friedman, published a collection of pieces on *Early American Jews* (1934) and has since brought out *Jewish Pioneers and Patriots* (1942) and *Pilgrims in a New Land* (1948), minor but usually interesting essays on a variety of themes. Anita L. Lebeson's *Jewish Pioneers in America* (1938), extending until 1840 but devoted mainly to the

period before 1800, is a competent survey of Jewish life and of prominent Jewish figures, based on data in the *PAJHS* and other published sources. A partial account of Jewish commercial activities is presented in Miriam K. Freund's *Jewish Merchants in Colonial America* (1939). Two brief monographs by S. Broches under the title *Jews in New England* (1942) bring to light a good deal of new source material on the Jews in Massachusetts from 1650 to 1750 and on Jewish merchants in Colonial Rhode Island. *American Overture* (1947) by Abram V. Goodman, offers a useful examination of the civic and political status of Jews in the individual colonies without, however, analyzing general trends or reaching conclusions on the evolution of policy. A contribution to economic history is to be found in Sidney M. Fish's monograph, *Aaron Levy, Founder of Aaronsburg* (1951), an account of the activities of an eighteenth-century frontier merchant and land speculator in Pennsylvania. Hannah R. London, who has specialized in the portraiture of early American Jews, has produced three excellent volumes on the subject.

Jacob R. Marcus, who has in the past decade concentrated on American Jewish history, made a major contribution in the two volumes of his *Early American Jewry* (1951-1953). The special value of this work lies in its felicitous exploitation of hitherto unpublished material, mainly letters and other personal documents, to illuminate many phases of Jewish life in the colonies. The second volume includes a particularly useful summary of the material and a general survey of the pattern of Jewish life in the Colonial period.

The period of Central European immigration and of the development of many new communities and communal forms in the nineteenth century has attracted only two specialists. Rudolf Glanz has published many useful essays in Yiddish and English. Several of his volumes, including one on Jewish peddlers in America, await publication. Bertram W. Korn has earned wide commendation for his excellent study, *American Jewry and the Civil War* (1951), in which he analyzed Jewish attitudes toward slavery, the impact of the conflict on the community, and the eruption of anti-Semitism on both sides under the stress of war. *Eventful Years and Experiences* (1954) contains a collection of Korn's essays on a variety of nineteenth-century historical topics. A good account of the cultural background and the contribution of Czechoslovak Jewish immigrants, usually lumped among Germans in American Jewish historiography, is to be found in Guido Kisch's volume *In Search of Freedom* (1949). Max J. Kohler is responsible for some useful essays on nineteenth-century German Jewry in America.

A fair number of congregational and local histories have been issued, but most of them are so parochial in scope and viewpoint and so amateurish methodologically as to have only peripheral historical interest and value. Among the better local histories the following are to be noted: *The Jews of Philadelphia* (1894) by Henry S. Morais (1860-1935); *The Jews of South Carolina* (1905) by Barnett A. Elzas (1867-1936), one of the best histories of a state community, though the mid-nineteenth century is rather sketchily treated; *The History of the Jews of Richmond* (1917) by Herbert T. Ezekiel and Gaston Lichtenstein; Morris A. Gutstein's *The Story of the Jews of Newport, 1658-1908* (1936), primarily devoted, however, to the Colonial Period; *Consider the Years* (1944) by Joshua Trachtenberg, an account of the Easton, Pa., community from 1752 to 1942; Hyman B. Grinstein's *The Rise of the Jewish Community of New York, 1654-1860* (1945); *The Jews of Charleston* (1950) by Charles Reznikoff and Uriah Z. Engelman; *The Pioneer Jews of Utah* (1952) by Leon L. Watters; Morris A. Gutstein's history of Chicago Jewry until the end of the nineteenth century, *A Priceless Heritage* (1953); *The Jews in American Alaska*

(1953) by Rudolph Glanz; Stuart E. Rosenberg's *The Jewish Community in Rochester* (1954), covering its history until 1925. Mention should also be made of the growing shelf of organizational histories, which contain much useful information, though it is too often buried in a mass of parochial detail. Of the scholarly literature on other Jewish communities of the Western Hemisphere, mention should be made of the following: *History of the Jews in Canada* (1945) by Benjamin B. Sack; *The Jewish Community of Cuba* (1948) by Boris Sapir; *The Records of the Earliest Jewish Community in the New World* (1954) by Arnold Wiznitzer.

Biographical and autobiographical studies, useful adjuncts to historiography when seriously undertaken, have been accumulating in recent years at a good pace. An annotated bibliography *American Jewish Biography* (1950) listing a considerable number of volumes of varying quality has been prepared by Isidore S. Meyer, the librarian of the AJHS, who has published several good papers on a variety of historical themes.

IX. SOCIAL AND CULTURAL STUDIES

1. ANTHROPOLOGY AND FOLKLORE

The entire area treated in this section is in general so new that it has only quite recently made inroads into Jewish scholarly concerns. Maurice Fishberg (1872-1934) was the American pioneer in the study of the physical anthropology of the Jews. His major contributions include *Physical Anthropology of the Jews* (1902-03), and *The Jews* (1911). Joseph Jacobs' articles in the *Jewish Encyclopedia* may also be included here as useful pioneer studies. And this is all. These two have had no successors.

Patai is the only scholar in America to have made a specialty of the cultural anthropology of the Jews. He is the author of a two-volume *Introduction to Anthropology* (1947) in Hebrew; he has also published a number of papers on Arab and Jewish communities and on culture problems of the Middle East, as well as on the Indian Jews of Mexico. *Israel Between East and West* (1953) is an interesting scholarly discussion of the collision and interaction of Western and Oriental cultures in that country within the framework of the general problem of cultural tension between the modern Western world and the traditional Middle East.

An interesting monograph by David Efron, *Gesture and Environment* (1941), gives the results of an investigation of the gestural behavior of East European Jews and Southern Italians in New York City. The writer found that the distinctive gestural patterns of the immigrant group tend to disappear as their descendants become "assimilated," and therefore concluded that group differences in behavior are determined by the environmental culture rather than by racial descent.

Some good studies in folklore have been published, but this field is still in an uncritical and undeveloped stage. Louis Ginzberg's outstanding compilation of literary materials in *Legends of the Jews*, which has been described above, is only tangentially folkloristic. Jacob Z. Lauterbach wrote several excellent essays on various Jewish customs in which he explored the Rabbinic literature with a fine critical sense; among his various studies *Tashlik, Breaking the Glass at Weddings*, and *The Naming of Children* are particularly noteworthy. Theodore H. Gaster, an expert on Semitic religion and folklore, has made a number of valuable contributions to the comparative study of Jewish and ancient Near Eastern materials, mainly in the field of myth and ritual. Raphael Patai's early studies in Biblical and Talmudic folklore have resulted in several outstanding works: *Water: A Study in Palestinian Folklore* (1936); *Jewish Seafaring in Ancient Times* (1938), much of which is devoted to the

folklore of the sea and seafaring; *Man and Earth in Jewish Custom, Belief and Legend* (2 vols., 1942-43); *Man and Temple in Ancient Jewish Myth and Ritual* (1947).

Only one work has appeared on medieval folklore, *Jewish Magic and Superstition* (1939) by Joshua Trachtenberg, a descriptive study of the beliefs and practices which made up the "folk religion" of Ashkenazic Jewry during the Middle Ages. Y. L. Cahan's posthumously published *Studies in Yiddish Folklore* (1952) contains a good deal of useful matter and is evidently the work of a pioneer in the field of Yiddish folklore. The volume as a whole falls short of appreciating the basic methodological problems. An excellent survey, "The Literature of Jewish Folklore," by Abraham Berger appeared in the *Journal of Jewish Bibliography* (I, 1938-39).

2. ART

Until the end of the nineteenth century there was virtually no serious interest in Jewish art anywhere. When such an interest finally developed it manifested itself first in the collecting of art objects, primarily ritual pieces, long before descriptive, analytical, or historical studies were undertaken. The assembling of such collections was an important contribution, not only for the value of the collections themselves, but because they provided the panoramic ensembles out of which critical studies could in time emerge.

Significantly, the pioneer approach in this country was made by a non-Jewish agency, the Smithsonian Institute, when it arranged an exhibit of Jewish ceremonial objects in 1889, as part of its program to illustrate the facets of human culture. The first collector of Jewish ritual objects in the United States was Hajji Ephraim Benguiat, who exhibited his collection at the World Columbian Exposition at Chicago in 1892-93, and subsequently turned it over as a loan to the National Museum in Washington. After Benguiat's death the JTS purchased his collection, which it put on display in 1931, and thereafter enlarged steadily under the direction of Paul Romanoff. These materials have been housed since 1947 in the Jewish Museum, the former home of Felix M. Warburg, bequeathed to the JTS for this purpose. The curator of the Museum is Stephen S. Kayser, an outstanding authority on Jewish art, who is assisted by Guido Schoenberger, an expert on Jewish ceremonial silver.

The HUC also began to form a systematic collection of ritual objects in 1913. In 1921 Adolph S. Oko, the librarian, acquired a large collection of coins and medals from Joseph Hamburger of Frankfurt, and in 1926 he purchased the great collection of Salli Kirschbaum of Berlin. This collection, too, has grown steadily since then, but only since 1948, when it was installed in the former Bernheim Library, has it been adequately displayed under the curatorship of the distinguished art historian, Franz Landsberger.

These are the two most important collections in the United States. In recent years a number of smaller ones, public and private, have come into being. Since the major concern in these activities has been religious, ritual objects have been assembled almost exclusively for demonstration purposes.

On the literary side the *Jewish Encyclopedia* made an important contribution by devoting considerable attention to various aspects of Jewish art, particularly through its many excellent illustrations. But not until the arrival, after 1933, of students trained in art history was a new critical field opened up, which concentrated on interpretation and research in the meaning and origins of Jewish art forms, and on dating, localizing and characterizing styles and types of ritual objects.

Rachel Wischnitzer has published a number of outstanding studies dealing mainly with the interpretation of symbols in early and medieval Jewish art. Her important volume *The Messianic Theme in the Paintings of the Dura Synagogue* (1948) is a description and analysis of the major theme of the series of wall paintings discovered in a third-century synagogue on the Euphrates. Franz Landsberger has published studies of illustrated Hebrew manuscripts and of ceremonial objects in American periodicals, and the first *History of Jewish Art* (1946) in the English language. His work *Rembrandt, the Jews and the Bible* (1946) offers an interesting historical and cultural sidelight on the work of the great Dutch painter. Jeanette W. Rosenbaum has just published an interesting study titled *Myer Myers* (1954), an eighteenth-century New York silversmith.

Although new synagogues are sprouting all over the land, the history of synagogue architecture has not received attention at all commensurate with its contemporary importance. Rachel Wischnitzer has published some useful studies of European and older American synagogue styles, and some articles by Alexander S. Kline have appeared. The situation is somewhat redressed by the issuance of *An American Synagogue for Today and Tomorrow* (1953) by the Union of American Hebrew Congregations, a splendid volume which is primarily concerned with current problems of synagogue construction but contains useful sections on the history of synagogue architecture and art.

Among the many studies of modern Jewish artists few have a specifically Jewish interest. A general survey is to be found in *Jewish Artists of the Nineteenth and Twentieth Centuries* (1949) by Karl Schwarz.

Numismatics has an important place in the history of Jewish art, for the ancient Palestinian coins reflect the attitude of Jews toward representation, and show how and when the use of various symbols became current. Paul Romanoff's description of *Jewish Symbols on Ancient Coins* (1944) throws light on Jewish religion and folklore as well as art. Bruno Kisch's articles on Jewish medals and community tokens deal mainly with their biographical and historical aspects, but they also possess interest for the art student.

3. MUSIC

The scientific study of Jewish music is also quite young in America, but has developed rapidly in recent years. The first step in the direction of serious study was an anthology of liturgical music, *A Collection of the Principal Melodies of the Synagogue* (1893), edited by W. Sparger and A. Kaiser.

Active research was inaugurated by two events: the purchase by the HUC Library, in 1919, of the great collection of Jewish music assembled by Cantor Eduard Birnbaum of Koenigsberg, and the arrival early in the Twenties of the eminent scholar Abraham Z. Idelsohn to teach at the HUC. His works exerted a profound and lasting influence upon the further development of this field. His ten-volume *Thesaurus of Hebrew Oriental Melodies* (1914-32) will not be surpassed, at least not as a great collective effort, for many years to come. With the unparalleled Birnbaum collection at his disposal, he prepared his *Jewish Music in its Historical Development* (1929), the first book in English on the subject, which is still, although in some parts dated, a valuable description and analysis of the elements and characteristics of Jewish music in all ages and countries.

Under Idelsohn's influence a number of students began to produce useful essays and monographs in musicology, turning for the first time to research in the music of East European Jewry, as well as to other phases of the subject, such as the synagogal modes, the cantorial art, instruments and music in the Biblical period, the influence of other cultures on Jewish music, analysis of the works of individual composers, Yiddish folk music, contemporary Palestinian music, and the like. This activity has continued unabated until today. Alfred Sendrey's valuable *Bibliography of Jewish Music* (1951) lists the contributions of a good many American students, among the more important of whom are Abraham W. Binder, David Ewen, Joseph Yasser, Judith K. Eisenstein, Israel Rabinovitch, and Lazare Saminsky. Saminsky's *Music of the Ghetto and the Bible* (1934), and Rabinovitch's *Of Jewish Music, Ancient and Modern* (1952, translated from the Yiddish *Musik bei Yidn*, 1940) are good examples of the work being done. Albert Weisser's *The Modern Renaissance of Jewish Music* (1954) is a comprehensive analytical account of the activity of a distinguished group of composers and scholars which investigated and utilized Jewish folk music in Russia in the early decades of this century, and greatly influenced the development of Jewish music in America. Johanna L. Spector is a leading specialist in Oriental Jewish folk and liturgical music.

Another major influence has been exerted, since 1933, by German and Austrian scholars who came to this country, some of whom had long before shown their active interest in the field of Jewish musical research. To this group belongs the undisputed master of classic musicology, Curt Sachs, whose books on *The History of Musical Instruments* (1940), and *The Rise of Music in the Ancient World* (1943), include sections on the music of ancient Israel, his main contributions to the Jewish field, constituting a basic text on the history of Jewish music of the ancient period. An outstanding member of this group is Eric Werner, who has written a number of valuable studies in specialized areas, particularly on the relationship between Jewish and Christian liturgical music.

4. SOCIOLOGY, ECONOMICS, SOCIAL PSYCHOLOGY

Interest in Jewish social research has risen sharply in recent years, concentrating mainly on problems of American Jewish life. The field is still in its infancy, and a good deal may be expected of it now that the community is maturing to the point of projecting long-range programs.

Good studies of immigration have been made by Oscar Handlin, who has specialized in this area, and by Jacob Lestschinsky, who is an expert in the statistical analysis and interpretation of immigration data. Rudolf Glanz has written on the German immigration of the mid-nineteenth century. Samuel Joseph's early study of *Jewish Immigration to the United States from 1881-1910* (1914) contains numerous statistical tables and documents in addition to a useful analysis of the causes of emigration, and the characteristics of the migrants. An evaluation of American immigration statistics was made by YIVO in *The Classification of Jewish Immigrants and its Implications* (1945). The only comprehensive study of the mass population movements since 1800 is Mark Wischnitzer's *To Dwell in Safety* (1948), probably the most complete collection of data on every phase of the subject.

There has been no comparably satisfactory analysis of the more complex processes of adjustment and integration, although a good number of short studies have appeared dealing with various limited themes. An early volume of essays, edited by Charles Bernheimer, *The Russian Jew in the United States* (1905), discussed social conditions in several large cities, and specific problems of philanthrophy, education, civic absorption, rural settlement, etc. Isaac B. Berkson's *Theories of Americanization* (1920) attempted a critical sociological analysis with special reference to the Jews of New York. *The American Jew* (1942), edited by Oscar I. Janowsky, comprises a series of papers describing and interpreting mainly the cultural and organizational aspects of Jewish life. Broader in scope, but still leaving much to be desired is *Jews in a Gentile World* (1942), a collection of essays edited by Isaque Graeber and Stuart

H. Britt. A competent survey, *Refugees in America* (1947), covering the period of Hitler migration, has been prepared by Maurice R. Davis. Probably the best sociological analysis available is to be found in *Social Systems of American Ethnic Groups* (1945), Volume III of the *Yankee City Series,* by Leo Srole and W. L. Warner, a study of a small New England city which is not devoted exclusively to its Jewish population. A useful study of acculturation, describing the social and cultural changes that have taken place in the Jewish community of Minneapolis, was carried out and published by Albert I. Gordon in *Jews in Transition* (1949). Abraham G. Duker has written several provocative essays in this field. A more ambitious attempt to survey the effects of the adaptive process on the American Jewish community in comparison with other ethnic groups has been made by Charles B. Sherman in his *Yidn un Andere Etnishe Grupn in di Fareinikte Shtatn* (Jews and Other Ethnic Groups in the United States, 1948).

An important phase of the Jewish experience in America which has had significant implications for American social development no less than for Jewish is the adaptation of Jewish labor to American life. The pioneer work on the history of Jewish labor was H. Burgin's exhaustive study, published in 1915. This work—*The History of the Jewish Labor Movement* (Yiddish)—was a comprehensive account of Jewish labor in America and Europe. A number of monographs on various aspects of Jewish labor have appeared since then, and among these mention must be made of Louis Levine's excellent *The Women's Garment Workers* (1924) and Joel Seidman's solid and basic study *The Needle Trades* (1942). Benjamin Stolberg's *Tailor's Progress* (1944) is at least a good popular account. These works contain a good deal of valuable information on the ideological and organizational development of Jewish labor organizations. Melech Epstein's *Jewish Labor in the United States*

(2 vols., 1950-53) is a competent account of highlights in American Jewish labor history. YIVO's *Geshikhte fun der Yiddisher Arbeter Bavegung in die Fareinikte Shtatn* (History of the Jewish Labor Movement in the United States, 2 vols., 1943-45), edited by Elias Tcherikover (1881-1943), a gifted researcher and writer, is undoubtedly one of the most valuable contributions to Jewish socio-economic literature. The scope of the work is indicated by the fact that these first two volumes contain a vast amount of introductory information on the social, economic and cultural background of Jewish immigration and the ideological, literary and organizational beginnings of the labor movement by such experts as Jacob Lestschinsky, E. Lipschutz, Raphael Mahler, Joseph Kissman, Nathan Goldberg, Judith Greenfeld, Abraham Menes and Herman Frank, not to mention the editor himself.

Another important contribution in the same area has been made by J. S. Hertz, whose survey *Di Yiddishe Sotsialistishe Bavegung in Amerike* (1954), embraces the entire panorama of the rise and fall of the Jewish socialist movement in the United States, including much valuable data on the Yiddish press and literature, and on the political and cultural interests of Jewish immigrants.

A number of excellent economic and sociological studies of contemporary Jewish life have been published in various journals by Jacob Lestschinsky, Nathan Reich, Nathan Goldberg and Bruno Blau (1885-1954). The Conference on Jewish Relations also has issued useful surveys of economic trends in the liberal professions.

Harry S. Linfield has been compiling estimates of the Jewish population in the United States—a most difficult task, due to the lack of official material. Demographic surveys have been conducted in a number of cities. A volume of ten such studies—edited by Sophia M. Robison—was issued by the Conference on Jewish

Relations, and some two score more have been made available since 1923 by the Bureau of Jewish Social Research and its successor Council of Jewish Federations and Welfare Funds. Stanley R. Brav, Uriah Z. Engelman and Julian Feibelman have also published demographic studies of individual communities, and Louis Rosenberg has produced statistical surveys of Winnipeg and of the entire Province of Canada.

An early work on the organization of the Jewish community, Boris D. Bogen's (1869-1929) *Jewish Philanthropy* (1917) has been superseded by Maurice J. Karpf's *Jewish Community Organization in the United States* (1938). The titles of these volumes by eminent social workers point to the change that has occurred in the philosophy of Jewish social service and in the conception of inner community relations. The excellent *JWB Survey* (1948) by Oscar I. Janowsky provides an outstanding example of institutional research, which probed many facets of the Jewish Welfare Board's program, particularly the nature and adequacy of the "Jewish content" proffered by the community centers which have sprung up in almost every city. The Council of Jewish Federations and Welfare Funds has sponsored many studies of social service facilities and functions all over the country which, although intended for on-the-spot practical planning, have a considerable cumulative value as an index to community structure and activity and thinking.

Jewish education has been studied and worried over endlessly, but objective analysis is rare, and undoubtedly peculiarly difficult in a realm where goals are poorly defined and always debatable. Among the writers who have made the most useful contributions, descriptively and analytically, are Isaac B. Berkson, Emanuel Gamoran, Samuel Dinin, Alexander Dushkin, Leibush Lehrer, and Zevi Scharfstein.

The recent brutal outbreak of anti-Semitism has stimulated the growth of a very large literature on its current manifestations, but surprisingly little serious attention has been paid to the manifestations and causes of this aberration in the past. Most of what has been written is of an ephemeral journalistic character, and it is not yet possible to evaluate the balance judiciously. A few of what appear to be the outstanding contributions by Jewish writers may, however, be mentioned.

Essays on Anti-Semitism (2nd ed., 1946) contains a collection of papers edited by Koppel S. Pinson on the historic background and economic and social implications by a number of academicians whose scholarly interests touch this theme only peripherally. A study of the medieval origins of anti-Semitic stereotypes is provided in *The Devil and the Jews* by Joshua Trachtenberg. Oscar Karbach and Hannah Arendt have written several good essays on nineteenth-century political anti-Semitism. The latter's study of *The Origins of Totalitarianism* (1951) is a brilliantly suggestive and important treatise on modern sociopolitical developments which surveys anti-Semitism within the frame of the growth of imperialism and totalitarianism.

The psychoanalytical basis of anti-Semitism as a social phenomenon has been explored in a number of studies by Ernst Simmel and Rudolf Loewenstein, and in three research projects which resulted in outstanding works: *Anti-Semitism and Emotional Disorder* (1950) by Nathan W. Ackerman and Marie Jahoda; *The Dynamics of Prejudice* (1950) by Bruno Bettelheim and Morris Janowitz; the most impressive and influential of the three is *The Authoritarian Personality* (1950) by T. W. Adorno, Else Frankel-Brunswick, Daniel J. Levinson and R. N. Sanford. This last work, which introduced a new conception into American social science, has been widely challenged on methodological grounds and stimulated a considerable literature, but has been generally upheld by subsequent studies.

How to utilize the findings of studies such as these in combatting anti-Semitism is an exceedingly difficult problem, apparently involving fundamental changes in social and cultural patterns. However, experiments have been made in attacking prejudice directly to test the effectiveness of current approaches. In one such experiment Henry E. Kagan tried out three methods—in *Changing the Attitude of Christian Toward Jew* (1952)—on groups of non-Jewish children attending church-sponsored summer camps and concluded that a "group therapy" type of technique can be most effective. How effective remains a moot question since it appears that expressed change of attitude does not readily carry over into actual life situations of an anti-Semitic character.

The application of current theories of group dynamics to the study of Jewish life is in its infancy. Some of the best contributions have been made by the noted social psychologist Kurt Lewin (1890-1947) whose theories and researches have had a profound and widespread influence. While devoting his attention primarily to problems of American social relations, he did not neglect those arising out of the Jewish group experience. His numerous essays include a classic study of Jewish "self-hate," and analyses of the psychological effects of Jewish minority status, the interrelationship between the individual and the group, Jewish education as a means of group identification, the problems of psychological security, etc. Some of these papers are to be found in the posthumous volume *Resolving Social Conflicts* (1948). Useful studies in Jewish social psychology and in the dynamics of child psychology have been written by Leibush Lehrer and Nisson Touroff (1877-1953).

Various facets of Jewish belief and practice, too, have been subjected to intensive psychological analysis in recent years, with interesting and instructive, if not always impressive, results. Abraham Cronbach, who has specialized in Jewish social ethics, has prepared an excellent survey of the literature of psychological and psychoanalytical investigation of Judaism.

These are of course only the beginnings of a field of research which seems to have infinite potentialities. The basic problem of Jewish scholarship today seems to be how to make it attractive for the many able young students who are engaged in or are planning to pursue academic careers. Its solution rests on a two-pronged question: can the community intensify the inherent values and satisfactions of Jewish identification to the point where Jewish interests and loyalties are paramount? Can the community provide the facilities and means whereby Jewish learning can be produc-

tively pursued and economically sustaining? But this brings us back to the question with which this survey began: Has the largest and wealthiest Jewish community in the world, which is proudly commemorating three centuries of settlement on American soil, matured sufficiently to appreciate its heritage, and therefore to devote its great capacities to enlarging the opportunities for a more meaningful application of mind and spirit to Jewish life in this fourth century of its history in America? To answer this question here would be no more than to project a wish into prophecy. The answer rests with the next century.

BIBLIOGRAPHY

ELBOGEN, ISMAR, "American Jewish Scholarship" — A survey, *American Jewish Year Book,* Vol. 45, 1943, pp. 47—65.

MARCUS, RALPH, "American Jewish Scholarship Today," *Chicago Jewish Forum,* VI, 1948, pp. 264—268.

OKO, ADOLPH S., "Jewish Book Collections in the United States," *American Jewish Year Book,* Vol. 45, 1943, pp. 67—96.

ROSENBACH, A. S. W., *An American Jewish Bibliography,* 1926.

WAXMAN MEYER, *A History of Jewish Literature,* IV, New York, 1941, pp. 1083—1191.

WEINRYB, BERNARD D., "American Jewish Historiography"—Facts and Problems, *Hebrew Union College Annual,* XXIII, 1950—1951, pp. 223—244.

INDEX

The letters a, b, c, d are for the reader's convenience in locating the reference in the proper quarter of the page. The letters a and b denote, respectively, the upper and lower half of the left-hand column; c and d, the upper and lower half of the right-hand column.